COMPETITION LAW AND THE WORLD TRADE ORGANISATION

AUSTRALIA
LBC Information Services—Sydney

CANADA AND USA
Carswell—Toronto

NEW ZEALAND
Brooker's—Auckland

SINGAPORE AND MALAYSIA
Sweet & Maxwell Asia
Singapore and Kuala Lumpur

COMPETITION LAW AND THE WORLD TRADE ORGANISATION: THE LIMITS OF MULTILATERALISM

Kevin C. Kennedy

Professor of Law
Michigan State University
Detroit College of Law
East Lansing, Michigan

LONDON
SWEET & MAXWELL
2001

Published in 2001 by
Sweet & Maxwell Limited of
100 Avenue Road
Swiss Cottage
London NW3 3PF
(http://www.sweetandmaxwell.co.uk)

Typeset by LBJ Typesetting Ltd of Kingsclere
Printed in Great Britain
by MPG Books Ltd, Bodmin, Cornwall

No natural forests were destroyed
to make this product, only farmed
timber was used and replanted

ISBN 0 421 824 506

A CIP catalogue record for this book
is available from the British Library

To my dear friend and good colleague, John Soave Jr. (1946–2000)

You are deeply missed by us all.

Acknowledgements

I want to offer my sincere thanks to several persons. First, my thanks to my outstanding research assistants, George Ivezaj (Michigan State University-Detroit College of Law, class of 2000) and Jun Kang (Michigan State University-Detroit College of Law, class of 2002). Their thoroughness was exemplary and invaluable.

Next, I want to offer a very special thank you to the scholars who graciously contributed their valuable time to review my manuscript: Professor Spencer Weber Waller, Loyola University-Chicago School of Law; Professor Daniel J. Gifford, University of Minnesota Law School; Professor Daniel Tarullo, Georgetown University Law Center; and Professor Raj Bhala, George Washington University Law School. I am eternally in their debt. All errors and omissions are, of course, mine alone.

Finally, I owe a debt of gratitude to the many legal scholars and policymakers who have worked so hard on the subject of trade and competition policy and upon whose work I have drawn. I learned so much from their contributions to literature on international competition law and policy. I have tried to recognise their many fine contributions to this subject throughout my book. My personal thanks to each and every one of them.

Preface

The World Trade Organisation (WTO) has been buffeted by a storm of criticism from almost every conceivable front. The 1999 street demonstrations in Seattle during the WTO's third ministerial conference showed the disdain of many groups and organisations—from environmental and human rights to labour and consumer—for the WTO and their disaffection in general with globalisation. The demonstrations also proved that the WTO and the trade agreements, which the Organisation administers, are poorly understood, if they are understood at all. Broadly, non-governmental organisations have criticised the WTO for being undemocratic, closed and secretive. Specifically, environmental and labour rights groups have condemned the WTO as being callous to environmental and labour rights issues, respectively. Consumer groups have blasted the WTO for being insensitive to food safety issues.

The debacle at the WTO's Seattle ministerial meeting in December 1999 was in part fuelled by myths and misinformation about the WTO, free trade and globalisation. It is true that accelerated trade liberalisation worldwide has led to the increased globalisation of business and the interdependence of national economies. Environmental fear mongers proclaim that we are on the brink of a global environmental collapse, thanks in large part to free trade. Labour unions condemn the labour rights record of developing countries. Many environmental and labour rights groups, however, view the world as a zero sum game: to the extent the WTO succeeds at promoting globalisation, then in equal measure do the environment and labour rights suffer. One can only pause and wonder whether they silently fear global economic interdependence and wish *sub rosa* for autarchy. In the words of former presidential economic adviser Murray Weidenbaum:

> If the full policy agenda of the anti-global activists were adopted, the long-run effect would be for the United States and other industrialized nations to lose the benefits of the specialization of labor, and suffer severe declines in standards of living. Ironically, the economic costs would soon be translated into environmental costs. Wealthier countries can afford to devote more resources to achieving a cleaner environment, and they do so. Poorer countries do far less to clean up the environment.[1]

Unilateralists/isolationists within national legislatures (here, read "some members of the U.S. Congress") view the WTO as a threat because to them it represents a loss of national sovereignty. "Dismantle the WTO" is the rallying cry for many of its critics. I have found most of the criticisms of the WTO to be the product of misinformation, distortion, and a lack of understanding of what the various WTO agreements actually provide. On the other side are the

[1] Murray Weidenbaum, "Globalization myths", Christian Sci. Monitor, Dec. 16, 1999, at 9.

WTO's supporters who sometimes fall into the trap of viewing the WTO as a panacea that should have its portfolio enlarged to include multilateral agreements on everything tangentially related to trade, including labour, the environment, foreign direct investment and competition policy.

What the critics fail to appreciate fully is that the WTO is not a top-down, supranational organisation that directs nations what to do. Rather, it is a bottom-up forum where member governments meet and occasionally reach agreement on the conduct of world trade. The main attraction of the WTO for many non-trade groups is the WTO's binding dispute settlement mechanism. When environmentalists criticise the WTO, they speak with the voice of the green-eyed monster of envy. The WTO's dispute settlement mechanism is coveted by environmental and labour rights groups that have been unsuccessful in creating their own parallel international dispute settlement body. As they have been unsuccessful in co-opting the WTO, they now want to trash it.

Calls for the dismantling of the WTO are incredibly shortsighted and shallow. They evidence no appreciation for the tremendous contribution that the WTO—and its predecessor organisation, the General Agreement on Tariffs and Trade—have made to increasing world wealth and improving the daily life of millions of person worldwide. To cite just one example, without an organisation like the WTO to defend liberal trade, and the legal and political commitment by WTO members to promoting free trade, developing countries would find markets in developed countries largely closed to their exports of textiles, clothing and other goods that are the product of labour-intensive industries. The critics would presumably prefer seeing the developing world locked into a state of perpetual economic stagnation and poverty, with the people of those countries working behind a water buffalo ploughing a malarial-infested field.

A December 1999 article in *The Economist* asks rhetorically, "Who needs the WTO?"[2] The article makes the following bold but highly defensible claim that "[f]or five decades the world's multilateral trade-liberalising machinery—known first as the General Agreement on Tariffs and Trade (GATT) and more recently as the World Trade Organisation (WTO)—has, in all likelihood, done more to attack global poverty and advance living standards right across the planet than has any other man-made device."[3] In answer to the question, "Who needs the WTO?" the answer is, of course, everyone. By increasing people's economic freedom, the WTO has enhanced people's political freedom and made most of them economically better off than they would have been in the absence of such an organisation.

In 1998, my good friend and collaborator, Professor Raj Bhala of the George Washington University Law School, and I co-authored a treatise entitled, *World Trade Law: The GATT-WTO System, Regional Arrangements, and U.S. Law*. Building on that earlier work, this book analyses the WTO's unfinished agenda and critiques the WTO's proposed new agenda in the area of competition policy. My personal motivation for writing this book is to shed

[2] "Who needs the WTO?" *The Economist*, Dec. 4, 1999 at 74.
[3] *id.*

light on an organisation that has done a miraculous job for over 50 years in increasing world wealth and global prosperity.

Structure of the Book

The book is divided into six chapters. Chapter One is an introduction to the trade and competition policy relationship. It describes the goals that the two policies share, as well as the points where the two policies collide and diverge. The Chapter also introduces the subject of trade and competition policy at the WTO, the arguments of those who support a WTO agreement on competition policy and the objections of those who oppose such a multilateral agreement.

Chapter Two examines the current mix of unilateral, bilateral, plurilateral, regional and multilateral approaches to resolving cross-border competition law and policy disputes. It spotlights the growth in bilateral co-operation agreements and the development of the principles of traditional comity and positive comity in transnational enforcement activities.

Chapter Three reviews the history of trade and competition policy at the WTO, beginning with the provisions of the General Agreement on Tariffs and Trade dealing with anti-competitive practices. The Chapter analyses the competition policy provisions of Uruguay Round and post-Uruguay Round agreements administered by the WTO. Trade and competition policy disputes in the WTO are also addressed.

Chapter Four details the recent work at the WTO on a possible multilateral agreement on competition policy, focusing on the submissions to the Working Group on the Interaction between Trade and Competition Policy established in 1997. Against the backdrop of the WTO work programme and the literature on competition law and policy, the Chapter describes the convergences and divergences among countries' competition laws and policies in the areas of horizontal restraints, vertical restraints, abuse of a dominant position (unlawful monopolisation) and mergers. It concludes that despite the many convergences among national competition laws, most of these are superficial and that critical divergences clearly outnumber the convergences.

Building on the convergences that do exist, Chapter Five outlines models for a WTO agreement on competition policy. It considers both an agreement on harmonised competition rules, as well as a framework agreement on competition policy.

Chapter Six concludes that, in the context of trade and competition policy, multilateralism has limits. In view of the many legal and policy differences dividing the WTO members in the field of competition law and policy, compounded by issues of national sovereignty, the time for a WTO agreement on competition policy is not yet ripe. The Chapter proposes ways in which anti-competitive practices that block market access can nevertheless be addressed under current GATT–WTO rules and the WTO dispute settlement mechanism.

Professor Kevin C. Kennedy
East Lansing, Michigan
November 2000

Contents

Acknowledgements vi
Preface vii
Contents xi
Table of Cases xvii
Table of Legislation xxiii
International Agreements and other formulations of International Trade Law xxvii
Table of Abbreviations xxxvii

Chapter 1: Trade and Competition Policy at the World Trade Organisation: An Introduction and Overview
I. What Is the Trade and Competition Policy Relationship? 1.05
A. Complementarities between Trade and Competition Policy 1.06
B. Divergences between Trade and Competition Policy 1.13
C. Summary 1.27
II. Competition Policy at the WTO: A First Look 1.31

Chapter 2: Unilateral, Bilateral, Regional, Plurilateral, and Multilateral Approaches to Competition Policy
I. Introduction 2.001
II. Unilateral Approaches 2.002
A. Self-Restraint: Comity 2.013
B. Other Self-Restraints on Unilateral Approaches 2.022
C. Anti-Competitive Conduct that may go Unchallenged Under a Unilateral Approach 2.027
D. Reactions to Unilateral Approaches: Foreign Non-disclosure Laws, Clawback Statutes, and Official Protests 2.029
E. The Limits of Unilateralism 2.032
III. Bilateral Approaches 2.037
A. Bilateral Co-operation Agreements on Competition Law Enforcement 2.041
1. The 1976 Germany-U.S. Antitrust Accord 2.042
2. The 1982 Australia-U.S. Antitrust Co-operation Agreement 2.044
3. The Canada-U.S. Co-operation Agreements 2.047
4. The E.U.-U.S. Co-operation Agreements 2.052
5. The 1999 Israel-U.S. Antitrust Co-operation Agreement 2.063

6. The 1999 Japan-U.S. Antitrust Co-operation Agreement 2.064
7. The 1999 Brazil-U.S. Antitrust Co-operation Agreement 2.068
8. The E.U.-Eastern and Central Europe Co-operation Agreements 2.069
9. The 1998 Canada-E.U. Co-operation Agreement 2.070
10. Other Bilateral Co-operation Agreements 2.071
B. Mutual Legal Assistance Agreements on Competition Law Enforcement 2.072
1. Bilateral Agreements on Antitrust Enforcement under the IAEAA 2.077
C. The Australia-New Zealand Closer Economic Relations Trade Agreement 2.088
IV. Regional Approaches 2.091
A. The European Union 2.091
1. Article 81 on Restrictive Agreements 2.094
2. Article 82 on Abuse of a Dominant Position 2.105
3. Article 86 on Government-Induced Distortions of Competition 2.107
4. The Regulation of Mergers and Acquisitions 2.108
5. Extraterritoriality and Comity 2.115
B. MERCOSUR 2.117
1. Introduction 2.117
2. Competition Policy 2.122
C. NAFTA 2.129
D. The Free Trade Area of the Americas 2.137
1. Introduction 2.137
2. The Negotiating Group on Competition Policy 2.142
E. CARICOM 2.149
V. Plurilateral Approaches 2.151
A. The Work of the OECD 2.151
1. Introduction 2.151
2. Studies and Recommendations on Trade and Competition Policy 2.152
3. Guidelines for MNEs on Competition Law and Policy 2.154
4. Co-operation on Competition Law Enforcement 2.160
5. Recommendation on action against Hard-Core Cartels 2.164
6. Notification of transnational Mergers 2.167
7. Technical assistance to developing countries 2.170
8. Summary 2.171
B. APEC 2.172
1. Introduction 2.172
2. Competition Policy 2.175

C. Other plurilateral initiatives 2.178
VI. Multilateral Approaches Outside of the WTO 2.188
A. The 1953 UN Draft Convention on Restrictive Business Practices 2.189
B. The UNCTAD Set of Principles on Restrictive Business Practices 2.193

Chapter 3: Trade and Competition Policy at the WTO: The Past and Present
I. The History of Competition Policy in the GATT-WTO System 3.001
A. The Havana Charter and the Stillborn International Trade Organisation 3.001
B. Competition Policy under GATT 1994 3.010
1. Provisions in GATT 1994 relating to Competition Policy 3.010
C. Proposals to add Competition Policy Provisions to GATT 1947 3.034
D. GATT Dispute Settlement Proceedings involving Competition Policy Issues 3.036
1. The Canadian Foreign Investment Review Act dispute 3.037
2. The Copper Cartel dispute 3.038
3. The Semiconductors dispute 3.039
4. Japanese *Keiretsu* 3.041
II. WTO Rules on Competition Policy 3.042
A. Competition Policy issues addressed in the Uruguay Round Agreements 3.044
1. The TRIPS Agreement 3.045
2. The GATS 3.060
3. The TRIMs Agreement 3.077
4. The Safeguards Agreement 3.087
5. The Agreement on Government Procurement 3.095
6. Other WTO Provisions 3.098
7. Summary 3.099
B. Competition Policy Disputes in the WTO 3.100
1. The *Kodak-Fuji Film* Dispute 3.101
2. The *Antidumping Act of 1916* Dispute 3.112
III. Cautious Steps Forward on Competition Policy Negotiations at the WTO 3.116

Chapter 4: The Search for Convergence, the Reality of Divergence
I. The WTO Work Programme on Competition Policy 4.001
A. The WGTCP's 1997 Work Programme 4.002
B. The WGTCP's 1998 Work Programme 4.016
C. The WGTCP's 1999 Work Programme 4.031

D. The WGTCP's 2000 Work Programme 4.044
E. Other WTO Activities on Trade and Competition Policy 4.050
II. Areas of Convergence and Divergence: threshold issues 4.051
III. Horizontal Restraints 4.057
A. Cartel Activity 4.059
1. Introduction 4.059
2. An example of Prohibited Cartel Activity: Price Fixing 4.061
3. Problems in Policing Export Cartel Activity 4.064
4. The OECD Recommendation on Hard-core Cartels 4.077
B. Import Cartels 4.078
C. Trading companies 4.080
IV. Vertical Restraints 4.082
A. Resale price maintenance 4.085
B. Vertical non-price restraints 4.088
C. Abuse of Intellectual Property rights in vertical agreements 4.091
D. Grey market goods and the Doctrine of Exhaustion 4.096
1. The regulation of grey market goods in the United States 4.100
E. Parent-subsidiary relationships 4.108
V. Abuse of a Dominant Position (Unlawful Monopolisation) 4.111
A. Definition of the relevant market 4.112
B. Predatory pricing 4.120
C. The fit of the Price Discrimination Laws and the Antidumping Duty Law 4.125
VI. Mergers and Acquisitions 4.143
VII. Residual Issues 4.157
VIII. Summary 4.173

Chapter 5: Trade and Competition Policy at the WTO: The Future
I. A WTO Multilateral Agreement on Competition Policy 5.01
A. A multilateral agreement on minimum RBP standards 5.02
1. Minimum Standards on Anti-Competitive Conduct 5.03
2. Non-Discrimination and Transparency 5.11
3. Dispute Settlement 5.12
4. Developing Countries 5.16
B. A WTO Framework Agreement on Core Principles 5.29
1. National Treatment 5.31
2. Most favoured-nation treatment 5.32
3. Transparency 5.34

4. The Content and Coverage of Competition Laws 5.35
5. Effective Enforcement Procedures and Meaningful Remedies 5.36
6. International Co-operation and Co-ordination 5.37
7. Developing Countries and Economies in Transition 5.38
8. Dispute Settlement 5.39
C. The Structure of Negotiations on a Multilateral Competition Policy Agreement 5.51
II. A WTO Plurilateral Agreement on Competition Policy 5.54
III. An OECD Agreement on Competition Policy 5.57

Chapter 6: The Limits of Multilateralism
I. Preconditions to Negotiations on a WTO Agreement on Competition Policy 6.01
II. Addressing Private RBPs under Existing GATT-WTO Rules 6.51
A. An Article XXIII: 1(a) Nullification or Impairment Complaint 6.53
1. An Article II: 4 Import Monopoly Complaint 6.55
2. A National Treatment Complaint 6.57
3. An Article XI Quantitative Restriction Complaint 6.64
4. Private import or export monopolies established under GATT Article XVII 6.68
5. GATS Competition Policy commitments 6.70
6. Abuse of Intellectual Property Rights 6.77
B. An Article XXIII: 1(b) Non-Violation Nullification or Impairment Complaint 6.78
C. An Article XXIII: 1(c) Non-Violation Nullification or Impairment Complaint 6.87
D. A post-mortem on and lessons from the *Kodak-Fuji Film* dispute 6.93
III. Summary and Conclusions 6.96

Index 333

Table of Cases

National Cases

Canada

Attorney General-Can. v. Fallbridge Holdings Ltd, 7 B.L.R. 275, 281 (Fed. Ct., Trail Div. 1979)........ 2.008
Director of Investigation & Research v. The Nutrasweet Co. (1990) 32 C.P.R. (3d) 1... 4.118
Director of Investigation and Research v. Consumers Glass Co. (1981) 33 O.R. (2d) 228, HCJ (Ont.)........ 4.123
Director of Investigation and Research v. Hoffman-La Roche (1980) 28 O.R. (2d) 164, *aff'd* (1981) 33 O.R. (3d) 694, CA (Ont.)........ 4.123
Director of Investigation and Research v. Laidlaw Waste Systems Ltd (1992) C.P.R. (3d) 289........ 4.118
General Motors of Canada Ltd v. City National Leasing, 1 S.C.R. 641 (1989)........ 4.161
R. v. Nova Scotia Pharmaceuticals Society, 2 S.C.R. 606 (1992)........ 4.063

United Kingdom

Rio Tinto Zinc Corp. v. Westinghouse Electric Corp. *See* Westinghouse Electric Corp. Uranium Contract Litigation MDL Docket 235 (No. 2).
Westinghouse Electric Corp. Uranium Contract Litigation MDL Docket 235 (No.2); *sub nom.* Rio Tinto Zinc Corp. v. Westinghouse Electric Corp. (Nos.1 and 2); RTZ Services Ltd v. Westinghouse Electric Corp. [1978] A.C. 547; [1978] 2 W.L.R. 81, HL........ 2.004

United States

A. Bourjois & Co. v. Katzel, 275 F.2d. 539 (1921), *rev'd* 260 U.S. 689 (1923)... 4.100, 4.102
AA Poultry Farms Inc. v. Rose Acre Farms Inc., 881 F.2d 1396 (7th Cir. 1989)........ 4.121
Accord NCAA v. Bd. of Regents of Univ. of Okla, 468 U.S. 85 (1984)........ 4.052
Alcoa Case. *See* United States v. Aluminum Co. of America.
American Banana Co. v. United Fruit Co., 213 U.S. 347 (1909)........ 2.003
Atlantic City Coin & Slot Service Co. v. IGT, 14 F. Supp. 2d 644 (D.N.J. 1998)........ 4.108
Atlantic Richfield Co. v. USA Petroleum Co., 495 U.S. 328 (1990)........ 4.052, 4.086
Banco Nacional de Cuba v. Sabbatino, 376 U.S. 398 (1964)........ 2.025
Bell & Howell: Mamiya Co. v. Masell Supply Co., 719 F.2d. 42 (2d Cir. 1983)........ 4.105
British Steel Corp. v. United States, 593 F. Supp. 405 (CIT 1984)........ 4.132
Brooke Group Ltd v. Brown Williamson Tobacco Corp., 509 U.S. 209 (1993)... 3.112, 4.122, 4.133
Brown Shoe Co. v. United States, 370 U.S. 294, 320 (1962)........ 4.052, 4.115
Brunswick Corp. v. Pueblo-O-Mat Inc., 429 U.S. 477 (1977)........ 4.132
Bulkferts Inc. v. Salatin Inc., 574 F. Supp. 6 (S.D.N.Y. 1983)........ 4.137
Business Elecs. Corp. v. Sharp Elecs. Corp., 485 U.S. 717 (1988)........ 4.083, 4.089
California Motor Transp. Co. v. Trucking Unlimited, 404 U.S. 508 (1962)........ 1.23
California Retail Liquor Dealers Ass'n v. Midcal Aluminum Inc., 445 U.S. 97 (1980).... 4.171
Caribbean Broadcast System Ltd v. Cable & Wireless plc, 148 F.3d 1080 (D.C. Cir. 1998)........ 2.017
Chemicor Drugs Ltd v. Ethyl Corp., 168 F.3d 119 (3d Cir. 1999)........ 4.124
City of Columbia v. Omni Outdoor Advertising Inc., 499 U.S. 365 (1991)........ 4.124

Coastal States Marketing Inc. v. Hunt, 694 F.2d 1358, 1364–66 (5th Cir. 1983)......... 1.23
Consumer Union of U.S. Inc. v. Kissinger, 506 F.2d 136 (D.C. Cir. 1974), *cert. denied*, 421 U.S. 1004 (1975).. 3.091
Continental Ore Co. v. Union Carbide & Carbon Corp., 370 U.S. 690 (1962)... 2.026, 4.109, 4.114
Continental T.V. Inc. v. GTE Sylvania Inc., 433 U.S. 36 (1977)..... 1.15, 4.083, 4.089, 4.090
Cook v. Arrowsmith Shelburne Inc., 69 F.3d 1235 (2d Cir. 1995)..................... 4.108
D.E. Rogers Assoc. Inc. v. Gardner-Denver Co., 718 F.2d 1431 (6th Cir. 1983).......... 1.28
Dr. Miles Medical Co. v. John D. Park & Sons Co., 220 U.S. 373 (1911).............. 4.086
Eastern R.R. Presidents Conf. v. Noerr Motor Freight, 365 U.S. 127 (1961)...... 1.23, 4.124, 4.137
Eastman Kodak Co. v. Image Technical Servs., 504 U.S. 451 (1992).................. 4.117
FTC v. Ticor Title Ins. Co., 504 U.S. 621 (1992).................................. 4.170
Filetech S.A.R.L. v. France Telecom S.A., 157 F.3d 922 (2d Cir. 1998).......... 2.016, 2.024
GAVCO Inc. v. Chem-Trend Inc., 81 F. Supp. 2d 633 (W.D.N.C. 1999)............... 4.108
Geneva Steel c. v. Ranger Steel Co., 980 F. Supp. 1209 (D. Utah 1997)................ 3.112
Gomez v. Toledo, 446 U.S. 635 (1980)... 5.42
Hartford Fire Insurance Co. v. California 509 U.S. 764 (1993).... 2.013, 2.015, 2.016, 2.035, 2.050
Henry v. Chloride Inc., 809 F.2d 1334 (8th Cir. 1987).............................. 4.132
Hilton v. Guyot, 159 U.S. 113, 164 (1895)... 2.013
Hunt v. Mobil Oil Corp., 550 F.2d 68 (2d Cir. 1977)............................... 4.109
Industrial Inv. Dev. Corp. v. Mitsui & Co., 671 F.2d 876, 884–85 (5th Cir. 1982)...... 2.015
Institut Merieux, Re, 113 F.T.C. 742 (1990)....................................... 4.154
Int'l Ass'n of Machinists & Aerospace Workers v. Organization of Petroleum Exporting Countries, 649 F.2d 1354 (9th Cir. 1979), *cert. denied* 454 U.S. 1163........... 2.025
K Mark Corp. v. Cartier Inc., 486 U.S. 281 (1988)................................. 4.102
Kiefer-Stewart Co. v. Joseph E. Seagram & Sons Inc., 340 U.S. 211 (1951)............. 4.086
Laker Airways Ltd v. Sabena Belgian World Airlines, 731 F.2d 909, 948–49 (D.C. Cir. 1984)... 2.015, 2034
Lever Bros. Co. v. United States, 981 F.2d 1330 (D.C. Cir. 1993)..................... 4.105
Lever Bros. Co. v. United States, 877 F.2d 101 (D.C. Cir. 1989)...................... 4.105
Liamuiga Tours v. Travel Impressions Ltd, 617 F. Supp. 920 (E.D.N.Y. 1985).......... 2.017
Liquor Corp. v. Duffy, 479 U.S. 335 (1987).. 4.086
McGlinchy v. Shell Chem. Co., 845 F.2d 802 (9th Cir. 1988)......................... 2.017
Mannington Mills Inc. v. Congoleum Corp., 595 F.2d 1287, 1297–98 (3d Cir. 1979)... 2.015
Matsushita Elec. Indus. Co. v. Zenith Radio Corp., 475 U.S. 574 (1986)............... 4.136
Maxwell Communications Corp. v. Societe Generale, 93 F.3d 1036 (2d Cir. 1996)...... 2.016
Metro Indus. Inc. v. Sammi Corp., 82 F.3d 839, 846 (9th Cir.), *cert. denied* 117 S. Ct. 181 (1996).. 2.016
Millicom Int'l Cellular S.A. v. Republic of Costa Rica, 995 F. Supp. 14 (D.D.C. 1998)... 2.024
Monsanto v. Spray-Rite Serv. Corp., 465 U.S. 752 (1984)........................... 4.086
Monte Carlo Shirt v. Daewoo Int'l (America) Corp., 707 F.2d 1054 (9th Cir. 1983)..... 4.105
Montreal Trading Ltd v. Amax Inc., 661 F.2d 864, 869–70 (9th Cir. 1981)............ 2.015
Music Center S.N.C. Di Luciano Pisoni & Cia. v. Prestini Musical Instruments Corp., 874 F. Supp. 543 (E.D.N.Y. 1995).. 4.124
NEC Electronics v. CAL Circuit Abco, 810 F.2d 1506 (6th Cir.) *cert. denied* 484 U.S. 851 (1987).. 4.105
Northern Pac. Ry. v. United States, 356 U.S. 1, 4 (1958)............................ 4.052
O.N.E. Shipping Ltd v. Flota Mercante Grancolombia S.A., 830 F.2d 449 (2d Cir. 1987).. 4.109S
O. Hommel Co. v. Ferro Corp., 659 F.2d 340 (3rd Cir. 1981)....................... 4.132
Occidental Petroleum Corp. v. Buttes Gas & Oil Co., 331 F. Supp. 92 (C.D. Cal. 1971), *aff'd* 461 F.2d 1261 (9th Cir.) *cert. denied* 409 U.S. 950 (1972)........... 1.23, 4.137
Original Appalachian Artworks v. Granada Elec. Inc., 816 F.2d 68 (2d Cir.), *cert. denied* 484 U.S. 847 (1987)... 4.105

Outboard Marine Corp. v. Pezetel, 461 F. Supp. 384, 395–96 (D. Del. 1978).......... 2.024
Outboard Marine Corp. v. Pezetel, 474 F. Supp. 168 (D. Del. 1979)................... 1.23
Parker v. Brown, 317 U.S. 341 (1943)... 4.171
Parklane Hosiery Co. v. Shore, 439 U.S. 322 (1979)............................... 4.158
Patrick v. Burget, 486 U.S. 94 (1988).. 4.171
Porters S.A. v. Hanes Printables Inc., 663 F. Supp. 494 (M.D.N.C. 1987).............. 2.017
Professional Real Estate Investors Inc. v. Columbia Pictures Ind. Inc., 508 U.S. 49, 60–61 (1993)... 1.23
Quality King Distributors Inc. v. L'Anza Research Int'l Inc., 118 S. Ct. 1125 (1998)..... 4.106
Real Estate Investors Inc. v. Columbia Pictures Industries Inc., 508 U.S. 49 (1993)...... 4.124
Sage Intern. Ltd v. Cadillac Gage Co., 507 F. Supp. 939 (E.D. Mich. 1981)............. 1.23
Societe Des Produits Nestle S.A. v. Casa Helvetia Inc., 982 F.2d 633 (1st F.2d 633 (1st Cir. 1992)... 4.105
Southern Motor Carriers Rate Conf. v. United States, 471 U.S. 48 (1985).............. 4.171
Southern Pac. Communications Co. v. Amer. Tel. & Tel. Co., 740 F.2d 980 (D.C. Cir. 1984).. 1.28
Spectrum Sport Inc. v. McQuillan, 506 U.S. 447 (1993)............................. 4.122
St. Joseph's Hosp. Inc. v. Hosp. Authority of America, 620 F. Supp. 814 (S.D. Ga. 1985) 1.23
Standard Oil Co. v. United States, 337 U.S. 293 (1949)............................. 4.090
State Oil v. Khan, 522 U.S. 3, 18 (1997).. 4.086
Sterling Drug Inc. v. Bayer AG, 14 F.3d 733 (2d Cir. 1994)......................... 2.016
Tampa Electric Co. v. Nashville Coal Co., 365 U.S. 320 (1961)...................... 4.090
Timberlane Lumber Co. v. Bank of Am., 549 F.2d 596, 611–12 (9th Cir. 1976) (Timberlane I)... 2.014, 2.016, 2.043, 2.052
Timberlane Lumber Co. v. Bank of Am. Nat'l Trust & Sav. Ass'n, 749 F.2d 1378, 1382 (9th Cir. 1984) (Timberlane II).. 2.014
United Air Lines v. Austin Travel Corp., 867 F.2d 737 (2d Cir. 1989)................ 4.117
United States v. Kanzakia Specialty Papers Inc., 6 Trade Reg. Rep. (CCH) 45,094, at 44,706–07 (D. Mass. August 3, 1994).. 2.075
United Mine Workers of America v. Pennington, 381 U.S. 657 (1965)................. 4.124
United Mine Workers v. Pennington, 381 U.S. 657 (1965)............................ 1.23
United States v. Izzi, 6 Trade Reg. Rep. (CCH) 45,094, at 44,696–97 (March 8, 16, 1995)... 2.075
United States v. Aluminum Co. of America, 148 F.2d 416, 443 (2d Cir. 1945)... 2.003, 2.017
United States v. AMAX Inc., 1977&1 Trade Cas. (CCH) 61,467, at 71,799 (N.D. Ill 1977)... 1.23
United States v. Amer. Tel. & Tel. Co., 401 F. Supp. 1310 (D. Minn. 1982)........... 3.006
United States v. Brown, 936 F.2d 1042, 1045 (9th Cir. 1991)........................ 4.062
United States v. Comet Prods. Inc., 6 Trade Reg. Rep. (CHH) 45,094, at 44,696–97 (October 4, 1994).. 2.075
United States v. E.I. du Pont Nemours & Co., 351 U.S. 316 (1961).................. 4.115
United States v. Eighty-Three Rolex Wates, 992 F.2d 508 (5th Cir. 1993)............. 4.103
United States v. Elof Hansson Paper & Bl. Inc., 6 Trade Reg. Rep. (CCH) 45,095, at 44,746–47 (June 9, 1995).. 2.075
United States v. General Dynamics Corp., 415 U.S. 486, 499–500 (1974).............. 1.15
United States v. General Elec. Co., 869 F. Supp. 1285 (S.D. Ohio 1994)......... 2.032, 2.037
United States v. Int'l Bus. Machines Inc., 887 F. Supp. 591 (S.D.N.Y. 1982)........... 3.006
United States v. Microsoft Corp., 87 F. Supp. 2d. 30 D.D.C. 2000).................. 3.006
United States v. Minnesota Mining & Manufacturing Co., 92 F. Supp. 947 (D. Mass. 1950)... 4.071
United States v. Mitsubishi Paper Mills Ltd, 6 Trade Reg. Rep. (CCH) 45,095, at 44,767–68 (September 26, 1995).. 2.075
United States v. New Oji Paper Co. Ltd, 6 Trade Reg. Rep. (CCH) 45,095, at 44–767–68 (September 26, 1995).. 2.075
United States v. Nippon Paper Indus. Co., 109 F.3d 1, 8–9 (1st Cir. 1997), *cert. denied*, 118 S. Ct. 685 (1998).................................. 2.015, 2.016, 2.034, 2.039

United States v. Plastics Inc., 6 Trade Reg. Rep. (CCH) 45,094, at 44,696–7 (October 4, 1994). 2.075
United States v. Polar Plastics Mfg. Ltd, 6 Trade Reg. Rep. (CCH) 45,094, at 44,696–97 (February 28, 1995). 2.075
United States v. Rock Royal Co-op Ass'n, 307 U.S. 533 (1939). 4.170
United States v. Scophony Corp. of America, 333 U.S. 795 (1948). 4.108
United States v. Socony-Vacuum Oil Co., 310 U.S. 150, 225 (1940). 4.062
United States v. Syufy Enters., 903 F.2d 659 (9th Cir. 1990). 4.117
United States v. U.S. Alkali Export Ass'n, 325 U.S. 196 (1945). 4.071
Uranium Antitrust Litigation, Re, 480 F. Supp. 1138 (N.D. Ill 1979). 2.034, 2.037
Uranium Antitrust Litigation, Re, 617 F.2d 1248, 1255 (7th Cir. 1980). 2.015
Velandra v. Regie Nationale des Usines Renault, 336 F.2d 292 (6th Cir. 1992). 4.108
W.S. Kirkpatrick & Co. v. Environmental Tectonics Corp., 493 U.S. 400 (1990). 2.025
Weil Ceramics & Glass Inc. v. Dash, 878 F.2d 659 (3d Cir.), *cert. denied* 493 U.S. 853 (1989). 4.105
Wheeling-Pittsburgh Steel Corp. v. Mitsui & Co. (U.S.A.) Inc., 2000 U.S. App. Lexis 17759 (6th Cir. July 27, 2000). 3.112
Williams v. Curtiss-Wright Corp., 694 F.2d 1287 (3rd Cir. 1982). 2.025
Zenith Radio Corp. v. Matsushita Elec. Indus. Co., 402 F. Supp. 244 (E.D. Pa. 1975). . . 3.112
Zenith Radio Corp. v. Matsushita Elec. Indus. Co., Ltd 494 F. Supp. 1190 (E.D. Pa. 1980). 3.112

CASES BEFORE THE EUROPEAN COURT OF JUSTICE

Ahlström Osakeyhtiö v. Commission (Cases 89, 104, 116–17, 125–9/85) [1988] E.C.R. 5193; [1988] 4 C.M.L.R. 901, ECJ. 2.005, 2.006, 2.115, 4.072, 4.075
British Leyland plc v. Commission (Case 226/84) [1986] E.C.R. 3263; [1987] R.T.R. 136; [1987] 1 C.M.L.R. 185; *The Times*, November 12, 1986, ECJ. 2.106
Bulk Oil (Zug) AG v. Sun International Ltd and Sun Oil Trading Co. (Case C–174/84) [1986] 2 All E.R. 744; [1986] E.C.R. 559; [1986] 2 C.M.L.R. 732, ECJ. 4.075
Commercial Solvents Corp. v. Commission of the European Communities (Case 6/74) [1974] E.C.R. 223; [1974] 1 C.M.L.R. 309, ECJ. 4.110
Consten SARL v. Commission (Case C–56/64). *See* Etablissements Consten SARL v. Commission (Case C–56/64).
Etablissements Consten SARL v. Commission (Case C–56/64) [1966] E.C.R. 299; [1966] E.C.R. 556, ECJ. 4.090
Europemballage Corp. and Continental Can Co. Inc. v. Commission (Case 6/72) [1973] E.C.R. 215; [1973] C.M.L.R. 199, ECJ. 2.106, 2.108
France v. Commission; *sub nom.* E.C.–USA Competition Laws Cooperation Agreement, Re (Case C–327/91) [1994] E.C.R. I–3641; [1994] 5 C.M.L.R. 517, ECJ. 2.052
Hoffmann La Roche & Co. AG v. Commission (Case 85/76) [1979] E.C.R. 461; [1979] 3 C.M.L.R. 211; [1980] F.S.R. 13, ECJ. 2.106
Imperial Chemical Industries Ltd v. Commission (Case 48/69) [1972] E.C.R. 619; [1972] C.M.L.R. 557, ECJ. 4.110
United Brands Co. v. Commission (Banana Market) (Case 27/76) [1978] E.C.R. 207; [1978] 1 C.M.L.R. 429, ECJ. 2.106, 4.126
Wood Pulp. *See* Ahlström Osakeyhtiö v. Commission.

E.C. COMMISSIONS DECISIONS

Aluminium Imports from Eastern Europe [1987] 3 C.M.L.R. 813; [1985] O.J. L92/1. . . . 2.115
Anglo American Corp./Lonrho (Case No. IV/M.754) [1998] O.J. L149/27; [1997] 4 C.M.L.R. 377 (IP). 4.154
Ball-bearing [1974] O.J. L343/19. . . . . 2.004

Boeing/McDonnell Douglas (Case IV/M.877) [1997] 5 C.M.L.R. 270 (IP); [1997] O.J. L336/16........ 2.054, 2.055, 2.112, 4.116, 4.151, 4.152, 4.153, 4.154, 4.155, 6.17, 6.42
Cable & Wireless plc (Case IV/M.1069), July 8, 1998........ 2.113
Cartel in Quinine, Re [1969] C.M.L.R. D41; [1969] O.J. Spec. Ed. L192/5........ 2.004
Duro-Dyne/Europair [1975] 1 C.M.L.R. D62; [1975] O.J. Spec. Ed. L29/11........ 2.004
Dyestuffs [1969] C.M.L.R. D23; [1969] O.J. Spec. Ed. L195/11........ 2.004
Gencor/Lonrho (Case IV/M.619) [1997] 4 C.M.L.R. 742........ 2.112, 4.154
Raymond/Nagoya [1972] C.M.L.R. D45; [1972] O.J. L143/39........ 2.004
Wood Pulp Cartel [1985] 3 C.M.L.R. 474; [1985] O.J. L85/1........ 2.005, 2.115

Table of Legislation

National Legislation

Australia

Trade Practices Act 1974
s. 46A 2.088

Canada

Competition Act 1999 4.053, 4.063, 4.149, 4.161
s. 1(1) 4.172
s. 45 .... 4.063
(5) 2.028, 4.069
(6) 2.028, 4.069
s. 46 .... 4.164
s. 47 .... 4.063
s. 50(1)(c) 4.123
s. 61 .... 4.087
(1)(a) 4.087
s. 77 .... 4.090
s. 82 .... 2.030
s. 83 .... 2.030
Foreign Extraterritorial Measures Act 1998 .... 2.029
Foreign Investment Review Act 1973 3.037, 3.077, 3.084
Investment Canada Act 1985 .... 3.037

Japan

Antimonopoly Law 1977 ...... 3.101, 4.169
Art. 25 .... 4.162
Art. 26 .... 4.162
Art. 89(1) 4.164

Mexico

Constitution 1917
Art. 28 .... 4.070
Federal Law on Economic Competition (Ley Federal de Competencia Economica) 1992 ..... 5.26, 5.27, 5.28
Art. 2 .... 5.27
Art. 6 .... 4.070
Art. 10 .... 5.27
Art. 12 .... 5.57
Art. 13 .... 5.27
Art. 16 .... 5.28
Federal Law on Economic Competition (Ley Federal de Competencia Economica) 1992—*cont.*
Art. 18 .... 5.28
Art. 20 .... 5.28
Art. 23 .... 5.28
Arts. 24–26 .... 5.28

New Zealand

Commerce Act 1986
s. 36A 2.088

United Kingdom

1978 State Immunity Act (c.33) 2.024
s. 5 .... 2.024
1980 Protection of Trading Interests Act (27 c.11) 2.029
1988 Competition Act (c.41) 4.159

United States

Antidumping Act 1916 3.021, 3.100, 3.112, 3.113, 3.114, 3.115, 4.128, 4.136, 4.142, 6.35, 6.39, 6.59, 6.63
Antitrust Civil Process Act 1962 ...... 2.078
Atomic Energy Act 1954 .... 3.057
Banking Merger Act 1960 .... 4.076
Capper-Volstead Act 1922 .... 4.076
Clayton Act 1914 ...... 2.017, 2.018, 4.158
s. 4 .... 4.158
s. 7 .... 2.017, 2.019, 4.071
Clean Air Act 1955 .... 3.057
Code of Federal Regulation 1994
16 C.F.R. ss. 801.1(a), 802.50–.52 (1995) 2.019
16 C.F.R. ss. 801.1(b) (1) & 802.20 .... 4.148
19 C.F.R. s. 133.21(a) 4.104
19 C.F.R. s. 133.21(c) 4.104
19 C.F.R. 133.21(c) (1)–(2) 4.103
Communications Act 1934 .... 4.076
Copyright Act 1976 .... 4.104
s. 109 .... 4.106
(a) 4.106
s. 602 .... 4.106
s. 602(a) 4.106

Defence Production Act 1950 .... 4.076
Energy Policy Act 1992 .... 3.057
Export Trading Company Act
1982 .... 2.028, 4.080, 6.66
Title III 4.073
Federal Trade Commission Act 1914 2.016, 2.078
Foreign Sovereign Immunities
Act 1976 .... 2.024
Foreign Trade Antitrust Improvements
Act 1982 .... 2.017, 2.036, 4.074
cl. 1(B) 2.017
Genuine Goods Exclusion Act 1930 ... 4.101
ss. 81–109 .... 4.101
Hart-Scott-Rodino Antitrust
Improvements Act 1976 .. 2.018, 2.081, 4.148, 6.43
International Antitrust Enforcement
Assistance Act 1994 ...... 2.054, 2.075, 2.076, 2.079, 2.080, 2.081, 2.083, 2.084, 2.085, 2.086, 2.087
Lanham Act 1946 .... 4.104
s. 32 .... 4.104
s. 42 .... 4.104, 4.105
McCarran-Ferguson Act 1945 .... 4.076
National Co-operative Research Act
1984 .... 4.076
National Co-operative Research and
Production Act 1993 .... 4.076
Norris-LaGuardia Act 1932 .... 4.076
Omnibus Trade and Competitiveness Act
1988 .... 3.049, 4.133
Reciprocal Trade Agreement Act
1934 .... 3.002
Restatement (Third) Foreign Relations
Laws of the United States (1987)
s. 403 .... 2.002, 2.004, 2.015
s. 441 .... 2.026
s. 443 .... 2.025
ss. 451–463 .... 2.024
Revenue Act 1916 .... 3.112
Title VIII 3.112
Robinson-Patman Act 1936 ... 3.112, 3.113, 4.132, 6.59, 6.63
Sherman Act 1890 ..... 2.003, 2.016, 2.017, 2.035, 4.074, 4.158, 6.43
s. 1 .... 2.093, 2.195, 4.079, 4.163
s. 2 .... 1.26, 2.093, 2.195, 4.122
Shipping Act 1984 .... 4.076
Telecommunications Act 1996 .... 3.074
Tariff Act 1930
Title VII 3.112
s. 337 ..... 3.019, 3.048, 6.60, 6.61, 6.62
(a) 6.60
s. 526 .... 4.101, 4.102, 4.104
Tariff Act 1922 .... 4.101
Trade Act 1974
s. 301 .... 3.101, 6.39
United States Code
12 U.S.C. s.1828 .... 4.076
15 U.S.C. s. 1 .... 4.060
15 U.S.C. ss. 1,2 .... 4.163
15 U.S.C. s. 6(a) 2.017
15 U.S.C. ss. 7a, 45(a) (3) 4.074
15 U.S.C. s. 8 .... 4.079
15 U.S.C. ss. 8–11 .... 4.079
15 U.S.C. s. 13(a) 3.112, 4.128, 6.59
15 U.S.C. s. 13(a), (b) 4.132
15 U.S.C. s. 15(a) 4.158
15 U.S.C. s. 17 .... 4.076
15 U.S.C. s. 18, ... 2.017
15 U.S.C. s. 18a 2.018
15 U.S.C. s. 18a(a) (3) 4.148
15 U.S.C. s. 18a(e), ... 4.148
15 U.S.C. ss. 61–66 .... 4.065
15 U.S.C. ss. 62, 65 .... 4.071
15 U.S.C. ss. 71–74 .... 6.59
15 U.S.C. s. 72 .... 3.112
15 U.S.C. s. 92(1) 4.148
15 U.S.C. s. 110 .... 3.148
15 U.S.C. s. 1011–1015 .... 4.076
15 U.S.C. s. 1114 .... 4.104
15 U.S.C. s. 1124 .... 4.104
15 U.S.C. ss. 4001–21 ...... 2.028, 4.073
15 U.S.C. 4013(a) 4.080
15 U.S.C. s. 4301 .... 4.076
15 U.S.C. ss. 4301–4305 .... 4.076
15 U.S.C. s. 6202(b) 2.079
15 U.S.C. s. 6204 .... 2.081
15 U.S.C. s. 6211(2) 2.080
15 U.S.C. s. 6211(2) (A) 2.079
15 U.S.C. s. 6211(2) (B) 2.079
18 U.S.C. s. 3571 .... 4.163
19 U.S.C. s. 526(a)-(c) 4.101
19 U.S.C. s. 1337(a) 6.60
19 U.S.C. s. 1526 .... 4.101
19 U.S.C. ss. 1673–1673g 6.59
19 U.S.C. s. 1673(2) 4.132
19 U.S.C. s. 1677(7) (A) 4.132
19 U.S.C. s. 2901(b)(10) 3.049
19 U.S.C. s. 3535 .... 1.46
28 U.S.C. ss. 1330, 1602–1611 .... 2.024
28 U.S.C. s. 1605(a) (2) 2.024
29 U.S.C. ss. 101–115 .... 4.076
42 U.S.C. s. 6272 .... 4.076
46 U.S.C. ss. 1701–1720 .... 4.076
47 U.S.C. ss. 151–156 .... 4.076
49 U.S.C. ss. 1382, 1384 .... 4.076
50 U.S.C. s. 2158a(j) 4.076
Uruguay Round Agreements Act 1994 .. 6.62
s. 101(a) 3.003

Uruguay Round Agreements Act 1994—*cont.*
s. 125 .... 1.46
s. 321(a) 6.62
Webb-Pomerene Act 1918 .... 2.028, 4.065, 4.071, 4.072, 4.073, 4.080, 6.66
Wilson Tariff Act 1894 .... 4.079

EUROPEAN AND INTERNATIONAL TREATIES & CONVENTIONS

Berne Convention for the Protection of Literary and Artistic Works 1886 3.050
E.C. Treaty (Treaty of Rome), March 25, 1957 .... 2.119, 4.053
Title V 2.093
Art. 3(g) 2.093
Art. 81 (ex 85) 2.005, 2.060, 2.093, **2.094**, 2.095, 2.096, 2.097, 2.098, 2.101, 2.104, 2.105, 2.107, 2.108, 2.115, 2.195, 4.053, 4.075, 4.083, 4.094, 4.160, 4.163
Art. 81(1) 2.094, 2.095, 2.096, 2.098, 2.104, 4.094
(2) 2.094, 4.094
(3) 2.094, 2.095, 2.104
Art. 82 (ex 86) 2.091, 2.093, 2.104, **2.105**, 2.106, 2.107, 2.108, 2.115, 2.185, 2.195, 4.111, 4.160, 4.163
Art. 82(c) 4.126
Art. 83 (ex 87) 2.093, 2.095
Art. 86 (ex 90) 2.093
Art. 189 .... 5.03
OECD Anti-Bribery Convention 1997 2.151
Protocol of the Defence of Competition in MERCOSUR 1996 .... 2.122, 2.124, 2.125, 4.126
Art. 2 .... 2.122, 2.127
Art. 6 .... 2.123
Art. 7 .... 2.122
Art. 14 .... 2.124
Art. 15 .... 2.125
Art. 16 .... 2.128
Art. 18 .... 2.125
Art. 19 .... 2.125
Art. 20 .... 2.126
Art. 22 .... 2.124
Protocol of the Defence of Competition in MERCOSUR 1996—*cont.*
Art. 23 .... 2.124
Art. 28 .... 2.127
Art. 29 .... 2.127
Art. 30 .... 2.128
Annex 2.127
Protocolo de Brasilia Para la Solucion de Controversias (Brasilia Protocol on the Settlement of Disputes), December 17, 1991 .... 2.119
Art. 21 .... 2.126
Art. 27 .... 2.127
Protocolo de Ouro Preto, December 17, 1994 .... 2.119
Art. 43 .... 2.119
Treaty Establishing a Common Market Between the Argentine Republic, the Federative Republic of Brazil, the Republic of Paraguay and the Eastern Republic of Uruguay, March 26, 1991 (Treaty of Asuncion) .. 2.117, 2.119
Art. 1 .... 2.117, 2.119
Art. 5 .... 2.119
(d) 2.119
Annex I 2.119
Treaty of Chaguaramas Establishing the Caribbean Community, July 4, 1973 ... 2.149
Protocol VIII 2.149, 2.150
Art. 30(a) 2.149
(b) 2.149
(c) 2.149
(e) 2.149
(g) 2.149
(11)—(12) 2.149
(i) 2.149
(k) 2.149
Treaty on Copyright Law 1996 ...... 3.050
Treaty on European Union, November 1, 1992 (Maastricht Treaty) 2.093
Art. 130 .... 2.093
Treaty on Performances and Phonograms 1996 .... 3.050
Treaty of Amsterdam, May 1, 1999
Art. 12 .... 2.093
UN Convention on Restrictive Business Practices (Draft) 1953 .... 2.188, 2.189, 2.190, 2.191, 2.192, 3.009
Preamble 2.189
Art. 1(1) 2.189
(3) 2.190
Art. 2(2)(b), (c) 2.190
Art. 3 .... 2.191

Preamble—*cont.*
Art. 5 .... 2.191
(1) 2.191
Arts. 10–17 .... 2.191
Art. 18(2) 2.191

E.C. DIRECTIVES

Dir. 89/104 on trade marks 4.099

E.C. REGULATIONS

Reg. 17/62 [1962] 5 O.J. Spec. Ed. Eur. Comm. 87 .... 2.093, 2.095, 2.104
Reg. 1983/83 on the application of Art. 85(3) of the Treaty to categories of exclusive distribution agreements [1983] O.J. L173/1 ...... 2.097, 2.100, 4.094
Reg. 1984/83 on the application of Art. 85(3) of the Treaty to categories of exclusive purchasing agreements [1983] O.J. L173/5 ...... 2.097, 2.100, 4.094
Reg. 2349/84 on the application of Art. 85(3) of the Treaty to certain categories of technology transfer agreements [1984] O.J. L219/15 2.097, 4.094, 4.095
Reg. 418/85 on the application of Art. 85(3) of the Treaty to categories of research and development agreements [1985] O.J. L53/5 ... 2.097, 4.095
Reg. 4087/88 on the application of Art. 85(3) of the Treaty to categories of franchise agreements [1988] O.J. L359/46 .... 2.097, 2.100, 4.094
Reg. 556/89 on the application of Art. 85(3) of the Treaty to certain categories of technology transfer agreements [1986] O.J. L61/1 ... 2.097, 4.094, 4.095
Reg. 4064/89 Merger Control Regulation [1989] O.J. L395/1 .. 2.054, 2.108, 2.109, 2.110, 2.112, 4.145, 4.146, 4.148, 6.41
Art. 1(2) 2.109, 4.146
(3) 2.109
Reg. 240/96 on the application of Art. 85(3) of the Treaty to certain categories of technology transfer agreements 2.097, 4.095
Art. 3(1) 4.095
(3) 4.095
(5) 4.095
Reg. 1310/97 amending Regulation 4064/89 on the control of concentrations between undertakings [1997] O.J. L180/1 2.109
Art. 2 .... 4.145
Reg. 2790/99 on the application of Art. 81(3) of the Treaty to categories of vertical agreements and concerted practices [1999] O.J. L336/21 .... 2.100

International Agreements and Other Formulations of International Trade Law

European and International Agreements

Agreement between the European Communities and the Government of Canada Regarding the Application of Their Competition Laws, 1998 .... 2.070
Art. IV 2.070
Art. V 2.070
Art. VII 2.070
Art. VI 2.070
Art. VI:2(ix) 2.070
Art. VIII 2.070
Art. IX 2.070
Agreement between the Government of the United States and the Government of the Federative Republic of Brazil, October 26, 1999 .... 2.068
Art. II 2.068
Art. III:1 .... 2.068
Art. III:3 .... 2.069
Art. IV 2.068
Art. VI:1 .... 2.068
Art. IX 2.068
Agreement between the Government of the United States of America and the Commission of the European Communities Regarding the Application of Their Competition Laws, September 23, 1991 ...... 2.047, 2.052, 2.054, 2.055, 2.056, 2.070, 2.112
Art. V(2) 2.055
Art. VI(3) 2.052, 5.37
Agreement between the Government of the United States of America and the European Communities on the Application of Positive Comity Agreement, June 4, 1998 2.056, 2.057, 2.059, 2.060
Art. I:1(b) 2.059
Agreement between the Government of the United States of America and the European Communities on the Application of Positive Comity Agreement, June 4, 1998—*cont.*
Art. IV:2 .... 2.056, 2.059
(a)(i) 2.056
(b) 2.057
(c) 2.058
Art. IV:4 .... 2.058
Agreement between the Government of the United States of America and the Government of Australia on Mutual Antitrust Enforcement Assistance, April 27, 1999 ...... 2.078, 2.083, 2.086
Art. II:E(2) 2.083
F 2.083
H 2.084
I 2.084
Art. IV:A(1)—(4) 2.084
Art. V 2.085
Art. VI 2.086
Art. VII 2.086
Art. IX 2.083
Art. X 2.083
Art. XI 2.086
Agreement between the Government of the United States of America and the Government of Australia Relating to Co-operation on Antitrust Matter, June 29, 1982 .... 2.044, 2.078
Art. 1 .... 2.044
Art. 2 .... 2.044
Art. 2.2(c) 2.063
Art. 2.5 .... 2.045
Art. 2.6(b) 2.044
Art. 3 .... 2.046
Art. 5.1 .... 2.046
Art. 6 .... 2.045

Agreement between the Government of the United States of America and the Government of Canada Regarding the Application of Their Competition and Deceptive Marketing Practices Laws, March 9, 1984 .... 2.047

Agreement between the Government of the United States of America and the Government of Canada Regarding the Application of Their Competition and Deceptive Marketing Practices Laws, August 3, 1995 ...... 2.047, 2.048, 2.051, 2.063, 2.067, 2.070
- Art. II 2.047
- Art. II.2(c) 2.047
- Art. III 2.047
- Art. V 2.048
- Art. VI 2.049, 2.063
- Art. VI:5(ii) 2.067
  - (iii) 2.067
  - (iv) 2.050
  - (v) 2.050
  - (vi) 2.067
  - (vii) 2.067
- Art. VII 2.051
- Art. VII:1 .... 2.051
  - 3 .... 2.051
  - 6 .... 2.063
- Art. IX 2.051
- Art. X 2.047

Agreement between the Government of the United States of America and the Government of the Federal Republic of Germany Relating to Mutual Cooperation Regarding Restrictive Business Practices, June 23, 1976 .... 2.042
- Art. 2(2) 2.042
  - (5) 2.042
- Art. 3 .... 2.042
- Art. 3(1)(b), (c) 2.042

Agreement between the Government of the United States of America and the Government of Hong Kong on Mutual Legal Assistance in Criminal Matters, with Annex, April 15, 1997, S. Treaty Doc. No. 6, 105; Cong., 3d Sess. (1997) 2.072

Agreement between the Government of the United States of America and the Government of Japan Concerning Cooperation on Anticompetitive Activities, October 7, 1999 .... 2.064, 2.066, 2.067
- Art. VI:3(b) 2.067
  - (c) 2.067
  - (d) 2.067
  - (g) 2.067

Agreement between the Government of the United States of America and the Government of the State of Israel Regarding the Application of Their Competition Laws, March 15, 1999 .... 2.063, 2.067, 2.068
- Art. I 2.063
- Art. II 2.063, 2.068
- Art. III 2.063, 2.068
- Art. III:3 .... 2.068
- Art. IV 2.063
- Art. V 2.063
- Art. VI 2.063
- Art. VI:5 .... 2.068
- Art. VII 2.063
- Art. VIII 2.063
- Art. IX 2.063

Agreement Establishing the World Trade Organisation 1994
- Art. III:3 .... 5.43
- Art. IV:1 .... 3.034
- Annex 3 .... 5.43

Annex 4 .... 3.095

Agreement on Basic Telecommunications 1997 ...... 3.007, 3.044, 3.073, 3.074, 3.075, 6.54, 6.73, 6.75

Agreement on Government Procurement, April 15, 1994 .... 3.095, 5.54
- Art. X 3.096
- Art. XV 3.097

Agreement on Implementation of Art. VI of the General Agreement on Tariffs and Trade 1994 .... 1.25, 3.021, 3.100, 3.113, 5.10
- Art. 1 .... 3.100
- Art. 2.2 .... 1.25
- Art. 3:5 .... 3.021
- Art. 4 .... 3.100
- Art. 5:4 .... 3.021, 3.100
- Art. 11:3 .... 3.021
- Art. 18:1 .... 3.114

Agreement on Sanitary and Phytosanitary Measures Agreement on Subsidies and Countervailing Measures 1994
Art. 15.5 .... 3.098
Agreement on Technical Barriers to Trade 1994 .... 3.098
Art. 3.1 .... 3.098
Art. 3.4 .... 3.098
Art. 4.1 .... 3.098
Art. 8.1 .... 3.098
Agreement on the Trade-Related Aspects of Intellectual Property Rights 1994 ... 1.35, 3.044, 3.045, 3.046, 3.050, 3.051, 3.053, 3.057, 3.077, 3.116, 4.039, 5.02, 5.17, 6.13, 6.54, 6.77
Agreement on Trade-Related Antitrust Measures 1994 .... 5.02
Agreement on Trade-Related Antitrust Principles 1994 .... 5.02
Agreement on Trade-Related Aspects of Competition Measures 1994 ...... 5.02
Art. 6 .... 3.055, 4.099
Art. 7 .... **3.052**
Art. 8 .... 1.34, 3.051, 3.052, 3.055, 6.77
(1) 3.053
(2) 3.005, **3.053**, 4.091
Art. 16 .... 3.056
Art. 22 .... 3.056
(2) 3.056
(3) 3.056
(4) 3.056
Art. 31 .... 1.34, 3.051, 3.053, 3.057
(b) 3.058
(c) 3.058
Art. 40 .... 1.34, 3.005, 3.051, 3.053, 3.054, 3.055, 6.11, 6.77
(1) 3.054
(2) 3.054, 3.055
(3) 3.054
Arts. 41–50 .... 5.03
Art. 41(1) 5.36
(2) 5.36
(4) 5.36
(5) 5.36
Art. 42 .... 5.36
Art. 43(1) 5.36
(2) 5.36
Art. 61 .... 5.35
Art. 65(2) 5.17
Art. 66(1) 5.17
Art. 67 .... 5.17, 5.38
Agreement on Trade-Related Investments Measures 1994 .... 3.037/1, 3.078, 3.079, 3.080, 3.081, 3.082, 3.083, 3.084, 3.085, 3.086, 4.001, 5.02, 5.20, 5.38
Art. 2.1 .... 3.079
Art. 2.2 .... 3.079
Art. 4 .... 3.082
Art. 5.2 .... 3.080, 5.38
Art. 5.5 .... 3.080
Art. 6.2 .... 3.080
Art. 9 .... 1.33, 3.081, 3.086, 6.11
Art. 14 .... 5.38
Annex 3.079
Annex 1(a) 3.037/1
(b) 3.085
Agreement with Hong Kong on Mutual Assistance in Criminal Matters, April 15, 1997, S. Treaty Doc. No. 6, 105th; Cong., 2d Sess. 1997 .... 2.072
Australia New Zealand Closer Economic Relations Trade Agreement on Acceleration of Free Trade on Goods, August 18, 1988
Art. 4 .... 2.088
Protocol, 1988 .... 2.088
Australia—New Zealand Closer Economic Relations Trade Agreement, March 28, 1983 .... 2.001, 2.088, 2.089, 2.090, 4.009, 6.24, 6.30
Convention for the Protection of Industrial Property 1883 .... 6.13
Art. 5 .... 3.059
Art. 10*bis* 3.056
Cooperation and Coordination Agreement Between the Australia Trade Practices Commission and the New Zealand Commerce Commission 1994 .... 2.088
E.U.—Eastern and Central Europe Co-operation Agreements 1995 .. 2.069
European Economic Area Agreement 1993 .... 2.112
European Free Trade Agreement 1960 ..... 4.126
Free Trade Agreement between Canada and Chile 1996, Chapter J 2.133
GATT Dispute Settlement Rules and Procedures, BISD, 36th Supp. 61 1989 .... 6.88

General Agreement on Tariffs 1947 ... 1.01, 1.06, 1.07, 1.09, 1.15, 1.19, 1.31, 1.32, 1.33, 1.41, 2.091, 2.179, 2.180, 2.189, 3.001, 3.002, 3.003, 3.008, 3.010, 3.014, 3.015, 3.016, 3.017, 3.019, 3.021, 3.024, 3.027, 3.030, 3.031, 3.032, 3.033, 3.034, 3.035, 3.036, 3.037, 3.037/1, 3.038, 3.039, 3.041, 3.042, 3.043, 3.044, 3.045, 3.046, 3.049, 3.077, 3.079, 3.082, 3.084, 3.090, 3.091, 3.092, 3.094, 3.099, 3.100, 3.101, 3.103, 3.105, 3.106, 3.108, 3.111, 3.113, 4.014, 4.032, 4.041, 4.140, 5.01, 5.02, 5.09, 5.10, 5.12, 5.13, 5.14, 5.30, 5.43, 5.44, 5.51, 5.53, 5.54, 6.01, 6.12, 6.13, 6.18, 6.20, 6.22, 6.23, 6.24, 6.28, 6.32, 6.35, 6.37, 6.51, 6.52, 6.53, 6.54, 6.57, 6.58, 6.59, 6.64, 6.67, 6.69, 6.74, 6.76, 6.78, 6.79, 6.87, 6.90, 6.92, 6.96, 6.97, 6.98

Pt. II ... 3.002
Art. I ... 6.69
Art. II ... 3.003
Art. II:4 ... 3.010, 3.011, 3.012, 3.012, 3.013, 3.014, 6.55, 6.56, 6.64
Art. III ... 3.010, 3.014, 3.015, 3.019, 3.077, 3.079, 3.113, 6.69
Art. III:1 ... **3.037**
Art. III:2 ... **3.016**
Art. III:4 ... **3.017**, 3.018, 3.019, 3.020, 3.037, 3.077, 3.079, 3.105, 3.106, 3.108, 3.112, 3.115, 6.57, 6.58, 6.59, 6.60, 6.62, 6.84
Art. III:5 ... 3.077
Art. III:7 ... 3.077
Art. V ... 2.140, 5.32
Art. VI 1.25, 3.021, 3.112, 3.113, 3.114, 3.115, 4.042, 4.127, 5.10, 6.85
Art. VI:1 ... 3.021, 3.100, 3.113, 3.114, 6.85
Art. VI:2 ... 3.021, 3.100, 3.113, 3.115
Art. IX ... 3.046
Art. IX:2 ... 3.046

General Agreement on Tariffs 1947—*cont.*
Art. IX:6 ... 3.046
Art. X 3.010, 3.022, 3.021, 3.024, 3.105, 5.34
Art. X:1 ... 3.022, 3.107, 3.109, 5.34
Art. XI ... 3.010, 3.025, 3.026, 3.037, 3.079, 3.094, 6.51, 6.64, 6.68
Art. XI:1 ... 3.025, 3.026, 3.029, 3.040, 3.079, 3.094, 6.65, 6.66
Art. XII ... 3.047
Art. XII:3(c)(iii) ... 3.047
Art. XVII ... 3.010, 3.027, 3.029, 4.028, 6.68, 6.69
Art. XVII:1(a) ... **3.027**
(b) ... 3.027, 6.68
Art. XVIII:10 ... 3.047
Art. XIX ... 1.17, 3.093, 3.094
Art. XX ... 3.028, 3.048
Art. XX(d) ... 3.010, 3.028, 3.029, 3.048
Art. XXII ... 3.006
Art. XXII:1(c) ... 6.89
Art. XXIII ... 1.15, 3.034, 3.035, 3.090, 6.78
Art. XXIII:1 ... 6.51, 6.52
(a) ... 3.030, 6.06, 6.53, 6.58, 6.64, 6.71, 6.73, 6.77, 6.80
(b) ... 3.010, 3.030, 3.032, 3.105, 3.106, 3.108, 6.06, 6.10, 6.78, 6.79, 6.80, 6.81, 6.84, 6.85, 6.89, 6.90
(c) ... 3.033, 6.78, 6.87, 6.88, 6.88
Art. XXIII:2 ... 3.034
Art. XXIV ... 1.17, 2.140, 5.32, 5.33
Art. XXVI:6 ... 3.003
Art. XXVIII:1(c) ... 3.010
Art. XXIX ... 3.002
Annex 1A ... 3.010
General Agreement on Tariffs 1947 .. 3.003, 3.008, 3.010, 3.034, 3.084, 6.88
Annex H ... 3.003
General Agreement on Trade in Services 1994 ... 3.007, 3.044, 3.045, 3.060, 3.065, 3.071, 3.073, 3.099, 3.116, 5.02, 6.13, 6.28, 6.31, 6.54, 6.70, 6.71, 6.76
Pt. III ... 3.070
Art. I:1 ... 3.060
Art. I:3 ... 3.060

General Agreement on Trade in Services 1994—*cont.*
Art. VII 3.061
Art. VII:2 .... 3.061
Art. VII:4 .... 3.061
Art. VII:5 .... 3.061
Art. VIII ... 1.34, 3.007, 3.062, 6.71, 6.86
Art. VIII:1 .... 3.062
Art. VIII:2 .... 3.062
Art. IX ... 1.34, 3.007, 3.062, 6.11, 6.31, 6.86
Art. XIII 3.071
Protocol 4 .... 3.073
Annex on Telecommunications 3.007, 3.044, 3.063, 3.064, 3.065, 3.067
Havana Charter on the International Trade Organisation, March 24, 1948 1.51, 2.189, 3.001, 3.002, 3.003, 3.004, 3.005, 3.007, 3.009, 6.22, 6.23
Chapter V 2.190, 3.005, 3.007, 3.008, 3.009, 3.034, 6.24
Art. 31 .... 6.56
(5) 6.56
Art. 46 .... 3.001, 3.004, 3.006, 3.007
(1) 3.004, 3.006, 3.007
(2) 3.004, 3.006, 3.007
(3) 3.005, 3.006, 3.007
Art. 47 .... 3.006, 3.008
Art. 48 .... 3.004, 3.006, 3.007
(1) 3.006
(4) 3.006
(7) 3.006, 3.007
(10) 3.006
Art 49 .... 3.008
Art. 50 .... 3.004, 3.007
Art. 50(1) 3.007
(3) 3.006
Art. 51 .... 3.008
Art. 52 .... 3.008
Art. 53 .... 3.007
Art. 54 .... 3.001, 3.008
International Antitrust Code (Draft) .. 2.178, 2.179, 2.180, 2.184, 2.186, 2.187
Pt 1 .... 2.179
Pt 2 .... 2.180
Pt 3 .... 2.184
Pt 6 .... 2.186
Pt 8 .... 2.186
Art. 4, 1 .... 2.180
Art. 4, 2 .... 2.180
Art. 5 .... 2.181
Art. 5, 1 .... 2.181
International Antitrust Code (Draft)—*cont.*
Art. 5, 2 .... 2.181
3(a) 2.181
4 .... 2.182
Art. 6 .... 2.182
Art. 6, 1 .... 2.182
2 .... 2.182
Art. 7 .... 2.182
Art. 9, 2(a) 2.184
Art. 10 .... 2.184
Art. 14 .... 2.185
Art. 15 .... 2.185
Art. 15, 1 .... 2.185
Art. 15, 6 .... 2.185
Art. 19 .... 2.186
International Antitrust Guidelines (1995) 2.007, 2.016, 2.019, 2.020, 2.034
Multilateral Agreement on Investment 1998 .... 1.42, 1.44, 2.151, 6.21
Multilaterally Agreed Equitable Principles and Rules for the Control of Restrictive Business Practices, April 22, 1980 .... 2.193, 2.194, 2.198
s. B(i)(1) 2.193
s. C(i)(1), (2) 2.194
s. D(1), (2) 2.194
(3)(a)—(g) 2.195
(4) 2.196
s. E 2.197
s. F 2.197
s. G 2.197
North American Free Trade Agreement 1992 ...... 2.092, 2.118, 2.129, 2.130, 2.131, 2.133, 2.134, 2.135, 2.136, 2.177, 4.038, 4.126, 6.24
Chapter 11 .... 2.133
Chapter 12 .... 2.131
Chapter 15 .... 2.129, 2.130, 2.133
Chapter 14 .... 2.131, 2.133
Art. 102 .... 2.130
Art. 102.1(b) 2.130
Art. 1501 .... 2.129
Art. 1501.1 .... 2.130
Art. 1501.2 .... 2.131
Art. 1501.3 .... 2.131
Art. 1502 .... 2.132
Art. 1502.3(a) 2.132
(b) 2.132
(c) 2.132
(d) 2.132

North American Free Trade Agreement 1992—*cont.*
Art. 1502.4 . . . . 2.132
Art. 1503 . . . . 2.133
Art. 1503.2 . . . . 2.133
Art. 1503.3 . . . . 2.133
Art. 1504 . . . . 2.130, 2.135
Art. 1505 . . . . 2.130
Art. 1704 . . . . **2.134**
Restrictive Business Practices Code (UNCTAD) 1980 . . . . 5.19
TRIPS Agreement. *See* Agreement on the Trade—Related Aspects of Intellectual Property Rights 1994
Treaty of Asuncion 1991 . . . . . 2.117, 2.118, 2.119, 2.120, 2.121, 2.122, 2.124, 2.126, 2.127, 2.128, 5.56
Treaty between the Government of the United States of America and the Government of Australia on Mutual Assistance in Criminal Matters, April 30, 1997, S. Treaty Doc. No. 27, 105th; Cong. 2d Sess. 1997 . . 2.072
Art. II:2 . . . . 2.072
Treaty between the United States of America and the Republic of Poland on Mutual Legal Assistance in Criminal Matters, July 10, 1996, S. Treaty Doc. No. 12, 105th; Cong., 1st Sess. 1996 . . . . 2.072
Treaty Concerning the Cayman Islands Relating to Mutual Legal Assistance in Criminal Matters, July 3, 1986; S. Treaty Doc. No. 100–8 . . . . 2.073
Art. 1(1) 2.073
Art. 2(1) 2.073
Art. 19(3) 2.073
Treaty of Mutual Legal Assistance in Criminal Matters between the United States and Canada, March 18, 1985, S. Treaty Doc. No. 14, 100th; Cong., 2d Sess. 1988 . . . . 2.073, 2.074, 2.075, 2.078
Art. I 2.074
Art. II:3 . . . . 2.072, 2.073
Art. VII 2.074
Annex 2.074
Treaty on Mutual Assistance in Criminal Matters between United States and Bahamas, June 12–Aug. 18, 1987, S. Treaty Doc. 100–17 . . . . 2.073
Treaty of Mutual Legal Assistance in Criminal Matters between the United States and Mexico, December 9, 1987, S. Treaty Doc. No. 100–13 (Mexico—U.S. MLAT) 2.073
Art. 1 . . . . 2.073
Uruguay Round Antidumping Agreement. *See* Agreement on Implementation of Art. VI of the General Agreement on Tariffs and Trade 1994.
Voluntary Export Restraint Agreements 1.50, 3.087, 3.089, 3.090, 3.091, 3.092, 3.093, 3.094
WTO Agreement on Competition Policy 1.42, 1.52, 5.42, 5.57, 6.01, 6.33
WTO Agreement on the Application on Sanitary and Phytosanitary Measures 1994 . . . . 6.35
WTO Antidumping Agreement. *See* Agreement on Implementation of Art. VI of the General Agreement on Tariffs and Trade 1994. . . . . 1.25
WTO Dispute Settlement Understanding 1994 . . . . 3.008, 3.033, 3.050, 4.006, 4.039, 5.15, 5.21, 5.29, 5.39, 5.40, 6.18, 6.80, 6.90, 6.91
Art. 4 . . . . 3.006
Art. 16(4) 6.88
Art. 22 . . . . 5.13, 6.53
Art. 26(1) 6.80
Art. 26.1(a) 6.79
(b) 5.13, 6.80
(d) 6.80
Art. 26.2 . . . . 6.88
WTO Framework Agreement on Core Principles 5.29
WTO Safeguards Agreement 1994 . . . . 1.50, 3.005, 3.087
Art. 2.1 . . . . 3.094
Art. 11.1(b) 3.005, 3.094
Art. 11.2 . . . . 3.094
Art. 11.3 . . . . 3.094
World Trade Organisation 1994 . . . . . . 1.01, 1.02, 1.03, 1.04, 1.06, 1.07, 1.09, 1.11, 1.19, 1.31, 1.32, 1.33, 1.35, 1.36, 1.37, 1.38, 1.40, 1.41, 1.42, 1.43, 1.44, 1.45, 1.46, 1.47, 1.52, 1.53, 2.039, 2.041, 2.066,

World Trade Organisation 1994—*cont.*
2.091, 3.001, 3.005, 3.010, 3.015, 3.021, 3.024, 3.030, 3.033, 3.042, 3.043, 3.045, 3.050, 3.061, 3.070, 3.076, 3.082, 3.094, 3.099, 3.101, 3.116, 4.001, 4.007, 4.008, 4.009, 4.011, 4.013, 4.014, 4.015, 4.030, 4.032, 4.034, 4.039, 4.040, 4.041, 4.050, 4.140, 4.168, 5.01, 5.02, 5.07, 5.09, 5.10, 5.12, 5.13, 5.14, 5.15, 5.25, 5.26, 5.30, 5.32, 5.43, 5.51, 5.53, 5.54, 6.01, 6.02, 6.03, 6.06, 6.07. 6.09, 6.10, 6.11, 6.12, 6.13, 6.14, 6.15, 6.20, 6.22, 6.24, 6.26, 6.28, 6.29, 6.30, 6.31, 6.32, 6.33, 6.34, 6.35, 6.36, 6.37, 6.38, 6.39, 6.41, 6.42, 6.46, 6.48, 6.50, 6.51, 6.52, 6.54, 6.67, 6.68, 6.69, 6.75, 6.76, 6.78, 6.79, 6.87, 6.91, 6.92, 6.95, 6.96, 6.97, 6.98, 6.99

TABLE OF GATT AND WTO REPORTS

Australian Subsidy on Ammonium Sulphate, Report of the Working Party, BISD II/188, 191 (1950) ... 5.45, 6.78, 6.82

Belgian Family Allowances, GATT Panel, BISD 1st Supp. 59, 60 (adopted November 7, 1952) 6.69

Canada—Administration of the Foreign Investment Review Act, GATT Panel, BISD 30th Supp. 140 (adopted February 7, 1984) 3.018, 3.037, 3.077, 6.85

Canada—Import, Distribution and Sale of Alcoholic Drinks by Canadian Provincial Marketing Agencies, GATT Panel, BISD, 35th Supp. 37 (adopted March 22, 1988) 3.012, 6.55, 6.68, 6.69

Canada—Import, Distribution and Sale of Alcoholic Drinks by Canadian Provincial Marketing Agencies, GATT Panel, BISD, 39th Supp. 37 (adopted February 18, 1992) 3.014, 3.023, 6.69

E.C.—Tariff Treatment on Imports of Citrus Products from Certain Countries in the Mediterranean Region, GATT Panel, GATT Doc. L/5576 (unadopted, February 7, 1985) 6.78, 6.83

EEC—Payments and Subsidies Paid to Processors and Producers of Oilseeds and Related Animal-Feed Proteins, GATT Panel, BISD 37th Supp. 86 (adopted January 25, 1990) 3.026, 3.030, 3.032, 6.78, 6.79

EEC—Production Aids Granted on Canned Peaches, Canned Pears, Canned Fruit Cocktail and Dried Grapes, GATT Panel, GATT Doc. L/5778 (unadopted, February 20, 1985) 6.78

EEC—Regulations on Imports of Parts and Components, GATT Panel, 37th Supp. 197 (1990) 3.018

EEC—Restrictions on Imports of Appeals, GATT Panel, BISD, 36th Supp. 135 (1989) 3.023

European Communities—Egime for the Importation, Sale and Distribution of Bananas, Report of the Appellate Body, WT/DS27/AB/R (1997) 5.14, 6.35, 6.39

European Communities—Measures Affecting Asbestos and Asbestos-Containing Products, WTO Panel, WT/DS135/R (2000) 6.78

European Communities—Measures Concerning Meat and Meat Products (Hormones), Report of the Appellate Body, WT/DS26/AB/R (1998) 5.14, 6.35, 6.39

International Competition Policy Advisory Committee to the Attorney General and Assistant Attorney General for Antitrust, Final Report 33 (2000) 1.03, 1.05, 1.28, 1.36, 1.37

International Competition Policy Advisory Committee to the Attorney General and Assistant Attorney General for Antitrust, Final Report 36 (2000) (final) 2.036, 2.056, 2.061, 2.072, 2.073, 2.078, 2.079, 2.082, 2.087, 2.192

International Competition Policy Advisory Committee to the Attorney General and Assistant Attorney General for Antitrust, Final Report 186 (2000) 4.059, 4.060, 4.116, 4.117, 4.144, 4.146, 4.148, 4.149, 4.150, 4.151, 4.155, 4.156, 4.164, 4.174, 6.04, 6.05, 6.11, 6.34, 6.37

International Competition Policy Advisory Committee to the Attorney General and Assistant Attorney General for Antitrust, Final Report 244 (2000) 2.012, 2.018, 2.019

Italian Discrimination against Imported Agricultural Machinery, GATT Panel, BISD 7th Supp. 60 (adopted October 23, 1958) 3.017, 6.57

Japan—Measures Affecting Consumer Photographic Film and Paper, WTO Panel, WT/DS44/R (adopted April. 22, 1998) 2.021, 2.065, 3.032, 3.033, 3.099, 3.101, 3.103, 3.105, 3.106, 3.108, 3.109, 3.111, 3.116, 4.167, 5.08, 5.34, 5.41, 5.47, 6.50, 6.51, 6.58, 6.66, 6.68, 6.78, 6.79, 6.83, 6.84, 6.93

Japan—Restriction on Imports of Certain Agricultural Products, GATT Panel, BISD, 35th Supp. 163 (1988) 3.029

Japan—Trade in Semi-Conductors, GATT Panel, BISD, 35th Supp. 116 (adopted May 8, 1988) ... 3.025, 3.040, 3.094, 6.65, 6.66, 6.78

Kodak-Fuji Film. *See* Japan—Measures Affecting Consumer Photographic Film and Paper (1998).

Report of the Group of Exports on restrictive Business Practices: Arrangements for Consultations, BISD, 9th Supp. 170 (1961) 3.034, 3.035

Republic of Korea—Restrictions on Imports of Beef, GATT Panel, BISD, 36th Supp. 202 (adopted November 7, 1989) 6.56, 6.68

Special Study on Trade and Competition Policy, WTO Annual Report 56 (December, 1997) 4.051, 4.161, 4.174, 5.07

Thailand—Restrictions on Importation of and Internal Taxes on Cigarettes, GATT Panel, BISD, 37th Supp. 200 (adopted November 7, 1990) 3.027, 6.69

Treatment by Germany of Imports of Sardines, GATT Panel, BISD, 1st Supp. 53 (adopted October 31, 1952) 6.78

United States—Agricultural Waiver, GATT Panel, BISD, 37th Supp. 228 (adopted November 7, 1990) 6.78

United States—Antidumping Act of 1916, Report of the Appellate Body, WT/DS136/AB/R, WT/DS162/AB/R (2000) 3.113, 3.114, 6.58, 6.59, 6.60

United States—Anti-Dumping Act of 1916, WTO Panel, WT/DS136/R (2000) 3.113

United States—Anti-Dumping Act of 1916, WTO Panel, WT/DS162/R (2000) 3.113

United States—Denial of Most-Favoured-Nation Treatment as to Non-Rubber Footwear from Brazil, GATT Panel, BISD, 39th Supp. 128 (1992) 3.019

United States—Imports of Certain Automotive Spring Assemblies, GATT Panel, BISD, 30th Supp. 107 (1984) 3.049

United States—Restrictions on Imports of Cotton and Man-Made Fibre Underwear, WTO Panel, WT/DS24/R (1997) 3.109

United States—Section 337 of the Tariff Act of 1930, GATT Panel, BISD, 36th Supp. 345 (adopted November 7, 1989) 3.019, 3.049, 6.58, 6.60, 6.61

United States—Taxes on Petroleum and Certain Imported Substances, GATT Panel, BISD, 34th Supp. 136 (adopted 27, 1987) 3.016

United States—Measures Affecting Alcoholic and Malt Beverages GATT Panel, BISD 39th Supp. 206 (adopted June 19, 1992) 3.016
Uruguayan Recourse to Article XXIII, GATT Panel, BISD, 11th Supp. 95 (adopted November 16, 1962) 6.78, 6.87
WTO, Report on Government Procurement, GPA/44 (November 2, 2000) 3.095
WTO, Working Group on the Interaction between Trade and Competition Policy Report to the General Council, WT/WGTCP/W/49 (November 25, 1997) 4.015
WTO, Working Group on the Interaction between Trade and Competition Policy Report to the General, WT/WGTCP/2 (December 8, 1998) 1.10, 1.33, 1.48, 3.042, 4.016, 4.017, 4.019, 4.020, 4.022, 4.024, 4.029, 4.050, 4.112, 4.142, 5.22, 5.23, 6.03, 6.15, 6.96
WTO, Working Group on the Interaction between Trade and Competition Policy Report to the General, WT/WGTCP/3 (October 11, 1999) . . . 1.41, 2.171, 4.032, 4.034, 4.035, 4.036, 4.037, 4.039, 4.040, 4.041, 4.042, 4.059, 4.129, 4.138, 4.140, 4.142, 5.17, 5.18, 5.25, 6.03, 6.04
World Trade Organisation, Annual Report (1999) 1.07, 6.75

List of Abbreviations

ACCC	Australian Competition and Consumer Commission
AD	antidumping
ALADI	Latin American Integration Association
Am. J. Int'l L.	American Journal of International Law
Am. U.J. Int'l L. & Pol'y	American University Journal of International Law and Policy
Am. U.L. Rev.	American University Law Review
Antitrust Bull.	Antitrust Bulletin
Antitrust L.J.	Antitrust Law Journal
Antitrust & Trade Reg. Rep.	Antitrust & Trade Regulation Reporter
ANZCERTA	Australian-New Zealand Closer Economic Relations Trade Agreement
APA	Administrative Procedure Act
APEC	Asia-Pacific Economic Co-operation forum
Ariz. J. Int'l & Comp. L.	Arizona Journal of International & Comparative Law
ASEAN	Association of Southeast Asian Nations
Asian Wall St. J.	Asian Wall Street Journal
Ass'n	Association
B.L.R.	Business Law Review
BOP	Balance-of-payments
Brooklyn J. Int'l L.	Brooklyn Journal of International Law
B.U.L. Rev.	Boston University Law Review
B.Y.U.L. Rev.	Brigham Young University Law Review
Canadian B. Rev.	Canadian Bar Review
Canadian Bus. L.J.	Canadian Business Law Journal
Can.-U.S. L.J.	Canada-U.S. Law Journal
CARICOM	Caribbean Community
Chi. J. Int'l L.	University of Chicago Journal of International Law
Chi.-Kent L. Rev.	Chicago-Kent Law Review
Christian Sci. Monitor	Christian Science Monitor
CLP	Competition Law and Policy
C.M.L.R.	Common Market Law Reports
Colo. L. Rev.	Colorado Law Review
Colum. J. Eur. L.	Columbia Journal of European Law
Colum. J. Transnat'l L.	Columbia Journal of Transnational Law
Comm'n	Commission
Common Mkt. Rep.	Common Market Report

Cong. Rec.	Congressional Record
Conn. J. Int'l L.	Connecticut Journal of International Law
Cornell Int'l L.J.	Cornell International Law Journal
Corp. Couns. Int'l Adviser	Corporate Counsel International Adviser
C.P.R.	Canada Patent Reporter
CTI	Committee on Trade and Investment
D.C. Cir.	Court of Appeals for the District of Columbia
Dep't	Department
Dep't St. Dispatch	Department of State Dispatch
DePaul L. Rev.	DePaul Law Review
DOJ	Department of Justice
DSU	Dispute Settlement Understanding
ECOSOC	United Nations Economic and Social Council
E.C.L.R.	European Competition Law Review
Econ. Perspectives	Economic Perspectives
E.C.R.	European Court Reports
EFTA	European Free Trade Area
FCC	Federal Competition Commission
Fordham Corp. L. Inst.	Fordham Corporate Law Institute
Fordham Intell. Prop., Media & Entertainment L.J.	Fordham Intellectual Property, Media and Entertainment Law Journal.
Food & Drug L.J.	Food and Drug Law Journal
Fordham Int'l L.J.	Fordham International Law Journal
Fordham L. Rev.	Fordham Law Review
FSIA	Foreign Sovereign Immunities Act
F. Supp.	Federal Supplement
FTAA	Free Trade Area of the Americas
FTAIA	Foreign Trade Antitrust Improvements Act
FTC	Federal Trade Commission
GATS	General Agreement on Trade in Services
GATT	General Agreement on Tariffs and Trade
Geo. L.J.	Georgetown Law Journal
Geo. Mason L. Rev.	George Mason Law Review
Geo. Wash. J. Int'l L. & Econ.	George Washington Journal of International Law and Economics
German Y.B. Int'l L.	German Yearbook of International Law
Global Comp. Rev.	Global Competition Review
Harv. Int'l L.J.	Harvard International Law Journal
Harv.L. Rev.	Harvard Law Review

Hastings Int'l & Comp. L. Rev.	Hastings International and Comparative Law Review
Hastings L.J.	Hastings Law Journal
Hous. J. Int'l L.	Houston Journal of International Law
H.R. Res.	House of Representatives Resolution
HSR	Hart-Scott-Rodino Antitrust Improvements Act of 1976
IAA	International Antitrust Authority
IAEAA	International Antitrust Enforcement Assistance Act of 1994
ICPAC	International Competition Policy Advisory Committee
Industry, Trade & Tech. Rev.	Industry Trade and Technology Review
Inter-Am. Legal Materials	Inter-American Legal Materials
Int'l Econ. Rev.	International Economic Review
Int'l Fin. L. Rev.	International Finance Law Review
Int'l Law.	International Lawyer
Int'l Leg. Materials	International Legal Materials
Int'l Rev. L. & Econ.	International Review Law & Economics
Int'l Trade Rep.	International Trade Reporter
IPRs	intellectual property rights
ITC	International Trade Commission
ITO	International Trade Organisation
J. Copyright Soc.	Journal of Copyright Society
JFTC	Japan Fair Trade Commission
J. Int'l Arb.	Journal of International Arbitration
J. Int'l L. & Econ.	Journal of International Law and Economics
J. Int'l L. & Prac.	Journal of International Law and Practice
J. Int'l Legal Studies	Journal of International Legal Studies
J. L. & Com.	Journal of Law and Commerce
J. L. & Econ.	Journal of Law and Economics
J. Reprints Antitrust L. & Econ.	Journal of Reprints of Antitrust Law and Economics
J. World Trade	Journal of World Trade
J. World Trade L.	Journal of World Trade Law
Law & Pol'y Int'l Bus.	Law and Policy in International Business
LCFE	Ley Federal de Competencia Economica
LDCs	Least Developed Countries
M&A	Merger and Acquisition
MAI	Multilateral Agreement on Investment

MERCOSUR	Common Market of the Southern Cone (in Spanish, "*Mercado Comun del Sur*" or "MERCOSUR" in Portuguese, "MERCOSUL")
MFN	most favoured nation
Mich. L. Rev.	Michigan Law Review
Minn. J. Global Trade	Minnesota Journal of Global Trade
MITI	Ministry of International Trade and Industry
MLATs	Mutual legal assistance treaties
MNEs	multinational enterprises
MOU	Memorandum of Understanding
MTN	Multilateral trade negotiation
N.C.J. Int'l & Com. Reg.	North Carolina Journal of International and Commercial Regulation
New Eng. L. Rev.	New England Law Review
NW. J. Int'l L. & Bus.	Northwestern Journal of International Law and Business
N.Y.U.L. Rev.	New York University Law Review
OECD	Organisation for Economic Co-operation and Development
OECD J. Competition L. & Pol'y	OECD Journal of Competition Law and Policy
O.J.	Official Journal of the European Communities
OPEC	Organisation of Petroleum Exporting Countries
O.R.	Ontario Reports
Pac. Econ. Rev.	Pacific Economic Review
Pac. Rim L. & Pol'y J.	Pacific Rim Law & Policy Journal
PECC	Pacific Economic Co-operation Council
PPEG	the Predatory Pricing Enforcement Guidelines
RBPs	Restrictive business practices
R.S.C.	Revised Statutes of Canada
RTAs	Regional trade arrangements
San Diego L. Rev.	San Diego Law Review
S.C.R.	Supreme Court of Canada
S. Cal. L. Rev.	Southern California Law Review
S. Ct.	Supreme Court Reporter
Seton Hall Legis. J.	Seton Hall Legislative Journal
SMEs	Small and medium-sized enterprises

Stan. J. Int'l L.	Stanford Journal of International Law
St. John's J. Legal Comment.	St. John's Journal of Legal Commentary
Sw. J. L. & Trade Am.	Southwestern Journal of Law & Trade in the Americas
Temp. L. Rev.	Temple Law Review
Tex. L. Rev.	Texas Law Review
TPRB	Trade Policy Review Body
TPRM	Trade Policy Review Mechanism
TRACLAP Agreement	Agreement on Trade-Related Aspects of Competition Law and Policy
Trade Reg. Rep.	Trade Regulation Reporter
Trademark Rep.	Trademark Reporter
TRAM Agreement	Agreement on Trade-Related Antitrust Measures
TRIMs Agreement	Agreement on Trade-Related Investment Measures
Transnat'l Law.	Transnational Lawyer
Transnat'l L. & Contemp. Prob.	Transnational Law and Contemporary Problems
TRAPS Agreement	Agreement on Trade-Related Antitrust Principles
TRIPs Agreement	Agreement on the Trade-Related Aspects of Intellectual Property Rights
UNCTAD	United Nations Conference on Trade and Development
U. Chi. L. Rev.	University of Chicago Law Review
U. Chi. Legal F.	University of Chicago Legal Forum
U. Cin. L. Rev.	University of Cincinnati Law Review
U.C.L.A. J. Int'l L. & For. Aff.	University of California-Los Angeles Journal of International Law and Foreign Affairs
U. Miami Inter-Am. L. Rev.	University of Miami Inter-American Law Review
U. Pa. J. Int'l Bus. L.	University of Pennsylvania Journal of International Business Law
U. Pa. J. Int'l Econ. L.	University of Pennsylvania Journal of International Economic Law
USTR	U.S. Trade Representative
U.S.-Mex. L.J.	U.S.-Mexico Law Journal
Va. J. Int'l L.	Virginia Journal of International Law
Vand. J. Transnat'l L.	Vanderbilt Journal of Transnational Law
VERs	Voluntary export restraint agreements
VRA	Voluntary restraint agreement
Wake Forrest L. Rev.	Wake Forrest Law Review

Wash. L. Rev.	Washington Law Review
Wash. & Lee L. Rev.	Washington & Lee Law Review
WGTCP	Working Group on the Interaction between Trade and Competition Policy
Whittier L. Rev.	Whittier Law Review
WIPO	World Intellectual Property Organisation
World Econ.	World Economy
World Econ. Affairs	World Economic Affairs
World Pol.	World Politics
WTO	World Trade Organisation
Yale L. J.	Yale Law Journal

CHAPTER ONE

Trade and Competition Policy at the World Trade Organisation: An Introduction and Overview

1.01 As the General Agreement on Tariffs and Trade (GATT) and its successor, the World Trade Organisation (WTO), have progressively removed or lowered government barriers to trade, the focus of policymakers has shifted to private barriers to market access that could undermine the progress of the GATT–WTO system. To what extent do private anti-competitive practices, as opposed to government barriers, block access to foreign markets? If they do inhibit market access to a significant extent, what should policymakers' response be?

1.02 The best method for removing these private barriers to market access, some argue, is through vigorous application of national competition laws.[1] National competition legislation directed at private anti-competitive conduct, the argument runs, is a natural complement to a set of international rules regulating government barriers to market access. Others state that a more appropriate response is to negotiate a multilateral agreement on binding rules and principles on competition policy. The proponents of a global response look to the World Trade Organisation as the forum for negotiating, administering, and enforcing these multilateral rules and principles.

Increased globalisation means that the effects of restrictive business practices are felt beyond national borders. Such practices can reduce the benefits of open trade and investment liberalisation in at least three ways. First, international cartels among multinational firms that fix prices or allocate world markets can have an adverse impact on several markets simultaneously. Secondly, import cartels, exclusionary practices of firms with a dominant position in a domestic market, and anti-competitive vertical agreements

[1] As used in this book, the term "competition laws" refers to that body of national legislation dealing with anti-competitive conduct in four broad areas: (1) horizontal restraints, *e.g.* agreements among competing firms to fix prices; (2) vertical restraints, *e.g.* agreements between a manufacturer and distributor on resale price maintenance; (3) abuse of a dominant position or, as described under U.S. antitrust law, unlawful monopolisation; and (4) mergers and acquisitions. The term "competition policy" refers to the goals that competition law is to designed to achieve, that is, competition law is the means to accomplishing the ends of competition policy. Competition policy thus informs the drafting, implementation and enforcement of competition law.

between domestic manufacturers and their parts suppliers can have anti-competitive effects in a domestic market by blocking market access to foreign goods and services. Thirdly, export cartels and firms with a dominant position can take action in a home market whose anti-competitive effects are felt in a foreign market.

1.03 At the turn of the nineteenth century, only one country had competition legislation—the United States. Until a few years ago, competition law was purely a domestic issue that arose in advanced economy countries. Today, it has a new name—competition policy, signifying a set of issues broader than the prescriptive rules of antitrust law—and has become a priority topic on policymakers' agendas. This change was triggered by several factors, including the simultaneous trends toward globalisation and regional integration, the creation of the World Trade Organisation, and the growing number of competition cases involving more than one country.[2] At the turn of the twentieth century, more than 80 countries have now enacted competition legislation, 60 per cent of which was introduced in the 1990s.[3] Another 20 or more countries are in the process of drafting and enacting competition laws. Those countries with competition laws account for nearly 80 per cent of total world output and 86 per cent of world trade.[4]

1.04 The question before the WTO is whether the mutually-reinforcing roles that international trade and competition policy play in opening markets to foreign goods, services, and capital, together with the 80-plus national competition laws, should be integrated into a WTO multilateral agreement on competition policy. This book answers that question in the negative. The reasons for doing so are developed in the following five chapters.

I. WHAT IS THE TRADE AND COMPETITION POLICY RELATIONSHIP?

1.05 International trade and competition policy share several common themes.[5] They also diverge at several critical points.

A. Complementarities between Trade and Competition Policy

1.06 Although nowhere explicitly stated in GATT or in any WTO agreement, the guiding economic premise that underlies the entire GATT–WTO system is open trade. One commentator has explained open trade (sometimes referred to as liberal trade) in the following terms:

---

[2] See UNCTAD, "Competition Cases Involving More Than One Country," Preliminary note prepared by the UNCTAD Secretariat from inputs received from Member States, TD/B/COM.2/CLP/9 (1999).

[3] See "International Competition Policy Advisory Committee to the Attorney General and Assistant Attorney General for Antitrust, Final Report" 33 (2000) (hereinafter "ICPAC Final Report").

[4] See "ICPAC Final Report", *supra* note 3, at 33 n.1; Mark R.A. Palim, "The Worldwide Growth of Competition Law: An Empirical Analysis", (Spring 1998) XLIII Antitrust Bull. 105, 109.

[5] See "ICPAC Final Report", *supra* note 3, at 201–81; OECD, "Trade and Competition Policies: Exploring the Ways Forward" (1999); Michael J. Trebilcock, "Competition Policy and Trade Policy, Mediating the Interface", (1996) 30 J. World Trade No. 4, at 71.

> In a liberal economic system, government does not thwart private parties in their attempts to enter voluntary transactions, and taxes are stable, predictable, and nonprohibitive. The General Agreement on Tariffs and Trade (GATT) is liberal in this sense. . . . Interventions [by governments] in liberal exchange across frontiers to make trade fair may be the political price of liberalism, but such interventions are themselves its antithesis.[6]

Why did open trade become GATT's desideratum? The answer is short but compelling: by exploiting the law of comparative advantage, liberal trade policies permit the unrestricted cross-border flow of the highest-quality goods and services at the lowest prices, thereby increasing total world wealth. Under the law of comparative advantage resources are allocated efficiently across and within industries in response to competitive pressures from imports. Both of these phenomena lead to product specialisation and increased firm size that in turn lowers the unit cost of goods and services.

1.07 The eight multilateral trade negotiation rounds sponsored by the General Agreement on Tariffs and Trade since 1947 have resulted in the progressive reduction of tariffs and non-tariff barriers to trade in goods and services and with it technological innovation, investment, lower prices for goods and services, and growth in world gross domestic product.[7] By reducing tariffs and non-tariff barriers to trade, the liberal trade policy embodied in GATT and the WTO agreements creates export opportunities and spurs international competition among businesses.

In sum, the role that multilateral trade rules play in fostering liberal trade manifests itself in two important ways. First, specialisation and economies of scale become possible because of secure access to a barrier-free international market. Secondly, increased international competition leads to product and process innovation, further reducing costs and expanding consumer choices.

1.08 This second point leads to an inquiry as to what the relationship between trade policy and competition policy is.[8] Like the goal of a liberal trade policy, the goal of competition policy is in general to promote the efficient allocation of resources by ensuring that markets are open and competitive. The objectives of a liberal trade policy closely match and complement those of competition policy. The reduction of government barriers to trade that shield domestic firms from import competition—the objective of a liberal trade policy—complements competition policy's goal of shielding consumers from private firms who either unilaterally or collectively set prices higher than those that would prevail under competitive market conditions. Firms are able to charge higher than competitive prices when they have market power, but firms are unlikely to have such power when barriers to market entry are low.

1.09 On the trade policy side, reducing or eliminating government-imposed barriers to market entry in the form of tariffs and non-tariff barriers

---

[6] Martin Wolf, "Why trade liberalization is a good idea", in *The Uruguay Round, A Handbook on the Multilateral Trade Negotiations* 14 (J. Michael Finger & Andrzej Olechowski eds. 1987).

[7] See World Trade Organisation, "Annual Report 1999", at 6.

[8] See OECD, "Joint Group on Trade and Competition", Complementarities Between Trade and Competition Policies, COM/TD/DAFFE/CLP(98)98/FINAL (Jan. 29, 1999).

makes markets more competitive through lower-cost imports, in turn making it more difficult for domestic firms to successfully charge abnormally high prices to consumers. On the competition policy side, trade liberalisation can succeed only if anti-competitive practices of private firms are checked through effective competition laws. Competition law thus complements trade policy by ensuring that the reduction or elimination of government barriers to trade are not negated by the anti-competitive behaviour of private firms through the abuse of market power or through collusive behaviour. Like a liberal trade policy that removes government barriers to competition at the border, competition policy removes private barriers to competition behind the border.[9]

1.10 The two policies strive to eliminate or reduce market distortions and barriers to market entry. They share the common objectives of promoting economic efficiency and welfare through non-discriminatory, transparent, rules-based regimes. In the absence of an effective competition law, the gains from liberalised trade may be undermined because of private restraints that deter or prevent access to foreign goods and services. Conversely, the absence of trade and investment liberalisation deters or prevents access to pro-competitive foreign goods and producers, hampering the ability of competition law to promote the contestability of markets.

The economics of competition policy and trade liberalisation are also quite similar. The overarching concern of competition policy is with economic efficiency—allocative and productive (referred to as static efficiency), as well as dynamic.[10] Allocative efficiency is concerned with the exchange and the distribution of resources to meet consumer demands. Productive efficiency assures that a given level of output is achieved at the lowest cost. Dynamic efficiency focuses on the process of innovation in technology, products, and processes to meet changing consumer tastes.[11]

1.11 A liberal trade policy also seeks to remove barriers to trade in order to achieve allocative, productive, and dynamic efficiencies. Professor Philip Marsden observes that the aim of both policies is to improve the efficient allocation of resources. Trade policy contributes to efficiency by removing barriers that impede the ability of foreign firms to access new markets. Competition policy contributes to efficiency by preventing firms from substantially lessening competition. Under competition policy analysis, however, foreign or domestic competitors may be lawfully excluded from a market, so long as competition is not thereby substantially lessened. In such cases, the objective of both policies to efficiently allocate resources is met and an efficient outcome achieved.[12] What must be guarded against, however, is a

[9] This distinction should not be overdrawn, however. One of the pillars of the GATT–WTO system is the national treatment obligation that addresses behind-the-border discrimination against imported products *vis-à-vis* the like domestic product.

[10] See OECD, Joint Group on Trade and Competition, "Consistencies and Inconsistencies Between Trade and Competition Policies", COM/TD/DAFFE/CLP(98)25/FINAL, at 6 (Feb. 25, 1999); Friedl Weiss, "From World Trade Law to World Competition Law", (2000) 23 Fordham Int'l L.J. 250, 256.

[11] See WTO, "Working Group on the Interaction between Trade and Competition Policy, Report to the General Council", WT/WGTCP/2, at 36 n.35 (Dec. 8, 1998).

[12] Philip Marsden, "The Impropriety of WTO 'Market Access' Rules on Vertical Restraints", (1998) 21 World Competition No. 6, at 5, 9.

"market access *über alles*" mindset that dominates thinking at the WTO and among trade policy officials.

1.12 In short, trade and competition policies share the common economic objective of removing barriers—governmental with trade policy, private with competition policy—to the competitive process, thereby ensuring that international markets are open to all entrants. The two policies are mutually reinforcing, but of the two a liberal trade policy that permits the free flow of goods and services across national borders arguably is more likely to cause domestic markets to become more competitive and in the process significantly advance the economic goals of competition policy.

B. Divergences Between Trade and Competition Policy

1.13 Despite their intimate interrelationship and common economic objective, these two policies have important points of departure as well. It cannot be forgotten that trade policy has several facets, just one which is trade promotion. Other objectives of trade policy include raising revenue, protecting producers from import competition, and saving workers' jobs.[13] Trade remedy laws and competition laws can work at cross-purposes. The former are designed to shield domestic producers from foreign competition, whereas the latter are designed to promote competition and thereby benefit domestic consumers and small businesses.

1.14 Competition policy, for example, has as its focus "behind the border" (national) issues, rather than international issues, whereas trade policy addresses "at the border" governmental measures. Moreover, competition policy deals with the efficient allocation of resources within that narrower, national market. Consequently, what might be an efficient allocation of resources within a national market might not be true at the global level. National antitrust laws also exempt certain sectors of the national economy from application of the antitrust laws on grounds of national security, food security, and sovereignty over natural resources. Similarly, international trade law permits the imposition of a temporary safeguard remedy to protect domestic industry from fairly traded imports, thus conflicting with the goal of allocative efficiency in the market.[14]

1.15 In short, allocative efficiency is not a shibboleth in trade or competition policy. A somewhat less charitable assessment is that these

[13] For a collection of the classical and contemporary arguments in support of free trade and the arguments for protectionism, see Raj Bhala, *International Trade Law* (1996) 5–78. See also "The miracle of trade", *The Economist*, Jan. 27, 1996 at 61–62; Richard B. Stewart, "International Trade and Environment: Lessons from the Federal Experience", (1922) 49 Wash. & Lee L. Rev. 1329, 1330.

[14] Economists speak of two kinds of efficiencies that are promoted by competition, static and dynamic efficiency. Static efficiency is subdivided into productive efficiency (operating efficiencies, together with transaction cost savings) and allocative efficiency (the allocation of products through the price system in the optimum manner to satisfy consumer demand). Dynamic efficiency refers to optimal introduction of new products, more efficient production processes, and superior organisational structures over time. See UNCTAD, Report by the UNCTAD Secretariat, "Empirical Evidence of the Benefits from Applying Competition Law and Policy Principles to Economic Development in Order to Attain Greater Efficiency in International Trade and Development" 6–11, TD/B/COM.2/EM/10/Rev.1 (May 25, 1998).

policies are at time contradictory and in a state of conflict. Take, for example, the auto parts negotiations between the United States and Japan in the mid-1990s to open the Japanese market for U.S.-manufactured auto parts. The United States, through the U.S. Trade Representative, complained that market access was virtually foreclosed because of the vertical relationships (*keiretsu*) between Japanese final assemblers and their suppliers. These relationships are long term in nature and cemented through cross-ownership of stock. Although the conduct blocking market access is private in nature, the United States nevertheless pressed its attack under Article XXIII of GATT, arguing that this was a market condition tolerated by the Japanese antitrust authorities that nullified or impaired trade benefits accruing to the United States under GATT. No one on the U.S. side stopped to question (at least publicly) whether this non-tariff barrier to U.S. auto parts trade was sheltering inefficient Japanese parts suppliers. Unless the exclusion from the Japanese auto parts market is inefficient does a misallocation of resources result. The unspoken assumption of U.S. trade negotiators apparently was that because *keiretsu* are exclusionary, they are necessarily inefficient. Market foreclosure was synonymous with market inefficiency. U.S. negotiators either conveniently ignored or were oblivious to Supreme Court jurisprudence that expressly recognises that long-term vertical relationships can have efficiency benefits.[15]

This episode puts in dramatic relief the disconnect between U.S. antitrust enforcement authorities (the Justice Department and the Federal Trade Commission) and U.S. trade authorities. It gives proof to the view that "trade policy is usually concerned with promoting the interests of specific competitors, whereas competition policy is usually concerned with promoting competitive markets."[16] It also fuels the fire of those who advocate a more coherent and integrated approach to the formulation of trade and competition policies.[17]

1.16 The advocates of integrating trade and competition policies argue that increased globalisation of production has made it difficult to identify the national origin of both products and firms. Consequently, under this view, what is important is devising policies that affect the operation of the national and international market, rather than the national identity of firms or imported goods.[18] The focus of such an approach in trade liberalisation negotiations would be on reforming national laws that discriminate between firms on the basis of nationality, national laws that unnecessarily distort the market, and international rules that are essential for the efficient operation of global markets.[19]

[15] See *Continental T.V., Inc. v. GTE Sylvania Inc.*, 433 U.S. 36 (1977); *United States v. General Dynamics Corp.*, 415 U.S. 486, 499–500 (1974).

[16] Daniel K. Tarullo, "Norms and Institutions in Global Competition Policy", (2000) 94 Am. J. Int'l L. 478, 483.

[17] See, *e.g.* Geza Feketekuty, "The Scope, Implication and Economic Rationale of a Competition-Oriented Approach to Future Multilateral Trade Negotiations", TD/TC(96)6 (OECD Apr. 22, 1996).

[18] See Feketekuty, *supra* note 17, at 3.

[19] See *id.* at 5.

Despite their mutually supportive roles, trade policy and competition policy often share an uneasy relationship, diverging and clashing at many points.[20] The underlying rationale of multilateral trade liberalisation is to increase global consumer welfare and achieve global productive efficiency. Competition policy is more focused on consumer welfare within national markets. Much of national trade policy is consumed with fashioning adequate trade remedy laws (*e.g.* safeguards, antidumping, countervailing duty).

1.17 National trade policy makers and legislators decide whether to sacrifice consumer welfare for other goals, including protecting producers or workers within an industry threatened by import competition.[21] The same may also be true for competition policy. For example, public choice theory posits that governments may deviate from a welfare-maximising competition policy for the sake of other non-economic ends, such as protecting "national champions," preventing industrial consolidation that would squeeze out politically-influential small producers, and dispersing control of economic resources.[22] Even when governments have welfare-maximisation in mind when they formulate their competition policy, it will be the welfare maximisation of their constituents, not of foreign consumers and producers who do not vote.

1.18 Competition policy thus reflects national concerns. Take the case of export cartels. Subject to certain qualifications, they are excepted under many countries' competition laws.[23] The upshot is that consumer welfare in the country of importation may be sacrificed for the benefit of producers in the country of exportation. If total global welfare is reduced as a consequence, then the optimal national policy of the country of exportation will not match the optimal global policy. Similarly, for a country exercising extraterritorial antitrust jurisdiction, its national welfare may be enhanced, but global welfare may be reduced. In such a policy environment, reaching an international agreement on competition policy seems unlikely.[24]

[20] See generally "Consistencies and Inconsistencies Between Trade and Competition Policies", *supra* note 10.

[21] For further reading on public choice models applied to international trade policy, see Warren F. Schwartz & Alan O. Sykes, "Toward a Positive Theory of the Most Favored Nation Obligation and Its Exceptions in the WTO/GATT System", (1996) 16 Int'l Rev. L. & Econ. 27 (analysing GATT Art. XXIV on regional trade arrangements using a public choice model); Alan O. Sykes, "Protectionism as a Safeguard: A Positive Analysis of the GATT 'Escape Clause' with Normative Speculations", (1991) 58 U. Chi. L. Rev. 255 (examining GATT Art. XIX on safeguard relief from a public choice perspective).

[22] For an analysis of antitrust policy from a public choice perspective, see *The Causes and Consequences of Antitrust: The Public-Choice Perspective* (Fred S. McChesney & William F. Shughart II eds., 1995).

[23] In addition to the United States, other countries which authorise export cartels include Germany, Japan, the United Kingdom and France, as well as the E.U. See Ulrich Immenga, "Export Cartels and Voluntary Export Restraints Between Trade and Competition Policy", in *Antitrust: A New Trade Remedy*? 93 (John O. Haley & Hiroshi Iyori eds. 1995); A. Paul Victor, "Export Cartels: An Idea Whose Time Has Passed", (1992) 60 Antitrust L.J. 571, 575–77; Nina Hachigan, "Essential Mutual Assistance in International Antitrust Enforcement", (1995) 29 Int'l Law. 117, 126–27.

[24] For an analysis of the welfare enhancing effects of national versus international antitrust legal regimes, see Andrew T. Guzman, "Is International Antitrust Possible?", (1998) 73 N.Y.U.L. Rev. 1501, 1511–21.

1.19 Competition policy can also clash with the market access goal of trade policy to the extent competition policy fails to regulate or actively encourages business practices that are anti-competitive. Such government-condoned business practices that affect market access include:

(1) export cartels,

(2) import cartels, and

(3) trading companies.[25]

Behaviour by domestic firms that are members of cartels, as well as behaviour by importing countries when acting through state trading enterprises, can be anti-competitive when that conduct blocks or impedes market access to imported goods from foreign competitors. The GATT–WTO system is a system built on reciprocity and mutually-beneficial concessions on market access. If competition policy allows private behaviour to erode the benefit of this negotiated bargain by foreclosing market access to exporters, then competition policy will undermine trade policy. If private anti-competitive behaviour is widely tolerated by national antitrust enforcement authorities and if such behaviour has a significant negative impact on market access to foreign producers, then support among exporters—the constituency with the most to lose—for a liberal trade policy will suffer.[26]

1.20 While competition policy and trade policy share the common goals of increasing efficiency and encouraging market access, could one policy replace the other? Although this suggestion might seem fanciful, just such a proposal has been floated in the case of the antidumping duty law.[27] Trade policy is at times schizophrenic, and the antidumping duty law is evidence of this schizophrenia. On the one hand, trade policy encourages opening of foreign markets to imports. On the other hand, trade remedy laws authorise the imposition of trade barriers to protect domestic producers from import competition. Thus, it is important to carefully distinguish the means by which these two policies are executed through the respective remedies available under trade and competition legislation. When examined in the light of law rather than policy, the two seem to work at cross-purposes, at least at the national level.

1.21 Competition law and unfair trade remedy laws differ in respect to the interests they are intended to protect. Take, for example, U.S. antitrust

[25] See generally OECD, "Competition and Trade Policies: Their Interaction" 11–14 (1984); Barry E. Hawk, "Overview", in *Antitrust and Market Access: The Scope and Coverage of Competition Laws and Implications for Trade* (OECD 1996); Eleanor M. Fox, "Competition Law and the Agenda for the WTO: Forging the Links of Competition and Trade", (1995) 4 Pac. Rim L. & Pol'y J. 1.

[26] Robert E. Hudec, "A WTO Perspective on Private Anti-Competitive Behavior in World Markets", (1999) 34 New Eng. L. Rev. 79, 83 (hereinafter Hudec, A WTO Perspective).

[27] See Harvey M. Applebaum, "The Interface of the Trade Laws and the Antitrust Laws", (1998) 6 Geo. Mason L. Rev. 479. An ABA Task Force considered such a convergence/substitution in the context of NAFTA, replacing the antidumping duty law in part with the Robinson-Patman Act on discriminatory pricing. *See* "Report of the ABA Antitrust Section Task Force on the Competition Dimension of the North American Free Trade Agreement", Chap. 6 (1994) (hereinafter "Report of the ABA Task Force").

and trade remedy law. U.S. trade remedy laws—from the countervailing and antidumping duty laws to escape clause relief—are designed to protect domestic industries and the workers in those industries from import competition. The last thing that U.S. trade remedy laws are concerned with is market contestability or the maximisation of consumer welfare. Trade remedy laws are not based on whether imports improve competition or lower inflation. Instead, trade remedy laws have as their *raison d'être* the protection of domestic industries and firms, not with the preservation of competition. Unfair trade remedy laws seek to protect domestic producers from unfair trade practices of foreign competitors that cause injury—and for that matter, from fairly traded imports that cause serious injury in the case of safeguard (escape clause) actions. The unfair trade remedy laws as administered in the United States do not take into account the effect of the targeted practices on competition or on consumers; these effects are neither elements of a *prima facie* case nor are they a defence.

1.22 Unfair trade remedy laws can also be abused by domestic producers who petition their government to initiate an unfair trade proceeding solely for the *in terrorem* effect such a petition might have on foreign competitors. Competitors might react by unilaterally raising their prices in the case of an antidumping proceeding, entering into a price undertaking or suspension agreement with the investigating authorities pursuant to which they agree to raise prices, limiting their exports, or exiting the market altogether. Unfair trade remedy proceedings, if abused, can permit collusion by domestic producers within an industry to restrain or eliminate foreign competition in the domestic market. Thus, the unfair trade remedy laws may themselves be the instrument of restrictive business practices. The filing of an unfair trade remedy petition is not *per se* an anti-competitive practice, but petitions that are baseless or are used to extract concessions from foreign competitors through price undertakings raise a serious question of whether domestic firms are abusing the unfair trade law process in order to restrict competition in their home market.

1.23 In the United States this problem has been addressed by the U.S. Supreme Court under the *Noerr-Pennington* doctrine. Under the *Noerr-Pennington* doctrine, firms that petition the government for enactment of favourable laws or the application of existing laws are not subject to the provisions of the antitrust laws prohibiting collusion or cartel-like behaviour.[28] However, under the sham exception to the doctrine, baseless claims filed as part of a conspiracy to harass a competitor are subject to prosecution under the antitrust laws.[29] To date, there has been only one case

[28] See *United Mine Workers v. Pennington*, 381 U.S. 657 (1965); *Eastern R.R. Presidents Conference v. Noerr Motor Freight*, 365 U.S. 127 (1961).

[29] See, *e.g. Professional Real Estate Investors, Inc. v. Columbia Pictures Ind., Inc.*, 508 U.S. 49, 60–61 (1993) ("sham" litigation must be objectively baseless and amount to an attempt to interfere directly with the business relationships of a competitor); *California Motor Transp. Co. v. Trucking Unlimited*, 404 U.S. 508 (1962). Lower courts are divided over whether the *Noerr-Pennington* doctrine extends to petitions filed with foreign governments. See, *e.g. Coastal States Marketing, Inc. v. Hunt*, 694 F.2d 1358, 1364–66 (5th Cir.1983) (doctrine applicable to suits

in which the applicability of the sham exception to an antidumping proceeding was raised.[30] Although the case was disposed of on other grounds, the court did suggest that a single, baseless antidumping petition was sufficient to state an antitrust claim.[31]

1.24 In contrast to the trade remedy laws, competition policy, at least as it is currently formulated in the United States, has at its goal the maintenance of competitive markets, thereby maximising and promoting consumer welfare. It is not concerned with protecting domestic producers from foreign competition. The overarching policy goal of competition law is to ensure competitive domestic market structures and the efficient allocation of resources by prohibiting practices that restrain competition or create barriers to new entrants. The principal concern is with protecting competition, not competitors. Competition policy generally offers no refuge for inefficient competitors against lower prices that are the product of efficiency, economies of scale, lower unit labour costs, or technological superiority, so long as the advantage is fairly obtained. Nor, in most countries, does competition law permit departure from these principles for firms that are caught in a recession, are faced with shrinking markets, or are technologically obsolete. A second point where the gears of competition law and unfair trade remedy laws do not mesh smoothly is the extent to which competition policy criteria are considered in the enactment and administration of the unfair trade laws, specifically, the antidumping law. The point of disconnect focuses on the role that price plays in the administration of these two sets of laws.

1.25 The antidumping law is triggered when sales in the country of importation are at prices below those charged in the home market of the foreign producer, provided those imports cause injury to the domestic industry as a whole (not to just one or two firms within a multi-firm industry). An alternative measure of dumping under U.S. law (permissible under the WTO Antidumping Agreement[32]) is if the imported goods are sold at prices that fail to cover the total cost of producing those goods in the home market. Such imports, if they cause injury, are subject to the assessment of antidumping duties as well. It is not an element of an antidumping case that the exporting firm intended to eliminate its competitors.

filed in foreign courts); *United States v. AMAX Inc.*, 1977–1 Trade Cas. (CCH) 61,467, at 71,799 (N.D. Ill. 1977) (doctrine inapplicable to efforts to influence Canadian government), and *Occidental Petroleum Corp. v. Buttes Gas & Oil Co.*, 331 F. Supp. 92, 108 (C.D. Cal. 1971), *aff'd per curiam*, 461 F.2d 1261 (9th Cir. 1972) (doctrine should not be applied abroad), *cert. denied*, 409 U.S. 950 (1972). The FTC and the Justice Department take the position that the doctrine is applicable to lawsuits and petitions filed with foreign governments to the same extent as if the lawsuit or petition was filed with the U.S. government. See "U.S. Dep't of Justice & Federal Trade Comm'n, Antitrust Enforcement Guidelines for International Operations" s. 3.34 (1995), *reprinted in* 4 *Trade Reg. Rep.* (CCH) 13,107 (1995). See also ABA "Section of Antitrust Law, Report of Special Committee on International Antitrust" 128–31 (1991).

[30] See, *e.g. St. Joseph's Hosp., Inc. v. Hosp. Authority of America*, 620 F. Supp. 814 (S.D. Ga. 1985); *Sage Intern., Ltd. v. Cadillac Gage Co.*, 507 F. Supp. 939 (E.D. Mich. 1981); *Outboard Marine Corp. v. Pezetel*, 474 F. Supp. 168 (D. Del.1979).

[31] See *Outboard Marine Corp. v. Pezetel*, 474 F. Supp. 168 (D. Del.1979).

[32] See Agreement on Implementation of Art. VI of the General Agreement on Tariffs and Trade 1994 (Antidumping Agreement), art. 2.2. See generally Raj Bhala, "Rethinking Antidumping Law", (1995) 70 Geo. Wash. J. Int'l L. & Econ. 141.

1.26 Competition law, on the other hand, encourages price competition and only intervenes where pricing is predatory, *i.e.* set below marginal cost or average variable cost,[33] or set on a discriminatory basis with the goal of restraining competition through the allocation or division of markets. Although a pricing practice may cause a rival's exit, it is predatory only if the pricing practice would prove to be unprofitable without the additional monopoly power (and the ability to capture monopoly rents) resulting from the rival's exit.

Another point of divergence between the antidumping and antitrust law are the defences that are available in the latter but not the former. For example, defences that would be available in an antitrust price discrimination case—meeting competition or other cost justification—are unavailable in antidumping proceedings.[34]

C. Summary

1.27 International trade and competition policy share several common themes. One overarching theme is increasing world wealth by opening markets to foreign goods, services, and capital. These policies can be mutually reinforcing when pursued with the common goal of opening markets and encouraging cross-border competition. To the extent trade liberalisation reduces entry barriers to foreign markets, it gives domestic firms less ability to engage in anti-competitive conduct. Competition policy focuses on private behaviour that acts as a barrier to market access for rival firms. Competition policy can undergird a liberal trade policy by reducing and eliminating private barriers to entry to foreign markets by making illegal cartels, abuse of a dominant market position (*i.e.* unlawful monopolisation), horizontal restraints of trade (*e.g.* price fixing), and vertical restraints of trade (*e.g.* certain exclusive distributorship arrangements).

1.28 To the extent that restrictive business practices by private firms act as non-tariff barriers to trade, they are a matter of concern to trade policymakers. Such private restraints and agreements can make it difficult, if not impossible for foreign firms to gain market access overseas for their goods and services. A strategy that foreign firms might pursue to penetrate an export market is to establish a physical presence in that market. One way of expanding into a new geographic market is to merge with an existing firm in that target market or to acquire such a firm. In 1999, cross-border merger

[33] In the United States, this is known as the Areeda-Turner test. See Philip E. Areeda & Donald F. Turner, "Predatory Pricing and Related Practices Under Section 2 of the Sherman Act", (1975) 88 Harv. L. Rev. 697; 3 Phillip E. Areeda & Donald F. Turner, *Antitrust Law* 711–721 (1978 & 1982 Supp.); *Southern Pac. Communications Co. v. Amer. Tel. & Tel. Co.*, 740 F.2d 980 (D.C. Cir. 1984); *D.E. Rogers Assoc., Inc. v. Gardner-Denver Co.*, 718 F.2d 1431 (6th Cir. 1983).

[34] For other procedural and substantive differences between antitrust and trade remedy laws, see Applebaum, see para. 1.20, n. 27.

activity was at an all-time high of $720 billion,[35] with $3.4 trillion in mergers announced worldwide.[36]

1.29 Transnational mergers and acquisitions as a mode of entry into a foreign market can in turn raise issues of:

(1) a reduction in the competitiveness or contestability of a market if too much market power is concentrated in a single, merged firm; and

(2) a loss of national sovereignty and adequate control over domestic enterprises.

The steady growth in foreign direct investment and cross-border mergers and acquisitions underscores the importance to some experts of crafting a competition policy that embraces global concerns.[37]

1.30 In theory, therefore, trade and competition policy ought to work in harmony. Their shared goals and objectives suggest teaming rules against private anti-competitive behaviour with rules on the elimination of government barriers to international trade. At the same time, however, unfair trade remedy laws have as their ostensible goal correcting market disequilibrium introduced by unfair and injurious import pricing practices, whether in the form of dumping or unlawful subsidisation. These trade remedy laws can also serve a protectionist purpose, however, by raising barriers to market entry by foreign competitors. Two areas of concern in this connection are first the extent to which domestic producers abuse unfair trade remedy laws by bringing actions that force foreign exporters to raise their prices or exclude them altogether from the domestic market and secondly, the extent to which unfair trade remedy laws take into account (or, more accurately, fail to take into account) the effects on competition of unfair trade law proceedings.

II. COMPETITION POLICY AT THE WTO: A FIRST LOOK

1.31 Over its 50-year history, the GATT–WTO system has had as its primary goal the elimination of government barriers, as opposed to private barriers, to international trade. The types of government conduct restricting international trade which have been of greatest interest to the GATT–WTO members include tariffs on imported goods, the use of import and export

[35] See *The Economist*, Oct. 7, 2000 at 124. Cross-border M&As totalled $468 billion in 1998 for developed countries. *See* "United Nations Conference on Trade and Development, World Investment Report" 1999, at xxi. In 1997, cross-border M&A activity totalled $342 billion. See "United Nations Conference on Trade and Development, World Investment Report 1998", at 19. In acquisitions exceeding $1 billion in the period 1995–97, financial services M&As accounted for 37% of the total. See *id.* at 21, Figure I.12. In Japan alone, foreign acquisitions of Japanese firms in fiscal year 1998 hit an all-time high, more than double the figure for FY 1997. See "Foreign Acquisitions of Japanese Firms Hit Record in FY 1998, Ministry Reports", (1999) 16 Int'l Trade Rep. (BNA) 863.

[36] See "ICPAC Final Report", see para. 1.03, n. 3, at 44. In 1998, the figure was $2.5 trillion, itself an all-time record. See *id.*

[37] See, *e.g.* "The new enforcers", *The Economist*, Oct. 7, 2000 at 79.

quotas, the lack of discipline on the imposition of safeguard measures, allowing state-run enterprises (*e.g.* transportation and mineral extraction industries) to ignore market disciplines in their purchasing decisions, the growing resort to antidumping actions, providing subsidies to sunset and sunrise domestic industries not otherwise internationally competitive and restricting imported goods on the basis of product standards. The GATT, and now the WTO, have pursued the goal of reining in these barriers to trade by negotiating trade liberalisation measures that have had the salutary effect of indirectly combating certain restrictive business practices engaged in by domestic firms, *e.g.* price fixing, by allowing greater import competition that tends to break up such illegal arrangements through price competition.

1.32 To a more limited degree the GATT–WTO system has had less to say about government-sponsored commodity cartels (*e.g.* Organisation of Petroleum Exporting Countries, OPEC), government-sponsored boycotts, government procurement laws that discriminate in favour of domestic suppliers and national laws that discriminate against or restrict foreign investment. The GATT–WTO portfolio, while ambitious, has been limited to addressing government conduct that restricts trade. It is not only governments that have the ability to restrict trade as both government and private actors can erect barriers to the free flow of goods and services across national borders. In partial recognition of the role that private conduct plays in restricting trade, three WTO agreements speak directly to the issue of private restrictive business practices.

1.33 First, Article 9 of the Agreement on Trade-Related Investment Measures directs the Council for Trade in Goods to consider whether the TRIMs Agreement should be complemented with provisions on investment and competition policy. Two Working Groups were established in 1997 to consider these questions. The Working Group on the Interaction between Trade and Competition Policy issued its first annual report in December 1998, recommending that its mandate be extended to study three areas more fully:

(1) the relevance of the core GATT principles of national treatment, most-favoured-nation treatment, and transparency to competition policy,

(2) possible approaches to promoting co-operation among WTO members, and

(3) the contribution of competition policy to achieving the WTO's objectives.[38]

As explored more fully in Chapter Four, the contributions of WTO members show that there are many areas of convergence and divergence in national legislation regulating restrictive business practices.

[38] See WTO, "Report of the Working Group on the Interaction of Trade and Competition Policy", WT/WCTCP/2 (1998), available at http://www.wto.org.

1.34 Secondly, Articles 8, 31, and 40 of the Agreement on the Trade-Related Aspects of Intellectual Property Rights (the TRIPS Agreement) address the abuse of intellectual property rights, restrictions on compulsory licensing, and anti-competitive practices in licensing agreements, respectively. Thirdly, Articles VIII and IX of the General Agreement on Trade in Services (GATS) prohibits monopoly service suppliers from discriminating against foreign firms when supplying their services and obligates WTO members to enter into consultations with other members on restrictive business practices of service suppliers.

1.35 Should the adoption of minimum standards on competition law and enforcement be required of all WTO members, just as minimum standards on intellectual property protection are mandated for all WTO members under the TRIPS Agreement? The absence of competition law in many WTO-Member countries does not necessarily present an insurmountable obstacle to a WTO agreement on competition policy, just as the absence of legislation on intellectual property protection in many WTO members did not prevent the conclusion of the TRIPS Agreement.

International merger and acquisition (M&A) activity is a general concern because it can reduce the competitiveness or contestability of a market. It is of special concern to the national authorities of the acquired firm because it represents a diminution of national sovereignty and control over domestic enterprises. Do the international dimensions of M&A activity support the argument for a WTO competition policy agreement? Would such an agreement reduce international frictions in the area of transnational M&As, an increasingly popular mode of entry into foreign markets?

1.36 Before its indefinite postponement in December 1999, several WTO members—including Australia, Canada, the E.U., Japan and Korea—academics, and other commentators urged that the WTO Millennium Round add to its agenda negotiations on multilateral rules on investment and competition policy.[39] Japan, for example, would like to see the WTO assume jurisdiction over international competition policy issues as a way of fending off the bullying tactics of the United States to push Japan to enforce its antimonopoly law more aggressively. The E.U. has proposed that WTO

[39] See, *e.g.* "The border of competition", *The Economist*, July 4, 1998 at 69; "Co-operate on competition", *The Economist*, July 4, 1998 at 16; "Prospects Diminishing for Talks on Rules Covering Investment, Competition", (1999) 16 Int'l Trade Rep. (BNA) 1598; "Canadian Government Urged to Push WTO for Action on Investment, Competition", (Dec. 16, 1998) 15 Int'l Trade Rep. (BNA) 2104; "U.S. Awaits Coming of 'Millennium Round' of WTO Negotiations", (Jan. 20, 1999) 16 Int'l Trade Rep. (BNA) 103. Canada renewed its call for a WTO multilateral framework agreement on co-operation in late 2000. See "Working Group on the Interaction between Trade and Competition Policy", Communication from Canada Co-operation in a Multilateral Setting, WT/WGTCP/W/155 (2000). Other countries supporting WTO negotiations on competition policy rules are Switzerland and the Central European Free Trade Agreement countries (Bulgaria, the Czech Republic, Hungary, Poland, Romania, Slovakia and Slovenia). See generally F.M. Scherer, *Competition Policies for An Integrated World Economy* (1994); Diane P. Wood, "The Internationalization of Antitrust Law: Options for the Future", (1995) 44 DePaul L. Rev. 1289; Mitsuo Matsushita, "Competition Law and Policy in the Context of the WTO System", (1995) 44 DePaul L. Rev. 1097; Eleanor M. Fox, "Competition Law and the Agenda for the WTO: Forging the Links of Competition and Trade", (1995) 4 Pac. Rim L. & Pol'y J. 1; ICPAC Final Report, see para. 1.03, n. 3 at 265–66.

members negotiate a plurilateral framework agreement on competition law that would include the following:

(a) Core principals and common rules relating to the adoption of a competition law (i.e., commitment to adopt a comprehensive competition law, limits on sectoral exclusions, application of principles of transparency and non-discrimination, rights of firms) and its enforcement (i.e., a combination of an active enforcement policy by competition authorities with well defined powers and enforcement through private action in national courts).
(b) Common approaches on anticompetitive practices with a significant impact on international trade and investment (i.e., hard-core cartels, criteria for assessment of vertical restrictions or abuses of dominance with a foreclosure effect, principles for cooperation on export cartels and international mergers).
(c) Provisions on international cooperation, which could include provisions on notification, consultation and surveillance in relation to anticompetitive practices with an international dimension as well as exchanges of non-confidential information. It could also incorporate concepts of negative and positive comity, while not imposing a binding obligation to investigate on behalf of another country.
(d) The basic function of dispute settlement would be to ensure that domestic competition law and enforcement structures are in accordance with the provisions agreed multilaterally. Dispute settlement modalities will have to be further considered in the light of the scope and nature of the commitments to be assumed, and need to be well adapted to the specifics of competition law. In any event, there should be no review of individual decisions.[40]

1.37 An even greater number of WTO members are either less enthusiastic or openly opposed to the call for WTO competition policy negotiations, including the United States, Mexico, India, Pakistan, Egypt, Hong Kong, Kenya (on behalf of the African Group), the member countries of the Association of Southeast Asian Nations (ASEAN) and several Central American countries.[41] Developing countries have expressed doubts about the value of negotiations on a competition policy agreement when many of them do not even have national competition legislation. U.S. business and labour groups are also opposed to any WTO negotiations on a competition policy agreement as unnecessary and potentially counterproductive.[42]

1.38 In the case of competition policy, the 140-member WTO is hardly of one mind as to what constitutes anti-competitive behaviour and what, if anything, should be done about it. First of all, although roughly half of the WTO membership has enacted some form of competition law, for many that

[40] Communication from the Commission to the Council and to the European Parliament, "The EU Approach to the WTO Millennium Round" (July 8, 1999); "EU Member States Eying Revision of WTO Negotiating Proposals", (2001) 18 Int'l Trade Rep. (BNA) 17.
[41] See "U.S. Outlines Priorities for WTO's Seattle Ministerial", (1999) 16 Int'l Trade Rep. (BNA) 1285.
[42] See ICPAC "Final Report", *supra* note 3, at 267–68.

have done so mechanisms and institutions to enforce it effectively are not yet in place. Secondly, of the countries that do have a competition law in force, some countries favour price fixing, while others condemn it. Some countries are suspicious of vertical agreements between wholesalers and retailers, and between manufacturers and suppliers, while others are not.

1.39 For the countries that have effective enforcement mechanisms in place, those mechanisms vary as well among countries. The process in the United States, for example, involves resolution of the issues in court when the Justice Department brings a complaint, whereas in the E.U. the process is more administrative in nature. Private parties may sue under U.S. antitrust law and may recover treble damages. In other countries the enforcement process is left to government authorities. Criminal prosecutions can be brought under U.S. antitrust law, which is not the case in other jurisdictions.

1.40 Suspicions exist in the United States that the E.U.'s call for a comprehensive trade negotiation round that includes negotiations on investment and competition policy agreements is nothing less than a red herring designed to draw attention away from negotiations on agricultural subsidies, a politically sensitive issue within the E.U.[43] In addition, in connection with negotiations on competition policy rules, the United States, speaking chiefly through the Justice Department, is of the opinion that reaching agreement on common competition rules within the WTO is doomed from the start given the diverse composition of the WTO membership.

Concern has also been expressed over trade-offs and compromises in WTO negotiations over common competition rules in order to conclude negotiations on, for example, agriculture. The Justice Department has no interest in seeing U.S. antitrust rules used as bargaining chips in WTO negotiations on trade in agriculture or services.[44] A related reservation is that WTO negotiations on harmonised competition rules could result not only in a ratcheting down that would weaken strong national rules, but also an ossification of any rules that are part of a multilateral agreement. The Justice Department has also questioned the wisdom of allowing WTO dispute settlement panels to possibly second-guess national competition law enforcement authorities in their handling of antitrust cases. A corollary objection is that businesses and national competition authorities will be reluctant or will flatly refuse to disclose confidential business information to a WTO panel for fear that such information will find its way into the hands of an unfriendly foreign competitor.[45]

1.41 Despite the many arguments arrayed against a WTO competition policy agreement, several benefits of having a WTO multilateral agreement on

[43] See "EU Official Says Support Growing for Comprehensive Trade Round", (1999) 16 Int'l Trade Rep. (BNA) 1284.

[44] See, *e.g.* A. Douglas Melamed, Principal Deputy Ass't Attorney General, Antitrust Division, U.S. Dep't of Justice, *Antitrust Enforcement in a Global Economy* (Oct. 22, 1998), available at http://www.usdoj.gov/atr/public/speeches/2043.htm.

[45] See Joel I. Klein, Acting Assistant Attorney General, Antitrust Division, "Address: A Note of Caution with Respect to a WTO Agenda on Competition Policy" (Nov. 18, 1996). The E.U. has responded to part of this criticism by advocating a competition policy agreement that is not covered by the WTO Dispute Settlement Understanding. See "Prospects Diminishing for Talks on Rules Covering Investment, Competition", (1999) 16 Int'l Trade Rep. (BNA) 1598.

competition policy have been identified.[46] First, although it is widely agreed that private anti-competitive practices can have an adverse impact on both international trade and investment, no multilateral mechanism exists for policing these practices. A WTO multilateral agreement on competition policy would fill this gap. Secondly, because private anti-competitive practices, as well as M&A activity, increasingly have an international dimension, there is a need for multilateral co-operation among national enforcement authorities to complement bilateral and regional efforts in this regard. Thirdly, a multilateral agreement on competition policy will foster a competition culture, thus reinforcing the GATT–WTO system overall. Finally, a multilateral agreement on competition policy could reduce transaction costs for businesses engaged in cross-border dealings that must comply with various countries' competition laws.

1.42 Despite the purported benefits of a WTO agreement on competition policy, whether the WTO will ever conclude a multilateral agreement on competition policy remains doubtful. Former U.S. Trade Representative Charlene Barshefsky stated in late 1998 that work on an agreed set of competition rules under WTO auspices was not yet sufficiently well advanced to warrant WTO negotiations on such an agreement.[47] She added in June 1999 that she saw no possibility of negotiations at the WTO comparable to the ill-fated Organisation for Economic Co-operation and Development (OECD) negotiations on the aborted Multilateral Agreement on Investment (MAI).[48] Several WTO members, led by the E.U., have championed a WTO framework agreement on competition policy, while others, following the lead of the United States, have expressed deep misgivings and great reluctance to move forward on competition policy negotiations.

1.43 Considering the diverse and broad WTO membership that includes developed, developing, and emerging economies, a strong argument can be made that the WTO is the proper forum for concluding such a multilateral framework agreement, not only because of its broad-based membership, but because of the close link between trade, liberalised investment rules, and international enforcement of mutually-agreed upon competition rules.

1.44 However, policy makers and government officials would be foolish to ignore the lesson of the OECD MAI fiasco.[49] Extrapolating from the collapse of the MAI negotiations, one lesson seems clear: if a small club of developed countries could not reach agreement on a foreign investment convention, where most of them have a relatively open investment climate to begin with and where their foreign investment laws are not dramatically far apart, then what chance is there of reaching agreement on competition policy

[46] See WTO, "Working Group on the Interaction between Trade and Competition Policy", Report (1999) of the Working Group on the Interaction between Trade and Competition Policy to the General Council, WT/WGTCP/3, at 24, para. 74 (Oct. 11, 1999) (hereinafter "WGTCP 1999 Report").

[47] See "U.S. Welcomes WTO Decision to Continue Antitrust Talks But Rules Out Negotiations", (1998) 15 Int'l Trade Rep. (BNA) 2087.

[48] See "WTO Trade Agenda Left Unresolved at Conclusion of OECD Ministerial", (1999) 16 Int'l Trade Rep. (BNA) 914.

[49] See UNCTAD, "Lessons from the MAI" (1999).

under WTO auspices—a subject that touches the sensitive and raw nerve of national sovereignty—among 140 economically, politically, and culturally diverse nations?

1.45 From the integration of national economies it does not inexorably follow that a multilateral approach to competition policy, let alone a multilateral approach under WTO auspices, is necessarily the right approach. Multilateralism is no desideratum. Indeed, it has limits that policymakers need to recognise. As explored in the following chapters, the legal and political arguments against such an approach are formidable. Strengthening domestic competition laws to eliminate restrictive business practices that close off market access to imported goods and services is in the end a far more preferable and effective approach, one that countries would more readily embrace than would be true of multilateral competition rules forced down their throats.

1.46 The WTO is a fragile institution. If you visit the WTO's web site, the WTO will remind you of its fragility with an image of an egg. As this book goes to press, the WTO's prestige, reputation, and authority are at an all-time low. The United States, its most powerful member, has been ambivalent at times in its support of the WTO and its goal of promoting liberal trade. The commitment of the United States to U.S. participation in the WTO is less than whole-hearted.[50] But even the most vocal government critics of the WTO have called for reform of the Organisation, not for U.S. withdrawal from in it.[51] At thc same time, intemperate and pandering remarks by President Clinton at the WTO Seattle Ministerial Conference, suggesting that the WTO conclude an agreement on core labour standards that would be enforced through trade sanctions, steeled the resolve of developing countries not to be steam rolled by the WTO's developed-country members at any new WTO trade negotiation round.

1.47 All of these developments are unfortunate because the WTO sets rules that bind rich countries and poor countries alike. Jeffrey Schott has noted that "as the weaker partners in the trading system, developing countries benefit the most when the major trading powers play by a common set of

[50] Despite the U.S. Trade Representative's ringing endorsement of continued U.S. membership in the WTO in her March 2000 Report, "2000 Trade Policy Agenda and the 1999 Annual Report of the President of the United States on the Trade Agreements Program", a resolution was introduced in Congress calling for U.S. withdrawal from the WTO pursuant to s. 125 of the Uruguay Round Agreements Act, 19 U.S.C. s. 3535 (mandating a five-year review of U.S. participation in the WTO). See Gary G. Yerkey, "USTR Sends Report to Congress Urging Continued U.S. Participation in WTO", (March 9, 2000) 17 Int'l Trade Rep. (BNA) 394. That resolution was defeated in the House of Representatives on June 21, 2000 by a vote of 363–56. See "House of Representatives Affirms American Membership in World Trade Organization", (2000) 17 Int'l Trade Rep. (BNA) 975; Office of the USTR, "USTR Barshefsky Hails Overwhelming House Vote on WTO, Bipartisan Vote Rejects U.S. Withdrawal from WTO", Press Release 00–49 (June 22, 2000). The House vote in June 2000 compares to a vote of 288–146 in Nov.1994 to join the Organisation and approve the Uruguay Round agreements.

[51] See Gary G. Yerkey, "USTR Set to Issue Report Defending Continued U.S. Participation in WTO", (Mar. 2, 2000) 17 Int'l Trade Rep. (BNA) 341 (Minority Leader Richard Gephardt continues to support U.S. participation in the organisation, but dispute settlement system needs to be reformed); Corbett B. Daly, "Ways and Means Panel Rejects Resolution Calling for U.S. Withdrawal from WTO", (June 15, 2000) 17 Int'l Trade Rep. (BNA) 923.

rules."[52] A liberal trade policy is a policy of increased competition and opportunity. Such a policy holds great promise for the world's developing countries. The big losers from the debacle in Seattle were developing countries.

1.48 It is unquestionably true that to the extent private firms engage in anti-competitive practices, they can impede international trade flows. Some observers contend that restrictive business practices may now constitute a more important barrier to market access than border controls.[53] While there is no empirical evidence to support this contention, few quarrel with the view that governmental barriers to market access remain the most significant impediment to the free flow of goods and services across national borders. Indeed, the point has been made in discussions at the WTO Working Group on the Interaction of Trade and Competition Policy that:

> although anti-competitive practices of enterprises might well have a detrimental impact on economic development, it was also important to consider the impact of anti-competitive policies and measures of governments. In many cases, this could be as great or greater than that of purely private anti-competitive practices. Furthermore, in many cases, ostensibly private anti-competitive behavior was itself prompted or facilitated by government actions.[54]

1.49 Whether governmental measures are more important than private RBPs in their impact on trade and competition is an empirical question, the answer to which could differ from country to country and from economic sector to economic sector. A closely-related question to the one of the impact of restrictive business practices on international trade flows is the extent to which governments erect similar barriers to trade by directly or indirectly supporting or condoning private RBPs. Protectionist pressures can lead governments to shelter weak industries and firms from foreign competition. Protectionist measures are introduced under the justification that certain domestic producers are to be preferred over their international competitors in the market in order to boost domestic employment and income. To take just one example, government procurement laws with buy-national directives discriminate against the lowest cost supplier of a good or service when the supplier is foreign.

1.50 Another anti-competitive governmental barrier to trade are the so-called "grey area" measures—voluntary export restraint agreements (VERs)—which are in essence a government-orchestrated, horizontal restraint of trade that sanctions a market-sharing arrangement among competing firms. The problem of VERs may now be of historical significance with the adoption of the WTO Safeguards Agreement that severely restricts the use of VERs, but

[52] Jeffrey Schott, "After Seattle", *The Economist*, Aug. 26, 2000, at 66.

[53] See Barry Hawk, "Overview, in Antitrust and Market Access: The Scope and Coverage of Competition Laws and Implications for Trade" 8 (OECD 1996).

[54] WTO, Working Group on the Interaction between Trade and Competition Policy, Report to the General Council, WT/WGTCP/2, at 15, para. 40 (Dec. 8, 1998) (footnote omitted).

the Agreement, and WTO members' resolve to abide by its terms, has yet to be tested in a period of a global economic recession.

1.51 Support for international disciplines on private RBPs came from the United States during the drafting of the ill-fated Havana Charter on the International Trade Organisation. The United States drafted the chapter in the Havana Charter on restrictive business practices. Whether the United States became disenchanted with multilateral efforts to resolve competition law disputes, or whether it simply saw no advantage in pursuing multilateralism when it could exercise extraterritorial antitrust jurisdiction, is not clear. Whatever the reasons, the United States dropped its support for international competition law disciplines and turned instead to unilateral and bilateral approaches to the problem. Still, the United States acknowledges the need for international co-operation and information sharing in competition investigations.

1.52 What are the prospects for a convention on international competition rules today? Has anything changed since the 1950s to make it realistic to think that we are any closer to reaching consensus on concluding an international competition policy agreement? Do the advantages of having a predictable, uniform legal environment for multinational corporations when they conduct transnational business—and thus, of having uniform, international competition policy standards—outweigh any disadvantages of such an international agreement?

The arguments of the proponents of a multilateral competition policy agreement are essentially twofold. First, more competition cases have a cross-border dimension, causing friction between national enforcement authorities and generating jurisdictional conflicts.[55] Secondly, private RBPs can undercut the trade liberalisation agenda of the WTO. The argument runs that an international framework agreement on competition law would have at least three salutary benefits:

- A WTO competition policy agreement would provide a more predictable legal environment within which multinational firms could operate.
- WTO dispute settlement would reduce duplication of enforcement efforts by national enforcement authorities.
- Harmonisation of national competition laws under WTO auspices would avoid conflicting jurisdictional disputes and potential conflicting decisions by national enforcement authorities.

[55] See, *e.g.* Sir Leon Brittan, "The Need for a Multilateral Framework of Competition Rules", in *Trade and Competition Policies: Exploring the Ways Forward* 29 (OECD 1999); Eleanor Fox, "Toward World Antitrust and Market Access", (1997) 91 Am. J. Int'l L. 1; Daniel Pruzin, "United Nations Calls for WTO Role in Checking Multinational Monopolies", (21 July, 1999) 16 Int'l Trade Rep. (BNA) 1209; "Japan FTC Proposes Global Rules in the WTO for Competition Policy", (Apr. 28, 1999) 16 Int'l Trade Rep. (BNA) 720; "WTO Cites Need for Competition Rules for Business Practices that Restrict Trade", (Dec. 24, 1997) 14 Int'l Trade Rep. (BNA) 2221; Daniel Pruzin, "EU Outlines Goals for WTO Talks on Services, IP, Competition Policy", (June 19, 1999) 16 Int'l Trade Rep. (BNA) 968.

1.53 Yet, business groups, other academics, the United States and other countries are moderately suspicious and highly sceptical of multilateral solutions calling for the harmonisation of national competition laws and the resolution of international competition law disputes in an international dispute settlement forum such as the WTO.[56] Harmonisation of national competition laws will not necessary address issues of efficiency in a global marketplace. Instead, national authorities will be focused on the impact to the domestic market of restrictive business practices. The E.U. and the United States, for example, would use international competition disciplines to promote exports and reduce conflict in cross-border merger approval. They are, however, probably less interested in exposing domestic firms to competition law disciplines when those firms are engaged solely in export activity. Smaller countries, on the other hand, are also interested in market access but would welcome an international agreement and enforcement mechanism that reaches anti-competitive practices engaged in abroad but with effects in their domestic market. In addition, not all countries will benefit equally from a multilateral competition policy agreement. Competition policy seeks generally to restrain the anti-competitive behaviour of firms and thereby increase consumer welfare. But firms that engage in restrictive business practices and consumers whose welfare is to be increased are distributed unequally among countries. Countries thus have different incentives at different times for regulating or not regulating firms that engage in RBPs. For these and other reasons that are developed more fully in the following chapters, the prospects for successfully concluding a multilateral agreement on competition policy seem remote.

[56] See, *e.g.* Joel I. Klein, "A Reality Check on Antitrust Rules in the World Trade Organization, and a Practical Way Forward on International Antitrust", in *Trade and Competition Policies: Exploring the Ways Forward* (OECD 1999) 37, 41–43; Bernard Hoekman & Peter Holmes, *Competition Policy, Developing Countries and the WTO* (1999); "OECD Antitrust/Trade Conference Shows Disparate Approaches Toward Reconciliation", (July 8, 1999) 77 Antitrust & Trade Reg. Rep. (BNA) 41 ("Judge Diane Wood . . . asserted that 'it is not the right time' and that the WTO is not the right place for negotiations"); Daniel Pruzin, "Business Groups Say Too Early for WTO to Set Framework for Competition Policy", (Sept. 15, 1999) 16 Int'l Trade Rep. (BNA) 1484; "U.S. Opposes Plan to Negotiate Agreement in WTO, Officials Say", (1997) 14 Int'l Trade Rep. (BNA) 2034; Joel Klein, "No Monopoly on Antitrust", *Financial Times*, Feb. 13, 1998, at 24; Merit Janow, "Unilateral and Bilateral Approaches to Competition Policy Drawing on Trade Experience", in *Brookings Trade Forum 1998* (Robert Z. Lawrence ed. 1998).

Chapter Two

Unilateral, Bilateral, Regional, Plurilateral, and Multilateral Approaches To Competition Policy

I. Introduction

2.001 The alternative legal approaches to mediating the relationship between trade and competition policy lie on a continuum from unilateral, bilateral, regional, plurilateral, to multilateral. The extent to which competition policy principles are covered in bilateral and regional agreements varies considerably, with coverage of competition policy under the Australia-New Zealand Closer Economic Relations Agreement (ANZCERTA) being comprehensive, but rules governing antitrust under NAFTA being threadbare. Many examples of non-multilateral approaches can be found in state practice, but few examples of such state practice can be found at the multilateral level.

II. Unilateral approaches

2.002 Under customary international law, legislative jurisdiction may be grounded on several bases, including territoriality, nationality, passive personality, national security (the protective principle), and effects.[1] Of these five bases of legislative jurisdiction, the territoriality and effects principles are the two bearing most directly on the question of international antitrust enforcement. The territoriality principle provides that a state has jurisdiction over individuals who violate the state's laws within the state's territory.[2] National enforcement authorities rely heavily, but not exclusively, on the territorial principle as the legal basis on which to address anti-competitive behaviour. The territorial principle provides a sufficient basis for adequately enforcing

---

[1] See *Restatement (Third) Foreign Relations Law of the United States*, s. 403 (1987).

[2] See *id.*; Ian Brownlie, *Principles of Public International Law* (1990) 300. The nationality principle can also be the basis for extending antitrust jurisdiction beyond national borders when nationals of the enforcing government engage in conduct overseas. A potential source of friction here is defining a firm's nationality.

national antitrust laws in most instances. However, in an increasingly integrated global economy, the territorial principle—if interpreted literally—falls short as a basis for jurisdiction in some, but not all, international antitrust cases.[3]

2.003 Restrictive business practices can have an effect in the territory of a state, but the conduct causing the effect may have occurred in another state. The United States refused to be jurisdictionally restricted in such a case and accordingly, developed what was at the time the controversial effects test. The most famous statement of the effects test is Judge Learned Hand's pronouncement in the *Alcoa* case:

> [A]ny state may impose liabilities, even upon persons not within its allegiance, for conduct outside its borders that has consequences within its borders which the state reprehends.[4]

The focus is thus on the location of the victim, not on that of the actor. Consequently, the U.S. effects test excludes conduct that harms only foreign competition, thereby excluding most export cartels.

2.004 A unilateral approach to resolving international antitrust disputes leaves with national authorities the sole responsibility for resolving such disputes through the extraterritorial application of national antitrust law. Although U.S. trading partners—most notably the UK[5]—have been outspoken in their criticism of the effects test as an exercise of extraterritorial (*i.e.* exorbitant) jurisdiction, "almost all of the industrialized nations apply some form of the effects test," including the E.U., many of its Member States, Canada, and Japan.[6] The practice of the European Commission and its Member States, for example, has been to exercise jurisdiction based on effects in their territories regardless of whether these effects have been caused by conduct within or without their territories.[7] The European Commission has relied on an effects test when imposing fines or ordering firms to desist from restrictive business practices when they are located in non-Member States. For

[3] See, *e.g.* A. Douglas Melamed, "International Antitrust in an Age of International Deregulation", (1998) 6 Geo. Mason L. Rev. 437 (observing that "[n]early 30% of the Antitrust Division's enforcement work involves international or transnational matters"); Diane P. Wood, "United States Antitrust Law in the Global Market", (1944) 1 Ind. J. Global Legal Stud. 409, 427 (observing that nearly one-third of pre-merger notifications under the Hart-Scott-Rodino Act involve foreign parties or significant foreign assets).

[4] *United States v. Aluminum Co. of America*, 148 F.2d 416, 443 (2d Cir. 1945). The view that prevailed in the United States for more than 30 years prior to the *Alcoa* case was the territorial approach. In *American Banana Co. v. United Fruit Co.*, 213 U.S. 347 (1909), Justice Holmes, writing for the Court, stated that "the character of an act as lawful or unlawful must be determined wholly by the law of the country where the act is done." *id.* at 356. Thus, even though the two parties were U.S. corporations, because the acts in question occurred in Panama and Costa Rica, they were beyond the reach of the Sherman Act.

[5] See, *e.g. Rio Tinto Zinc Corp. v. Westinghouse Elec. Corp.*, [1978] A.C. 547 (House of Lords); Kurt Stockmann, "Foreign Application of European Antitrust Laws", (1985) Fordham Corp. L. Inst. 251, 254 n.7.

[6] ABA Section of Antitrust Law, "Report of the Special Committee on International Antitrust" (1991) 148 (hereinafter ABA Special Committee Report). See Restatement (Third) Foreign Relations Law of the United States, s. 403, Reporter's note 3 (1987).

[7] See Stockmann, *supra* note 5, at 253.

the Commission, the application of Article 81 turns on whether the practices under investigation have as their object or effect the prevention, restriction, or distortion of competition within the Community.[8] Some Commission decisions merely require that a restrictive business practice "have a noticeable effect on competition within the common market."[9] It is irrelevant whether a firm is located within or outside the Community, where the contract is entered into, or whether acts were committed or business conducted within the territory of a Member State.[10]

2.005 Although the European Commission has endorsed the effects test, the European Court of Justice has adopted a version of the effects test from the *Wood Pulp* decision in 1988 known as the implementation test instead.[11] In that case a group of non-E.U. suppliers of wood pulp physically met outside the E.U. in order to reach agreement on the price of imports of wood pulp into the E.U. In answering the question whether the E.U. had jurisdiction to punish the price fixing, the European Court of Justice adopted the effects test in all but name:

> It should be observed that an infringement of Article 85 [now Article 81], such as the conclusion of an agreement which has the effect of restricting competition within the Common Market, consists of conduct made up of two elements, the formation of the agreement, decision or concerted practice and the implementation thereof. If the applicability of prohibitions laid down under competition law were made to depend on the place where the agreement, decision or concerted practice was formed, the result would obviously be to give undertakings as easy means of evading these prohibitions. The decisive factor is therefore the place where it is implemented.

The producers in this case implemented their pricing agreement within the Common Market. It is immaterial in that respect whether or not they had recourse to subsidiaries, agents, sub-agents, or branches within the Community in order to make their contacts with purchasers within the Community.

Accordingly, the Community's jurisdiction to apply its competition rules to such conduct is covered by the territoriality principle as universally recognized in public international law.[12]

2.006 While invoking the territoriality principle as the basis for exercising jurisdiction to cover conduct outside the E.U., the Court stated that jurisdiction may be exercised over any practice that is implemented within the E.U.

[8] See, *e.g.* Commission Decisions, *Quinine*, July 16, 1969, [1969] O.J. Spec. Ed. L192/5, 16; *Ballbearings*, 25 Nov. 29, 1974, O.J. Spec. Ed. L343/19; *Duro-Dyne/Europair*, Dec. 19, 1974, [1974] O.J. L29/11, 12.

[9] Commission Decision, *Raymond/Nagoya*, June 9, 1972, [1972] O.J. L143/39, 41.

[10] See Commission Decision, *Dyestuffs*, July 24, 1969, [1969] O.J. Spec. Ed. L195/11, 14.

[11] *Ahlström Osakeyhtiö v. Commission*, Cases 89, 104, 116–17, 125–9/85, [1988] E.C.R. 5193, [1988] 4 C.M.L.R. 901 [hereinafter *Wood Pulp*]. See Ivo E. Schwartz, "The International Antitrust Law of the European Community", in *International Harmonization of Competition Laws* 97, 101 (Chia-Jui Cheng, Lawrence S. Liu, & Chih-Kang Wang eds. 1995).

[12] Wood Pulp Cartel [1985] 3 C.M.L.R. 474, aff'd sub nom., Case 89/85, *A. Ahlström Osakeyhitö v. Comm'n* [1988] E.C.R. 5193, 5242–43, [1988] 4 C.M.L.R. 901.

regardless of the location of the parties. A recent example of the E.U.'s implementation test in operation centres on the Boeing/McDonnell Douglas merger. Neither firm had production facilities in the E.U.; however, the European Commission still exercised competition law jurisdiction over the proposed merger. Thus, not unlike the effects test in the United States, the jurisdictional nexus in the *Wood Pulp* decision was the place where the anti-competitive conduct was implemented, *i.e.* the place where the restraint causes anticompetitive effects.[13]

2.007 Joseph Griffin noted, however, that while the E.U.'s implementation test and the U.S. effects test often produce similar results, the two tests could reach different results where an import cartel of U.S. purchasers refused to buy goods from E.U. sellers. In this situation, "it is doubtful that the purchasers would be deemed to have 'implemented' their conduct within the European Union."[14] The Justice Department has acknowledged this difference in a footnote to its International Antitrust Guidelines where it states that:

> in the context of import trade, the 'implementation' test adopted in the European Court of Justice usually produces the same outcome as the 'effects' test employed in the United States.[15]

2.008 Mexico also uses a version of the effects test for reaching transactions or agreements entered into abroad with effects on domestic competition.[16] Canadian competition law, however, while capable of extraterritorial application, has rarely been applied in such a fashion. Canadian courts have generally opposed extraterritorial jurisdiction based on effects and have favoured the "moderation and restraint" comity approach to extraterritorial competition law enforcement advocated by the OECD instead.[17] Canadian courts, like their American counterparts, have recognised that principles of international comity may restrict the extraterritorial reach of national laws.[18]

2.009 With the effects test, or variations thereof, gaining ground in jurisdictions other than the United States,[19] protests raised over the extraterritorial application of national competition laws is more a minor argument

[13] See Lennart Ritter, W. David Braun & Francis Rawlinson, *European Competition Law: A Practitioner's Guide* 61–62 (2d ed. 2000).

[14] Joseph P. Griffin, "Foreign Governmental Reactions to U.S. Assertions of Extraterritorial Jurisdiction", (1998) 6 Geo. Mason L. Rev. 505, 513.

[15] U.S. Dep't of Justice & Federal Trade Comm'n, "Antitrust Enforcement Guidelines for International Operations" 12 n.51 (1995), reprinted in 4 Trade Reg. Rep. (CCH) 13,107 (1995), available at http://www.usdoj.gov/atr/public/guidelines/internat.tx (hereinafter "1995 International Antitrust Guidelines").

[16] See American Bar Ass'n, The *Competition Laws of NAFTA, Canada, Mexico, and the United States, A Practitioner's Guide* 161 (1997) (hereinafter "The Competition Laws of NAFTA").

[17] See *The Competition Laws of NAFTA, supra* note 16, at 161; OECD Committee on International Investment and Multinational Enterprises, *Minimizing Conflicting Requirements: Approaches of Moderation and Restraint* (1987).

[18] See, *e.g. Attorney General-Can. v. Fallbridge Holdings Ltd.*, 7 B.L.R. 275, 281 (Fed. Ct., Trial Div. 1979).

[19] Other countries that take the view that their domestic laws can apply to conduct abroad having adverse effects at home include Austria, Belgium, Denmark, Finland, France, Germany, Greece, Luxembourg, Norway, Portugal, Spain, Sweden and Switzerland. See Merit E. Janow, "Unilateral and Bilateral Approaches to Competition Policy Drawing on the Trade Experience", *in Brookings Trade Forum* 1998, 253, 265 n.29 (Robert Z. Lawrence ed.1998). The same holds true for virtually every merger control law as well.

that is typically invoked when one's nationals are defendants in a foreign proceeding than it is a principled objection. A sense of loss of sovereignty premised on the territoriality principle is probably one objection to the unilateral and extraterritorial enforcement of national competition laws. With extraterritoriality, the toughest national antitrust law will govern international activities. In marked contrast to the section 301 mechanism where the U.S. Trade Representative (USTR) acts as prosecutor, judge and jury, under U.S. antitrust law every foreign defendant receives complete due process protections in U.S. courts—the final arbiters of whether U.S. antitrust law has been violated. Given that U.S. case law firmly supports the extraterritorial application of U.S. antitrust law, the United States would seem to have little incentive to enter into international agreements on competition law that might weaken its ability to enforce its laws extraterritorially. Further, if the United States and the E.U., the two jurisdictions with the most active enforcement of international antitrust law, have in essence bridged the conceptual gap in the extraterritorial enforcement of their competition laws, then the matter should be left there.

2.010 In a world of only two countries, an affirmative answer to the question, "why not leave matters where they are?" might be appropriate. Judge Diane Wood has argued, for example, that "the optimal enforcer for any competition case is the country whose consumers are harmed by the particular practice in question."[20] Professor Andrew Guzman, however, has demonstrated that:

> a country that can apply its law extraterritorially will underregulate anticompetitive behavior if it is a net exporter and overregulate such behavior if it is a net importer.[21]

Japan would be an example of the former, the United States an example of the latter. According to Professor Guzman, Judge Wood's proposal would result in over-regulation.

2.011 A negative response to this question was offered by U.S. trading partners other than the E.U., but at a time when bilateral co-operation agreements were rare. A Canadian government official, for example, identified the policy conflict in cross-border competition law enforcement as a reason for abstaining from unilateral competition law enforcement in cross-border cases:

> Where a transnational antitrust issue is really a manifestation of a policy conflict between governments, it should be recognized that there may be no applicable international law to resolve the conflict. In such cases, resolution should be sought through the normal methods of consultation and negotiation. For one government to seek to resolve the conflict in its favor by invoking its national law before its domestic tribunals is not the

[20] Wood, A Cooperative Framework, see para. 2.002, n. 3, at 530.

[21] Andrew T. Guzman, "Is International Antitrust Possible?", (1998) 73 N.Y.U.L. Rev. 1501, 1520.

> rule of law but an application, in judicial guise, of the principle that economic might is right.[22]

This view is probably out-of-date given the development of co-operation agreements not only between Canada and the United States, but between the United States and its other major trading partners, as well as between Canada and the E.U. These bilateral co-operation agreements are explored in detail below.

2.012 In practice, athe extraterritorial application of U.S. antitrust law in cases involving market closure to U.S. exports has been restrained. Since 1912, the Justice Department has filed only 44 cases in which the United States claimed that the defendants were engaged in conduct that restrained market access for U.S. exports.[23] In the view of the International Competition Policy Advisory Committee (ICPAC), "unilateral government enforcement cannot be considered to have played a major role in opening foreign markets."[24] Moreover, extraterritoriality has two sides, as seen in the *Boeing/McDonnell Douglas* merger. Thus, enlightened self-interest has provided the necessary incentive for the United States to conclude bilateral antitrust co-operation agreements, holding in reserve the ability to apply U.S. antitrust law unilaterally and extraterritorially when co-operation with sister agencies fails.[25] Moreover, effective competition law enforcement often requires information gathering abroad and co-operation from foreign governments.

A. Self-Restraint: Comity

2.013 Traditional comity refers to

> the recognition which one nation allows within its territory to the legislative, executive, or judicial acts of another nation, having due regard both to international duty and convenience and to the rights of its own citizens or of other persons who are under the protection of its laws.[26]

The OECD Committee of Experts on Restrictive Business Practices concluded in 1984 that:

> [a]lthough there seems to be growing observance of moderation and self-restraint, in the absence of multilaterally agreed upon criteria, unilateral approaches are not likely to be successful in resolving all conflicts which may arise.[27]

[22] J.S. Stanford, "The Application of the Sherman Act to Conduct Outside the United States: A View from Abroad", (1978) 11 Cornell Int'l L.J. 195, 213 n.46.

[23] See "International Competition Policy Advisory Committee to the Attorney General and Assistant Attorney General for Antitrust, Final Report" 244 (2000) [hereinafter ICPAC "Final Report"].

[24] *id.*

[25] For background on the extraterritorial enforcement of competition laws, see generally Spencer Weber Waller, *Antitrust and American Business Abroad* (1997).

[26] *Hilton v. Guyot*, 159 U.S. 113, 164 (1895).

[27] OECD, "Report of the Committee of Experts on Restrictive Business Practices, Export Cartels 16 (1974).

While this is a view shared by many,[28] the conclusion raises the issue of whether a multilateral approach will succeed in resolving conflicts in the enforcement of competition rules that have transnational effects where unilateral self-restraint has failed. As enforced in U.S. courts, one objection to self-restraint is the lack of a consistent application of principles of international comity. As explained in more detail below, the role of comity principles in the extraterritorial application of U.S. antitrust law remains an unsettled area of law after the U.S. Supreme Court's decision in *Hartford Fire Insurance Co. v. California*.[29]

2.014 Principles of international comity that are overlaid on national law reflect sensitivity towards the interests of other countries and foreign nationals of those countries. For example, at the administrative level in the United States the Federal Trade Commission (FTC) has worked closely with the European Commission to ensure expeditious approval of international mergers where the FTC did not see any significant antitrust concerns (*e.g.* Daimler/Chrysler and Lucas/Varity), as well as in cases where the Commission and the FTC did not agree (*e.g.* AOL/Time Warner and *Boeing/McDonnell Douglas*).[30] In addition, the jurisdictional rule of reason tempers the extraterritorial reach of U.S. antitrust law in U.S. judicial proceedings.[31] First announced in 1976 in the *Timberlane* case,[32] a court examined "the appropriateness of exercising extraterritorial jurisdiction in light of considerations of international comity and fairness."[33] The considerations include:

> [t]he degree of conflict with foreign law or policy, the nationality or allegiance of the parties and the locations or principal places of business of corporations, the extent to which enforcement by either state can be expected to achieve compliance, the relative significance of effects on the United States as compared with those elsewhere, the extent to which there is explicit purpose to harm or affect American commerce, the foreseeability of such effect, and the relative importance to the violations charged of conduct within the United States as compared with conduct abroad.[34]

[28] See, *e.g.* Diane P. Wood, "The Impossible Dream: Real International Antitrust", 1992 U. Chi. Legal F. 277, 280–81 (hereinafter Wood, "The Impossible Dream"); Ernest-Ulrich Petersmann, "International Competition Rules for Governments and for Private Business: A "Trade Law Approach" for Linking Trade and Competition Rules in the WTO", (1996) 72 Chi.-Kent L. Rev. 545; Philip Marsden, "'Antitrust' at the WTO", (1999) 13 Antitrust 28; Eleanor M Fox, "Toward World Antitrust and Market Access", (1997) 91 Am. J. Int'l L. 1.

[29] 509 U.S. 764 (1993).

[30] See "FTC Testifies before Senate Subcommittee on International Antitrust Issues", Federal Trade Comm'n, News Release, *available at* 1998 WL 683460 (Oct. 2, 1998).

[31] The phrase "jurisdictional rule of reason" was first coined by Kingman Brewster. See Kingman Brewster, "Antitrust and American Business Abroad" 446 (1st ed. 1958).

[32] *Timberlane Lumber Co. v. Bank of Am.*, 549 F.2d 597, 611–12 (9th Cir. 1976) (*Timberlane I*).

[33] *Timberlane Lumber Co. v. Bank of Am. Nat'l Trust & Sav. Ass'n*, 749 F.2d 1378, 1382 (9th Cir. 1984) (*Timberlane II*).

[34] *Timberlane I*, 549 F.2d at 614.

2.015 The jurisdictional rule of reason has been approved by the Third, Fifth, and Tenth Circuits.[35] Nevertheless, even where moderation and self-restraint are exercised, the courts of one country have a difficult task ensuring that all relevant interests are properly considered and given appropriate weight, particularly in private litigation where the interests of foreign countries can only be known if:

(1) the private litigants understand and fairly present those interests to the court; or

(2) the foreign governments themselves make known those interests through the submission of *amicus curiae* briefs to the court.

It is also debatable whether it is a proper judicial function at all to use a test that weighs the policies of another country and then balances them against the interests of the United States.[36] Nevertheless, in a somewhat controversial move, in 1987 the American Law Institute added the jurisdictional rule of reason to the Restatement (Third) Foreign Relations Law of the United States.[37]

2.016 In 1993, the U.S. Supreme Court had an opportunity to express its view on the validity of the jurisdictional rule of reason in *Hartford Fire Insurance Co. v. California*.[38] The majority of the Court declined to express an opinion, concluding instead that the case was not a factually proper one for considering the applicability of the jurisdictional rule of reason because, in the majority's view, there was no "true conflict" between U.S. and U.K. competition law, *i.e.* the defendants could comply with both bodies of law.[39]

[35] See *Mannington Mills, Inc. v. Congoleum Corp.*, 595 F.2d 1287, 1297–98 (3d Cir. 1979); *Industrial Inv. Dev. Corp. v. Mitsui & Co.*, 671 F.2d 876, 884–85 (5th Cir. 1982); *Montreal Trading Ltd. v. Amax, Inc.*, 661 F.2d 864, 869–70 (9th Cir. 1981). But see *Laker Airways Ltd. v. Sabena, Belgian World Airlines*, 731 F.2d 909, 948–49 (D.C. Cir. 1984); *Re Uranium Antitrust Litig.*, 617 F.2d 1248, 1255 (7th Cir. 1980); *United States v. Nippon Paper Indus. Co.*, 109 F.3d 1, 8–9 (1st Cir. 1997), *cert. denied*, 118 S. Ct. 685 (1998).

[36] It is for this reason that the D.C. Circuit has rejected the jurisdictional rule of reason. See *Laker Airways Ltd. v. Sabena, Belgian World Airlines*, 731 F.2d 909, 948–49 (D.C. Cir. 1984). See also *Hartford Fire Ins. Co. v. California*, 509 U.S. 764 (1993) (principles of international comity should be used only where there exists a true conflict between U.S. and foreign law such that a party cannot simultaneously comply with both laws).

[37] *Restatement (Third) Foreign Relations Law of the United States*, s. 403 (1987). S. 403 lists eight factors that a court should consider when applying the jurisdictional rule of reason:
(1) the extent to which the activity takes place within the territory of the regulating state, or has a substantial, direct, and foreseeable effect upon or in the territory; (2) the connection between the regulating state and the person principally responsible for the activity to be regulated, or between the state and those whom the regulation is designed to protect; (3) the character of the activity to be regulated, the importance of regulation to the regulating state, the extent to which other states regulates such activities, and the degree to which the desirability of such regulation is generally accepted; (4) the existence of justified expectations that might be protected or hurt by the regulation; (5) the importance of the regulation to the international political, legal, or economic system; (6) the extent to which the regulation is consistent with the traditions of the international system; (7) the extent to which another state might have an interest in regulating the activity; and (8) the likelihood of conflict with regulation by another state.

[38] 509 U.S. 764 (1993).

[39] See Joseph P. Griffin, "Extraterritoriality in U.S. and EU Antitrust Enforcement", 67 Antitrust (1999) L.J. 159, 164–66; Joseph P. Griffin, "Regulation of Competition in the Canada/U.S. Context—Extraterritorial Reach of U.S. Antitrust Law—A U.S. Perspective", (1998) 24 Can.—U.S. L.J. 315; Gary B. Born, *International Litigation in United States Courts* (1996) 603–06.

By declining to apply a comity analysis, the Court in effect extended the extraterritorial reach of U.S. antitrust law. For that reason, the opinion has been criticised by U.S. trading partners.[40]

Whether *Hartford Fire Insurance* signals an end to a jurisdictional rule of reason analysis by the courts in future antitrust cases where the defendant is not confronted with a "true conflict" remains an open question.[41] At least three post-*Hartford Fire Insurance* cases—one of them the first Sherman Act criminal antitrust action involving acts outside the United States[42]—refused to apply the jurisdictional rule of reason except in "true conflict" cases as described by the Supreme Court in *Hartford Fire Insurance*.[43] In any event, the Justice Department and the FTC have stated that they will continue to use a comity analysis even if there is no "true conflict."[44] Moreover, as explained below, comity principles are a part of every bilateral co-operation agreement to which the United States is a party. They are also recognised in the preamble to the 1995 revised OECD recommendation concerning co-operation between member countries (also discussed later in this chapter).

In the legislative environment, a rigid approach to the unilateral enforcement of national antitrust rules with a trans-border impact has been softened through what might be described as enlightened self-restraint by Congress, despite the unsettled status of comity principles in U.S. courts in cases involving private party enforcement.

2.017 In 1982 Congress amended the Sherman and Federal Trade Commission Acts with passage of the Foreign Trade Antitrust Improvements Act (FTAIA) with respect to export trade and wholly foreign conduct.[45] Legislative jurisdiction was extended to reach alleged anti-competitive conduct that has a "direct, substantial, and reasonably foreseeable" effect on U.S. domestic commerce or on U.S. export commerce.[46] The legislative history to the FTAIA does nothing to prevent courts interested in employing the

---

[40] See Griffin, see para. 2.005, n. 12, at 522.

[41] See, *e.g.* Russell J. Weintraub, "Globalization's Effect on Antitrust Law", (1999) 34 New Eng. L. Rev. 27, 28–30.

[42] See *United States v. Nippon Paper Industries Co.*, 109 F.3d 1 (1st Cir. 1997) (no true conflict between Japanese and U.S. law), cert. denied, 118 S. Ct. 685 (1998). For an analysis of the *Nippon Paper* decision, see Michael Bishop, "*United States v. Nippon Paper Industries Co.*: Criminal Application of the Sherman Act Abroad", (1999) 32 Geo. Wash. J. Int'l L. & Econ. 271.

[43] See, *e.g. Filetech S.A.R.L. v. France Telecom S.A.*, 157 F.3d 922 (2d Cir. 1998) (insufficient showing of a true conflict between U.S. and French law such that compliance with the regulatory law of both countries would be impossible); *Maxwell Communications Corp. v. Societe Generale*, 93 F.3d 1036 (2d Cir. 1996). But see *Metro Indus. Inc. v. Sammi Corp.*, 82 F.3d 839, 846 n. 5 (9th Cir.) (*Hartford Fire* "did not question the propriety of the jurisdictional rule of reason or the seven comity factors set forth in Timberlane I."), cert. denied, 117 S. Ct. 181 (1996); *Sterling Drug, Inc. v. Bayer AG*, 14 F.3d 733 (2d Cir. 1994) (noting that *Hartford Fire* might be limited to the antitrust setting). For an analysis of the case law since *Hartford Fire Insurance*, see Spencer Weber Waller, "From the Ashes of *Hartford Fire*: The Unanswered Questions of Comity", 1998 Fordham Corp. L. Inst. 33.

[44] See 1995 "International Antitrust Guidelines", see para. 2.007, n. 15, at 21.

[45] 15 U.S.C., s. 6(a) (hereinafter FTAIA).

[46] See, *e.g. Caribbean Broadcast System, Ltd. v. Cable & Wireless PLC*, 148 F.3d 1080 (D.C. Cir. 1998) (plaintiff alleged a "direct, substantial, and reasonably foreseeable effect" on export trade or commerce sufficient to establish jurisdiction under clause 1(B) of FTAIA).

jurisdictional rule of reason from doing so, however. The House Report states that:

> the bill is intended neither to prevent nor to encourage additional judicial recognition of the special international characteristics of transactions. If a court determines that the requirements for the subject matter jurisdiction are met, this bill would have no effect on the courts' ability to employ notions of comity . . . or otherwise to take account of the international character of the transaction.[47]

Courts have relied on the FTAIA to dismiss antitrust actions.[48] Several courts have also concluded that the FTAIA's effects test is more difficult to satisfy, and thus more protective of foreign interests, than the *Alcoa* standard.[49]

Similar self-restraint has been exhibited by the executive branch and also at the administrative level. Section 7 of the Clayton Act prohibits mergers or acquisitions that have the effect of substantially lessening competition or tend to create a monopoly.[50] Merger activities by firms outside the United States are subject to the Clayton Act's prohibition if they have an anti-competitive affect on U.S. commerce.

2.018 In 1976 amendments to the Clayton Act, the Hart-Scott-Rodino Antitrust Improvements Act of 1976 requires parties to certain mergers, acquisitions, and joint ventures to notify the Justice Department and the Federal Trade Commission of their proposed agreement and observe a waiting period before closing the deal.[51] The implementing regulations exempt two categories of transaction:

(a) certain transactions with foreign elements if they fail to meet the minimum dollar thresholds of assets and/or sales, and

(b) certain transactions by firms owned by foreign governments or acquisitions of firms by a foreign government.[52]

2.019 Furthermore, the 1995 Antitrust Enforcement Guidelines for International Operations, published jointly by the Antitrust Division of the Justice Department and the Federal Trade Commission, reiterate the agencies' position that section 7 of the Clayton Act applies to a merger of two or more foreign firms if the merger affects U.S. commerce (for example, when at least

[47] H.R. Rep. No. 686, 97th Cong., 2d Sess. 10 (1982).

[48] See, *e.g. McGlinchy v. Shell Chem. Co.*, 845 F.2d 802 (9th Cir. 1988); *Liamuiga Tours v. Travel Impressions, Ltd.*, 617 F. Supp. 920 (E.D.N.Y. 1985).

[49] See, *e.g.* The "In" *Porters, S.A. v. Hanes Printables, Inc.*, 663 F. Supp. 494 (M.D.N.C. 1987); *Liamuiga Tours v. Travel Impressions, Ltd.*, 617 F. Supp. 920 (E.D.N.Y. 1985).

[50] 15 U.S.C., s. 18.

[51] 15 U.S.C., s. 18a. In 1999, U.S. antitrust authorities received notifications for 4,679 transactions. See ICPAC "Final Report", see para. 2.012, n. 23, at 45. See generally Stephen M. Axinn, Blaine V. Fogg & Neal R. Stoll, *Acquisitions Under the Hart-Scott-Rodino Antitrust Improvements Act* (2d ed. 1988); Deborah P. Herman, "The Effect of Twenty Years of Hart-Scott-Rodino on Merger Practice: A Case Study in the Law of Unintended Consequences Applied to Antitrust Legislation", (1997) 65 Antitrust L.J. 865.

[52] See 16 C.F.R. ss. 801.1(a), 802.50–.52 (1995).

one of the firms has distribution facilities in the United States or exports its products to the U.S. market).[53] The 1995 International Antitrust Guidelines also introduce notions of international comity in order to temper the rigid, unilateral approach to the enforcement of national antitrust rules with a transborder impact. The Guidelines provide that the comity analysis should consider all relevant factors, including

(a) the relative significance to the alleged violation of conduct within the United States, as compared to conduct abroad;

(b) the nationality of the persons involved in, or affected by, the conduct;

(c) the presence or absence of a purpose to affect U.S. consumers, markets, or exporters;

(d) the relative significance and foreseeability of the effects of the conduct on the United States as compared to the effects abroad;

(e) the existence of reasonable expectations that would be furthered or defeated by the action;

(f) the degree of conflict with foreign law or articulated foreign economic policies;

(g) the extent to which the enforcement activities of another country with respect to the same persons, including remedies resulting from those activities, may be affected; and

(h) the effectiveness of foreign enforcement as compared to U.S. enforcement action.[54]

2.020 The Guidelines add that other relevant factors to the comity analysis are whether another country encourages a certain course of conduct or leaves the parties free to choose among various business strategies, while another country prohibits those strategies. The Guidelines also take the position that courts should refrain from engaging in a comity analysis in an antitrust action filed by the Justice Department because of the delicate judgments affecting foreign relations that must be made in any comity analysis, judgments that the executive branch has already presumably made when it decided to bring an enforcement action.[55] The Guidelines encourage

[53] See 1995 "International Antitrust Enforcement Guidelines", see para. 2.007, n. 15, s. 3.14, illustrative example H. In the decade 1987–1997, merger filings in the United States involving either a foreign acquiring person or a foreign acquired entity ranged from 15.5% to 51% of total filings annually. See ICPAC "Final Report", see para. 2.012, n. 23, at 45. See generally Joseph P. Griffin, *U.S. International Antitrust Enforcement: A Practical Guide to the Agencies' Guidelines* (1997); Dean Brockbank, "The 1995 International Antitrust Guidelines: The Reach of U.S. Antitrust Law Continues to Expand", (1996) 2 J. Int'l Legal Studies 1.

[54] 1995 "International Antitrust Enforcement Guidelines", see para. 2.007, n. 15, s. 3.2.

[55] For criticisms of the Justice Department's position, see Griffin, *supra* note 53, at 190–92; ABA "Special Committee Report", see para. 2.004, n. 6, at 164; Spencer Weber Waller, "The Internationalization of Antitrust Enforcement", (1997) 77 B.U.L. Rev. 343 (hereinafter Waller I).

international notification, co-operation, information exchange, and comity with foreign enforcement authorities as an alternative to redressing trans-border restrictive business practices through extraterritorial, unilateral enforcement. Practice indicates that these are more than just hollow words. For example, in 1996 the Justice Department acceded to the remedy imposed by the European Commission on A.C. Nielsen's marketing practices and did not bring its own enforcement action in U.S. courts.[56]

2.021 The Justice Department's focus on process, caution, respect, self-restraint, and co-operation—in short, comity—in international antitrust enforcement stands in sharp contrast to the USTR's focus on results as exemplified by the *Kodak-Fuji Film* dispute. The USTR allowed Kodak to circumvent filing a petition with the Japan Fair Trade Commission (JFTC) before proceeding with a section 301 petition. This failure to require exhaustion of administrative remedies incensed the Japanese. The JFTC was obstinate by refusing initially to take action on the petition that Kodak did eventually file with the JFTC and by refusing to co-operate with the USTR in resolving the dispute. To have done otherwise, from the Japanese viewpoint, would have been equal to conceding that the USTR may replace the JFTC at the discretion of the former, a *de facto* surrender of sovereignty to which the Federal Trade Commission or the Justice Department would never have acceded to had circumstances been different.

The outcome was an absence of meaningful dialogue between the USTR and the Ministry of International Trade and Industry (MITI) on resolving Kodak's complaint. This episode also delayed conclusion of the bilateral Japan-U.S. antitrust co-operation agreement that was ultimately signed in 1999. It is likely that the Justice Department would have handled the matter differently. Whether it would have obtained a different result is subject to conjecture. Whatever the ultimate outcome, the relationship would probably not have been damaged; on the contrary, it probably would have been strengthened through constructive dialogue.

B. Other Self-Restraints on Unilateral Approaches

2.022 Three legal doctrines: foreign sovereign immunity, the act of state doctrine, and foreign sovereign compulsion may restrain competition law enforcement in cases where governments are involved in commercial activities. Indeed, these doctrines may exempt the anti-competitive conduct of foreign firms from the reach of domestic competition law altogether. The first two doctrines hold that certain actions of governmental bodies are not subject to legal challenge. While the foreign sovereign immunity and act of state doctrines developed outside the antitrust context (although they apply to it), the doctrine of foreign sovereign compulsion has its origins in the antitrust setting.

[56] See U.S. Dep't of Justice, Press Release, "Justice Department Closes Investigation into the Way A.C. Nielsen Co. Contracts Its Services for Tracking Retail Sales" (Dec. 3, 1996). The Justice Department also acquiesced in the SABRE case concerning airline computer reservation systems, discussed below.

2.023 First, the doctrine of foreign sovereign immunity has been a staple of public international law.[57] Under the traditional view, the acts of a foreign sovereign were absolutely immune from lawsuits, regardless of the circumstances. In the twentieth century, with the increasing involvement of governments in commercial activities, the traditional view of absolute immunity was replaced by the principle of restrictive immunity. States are immune from suit only when exercising their sovereign functions (legislative, judicial, or administrative authority) and not when they engage in commercial activities. Thus, when a state engages in essentially commercial activities it is potentially subject to the laws of other countries, including those countries' competition laws.[58]

2.024 The doctrine of restrictive immunity is observed by most developed countries, although differences remain over what constitutes a "commercial" activity. In the United States, the Foreign Sovereign Immunities Act (FSIA) codifies these principles, including the commercial activity exception.[59] Under the FSIA, the test of whether conduct is "commercial activity" depends on the nature of the conduct rather than its purpose.[60] If the nature of the activity is one that a private person could engage in, *e.g.* entering into a contract for the construction of a building, then the purpose for which the building is being constructed is irrelevant. Although the U.S. Supreme Court has never considered the commercial activity exception in an antitrust context, the FSIA does require that the commercial activity of a foreign state have a sufficient nexus with the United States before immunity under the Act is lifted. The activity must occur in the United States; an act by the foreign state must occur in the United States in connection with commercial activity elsewhere; or the commercial activity must have a "direct effect" within the United States.[61] In the United Kingdom, the State Immunity Act lists the commercial activities of governmental entities that do not enjoy immunity. In Canada, the Canadian State Immunity Act provides in section 5 that a state does not enjoy immunity for any commercial activity of the foreign state.

2.025 A second form of self-restraint in the exercise of extraterritorial jurisdiction is the act of state doctrine. Under the act of state doctrine, courts refrain from passing judgment on the legality of the acts of a foreign sovereign

[57] See generally Gary B. Born, *International Litigation in United States Courts* (1996) 199–286.
[58] See ABA "Special Committee Report", see para. 2.004, n. 6, at 132–36.
[59] 28 U.S.C. ss. 1330, 1602–1611. Before enactment of the Foreign Sovereign Immunities Act, the United States adopted the restrictive theory of immunity in the so-called Tate Letter. See Letter from Jack B. Tate, Acting Legal Advisor, U.S. Department of State, to Department of Justice, 26 Dep't State Bull. 984 (May 1952). See also Born, *supra* note 57, at 207–85; Restatement (Third) Foreign Relations Law of the United States, ss. 451–463 (1987).
[60] See, *e.g. Outboard Marine Corp. v. Pezetel*, 461 F. Supp. 384, 395–96 (D. Del. 1978) (sovereign immunity does not shield state-controlled Polish golf cart manufacturer); *Millicom Int'l Cellular, S.A. v. Republic of Costa Rica*, 995 F. Supp. 14 (D.D.C. 1998) (commercial activity exception not available because the Costa Rican government's activities did not take place in the United States, nor did they have a direct effect on the United States); *Filetech S.A.R.L. v. France Telecom S.A.*, 157 F.3d 922 (2d Cir. 1998) (insufficient factual findings to establish that subject matter jurisdiction exists over antitrust claims against France Telecom, a corporation in which the French government is a majority shareholder, under the FTAIA and the FSIA).
[61] See 28 U.S.C., s. 1605(a) (2).

when taken in its sovereign capacity.[62] It is a doctrine of judicial restraint that reflects the view that sensitive political judgments are best left to the political branches of government rather than the judicial branch. Although today the act of state doctrine is a very modest check on private and public competition law enforcement activities, the doctrine can be a significant barrier to competition law enforcement, as illustrated in the antitrust lawsuit brought against OPEC in the 1970s.[63] In that case the 9th Circuit affirmed the dismissal of an antitrust lawsuit brought against OPEC on the ground of the act of state doctrine.

In *Williams v. Curtiss-Wright Corp.*,[64] however, the 3rd Circuit refused to dismiss an antitrust lawsuit on act of state doctrine grounds. The court reasoned that suit was based on the acts of a competitor in the sale of jet aircraft abroad and not the validity of the decisions of foreign governments in refusing to purchase from the plaintiff. The U.S. Supreme Court gave the act of state doctrine a severely restricted construction in *W.S. Kirkpatrick & Co. v. Environmental Tectonics Corp.*, where it held that the act of state doctrine does not preclude judicial inquiry into a government's motives for performing certain acts.[65]

2.026 Thirdly, under the doctrine of foreign sovereign compulsion conduct by a private firm that is compelled or required by a foreign government within its territory does not give rise to liability under U.S. antitrust law.[66] The defence has been narrowly construed by U.S. courts. It will lie only where direct and specific compulsion can be demonstrated.[67] The defence is not available if the conduct is based on mere encouragement or acquiescence by the foreign government.[68] The doctrine has had important consequences for international trade. For example, to avoid potential liability of its auto manufacturers under U.S. antitrust law following the conclusion of the 1981 voluntary restraint agreement (VRA) on exports of automobiles from Japan to

[62] For the contemporary formulation of the act of state doctrine in U.S. courts, see *Banco Nacional de Cuba v. Sabbatino*, 376 U.S. 398 (1964); *W.S. Kirkpatrick & Co. v. Environmental Tectonics Corp.*, 493 U.S. 400 (1990). See Restatement (Third) Foreign Relations Law of the United States, s. 443 (1987); Ulrich Immenga, "Export Cartels and Voluntary Export Restraints Between Trade and Competition Policy", in *Antitrust: A New Trade Remedy* (John O. Haley & Hiroshi Iyori eds. 1995) 93, 109–10. See also Born, see para. 2.019, n. 53, at 685–744; ABA "Special Committee Report", see para. 2.004, n. 6, at 137–42; Lawrence A. Sullivan & Warren S. Grimes, *The Law of Antitrust: An Integrated Handbook* 993–95 (2000).

[63] See *Int'l Ass'n of Machinists & Aerospace Workers v. Organization of Petroleum Exporting Countries*, 649 F.2d 1354 (9th Cir. 1979), *cert. denied*, 454 U.S. 1163 (1982).

[64] 694 F.2d 1287 (3rd Cir. 1982).

[65] See *W.S. Kirkpatrick & Co. v. Environmental Tectonics Corp.*, 493 U.S. 400 (1990).

[66] See Born, see para. 2.019, n. 53, at 745–52; Restatement (Third) Foreign Relations Law of the United States, s. 441 (1987); Immenga, see para. 2.025, n. 62, at 111–12. As noted in the 1991 ABA Special Committee Report, "[i]t is a generally accepted legal proposition that persons lacking free will should not be held responsible for something they were forced to do. Thus, it follows that a defendant should not be subject to antitrust liability for conduct compelled by a foreign sovereign." ABA "Special Committee Report", see para. 2.004, n. 6, at 117 (footnote omitted).

[67] See, *e.g. Continental Ore Co. v. Union Carbide & Carbon Corp.*, 370 U.S. 690, 707–08 (1962).

[68] See ABA "Special Committee Report", see para. 2.025, n. 62, at 118–21. The defence has been criticised as being too restrictive in the case of Japan where "administrative guidance" by the government is the functional equivalent of compulsion. See *id.* at 120.

the United States, the Japanese government administered the VRA and ordered the division of markets among the Japanese firms.

C. Anti-Competitive Conduct that May go Unchallenged under a Unilateral Approach

2.027 As a policy matter most countries only prosecute conduct that causes anti-competitive effects in the domestic market. Although this policy is consistent with the view that competition law is concerned with the effects of RBPs on the domestic market, it does not prevent domestic firms from engaging in collusive activity in the field of foreign trade. Consequently, practices such as export cartels (which could be prosecuted if executed in domestic markets) will go unchallenged when used to promote export trade, in addition to certain joint ventures on research and development, absent anti-competitive effects in the domestic market.[69] As a matter of policy, therefore, firms are often given a wide berth when they engage in export trade, leaving the task of pursuing any anti-competitive effects to the importing country.

2.028 In Canada, for example, export cartels are exempt from prosecution under the competition laws for conspiracy, subject to certain qualifications.[70] In the United States, the Export Trading Company Act of 1982 was passed in order to reduce the exposure and uncertainty of firms engaged in export trade.[71] The Act permits U.S. companies to obtain advance certification from the government that enumerated activities in export trade will not be subject to treble damages awards, although private persons injured as a result of violations of the Act may recover compensatory damages. Such certification obviously does not shield an export trading company from competition law enforcement by other countries. Depending upon the jurisdictional principles that inform an importing country's competition laws, an importing country may find actionable conduct of an export cartel that occurs in the country of exportation, not in the import market. If the importing country exercises effects jurisdiction (*e.g.* the United States), it can challenge the collusive behaviour on the basis of the effects it causes in the import market, despite the fact that the conduct occurred abroad. If the importing country's practice is to adhere to the territoriality principle, however, it may find itself hamstrung in its ability to take action against anti-competitive export cartel activity.

D. Reactions to Unilateral Approaches: Foreign Nondisclosure Laws, Clawback Statutes, and Official Protests

2.029 There was a legislative backlash to the extraterritorial application of U.S. antitrust laws by Australia, Canada, France, New Zealand, and the

[69] See Kung Wang & Jyh—Feng Ho, "Research Joint Venture, Production Joint Venture and Competition Policy", in *International Harmonization of Competition Laws* (Chia-Jui Cheng, Lawrence S. Liu, & Chih-Kang Wang eds. 1995) 35 (noting the regulatory exemption from competition law for research and development joint ventures in the E.U., Japan the United States).

[70] See Competition Act, ss. 45(5), 45(6).

[71] See 15 U.S.C., ss. 4001–21. The Export Trading Company Act was enacted to breath new life into the moribund Webb-Pomerene Act. Both of these Acts are discussed in Chapter Four.

U.K. in the 1970s.[72] Each country enacted one or more pieces of legislation or adopted regulations aimed at controlling or preventing the communication of business and commercial information to foreign officials. These nondisclosure laws and regulations, popularly known as blocking statutes, were drafted without reference to any particular foreign country, but the clear target of these blocking statutes was the United States.[73] These prohibitory measures were motivated by the perceived need by these countries to protect their sovereign interests. The measures reflect the differences, perhaps the gulf, that separates the United States and some of its trading partners over jurisdictional, substantive, and procedural issues involving international competition law enforcement.

2.030 Most of these statutes contain discretionary provisions which allow government officials to permit or restrict the disclosure of information where important national interests are deemed to be affected.[74] Although they are an irritant to U.S. antitrust enforcement authorities, as well as to private parties who have filed an antitrust action in U.S. district court, blocking statutes do not invariably erect an insurmountable barrier to the discovery of information located abroad.[75] One explanation for this is that plaintiffs, both public and private, seek and are successful in obtaining information that is physically located within the United States. In addition, further mitigating the impact of blocking statutes, antitrust enforcement authorities seek the co-operation of foreign authorities in obtaining information that is physically located abroad.[76]

2.031 In recent years blocking and clawback statutes have been rarely

[72] The legislative backlash was large part a response to the uranium antitrust cases pursued by the Justice Department in the 1970s. See Daniel K. Tarullo, "Norms and Institutions in Global Competition Policy", (2000) 94 Am. J. Int'l L. 478, 481; Joseph P. Griffin, "Extraterritoriality in U.S. and EU Antitrust Enforcement", (1999) 67 Antitrust L.J. 159; Joseph P. Griffin, "Foreign Governmental Reactions to U.S. Assertions of Extraterritorial Jurisdiction", (1998) 6 Geo. Mason L. Rev. 505.

[73] See, *e.g.* Protection of Trading Interests Act, 1980, (c. 11), reprinted in (1982) 21 Int'l Leg. Materials 834; Foreign Extraterritorial Measures Act, R.S.C., Chap. F—29 (1985) (Canada), reprinted in (1985) 24 Int'l Leg. Materials 794. In addition to Canada and the United Kingdom, other countries which have enacted blocking statutes include Australia, Bermuda, the Bahamas, the Cayman Islands, France, Germany, Liechtenstein, New Zealand, Panama, Singapore, South Africa and Switzerland. See also Born, see para. 2.019, n. 53, at 849–60; Joseph P. Griffin, "United States Antitrust Laws and Transnational Business Transactions: An Introduction", (1987) 21 Int'l Law. 307, 308–309 (more than 15 blocking statutes designed to impede or thwart the extraterritorial application of the U.S. antitrust laws have been enacted by some of America's closest allies, including Australia, Canada, England, France, Switzerland and West Germany). Some of these statutes provide for non-recognition of U.S. antitrust judgments or allow the judgment-debtor to "clawback" the trebled portion of the judgment. See *id.* In addition to the enactment of blocking statutes, some countries also passed "clawback" laws that authorise recovery of the trebled portion of any U.S. antitrust judgment by the U.S. judgement debtor.

[74] For example, s. 82 and s. 83 of the Canadian Competition Act authorises the Canadian Competition Tribunal to issue orders blocking the implementation in Canada of foreign laws or other directives, and foreign judgments, decrees, orders or other processes, that would adversely affect competition in Canada, the efficiency of trade or industry in Canada, or the foreign trade of Canada, without compensating advantages. See Competition Act, R.S.C. 1985, c. S-15, as amended, ss. 82, 83.

[75] See Born, see para. 2.019, n. 53, at 849–60.

[76] *See* OECD, "Competition Law Enforcement: International Cooperation in the Collection of Information" (1984).

used, although they remain in effect. Other devices used by foreign governments to resist or to object to the extraterritorial application of U.S. antitrust law include filing diplomatic protests, submitting *amicus curiae* briefs in pending U.S. antitrust litigation, and refusing to recognise and enforce U.S. court judgments for treble damages. Further mitigating or eliminating the impact of blocking statutes are the bilateral co-operation agreements entered into in the 1980s and 1990s.

E. The Limits of Unilateralism

2.032 Applying antitrust law extraterritorially via the effects test is controversial because it is viewed as an infringement on state sovereignty.[77] The reaction of foreign governments to the extraterritorial application of another jurisdiction's competition law has been diplomatic protests, the enactment of blocking statutes and the implementation of related forms of resistance and non co-operation. In the absence of co-operation in international investigations, the Justice Department and the Federal Trade Commission know that bringing a successful antitrust case can be problematic. The aborted industrial diamonds prosecution involving General Electric and De Beers demonstrates the need for co-operation in cross-border enforcement actions.[78] As the trial judge observed in entering a judgment of acquittal:

> It would have been difficult for the government to prove its case even in the best of circumstances. Here, however, the government's usual burden of investigating and proving its case was made more difficult because three of the four named defendants, and many potential witnesses, are foreign nationals beyond the jurisdiction of this Court.[79]

2.033 Besides the difficulties encountered in extraterritorial competition law enforcement, unilateral efforts to impose U.S. competition policy principles on other nations has met with mixed results. The U.S.-Japan Enhanced Initiative on Deregulation and Competition Policy (discussed below) is arguably an example of a successful effort to re-invigorate Japan's competition law enforcement activities. Resistance to U.S. competition enforcement authorities' efforts to push countries toward a more aggressive enforcement stance in their domestic markets is based on at least two factors. First, U.S. antitrust law does not purport to advance foreign consumer welfare and secondly, a claim that nations have an obligation under international law to restrict anti-competitive behaviour within their domestic economy runs up against both widespread practice to the contrary and the absence of any specific instrument spelling out such an obligation, other than the positive comity provisions of bilateral co-operation agreements, discussed in the next part. Any attempt by the United States to create such an obligation through a

---

[77] See Tony A. Freyer, "Restrictive Trade Practices and Extraterritorial Application of Antitrust Legislation in Japanese-American Trade", (1999) 16 Ariz. J. Int'l & Comp. L. 159, 176.
[78] See *United States v. General Elec. Co.*, 869 F. Supp. 1285 (S.D. Ohio 1994); Waller I, see para. 2.020, n. 55, at 376–77.
[79] *United States v. General Elec. Co.*, 869 F. Supp. at 1300.

naked assertion of power risks provoking retaliation and upsetting the bilateral arrangements currently in place with which the United States largely is satisfied.

2.034 Against the backdrop of formal barriers to effective, unilateral competition law enforcement arrayed against a country, the incentives for co-operation are, in the words of Professor Merit Janow, "quite compelling."[80] Today, as a matter of policy, the United States espouses comity, both traditional and positive, as reflected in its 1995 International Antitrust Guidelines and in the bilateral co-operation agreements it has negotiated with its major trading partners (Canada, the E.U., Japan, and Mexico). The United States favour co-operation, as exemplified in the *Uranium* antitrust litigation,[81] where the Justice Department elected not to indict foreign parties, and in the *Laker Airways* case, where President Reagan directed the Attorney General to terminate a grand jury investigation on foreign policy grounds.[82] It is difficult, however, to reconcile these cases with the *Nippon Paper* case where the differences between the Governments of Japan and the United States could not have been more diametrical. In its *amicus curiae* brief, Japan stated: "extraterritorial application of the Sherman Act is invalid under international law and runs counter to the spirit of international comity."[83]

2.035 On the strength of the *Hartford Fire Insurance* decision, the First Circuit concluded that:

> the current state of the case law conclusively establishes that civil antitrust actions predicated on wholly foreign conduct which has an intended and substantial effect in the United States come within Section One's jurisdictional reach.[84]

As the language of the civil and criminal provisions of the Sherman Act are identical, the court was compelled to interpret the civil and criminal provisions in the same manner.[85] The court also rejected the comity arguments advanced by the Government of Japan. Following remand and reinstatement of the indictment, the case ended in a hung jury after a four-week trial. The district court thereafter dismissed the indictment and entered a judgment of acquittal. Perhaps the case is aberrational. Perhaps it signals a trend. The truth probably lies somewhere in between. What is safe to say is that the Antitrust Division of the Justice Department has earned a reputation for being independent, for being above politics, and for bringing cases based on their merits. Federal judges enjoy even greater independence, "enhanc[ing] confidence in their ability to proceed objectively while providing ample due process for all participants."[86]

---

[80] See Janow, see para. 2.009, n. 19, at 270.

[81] For a discussion of the *Uranium* antitrust litigation, see James R. Atwood & Kingman Brewster, *Antitrust and American Business Abroad*, ss. 6.16–6.17 (2d ed. 1981).

[82] See U.S. Dep't of Justice, Press Release, Nov. 19, 1984.

[83] Brief of *Amicus Curiae*, the Government of Japan, *United States v. Nippon Paper Indus.*, 109 F.3d 1 (1st Cir. 1997).

[84] *Nippon Paper*, 109 F.3d at 4.

[85] See *id.* at 5 (the case for interpreting the two provisions in the same manner is "irresistible").

[86] American Bar Ass'n, "Report of the Sections of Antitrust Law and International Law and Practice Concerning Private Anticompetitive Practices as Market Access Barriers" 18 (2000) (hereinafter "Report Concerning Private Anticompetitive Practices").

2.036 As previously noted, Congress has also reined in extraterritorial exercises of antitrust jurisdiction through enactment of the Foreign Trade Antitrust Improvements Act. Moreover, the International Competition Policy Advisory Committee (ICPAC) reports that:

> [t]oday, there is far less conflict between jurisdictions, and in the last decade there have been few, if any, instances of countries invoking statutes such as blocking or clawback laws to impede the United States in its efforts to prosecute transnational antitrust cases.[87]

Despite the blandishments of bilateral co-operation and the formal barriers, both jurisdictional and evidentiary, to international enforcement efforts, unilateral enforcement activities can still achieve successful results when targets of an antitrust investigation are encouraged to co-operate. In that connection, the Justice Department has in place a Corporate Leniency Policy that has enabled it:

> to vault a number of the more traditional barriers to international enforcement efforts. . . [I]t appears that unilateral policy measures undertaken by U.S. antitrust authorities . . . are succeeding in overcoming traditional barriers to international law enforcement . . . .[88]

III. BILATERAL APPROACHES

2.037 Problems stemming from differences in competition policy have been mitigated by the exercise of self-restraint in national competition law enforcement and the negotiation of bilateral co-operation agreements. Regardless of one's views on the merits of a unilateral approach to resolving international antitrust violations, resolving competing claims of jurisdiction between national competition enforcement authorities frequently requires co-operation. As a practical matter, national enforcement authorities often need access to information and evidence located outside the territory of an enforcement authority and thus beyond its jurisdictional reach.[89]

2.038 The inability to obtain personal jurisdiction over foreign defendants can also impede or block cross-border antitrust cases. Co-operation between national enforcement authorities can be a prerequisite to a successful competition law enforcement action involving foreign parties and the interests of

[87] International Competition Policy Advisory Committee to the Attorney General and Assistant Attorney General for Antitrust, "Final Report" 36 (2000) (hereinafter "ICPAC Final Report"). ICPAC adds that "even when U.S. agencies do not receive any overt co-operation from another jurisdiction, they have been relatively unhindered during the last two or more decades by application of blocking statutes and other affirmative tools in opposition to U.S. international investigations." *id.* at 180–81.

[88] See "ICPAC Final Report", *supra* note 87, at 184–85. For a summary of the DOJ's leniency programme, see *id.* Annex 4–B.

[89] See, *e.g. United States v. General Elec. Co.*, 869 F. Supp. 1285 (S.D. Ohio 1994); *Re Uranium Antitrust Litigation*, 480 F. Supp. 1138 (N.D. Ill. 1979) (ordering 11 foreign defendants to produce documents).

more than one country.[90] A constructive counter-response to blocking statutes has been mutual legal assistance agreements and antitrust co-operation agreements. The need at times for co-operation among national enforcement authorities lends support to the argument that bilateral co-operation agreements are desirable, if only because they are a practical necessity. As noted, the 1994 investigation by the U.S. Justice Department into allegations that General Electric and De Beers had fixed the price of industrial diamonds hit a stone wall when national authorities in most other countries refused to co-operate with the Justice Department's investigation. (Belgium was an exception, but the evidence it proffered was held inadmissible.)

2.039 Bilateral co-operation agreements, however, (other than perhaps mutual legal assistance agreements) are not legally enforceable, so when strong national interests enter the picture, co-operation could easily stall or evaporate. In addition, bilateral co-operation agreements do not address collaborative efforts in the area of transnational mergers and acquisitions. Still, these shortcomings do not necessarily lead to the conclusion that a multilateral co-operation agreement or a multilateral agreement on competition policy is the preferred alternative. To be effective, a necessary but not sufficient condition to a multilateral solution is that the organisation tapped to deal with these issues has the resources and the expertise to address them and resolve them creditably. At present, neither the WTO nor any other international organisation meets either of these conditions.

2.040 Other than through informal co-operation between national enforcement authorities,[91] international co-operation in the area of competition law enforcement takes place pursuant to some kind of international agreement. Currently, five types of such agreements exist:

(1) bilateral agreements dealing exclusively with co-operation on competition law enforcement;

(2) bilateral agreements relating to mutual legal assistance in criminal matters, including criminal antitrust cases;

(3) bilateral agreements providing for technical co-operation on competition policy;

[90] The process of simultaneously pursuing unilateral and bilateral approaches to cross-border competition law enforcement has been described as "cooperative unilateralism." See Edward M. Graham & J. David Richardson, "A U.S.-EU Road Toward Multilateralism in International Competition Policy", (Feb. 1999) 4 Econ. Perspectives, USIA Electronic Journal No. 1, http://www.usia.gov/journals/ites/0299/ijee/iie.htm. This approach has also been advocated by Judge Diane Wood. See Diane P. Wood, "The Internationalization of Antitrust Law: Options for the Future", (1995) 44 DePaul L. Rev. 1289, 1298–99 (recommending that the United States pursue vigorous unilateral enforcement and co-operation rather than harmonisation). But see Waller I, see para. 2.020, n. 55, at 378 (co-operation agreements are in vogue because they increase national power; they are a dead end to substantive harmonisation of international antitrust).

[91] An example of such informal co-operation is the assistance that Japanese prosecutors gave to Justice Department officials in the *Nippon Paper* criminal prosecution in 1995. See Freyer, see para. 2.032, n. 77, at 175–76.

(4) regional agreements or bilateral agreements concluded within a regional framework agreement, such as an agreement creating a free trade area or customs union; and

(5) non-binding multilateral instruments.

As noted in a 1998 United Nations Conference on Trade and Development (UNCTAD) report, "In practice, the borderlines between these different types of agreements are sometimes blurred."[92] Each of these agreement will be discussed in turn.

A. Bilateral Co-operation Agreements on Competition Law Enforcement

2.041 The principle of international comity that has worked its way into antitrust jurisprudence and the administrative practice of the United States has also found a home in bilateral co-operation agreements to which the United States and other countries are parties.[93] While some of the older bilateral co-operation agreements were concerned mostly with avoiding jurisdictional conflicts through principles of traditional comity, the newer agreements add provisions on co-operation in antitrust enforcement, including the principle of "positive comity". This principle allows a party to an agreement to request the other party to initiate antitrust enforcement proceedings against anti-competitive activities in the latter's territory that cause injury and other anti-competitive effects in the requesting party's territory. The bilateral co-operation agreements to which the United States is a party are dominated by two themes: enforcement co-operation, and avoidance and management of jurisdictional disputes between national enforcement authorities. The most recent agreements have a third theme of technical co-operation.

1. *The 1976 Germany-U.S Antitrust Accord*

2.042 The 1976 Germany-U.S. antitrust co-operation agreement represents the first generation of bilateral antitrust co-operation agreements entered

[92] UNCTAD, "Experiences Gained So Far With International Cooperation on Competition Policy Issues and the Mechanisms Used", TD/B/COM.2/CLP/3 (1998), available at http://www.unctad.org. See See OECD, Joint Group on Trade and Competition, "Outline of (A) Core Principles, Common Approaches and Common Standards and (B) Bilateral and Multilateral Approaches", at 11, COM/TD/DAFFE/CLP(98)97/Final (Oct. 13, 1999) (describing 5 models of bilateral co-operation agreements).

[93] Under U.S. law, bilateral co-operation agreements are executive agreements. As such, they are binding international agreements for U.S. authorities, but they do not have the legal status of treaties under U.S. law and do not supersede domestic law. Consequently, the bilateral agreements do not supplant U.S. statutes that prohibit sharing confidential information without the submitter's consent. See WTO, Working Group on the Interaction between Trade and Competition Policy, Communication from the United States, "Approaches to Promoting Cooperation and Communication among Members including in the Field of Technical Cooperation", WT/WGTCP/W/129, at 3 (May 25, 1999). For a summary of U.S. bilateral co-operation agreements, see Janow, see para. 2.009, n. 19, at 271–78; WTO, Working Group on the Interaction between Trade and Competition Policy, Submission from the United States, "US Experience with Antitrust Cooperation Agreements", WT/WGTCP/W/48 (Nov. 24, 1997).

into by the United States.[94] The agreement primarily focuses on enforcement co-operation. The agreement calls on the parties broadly to co-operate and render assistance to antitrust enforcement authorities of the other party in connection with antitrust investigations or proceedings. Co-operation includes providing the other party with any significant information involving restrictive business practices that have a "substantial effect on the domestic or international trade of such other party."[95] The parties are also to attempt to co-ordinate concurrent enforcement investigations or proceedings in the two countries that are related to each other.[96] However, despite the calls for co-operation, co-ordination, and consultation, Article 3 relieves the parties of these obligations when, *inter alia*, "compliance would be inconsistent with its security, public policy or other important national interests," or if compliance would breach national laws on confidentiality of information.[97] These exceptions have the potential for punching a large hole in the norms which the agreement attempts to establish.

2.043 Notably absent from the agreement are provisions on conflict avoidance and comity in those cases where enforcement authorities exercise extraterritorial jurisdiction. Given the agreement's relatively early date (1976), and considering that notions of comity in the exercise of extraterritorial jurisdiction where still nascent (the 9th Circuit's *Timberlane* case was decided in 1976), this lacuna is not surprising. In all future bilateral co-operation agreements entered into by the United States, however, provisions incorporating principles of traditional comity and later positive comity would become standard.

2. *The 1982 Australia-U.S. Antitrust Co-operation Agreement*

2.044 The 1982 co-operation agreement on antitrust matters between the United States and Australia focuses on conflict avoidance and recognises the close relationship between trade policies and competition law enforcement.[98] First, the agreement requires each party to notify and consult with the other party if a policy it has adopted or an investigation it has undertaken may have ramifications for the laws, policies, or national interests of the other party.[99] This provision was adopted with a special view to identifying and resolving potential difficulties for Australian exporters before they have made a substantial commitment to foreign markets—a commitment that could become the target of an antitrust investigation by the Justice Department.[1]

[94] See Agreement Between the Government of the United States of America and the Government of the Federal Republic of Germany Relating to Mutual Cooperation Regarding Restrictive Business Practices, done at Bonn, Germany, June 23, 1976, U.S.-FRG, 27 U.S.T. 1956, available at http://www.usdoj.gov.

[95] *id.* Art. 2(2).

[96] See *id.* Art. 2(5).

[97] *id.* Art. 3(1) (b)–(c).

[98] See Agreement Between the Government of the United States of America and the Government of Australia Relating to Co-operation on Antitrust Matters, done at Washington, D.C., June 29, 1982, available at http://www.usdoj.gov, reprinted in (1984) 21 Int'l Leg. Materials 275.

[99] See *id.* arts. 1, 2.

[1] See *id.* Art. 2.6(b).

2.045 Secondly, the parties agree that during consultations they:

> shall seek earnestly to avoid a possible conflict between their respective laws, policies and national interests and for that purpose to give due regard to each other's sovereignty and to considerations of comity.[2]

In those courts in the United States that use the jurisdictional rule of reason, the United States has agreed to intervene in private antitrust litigation and to present to the courts the outcome of discussions between the two countries in such litigation.[3] In such circumstances, the enforcement authorities will be able to inform the courts as to Australia's interests and the reason why it declined to take enforcement action, thereby enabling a judge to better assess the interests of the affected country when applying the jurisdictional rule of reason in private antitrust litigation.

2.046 Thirdly, the Agreement provides that documents and information provided by the parties is to be treated as confidential and not to be used as evidence in any judicial or administrative proceeding without the consent of the disclosing party.[4] Fourthly, the parties agree to co-operate with each other in antitrust enforcement, provided a proposed antitrust investigation or enforcement action does not adversely affect the laws, policies, or national interests of the other.[5]

3. *The Canada-U.S. Co-operation Agreements*

2.047 In 1995, the United States and Canada signed a new antitrust co-operation agreement.[6] This agreement effectively supersedes the 1984 Memorandum of Understanding (MOU), which both countries recognised had grown obsolete given its emphasis on conflict avoidance and its relative neglect of enforcement co-operation that had become the main theme in antitrust dealings between Canada and the United States.[7]

---

[2] *id.* Art. 2.5.
[3] See *id.* Art. 6.
[4] See *id.* Art. 3.
[5] See *id.* Art. 5.1.
[6] "Agreement Between the Government of the United States of America and the Government of Canada Regarding the Application of Their Competition and Deceptive Marketing Practices Laws", Aug. 3, 1995, U.S.-Canada, reprinted in 4 Trade Reg. Rep. (CCH) 13,503, available at http://www.sice.oas.org/cp_comp/english/cpa/cpa1_e.asp. See Sanford Yosowitz, "Regulation of Competition in the Canada/U.S. Context—Extraterritorial Reach of U.S. Antitrust Law", (1998) 24 Can.-U.S. L.J. 297; John Gero, "The View from North of the Border: A Canadian Perspective on Trade and Competition Views in North America", (1996) 4 U.S.-Mex. L.J. 55. Canada has entered into only one other bilateral antitrust co-operation agreements, the 1998 agreement with the E.U., discussed below.
[7] See "Agreement Between the Government of the United States of America and the Government of Canada Regarding the Application of Their Competition and Deceptive Marketing Practices Laws', Mar. 9, 1984, U.S.-Canada, reprinted in (1984) 23 Int'l Leg. Materials 275. For more on the 1984 MOU, see Waller I, see para. 2.020, n. 55, at 363–65. See also Crystal L. Witterick, "Regulation of Competition in the Canada/U.S. Context—Extraterritorial Reach of U.S. Antitrust Law—A Canadian Perspective", 24 Can.-U.S. L.J. 299 (1998); Lawson A.W. Hunter & Susan M. Hutton, "Where There Is a Will, There Is a Way: Cooperation in Canada-U.S. Antitrust Relations", (1994) 20 Can.-U.S. L.J. 101 (describing the history of Canada-U.S. competition law relations).

The new agreement is similar in many respects to the 1991 agreement between the United States and the European Community (discussed below).[8] It provides for notification with respect to enforcement activities "that may affect important interests of the other Party."[9] One of the more important additions to the 1995 Agreement, which improves significantly upon the 1984 MOU, is a notification obligation covering mergers and acquisitions in which one or more parties to the transaction, or a company controlling one or more parties to the transaction, is incorporated or organised under the laws of Canada or the United States.[10] This provision is an important one, given the boom in M&A activity and is unique to bilateral co-operation agreements to which the United States is a party.

2.048 The Agreement provides for co-operation and co-ordination in cross-border enforcement efforts whenever there is a potential for mutual assistance and reinforcement. To that end, enforcement co-operation includes assistance in locating and securing evidence and witnesses.[11] However, neither party is required to disclose confidential information to the other party if such disclosure is prohibited by law or would otherwise be incompatible with that party's important interests.[12] Under Article V of the Agreement dealing with positive comity, each party can ask the other to enforce its antitrust laws against local conduct that adversely affects the other's interests.

2.049 Adopting the principle of traditional comity, Article VI directs the parties to avoid conflicts in the enforcement of their respective antitrust laws. When it appears that one party's enforcement activities may adversely affect the important interests of the other party, the following non-exhaustive list of nine factors is to guide the parties in the exercise of their jurisdiction:

(1) the relative significance to the anticompetitive activities involved of conduct occurring within one Party's territory as compared to conduct occurring within that of the other;

(2) the relative significance and foreseeability of the effects of the anti-competitive activities on one Party's important interests as compared to the effects on the other Party's important interests;

(3) the presence or absence of a purpose on the part of those engaged in the anti-competitive activities to affect consumers, suppliers or competitors within the enforcing Party's territory;

(4) the degree of conflict or consistency between the first Party's enforcement activities (including remedies) and the other Party's laws or other important interests;

[8] See "Agreement Between the Government of the United States of America and the Commission of the European Communities Regarding the Application of Their Competition Laws", Sept. 23, 1991, U.S.-E.C., (1991) 30 Int'l Leg. Materials 1491, reprinted in 4 Trade Reg. Rep. (CCH) 13,504.

[9] *id.* Art. II.

[10] See *id.* Art. II:2(c).

[11] See *id.* Art. III.

[12] See *id.* Art. X.

(5) whether private persons, either natural or legal, will be placed under conflicting requirements by both Parties;
(6) the existence or absence of reasonable expectations that would be furthered or defeated by the enforcement activities;
(7) the location of relevant assets;
(8) the degree to which a remedy, in order to be effective, must be carried out within the other Party's territory; and
(9) the extent to which enforcement activities of the other Party with respect to the same persons, including judgments or undertakings resulting from such activities, would be affected.[13]

2.050 While these comity factors are similar to the ones listed in the joint Justice Department/FTC Antitrust Enforcement Guidelines for International Operations, the Agreement does not require consideration of the "nationality of the persons involved in or affected by the conduct" or "the degree of conflict with foreign law or articulated foreign economic policies."[14] Instead, the Agreement directs the parties to take into account "whether private persons, either natural or legal, will be placed under conflicting requirements by both Parties," and "the degree of conflict or consistency between the first Party's laws enforcement activities (including remedies) and the other Party's laws or other important interests."[15] The Agreement's focus on whether private persons will be placed under conflicting requirements reflects the *Hartford Fire Insurance* view that the jurisdictional rule of reason is triggered only after a person is subject to conflicting legal requirements in two jurisdictions. The Agreement's eighth comity factor: "the degree to which a remedy, in order to be effective, must be carried out within the other Party's territory" also differs from the DOJ/FTC Guidelines which focuses on "the effectiveness of foreign enforcement as compared to [domestic] enforcement action."[16]

2.051 Article VII of the Agreement for the first time establishes a framework for co-operation and co-ordination with respect to enforcement of deceptive marketing practices laws, including notification and the sharing of information in the enforcement of the parties' deceptive marketing practices laws.[17] Finally, Article IX requires U.S. and Canadian authorities to meet semi-annually to exchange information on enforcement activities and to discuss policy changes. The 1995 Canada-U.S. Antitrust Co-operation Agreement served as a model for the two co-operation agreements concluded in 1999 between the United States and Israel, and between the United States and Japan.

4. *The E.U.-U.S. Co-operation Agreements*

2.052 **a. The 1991 Co-operation Agreement** The potential for international conflict in the regulation of anti-competitive business activities is at

[13] *id.* Art. VI.
[14] "1995 International Antitrust Guidelines", see para. 2.007, n. 15, ss. 3.2(2), 3.2(5).
[15] Canada-U.S. Cooperation Agreement, see para. 2.047, n. 6, Art. VI, ss. 5(v), 5(iv).
[16] "1995 International Antitrust Guidelines", see para. 2.007, n. 15, s. 3.2(8).
[17] "Canada-U.S. Cooperation Agreement", see para. 2.047, n. 6, Art. VII, ss. 1, 3.

its greatest where two countries have overlapping jurisdiction. In appreciation of the transatlantic effects on business arising out of these jurisdictional conflicts, in September 1991 the European Commission and the United States concluded an Antitrust Co-operation Agreement.[18] The Agreement has resulted in a significant increase in the exchange of information between enforcement authorities.[19] A key provision of the agreement recognises the principle of traditional comity that calls upon both parties to take account of the other's important interests at all phases of enforcement activities. Article VI(3) sets forth six factors to guide the parties' comity analysis, factors that are similar to, but not identical with, those announced in the *Timberlane* decision:

(1) the relative significance to the anti-competitive activities involved of conduct within the enforcing Party's territory as compared to conduct within the other Party's territory;

(2) the presence or absence of a purpose on the part of those engaged in the anti-competitive activities to affect consumers, suppliers, or competitors within the enforcing Party's territory;

(3) the relative significance of the effects of the anti-competitive activities on the enforcing Party's interests as compared to the effects on the other Party's interests;

(4) the existence or absence of reasonable expectations that would be furthered or defeated by the enforcement activities;

(5) the degree of conflict or consistency between the enforcement activities and the other Party's laws or articulated economic policies; and

(6) the extent to which enforcement activities of the other Party with respect to the same person, including judgments or undertakings resulting from such activities, may be affected.

2.053 Notifications of merger and enforcement activities with an E.U./U.S. dimension has steadily increased since 1991. For example, in 1997, the E.U. notified U.S. enforcement authorities of 42 cases involving competition law enforcement and merger regulation, while the United States notified the E.U. of 36 combined antitrust/merger cases. In 1998, the figures were 52 combined competition law/merger cases notified to the United States by the

[18] "Agreement between the Government of the United States and the Commission of the European Communities Regarding the Application of Their Competition Laws", Sept. 23, 1991, U.S.-EC, reprinted in (1991) 30 Int'l Legal Materials 1491. France successfully challenged the legality of the 1991 Agreement on the ground that the Commission acted *ultra vires*. See *France v. Commission* [1994] E.C.R. I—3641, I—3678. Shortly thereafter, the E.U. approved an identical agreement utilising proper procedure.

[19] By one report, approximately 10% of the Hart-Scott-Rodino pre-merger notification filings have involved at least one company headquartered in the E.U. and, conversely, more than 20% of the mergers notified under the Merger Regulation have been notified simultaneously under Hart-Scott-Rodino. See Griffin, see para. 2.016, n. 39, at 181–82.

E.U., and 46 combined antitrust/merger cases notified to the E.U. by the United States.[20]

2.054 In its 1999 status report on the 1991 E.U.-U.S. Co-operation Agreement,[21] the European Commission painted a picture of calm seas and smooth sailing for calendar year 1998.[22] In all cases of mutual interest, the Commission reported, it is the parties' norm to establish contacts at the outset in order to exchange views and, in appropriate cases, to co-ordinate enforcement activities. In connection with the latter, co-operation has involved the synchronisation of investigations in order to prevent the destruction of evidence by companies suspected of cartel activity.[23] The Report also noted that with regard to combating hard-core cartels, E.U.-U.S. co-operation would be more effective if the parties could share confidential information.[24] With regard to merger activity, the 1999 Commission Report noted that "[i]nternational co-operation has proved effective in the context of individual cases."[25] Commenting on the WorldCom/MCI merger, the Report described it as an example of the best co-operation practices. With the *Boeing/McDonnell Douglas* merger the Report focused on the positive aspects of trans-Atlantic co-operation, noting the co-operation between the Commission and the FTC on timing, market definition, remedies, and the assessment of anti-competitive effects.[26] As one of four conditions of its approval of the merger, the Commission demanded that Boeing abandon exclusive supply contracts it had with three U.S. airlines.[27] The contracts were unrelated to the merger,

---

[20] See WTO, Working Group on the Interaction between Trade and Competition Policy, Communication from the European Community and Its Member States, "Approaches to promoting co-operation and communication among WTO Members, including in the field of technical cooperation", WT/WGTCP/W/129, at 6 (July 12, 1999).

[21] European Commission, "XXVIIIth Report to the Council and the European Parliament on the Application of the Agreement Between the European Communities and the Government of the United States of America regarding the Application of Their Competition Laws", Com(99) final (1999) (hereinafter "XXVIIIth Report"), available at http://www.europa.eu.int/comm/dg04/interna/bilateral.htm.

[22] For a contrary view, see Laura E. Keegan, "The 1991 U.S./EC Competition Agreement: A Glimpse of the Future Through the *United States v. Microsoft Corp.* Window, (1996) 2 J. Int'l Legal Stud. 149.

[23] "XXVIIIth Report", see para. 2.054, n. 21, at 2–3.

[24] See *id.* at 4. The International Antitrust Enforcement Assistance Act of 1994, discussed below, attempts to repair this defect in antitrust co-operation agreements. The lack of co-operation in information sharing has been noted as a major obstacle to combating hard-core cartels on price fixing, bid rigging, and market allocation. See Report by the OECD Competition Law and Policy Committee, "New Initiatives, Old Problems: A Report on Implementing the Hard Core Cartel Recommendation and Improving Co-operation", in (2000) OECD, Hard Core Cartels 28–43 (hereinafter Report of the CLP Committee).

[25] "XXVIIIth Report", see para. 2.054, n. 21, at 3.

[26] See *id.*

[27] See Commission of the European Communities, "The Commission Clears the Merger Between Boeing and McDonnell Douglas Under Certain Conditions and Obligations", RAPID Press Release, July 30, 1997, available in LEXIS, Intlaw Library, E.C. News File, reported in [1997] O.J. L336 16. Boeing reluctantly agreed to the following list of conditions in order to ensure Commission approval of the merger:

(1) Refrain from entering exclusive supply contracts until 2007, and not enforce the exclusivity rights in its existing contracts with three U.S. airlines. (2) License to competitors non-exclusive patents developed from publicly financed research and development. (3) Maintain DAC, the

therefore critics charged that the Commission's remedy exceeded its authority under the Merger Regulation.[28] The critics claimed the E.C. was not analysing the impact of the merger on competition, but was merely acting to protect Boeing's European rival, Airbus Industrie.

2.055 The *Boeing/McDonnell Douglas* case illustrates that advancing the goal of bilateral co-operation can soon reach its limits when deep-seated national (or in the case of the E.U., regional) economic interests enter the analysis. The strong desire by the Commission to defend the interests of its local civil aircraft champion, Airbus Indsutrie, undoubtedly overwhelmed any sentiment on the part of the Commission to rollover by acceding to the determination of the Federal Trade Commission that the Boeing/McDonnell Douglas merger did not, on balance, represent a threat to competition in the civil aircraft industry.[29] Despite the Boeing/McDonnell Douglas imbroglio, the Commission's 1999 Report concluded, "It is clear that the 1991 Agreement has provided a solid and quite satisfactory framework for cooperation."[30] This sentiment has been echoed by the chairman of the Federal Trade Commission, Robert Pitofsky.[31]

The 1991 E.U.-U.S. Co-operation Agreement also includes positive comity principles, a significant departure from first-generation bilateral co-operation agreements. Although the Agreement does not use the term "positive comity" *in haec verba*, Article V(2) of the Agreement provides that a party affected by anti-competitive practices occurring within the territory of the other party may request that it commence appropriate enforcement action. The requested party retains the discretion to initiate an investigation and any enforcement action. The parties' follow-on 1998 co-operation agreement expands on the positive comity principle.

2.056 b. The 1998 Positive Comity Agreement With the increased integration of national economies, especially the transatlantic economies, a

commercial aircraft manufacturing unit of McDonnell Douglas, as a separate legal entity for a period of 10 years. (4) Refrain from using its dominant position to abuse relationships with customers and suppliers.
See *id.*

[28] Both the House of Representatives and the Senate passed resolutions opposing the European Commission's "interference" in a U.S. business transaction. See H.R. Res. No. 191, 105th Cong. (1997), 143 Cong. Rec. 5550 (1997); S. Res. No. 108, 105th Cong. (1997), 143 Cong. Rec. 7609 (1997).

[29] For scholarly criticisms of the European Commission's handling of the *Boeing/McDonnell Douglas* merger, see Sondra Roberto, "The Boeing/McDonnell Douglas Merger Review: Serious Stretch of European Competition Powers", (1998) 24 Brooklyn J. Int'l L. 593; Brian Peck, "Extraterritorial Application of Antitrust Laws and the U.S.-EU Dispute Over the Boeing and McDonnell Douglas Merger: From Comity to Conflict? An Argument for a Binding International Agreement on Antitrust Enforcement and Dispute Resolution", (1998) 35 San Diego L. Rev. 1163. But see Tarullo, see para. 2.030, n. 72, at 481 ("The Boeing-McDonnell Douglas was highly unusual, since it involved what has now become a worldwide duopoly, with one company in the United States and the other in Europe.").

[30] "XXVIIIth Report", see para. 2.054, n. 21, at 5.

[31] See Robert Pitofsky, Chairman, U.S. Federal Trade Comm'n, "Competition Policy in a Global Economy—Today and Tomorrow", Remarks before the European Institute's Eighth Annual Transatlantic Seminar on Trade and Investment (Nov. 4, 1998), *available at* http://www.ftc.gov/speeches/speech1.htm.

need was identified to broaden and deepen the 1991 E.U.-U.S. Co-operation Agreement. In the spirit of the 1998 OECD Recommendation Concerning Effective Action Against Hard Core Cartels (discussed below), in June 1998, the United States and the E.C. signed a milestone antitrust co-operation agreement supplementing their 1991 agreement.[32] By formally adopting the principle of "positive comity," the 1998 Positive Comity Agreement creates a presumption that when anti-competitive activities occur in whole or substantial part in the territory of one of the parties and affect the interests of the other party, the latter "will normally defer or suspend its enforcement activities in favor of" the former.[33] For example, such deferral would be expected when these anti-competitive activities do not have a direct, substantial, and reasonably foreseeable impact on consumers in the territory of the party deferring or suspending its investigation.[34]

2.057 The principle of traditional comity calls for restraint and moderation on the part of antitrust enforcement authorities when engaged in the extraterritorial application of their antitrust laws. Under the positive comity principle if either the United States or the E.U. believes that their "important interests" are being adversely affected by restrictive business practices taking place in the territory of the other that violate the latter's antitrust laws, the adversely affected authority may request that the other initiate enforcement proceedings.[35] The Positive Comity Agreement envisions that in cases where anti-competitive conduct in the territory of the requested party harms the requesting country's consumers, the requesting country will still defer or suspend enforcement and the requested party will investigate and take appropriate remedial measures in conformity with its own laws.

2.058 In conducting its investigation, the requested party will also report back to the requesting party on the status of the investigation, notify any changes in enforcement intentions and comply with any reasonable suggestions of the requesting party.[36] Notwithstanding the presumption, the agreement contemplates that parties may pursue separate and parallel enforcement activities where anti-competitive conduct, such as international price fixing cartels, affects both territories and justifies the imposition of penalties within both jurisdictions.[37]

2.059 The Positive Comity Agreement does not impose an affirmative obligation to act upon a request or to suspend an ongoing investigation in

---

[32] "Agreement between the Government of the United States of America and the European Communities on the Application of Positive Comity Principles in the Enforcement of Their Competition Laws", June 4, 1998, U.S.-EC, reprinted in (1998) 37 Int'l Legal Materials [hereinafter "Positive Comity Agreement"], available at http://www.usdoj.gov/atr/public/international/docs/1781.htm. See also U.S. Department of Justice, Press Release, U.S. and European Communities Sign Antitrust Consideration Agreement, available at http://www.usdoj.gov/public/press_releases/1998/1782.htm.

[33] See "Positive Comity Agreement", *supra* n. 32, Art. IV:2.

[34] See *id.* Art. IV:2(a) (i). For an analysis and assessment of positive comity, see "ICPAC Final Report", see para. 2.036, n. 87, at 226–41; OECD, "Committee on Competition Law and Policy Report on Positive Comity", DAFFE/CLP(99)19 (June 14, 1999) (hereinafter "OECD Report on Positive Comity").

[35] See Positive Comity Agreement, *supra* note 32, Art. IV:2(b).

[36] See *id.* Art. IV:2(c).

[37] See *id.* Art. IV:4.

deference to the party on whose territory the anti-competitive conduct has occurred. At most, the requesting party is required to give the requested party its reasons for not suspending an investigation should it choose to pursue its own enforcement action.[38] Importantly, positive comity only applies when the challenged conduct violates the antitrust laws of the host country. Consequently, as a general matter export activity that is permitted by the host country cannot be the subject of a positive comity request, even if that activity adversely affects the important interests of the requesting state.[39] There could be instances, however, where a U.S. export cartel would violate the FTAIA and hence be subject to a positive comity request from the E.U. Moreover, informal co-operation is still possible.

2.060 One of the E.U.'s motives for entering into the Positive Comity Agreement was to parry and blunt U.S. extraterritorial enforcement of its antitrust laws in order to open the E.U. market when it is closed by private RBPs.[40] Sceptics of positive comity warn that it is unrealistic to expect that a government will prosecute its own nationals for the benefit of another country.[41] The E.U.'s 1999 status report notes that no requests had been submitted by the E.U. or the United States under the 1998 Positive Comity Agreement.[42] However, one formal referral was made by the United States under the 1991 E.U.-U.S. Agreement in April, 1997, requesting the E.U. to investigate alleged anti-competitive conduct involving airlines' computer reservation systems.[43] The European Commission initiated an investigation against the competing E.U. reservation system, Amadeus, and eventually issued a Statement of Objections some 26 months after the U.S. referral. In the meantime, SABRE, the U.S.-based computer reservation system, and two European airlines, Lufthansa and SAS, reached a private settlement. In September 1999, the Commission closed its investigation on the basis that it had discovered no violation of Article 81.

2.061 FTC Chairman Robert Pitofsky has put the purported benefits of positive comity into the following perspective:

> [it is] a small and modest element that you use in unusual cases to try to protect American firms doing business abroad or foreign firms doing business in the United States. It's hardly a common resort.[44]

Putting it more bluntly, E.C. Competition Director Alexander Schaub stated in January 1999 that the concept of positive comity has been "oversold" at its

[38] See *id.* Art. IV:(2).
[39] See *id.* Art. I:1(b).
[40] See Karl van Miert, "International Cooperation in the Field of Competition: A View from the EC", 1997 (1998) Fordham Corp. L. Inst., Ch. 2, at 23.
[41] See Robert D. Shank, "The Justice Department's Recent Antitrust Enforcement Policy: Toward A 'Positive Comity' Solution to International Competition Problems?" (1996) 29 Vand. J. Transnat'l L. 155; James R. Atwood, "Positive Comity—Is It a Positive Step?", 1992 (1993) Fordham Corp. L. Inst. 79, 87 (1993) ("laws are written and enforced to protect national interests").
[42] "XXVIIIth Report", see para. 2.056, n. 32, at 7.
[43] See U.S. Dep't of Justice, Press Release, "Justice Department Asks European Communities to Investigate Possible Anticompetitive Conduct Affecting U.S. Airlines' Computer Reservation Systems" (Apr. 28, 1997).
[44] "ICPAC Final Report", see para. 2.036, n. 87, at 235.

inception.[45] Assistant Attorney Joel Klein has added that positive comity is no panacea for all antitrust-related trade problems.[46] In a more pragmatic assessment, the OECD concludes that even though the ultimate viability of positive comity has yet to be tested, there are no apparent downside risks in using it.[47]

2.062 In a 2000 report, the ABA Sections of Antitrust Law and International Law and Practice offered some preliminary conclusions on the potential efficacy of positive comity agreements. First, in order to increase transparency and build confidence, the requesting party must be kept fully informed about the process undertaken by the investigating party. Secondly, positive comity can be beneficial if the requesting party is allowed to play an advisory role in the investigatory process undertaken by the requested party.[48] Finally, neither the 1991 nor the 1998 agreements apply specifically to merger enforcement because of different mandatory deadlines for pre-merger investigations, and neither agreement provides for the exchange of business confidential information unless the information source consents.

5. *The 1999 Israel-U.S. Antitrust Co-operation Agreement*

2.063 The Israel-U.S. Antitrust Co-operation Agreement closely tracks the format, language, and scope of the 1995 Canada-U.S. Agreement.[49] Its various articles cover purpose (Article I), notification (Article II, but with no reference to notification of merger and acquisition activity as does Article II:2(c) of the Canada-U.S. Agreement), enforcement co-operation (Article III), co-ordination with regard to related enforcement matters (Article IV), positive comity (Article V), avoidance of conflicts (Article VI, which identifies the same nine comity factors as are listed in the Canada-U.S. Agreement), consultations (Article VII), meetings (Article VIII), and confidentiality of information (Article IX). This co-operation agreement represents one of the first co-operation agreements between a country new to competition law enforcement and the country with the most experience in that regard.

6. *The 1999 Japan-U.S. Antitrust Co-operation Agreement*

2.064 The 1999 Japan-U.S. Antitrust Co-operation Agreement was concluded against a backdrop of a longstanding dialogue on competition policy

[45] See *id.*

[46] See Assistant Attorney General Joel I. Klein, "A Reality Check on Antitrust Rules in the World Trade Organization, and A Practical Way Forward on International Antitrust", in OECD, *Trade and Competition Policies: Exploring the Ways Forward* (1999) 37, 41.

[47] See "OECD Report on Positive Comity", see para. 2.056, n. 34, at 16.

[48] See "Report Concerning Private Anticompetitive Practices", see para. 2.034, n. 86, at 23.

[49] See "Agreement Between the Government of the United States of America and the Government of the State of Israel Regarding the Application of Their Competition Laws", done at Washington, D.C., Mar. 15, 1999 available at http:/www.usdoj.gov. The one substantive difference concerns Article VI of the Canada-U.S. Co-operation Agreement. That Article calls for co-operation and co-ordination with respect to enforcement of deceptive marketing practices laws. However, the provisions of the Agreement dealing with notification, consultation, traditional comity and positive comity do not apply to deceptive marketing practices. See "Agreement Between the Government of the United States of America and the Government of Canada Regarding the Application of Their Competition and Deceptive Marketing Practices Laws", see para. 2.047, n. 6, Art. VII:6.

and law enforcement between U.S. and Japanese government officials. Informal meetings between the countries' respective antitrust authorities date back to the 1980s. Annual meetings between competition and trade authorities were held during the 1990s under the 1989 Structural Impediments Initiative and the 1993 U.S.-Japan Framework for a New Economic Partnership.[50] Under the Framework, the two countries have agreed to address reform of relevant government laws, regulations, and guidance that have the effect of substantially impeding market access for competitive goods and services.[51]

2.065 Building on the Framework and in the aftermath of the *Kodak-Fuji Film* dispute, the United States and Japan launched the Enhanced Initiative on Deregulation and Competition Policy in June 1997. The Enhanced Deregulation Initiative creates a bilateral process to address regulatory and anti-competitive barriers for both foreign and domestic firms in Japan in the telecommunications, housing, medical devices, pharmaceuticals, and financial services markets.[52] Japan and the United States have discussed structural issues, including competition policy, distribution, and issues related to transparency and government practices.[53] An item of special interest is access to Japan's photographic film market in light of Japan's representations at the WTO that its market to imports of photographic film is open.[54]

2.066 In support of the Enhanced Deregulation Initiative, Japan and the United States concluded an antitrust co-operation agreement in October

---

[50] See Kristin Leigh Case, "An Overview of Fifteen Years of United States-Japanese Economic Relations", (1999) 16 Ariz. J. Int'l & Comp. L. 1; Mitsuo Matsushita, "The Structural Impediments Initiative: An Example of Bilateral Trade Negotiation", (1991) 12 Mich. J. Int'l L. 436.

[51] For the text of the Joint Statement on the United States-Japan Framework for a New Economic Partnership, see U.S.-Japan Framework for a New Economic Partnership, Dep't St. Dispatch (July 12, 1993), *available in* LEXIS, Itrade Library, Dstatc File.

[52] See Office of the U.S. Trade Representative, "United States and Japan Reach Agreement on Deregulation Initiative", Press Release (June 19, 1997); Submission by the Government of the United States to the Government of Japan Regarding Deregulation, Competition Policy, and Transparency and Other Government Practices in Japan (Nov. 7, 1997); Office of the USTR, Fact Sheet: "U.S.-Japan Enhanced Initiative on Deregulation and Competition Policy", Press Release (May 15, 1998); Office of the U.S. Trade Representative, "First Joint Status Report on the U.S.-Japan Enhanced Initiative on Deregulation and Competition Policy", May 15, 1998, available at www.ustr.gov/releases/1998/05/index.html; Office of the U.S. Trade Representative, Second Joint Status Report on the U.S.-Japan Enhanced Initiative on Deregulation and Competition Policy, May 3, 1999, available at www.ustr.gov/releases/1999/05/index.html; Office of the U.S. Trade Representative, "United States Calls on Japan to Undertake Sweeping Reforms in Fourth Annual Submission on Deregulation and Competition Policy", Press Release 00–72 (Oct. 12, 2000), available at www.ustr.gov/releases/2000/10/index.html. For further analysis of competition policy disputes between Japan and the United States, see Freyer, see para. 2.032, n. 77.

[53] See Office of the U.S. Trade Representative, "Submission by the Government of the United States to the Government of Japan Regarding Deregulation, Competition Policy, and Transparency and Other Government Practices in Japan" (Oct. 6, 1999); Office of the U.S. Trade Representative, "Fact Sheet: Third Joint Status Report Under the U.S.-Japan Enhanced Initiative on Deregulation and Competition Policy" (July 19, 2000); Office of the U.S. Trade Representative, "Annual Submission by the Government of the United States to the Government of Japan Under the U.S.-Japan Enhanced Initiative on Deregulation and Competition Policy" (Oct. 12, 2000). These submissions are available at http://www.ustr.gov/releases.

[54] See Office of the USTR, "Access to Japan's Photographic Film and Paper Marker: Report on Japan's Implementation of Its WTO Representations", Press Release 99–49 (June 9, 1999).

1999.[55] The preamble cites as inspiration the 1995 OECD Recommendation on Co-operation on Anti-competitive Practices Affecting International Trade, and the 1998 OECD Recommendation on Effective Action Against Hard Core Cartels. A Justice Department press release notes the highlights of the agreement:

> *Agreement on the Importance of Cooperation*: The parties acknowledge the importance of antitrust co-operation in enhancing enforcement of each party's competition laws, and that the sound and effective enforcement of competition law is important both for the efficient functioning of each market and trade between the U.S. and Japan.
> *Notification of Enforcement Activities*: Each antitrust agency will notify the other of antitrust enforcement activities that may affect the other's important interests.
> *Enforcement Cooperation and Coordination*: The antitrust agencies agree to provide assistance to the other in its antitrust enforcement activities and to consider coordination of investigations involving both the U.S. and Japanese markets. In any coordinated arrangement, they will seek to conduct their activities consistently with the other party's enforcement interests.
> *Positive Comity*: The antitrust agencies also agree to a "positive comity" provision whereby each antitrust agency would give careful consideration to a request by the other to take antitrust enforcement action against illegal behavior occurring within its jurisdiction that injures the other party's interests.
> *Conflict Avoidance*: The parties agree to consider carefully one another's interests in carrying out enforcement activities, and the agreement includes a non-exhaustive list of factors to be considered in this regard.
> *Consultations and Exchange of Information*: The antitrust agencies, and the parties, agree to consult with each other on matters which arise under the agreement. The parties agree to exchange antitrust-related information, within applicable confidentiality constraints.
> *Existing Laws*: The parties recognize that the agreement will be implemented in accordance with existing laws in each country.[56]

2.067 With the exception of minor format and drafting changes, the Japan-U.S. Antitrust Co-operation Agreement follows the 1995 Canada-U.S. Agreement in substance. The press release is silent on the differences in the traditional comity factors between the Japan-U.S. Agreement and those in both the Canada-U.S. and the Israel-U.S. Agreements. The traditional comity factors are similar to those listed in the Canada-U.S. Agreement, but make some additions, deletions, and refinements. (The Israel-U.S. Agreement,

[55] See "Agreement Between the Government of the United States of America and the Government of Japan Concerning Cooperation on Anticompetitive Activities, done at Washington", D.C, Oct. 7, 1999, available at http:/www.usdoj.gov. The Japan-U.S. antitrust Co-operation Agreement is the only bilateral antitrust co-operation agreement to which Japan is a party. More information on the international antitrust activities of the Japan Fair Trade Commission is available at http:www.jftc.admix.go.jp/.

[56] U.S. Dep't of Justice, "United States and Japan Sign Antitrust Cooperation Agreement", Press Release (Oct. 7, 1999), available at http://www.usdoj.gov.

concluded just eight months earlier, tracks the nine comity factors of the Canada-U.S. Agreement verbatim.) For example, the Canada-U.S. Agreement mentions "the relative *significance* and foreseeability of the effects of the anticompetitive activities" on one party's important interests, whereas the Japan-U.S. Agreement refers to the "relative *impact* of the anticompetitive activities" and deletes the reference to the "foreseeability of such effects."[57] The Canada-U.S. Agreement refers to "the presence or absence of a purpose" to affect competitors, while the Japan-U.S. Agreement mentions "the presence or absence of evidence of an intention" to affect competitors.[58] The Canada-U.S. Agreement identifies "the location of relevant assets" as a factor; the Japan-U.S. Agreement looks to "the location of relevant assets and parties to the transaction."[59] Finally, the Japan-U.S. Agreement adds a factor, "the extent to which the anticompetitive activities substantially lessen competition in the market of each country,"[60] and drops the factor of "the existence or absence of reasonable expectations that would be furthered or defeated by the enforcement activities."[61]

7. *The 1999 Brazil-U.S. Antitrust Co-operation Agreement*

2.068 In October 1999, the United States and Brazil concluded the first bilateral antitrust co-operation agreement between the United States and a developing country.[62] Like the co-operation agreements with Australia, Canada, Israel, and Japan, the Brazil-U.S. Agreement includes provisions on positive comity (Article IV) and confidentiality of information (Article IX). While substantively similar to the other U.S. co-operation agreements in most other respects, the Brazil-U.S. Agreement does omit a number of provisions that are common to the other bilateral agreements. For example, in Article II, *Notification*, the Brazil-U.S. Agreement closely tracks the Israel-U.S. Agreement but the latter agreement imposes more detailed notification requirements.[63] Under Article III of the Israel-U.S. Co-operation Agreement on enforcement co-operation, the parties have an affirmative obligation to assist one another in obtaining and sharing information.[64] Under the Brazil-U.S. Agreement, however, the parties "agree that it is in their common interest to cooperate" in enforcement activities, which is a mere exhortation.[65] With

[57] Compare Canada-U.S. Agreement, Art. VI:5(ii), with Japan-U.S. Agreement, Art. VI:3(b) (emphasis added).
[58] Compare Canada-U.S. Agreement, Art. VI:5(iii), with Japan-U.S. Agreement, Art. VI:3(c).
[59] Compare Canada-U.S. Agreement, Art. VI:5(vii), with Japan-U.S. Agreement, Art. VI:3(g).
[60] Japan-U.S. Agreement, Art. VI:3(d).
[61] Canada-U.S. Agreement, Art. VI:5(vi).
[62] See "Agreement Between the Government of the United States and the Government of the Federative Republic of Brazil", Oct. 26, 1999 (hereinafter "Brazil-U.S. Co-operation Agreement"), available at http://www.usdoj.gov/atr/public/international/3776.htm. With a gross domestic product of over $750 billion in 1998, Brazil is the world's eighth largest economy, and the third largest U.S. export market in the Western Hemisphere after Canada and Mexico. See U.S. Dep't of Justice, Press Release, "Attorney General Signs Antitrust Cooperation Agreement with Brazil", http://www.usdoj.gov/atr/public/press_releases/1999/3780.htm.
[63] Compare "Brazil-U.S. Cooperation Agreement", *supra* note 62, Art. II, with "Israel-U.S. Cooperation Agreement", see para. 2.063, n. 49, Art. II.
[64] See "Israel-U.S. Cooperation Agreement", see para. 2.063, n. 49, Art. III:3.
[65] See "Brazil-U.S. Cooperation Agreement", see para. 2.068, n. 62, Art. III:1.

regard to traditional comity, while the Israel-U.S. Agreement itemises nine non-exclusive factors the parties are to consider in order to avoid jurisdictional conflicts, the Brazil-U.S. Agreement's traditional comity provision states broadly that each party shall "give careful consideration to the other Party's important interests throughout all phases of its enforcement activities. . .."[66]

8. *The E.U.-Eastern and Central Europe Co-operation Agreements*

2.069 The E.U. has entered into 20 bilateral competition law co-operation agreements, divided into two groups. One group are agreements—the so-called "Europe Agreements" that are best be described as skeletal—between 10 Eastern European countries which have applied for E.U. membership (Bulgaria, the Czech Republic, Estonia, Hungary, Latvia, Lithuania, Poland, Romania, the Slovak Republic, and Slovenia), and with eight other countries, some of which have also applied for E.U. membership (Cyprus, Israel, Moldova, Kazakhstan, the Russian Federation, Switzerland, Turkey, and Ukraine).[67] These agreements contain provisions that direct the non-E.U. countries to harmonise and make their domestic competition laws compatible with those of the Community. In terms of trade flows, however, the most important set of bilateral antitrust co-operation agreements are those with the United States and Canada.

9. *The 1998 Canada-E.U. Co-operation Agreement*

2.070 In 1998, Canada and the E.U. concluded a competition law co-operation agreement similar in style, format, and content to the 1995 U.S.-Canada Co-operation Agreement and the 1991 U.S.-E.U. Co-operation Agreement.[68] The main features of the Canada-E.U. Agreement include co-ordination of enforcement activities (Article IV), positive comity (Article V), comity (Article VI), exchange of information (Article VII), semi-annual meetings (Article VIII), and confidentiality and restricted use of information (Article IX). The Agreement lists 10 factors the parties are to consider when jurisdictional conflicts arise, nine of which track verbatim the comity factors listed in the U.S.-Canada Co-operation Agreement. The Canada-E.U. Agreement adds a tenth factor: the need to minimise the negative effects on the other Party's important interests, in particular when implementing remedies to address anti-competitive effects within the Party's territory.[69]

10. *Other Bilateral Co-operation Agreements*

2.071 Within the E.U., several competition law enforcement agreements are in place among the member countries *inter se*. Australia and New Zealand

[66] Compare "Israel-U.S. Cooperation Agreement", see para. 2.063, n. 49, Art. VI:5, with "Brazil-U.S. Cooperation Agreement", see para. 2.068, n. 62, Art. VI:1.

[67] These agreements are available at the E.U.'s web site http://www.europa.eu.int/comm/dg04/interna/bilateral.htm.

[68] See "Agreement Between the European Communities and the Government of Canada Regarding the Application of Their Competition Laws" (1998), available at http://www.europa.eu.int/comm/dg04.

[69] See "Agreement Between the European Communities and the Government of Canada Regarding the Application of Their Competition Laws", Art. VI:2(ix). 1.

entered into a competition law enforcement agreement in 1994 (discussed below). Australia and New Zealand have also entered into separate bilateral co-operation agreements with Taiwan, Australia in 1996, and New Zealand in 1997.

B. Mutual Legal Assistance Agreements on Competition Law Enforcement

2.072 Mutual legal assistance treaties (MLATs) are bilateral treaties pursuant to which the two signatory nations agree to assist one another in criminal law enforcement. The scope of MLATs to which the United States is a party (approximately 30 as of January 1, 2000, with another 21 pending ratification[70]) provides for assistance in the prosecution of a wide variety of crimes.[71] MLATs create a routine channel for obtaining a broad range of legal assistance.[72] Mutual assistance available under MLATs includes taking testimony or statements of persons; providing documents, records, and other articles of evidence; serving documents; locating or identifying persons; transferring persons in custody for testimony or other purposes; executing requests for searches and seizures; executing requests for restitution; immobilising instrumentalities and proceeds of crime; assisting in proceedings related to forfeiture or confiscation; and rendering any other form of assistance not prohibited by the laws of the requested state.

2.073 With few exceptions, MLATs cover mutual assistance in criminal matters involving drug trafficking, terrorism, other violent crime, money laundering, fiscal fraud (tax evasion), and other "white-collar" crime, but do not cover U.S. criminal antitrust prosecutions. According to a U.S. antitrust practitioner,

---

[70] See "ICPAC Final Report", see para. 2.036, n. 87, at 181 n.57. See, *e.g.* "Agreement with Hong Kong on Mutual Legal Assistance in Criminal Matters, With Annex, signed at Hong Kong", Apr. 15, 1997, S. Treaty Doc. No. 6, 105th Cong., 2d Sess. (1997); "Treaty Between the United States of America and the Republic of Poland on Mutual Legal Assistance in Criminal Matters", signed at Washington, July 10, 1996, S. Treaty Doc. No. 12, 105th Cong., 1st Sess. (1996).

[71] The MLAT between the United States and Australia entered into in 1997 is typical of the scope of these agreements. It provides: 1. The Contracting Parties shall provide mutual assistance, in accordance with the provisions of this Treaty, in connection with the investigation, prosecution, and prevention of offences, and in proceedings related to criminal matters. "Treaty Between the Government of the United States of America and the Government of Australia on Mutual Assistance in Criminal Matters", signed at Washington, Apr. 30, 1997, Art. II:1, S. Treaty Doc. No. 27, 105th Cong., 2d Sess. See A. Paul Victor, "The Growth of International Criminal Antitrust Enforcement", (1998) 6 Geo. Mason L. Rev. 493.

[72] For example, the Australia-U.S. MLAT provides: 2. Assistance shall include: (a) taking the testimony or statements of persons; (b)providing documents, records, and other articles of evidence; (c) serving documents; (d) locating or identifying persons; (e) transferring persons in custody for testimony or other purposes; (f) executing requests for searches and seizures and for restitution; (g) immobilizing instrumentalities and proceeds of crime; (h) assisting in proceedings related to forfeiture or confiscation; and (i) any other form of assistance not prohibited by the laws of the Requested State.

Id. Art. II:2. For the history of MLATs, see Bruce Zagaris & Jessica Resnick, "The Mexico-U.S. Mutual Legal Assistance in Criminal Matters Treaty: Another Step Toward the Harmonization of International Law Enforcement", (1997) 14 Ariz. J. Int'l & Comp. L. 1, 8–10.

> Although MLATs are beginning to play an increasingly important role in multinational criminal antitrust enforcement, especially vis-a-vis the U.S. and Canada, they traditionally have not been very useful in the antitrust area because most of the U.S.'s MLAT partners have not yet criminalized their antitrust offenses and, therefore, they are not obligated to assist the U.S. in criminal antitrust investigations.[73]

2.074 The 1985 Treaty of Mutual Legal Assistance in Criminal Matters between the United States and Canada provides much broader international assistance. The Canada-U.S. MLAT includes within its scope co-operation in criminal proceedings against cartels. Both the United States and Canada treat hard-core cartels, such as price fixing, bid-rigging, and market division, as criminal offences under their respective antitrust laws. Under the MLAT, either country may request the assistance of compulsory process in the other country, including the use of search warrants and grand juries.[74] The MLAT between the United States and Canada includes co-operation in investigating antitrust violations, therefore it enables the United States to obtain information directly from persons in Canada, regardless of whether charges have been filed in the United States.[75]

2.075 Canada-U.S. antitrust co-operation received a huge boost in 1990 when the U.S.-Canada MLAT went into effect.[76] Both countries have seized on the MLAT's potential for antitrust enforcement and have made good use

[73] Victor, see para. 2.072, n. 71, at 497. Many MLATs have a requirement of dual criminality, *i.e.* in order to be the subject of a request for assistance, the activity being investigated must be criminal in both the requesting and requested state. See, *e.g.* Treaty Concerning the Cayman Islands Relating to Mutual Legal Assistance in Criminal Matters, July 3, 1986, U.S.-U.K., S. Treaty Doc. No.100–8, arts. 1(1), 19(3) (1987); Treaty on Mutual Assistance in Criminal Matters, June 12–Aug. 18, 1987, U.S.-Bahamas, S. Treaty Doc. No. 100–17 Art. 2(1) (1988).

Two important exceptions to the dual criminality requirement are the Canada-U.S. and Mexico-U.S. MLATs. The Canada-U.S. MLAT provides, "Assistance shall be provided without regard to whether the conduct under investigation or prosecution in the Requesting State constitutes an offence or may be prosecuted by the Requested State." "Treaty with Canada on Mutual Legal Assistance in Criminal Matters, Mar. 18, 1985", Art. II:3 U.S.-Can., S. Treaty Doc. No. 14, 100th Cong., 2d Sess. (1988), reprinted in (1985) 24 Int'l Leg. Materials 1092. The Mexico-U.S. MLAT also dispenses with the dual criminality requirement. See Mexico-United States: Mutual Legal Assistance Cooperation Treaty, Dec. 9, 1987, U.S.-Mex., S. Treaty Doc. No. 100–13, Art. 1 (1988). Other MLATs supplement such offences with a list of offences for which both countries agree to render assistance in the absence of dual criminality. See Zagaris & Resnick, *supra* note 72, at 26–27.

For examples of interagency co-operation that the Justice Department has received in international cartel investigations through MLATs, see "ICPAC Final Report", see para. 2.036, n. 87, at 182.

[74] Canada-U.S. MLAT, *supra* note 73, Art. VII.

[75] The Canada-U.S. MLAT defines the term "offence" broadly to include: a) for Canada, an offence created by a law of Parliament that may be prosecuted upon indictment, or an offence created by the Legislature of a Province specified in the Annex; b) for the United States, an offence for which the statutory penalty is a term of imprisonment of one year or more, or an offence specified in the Annex; . . .

Canada-U.S. MLAT, *supra* note 73, Art. I. The Annex provides:

The definition of offence includes offences created by the Legislature of a Province of Canada or offences under the law of the United States in the following categories: (1) securities; (2) wildlife protection; (3) environmental protection; and (4) consumer protection.

[76] See Laurie N. Freeman, "U.S.-Canadian Information Sharing and the International Antitrust Enforcement Assistance Act of 1994", (1995) 84 Geo. L.J. 339.

of it, in both directions, over the past few years. In *United States v. Kanzaki Specialty Papers, Inc.*,[77] for example, the U.S. Justice Department indicted Japanese firms for conspiring to fix the price of thermal fax paper, based in part on information from the Canadian government.[78] The joint investigation efforts of the Canadian Bureau of Competition and the DOJ Antitrust Division were critical in breaking up this $120 million a year international cartel.[79] In a second investigation, Canadian assistance in conducting document raids enabled the DOJ to indict plastic dinnerware manufacturers for price fixing. This investigation led to multimillion dollar fines and substantial jail terms.[80] In a third case involving ductile pipe, the Justice Department and the Canadian Bureau of Competition conducted parallel investigations into anti-competitive behaviour in the ductile pipe industry.[81] While the DOJ concluded that it did not have sufficient evidence to prosecute under U.S. law, the Canadian authorities assembled a different body of evidence that was sufficient to obtain a guilty plea and a record criminal fine in September, 1995 from a Canadian subsidiary of a U.S. firm. The fax paper, plastic dinnerware, and ductile pipe cases are the first criminal cases investigated jointly with the full co-operation of a foreign enforcement agency, here the Canadian Bureau of Competition.

2.076 The MLAT does, however, limit the potential for U.S.-Canadian co-operation. First, because the MLAT is limited to criminal enforcement, it does not enable authorities to co-operate in civil antitrust investigations. This lacuna was filled by the 1995 Canada-U.S. Co-operation Agreement but not where confidential business information needs to be exchanged. In the absence of a co-operation agreement concluded under the International Antitrust Enforcement Agreement Act, discussed next, or an amendment to Canadian law permitting such exchanges, gaps still exist in Canadian-U.S. civil antitrust enforcement assistance. Secondly, although the United States has

---

77 Crim. No. 94–10176NMG (D. Mass., filed July 14, 1994).

78 See *United States v. Kanzaki Specialty Papers, Inc.*, 6 Trade Reg. Rep. (CCH) 45,094, at 44,706–07 (D. Mass. Aug. 3, 1994) (defendant acquitted). For related cases, see *United States v. Mitsubishi Paper Mills, Ltd.*, 6 Trade Reg. Rep. (CCH) 45,095, at 44,767–68 (Sept. 26, 1995); *United States v. New Oji Paper Co., Ltd.*, 6 Trade Reg. Rep. (CCH) 45,095, at 44,767–68 (Sept. 26, 1995); *United States v. Elof Hansson Paper & Bd., Inc.*, 6 Trade Reg. Rep. (CCH) 45,095, at 44,746–47 (June 9, 1995). See also Freeman, *supra* note 76, at 353–54; Victor, see para. 2.072, n. 71, at 494–95.

79 See "International Antitrust Enforcement Assistance Act of 1994: Hearings on H.R. 4781 Before the Subcomm. on Economic and Commercial Law of the House of Representatives Comm. on the Judiciary", 103d Cong., 2d Sess. 28 (1994) (statement of Anne K. Bingaman, Assistant Attorney General, Antitrust Division, Department of Justice); Janow, see para. 2.009, n. 19, at 275–76 ("It has been said that absent Canadian assistance in the fax paper cartel, the Department of Justice would have been unable to prosecute that conspiracy because key evidence was located in Canada and beyond the reach of U.S. investigative capabilities.").

80 See *United States v. Izzi*, 6 Trade Reg. Rep. (CCH) 45,094, at 44,696–97 (Mar. 8, 16, 1995); *United States v. Polar Plastics Mfg., Ltd.*, 6 Trade Reg. Rep. (CCH) 45,094, at 44,696–97 (Feb. 28, 1995); *United States v. Comet Prods., Inc.*, 6 Trade Reg. Rep. (CCH) 45,094, at 44,696–97 (Oct. 4, 1994); *United States v. Plastics, Inc.*, 6 Trade Reg. Rep. (CCH) 45,094, at 44,696–97 (Oct. 4, 1994). See also Freeman, *supra* note 76, at 354.

81 See "International Cooperation and the Future of U.S. Antitrust Enforcement", Address by Anne K. Bingaman, Assistant Attorney General, Antitrust Division, U.S. Department of Justice (May 16, 1996), available at http://www.usdoj.gov/atr/public/speeches/96–05–16.ali.

been able to obtain information directly from persons in Canada with the assistance of Canadian authorities, the MLAT permits the Canadian government to refuse assistance deemed contrary to the public interest.

1. Bilateral Agreements on Antitrust Enforcement under the International Antitrust Enforcement Assistance Act of 1994 (IAEAA)

2.077 Provisions in national laws designed to protect the confidentiality of business information often impedes cross-border competition law enforcement. Even though enforcement assistance is formally available under the bilateral co-operation agreements described above, these agreements do not permit competition enforcement authorities to compel production of documents located abroad, nor do they authorise access to confidential business information in the possession of a sister enforcement agency.

2.078 The United States, for example, maintains a web of confidentiality laws and procedures that protect the confidentiality of antitrust evidence, backed up by laws and procedures that provide sanctions for breaches of those confidentiality provisions.[82] Thus, if the U.S. Department of Justice and a foreign antitrust enforcement authority are investigating the same international cartel, the agencies cannot share the most important fruits of their respective investigations, absent a waiver of confidentiality from the firms under investigation.[83] This information is typically obtained through the grand jury process in the United States and through search and seizures or what are sometimes called "dawn raids" in other jurisdictions. Confidentiality provisions in national laws serve legitimate purposes, but they also are an impediment to the kind of cross-border co-operation required in a global economy. The OECD Committee on Competition Law and Policy has assessed the benefits and costs of sharing confidential information and has concluded that the benefits far outweigh the costs.[84]

Bilateral co-operation agreements are not a fully satisfactory mechanism to deal with the increasingly frequent need for foreign-located evidence in the hands of firms or individuals because they do not address the problem of access to confidential information. As noted by the OECD Committee on Competition Law and Policy:

---

[82] The International Antitrust Enforcement Assistance Act, 15 U.S.C., s. 6207(b), prohibits the DOJ and FTC from disclosing, in violation of an antitrust mutual assistance agreement, any antitrust evidence received under such agreement, except to the extent such disclosure is required by law to be made to a defendant or respondent in an action brought by the DOJ or FTC.

The Antitrust Civil Process Act see also 15 U.S.C., s. 1313(1) (requiring consent of producing party to disclose information obtained by DOJ through compulsory puchase); Federal Trade Commission Act 15 U.S.C., ss. 46(f), 576–2(b), 576–2(c), 576–2(f), 250 (confidentiality provisions).

[83] For example, Australia has a number of laws on confidentiality of information. See Agreement Between the Government of the United States of America and the Government of Australia on Mutual Antitrust Enforcement Assistance, done at Washington, D.C., April 27, 1999, Annex A, available at http://www.usdoj.gov.

With the exception of multi-jurisdictional merger review cases, the business community typically sees the disadvantages outweighing the advantages of waiving confidentiality. See "ICPAC Final Report", see para. 2.036, n. 87, at 71–72.

[84] See Report of the CLP Committee, see para. 2.054, n. 24, at 34–41. Other authorities have made a similar assessment. See "ICPAC Final Report", see para. 2.036, n. 87, at 67.

> [E]xcept in the context of a few special relationships and situations, no competition agencies have the legal authority to use compulsory process in gathering information on behalf of a foreign agency or to share any confidential business information, and most cannot even share any non-public but non-confidential information they have obtained in connection with their law enforcement activities.[85]

2.079 In the United States, the increasing need for sharing of confidential business information between sister competition law enforcement agencies led to the enactment of the International Antitrust Enforcement Assistance Act of 1994 (IAEAA).[86] The IAEAA follows the basic outline of earlier legislation that authorises U.S. securities regulators to co-operate with their foreign counterparts. The IAEAA permits U.S. antitrust agencies to enter into agreements with foreign enforcement authorities to exchange information with one another whose disclosure would otherwise be prohibited by confidentiality laws and allows use of their investigative powers at the request of a foreign authority to obtain evidence from private parties in their respective territories.[87] These provisions are similar to the type of assistance that is available to U.S. agencies in criminal matters under MLATs. Before the U.S. agencies can provide confidential information they must receive assurances that the sister competition law enforcement authority can and will afford protection to the information comparable to that afforded by the U.S.

[85] Report of the CLP Committee, see para. 2.054, n. 24, at 28 (footnote omitted). OECD-member countries have identified the major obstacle to effective co-operation in information sharing as being the legal restrictions on sharing information with, and gathering information on behalf of, foreign competition authorities. See *id.* at 29. The OECD Competition Law Committee has never found any reason why confidential information could not be protected and shared. See *id.* at 32. To the extent that lack of resources prevents honouring requests for information, the Australia-U.S. Cooperation Agreement and the Canada-U.S. MLAT both provide for payment of compensation to cover the costs of complying with a request for information.

For a survey of the tools available for information gathering in the international antitrust setting, see Nina Hachigian, "Essential Mutual Assistance in International Antitrust Enforcement", (1995) 29 Int'l Law. 117.

[86] 15 U.S.C., ss. 6200–6212. See John H. Chung, "The International Antitrust Enforcement Assistance Act of 1994 and the Maelstrom Surrounding the Extraterritorial Application of the Sherman Act", (1996) 69 Temp. L. Rev. 371; Charles S. Stark, "International Antitrust Cooperation in NAFTA: The International Antitrust Assistance Act", (1996) 4 U.S.-Mex. L.J. 169; Freeman, see para. 2.075, n. 76, at 356–60.

According to former Assistant Attorney General Anne K. Bingaman, mutual assistance agreements prior to the IAEAA were inadequate because they did not (1) alter existing U.S. law, (2) permit the sharing of information protected under U.S. confidentiality laws, and (3) enable agencies to use compulsory powers to obtain information from private parties to assist a foreign antitrust investigation.

In her view, the IAEAA would remove these important barriers to investigating anti-competitive conduct abroad. See International Antitrust Enforcement Assistance Act of 1994: Hearings on H.R. 4781 Before the Subcomm. on Economic and Commercial Law of the House of Representatives Comm. on the Judiciary, 103d Cong., 2d Sess. 29 (1994) [hereinafter Hearings] (statement of Anne K. Bingaman, Assistant Attorney General, Antitrust Division, Department of Justice). See also Douglas E. Rosenthal, "Equipping the Multilateral Trading System with a Style and Principles to Increase Market Access", (1998) 6 Geo. Mason L. Rev. 543, 568.

[87] See 15 U.S.C., s. 6202(b).

agencies.[88] Section 6211(2)(A) provides that any mutual assistance agreement must include an:

> assurance that the foreign antitrust authority will provide to the Attorney General and the [Federal Trade] Commission assistance that is comparable in scope to the assistance the Attorney General and the Commission provide under such agreement or such memorandum.[89]

Evidence that is obtained pursuant to an IAEAA request may only be used or disclosed for the purpose and the investigation for which it was requested, with two exceptions:

(1) if the information is essential to a significant law enforcement objective and the authority providing the information consents, and

(2) if the information has been made public through a use consistent with that for which it was requested under the IAEAA agreement.

2.080 The IAEAA also requires that the U.S. agencies determine in each case that providing assistance is consistent with the interests of the United States.[90] Presumably, agreements reached under the IAEAA will afford comparable discretion to the other party, as is the case in the one IAEAA agreement concluded to date with Australia. By allowing this discretion, the IAEAA deals with concerns that the United States or the other party to an agreement might be required to give assistance in a case it viewed as antithetical to its interests. Thus, agreements under the IAEAA provide a framework for co-operation that would not otherwise be possible, provided there is a mutual desire to co-operate. Importantly, an IAEAA agreement dispenses with the dual criminality requirement that is a feature of some MLATs. Accordingly, assistance under an IAEAA agreement may be provided regardless of whether the conduct under investigation would constitute a violation of the competition laws of the requested country.

2.081 There are exceptions to the kinds of information that can be provided under the IAEAA. The principal exception is that information obtained by U.S. authorities as a result of the Hart-Scott-Rodino Act pre-merger notification requirements cannot be given to foreign authorities.[91] While the IAEAA does not exclude co-operation in pre-merger investigations, it does prohibit disclosure of pre-merger filings and information obtained through "second requests" in merger investigations. Nevertheless, at the

[88] s. 6211(2) (B) provides that any IAEAA agreement must contain an "assurance that the foreign antitrust authority is subject to laws and procedures that are adequate to maintain securely the confidentiality of antitrust evidence that may be received [from the Justice Department and the Federal Trade Commission] . . . and will give protection to antitrust evidence received . . . that is not less than the protection provided under the laws of the United States to such antitrust evidence." For a summary of the safeguards for confidential and privileged information under IAEAA agreements, see "ICPAC Final Report", see para. 2.036, n. 87, Annex 1–C, at x.

[89] 15 U.S.C., s. 6211(2) (A).

[90] See 15 U.S.C., s. 6211(2).

[91] See 15 U.S.C., s. 6204.

request of a sister competition law enforcement authority U.S. agencies may address a request to the merging companies on the foreign authority's behalf, and the companies may be obliged to comply with the request.

2.082 The benefits of this kind of information sharing are clear. Competition law enforcement authorities in two or more jurisdictions that are looking into the same conduct will be able to co-operate and co-ordinate their investigations fully, sharing critical evidence without being limited to what is publicly known. Evidence located in another country can be obtained through co-operation with the authorities of that country, eliminating disputes over unilateral methods of obtaining foreign-located evidence. Finally, there will be fewer cases in which competition law enforcement authorities will be unable to deal with anti-competitive transnational conduct because the necessary facts are beyond their reach.[92] Nevertheless, ICPAC concludes that "while foreign assistance has and can facilitate antitrust enforcement efforts, only periodically does it prove crucial to their outcome."[93]

2.083 a. The Australia-U.S. IAEAA Agreement. In 1999, Australia and the United States negotiated the first mutual assistance enforcement agreement pursuant to the IAEAA.[94] The agreement has four main features. First, the United States and Australia agree to assist one another and to co-operate on a reciprocal basis in providing or obtaining antitrust evidence pursuant to their respective mutual assistance legislation, and regardless of whether the conduct underlying a request would violate the laws of the requested party.[95] Evidence may be obtained through several means, including taking testimony or statements of persons, obtaining documents, locating or identifying persons or things and executing searches and seizures.[96] The agreement provides for assistance in both civil and criminal antitrust matters.

2.084 Secondly, evidence obtained under the agreement may be used only for antitrust enforcement purposes, except in certain narrow circumstances consistent with the Act.[97] A party may deny assistance if it determines that

(1) a request is not made in accordance with the Agreement;

(2) execution of a request would exceed reasonably available resources;

---

[92] For arguments that the IAEAA is an illusory promise of greater cross-border co-operation in competition law enforcement, see Waller I, see para. 2.020, n. 55, at 378 (only countries with an interest in investigating the anticompetitive conduct of U.S. firms on U.S. soil will enter into IAEAA agreements; the IAEAA is surplusage because foreign competition enforcement authorities can obtain evidence in the United States through letters of request).

[93] "ICPAC Final Report", see para. 2.036, n. 87, at 184. For a summary of U.S. experience with international antitrust enforcement co-operation, as well as an analysis of the IAEAA, see *id.* Annex 1–C, at iv–ix.

[94] See Agreement Between the Government of the United States of America and the Government of Australia on Mutual Antitrust Enforcement Assistance, done at Washington, D.C., Apr. 27, 1999, entered into force Nov. 5, 1999, available at http://www.usdoj.gov/atr/public/international/docs/usaus7.htm. See also U.S. Dep't of Justice, Press Release, Attorney General Signs Antitrust Assistance Agreement with Australia, Apr. 27, 1999, available at http://www.usdoj.gov.

[95] Australia-U.S. Mutual Assistance Agreement, *supra* note 94, Art. II:F.

[96] See *id.* arts. II:E(2), IX, X.

[97] See *id.* Art. II:H.

(3) execution of a request would not be authorised by the requested party's domestic law; or

(4) execution of a request would be contrary to the requested party's public interest.[98]

The Agreement also provides that nothing in it "compels a person to provide antitrust evidence in violation of any legally applicable right or privilege."[99]

2.085 Third, all Australian requests for assistance are to be channelled through the Department of Justice, as required by the Act. However, requests may be executed by either the Department of Justice or the FTC, or both, as appropriate under the circumstances. Both the Justice Department and the FTC may make requests for assistance directly to the Australian Competition and Consumer Commission (ACCC) and U.S. requests will be executed by the ACCC, the Attorney General's Department, or both, as appropriate.[1]

2.086 Fourthly, striking a proper balance between maintaining the confidentiality of sensitive business information that might be exchanged, against effective antitrust law enforcement across national borders, has been a problem that has plagued bilateral antitrust co-operation agreements. Under the Agreement, the ACCC, DOJ, and FTC are authorised to obtain information within their respective jurisdiction for the purpose of assisting an agency in the other jurisdiction to enforce its competition laws. However, consistent with the IAEAA, the Agreement permits the exchange of such information between the United States and Australia *inter se* for the sole purpose of enforcing the antitrust laws of the requesting party,[2] but contains strict confidentiality requirements that will protect such information from being disclosed to third parties.[3]

2.087 b. Future Agreements under the IAEAA. Competition officials in other jurisdictions have expressed an interest in expanding the bilateral co-operation agreements they have with the United States. At ICPAC hearings held in 1998, Canadian, E.U., and other officials indicated that they were interested in exploring possibilities for IAEAA agreements with the United States.[4] The likelihood of concluding future agreements with the E.U. and Canada would appear to be good, given their history of close co-operation over the past decade or more. However, the probability of concluding an IAEAA agreement with Japan would seem to be low at present, through no fault of either the DOJ or FTC, but rather due to the adversarial relationship created by the USTR with the JFTC.

---

[98] See *id.* Art. IV:A(1)–(4).

[99] See *id.* Art. II:I.

[1] See *id.* Art. V.

[2] See *id.* Art. VII.

[3] See *id.* Art. VI. The Agreement also requires the return of all antitrust evidence at the conclusion of an investigation or proceeding. See *id.* Art. XI.

[4] See "ICPAC Final Report", see para. 2.036, n. 87, at 184.

C. The Australia-New Zealand Closer Economic Relations Trade Agreement

2.088 The one, and perhaps only, successful experience at addressing on a bilateral basis anti-competitive practices at their source, *i.e.* in the firm's home territory, has been that of Australia and New Zealand pursuant to their free trade area framework agreement of 1983, the Australian-New Zealand Closer Economic Relations Trade Agreement (ANZCERTA).[5] Recognising that legally separating the New Zealand and Australian markets for the purpose of competition law enforcement was an artificial distinction in economic terms, ANZCERTA established a mandate for the harmonisation of laws on restrictive business practices. This mandate resulted in New Zealand's adoption in 1986 of a new competition law similar to Australia's.

In 1988, Australia and New Zealand adopted a protocol that eliminated the application of antidumping measures to their respective trade, effective July 1, 1990.[6] In 1994, a parallel agreement also was reached regarding the application of competition laws regulating conduct affecting trade between the countries.[7] Australia and New Zealand simultaneously extended the application of their competition law prohibitions on the abuse of market power. The new provisions (section 46A of the Australian Trade Practices Act 1974 and section 36A of the New Zealand Commerce Act 1986) prohibit the use of substantial market power or dominant position in the trans-Tasman market for certain anti-competitive purposes.[8] The trans-Tasman market is defined as a market in Australia, New Zealand, or Australia and New Zealand. Thus, the two governments agreed to abolish the application of anti-

[5] "Closer Economic Relations—Trade Agreement", Mar. 28, 1983, N.Z.-Austl., reprinted in (1983) 22 Int'l Legal Materials 945, 948–49. *See* Kerrin M. Vautier, "Trans-Tasman Trade and Competition Law", in *CER and Business Competition—Australia and New Zealand in a Global Economy* (1990) 73; Bernard M. Hoekman, "Preferential Trade Agreements" in Brookings Trade Forum 1998, at 310–313 (Robert Z. Lawrence ed. 1998); Waller I, see para. 2.020, n. 55, at 355–56. Additional information on ANZCERTA is available from the following two web sites: http://dfat.gov.au/geo/spacific/nz/; http://www.austlii.edu.au/au/other/dfat/treaties.

[6] See Protocol to the Australia New Zealand Closer Economic Relations Trade Agreement on Acceleration of Free Trade in Goods, Australia T.S. 1988, no.18, done at Canberra, Australia, entered into force Aug.18, 1988. Art. 4 of the 1988 Protocol provides in part:

(1) The Member States agree that anti-dumping measures in respect of goods originating in the territory of the other Member State are not appropriate from the time of achievement of both free trade in goods between the Member States on 1 July 1990 and the application of their competition laws to relevant anti-competitive conduct affecting trans-Tasman trade in goods. (2) From 1 July 1990, neither Member State shall take anti-dumping action against goods originating in the territory of the other Member State. In particular: (a) neither Member State shall initiate or continue any investigations into anti-dumping complaints made in respect of goods originating in the territory of the other Member State; (b) neither Member State shall levy new anti-dumping duties or impose other new anti-dumping measures in respect of such goods; (c) each Member State shall revoke all existing instruments levying anti-dumping duties or imposing other anti-dumping measures in respect of such goods; (d) each Member State shall release any exporter who has given undertakings in respect of such goods in connection with an anti-dumping investigation by that Member State from such undertakings; and (e) each Member State shall terminate any anti-dumping investigations underway in respect of such goods and shall return any securities provided in connection with such investigations.

[7] See "Cooperation and Coordination Agreement Between the Australia Trade Practices Commission and the New Zealand Commerce Commission" (1994), available at http://www.accc.gov.au.

[8] For a comparative analysis of these two provisions, see Vautier, see para. 2.088, n. 5, at 80–88.

dumping laws between the two countries and further agreed to amend their respective competition laws on abuse of dominant position in order to allow complainants in one country to initiate proceedings against the conduct of producers in the other country. In 1991, New Zealand amended its mergers and acquisitions law by repealing the mandatory pre-notification and pre-clearance rules for mergers and acquisitions, thereby bringing its law into line with Australia's. As a consequence, both countries rely on voluntary compliance with statutory market power thresholds, or private or government enforcement action, to ensure that mergers and acquisitions do not result in an acquisition of or increase in a dominant market position.[9]

2.089 The powers of inquiry of the Australian Competition and Consumer Commission[10] and the New Zealand Commerce Commission also were extended. Each authority is authorised to issue subpoenas to companies in the other country. The 1988 Protocol and its subsidiary agreements allow the enforcement authorities to apply their respective domestic competition laws to conduct in the other country that affects markets in the enforcing country. This arrangement permits each body to hold hearings, compel evidence and have its orders enforced in the other country.[11]

The explicit recognition of extraterritorial jurisdiction based on the "effects test" in ANZCERTA, together with the mutual recognition of the decisions of each country's competition authority, is an innovative, but arguably case specific, approach for addressing trade distorting, private anti-competitive conduct. Necessary pre-conditions include similar substantive laws (*i.e.* harmonisation) and a high degree of mutual confidence in the legal and administrative institutions of each country within the government and business communities.[12] This approach has good prospects for long-term success due to the high degree of substantive and procedural convergence between the two countries' competition laws and their enforcement institutions.

2.090 Given the commonalities in the legal and economic systems of Australia and New Zealand, their similar level of economic development and their common culture, the ANZCERTA experience is not necessarily transferable to other free trade agreements.[13] The case of Australia and New Zealand could provide useful lessons for regional trade arrangements (RTAs) and competition policy agreements that do not depend upon supranational enforcement authorities, as is the case of MERCOSUR, discussed below.[14] However, the greater substantive and procedural divergence among various

[9] See *id.* at 75.

[10] Additional information on the activities of the Australian Competition & Consumer Commission is available from its web site at http://www.accc.gov.au (last visited May 16, 2000).

[11] For a discussion of trans-Tasman competition law, see *CER. and Business Competition—Australia and New Zealand in a Global Economy* (K.M. Vautier, J. Farmer & R. Baxt eds. 1990).

[12] See Paul Crampton & Milos Barutciski, "Trade Distorting Private Restraints: A Practical Agenda for Future Action", (1999) 6 Sw. J.L. & Trade Am. 3, 48–49.

[13] See WTO, "Working Group on the Interaction between Trade and Competition Policy, Submission from New Zealand", *New Zealand's Experience with Trade and Competition Policy Under the Australia-New Zealand Closer Economic Relations Agreement*, WT/WGTCP/W/47, at 6, para. 26 (Nov. 25, 1997).

[14] See generally Terence P. Stewart & Timothy C. Brightbill, "Trade Law and Competition Policy in Regional Trade Arrangements", (1996) 27 Law & Pol'y Int'l Bus. 937.

countries' competition laws and institutions outside ANZCERTA makes it highly unlikely that such an approach could be implemented successfully at the multilateral level at the present time. In the view of two close observers of the subject,

> Although this may be a realistic long-term objective for a small group of countries in the context of a regional trade agreement, such an approach is not feasible in the multilateral context for the near to medium term.[15]

IV. REGIONAL APPROACHES

A. The European Union

2.091 In the opinion of some observers, a free trade area or customs union is only partially complete if it regulates government intervention in the market, but leaves private businesses free to engage in anti-competitive behaviour.[16] While most of the common policies developed by the E.U. are noteworthy achievements, the tremendous effort the E.U. has made to develop a comprehensive policy on restrictive business practices is unique and therefore, warrants a particularly close look.[17] With the WTO having made the topic of competition law and restrictive business practices part of its work programme in 1997,[18] the E.U.'s competition policy was considered by some as a useful supranational model.

Out of the many hallmarks of the E.U. that distinguish it not only from other RTAs, including NAFTA, and from the GATT-WTO system, none stands out more than the E.U.'s competition policy. As explained below, NAFTA leaves it to each NAFTA Party to apply its own domestic antitrust rules to curb anti-competitive business practices. In contrast, the E.U. has concrete rules and enforcement mechanisms for developing a co-ordinated competition policy that promotes completion of E.U. economic integration.[19]

2.092 As the principal institution of the E.U. and its "guardian," the European Commission is responsible for ensuring the proper functioning and development of the common market, execution of the budget and enforcement of E.U. rules. The Commission is in effect the executive body of the

---

[15] See para. 2.088, n. 5, at 49. For additional views on the unique and non-transferable nature of ANZCERTA, see Rex J. Ahdar, "The Role of Antitrust Policy in the Development of Australian-New Zealand Free Trade", (1991) 12 Nw. J. Int'l L. & Bus. 317, 318 & n.3; Maureen Brunt, "The Role of Antitrust Policy in the Development of Australian-New Zealand Free Trade", 1992 Fordham Corp. L. Inst. 131.

[16] For further reading on competition rules in free trade areas, see generally Gabrielle Marceau, *Anti-Dumping and Anti-Trust Issues in Free-Trade Areas* (1995); Therese Blanchet, Risto Piipponen, & Maria Westman-Clement, *The Agreement on the European Economic Area: A Guide to the Free Movement of Goods and Competition Rules* (1994).

[17] See generally David J. Gerber, *Law and Competition in Twentieth Century Europe* (1998).

[18] See Singapore Ministerial Declaration, adopted on Dec. 13 1996, WT/MIN(96)/DEC.

[19] For a description of E.U. competition policy, see generally Ritter, Braun & Rawlinson, see para. 2.007, n. 13; David J. Gerber, "The Transformation of European Community Competition Law?", (1994) 35 Harv. Int'l L.J. 97; Per Jebsen & Robert Stevens, "Assumptions, Goals, and Dominant Undertakings: The Regulation of Competition Under Article 86 of the European Union", (1996) 64 Antitrust L.J. 443; Philip Marsden, "'Antitrust' at the WTO", (1999) 13 Antitrust 28.

Union. Headquartered in Brussels, the Commission is comprised of 20 Commissioners, two each from France, Germany, Spain, Italy and the U.K. and one from each of the remaining 10 Member States. It has a full-time staff of 16,000.[20]

2.093 The foundation of E.U. competition policy is Title V of the E.C. Treaty: Common Rules on Competition, Taxation and Approximation of Laws. The policy is embodied in the tetrad of Articles 81, 82, 83, and 86,[21] which has many parallels in U.S. antitrust law.[22] Article 81 prohibits agreements in restraint of trade, such as price fixing, limitations on production, market division, and tying arrangements, subject to certain exceptions. It is analogous to section 1 of the U.S. Sherman Act.[23] Article 82 prohibits abuse of a dominant position, and reaches the same conduct that is prohibited under section 2 of the U.S. Sherman Act.[24] Article 83 is a specific charge to the European Council and Commission to promulgate regulations and directives to give effect to the principles set out in Articles 81 and 82. The most important of these regulations and directives is Regulation 17, issued in 1962, and substantially revised in 1999.[25] Article 86 prohibits Member States from taking measures contrary to the competition rules of the Treaty with regard to public undertakings or undertakings vested with special or exclusive rights.

1. *Article 81 on Restrictive Agreements*

2.094 Article 81 regulates anti-competitive agreements, decisions, and concerted practices.[26] All agreements, decisions, or concerted practices prohibited under Article 81(1) are automatically void pursuant to Article 81(2),

[20] See "European Commission: The big squeeze", *The Economist*, Feb. 8, 1997, at 55.

[21] See Treaty Establishing the European Economic Community, Mar. 25, 1957, Arts. 85, 86, 87, 298 U.N.T.S. 11, 47–50 (the Treaty of Rome). Art. 12 of the Treaty of Amsterdam, which entered into force on May 1,1999, provides, *inter alia*, for the renumbering of the Articles of the E.C. Treaty. Art. 85, 86, 87, and 90 are now renumbered Art. 81, 82, 83, and 86, respectively. This book employs the new numbering. In 1992, the Treaty of Rome was amended substantially by the Maastricht Treaty on European Union (TEU or Maastricht Treaty). See Maastricht Treaty on European Union, [1992] O.J. (CC 191) 1, [1992] 1 C.M.L.R. 719. A cosmetic change is that the Treaty of Rome is officially retitled Treaty Establishing the European Community (the E.C. Treaty), and the resulting combined treaty is entitled Treaty on European Union together with the Treaty Establishing the European Community. Treaty on European Union, Nov. 1, 1992, entered into force Jan. 1, 1993, reprinted in [1992] 1 C.M.L.R. 719 [hereinafter the E.C. Treaty]. Art. 81–83 of the E.C. Treaty have been the subject of numerous commentaries. See, *e.g.* Ritter, Braun & Rawlinson, see para. 2.007, n. 13.

[22] Art. 3(g) of the E.C. Treaty empowers the E.U. to institute "a system insuring that competition in the common market is not distorted . . . ." The Maastricht Treaty on European Union revises the E.C. Treaty to create an industrial policy aimed at accelerating adjustment, but abjures "any measure which could lead to a distortion of competition." Maastricht Treaty Art. 130.

[23] S. 1 of the Sherman Antitrust Act makes illegal "[e]very contract, combination . . . or conspiracy, in restraint of commerce or trade among the several States, or with foreign nations." 15 U.S.C., s. 1.

[24] S. 2 of the Sherman Antitrust Act provides that no person shall "monopolize, or attempt to monopolize, or combine or conspire with any other person or persons, to monopolize . . . ." 15 U.S.C., s. 2.

[25] [1962] 5 O.J. Spec. Ed. Eur. Comm. 87.

[26] See E.C. Treaty, Art. 81, Nov. 10, 1997 [1997] O.J. C340/173–308. Article 81 provides: The following shall be prohibited as incompatible with the common market: all agreements between undertakings [i.e., firms or business entities], decisions by associations of undertakings and

at least to the extent the anti-competitive provisions are non-severable from the balance of the agreement, decision, or practice. Under Article 81(3), an agreement, decision, or concerted practice may be exempted from the prohibition of paragraph 1 if it contributes to improving the economic welfare of consumers, or if it helps the common market overall even though certain consumer interests might be hurt.

2.095 **a. Individual Exemptions.** Under Article 81(3), Articles 83, and Regulation 17, the Commission may declare the Article 81(1) prohibitions inapplicable to a specific agreement, decision, or practice either through a "negative clearance" or an individual exemption. Generally, any party seeking an exemption under Article 81 must submit their request to the Commission, which has exclusive jurisdiction to grant a "negative clearance" or an individual exemption. Under an individual exemption, the parties admit that their agreement, decision, or practice violates Article 81(1), but nevertheless seek an exemption under Article 81(3). Under a negative clearance, the parties contend that their agreement, decision, or practice does not violate Article 81(1) whatsoever. If the Commission grants a negative clearance, it certifies that based on the facts in its possession, no grounds for action exist under Article 81(1). However, a negative clearance does not bind E.U.-members' national courts and the Commission is not estopped from intervening at a later time if the facts change.

2.096 In some cases where the parties desire a Commission opinion on the legality of a proposed agreement, decision, or practice under Article 81 (*e.g.*, a technology transfer, franchise, or licencing agreement), the Commission issues a "comfort letter" stating that it sees no reason to investigate the agreement, decision, or practice in question under Article 81(1). In the absence of changed circumstances, the Commission is estopped from later challenging the proposed agreement, decision, or practice. Comfort letters do not, however, bar national courts from entertaining antitrust challenges to

concerted practices which may affect trade between Member States and which have as their object or effect the prevention, restriction or distortion of competition within the common market, and in particular those which: (a) directly or indirectly fix purchase or selling prices or any other trading conditions; (b) limit or control production, markets, technical development, or investment; (c) share markets or sources of supply; (d) apply dissimilar conditions to equivalent transactions with other trading parties, thereby placing them at a competitive disadvantage; (e) make the conclusion of contracts subject to acceptance by the other parties of supplementary obligations which, by their nature or according to commercial usage, have no connection with the subject of such contracts. 2. Any agreements or decisions prohibited pursuant to this Article shall be automatically void. 3. The provisions of paragraph 1 may, however, be declared inapplicable in the case of:—any agreement or category of agreements between undertakings;—any decision or category of decisions by associations of undertakings;—any concerted practice or category of concerted practices; which contributes to improving the production or distribution of goods or to promoting technical or economic progress, while allowing consumers a fair share of the resulting benefit, and which does not: (a) impose on the undertakings concerned restrictions which are not indispensable to the attainment of these objectives; (b) afford such undertakings the possibility of eliminating competition in respect of a substantial part of the products in question. See generally Ritter, Braun & Rawlinson, see para. 2.007, n. 13, at 75–326.

such agreements. Over 90 per cent of all clearances come by way of a comfort letter due to its informality and speed.[27]

2.097 **b. Block Exemptions.** In addition to the agreement-specific negative clearance, individual exemption and comfort letter, the Commission has the power to grant "block exemptions" for classes of agreements. Commonly applied block exemptions include research and development agreements (Regulation 418/85), exclusive distribution agreements (Regulation 1983/83), exclusive purchasing agreements (Regulation 1984/83), franchising agreements (Regulation 4087/88), and technology transfer agreements (Regulation 240/96). In each of the regulations on these block exemptions, the Commission lists contract terms that are permitted and prohibited under these agreements.[28] A franchiser planning to license franchisees on an E.U.-wide basis would be interested in obtaining a block exemption for all its intended franchise agreements. A negative clearance would be of little value to the franchiser because each franchise agreement would have to be submitted for Commission review. The block exemption dispenses with the requirement of notifying the Commission of each proposed agreement. Provided the agreements meet the criteria outlined in the Commission's regulations for qualifying for the block exemption, they are presumptively valid under Article 81.

2.098 **c. Agreements of Minor Importance.** The Commission will not apply Article 81 to agreements, decisions, or concerted practices that fall below certain thresholds. For horizontal agreements, the threshold is five per cent of the relevant market; for vertical agreements, the threshold is 10 per cent.[29] In addition, the Commission generally will not investigate agreements between small and medium-sized enterprises (SMEs) where annual turnover and balance sheet totals do not exceed 40 million Euros and 27 million Euros, respectively, and which have a maximum of 250 employees. If an agreement falls below the thresholds, national courts and competition enforcement authorities are responsible for taking action first, unless the Community requires intervention by the Commission. Horizontal agreements on price fixing, output restrictions, or market sharing are not excepted under the *de minimis* rule. Similarly, vertical agreements that fix resale prices or contain territorial protection clauses are not excepted.

2.099 **d. Fines.** The Commission not only has broad investigatory powers, but it also may punish parties to illegal agreements by imposing a

[27] See W. David Braun, "Sales and Distribution Practices: Dealing with Sales Agents, Distributors and a Vigilant Competition Directorate", in *Introduction to European Law: How to Comply and Compete in the European Union* (Global Law and Policy Initiative 1999).

[28] See, *e.g.* Commission Regulation 1983/83, [1983] O.J. L173/1 (exclusive distribution agreements); Commission Regulation 1984/83, [1983] O.J. L173/5 (exclusive purchasing agreements); Commission Regulation 418/85, [1985] O.J. L53/5 (joint research and development); Commission Regulation 2349/84, [1984] O.J. L219/15; [1985] O.J. L113/34 (patent licensing); Commission Regulation 556/89, [1989] O.J. L61/1 (know-how licensing); Commission Regulation 4087/88, [1988] O.J. L359/46 (franchise agreements).

[29] See Notice on agreements of minor importance which do not fall under Art. 81(1) of the Treaty Establishing the European Community, available at http://europa.eu.int/en/comm/dg04/lawenten/en/s971799.htm.

maximum fine of 1,000,000 Euros ($1.2 million), or 10 per cent of a company's annual worldwide turnover (sales), whichever is greater. Fines imposed by the Commission are subject to review by the Court of First Instance, as are all Commission decisions in the competition law enforcement field.

2.100 **e. The 1999–2000 Reforms Affecting Vertical Restraints.** On September 30, 1998, the Commission issued a communication recommending that a single block exemption Regulation be adopted that will cover virtually all vertical restraints concerning intermediate and final goods and services.[30] Under Guidelines issued by the Commission on May 24, 2000[31] which complement the block exemption Regulation issued in December, 1999[32] the amended regulation defines what is not block-exempted instead of defining what is exempted, thus giving firms that lack market power a safe haven within which to conduct business operations. The new rules apply from June 1, 2000 and replace three old block exemption regulations applicable to exclusive distribution, exclusive purchasing, and franchising agreements respectively.[33] Existing agreements will continue to benefit from the old block exemption regulations until the end of 2001. The basic aim of the new approach is to simplify the rules applicable to supply and distribution agreements and to reduce the regulatory burden, especially for companies lacking market power like SMEs, while ensuring a more effective control of agreements entered into by companies holding significant market power.

2.101 The new policy is based on a single regulation with a wide scope of application that block-exempts supply and distribution agreements concerning final and intermediary goods as well as services. The new block exemption Regulation allows companies whose market share is below 30 per cent to benefit from a so-called safe harbour under the Community competition rules. The safe harbour below 30 per cent market share offers companies the freedom to create supply and distribution arrangements best suited to their individual commercial interests and to adapt to changing economic conditions. Above the 30 per cent market share threshold, vertical agreements will not be covered by the new block exemption Regulation, but they are not automatically presumed to be illegal either. They may require an individual examination under Article 81 which spells out the conditions under which agreements between companies may be exempted from E.C. competition rules. Companies in that situation are asked to do a self-assessment of the

---

30 See European Commission, Communication from the Commission on the Application of the Community Competition Rules to Vertical Restraints: Follow-up to the Green Paper on Vertical Restraints, COM(98)522 Final (Sept. 30, 1998), available at http://europa.eu.int/en/comm/dg04/index_en.htm. See also Alexander Schaub, "EC Competition System—Proposals for Reform", (1999) 22 Fordham Int'l L.J. 853, 869–73.

31 See Commission Notice, Guidelines on Vertical Restraints (May 24, 2000).

32 See Commission Regulation 2790/1999 of 22 Dec.1999 on the application of Art. 81(3) of the Treaty to categories of vertical agreements and concerted practices, 29 Dec.1999 [1999] O.J. L336, p.21–25. The texts of the new block exemption regulation and Guidelines are available at http://europa.eu.int/comm/dg04/lawenten/en/entente3.htm#iii_1.

33 See Commission Regulations 1983/83, [1983] O.J. L173, p. 1; 1984/83, [1983] O.J. L173, p. 5; and 4087/88, [1988] O.J. L359, p. 46.

possible consequences of their vertical agreements under the law. The Guidelines assist them in carrying out such an assessment.

2.102 The block exemption Regulation does not apply to two sets of restrictions. The first set concerns hard-core restrictions. Companies are not allowed to use the following restrictions in their agreements:

- A producer may not impose on its distributors the price at which to resell its products. However, maximum and recommended prices are normally permissible.
- A producer may not restrict its distributors selling to any customer if it is an unsolicited order (a passive sale). This means that each distributor must be free to respond to a request for the product or service made by any customer inside the Community. Distributors must be left free to also use the Internet to respond to such requests.
- A producer applying a selective distribution system, for instance in the field of cosmetics, may neither restrict active nor restrict passive selling by the authorised distributors to end-users or other authorised distributors.
- A producer buying components for incorporation in its own products, for instance a component for the manufacture of a household appliance, may not prevent the supplier of the components from selling these as spare parts to end-users or independent repairers.

These restrictions are prohibited in order to maintain free price competition between distributors for the benefit of consumers and to guarantee the consumers' right to purchase goods and services wherever they want inside the Community. These rules can also be applied directly by national competition authorities and national courts. Violations of these rules can be fined and give rise to claims for damages.

2.103 The second set of restrictions not covered by the new regulation concerns certain restrictions which are not exempted but which may, under certain circumstances, be compatible with the E.C. competition rules. The most important concerns non-compete obligations requiring distributors to resell only the brands of one supplier when their duration exceeds five years. Such agreements are not covered by the new block exemption Regulation as they may have a strong foreclosure effect on the market. The Guidelines describe under which circumstances long-term investments may justify a longer duration of non-compete obligations.

The Commission plans to revise the Guidelines in 2004 in order to take account of market developments and the experience gained by the Commission in applying the new policy.

2.104 f. The 2001 Reforms Affecting Regulation No. 17. In order to alleviate a portion of its crushing and ever-expanding workload, the Commission issued a White Paper on May 12, 1999 outlining reform of Regulation No. 17 implementing Articles 81 and 82 of the E.C. Treaty.[34] The proposed

[34] See European Commission, White Paper on Modernisation of the Rules Implementing Art. 81 and 86 of the E.C. Treaty, [1999] O.J. C132/1.

reforms will decentralise the application of the E.U. competition rules and end the notification and authorisation system established under Regulation No. 17. The result would be that RBPs that are prohibited under Article 81(1), but which meet the tests of Article 81(3) are lawful without the need for any prior decision or clearance from the Commission. National competition enforcement authorities would be given lead responsibility for policing vertical and horizontal RBPs that might violate Article 81.[35]

2. *Article 82 on Abuse of a Dominant Position*

2.105 Article 82 of the E.C. Treaty prohibits abuse of a dominant position, but monopolies are not unlawful *per se*.[36] Unlike Article 81, Article 82 makes no provision for individual or block exemptions. The Commission may, however, grant negative clearances.

2.106 The Commission and the Court of Justice have adopted a broad definition of "dominant position."[37] The Court of Justice has defined dominant position as:

> a position of economic strength enjoyed by an undertaking which enables it to prevent effective competition being maintained on the relevant market by affording it the power to behave to an appreciable extent independently of its competitors, its customers and ultimately of the consumers.[38]

The definition of "dominant position" has been expanded by defining the relevant market narrowly.[39]

Once the existence of a dominant position is established, the next question is whether that position has been abused.[40] The Commission uses Article 82 as an opening wedge for investigating a wide range of practices it considers an abuse of a dominant position. The Commission has found such abuse in refusals to deal; pricing at below average total or variable cost if there is an

---

[35] See *id.*; Joseph Kirwin & Catherine DeW. Sullivan, "EU Proposes Overhauling Competition Rules Enforcement", (May 5, 1999) 16 Int'l Trade Rep. (BNA) 777.

[36] Art. 82 provides: Any abuse by one or more undertakings of a dominant position within the Common Market or in a substantial part of it shall be prohibited as incompatible with the Common Market in so far as it may affect trade between Member States. Such abuse may in particular consist in: (a) directly or indirectly imposing unfair purchase or selling prices or other unfair trading conditions; (b) limiting production, markets or technical development to the prejudice of consumers; (c) applying dissimilar conditions to equivalent transactions with other trading parties, thereby placing them at a competitive disadvantage; (d) making the conclusion of contracts subject to acceptance by the other parties of supplementary obligations which, by their nature or according to commercial usage, have no connection to the subject of such contracts. See generally Ritter, Braun & Rawlinson, see para. 2.007, n. 13, at 327–404.

[37] *See* David J. Gerber, *Law and Competition in Twentieth Century Europe: Protecting Prometheus* (1998); Per Jebsen & Robert Stevens, "Assumptions, Goals and Dominant Undertakings: The Regulation of Competition Under Article 86 of the European Union", (1996) 64 Antitrust L.J. 443.

[38] *Hoffmann–La Roche & Co. AG v. Commission*, [1979] E.C.R. 461; [1979] 3 C.M.L.R. 211.

[39] See, *e.g. Europemballage Corp. v. Commission*, [1973] E.C.R. 215; [1973] C.M.L.R. 199. See also Ritter, Braun & Rawlinson, para. 2.007, n. 13, at 24–39.

[40] See, *e.g. United Brands Co. v. Comm'n*, [1978] E.C.R. 207; [1978] 1 C.M.L.R. 429; [1973] C.M.L.R. 199.

intent to eliminate a competitor, thereby making such pricing predatory; and excessive pricing, where prices bear little relation to the economic value of the goods sold.[41] Whereas in the United States exploiting market power that was innocently obtained does not violate the antitrust laws, in the E.U. excessive pricing by a dominant firm can be an Article 82 violation.[42] In the view of two U.S. authorities, the concept of "abuse" in Article 82 is a hair trigger.[43]

3. *Article 86 on Government-Induced Distortions of Competition*

2.107 In order to ensure that the Article 81 and Article 82 prohibitions on private anti-competitive conduct are not undercut by government anti-competitive behaviour in the market, Article 86 of the E.C. Treaty prohibits Member States from taking measures contrary to the competition rules of the Treaty with regard to public undertakings or undertakings vested with special or exclusive rights.[44] As noted by Ritter, Braun, and Rawlinson:

> Private firms determine their industrial and commercial strategy mainly by reference to requirements of profitability. Decisions of public enterprises, on the other hand, may, under the influence of the government, be affected by considerations related to the pursuit of public interest objectives, and such decisions may distort competition no less than agreements between private enterprises.[45]

Member States are, in short, obligated to refrain from government-induced distortions of competition. The European Court of Justice has ruled that Article 86 is violated if a member's conferral of exclusive rights on an enterprise results in discriminatory purchases of domestic over imported goods or otherwise infringes E.U. competition rules on abuse of a dominant position.[46]

4. *The Regulation of Mergers and Acquisitions*

2.108 Articles 81 and 82 give no clear authority to the Commission to regulate mergers and acquisitions. The Court of Justice has nevertheless concluded that the Commission possesses such authority in order to prevent "distorted competition."[47] If businesses could merge and *eliminate* (as opposed to *restrict*) competition, then the entire E.U. enterprise would be in jeopardy. Having thus filled in part the "merger" gap, the Court of Justice still did not find in Articles 81 and 82 a mechanism requiring pre-merger notification to the Commission. If a merger were presented as a *fait accompli*,

[41] See, *e.g. British Leyland PLC v. Commission*, [1986] E.C.R. 3263; [1987] 1 C.M.L.R. 185 (excessive pricing exists where a fee is clearly disproportionate to the economic value of the service provided); *Instituto Chemioterapico Italiano SpA v. Commission*, [1974] E.C.R. 223 (refusal to deal).

[42] See Sulivan & Grimes, see para. 2.025, n. 62, at 997.

[43] See *id.*

[44] See generally Ritter, Braun & Rawlinson, see para. 2.007, n. 13, at 749–99.

[45] See *id.* at 757.

[46] See Greek Television Monopoly, [1991] E.C.R. I–2925, paras. 15–16, 34–36.

[47] See *Europemballage Corp. v. Commission*, 1973 E.C.R. 215; C.M.L.R. 199.

courts understandably might be reluctant to unravel the deal. This gap was filled in 1989 with the unanimous adoption by the Council of Ministers of Merger Control Regulation 4064, effective in 1990.[48]

2.109 Significant amendments to the E.C. Merger Regulation entered into force in March 1998.[49] One of the more important changes is that notification thresholds are lowered. Under the Merger Control Regulation's initial test, a merger has a "Community dimension"—and thus subject to Commisison review—if:

(1) the undertakings concerned have combined worldwide sales of 5 billion Euros (approximately $5.75 billion), and

(2) at least two of the undertakings concerned each has sales in the E.U. of 250 million Euros (approximately $287 million).[50]

If each of the undertakings concerned made more than two-thirds of its E.U. sales in only one Member State, then the merger does not have a Community dimension. Under the Merger Control Regulations's amended supplementary test, a merger has a Community dimension and must be notified where:

(1) the combined aggregate worldwide turnover of all the firms concerned is at least 2.5 billion Euros (approximately $2.9 billion; formerly 5 billion Euros);

(2) the combined aggregate turnover of all the firms concerned is more than 100 million Euros in each of at least three Member States (approximately $115 million);

(3) the combined aggregate turnover of each of at least two of the firms concerned is more than 25 million Euros in each of at least three Member States (approximately $30 million; formerly 250 million Euros); and

(4) the aggregate Community-wide turnover of each of at least two of the firms concerned is more than 100 million Euros.

If each of the firms concerned made more than two-thirds of its E.U. sales in only one Member State, then the merger does not have a Community dimension.[51] These changes are recognition that mergers with effects in a

[48] Council Reg. 4064/89, [1989] O.J. L395 1, as amended, [1990] O.J. L257 13, [1997] O.J. L180 1, [1998] O.J. L61. For a discussion of the Merger Control Regulation, see Volker Hirsch, "EU Merger Control—The Latest Developments", (1995) 4 J. Int'l L. & Prac. 43; Griffin, see para. 2.029, n. 72, at 177–80; Andre Fiebig, "The Extraterritorial Application of the European Merger Control Regulation", (1998) 5 Colum. J. Eur. L. 79.

[49] See Council Regulation 1310/97 of 30 June 1997, amending Council Regulation 4064/89 on the Control of Concentrations between Undertakings, [1997] O.J. L180 1.

[50] See Merger Control Regulation, Art. 1(2). See generally Ritter, Braun & Rawlinson, see para. 2.007, n. 13, at 405–54.

[51] See Merger Control Regulation, Art. 1(3). See also Andre R. Fiebig, "Joint Ventures and Mergers", in *Introduction to European Law: How to Comply and Compete in the European Union* (Global Law and Policy Initiative 1999).

number of Member States are best handled at the Commission level rather than at the individual member-state level.[52] For businesses desirous of "one-stop shopping" within the E.U., the lower thresholds are an attractive alternative to seeking a pre-merger review in up to15 E.U.-member states.[53]

2.110 The Commission retains exclusive jurisdiction to review mergers and acquisitions when the financial thresholds that establish a "Community dimension" are met, although it may refer the case to a Member State in appropriate circumstances. The Commission's jurisdiction rests on meeting the financial thresholds on worldwide and E.U. sales; a physical presence in the E.U. is not required in order to trigger Commission review. Pursuant to Regulation 4064, if either the initial financial test or the supplementary test is met, then firms are under an affirmative duty to notify the Commission within one week of the signing of a merger or acquisition agreement.

2.111 Once a proposed merger or acquisition is notified, its effective date is suspended while the Commission investigates the agreement. The Commission has four months within which to complete its investigation and challenge or approve the agreement. Given the high thresholds established under the Merger Regulation, most mergers are not subject to its notification and approval requirements. Nevertheless, even if the thresholds are not met, a Member State can still request the Commission to investigate a merger.

2.112 Does the Merger Regulation give the Commission extraterritorial enforcement power?[54] While the Regulation is silent on this question, in practice the answer is "yes". For example, in 1996 the Commission blocked the merger of two South African mining companies with no physical presence in the E.U. because it would have created a duopoly in the platinum and rhodium markets.[55] In 1997, the Commission undertook its most high-profile merger examination involving *Boeing and McDonnell Douglas*;[56] another case involving two companies with no physical presence in the E.U. Does the Commission take into account international comity when exercising its authority under the Merger Regulation? In the *Boeing/McDonnell Douglas* case, the Commission asserted that it does:

> In particular, as far as U.S. defence interests were concerned, the Commission has limited the scope of its action to the civil side of the operation. The Commission has not pursued further the concerns it expressed in its Statement of Objections concerning the effect of the concentration on the international market for fighter aircraft. As far as [Douglas Aircraft] is concerned, the Commission has not considered a divestiture as a remedy to resolve the competition problems created by the concentration.[57]

---

[52] For additional analyses of Council Regulation 1310/97, see Yvonne Regn, "Legislative Development: Merger Regulation Amendments", (1998) 4 Colum. J. Eur. L. 687.

[53] See Waller I, see para. 2.020, n. 55, at 386.

[54] See Fiebig, see para. 2.108, n. 48.

[55] *Gencor/Lonrho*, Case IV/M 619 [1997] 4 C.M.L.R. 742.

[56] See Thomas P. O'Toole, "'The Long Arm of the Law'—European Merger Regulation and Its Application to the Merger of Boeing and McDonnell Douglas", (1998) 11 Transnat'l Law. 203.

[57] "Commission Report to the Council on the Application of the Agreement Between the European Communities and the Government of the United States Regarding the Application of Their Competition Laws", reprinted in European Comm'n, Twenty-Seventh Report on Competition Policy 317, 323 (1998).

Even though the Federal Trade Commission had approved the proposed *Boeing/McDonnell Douglas* merger, the Commission threatened to disapprove it unless Boeing addressed specific Commission concerns, including indirect subsidisation of Boeing through McDonnell Douglas' defence contracts. Rather than risk Commission fines of up to 10 per cent of its total revenues or being shut out of the E.U. market altogether, Boeing acceded to three Commission demands:

(1) it agreed not to abuse its position in the civil aircraft industry by maintaining the civil aircraft business of McDonnell Douglas as a separate entity for 10 years;

(2) it agreed to license any patents it obtains from McDonnell Douglas' defence contracts; and

(3) it agreed not to enforce the 20–year exclusive supplier contracts it has with Delta, Continental, and American Airlines and not to conclude any future exclusive supplier contracts for 10 years.[58]

While the handling of the *Boeing/McDonnell Douglas* merger was not a model of transatlantic agreement at the agency level, the FTC and the Commission actually worked together quite closely during their respective investigations. In the end, they simply failed to agree on the effect of the merger on competition.

2.113 The 1998 MCI/WorldCom merger reflected not only close antitrust co-operation, but also agency agreement. The Department of Justice and the European Commission were in regular contact, exchanged views, co-ordinated information gathering with the parties' consent and held joint meetings and settlement negotiations.[59] The merger was cleared after MCI agreed to divest its interest in certain Internet assets to Cable & Wireless PLC.[60] In 1999, both U.S. and E.U. regulators approved the $77.4 billion merger of Exxon and Mobil. In 2000, they approved Alcoa's $5.6 billion purchase of Reynolds Metals Co. Also in 2000, the Commission blocked the proposed merger of WorldCom and Sprint (the first time it has objected to a

[58] See Commission Decision IV/M.877 of 30 July 1997 declaring the concentration compatible with the Common Market and the Functioning of the EEA Agreement, [1997] O.J. L336 16; European Union, Press Release, "The European Commission Takes a Favorable Decision in Principle on the Merger of Boeing and McDonnell Douglas after Concessions Offered by Boeing" (July 23, 1997), Case IV/M 877, [1997] 5 C.M.L.R. 270; "*Boeing v. Airbus*, Peace in our time", *The Economist*, July 26, 1997, at 59–61. See generally Spencer Weber Waller, "Understanding and Appreciating EC Competition Law", (1992) 61 Antitrust L.J. 55, 57.

[59] See "Justice Department Clears WorldCom/MCI Merger After MCI Agrees to Sell Its Internet Business", Dept. of Justice, July 15, 1998, available at 1998 WL 389299.

[60] See Commission Decision IV/M 1069 of July 8, 1998.

proposed merger between two non-European companies).[61] The Justice Department filed a lawsuit to block the proposed Sprint/WorldCom merger as well.[62] In June 2000, the Commission and the Justice Department established a working group on mergers with the aim of extending their co-operation efforts.[63] In sum, transatlantic co-operation in the merger control area appears to be working, despite the absence of a multilateral agreement on the subject.

2.114 Given the time pressures under which the Commission must make a decision on a proposed merger (a final ruling must be made within four months of the notification) there is a growing perception among U.S. businesses that the Commission would rather block a merger than wave it through.[64] Historically, however, the Commission has blocked less than one per cent of the more than 1,100 mergers it has reviewed since 1990 and has required some action by notifying firms prior to approving a merger in only 7.2 percent of the cases.[65]

5. *Extraterritoriality and Comity*

2.115 Although neither Article 81 nor Article 82 expressly authorises the Commission to exercise jurisdiction over commerce with foreign nations, the Commission does apply E.U. competition rules to conduct occurring outside the E.U. if the challenged conduct is implemented within the E.U.[66] The European Commission, in theory, follows the OECD's revised recommendation that countries recognise:

> the principles of international law and comity and . . . use moderation and self-restraint in the interest of cooperation in the field of anticompetitive practices.[67]

Nevertheless, the Commission appears to be of the opinion that principles of international comity may be trumped easily by the fundamental Community interest that competition within the common market not be distorted.[68] Likewise, the European Court of Justice has rejected the argument that principles of international comity must be considered by the Commission when exercising extraterritorial jurisdiction.[69] In short, whether principles of

[61] See Brandon Mitchener, "EC Regulators Leave Deal Makers Bitter", *Wall Street Journal* at A21, col. 1, June 29, 2000.
[62] See "Sprint Retains Hope in WorldCom Deal", *Wall Street Journal* at A3, col. 1, June 29, 2000.
[63] See "EC Regulators Leave Deal Makers Bitter", *supra* note 61.
[64] See "Sprint Retains Hope in WorldCom Deal", *supra* note 62.
[65] See "EC Regulators Leave Deal Makers Bitter", *supra* note 61.
[66] See *Re Wood Pulp Cartel: A. Ahlström Osakeyhtiö v. E.C. Commission*, [1988] E.C.R. 5193, [1988] 4 C.M.L.R. 901, Common Mkt. Rep. (CCH) 14,491 (1988). See also Walter Van Gerven, "EC Jurisdiction in Antitrust Matters: The Wood Pulp Judgment", 1989 (1990) Fordham Corp. L. Inst. 451); Jose Perez Santos, "The Territorial Scope of Article 85 of the EEC Treaty", 1989 (1990) Fordham Corp. L. Inst. 571.
[67] "Revised Recommendation of the OECD Council Concerning Cooperation Between Member Countries on Anticompetitive Practices Affecting International Trade", OECD Doc. No. C (95) 130 (July 27, 1995), available at http://www.oecd.org.
[68] See *Aluminium Imports from Eastern Europe*, [1985] O.J. L92/1, at 14.7.
[69] See *Wood Pulp*, see para. 2.115, n. 66, [1988] C.M.L.R. at 22.

international comity should play any role in the Commission's decision to exercise jurisdiction in a case involving non-E.U. parties is left to its discretion.

2.116 Whether the E.U.'s "implemented" test is the same as or different from the "effects" test used in the United States remains a matter of some controversy. As summed up by one expert:

> Any practical importance of the distinction between anti-competitive conduct outside the EU 'implemented' in the Common Market and the 'effect' of such conduct in the Common Market likely is limited to a few, rare situations—such as concerted refusals to buy from, or export to, the EU or agreements to restrict non-EU production to create a scarcity outside the EU that would have the effect of raising prices within the EU.[70]

B. Mercosur

1. *Introduction*

2.117 The most ambitious of the world's new RTAs is the Common Market of the Southern Cone (in Spanish, "*Mercado Comun del Sur*" or "MERCOSUR," in Portuguese, "MERCOSUL").[71] On March 26, 1991 the governments of Argentina, Brazil, Paraguay and Uruguay signed the Treaty of Asuncion, which entered into force on November 29, 1991.[72] In the near term, the Treaty establishes a customs union. Behind Brazil's leadership, MERCOSUR's long-term goal is to establish itself as common market that serves as a regional economic hub and as a counterbalance to NAFTA.

2.118 After NAFTA and the E.U., MERCOSUR is the third largest RTA in the world. Its long-term goal is to form a common market among its members that permits the free movement of goods, services, and capital. Despite a population of over 200 million persons and a combined gross domestic product (GDP) in excess of $1 trillion, the MERCOSUR market still is significantly smaller than the combined NAFTA and E.U. markets. Nevertheless, MERCOSUR is nearly twice as large as the next largest Latin American RTA.

Unlike other earlier Latin America RTAs that were predicated on achieving regional economic growth through import-substitution, MERCOSUR's underlying economic premise is market openings and export promotion as the bases for economic growth. Still, economists remain divided over whether MERCOSUR is a trade-creating or trade-diverting RTA.[73]

---

[70] Griffin, see para. 2.029, n. 72, at 187. See also Roger P. Alford, "The Extraterritorial Application of Antitrust Laws: The United States and European Community Approaches", (1992) 33 Va. J. Int'l L. 1.

[71] See generally Thomas Andrew O'Keefe, "An Analysis of the Mercosur Economic Integration from a Legal Perspective", (1994) 28 Int'l Law. 439; Ana Maria de Aguinis, "Can MERCOSUR Accede to NAFTA? A Legal Perspective", (1995) 10 Conn. J. Int'l L. 597.

[72] See Treaty Establishing a Common Market Between the Argentine Republic, the Federative Republic of Brazil, the Republic of Paraguay and the Eastern Republic of Uruguay, Mar. 26, 1991, Art. 1, reprinted in (1991) 30 Int'l Legal Materials 1044 (hereinafter Treaty of Asuncion).

[73] See "Remapping South America: A Survey of MERCOSUR", *The Economist*, Oct. 12, 1996, at 6; "A Closer Look at MERCOSUR", (USITC Feb./Mar. 1977) Int'l Econ. Rev. 10–11.

2.119 The Treaty of Asuncion is a framework agreement, much like the E.C. Treaty, that contains guidelines and objectives for the MERCOSUR members. The Treaty's key obligations are:

(1) the establishment of a free trade area where tariffs and non-tariff barriers to trade among the MERCOSUR members are progressively eliminated;[74]

(2) co-ordination of macroeconomic policies and the harmonisation of laws;

(3) implementation of a common external tariff and a common trade policy in relations with third parties; and

(4) adoption of sectoral agreements.[75]

The Treaty provides for the establishment of a common market with the free movement of goods, services, and capital beginning January 1, 1995; a date that has been pushed back to 2006.[76] Dispute settlement and the interpretation of MERCOSUR rules are governed by the Protocol of Brasilia. A protocol signed in 1991[77] obligates MERCOSUR members to resolve disputes through a 15–day period of direct negotiations. If no settlement is reached, the matter is referred to the Common Market Group for a 30–day period of review. The Group may in turn refer the matter to a three-member arbitral panel and panel proceedings are strictly member-to-member. The panel's decision is confidential, final nonappealable and must be unanimous. If the responding member does not comply with the panel's decision, then the complaining member may take appropriate compensatory measures. In late 1994, the members signed the Ouro Preto Protocol that reaffirms the Protocol of Brasilia and gives binding legal status to the directives of the MERCOSUR Trade Commission, a new MERCOSUR intergovernmental body.[78]

---

[74] See Treaty of Asuncion, see para. 2.118, n. 72, Annex I. Annex I contains a timetable for the elimination of tariffs among the MERCOSUR members, with exceptions for certain goods. The original list of exceptions included 394 items for Argentina, 324 for Brazil, 439 for Paraguay, and 960 for Uruguay.

[75] See *id.* Art. 5. The Treaty of Asuncion calls for "the adoption of sectoral agreements in order to optimize the use and mobility of factors of production and to achieve efficient scales of operation." *id.* art 5(d). However, consistent with MERCOSUR's free market approach, no *supra*national body was created to direct this process. *See* Thomas Andrew O'Keefe, "The Legal Framework and Institutions of Mercosur: The Newly Emerging Economic Bloc in South America's Southern Cone", (1992) 6 Inter–Am. Legal Mat. 90, 100–01.

[76] See Treaty of Asuncion, see para. 2.118, n. 72, Art. 1.

[77] See Protocolo de Brasilia Para la Solucion de Controversias, Dec. 17, 1991 reprinted in 6 Inter-Am. Legal Materials (1992) 1.

[78] See Protocolo de Ouro Preto, Dec. 17, 1994, Art. 43. See also Aguinas, *supra* note 77, at 608–17.

2.120 In 1996, MERCOSUR expanded its membership to include Chile as an associate member.[79] As an associate member, Chile joins the MERCOSUR free trade area, but not its customs union.[80] With Chile's accession, MERCOSUR represents a market of 220 million people with a combined GDP of nearly $1 trillion and total world trade of $175 billion. The Chilean economy will add little to MERCOSUR's internal market, at least initially, given that most interregional trade already occurs at preferential terms under the auspices of the Latin American Integration Association (ALADI) RTA. However, the addition of Chile to the group could add significant momentum for other Latin American countries to seek membership in MERCOSUR.

2.121 Bolivia joined MERCOSUR as an associate member on January 1, 1997 and in August 2000 announced that it would seek full membership.[81] Mexico, Peru, and Venezuela have expressed interest in joining MERCOSUR as associate members.[82] MERCOSUR has approached members of the Andean Group (Bolivia, Colombia, Ecuador, Peru and Venezuela) to begin accession negotiations. At a two-day conference held in August 31–September 1, 2000 and attended by the leaders of all 12 South American countries, the participants agreed in principal on a continent-wide free trade area by the end of 2002.[83]

2. *Competition Policy*

2.122 The main provisions of MERCOSUR relating to competition policy are contained in the Protocol of the Defence of Competition in MERCOSUR.[84] The Protocol has two main features. First, it creates a mechanism for investigating and punishing anti-competitive practices of MERCOSUR firms and reaches both private and public conduct. Article 2 of the Protocol provides that it applies to the acts of natural and legal persons under public

[79] See "MERCOSUR: Now they are six", *The Economist*, Dec. 21, 1996.

[80] See "Chile-MERCOSUR Association Agreement", (USITC Oct./Nov. 1996) Int'l Econ. Rev. 24; "MERCOSUR and Chile Sign Free-Trade Pact", 13 Int'l Trade Rep. (BNA) 1096 (1996). Chile did not join the MERCOSUR customs union because its average tariff level is 11%, 3 percentage points lower than MERCOSUR's average common external tariff. Even with Chile's open economy, Chilean officials nevertheless bowed to pressure from farm groups that wanted greater protection from more efficient Argentine grain farmers by negotiating an 18–year exception for wheat and flour. In June 2000, Chile announced that it would seek full integration with MERCOSUR on political, economic, and financial matters, but that joining the MERCOSUR customs union would have to wait. See James Langman, "Chile Shifts Strategy for Achieving Full Membership in MERCOSUR Bloc", (June 22, 2000) 17 Int'l Trade Rep. (BNA) 983.

[81] See "Bolivia to Sign Free-Trade Accord with MERCOSUR", (1996) 13 Int'l Trade Rep. (BNA) 1647; James Langman, "Bolivia Trade Minister Says Nation Wants to be Full Member of MERCOSUR", (Aug. 24, 2000) 17 Int'l Trade Rep. (BNA) 1315.

[82] See "Pan-American free trade: Slow, but ahead", *The Economist*, May 24, 1997 at 35.

[83] See Rosella Brevetti & Ed Taylor, "MERCOSUR, Andean Pact Nations Agree at Summit to Negotiate An Economic Zone", (Sept. 7, 2000) 17 Int'l Trade Rep. (BNA) 1359; "South American dreams", *The Economist*, Sept. 9, 2000 at 19.

[84] See Protocol of the Defence of Competition in MERCOSUR, Decision 17/96, Dec. 17, 1996 available at http://www.sice.oas.org/cp_comp/english/cpa/cpa3_e.asp. For an analysis of competition law enforcement within MERCOSUR, see Jose Tavares de Araujo, Jr. & Luis Tineo, "The Harmonization of Competition Policies Among Mercosur Countries", (1998) 24 Brooklyn J. Int'l L. 441.

and private law. Included in this definition are state monopolies. Secondly, the Protocol calls for the harmonisation of the national competition laws of MERCOSUR members.[85]

2.123 Article 6 provides the following non-exhaustive list of 17 types of conduct that constitute a prohibited restrictive business practice:

(1) to fix, impose, or practice, directly or indirectly, in collaboration with competitors or individually, in any form, the prices and conditions of the purchase or sale of goods or services;

(2) to procure or to contribute to the adoption of uniform business practices or concerted action by competitors;

(3) to enter into agreements to limit or control research and technological development, the production of goods or the supply of services, or to hinder investments intended for the production of goods or services or their distribution;

(4) to divide up the markets of finished or semi-finished goods or services, or the supply source of raw materials and intermediate products;

(5) to limit or prevent access of new enterprises to the market;

(6) to agree on prices or advantages which may affect competition in public bids;

(7) to adopt unequal conditions for equivalent services with regard to third parties, thus placing them at a competitive disadvantage;

(8) to tie the sale of one good to the purchase of another good or to the use of a service, or to tie the supply of a service to the use of another or to the purchase of a good;

(9) to prevent the access of competitors to raw materials, goods, technologies, or distribution channels;

(10) to require or to grant exclusivity with respect to the dissemination of publicity in the communication media;

(11) to tie buying or selling to the condition of not using or acquiring, selling, or supplying goods or services which are produced, processed, distributed, or marketed by a third party (*i.e.* boycotts);

(12) to sell merchandise, for reasons unfounded on business practices, at prices below the cost of the goods;

(13) to reject without good reason the sale of goods or the supply of services;

[85] See Protocol of the Defence of Competition in MERCOSUR, Art. 7. Art. 7 obligates MERCOSUR members to adopt common rules for the control of conduct that may limit or prejudice free trade, or that may result in regional market domination.

(14) to interrupt or to reduce production on a large scale, without any justifiable cause;

(15) to destroy, render useless, or accumulate raw materials, intermediate or finished goods, as well as to destroy, render useless, or obstruct the functioning of equipment designed to produce, transport, or distribute them;

(16) to abandon, cause to be abandoned, or destroy crops and plantations without just cause; and

(17) to manipulate the market in order to impose prices.

2.124 The Competition Protocol is enforced by the Trade Commission and the Committee for the Defence of Competition. The Committee is responsible for the investigation and evaluation of cases referred to it, while the Commission performs adjudicative functions. Proceedings are conducted in three stages. First, proceedings are initiated at the instance of a MERCOSUR member with the national enforcement authorities of the defendant's domicile. The national enforcement authority conducts an investigation of any alleged RBP in the first instance. In each case investigated, the Committee is responsible for establishing guidelines for the definition of the relevant market and criteria for the economic effects of the investigated practice.[86]

2.125 Secondly, once the investigation has been concluded, the national enforcement authority responsible for the investigation must present a conclusive ruling on the matter to the Committee.[87] Taking into account the ruling of the national enforcement authority, the Committee makes an evaluation of whether the business practice violates the Protocol.[88] If the Committee concludes that the business practice in issue violates the Protocol, it recommends the sanctions to be imposed.[89]

2.126 Thirdly, the Committee's evaluations and recommendations are forwarded to the Trade Commission. Taking into account the Committee's evaluation and recommendations, the Trade Commission makes a ruling through the adoption of a Directive setting forth the sanctions to be applied to the infringing party or other appropriate measures.[90] The sanctions are applied by the national enforcement authority of the MERCOSUR member in whose territory the infringing party is domiciled. If the Trade Commission

[86] See *id.* Art. 14. At any stage of the proceeding, the Committee may ratify an undertaking of cessation of the practice under investigation, which shall not constitute an admission of any facts or an acknowledgement of the illegal nature of the conduct under investigation. See *id.* Art. 22. The cessation undertaking must include the following terms: (1) the agreement of the defendant to cease the practice being investigated; (2) the value of the daily fine to be imposed in case of noncompliance with the undertaking; and (3) the obligation of the defendant to submit regular reports on its activities in the market, including keeping the national enforcement authority informed of changes in the company's structure, control, activities, and location. See *id.* Art. 23.

[87] See *id.* Art. 18.

[88] See *id.* Art. 15.

[89] See *id.* Art. 19.

[90] See *id.* Art. 20.

does not reach a consensus, it is to bring the different proposed solutions before the Common Market Group. The Common Market Group makes a ruling upon the matter through adoption of a resolution. If the Common Market Group cannot reach consensus, the interested member may resort directly to the dispute settlement panel procedure set forth in the Brasilia Protocol on the Settlement of Disputes.[91]

2.127 Sanctions may include one or more of the following:

(1) a cease-and-desist order;

(2) a fine, based on the earnings, gross revenues, or assets obtained from commission of the infringing practice, to be paid to the national enforcement authority of the MERCOSUR member in the territory of which the infringing party is domiciled;[92]

(3) in the case of non-compliance with a cease-and-desist order, a daily fine of up to one per cent of the company's gross billing for the previous financial period;[93] and

(4) debarment from participating in government procurement contracts.[94]

When determining the level of the fine to be imposed, the Commission is to consider the seriousness of the RBP and the amount of the damage caused to competition in MERCOSUR.[95] The national enforcement authority of the member in the territory of which the infringing party is domiciled executes the cease-and-desist order, as well as imposition of the fine.

2.128 In order to ensure the proper functioning of the Protocol, members are to adopt co-operation and consultation mechanisms, including mechanisms for the joint investigation of practices harmful to competition within MERCOSUR.[96] The Protocol represents, in sum, a blend of national and supranational competition law enforcement, supported by co-operation from the other MERCOSUR members.[97] The potential for friction in its operation is high. At each stage of an investigation—from the national authorities, to the Committee, to the Trade Commission—the latter agency has the power to

---

[91] See *id.* Art. 21.

[92] See *id.* Art. 27. In the Annex to the Protocol of Defence of Competition in MERCOSUR, adopted in 1997, the MERCOSUR members established the following criteria for the determining the amount of fines to be imposed under the Protocol. Fines may equal: (1) up to 150% of the profits obtained through the illegal practice, (2) up to 100% of the value of the assets involved; or (3) up to 30% of the value of the company's gross billing for its previous financial year, net of tax.
Such fines may not be less than the advantage obtained, if quantifiable. Twelfth Meeting of the Common Market Council, Asuncion, Decision 18/VI/97, Art. 1, available at http://www.sice.oas.org/cp_comp/english/cpa/cpa3_e.asp.

[93] See Annex to the Protocol of the Defence of Competition in MERCOSUR, see para. 2.122, n. 85, Art. 2.

[94] See Protocol for the Protection of Competition, Art. 28.

[95] See *id.* Art. 29.

[96] See *id.* Art. 30.

[97] See *id.* Art. 16.

overrule the decisions of the former. Given the critical roles that the two intergovernmental bodies play in the process, ensuring that investigations remain politically neutral will be a challenge. In that regard, harmonising national competition laws will be key to politically neutral decision making by the two intergovernmental bodies.[98]

C. NAFTA

2.129 Neither antitrust enforcement nor antitrust co-operation were new ideas among the NAFTA partners.[99] As noted above, the United States and Canada have a history of co-operation in antitrust enforcement activities. Both the United States and Canada have antitrust histories that go back more than a century. Mexico's antitrust regime is newer, having been substantially revised in 1993.[1] Effective antitrust enforcement that opens markets and makes them competitive can complement and promote the reduction of governmental barriers to cross-border trade in goods and services. This is the basic premise behind NAFTA Chapter Fifteen, "Competition Policy, Monopolies and State Enterprises".[2] NAFTA Chapter Fifteen's second premise, set out in Article 1501, is that co-operation and co-ordination in enforcing national antitrust laws is essential among the NAFTA parties' antitrust enforcement authorities. However, the parties adopted a minimalist approach to transborder co-operation on competition policy and law enforcement.

2.130 NAFTA Chapter Fifteen consists of three substantive articles.[3] First, the parties recognise that preventing anti-competitive activity would enhance the NAFTA objectives. NAFTA Article 102 identifies several objectives of the Agreement, including to "promote conditions of fair competition in the free trade area."[4] Accordingly, Article 1501.1 sets out a core commitment by each of the NAFTA parties to adopt, maintain, and enforce laws "to proscribe anti-competitive business conduct and take appropriate actions with respect thereto." Although it requires the parties to adopt and maintain legislation prohibiting "anti-competitive business conduct," the Agreement does not specifically describe the kinds of business conduct to be proscribed.

2.131 Article 1501.2 calls upon the parties to co-operate in competition law enforcement. To that end, the parties agree to co-operate in administering

---

[98] See de Araujo & Tineo, see para. 2.122, n. 84. Unlike ANZCERTA, which abolished the application of antidumping measures to Australia-New Zealand trade *inter se*, MERCOSUR countries have retained their antidumping duty laws and assess antidumping duties on dumped goods imported from other MERCOSUR members. See Ed Taylor, "MERCOSUR's Brazil, Argentina Embroiled in Dispute over Dumped Poultry Products", (Aug. 3, 2000) 17 Int'l Trade Rep. (BNA) 1221.

[99] See generally American Bar Ass'n, *The Competition Laws of NAFTA, Canada, Mexico, and the United States: A Practitioner's Guide* (1997).

[1] See Ley Federal de Competencia Economica (Federal Law of Economic Competition), Diario Ofical de La Federacion (Official Gazette of the Federation) (Dec. 24, 1992). For an English translation of the Mexican competition law, see "Report of the ABA Antitrust Section Task Force on the Competition Dimension of the North American Free Trade Agreement", Appendix Two (1994).

[2] See Charles S. Stark, "International Antitrust Cooperation in NAFTA: The International Antitrust Assistance Act of 1994", (1996) 4 U.S.-Mex. L.J. 169.

[3] Outside of Art. 1505 on definitions, the one procedural article is Art. 1504 which establishes a Working Group on Trade and Competition, discussed below.

[4] NAFTA Art. 102.1(b).

their own antitrust legislation by exchanging information, providing mutual assistance among enforcement agencies and notifying the other signatories as to actions taken against foreign companies. Importantly, however, pursuant to Article 1501.3, the failure of a NAFTA party to fulfil its obligations under either Article 1501.1 or 1501.2 may not be the subject of dispute settlement. Nevertheless, ways exist to "backdoor" competition disputes under other NAFTA provisions. For example, a party's failure to honour market access commitments in the financial services or telecommunications sectors stemming from the unchecked conduct of a monopoly service supplier could be the subject of a NAFTA Chapter Fourteen or Twenty dispute settlement proceeding, respectively.

2.132 Next, Article 1502 reserves the right of the parties to designate state monopolies (*e.g.* enterprises that provide transportation or energy services) but such monopolies are subject to four conditions relating to abuse of monopoly power. First, state monopolies are required to act in a manner that is not inconsistent with the party's obligations under the Agreement wherever such a monopoly exercises any regulatory, administrative, or other governmental authority that the party has delegated to it in connection with the monopoly good or service.[5] Secondly, state monopolies are to act in accordance with commercial considerations with regard to price, quality, availability, marketability, transportation, and other terms and conditions of purchase or sale when selling or buying the monopoly good and service.[6] Thirdly, they are not to discriminate against the investors of other parties in the purchase or sale of their monopoly good or service.[7] Fourthly, state monopolies must not use their monopoly position to engage in anti-competitive practices, either directly or indirectly through a parent, subsidiary, or other enterprise with common ownership, in a non-monopolised market that adversely affects another party's investors, including through the discriminatory provision of a monopoly good or service, cross-subsidisation, or predatory conduct.[8] Excepted conduct is government procurement of goods and services "for governmental purposes and not with a view to commercial resale.[9]

2.133 The final substantive provision, Article 1503, reserves the right of parties to maintain or establish state enterprises. However, a state enterprise is prohibited from acting in a manner that is inconsistent with the parties' obligations under Chapter Eleven on investment and Chapter Fourteen on financial services wherever such enterprise exercises regulatory, administrative, or other governmental authority that a party has delegated to it.[10] State enterprises must also refrain from discriminating against the investors of other NAFTA parties in the sale of its goods and services.[11]

[5] See *id.* Art. 1502.3(a).
[6] See *id.* Art. 1502.3(b).
[7] See *id.* Art. 1502.3(c).
[8] See *id.* Art. 1502.3(d).
[9] See *id.* Art. 1502.4.
[10] See *id.* Art. 1503.2.
[11] See *id.* Art. 1503.3. The Canada-Chile Free Trade Agreement contains competition policy rules that track those of NAFTA Chapter Fifteen practically verbatim. See Free Trade Agreement between Canada and Chile, Chapter J, available at http://www.sice.oas.org/cp_comp/english/cpa/cpa2_e.asp.

2.134 A final NAFTA provision dealing with restrictive business practices is Article 1704 of the Chapter on Intellectual Property Rights, entitled Control of Abusive or Anti-competitive Practices or Conditions". Article 1704 provides:

> Nothing in this Chapter shall prevent a Party from specifying in its domestic law licensing practices or conditions that may in particular cases constitute an abuse of intellectual property rights having an adverse effect on competition in the relevant market. A Party may adopt or maintain, consistent with the other provisions of this Agreement, appropriate measures to prevent or control such practices and conditions.

In the view of Professor Spencer Weber Waller:

> [t]his section's broad language will ultimately require the parties to develop continental standards for the application of competition rules in the intellectual property area.[12]

2.135 Canada, Mexico, and the United States have also participated in a Working Group established under NAFTA Article 1504 to examine the relationship between trade and competition policies in the free trade area. Its mandate was to develop a recommendation to the NAFTA Commission on these issues and issue a report by the end of 1998. The Working Group's mandate expired on January 1, 1999 and no final report was issued.[13] In its 1996 interim report, the Working Group studied the differences and similarities between the competition laws and policies of the three NAFTA parties and considered which, if any, differences had implications for trade among the parties.[14] In a parallel study, an ABA Task Force proposed eight framework principles for developing the competition principles of NAFTA and elaborated on how they might be implemented.[15]

2.136 In sum, unlike the well-developed competition legal regime of the E.U., NAFTA has no harmonised body of competition law applicable to all members and has no supranational enforcement authority. Nevertheless, the parties' competition laws are quite similar, at least textually. Waller attributes the similarities among the three NAFTA parties' competition laws to U.S. dominance. "This regional harmonization appears to be driven by U.S. hegemony," he writes, "and any future NAFTA partners likely would have to

[12] Waller I, see para. 2.020, n. 55, at 359.
[13] See American Bar Ass'n, "Report of the Sections on Antitrust Law and International Law and Practice on the Internationalization of Competition Law Rules: Coordination and Convergence" 17–48 (2000) (the NAFTA Working Group made "little contribution") (hereinafter "Report on Coordination and Convergence").
[14] See "Interim Report of the NAFTA 1504 Working Group on Trade and Competition to the NAFTA Commission" (1996), available at http://www.sice.oas.org/trade/nafta/reports/comp_e.asp.
[15] See American Bar Ass'n, "Report of the Task Force of the ABA Section of Antitrust Law on the Competition Dimension of NAFTA" (1994). The analysis and recommendations of the American Bar Association and its Canadian and Mexican counterparts were relied upon by the Working Group in the preparation of its interim report.

accept similar changes to their competition laws as a condition of membership."[16]

D. The Free Trade Area of the Americas

1. *Introduction*

2.137 A proposal to integrate the economies of the countries of the Western Hemisphere was launched by President Bush in 1990 in his Enterprise for the Americas Initiative. The Bush initiative was championed by the Clinton administration and restyled as the Free Trade Area of the Americas (FTAA).[17] The goal of the FTAA, as articulated at the Summit of the Americas held in Miami in December 1994, and renewed at the Third Ministerial meeting at Belo Horizonte, Brazil in May 1997, is a free trade area stretching from Alaska to Tierra del Fuego by 2005.[18] The 34 heads of the democratic nations in the Western Hemisphere (*i.e.* all countries in the hemisphere with the exception of Cuba) launched FTAA negotiations at the 1994 Summit of the Americas in Miami, calling for the completion of an FTAA by 2005. The leaders committed themselves to integrate the patchwork quilt of bilateral and regional trade agreements (at least six regional trade arrangements and more than 25 bilateral trade agreements) that exist in the Western Hemisphere. Upon its completion, the FTAA will integrate a population of 850 million people into a $13 trillion market.

2.138 In the Declaration of Principles, the countries committed to "begin immediately" the construction of the FTAA. It calls for building on existing bilateral and sub-regional arrangements "in order to broaden and deepen hemispheric economic integration". In the Plan of Action accompanying the Declaration of Principles, "Promoting Prosperity through Economic Integration and Free Trade" the parties are to:

---

[16] Waller I, see para. 2.020, n. 55, at 360.

[17] See generally Richard L. Bernal, "Regional Trade Arrangements and the Establishment of a Free Trade Area of the Americas", (1996) 27 Law & Pol'y Int'l Bus. 945; Frank J. Garcia, "'Americas Agreements'—An Interim Stage in Building the Free Trade Area of the Americas", (1997) 35 Colum. J. Transnat'l L. 63; Paul A. O'Hop, "Hemispheric Integration and the Elimination of Legal Obstacles Under a NAFTA-Based System"(1995) 36 Harv. Int'l L.J. 127; Carol Stump, "Free Trade Area of the Americas (FTAA)", (1995) 4 J. Int'l L. & Prac. 153; Ruperto Patino Manffer, "The Future of Free Trade in the Americas", (1995) 10 Conn. J. Int'l L. 639; Kenneth W. Abbott & Gregory W. Bowman, "Economic Integration in the Americas: 'A Work in Progress'", (1994) 14 Nw. J. Int'l L. & Bus. 493; David A. Pawlak, "Learning from Computers: The Future of The Free Trade Area of the Americas", (1995) 27 U. Miami Inter-Am. L. Rev. 107; Frank J. Garcia, "NAFTA and the Creation of the FTAA: A Critique of Piecemeal Accession", (1995) 35 Va. J. Int'l L. 539; Charles M. Gastle, "Policy Alternatives for Reform of the Free Trade Agreement of the Americas: Dispute Settlement Mechanisms", (1995) 26 L. & Pol'y Int'l Bus. 735; "The Evolution of Free Trade in the Americas: NAFTA Case Studies", (1996) 11 Am. U.J. Int'l Law & Pol'y 687 (conference papers).
The FTAA maintains a website at http://www.alca-ftaa.org. Other FTAA web sites are http://www.itaiep.doc.gov and http://americas.fiu.edu.

[18] "See Summit of the Americas, Declaration of the Principles and Plan of Action", Dec. 11, 1994, reprinted in 34 Int'l Legal Materials (1995) 808; Summit of the Americas, Third Ministerial Trade Meeting, Belo Horizonte, Minas Gerais, Brazil, May 16, 1997 Joint Declaration, para. 2.

determine areas of commonality and divergence in the particular agreements under review and the consideration of the means of bringing them together.[19]

2.139 The 1994 Miami Summit Action Plan called on the trade ministers of the FTAA participants to meet in 1995 to draft a more complete plan for FTAA negotiations and to meet in 1996 to develop a timetable for future work.[20] Trade ministers met in Denver in June 1995, and issued a Joint Declaration and Work Plan. The ministers agreed to set up FTAA Working Groups on investment, customs procedures and rules of origin, technical standards, sanitary and phytosanitary standards, subsidies and antidumping duties, market access, services, smaller economies, intellectual property, government procurement and competition policy. Dispute settlement was the only issue that was neither taken up at the June 1995 ministerial meeting nor mentioned as an item to be considered at the March 1996 meeting. Several sources reported that there was a widespread feeling that efforts at this stage should support the WTO dispute settlement procedures and not attempt to create new procedures in the FTAA context. In addition, working groups have not been established for the areas of labour and the environment, notwithstanding the call in the Miami Summit's Action Plan to "further secure the observance and promotion of worker rights" and to make trade liberalisation and environmental policies "mutually supportive."

2.140 Several Latin American representatives, as well as private groups, have voiced reservations over a U.S. proposal to include labour and environmental ministers in the FTAA process. Opposition to the U.S. proposal has mounted on the ground that neither issue merits inclusion in the immediate action plan required to advance the FTAA process. Moreover, some participants argue that the proposed U.S. language on labour and the environment departs from the more vaguely worded language on labour and the environment in the Miami Summit's Action plan. Sources monitoring the pre-Denver consultations reported that the United States agreed to soften its proposed language to achieve consensus at the June ministerial.

At the March 1996 ministerial meeting in Cartagena, the trade ministers agreed on: "the importance of further observance and promotion of worker rights and the need to consider appropriate processes in this area, through our respective governments".[21]The ministers also agreed to establish a Working Group on Dispute Settlement, but postponed the establishment of a Working Group on the environment. The initially slow pace of FTAA negotiations was accelerated at the 1997 Belo Horizonte summit in Brazil. In their Joint Declaration,[22] the trade ministers reiterated that:

---

[19] The texts of all FTAA documents are available from the FTAA's website at http://www.alca-ftaa.org.

[20] See "Free Trade Area for the Americas: Chile Is the Linchpin", Int'l Econ. Rev. 11 (USITC Pub. 2934 Nov. 1995).

[21] See Summit of the Americas Second Ministerial Trade Meeting Joint Declaration, adopted March 21, 1996. The text of the Joint Declaration is available from the FTAA's website http://www.alca-ftaa.org and from the USTR's website at http://www.ustr.gov.

[22] See Summit of the Americas Third Ministerial Trade Meeting, Belo Horizonte, Minas Gerais, Brazil, May 16, 1997 Joint Declaration. The text of the Joint Declaration is available from the FTAA's website http://www.alca-ftaa.org and from the USTR's website at http://www.ustr.gov.

(1) FTAA negotiations will be completed no later than 2005;

(2) the FTAA will be consistent with GATT Article XXIV and GATS Article V on regional trade arrangements; and

(3) the FTAA will be trade creating, not trade diverting.[23]

The FTAA participants held their fourth ministerial meeting in San Jose, Costa Rica, in March 1998.[24] The trade ministers outlined the structure and organisation of the negotiations into nine negotiating groups: market access; investment; services; government procurement; dispute settlement; agriculture; intellectual property rights; subsidies, antidumping, and countervailing duties; and competition policy.[25] This restructuring converted the original 12 FTAA working groups to nine negotiating groups.

2.141 At the Second Summit of the Americas held in Santiago, Chile, in April 1998, the 34 heads of state participating in the FTAA negotiations accepted the recommendations made by their trade ministers in San Jose and officially launched negotiations on a Free Trade Area of the Americas.[26] The Santiago Declaration reiterates the negotiators' commitment to complete FTAA negotiations by 2005. The Declaration also states that the FTAA will be balanced, comprehensive, WTO-consistent, and will constitute a single undertaking (*i.e.* will be an all-or-nothing, package deal, identical to the Uruguay Round single undertaking).

2. *The Negotiating Group on Competition Policy*

2.142 The FTAA Working Group on competition policy was established on May 1996 and was renamed in 1998 to the Negotiating Group on Competition Policy.[27] Its mandate includes, among other initiatives, the exchange of views on the operation of competition policy regimes in the region, the identification of co-operation mechanisms among governments and the elaboration of specific recommendations on how to proceed in this matter.

2.143 At a competition policy workshop held at the 1997 Belo Horizonte Summit, the group reached consensus on general substantive and procedural principles. The overwhelming sentiment was that the current inventory of competition laws and policies within the hemisphere must be studied and discussed with the goals of

[23] See Joint Declaration, see para. 2.140, n. 21, paras. 1–2.

[24] See U.S. International Trade Community, "Free Trade Area of the Americas", Int'l Econ. Rev., at 1–5 (Mar./Apr./May 1998).

[25] See San Jose Ministerial Declaration, Summit of the Americas, Fourth Trade Ministerial, San Jose, Costa Rica, March 19, 1998, paras. 8, 11, available at http://www.alca_ftaa.org/EnglishVersion/costa_e.htm.

[26] See Second Summit of the Americas, Santiago Declaration, Apr. 19, 1998, available at http://www.sice.oas.org/ftaa/santiago/sadop_e.htm. The heads of state also issued a Plan of Action, a body of concrete initiatives intended to promote the overall development of FTAA countries. *See* Second Summit of the Americas, Plan of Action, Apr. 19, 1998, available at http://www.sice.oas.org/ftaa/santiago/sapoa_e1.stm.

[27] Additional information on the activities of the FTAA Working Group on Competition Policy are available at http://www.ftaa-alca.org/ngroups/ngcomp_e.asp.

(1) educating those countries that do not now have competition regimes; and

(2) co-ordinating, to the extent possible, competition policies and enforcement actions of those countries that do have them and those that will develop them in the future.[28]

The group made the following recommendations:

- The FTAA should adopt as its goal the creation of an integrated market based on principles of free competition.
- FTAA negotiations on competition policy must be within the framework of existing multilateral agreements. FTAA provisions must not abrogate existing multilateral obligations, but they may and should produce a more completely integrated market.
- In the formation of free trade areas, the development of a competition law framework is indispensable to facilitating and attracting business and to promoting a sense of security and certainty to investors.
- The FTAA negotiating process should concentrate on educating and spreading information on competition legislation and policy. Hemispheric agreements should be negotiated gradually and should seek harmonisation to the extent possible, recognising national differences. To that end, the FTAA Working Group should co-ordinate the provision of technical assistance in educating and promoting the adoption of competition laws throughout the hemisphere.
- Competition laws and policy should be applied through specialised independent agencies that employ transparent, non-discriminatory methods defined in law and that guarantee a forum where agency decisions can be reviewed.
- The competition laws of the FTAA countries must be transparent and non-discriminatory. For example, there should be no exemptions for export cartels in the FTAA.
- The FTAA Working Group should promote co-operation among the competition law enforcement agencies of the FTAA countries. While recognising the continued vitality of the "effects test" in determining

[28] At the request of the FTAA Working Group on Competition Policy, in 1999 the Organisation of American States (OAS) completed a report on developments in competition policies and laws in the Western Hemisphere. See OAS, "Report on Developments and Enforcement of Competition Policy and Laws in the Western Hemisphere" (1999), available at http://www.ftaa-alca.org. The OAS also compiled an inventory of domestic competition policies and laws in the Western Hemisphere in 1997. See OAS, "Inventory of Domestic Laws and Regulations Relating to Competition Policy in the Western Hemisphere" (Final Version), SG/TU/WG.COMPOL/DOC.1/97/Rev.5/Corr.1 (Aug. 30, 1997). It is available from the FTAA web site http://www.alca-ftaa.org/publications/covcome.asp. Of the 34 countries participating in the FTAA negotiations, only 15 had a competition law as of 1999.

jurisdiction to enforce national competition laws, the FTAA countries should strive to adopt a philosophy of positive comity in which one member country can appeal to another to enforce its own competition laws to restrain anti-competitive conduct within its borders that affects other member countries.

- State and private monopolies, if they cannot be prevented, should be controlled so as to distort competition as little as possible.
- National and international rules for the protection of intellectual property must take competition policy into consideration to prevent patent and copyright abuse.[29]

2.144 At least two areas of divergence surfaced at the Belo Horizonte workshop. First, some participants suggested that a supranational hemispheric body be created to develop and promote at least the basic principles of competition policy, such as the prevention of hard-core cartels and abuse of monopoly power and/or dominant position. This supranational body would also settle disputes between countries, as well as between private parties. Most participants, however, felt it was premature to consider creating a supranational body.

2.145 Secondly, some participants recommended that antidumping laws be eliminated and replaced by enforcement of predatory pricing rules. At a minimum, application of antidumping rules should take into consideration competition policy concerns for the welfare of consumers in the FTAA countries. Others, noting the need to protect local industries, particularly in developing countries, pointed out that antidumping laws serve policy considerations that should remain apart from competition policy.[30]

2.146 In contrast to the sweeping and broad goals announced in Belo Horizonte, at its March 1998 meeting in San Jose, Costa Rica, the Working Group narrowed its focus. It generally recommended that in the negotiation of competition policy rules, FTAA participants focus on the development of general principles, including the following:

(1) the general economic interest (which the Working Group did not define) should be the guiding principle when targeting conduct which significantly restricts competition;

(2) national legislation dealing with competition policy and its relation to international trade should not become a barrier to flows of investment and services;

(3) national legislation must include general principles prohibiting abuse of dominant position, regulating vertical and horizontal practices that restrain competition, and controlling mergers and concentrations;

[29] See Meeting of the Americas, Third Business Forum of the Americas, Belo Horizonte, Brazil, May 1997, Workshop 5: Competition Policy, available at http://www.sice.oas.org/ftaa/belo/forum/workshops/sucon5%5Fe.asp.

[30] See *id.*

(4) national legislation should contain precise rules as to when and which acts constitute abuse of dominant position or an anti-competitive practice; and

(5) national authorities should develop clear and predictable rules on mergers, joint ventures, strategic alliances, and vertical arrangements so that, when enforced, these rules do not act as a barrier to trade and investment and do not hinder the economic growth of individual countries.[31]

With regard to the interface of competition law and the antidumping duty law, Chile advocated the elimination of the antidumping duty law once a free trade area is created, to be replaced by competition law.

2.147 Whereas the Costa Rica meeting of the competition policy working group focused on the framework of competition law at the national level, at the fifth FTAA trade ministers meeting held in Toronto in November 1999, the participants in the competition policy workshop took a more hemispheric approach, including a recommendation that the private sector be actively engaged in the negotiation process. The working group made the following specific recommendations:

- The private business sector should be actively involved in and informed of any development in the FTAA process. As competition policy affects the core of business practice, governments must carefully consider the recommendations of the private sector. Mechanisms should be developed to ensure the success and effectiveness of this consultative process. As a suggestion, the Americas Business Forum should be scheduled sufficiently in advance of the Ministerial meeting so that the recommendations of the private sector are thoroughly considered and discussed by negotiating governments. Further, experts from the private sector should assist government officials during the negotiation process.
- FTAA member-countries should be guided by policies that would restrain all forms of anti-competitive behaviour. Co-operation among FTAA member-countries would be facilitated by an effective and constant exchange of information. The FTAA negotiation process should identify competition principles common to all FTAA-member countries. A priority should be the prohibition of agreements related to price fixing, market division, bid rigging and output restriction. All other practices, such as predatory pricing, price discrimination, or resale price maintenance should be deemed illegal only if a structural analysis of the market suggests that, in the particular case investigated, the anti-competitive effect outweighs the

[31] See Fourth Business Forum of the Americas, San Jose, Costa Rica, March 1998, Workshop 9: Competition Policy, Subsidies, Anti-dumping, Countervailing Duties and Safeguards, available at http://www.sice.oas.org/ftaa/costa/forum/workshops/conclus/wks9%5Fe.asp.

positive competitive benefits. Further, mechanisms should be created that clearly spell out the rules for mergers and acquisitions.

- A hemispheric agreement should consider issues related to the interaction between trade and competition policy. Further, it should promote mechanisms for handling anti-competitive practices with cross-border effects within the hemisphere. The hemispheric agreement should establish basic principles for fair competition in order to facilitate the negotiation process and enhance investors' security and certainty with respect to conducting business in the hemisphere. This agreement should take into consideration the various levels of development of the different economies.
- All FTAA countries should enact national legislation before 2005 promoting competition and the enhancement of market access for all businesses. Such legislation should be transparent and non-discriminatory. Further, existing national legislation should be harmonised.
- FTAA countries should establish a legal and institutional framework at the national, sub-regional, or regional levels to deal with anti-competitive trade practices with cross-border effects. Co-operation among FTAA countries would be facilitated by an effective exchange of information regarding the application and enforcement of competition.[32]

2.148 On October 9, 1998, the competition authorities of 11 Western Hemisphere countries: Argentina, Brazil, Canada, Colombia, Costa Rica, Jamaica, Mexico, Panama, Peru, the United States and Venezuela adopted a policy statement expressing strong disapproval of cartel behaviour and a commitment to co-operate in international enforcement against such behaviour.[33] The delegates agreed to advance these principles in the FTAA Negotiating Group on Competition Policy.

E. CARICOM

2.149 In 2000, the Caribbean Community (CARICOM), a common market of English-speaking Caribbean nations formed in 1973, established one of the newest regional competition policy regimes.[34] Protocol VIII to the Treaty of Chaguaramas Establishing the Caribbean Community sets forth regional rules on competition policy, consumer protection, dumping and subsidies.[35] The basic goal of the CARICOM competition policy regime is to

[32] See Recommendations and Conclusions from the Competition Policy Workshop, Fifth Western Hemisphere Trade Ministerial and Business Forum, Toronto, Canada, Nov. 1999, available at http://www.sice.oas.org/ftaa/toronto/forum/wksrec/rcomp%5Fe.asp.

[33] See Communique issued at Panama City, Panama, Oct. 9, 1998 available at http://www.ftc.gov/opa/1998/9810/communique.htm.

[34] The 13 members of CARICOM are Antigua and Barbuda, Barbados, Belize, Dominica, Grenada, Guyana, Jamaica, Montserrat, St. Kitts and Nevis, Saint Lucia, St. Vincent and the Grenadines, Suriname, and Trinidad and Tobago. Information on CARICOM is available at http://www.caricom.org.

[35] See Treaty Establishing the Caribbean Community, signed at Chaguaramas July 4, 1973 amended by Protocol VIII: Competition Policy, Consumer Protection, Dumping and Subsidies (2000), available at http://www.caricom.org/protocolviii.htm (hereinafter Protocol VIII).

ensure that private anti-competitive conduct does not subvert the establishment of the CARICOM Single Market and Economy.[36] The competition regime covers horizontal restraints (*e.g.* price fixing, restrictions on output, market division, bid rigging), exclusionary vertical restraints, and abuse of dominance (*e.g.* predatory pricing and price discrimination).[37] The Protocol does not cover merger activity. CARICOM members are required to enact harmonised competition laws and to establish national competition authorities.[38] The Protocol calls for the creation of a CARICOM Competition Commission, whose responsibilities include investigating alleged RBPs and applying competition rules to cross-border RBPs following a complaint from a CARICOM member.[39] If a CARICOM member and the Commission disagree over questions of jurisdiction, the matter may be referred to the CARICOM Council for Trade and Development for its decision. Adverse decisions of the Commission may be appealed to the Caribbean Court of Justice.[40]

2.150 As a group of poor, developing countries, the challenges faced by CARICOM members in implementing Protocol VIII are formidable. They include developing skilled human resources; finding the financial resources to administer and implement competition legislation; promoting a culture of competition so that firms and consumers are aware of competition law and its impact on their interests; and training lawyers and economists to staff national competition authorities and the CARICOM Competition Commission.[41]

V. PLURILATERAL APPROACHES

A. The Work of the OECD

1. *Introduction*

2.151 The leading institution for the promotion of multilateral co-operation in competition law and policy has been the Organisation for Economic Co-operation and Development (OECD). The OECD groups 29 member countries[42] in an organisation that provides governments a setting in which to discuss, develop and perfect economic and social policy. Founded in 1960 as the successor organisation to the Organisation for European Economic Co-operation, the OECD was created to encourage the expansion of world trade and to promote the development of economic expansion in

[36] See Protocol VIII, Art. 30(a).
[37] See *id.* Arts. 30(i), 30(k).
[38] See *id.* Art. 30(b).
[39] See *id.* Arts. 30(c), 30(e), 30(g).
[40] See *id.* Art. 30(g) (11)–(12).
[41] See WTO, "Working Group on the Interaction between Trade and Competition Policy, Communication from Trinidad and Tobago", *Developing and Implementing a Competition Regime: Challenges Faced by Small Open Economies*, WT/WGTCP/W/143, at 2 (Aug. 2, 2000).
[42] The OECD member countries, while economically diverse, are market economies and pluralist democracies which respect for human rights. The 20 charter members of the OECD are located in Western Europe and North America. Next to join were Japan, Australia, New Zealand and Finland. Most recently, Mexico, the Czech Republic, Hungary, Poland and Korea have joined.

developing countries. It works to co-ordinate domestic and international policies in order to develop a web of even practice across nations. OECD members' exchanges may lead to agreements to act in a formal way (*e.g.* the OECD Anti-Bribery Convention and the aborted Multilateral Agreement on Investment). More typically, their discussions lead to non-binding recommendations. Exchanges between OECD governments flow from information and analysis provided by a Secretariat in Paris. Parts of the OECD Secretariat collect data, monitor trends, analyse and forecast economic developments, while others research social changes or evolving patterns in trade, environment, agriculture, technology, taxation and more. This work, in areas that mirror the policy-making structures in ministries of governments, is done in close consultation with policymakers who regularly make use of the analyses. The Organisation facilitates discussion among member countries when they meet in specialised committees of the OECD.

2. *Studies and Recommendations on Trade and Competition Policy*

2.152 The OECD has been a principal forum for extended discussion and study of the relationship between trade and competition policy. In 1961, the OECD Competition Law and Policy Committee was formed to collect and distribute information relating to national legislation on restrictive business practices, and to study and promote harmonisation of national laws and co-ordination of national enforcement actions. The OECD Committee on Trade has also looked at the issue of the interaction between trade and competition policies. In the 1990s, the two Committees carried out joint work as the Joint Group on Trade and Competition. The Joint Group's activities are based on three premises:

(1) that private RBPs can restrain market access,
(2) that trade measures can restrain competition, and
(3) that government regulation can restrain both market access and competition.

The Joint Group's work programme includes studies of issues relevant to the interface of trade and competition policy.

2.153 The OECD has not only published outstanding studies and reports in the area of competition policy, but it also has been instrumental in promoting co-operation among national authorities in competition law enforcement. Among the OECD's most important work are the non-binding recommendations and guidelines it has developed in the field of competition law and policy. It has issued Guidelines for Multinational Enterprises in 1976 (revised in 1997 and again in 2000), a non-binding, consensus document instructing multinational firms that engage in foreign direct investment to refrain from certain restrictive business practices in host countries. The OECD has also drafted two other instruments of note:

(1) the 1995 Revised Recommendation Concerning Co-operation between Member Countries on Anti-competitive Practices Affecting International Trade, and

(2) the 1998 recommendation concerning effective action against hard-core cartels.

3. *Guidelines for MNEs on Competition Law and Policy*

2.154 The OECD first developed its Guidelines for Multinational Enterprises in 1976 as a voluntary code of conduct for multinational corporations with facilities in developing nations. The Guidelines were republished 1997 in a substantially unchanged form.[43] The competition Chapter of the 1997 revised OECD Guidelines provided:

> Enterprises should, while conforming to official competition rules and established policies of the countries in which they operate:
>
> (1) Refrain from actions which would adversely affect competition in the relevant market by abusing a dominant position of market power, by means of, for example:
>
> a) Anti-competitive acquisitions;
> b) Predatory behaviour toward competitors;
> c) Unreasonable refusal to deal;
> d) Anti-competitive abuse of industrial property rights;
> e) Discriminatory (*i.e.* unreasonably differentiated) pricing and using such pricing transactions between affiliated enterprises as a means of affecting adversely competition outside these enterprises;
>
> (2) Allow purchasers, distributors and licensees freedom to resell, export, purchase and develop their operations consistent with law, trade conditions, the need for specialisation and sound commercial practice;
>
> (3) Refrain from participating in or otherwise purposely strengthening the restrictive effects of international or domestic cartels or restrictive agreements which adversely affect or eliminate competition and which are not generally or specifically accepted under applicable national or international legislation;
>
> (4) Be ready to consult and co-operate, including the provision of information, with competent authorities of countries whose interests

[43] See OECD Guidelines for Multinational Enterprises, OCDE/GD(97)40 (1997), available at http://www.oecd.org/daf/investment/guidelines/freeonline.htm . The Guidelines establish standards in fairly general terms, covering information disclosure, competitive practices, tax compliance, employment and industrial relations policies, environmental protection, and technology transfer. For additional analyses of the 1976 OECD Guidelines, see *The OECD Guidelines for Multinational Enterprises: A Business Appraisal* (Philip Coolidge, George C. Spina & Don Wallace, Jr., eds., 1977); Henri Schwamm, "The OECD Guidelines for Multinational Enterprises", (1978) 12 J. World Trade L. 342; Barry E. Hawk, "The OECD Guidelines for Multinational Enterprises: Competition", (1977) 46 Fordham L. Rev. 241 (discussing how OECD Guidelines affect concerns about restrictive business practices internationally); Joel Davidow, "Some Reflections on the OECD Competition Guidelines", (1977) 22 Antitrust Bull. 441.

> are directly affected in regard to competition issues or investigations provisions of information should be in accordance with safeguards normally applicable in this field.

2.155 The Guidelines in short identify three categories of horizontal and vertical restraints that MNEs are to avoid in their operations. First, the Guidelines admonish MNEs to refrain from abusing their dominant position in a market by, for example, engaging in the following activities:

(1) anti-competitive acquisitions,

(2) predatory behaviour toward competitors,

(3) unreasonable refusals to deal,

(4) anti-competitive abuse of industrial property rights, or

(5) discriminatory (*i.e.* unreasonably differentiated) pricing and using such discriminatory pricing between affiliated enterprises as a means of adversely affecting competition outside these enterprises.

Secondly, the Guidelines direct MNEs not to restrict their buyers, distributors, and licensees in the resale, export, and purchase of goods, and to allow them to develop their operations consistent with law, trade conditions, the need for specialisation, and sound commercial practice.

2.156 Third, MNEs are to refrain from participating in, or otherwise purposely strengthening, the restrictive effects of international or domestic cartels or restrictive agreements that adversely affect or eliminate competition and that are not generally or specifically accepted under applicable national or international legislation.

The 1997 Revised OECD Guidelines on competition instruct MNEs to be ready to consult, co-operate, and provide information to competent authorities of countries whose interests are directly affected in regard to competition issues or investigations.

The competition guidelines make specific reference to conflicting requirements that might be imposed on multinational enterprises as a result of different jurisdictional approaches by OECD member countries. Paragraph 11 of the Introduction to the Guidelines provides that when

> [m]ultinational enterprises are made subject to conflicting requirements by Member countries, the Governments concerned will co-operate in good faith with a view to resolving such problems either within the Committee on International Investment and Multinational Enterprises established by the OECD Council on 21st January, 1975 or through other mutually acceptable arrangements.

2.157 The OECD has noted the significant amount of co-operation between countries in cases of conflicting jurisdiction. Even in cases where blocking legislation might make such co-operation problematic, the OECD has observed that most such legislation gives responsible authorities discretion to release requested information where significant national interests would not be jeopardised.[44] The OECD has also concluded that:

> [o]ne of the principal virtues of . . . bilateral agreements appears to be that through notification and consultation they allow countries to discuss problems in their incipiency before conflicts and costs escalate.[45]

In June 2000, the OECD revised its Guidelines for MNEs and made significant changes to the Chapter on competition. The revisions reflect two developments in international competition law and policy:

(1) greater convergence as to what constitutes prohibited RBPs, and

(2) the conclusion of bilateral co-operation agreements.

The 2000 revised Guidelines provide:
Enterprises should, within the framework of applicable laws and regulations, conduct their activities in a competitive manner. In particular, enterprises should:

(1) Refrain from entering into or carrying out anti-competitive agreements among competitors:

  (a) to fix prices;
  (b) to make rigged bids (collusive tenders);
  (c) to establish output restrictions or quotas; or
  (d) to share or divide markets by allocating customers, suppliers, territories or lines of commerce.

(2) Conduct all of their activities in a manner consistent with all applicable competition laws, taking into account the applicability of the competition laws of jurisdictions whose economies would be likely to be harmed by anti-competitive activity on their part.

(3) Co-operate with the competition authorities of such jurisdictions by, among other things and subject to applicable law and appropriate safeguards, providing as prompt and complete responses as practicable to requests for information.

(4) Promote employee awareness of the importance of compliance with all applicable competition laws and policies.[46]

2.158 The Commentaries to the 2000 revisions note that the goal of competition policy is to contribute to overall social welfare and economic growth by creating and maintaining market conditions in which the nature,

[44] See "Trade and Competition Policies", see para. 2.061, n. 46, at 113.
[45] *id.*
[46] OECD "Guidelines for Multinational Enterprises" (2000), available at http://www.oecd.org/investment/guidelines/mnetext.htm.

quality, and price of goods and services are determined by market forces, "except to the extent a jurisdiction considers necessary to achieve other goals."[47] The Commentaries add that the Guidelines are intended to emphasise the importance of competition laws and policies to the efficient operation of both domestic and international markets. The Guidelines should reaffirm the importance of compliance with those laws and policies by domestic and multinational enterprises and ensure that all enterprises are aware of developments concerning the number, scope, and severity of competition laws, and the extent of co-operation among competition authorities.

Regarding the convergence of national competition laws, in general the Commentaries state that national competition laws and policies prohibit the following:

(1) hard core cartels;

(2) other agreements that are deemed to be anti-competitive;

(3) conduct that exploits or extends market dominance or market power; and

(4) anti-competitive mergers and acquisitions.

The anti-competitive agreements and conduct referred to in (2) and (3) are more general because the effects of these kinds of agreements and of unilateral conduct are more ambiguous, and there is less consensus on what should be considered anti-competitive.

2.159 Moreover, the Commentaries note, the growth of cross-border trade and investment makes it more likely that anti-competitive conduct taking place in one jurisdiction will have harmful effects in other jurisdictions. As a result, anti-competitive unilateral or concerted conduct that is or may be legal where it occurs is increasingly likely to be illegal in another jurisdiction. Enterprises are admonished to take into account both the law of the country in which they are operating and the laws of all countries in which the effects of their conduct are likely to be felt.[48]

Finally, the revised Guidelines advise enterprises that they should understand that competition authorities are engaging in more and deeper co-operation in investigating and challenging anti-competitive activity.[49] Accordingly, the Guidelines conclude that when the competition authorities of various jurisdictions are reviewing the same conduct, enterprises' facilitation of co-operation among national enforcement authorities promotes consistent and sound decision-making while also permitting cost savings for governments and enterprises.

[47] Commentary on the OECD "Guidelines for Multinational Enterprises: Review 2000", at 57 (June 27, 2000) available at http://www.oecd.org/daf/investment/guidelines/mnecome.pdf.

[48] See *id.* 58.

[49] See *id.* 59. See generally OECD, "Revised Recommendation of the Council Concerning Co-operation between Member Countries on Anticompetitive Practices Affecting International Trade", C(95)130/Final (1995); OECD, "Making International Markets More Efficient Through "Positive Comity" in Competition Law Enforcement", Report of the OECD Committee on Competition Law and Policy, DAFFE/CLP(99) (1999).

4. *Co-operation on Competition Law Enforcement*

2.160 The OECD Recommendation on Co-operation on Anti-Competitive Practices has contributed importantly to enforcement co-operation and conflict management among OECD-member countries.[50] This Recommendation dates back to 1967, and was revised and strengthened in 1995 to emphasise how important co-ordination and information sharing among antitrust authorities is to effective competition law enforcement.

2.161 The 1995 revised Recommendation recognises that antitrust investigations by one country may affect important interests of other OECD-member countries. In recognition of the potential for cross-border conflict, the 1995 OECD recommendation encourages closer co-operation between member countries in the form of notification, exchange of information, co-ordination of action, and consultation and conciliation on a fully voluntary basis,

> it being understood that such co-operation should not, in any way, be construed to affect the legal positions of Member countries with regard to questions of sovereignty, and in particular, the extra-territorial application of laws concerning anticompetitive practices, as may arise.[51]

The preamble to the 1995 recommendations also recognises:

> the need for Member countries to give effect to the principles of international law and comity and to use moderation and self-restraint in the interest of co-operation on the field of anticompetitive practices.

2.162 The OECD Recommendation encourages:

(1) notification, exchange of information, and co-ordination of action when a member country undertakes an antitrust investigation that may affect important interests of another member country, and

(2) consultation between member countries when a member country believes that another member's antitrust investigation may affect its important interests.

An appendix to the Recommendation lists "Guiding Principles" for notifications, exchange of information, co-operation in investigations and proceedings and consultations and conciliation of anti-competitive practices affecting

[50] "Revised Recommendation of the Council Concerning Co-operation Between Member Countries on Anti-Competitive Practices Affecting International Trade, C(95)130/Final (1995), reprinted in (1996) 35 Int'l Legal Materials 1313, 1314.
In 1986 the OECD Council for Consultation and Conciliation of Competition with Trade Policies issued a Recommendation urging members "(1) not to misuse unfair trade laws as a way of lessening competition, (2) to take into account the impact of export and import restraints on competition, (3) to make trade restraints and the provisions of subsidies transparent, and (4) to allow members to communicate concerns about alleged breaches of the Recommendation to other members. See OECD, Recommendation of the Council for Co-Operation between Member Countries in Areas of Potential Conflict between Competition and Trade Policies, C(86)65(Final) (adopted by the Council, Oct. 23, 1986)".

[51] *id.* Preamble.

international trade. These guiding principles provide greater clarity on the procedures to be observed by OECD members when utilising the Recommendation. With regard to confidentiality of information, however, paragraph 10 of the Guiding Principles provides that exchange of information is subject to the laws of participating member countries governing the confidentiality of information. Paragraph 10 further provides that a member country may specify the protection to be accorded the information provided and the limitations that may apply to the use of such information.[52]

2.163 It has been observed that to the extent that "soft law" co-operation agreements, such as the 1995 OECD Recommendation, are subject to the domestic confidentiality laws of the signatory parties and do not provide a mechanism for one party to obtain information located in the latter's jurisdiction, they fail to provide the tools necessary to permit enforcement authorities to effectively pursue a broad range of international anti-competitive, trade distorting conduct.[53] In the opinion of Professor Spencer Weber Waller:

> The Recommendation remains a modest affair. . . . If this is law, it is of the softest variety. Nonetheless, over time, the OECD recommendations have established a framework that has been reasonably successful and have set the stage for more binding commitments on a bilateral basis.[54]

Since the OECD's membership consists of nations with the most fully developed competition laws and extensive enforcement experience, it would naturally fall to the OECD to play the lead role in promoting international co-operation on antitrust enforcement issues.[55]

---

[52] In 1997, U.S. antitrust enforcement agencies made over 70 notifications to other countries' competition agencies pursuant to the OECD recommendation. See Michael Wise, "Review of United States Competition Law and Policy", (1999) 1 OECD J. Competition L. & Pol'y 7, 14.

[53] See Paul Crampton & Milos Barutciski, "Trade Distorting Private Restraints: A Practical Guide for Future Action," (1999) 6 Sw. J.L. & Trade Am. 3, 40. Crampton and Barutciski add that "soft law" agreements are a step in the direction of mitigating cross-border tensions that arise from international antitrust enforcement: "[T]hese types of agreements play a useful role in creating a framework for international co-operation. The agreements can provide countries with an opportunity to gain a level of comfort and familiarity with the fundamentals of international co-operation and establish important contacts with sister agencies in other jurisdictions. This first step is necessary, particularly for those nations that have relatively new competition laws and enforcement agencies. Once those agencies gain sufficient experience with sophisticated enforcement techniques and safeguards at the domestic level, along with "soft" international co-operation, they will be in a better position to begin engaging in the more extensive co-operation contemplated by agreements such as the Canada-U.S. MLAT. More importantly, a country can use this initial period to establish credibility with the international business and enforcement community and cultivate a level of comfort regarding their procedures for maintaining the confidentiality of information received from private parties. At the same time, they can build support among domestic business, legal and political communities to enter into bilateral co-operation agreements with other nations. To further increase the prospects for the adoption of some form of "hard" agreement in the mid to longer term, such nations may also wish to consider entering into "positive comity" arrangements, such as the 1998 Agreement between the Government of the United States and the European Communities on the Application of Positive Comity Principles in the Enforcement of their Competition Laws. Id. at 40–41.

[54] See Waller I, see para. 2.02, n. 55, at 362.

[55] See James F. Rill, "A Framework for Cooperation: The Status of International Antitrust", (1997) 18 Whittier L. Rev. 321, 328.

5. *Recommendation on Action Against Hard-Core Cartels*

2.164 In February 1998 the OECD, building on its 1976 Guidelines and its 1995 Recommendation on Co-operation, adopted a non-binding recommendation against hard-core cartels.[56] The Recommendation seeks to foster co-operation among nations through the exchange of documents and information, and encouraging countries to "consider bilateral and multilateral agreements to facilitate cooperation and to review all obstacles to effective cooperation."

The Recommendation defines a "hard core" cartel as an anti-competitive agreement, anti-competitive concerted practice, or anti-competitive arrangement by competitors to fix prices, rig bids (collusive tenders), establish output restrictions or quotas, or share or divide markets by allocating customers, suppliers, territories, or lines of commerce.[57] Hard-core cartels do not include agreements, concerted practices, or arrangements that:

(1) are reasonably related to lawful realisation of cost-reducing or output-enhancing efficiencies,

(2) are excluded directly or indirectly from the coverage of a member country's own laws, or

(3) are authorised in accordance with those laws.

However, all exclusions and authorisations of what would otherwise be hard-core cartels should be transparent and should be reviewed periodically to assess whether they are no broader than necessary to achieve their overriding policy objectives.[58]

2.165 The heart of the Recommendation is Section B, "International Co-operation and Comity in Enforcing Laws Prohibiting Hard Core Cartels".[59] It recognises that OECD members have a common interest in preventing hard-core cartels—assuming agreement on whether one exists can be reached—and encourages them to seek ways in which co-operation:

> might be improved by positive comity principles applicable to requests that another country remedy anticompetitive conduct that adversely affects both countries, and should conduct their own enforcement activities in accordance with principles of comity when they affect other countries' important interests.

---

[56] See OECD, Recommendation Concerning Effective Action Against "Hard Core" Cartels, OECD C(98)35/Final (March 30, 1998), available at http://www.oecd.org/daf/clp/Recommendations/Rec9com.htm.

[57] See *id.* Part I.A.2(b).

[58] See *id.* See also Mark A.A. Warner, "Restrictive Trade Practices and the Extraterritorial Application of U.S. Antitrust and Trader Legislation", (1999) 19 Nw. J. Int'l L. & Bus. 330.

[59] Part I.B.1 provides: "1. Member countries have a common interest in preventing hard core cartels and should co-operate with each other in enforcing their laws against such cartels. In this connection, they should seek ways in which co-operation might be improved by positive comity principles applicable to requests that another country remedy anticompetitive conduct that adversely affects both countries, and should conduct their own enforcement activities in accordance with principles of comity when they affect other countries' important interests".

Section B continues with exhortations on co-operation, consultation, comity, and information exchange.[60]

The Recommendation adds that in order to establish a framework for their co-operation in dealing with hard-core cartels, member countries are encouraged to consider entering into bilateral or multilateral agreements or other instruments consistent with these principles. As previously mentioned, under the influence of this OECD Recommendation a bilateral agreement on positive comity was entered into between the United States and the E.U. in 1998.

2.166 What the Recommendation giveth with the right hand (by incorporating the principle of positive comity, not recognised in the 1995 OECD Recommendation), it taketh away with the left (by allowing non co-operation in information sharing on the ground of confidentiality). In addition, the practical utility of the Recommendation in resolving import boycotts remains untested, given that the OECD Recommendation's definition of a hard-core cartel excludes boycotts. Similarly, while the members are urged to enact laws with "effective sanctions, of a kind and at a level adequate to deter firms and individuals from participating in such cartels,"[61] it is not clear that the OECD Recommendation will help resolve disputes over the appropriateness of criminal sanctions, especially those applied extraterritorially.[62]

Recognising the shortcomings of the Recommendation and in light of a report and a recommendation by the OECD Competition Law and Policy (CLP) Committee,[63] the OECD expanded its anti-cartel programme for an additional three years beginning in 2000.[64] Specifically, the CLP Committee has been charged with the task of assisting competition enforcement authorities to increase opportunities for information sharing. The CLP Committee is to address the extent of cartel overcharges, the impact of restrictions on

---

[60] Part I.B.2 provides: "2. Co-operation between or among Member countries in dealing with hard core cartels should take into account the following principles: a) the common interest in preventing hard core cartels generally warrants co-operation to the extent that such co-operation would be consistent with a requested country's laws, regulations, and important interests; b) to the extent consistent with their own laws, regulations, and important interests, and subject to effective safeguards to protect commercially sensitive and other confidential information, Member countries' mutual interest in preventing hard core cartels warrants co-operation that might include sharing documents and information in their possession with foreign competition authorities and gathering documents and information on behalf of foreign competition authorities on a voluntary basis and when necessary through use of compulsory process; c) a Member country may decline to comply with a request for assistance, or limit or condition its co-operation on the ground that it considers compliance with the request to be not in accordance with its laws or regulations or to be inconsistent with its important interests or on any other grounds, including its competition authority's resource constraints or the absence of a mutual interest in the investigation or proceeding in question; d) Member countries should agree to engage in consultations over issues relating to co-operation."

[61] *id.* Part I.A.1(a).

[62] See Warner, see para. 2.164, n. 58, at 358.

[63] See Report by the OECD Competition Law and Policy Committee, "New Initiatives, Old Problems: A Report on Implementing the Hard Core Cartel Recommendation and Improving Co-operation", in (2000) OECD, Hard Core Cartels 11–48.

[64] See OECD, Hard Core Cartels 6–7 (2000).

international co-operation in cartel cases, and optimal investigatory tools and sanctions in cartel cases. The Committee is to report its findings in 2003.[65]

6. *Notification of Transnational Mergers*

2.167 In February 1999, the CLP Committee issued a report on notification of transnational mergers.[66] The Report notes the increase in merger activity and that many mergers are likely to be subject to the merger control laws of more than one country. The Report adds that the merger control procedures of most countries provide for some form of notification to national antitrust enforcement authorities. While the form and quantity of information requested is never identical among countries, there does tend to be a common core of information that is reported. These inconsistencies, the Committee has concluded, interfere with efficient review of transnational mergers and impose significant transaction costs. Harmonisation of merger reporting requirements, therefore, could have at least two salutary benefits:

(1) transaction costs for the merging parties would be reduced by avoiding duplication in the presentation of the same information to the enforcement authorities of more than one country; and

(2) co-operation among enforcement authorities would be enhanced to the extent that are reviewing the same or similar information.

2.168 Nevertheless, the differences among national pre-merger reporting requirements are largely a reflection of the substantive differences in national competition laws. For example, the United States has relatively low thresholds triggering the obligation to report a proposed merger. The E.U., by comparison, has much higher thresholds, resulting in fewer notifications. In 1998, 3,700 mergers were notified in the United States, while in the E.U. the number was 200.[67] In the United States, a two-step process is utilised, while in the E.U. the process is one-step notification. Thus, complete harmonisation of reporting requirements is not possible, given the disharmony among national laws.

2.169 The Committee reviewed all OECD members' notification practices and synthesised the common elements of notification forms into a model notification form, "Framework for Notification and Report Form for Concentrations".[68] It specifies the information that many countries currently require and is accompanied by an explanatory text. Recognising the differences that exist among some countries' forms, alternative provisions are provided where appropriate. The Framework consists of six parts that request the following information:

---

[65] See *id.* at 7–8.

[66] See OECD "Committee on Competition Law & Policy, Report on Notification of Transnational Mergers", DAFFE/CLP(99)2/Final (Feb. 24, 1999) available at http://www.oecd.org/daf/clp/law_enforcement.htm.

[67] See *id.* para. 6.

[68] See *id.* Appendix.

(1) the identity of the parties to the transaction,

(2) a description of the transaction that is the subject of the notification,

(3) a description of the operations of the parties in the notified country,

(4) a description of the markets in which the transaction could have horizontal or vertical effects,

(5) a request for the documentation constituting the transaction and the parties' annual reports, and

(6) a waiver of confidentiality of the information submitted for the purpose of facilitating the notification process with other interested national authorities.

It remains to be seen whether the Committee's work will be bear fruit in the form of increased co-operation among national antitrust enforcement authorities in the field of merger notification.

7. *Technical Assistance to Developing Countries*

2.170 The OECD, in collaboration with the World Bank, prepared a publication entitled "A Framework for the Design and Implementation of Competition Policy".[69] It provides a comprehensive overview of issues concerning the application of competition policy in developing countries and in countries whose economies are in transition. It suggests best practices for developing countries to follow when designing and implementing a competition policy.

8. *Summary*

2.171 Through 1998, the OECD has conducted and participated in over 90 programmes on competition policy for both member and non-member countries. However, the OECD work programme does not go beyond issuing non-binding guidelines and recommendations. This self-imposed limitation, some argue, suggests that the WTO is the forum best-suited for negotiating a multilateral agreement on competition policy, given the WTO's extensive experience with multilateral negotiations that include developed and developing countries, as well as its binding dispute settlement mechanism.[70]

B. APEC

1. *Introduction*

2.172 At its founding in 1989 in Canberra, Australia, the Asia-Pacific Economic Co-operation forum (APEC) held a ministerial meeting as a small

[69] See OECD & World Bank, *A Framework for the Design and Implementation of Competition Policy* (1999).

[70] See WTO, "Working Group on the Interaction between Trade and Competition Policy, Report (1999) of the Working Group on the Interaction between Trade and Competition Policy to the General Council", WT/WGTCP/3, at 16, para. 51 (Oct. 11, 1999)

(12-member),[71] loosely organised forum for consultation and co-operation on a range of economic issues.[72] Since then, APEC has grown to a membership of 21 countries[73]: Australia, Brunei, Canada, Chile, China, Taiwan, Hong Kong, Indonesia, Japan, Malaysia, Mexico, New Zealand, Papua New Guinea, Peru, the Philippines, Russia, Singapore, South Korea, Thailand, the United States and Vietnam—and has adopted an ambitious action agenda. Interestingly, APEC is the only supranational forum in which China and Taiwan are both members.

APEC is unique among regional trade arrangements. Even though it has established working groups, ad hoc groups, committees, a secretariat and action plans, APEC remains nominally an informal organisation. It has no written treaty or other organic document creating institutions, rules of procedure, or mechanisms for dispute settlement. Rather, APEC members reach agreement by consensus, with decisions implemented directly or through the working groups.[74] An organisation built on decision making by consensus effectively gives each member a veto, thereby making aggressive action by APEC a remote possibility. APEC, as an organisation, can take no action that is not supported by all its members. It chief value, therefore, is as a forum for consultation.

2.173 A small but important step in APEC's evolution was the establishment of a permanent APEC Secretariat in 1992, headquartered in Singapore. The creation of an APEC Secretariat was widely perceived as marking APEC's transition from an experiment in international economic relations to an organisation. Despite its permanent Secretariat, APEC remains institutionally decentralised, with no central decision-making body. APEC is not a negotiating body or a free trade bloc. It does not impose any legal obligations on its

---

[71] Japan played a significant role in originating the concept but Australia took the lead in calling together 12 nations of the Asia-Pacific region to found the organisation.

[72] For background and additional reading on APEC, see Norman D. Palmer, *The New Regionalism in Asia and the Pacific* (1991); Diane L. Manifold, "APEC: Organization, Goals and Approach" (USITC Working Paper Mar. 7, 1997); Merit E. Janow, "Assessing APEC's Role in Economic Integration in the Asia-Pacific Region", (1996–97) 17 Nw. J. Int'l L. & Bus. 947; C. Fred Bergsten, "APEC and World Trade: A Force for Worldwide Liberalization", (May/June 1994) Foreign Affairs 20. Additional information on APEC and texts of APEC documents are available from the APEC's website at http://www.apecsec.org.sg, and from the U.S. Information Agency's website at http://usinfo.state.gov/regional/ea/apec.

[73] The 12 original members were Brunei, Indonesia, Japan, Malaysia, the Philippines, Singapore, South Korea, Thailand, Australia, Canada, New Zealand and the United States. See "APEC Meeting in Singapore Said to Establish Group as Major Forum for Region's Interests", (1990) 7 Int'l Trade Rep. (BNA) 1245. The 3 Chinas—the People's Republic of China, Hong Kong and Taiwan (referred to within APEC as Chinese Taipei)—were admitted in 1991. See Fact-Sheet: Asia-Pacific Economic Cooperation (APEC), 4 Dep't St. Dispatch 555 (1993). Papua New Guinea was admitted in 1993. See Janow, "Assessing APEC's Role", see para. 2.009, n. 19; "Asia-Pacific Leaders Make Commitments to Freer Trade, GATT, Another Meeting", 10 Int'l Trade Rep. (BNA) 1978 (1993); David K. Linnan, "APEC: Quo Vadis?", 89 Am. J. Int'l L. 824 (1995). Mexico became a member of APEC in 1993, during the summit meeting of Asia-Pacific heads of government held in Seattle, Washington. Chile was admitted to membership at the November 1994 summit meeting in Jakarta, Indonesia. Russia, Peru and Vietnam joined in 1998. Countries that have applied for membership include Colombia, India, Mongolia, Pakistan, Panama and Sri Lanka.

[74] For an analysis of APEC's evolving institutional structure, see Yoshi Kodama, "Asia-Pacific Region: APEC and ASEAN", (1996) 30 Int'l Law. 367, 379–82.

members. All timetables are voluntary, not mandatory.[75] Nevertheless, action plans adopted by APEC at its annual ministerial meetings contain concrete and substantive blueprints for closer economic integration.

The 21-member APEC today carries out its substantive work through 10 sectoral working groups and an ad hoc group dealing with wider regional trade liberalisation and economic policies. The 10 working groups are assigned the tasks of gathering trade and investment data, developing proposals and conducting studies on trade promotion, investment and technology transfer, human resource development, regional energy co-operation, marine resource co-operation, telecommunications, transportation, tourism and fisheries.[76]

2.174 A milestone in APEC's development was reached in 1994 when APEC leaders agreed in Indonesia to achieve free and open trade and investment in the Asia-Pacific region no later than 2010 for industrialised economies and 2020 for developing economies.[77] The agreement was reinforced by APEC's 1995 action plan adopted in Osaka for achieving these trade liberalisation goals.[78] Included in the Osaka Action Agenda are three objectives for competition policy:

(1) enhancing the competitive environment in the Asia-Pacific region by introducing or maintaining effective and adequate competition law and policies,

(2) ensuring the transparency of competition laws and policies, and

(3) promoting competition among APEC economies.[79]

In addition at their 1996 meeting in New Zealand, the APEC trade ministers issued a statement expressing their determination to make definitive progress in negotiations on financial services, basic telecommunication services and maritime transport services.[80] APEC members also submitted individual

---

[75] See Harold Dichter, "Legal Implications of an Asia-Pacific Grouping", (1995) 16 U. Pa. J. Int'l Bus. L. 99.

[76] "East Asia Regional Economic Integration", see para. 2.172, n. 72, at 55.

[77] For a more detailed discussion of APEC, see Kenneth W. Abbott & Gregory W. Bowman, "Economic Integration for the Asian Century: An Early Look at New Approaches", (1994) 4 Transnat'l L. & Contemp. Prob. 187, 208–25; Norman D. Palmer, *The New Regionalism in Asia and the Pacific* 2–5 (1991); Peter Drysdale & Ross Garnaut, "The Pacific: An Application of a General Theory of Economic Integration", in *Pacific Dynamism and the International Economic System* 183, 186 (C. Fred Bergsten & Marcus Noland eds., 1993); "Declaration on an APEC Trade and Investment Framework", 4 Dep't St. Dispatch 832 (1993) (joint statement of APEC leaders at Seattle summit, proclaiming determination to work through APEC toward the further development of open regionalism and market-driven economic interdependence in the Asia Pacific region) (hereinafter "Declaration on APEC"). See also APEC, "Achieving the APEC Vision: Free and Open Trade in the Asia Pacific" 2–3, 29–35 (1994) (Second Report of APEC Eminent Persons Group).

[78] See generally "Pacific Business Forum, The Osaka Action Plan: Roadmap to Realising the APEC Vision" (1995).

[79] See WTO, "Working Group on the Interaction between Trade and Competition Policy, Communication from APEC", WT/WGTCP/W/18 (July 4, 1997).

[80] See "APEC Trade Ministers Seek Progress in Services, Telecom, and Maritime Talks", (1996)13 Int'l Trade Rep. (BNA) 1172.

actions plans in 1996 laying out the steps they propose to take to achieve greater liberalisation in 15 trade and investment areas and in 13 areas of economic and technical co-operation.[81] The measures announced in the APEC members' individual action plans are analogous to offers made in more formal trade negotiations. However, they are non-binding and voluntary in nature and only loosely connected insofar as the timing of their implementation. [82] These features of the individual action plans reflect Japan's desire to keep APEC an organisation that builds harmony and fosters policy co-ordination.

2. *Competition Policy*

2.175 APEC has three permanent Committees. In 1993, a Committee on Trade and Investment was created to assume the duties of the working group formerly assigned to that task. The work programme of the Committee includes reviewing the results of the Uruguay Round and its implications for the region, pursuing efforts to simplify and harmonise customs procedures in the region and examining the investment environment within APEC.[83] (The Ad Hoc Group on Economic Trends and Issues became the Economic Committee in 1994. In 1994, the APEC ministers also created a Budget and Administrative Committee.[84])

The globalisation of business has highlighted the importance of competition issues. APEC's objective in this work area is to enhance the competitive environment of the region. In November 1994, APEC Ministers agreed that the Committee on Trade and Investment (CTI) would develop an understanding on the competition laws and policies of economies in the region. They agreed that the CTI should learn how competition laws and policies affect flows of trade and investment in the APEC region and identify potential areas of technical co-operation among member economies. In 1996, the Osaka Action Agenda work programmes for competition policy and deregulation were combined, in view of the linkages between the two issues. The competition policy/deregulation work area has been a key component of work on the strengthening-of-markets theme.

[81] See "APEC Ministers Urge Transparency, Dynamism in Individual Action Plans", 13 (1996) Int'l Trade Rep. (BNA) 1173; "APEC Officials Make Progress on Action Plans to Liberalize Trade", (1996) 13 Int'l Trade Rep. (BNA) 1384–85.

[82] For a summary of the developments at the preceding seven APEC ministerial meetings, see Kodama, see para. 2.172, n. 74, at 371–77.

[83] Joint Statement of APEC Ministers, "Declaration on an APEC Trade and Investment Framework", Annex 1, Nov. 20, 1993. The APEC Non-Binding Investment Principles were adopted in 1994. They deal with transparency, non-discrimination among investor nations, national treatment, investment incentives, performance requirements, expropriation and compensation, repatriation and convertibility, dispute settlement, temporary entry of personnel, and avoidance of double taxation. See World Trade Organization, "Trade and Foreign Direct Investment: Report by the WTO Secretariat" 30–31 (1996); "United Nations Conference on Trade and Development, World Investment Report 1996: Investment, Trade and International Policy Arrangements" 140–42 (1996).

[84] In the evolution of APEC's institutions, a working group progresses to an *ad hoc* group, and an *ad hoc* group develops into a committee. See Kodama, see para. 2.172, n. 74, at 376.

2.176 Through 1999, five annual workshops have been held, covering issues such as: approaches and exemptions to competition policies and law, technical assistance, linkages between competition policy and trade policy, objectives and mechanisms of competition policy, the inter-relationship between competition policy and deregulation, regulation of national monopolies, occupational regulation and regulatory reform.[85]

At the APEC Competition Policy and Deregulation Workshop held in 1999, it was agreed to develop a set of APEC competition and regulatory principles. The "APEC Principles to Enhance Competition and Regulatory Reform" were endorsed by APEC ministers in September 1999.[86] Four non-binding, core principles were approved: non-discrimination, comprehensiveness, transparency and accountability. As far as implementing the core principles, the aim is to provide a basis for policy development rather than a rigorous set of specific rules. APEC members are to make efforts to address anti-competitive behaviour by implementing competition policy and to take practical steps to promote the consistent application of competition policies and rules.

2.177 The members of APEC agree that APEC is to be a catalyst for trade liberalisation, but not a substitute for any existing RTAs. APEC will not supersede or have any formal role in any of the other regional or sub-regional organisations within the Pacific Rim, such as the Pacific Economic Co-operation Council (PECC), ASEAN, or NAFTA. Instead, APEC will co-ordinate its activities with these other organisations. PECC, for example, already has established task forces that concentrate on specific areas of economic co-operation in the region and that participate in APEC's working groups.[87] APEC agreements, if any, will in all probability resemble OECD recommendations.[88]

C. Other Plurilateral Initiatives

1. *The Draft International Antitrust Code*

2.178 In 1991, a dozen experts in the field of international competition law formed a working group that met in Munich for the purpose of drafting an international antitrust code.[89] In 1993, the expert group released their proposed code as a plurilateral agreement to be adopted by and administered under the auspices of the WTO. The drafters followed five principles in preparing the Draft Code:

---

[85] An APEC competition policy and law database is available at http://www.apeccp.org.tw/index.html.

[86] For the text of this document, see WTO, Working Group on the Interaction between Trade and Competition Policy, Communication from New Zealand, WT/WGTCP/W/139 (Oct. 12, 1999).

[87] See Fact Sheet: APEC Working Groups, 4 Dep't St. Dispatch 837 (1993) (Tourism Working Group). See *U.S. Int'l Trade Comm'n, The Year in Trade 1993, Operation of the Trade Agreements Program* 67 (USITC Pub. 2769 1994). See also Donald Crone, "Does Hegemony Matter? The Reorganization of the Pacific Political Economy", (1993) 45 World Pol. 501, 523.

[88] See "APEC Trade Ministers Review Progress on Liberalization", Int'l Econ. Rev. 8, 10 (USITC Pub. 2986 Aug. 1996).

[89] See Wolfgang Fikentscher & Ulrich Immenga, *Draft International Antitrust Code* (1995); Wolfgang Fikentscher, "The Draft International Antitrust Code ('ADIAC') in the Context of International Technological Integration", (1996) 72 Chi.-Kent L. Rev. 533.

- Do not replace national law with a uniform international rule, but instead harmonise national laws.
- National laws should accord national treatment to foreign firms doing business in that country.
- Every national law should adopt a set of minimum standards using the 1980 UNCTAD Principles on Restrictive Business Practices as a guide.
- Standing under national law would be given to a WTO official (an "International Antitrust Authority") to plead international competition law cases before the responsible national competition law enforcement authorities under national law (referred to by the drafters as "the international procedural initiative").
- The Code would only apply to transborder antitrust cases.[90]

2.179 The Code is comprised of 21 articles, divided into seven parts.[91] Part One, "General Provisions and Basic Principles" covers acceptance of the Code by GATT (now WTO) members on a plurilateral basis, implementation in member countries on a non-discriminatory basis (national treatment) and scope of application (only transborder cases).

2.180 Part Two, "Horizontal and Vertical Restraints" divides horizontal restraints into two categories. In the first category are practices that are deemed unlawful *per se*. The *per se* offences are agreements, understandings and concerted practices between two or more competitors to fix prices, divide customers or territories (allocate markets), or assign quotas.[92] The *per se* offences are irrebutably presumed to restrict competition.[93] Other horizontal agreements are declared illegal if they unreasonably restrict competition and are presumed to do so.[94] Unreasonable horizontal restraints are defined as those whose purpose or effect is the lessening of competition.[95] The burden rests with the responding firm(s) to prove the reasonableness of a horizontal agreement by showing that its anti-competitive effects are outweighed by:

(1) the pro-competitive effects or efficiencies that are likely to increase rivalry or inventiveness, or

(2) the assistance it gives the firms to the agreement to produce a better or lower-cost good or service.[96]

[90] See F.M. Scherer, *Competition Policies for An Integrated World Economy* (1994) (hereinafter Scherer); Ernest-Ulrich Petersmann, "International Competition Rules for Governments and for Private Business: A 'Trade Law Approach' for Linking Trade and Competition Rules in the WTO", (1996) 72 Chi.-Kent L. Rev. 545, 573.

[91] See Draft International Antitrust Code of July 10, 1993 reprinted in 64 Antitrust & Trade Reg. Rep. (BNA) No. 1628 (Special Supp. Aug. 19, 1993) (hereinafter Draft Code). For a thorough critique of the Draft Code, see Daniel J. Gifford, "The Draft International Antitrust Code Proposed at Munich: Good Intentions Gone Awry", (1997) 6 Minn. J. Global Trade 1, 3.

[92] See Draft Code, *supra* n. 91, Art. 4, s. 1.

[93] See *id.*

[94] See *id.* Art. 4, s. 2.

[95] See *id.* Art. 4, s. 2.

[96] See *id.*

By placing the burden of showing reasonableness on the defendant firms, rather than on the plaintiff to show that the agreement is unreasonable, the Code does not follow the rule-of-reason jurisprudence that has developed under U.S. antitrust law.[97]

2.181 Article 5 of the Code deals with vertical restraints and places them into three groups. Restraints in the first group are irrebutably presumed to be unlawful, namely, distribution agreements that create or facilitate a producer or distributor cartel and distribution agreements fixing resale prices or price levels.[98] Restraints in the second group are presumed to be illegal, but the presumption of illegality may be rebutted under the rule of reason. As is the case with horizontal restraints, the defendant carries the burden of showing reasonableness. In this second group are vertical restraints preventing or restricting the free movement of goods or services across national borders, discriminating against goods and services of non-nationals, or distribution agreements prohibiting discounting or transshipping.[99]

2.182 All other vertical restraints fall into the third group and are presumed legal, but their reasonableness may be rebutted by the complaining party if it can be shown

(1) that they confer or increase market power; or

(2) that they deny the complaining party market access, and

(a) the restraint is not reasonably necessary to improve production or distribution, and

(b) a fair share of the benefits will not be passed on to consumers.[1]

Agreements in this third category include tying agreements, exclusive supply contracts, and exclusive purchasing agreements.

Article 6 deals with abuse of intellectual property rights (IPRs). Abuse of a dominant position in the acquisition or exercise of IPRs is prohibited, as are patent pools designed to suppress technology or raise prices. In connection with other IPRs, Article 6 provides:

> When the exploitation of an intellectual property right exceeds the limits of its legal content, any resulting restraint of competition may be illegal under the provisions of this Agreement.[2]

However, Article 6, section 2 defines exclusive, non-exclusive and territorially restricted licenses as forming part of the legal content of an intellectual

[97] See Wolfgang Fikentscher, "Collaborative Activities Among Industrial Competitors—In German, European, and U.S. Antitrust Law, and in the Draft International Antitrust Code in the GATT/WTO System", in *International Harmonization of Competition Laws* 109, 111, 123 (Chia-Jui Cheng, Lawrence S. Liu, & Chih-Kang Wang eds. 1995) (hereinafter International Harmonization).

[98] See Draft Code, Art. 5, ss. 1, 2.

[99] See *id.* Art. 5, s. 3(a).

[1] See *id.* Art. 5, s. 4.

[2] *id.* Art. 6, s. 1.

property right, thus apparently permitting IPR owners to impose vertical restraints on their licensees in the form of territorial and exclusivity restrictions.[3]

2.183 Article Seven provides that "[u]ndertakings may neither solicit nor inflict disadvantages upon other undertakings."As Professor Daniel Gifford notes:

> [A] prohibition against inflicting disadvantages upon other undertakings appears radically imprecise and . . . extremely dangerous. . . . Firms are constantly struggling to find more efficient production and distribution methods, develop superior products, and acquire superior technology. All of these efforts can be described as attempts to gain advantages over rivals.[4]

If this provision means that the Code protects competitors and not competition, then it goes against U.S. antitrust law and policy.

2.184 Part Three, "Control of Concentration and Restructuring" deals with mergers (although the Code opts for the term "concentrations"). Article 10 requires notification of mergers with an international dimension. Under the financial threshold test, a proposed merger has an "international dimension" if the aggregate, annual worldwide turnover of all the firms concerned is at least 0.1 per cent of the gross national product of the member affected by the merger, or no more than 90 per cent of the aggregate worldwide turnover of all the firms concerned is made outside the territory of the affected member.[5] If a proposed merger would increase the power of one or more of the firms concerned to impede effective competition in the relevant market, then national competition law authorities are to disapprove it. If more than one national authority is involved, then the matter is to be referred to the international antitrust authority established under the Code, subject to certain exceptions.

2.185 Part Four addresses abuse of a dominant position. Article 14 follows the language of Article 82 of the E.C. Treaty, but does not exhaustively list instances of such abuse. Part Five, "Remedies" requires members to adopt effective remedies. Article 15 establishes a private right of action to recover damages.[6] Minimum remedies are to include injunctive relief, fines, disgorgement of profits, damages, and publication of judgments. Members are free to provide additional remedies and penalties if they so desire, including imprisonment, multiple damages, punitive damages, and suspension or termination of business.[7]

---

[3] It has been suggested that the scope of Article 6, s. 2 be narrowed in this regard. See Yun-Peng Chu, "Towards the Establishment of an Order of Competition for the International Economy: With References to the Draft International Antitrust Code, The Parallel Imports Problem, and the Experience of Taiwan, ROC, in" *International Harmonization*, see para. 2.180, n. 97, at 453, 465.

[4] Gifford, see para. 2.179, n. 91, at 16.

[5] See Draft Code, Art. 9, s. 2(a).

[6] See *id.* Art. 15, s. 6.

[7] See *id.* Art. 15, s. 1.

2.186 Part Six, "Public Undertakings and State Authorisation" requires that state enterprises be treated the same as private firms under national competition law.
Part Seven covers institutional provisions. The most important of these creates the International Antitrust Authority (IAA) within the WTO. The investigation of individual cases and the administration of remedies remains the responsibility of national authorities. The IAA, however, is vested with five residual rights:

(1) the right to request national authorities to initiate an investigation,

(2) the right to bring actions for mandamus relief against national authorities in national courts whenever the former refuses to take appropriate measures against individual restraints of competition,

(3) the right to sue private persons in national courts for injunctive relief against RBPs,

(4) the right to appeal adverse judicial decisions, and

(5) the right to sue a WTO member before a WTO international authority panel whenever the IAA believes that a member has violated its obligations under the Code.[8]

Finally, Part Eight deals with the future development of the Draft Code. Two of the more important topics that the drafters chose not to tackle are predatory pricing and price discrimination, apparently appreciating the lack of consensus on these issues and not wishing to antagonise already sceptical national enforcement authorities further.
2.187 The drafters acknowledged the lack of political consensus for such an international code generally, but forged ahead in the belief that:

> an ambitious academic model agreement can assist in stimulating world-wide reflection and debate on the need for international competition rules.[9]

The minimum-standards approach of the Draft Code yields a document that represents a common denominator in international competition policy principles, but not necessarily the lowest common denominator. In addition, for countries desiring higher competition law standards, national laws could be drafted to reflect a two-tiered system, provided, of course, that the higher national standards were more pro-competitive than the minimum standards of the Code. Nevertheless, the Draft Code has been criticised for the vagueness and ambiguity of key provisions and for leaving it to a supranational authority to iron out the wrinkles of the Code.[10] Finally, there is always a risk that the

[8] See *id.* Art. 19.
[9] Petersmann, see para. 2.013, n. 28, at 572.
[10] See Gifford, para. 2.179, n. 91, at 4–5.

minimum standards of the Draft Code could ossify over time and become the maximum standards at both the national and international levels, one of the major reservations to a WTO competition policy agreement voiced by Assistant Attorney General Joel Klein and others.[11]

VI. MULTILATERAL APPROACHES

2.188 Although the subject has been closely examined and debated at the League of Nations since the end of World War I, efforts to reach a multilateral agreement on competition law and policy have not been successful.[12] So far a consensus has failed to build on adopting either uniform national competition legislation or an international convention on RBPs. Sigmund Timberg, the Secretary of the United Nations Ad Hoc Committee on Restrictive Business Practices, which was responsible for the 1953 UN Draft Convention on Restrictive Business Practices, was of the opinion in 1973 that "[t]he notion that national antitrust legislation and administration can be modified so as to achieve uniform national standards is quite unrealistic."[13] This view was echoed in 1999 by the OECD's Joint Group on Trade and Competition which agreed that "the idea of a uniform competition law has never been considered realistic or relevant".[14] Instead unilateral, bilateral, and regional approaches have carried the day.[15] Nevertheless, international organisations, including UNCTAD and the OECD, have made valuable contributions to the international competition policy debate.

A. The 1953 UN Draft Convention on Restrictive Business Practices

2.189 Following unsuccessful attempts to reintroduce the stillborn Havana Charter's competition policy principles by making them a part of GATT,[16] the ball was passed to the United Nations to try its hand at drafting a convention on RBPs affecting international trade. In 1953, the United Nations Ad Hoc Committee on Restrictive Business Practices reported to the UN Economic and Social Council a draft convention on the prevention and control of restrictive business practices in international trade (the UN Draft

[11] See also Joanna Shelton, "Competition Policy: What Chance for International Rules?" (1999) 2 OECD J. Competition L. & Pol'y 57, 62.
[12] See Dale B. Furnish, "A Transnational Approach to Restrictive Business Practices", (1970) 4 Int'l Law. 317, 318–22 (describing the work of the League of Nations to create international competition rules); Waller I, see para. 2.020, n. 55, at 350–51.
[13] Sigmund Timberg, "An International Antitrust Convention: A Proposal to Harmonize Conflicting National Policies Towards the Multi-National Corporation", (1973) 30 J. Int'l L. & Econ. 157, 164.
[14] See OECD, Joint Group on Trade and Competition, "Outline of (A) Core Principles, Common Approaches and Common Standards and (B) Bilateral and Multilateral Approaches", at 3, COM/TD/DAFFE/CLP(98)97/Final (Oct. 13, 1999).
[15] See Waller I, see para. 2.020, n. 55, at 360–70.
[16] The Havana Charter's provisions on RBPs and the initiatives taken within GATT to adopt rules on RBPs are discussed in the next Chap.

Convention).[17] The draft Convention would have established a new international agency to receive and investigate complaints of RBPs.[18] The application of the Draft Convention was limited to restrictive business practices on the part of one or more commercial enterprises possessing

> effective control of trade among one or more countries in one or more products . . . affecting international trade which restrain competition, limit access to markets, or foster monopolistic control, whenever such practices have harmful effects on the expansion of production or trade, in the light of the objectives set forth in the Preamble to this Agreement.[19]

The Preamble to the UN Draft Convention set forth the following four objectives:

> (1) To promote the reduction of barriers to trade, governmental and private, and to promote on equitable terms access to markets, products, and productive facilities;
>
> (2) To encourage economic development, industrial and agricultural, particularly in under-developed areas;
>
> (3) To contribute to a balanced and expanding world economy through greater and more efficient production, increased income and greater consumption, and the elimination of discriminatory treatment in international trade;
>
> (4) To promote mutual understanding and co-operation in the solution of problems arising in the field of international trade in all its aspects.[20]

As the Preamble embraced more than just the traditional issues that are the focus of competition law and policy, the U.S. delegation responded by insisting that developed countries be free to enforce their own national laws.[21]

2.190 An important limitation on the scope of the Draft Convention was set out in Article 2.2(b) and (c) which limited the scope of the Convention to practices affecting international trade "which restrain competition, limit access to markets or foster monopolistic control".[22]

This jurisdictional limitation was deemed necessary in order to exclude RBPs with only national effects, which would be left to national competition

[17] See "Report of the Ad Hoc Committee on Restrictive Business Practices to the Economic and Social Council, Annex 2", 16 U.N. ECOSOC, Supp. 11 (1953) (hereinafter "Report of the Ad Hoc Committee"). The 20 articles of the UN Draft Convention are found in Annex 2 to the Report of the Ad Hoc Committee.

[18] See Scherer, see para. 2.178, n. 90, at 39; Wood, "The Impossible Dream", see para. 2.013, n. 28, at 284–85.

[19] UN Draft Convention Art. 1.1.

[20] *id.* preamble.

[21] See "Report of the Ad Hoc Committee", see para. 2.189, n. 17, at 15.

[22] "Report of the Ad Hoc Committee", see para. 2.189, n. 17, at 12–18.

law enforcement agencies.The list of prohibited RBPs was almost identical to those listed in the Chapter V of the Havana Charter: vertical or horizontal price fixing; restrictions on output, distribution, or investment; the division of markets or sources of supply; and tying arrangements and full-line forcing.[23]

2.191 The Draft Convention contemplated that investigations would be undertaken by an international authority in an adversarial procedure initiated by a complaint filed by an aggrieved party to the Convention.[24] However, the complaining party was responsible for conducting its own investigation and making available to the international authority the reports and information requested by the authority.[25] The investigating agency would have been properly staffed with experts in the competition law field.[26] However, the investigating authority was not responsible for executing the remedial measures recommended by it; rather, that task was left to national authorities.[27] Under Article 5.1, a member government would have been obligated to

> take all possible measures by legislation or otherwise, in accordance with its constitution or system of law and economic organization, to ensure, within its jurisdiction, that private and public commercial enterprises do not engage in harmful RBPs.

Participation in the Draft Convention was not limited to developed countries—as a UN project, such a limitation would have been unthinkable. However, the Draft Convention would not enter into force until it had been accepted either by

(1) 20 or more countries accounting for 65 per cent or more of the total value of world imports and exports, or

(2) countries accounting for 65 per cent or more of the total value of world imports and exports, including six countries which individually accounted for three percent or more of such total value.[28]

This membership requirement was an acknowledgement that any convention regulating international RBPs had to have the participation of the major developed countries.

2.192 The fear that small countries would be passing judgment on U.S. business practices was one of the factors that alienated the U.S. business community. It was feared that the Draft Convention's one-nation, one-vote provision would give small nations that were hostile to the United States the opportunity to harass it through frivolous complaints. The American business community eventually withdraw its support for the Draft Convention.[29]

---

[23] See UN Draft Convention Art. 1, para. 3.
[24] See *id.* Art. 3.
[25] See *id.* Art. 5.
[26] See *id.* Arts. 10–17.
[27] See *id.* Art. 5.1
[28] See *id.* Art. 18.2.
[29] See "Statement of Gilbert H. Montague", in Report of the Attorney General's National Committee to Study Antitrust Laws 107 (1955). See also para. 2.188, n. 13, at 173.

Ultimately, the State Department also withdrew its support in 1955 on the grounds that national competition laws, policies, and enforcement mechanisms were not sufficiently comparable, therefore, making any new international organisation ineffective.[30]

B. The 1980 UNCTAD Principles on Restrictive Business Practices

2.193 In 1980, the UNCTAD held a conference on restrictive business practices that yielded a document, *The Set of Multilaterally Agreed Principles and Rules for the Control of Restrictive Business Practices*,[31] "[t]he sole universally applicable multilateral instrument in this area".[32] The goal of the document is the elimination and control of RBPs that have a negative impact on international trade liberalisation, especially within developing countries.[33] The 1980 UNCTAD Principles define RBPs as:

> acts or behaviour of enterprises which, through an abuse or acquisition and abuse of a dominant position of market power, limit access to markets or otherwise unduly restrain competition, having or being likely to have adverse effects on international trade, particularly that of developing countries, and on the economic development of these countries, or which, through formal, informal, written or unwritten agreements or arrangements among enterprises, have the same impact.[34]

2.194 Being precatory in nature, the UNCTAD Principles recommend that:

(1) appropriate action should be taken in a mutually reinforcing manner at national, regional, and international levels to eliminate, or effectively deal with, restrictive business practices, including those of transnational corporations, adversely affecting international trade, particularly that of developing countries and the economic development of these countries; and

(2) collaboration between governments at bilateral and multilateral levels should be established and, where such collaboration has been established, it should be improved to facilitate the control of restrictive business practices.[35]

---

[30] See Timberg, see para. 2.188, n. 13, at 176; "ICPAC Final Report", see para. 2.012, n. 23, at 256.

[31] Set of Multilaterally Agreed Equitable Principles and Rules for the Control of Restrictive Business Practices, Apr. 22, 1980, UN Doc. TD/RBP/CONF/10 (1980), reprinted in 9 Int'l Legal Materials 813 (1980) [hereinafter UNCTAD Principles].

[32] "Experiences Gained So Far", see para. 2.040, n. 92, at 4.

[33] The Set of Principles also contain a number of hortatory provisions calling for special attention to the problems of developing countries. See, *e.g. id.* s. A(4), s. C, Equitable Principle 1. See generally Timothy B. Atkeson & David G. Gill, "The UNCTAD Restrictive Business Practice Code: A Step in the North-South Dialogue", (1981) 15 Int'l Law. 1; Joel Davidow, "The UNCTAD Restrictive Business Practice Code", (1979) 13 Int'l Law. 587; Wood, "The Impossible Dream", see para. 2.013, n. 28, at 300 (observing that the Code's practical effect has been minimal). For an analysis of the Code from a developing-country perspective, see Susan K. Sell, *Power and Ideas: North-South Politics of Intellectual Property and Antitrust* (1998) 141–73.

[34] UNCTAD Principles, *supra* n. 31, s. B(i)(1).

[35] See *id.* s. C(i) (1)–(2).

As threshold matters, the Principles direct enterprises to comply with the restrictive business practices laws of the countries in which they operate, and, in the event of proceedings under these laws, to be subject to the competence of the courts and relevant administrative bodies therein. Enterprises should co-operate with national enforcement authorities by providing information, in particular details of restrictive arrangements, required for this law enforcement purpose, including information that may be located in foreign countries, to the extent that in the latter event such production or disclosure is not prevented by applicable law or established public policy.[36]

2.195 The principles on competition which multinational enterprises are to observe cover the core prohibitions on vertical and horizontal restraints, and resemble Sections 1 and 2 of the Sherman Act and Articles 81 and 82 of the E.C. Treaty.[37] First, competitors should refrain from the following anti-competitive practices having or being likely to have adverse effects on international trade, particularly that of developing countries:

(1) agreements fixing prices, including as to exports and imports;

(2) collusive tendering;

(3) market or customer allocation arrangements;

(4) allocation by quota as to sales and production;

(5) collective action to enforce arrangements, *e.g.* by concerted refusals to deal;

(6) concerted refusal of supplies to potential importers; and

(7) collective denial of access to an arrangement, or association, which is crucial to competition.[38]

2.196 With regard to certain monopolistic practices, enterprises should refrain from the following acts or behaviour in a relevant market when, through an abuse or acquisition and abuse of a dominant position of market power, they limit access to markets or otherwise unduly restrain competition, having or being likely to have adverse effects on international trade, particularly that of developing countries, and on the economic development of these countries:

(1) predatory behaviour towards competitors, such as using below-cost pricing to eliminate competitors;

(2) discriminatory pricing or terms or conditions in the supply or purchase of goods and services;

(3) mergers, take-overs, joint ventures or other acquisitions of control, whether of a horizontal or vertical nature;

[36] See *id.* s. D (1)–(2).

[37] See "Report on Coordination and Convergence", see para. 2.135, n. 13, at 6.

[38] See UNCTAD Principles, *supra* n. 31, s. D(3) (a)–(g).

(4) fixing the prices at which goods exported can be resold in importing countries;

(5) restrictions on parallel imports which have been legitimately marked abroad with a trademark identical with or similar to the trademark protected as to identical or similar goods in the importing country where the trademarks in question belong to the same owner or are used by enterprises which are legally interdependence and where the purpose of such restrictions is to maintain artificially high prices;

(6) refusals to deal on the enterprise's customary commercial terms; and

(7) making the supply of particular goods or services dependent upon

(a) the acceptance of restrictions on the distribution or manufacture of competing or other goods, or
(b) the purchase of other goods or services from the supplier or his designee.[39]

2.197 Sections E and F of the UNCTAD Principles direct states to adopt and enforce antitrust laws that have as their goal the elimination of practices to limit access to markets or unduly restrain competition. States are also encouraged to enter into co-operative and collaborative arrangements with other states to facilitate cross-border antitrust enforcement. Finally, Section G establishes the Intergovernmental Group of Experts on Restrictive Business Practices (the General Assembly changed its name in 1997 to the Intergovernmental Group of Experts on Competition Law and Policy). The Intergovernmental Group is a forum for multilateral discussions on competition policy. Its functions include undertaking studies and making reports on matters relating to the implementation of the set of multilaterally agreed equitable principles and rules.

2.198 At its first session in 1998—more than 18 years after the adoption of the 1980 Principles—the Intergovernmental Group agreed to continue UNCTAD's work programme on competition law and policy, capacity building for individual countries, and the promotion of international co-operation.[40] At its second session in 1999, the Intergovernmental Group noted that UNCTAD has an important role to play in promoting a competition culture in developing countries and countries with economies in transition.[41] It encouraged the UNCTAD Secretary-General to co-operate with the

[39] See *id.* s. D(4).
[40] UNCTAD has prepared a "Handbook on Competition Legislation and a Directory of Competition Authorities". These are available at http://www.unctad.org/en/subsites/cpolicy/cpindex.htm. UNCTAD also has drafting a model law on RBPs that will be of assistance to those developing countries which do not yet have a competition law in place. The Model Law has had some influence in less-developed countries. See Model Law and Commentaries to Possible Elements for Articles of a Model Law or Laws, TD/RBP/CONF.5/7, TD/B/RBP/81/Rev.5, available at http://www.unctad.org/en/subsites/cpolicy/index.htm.
[41] See UNCTAD, "Report of the Intergovernmental Group of Experts on Competition Law and Policy on its Second Session", TD/B/COM.2/CLP/14 (June 1999), available at http://www.unctad.org.

WTO and other organisations working in the area of competition law and policy. On the twentieth anniversary of the adoption of the UNCTAD Principles, at its 2000 meeting the Intergovernmental Group reviewed all aspects of the Principles, reaffirmed their validity, and called upon all UN members to adopt them.[42]

For better or for worse, the UNCTAD Code has had little impact on either competition law enforcement or on MNEs at which the Code is directed.[43]

[42] See UNCTAD, Fourth United Nations Conference to Review All Aspects of the Set of Multilaterally Agreed Equitable Principles and Rules for the Control of Restrictive Business Practices, Sept. 25, 2000 Resolution, TD/RBP/CONF.5/15 (Oct. 5, 2000).

[43] See Tarullo, see para. 2.029, n. 72, at 485 n.33; Waller I, see para. 2.020, n. 55, at 351–52. Urged on by developing countries, UNCTAD also considered a code on the transfer of technology in the 1970s. Proponents of a technology transfer code wished to ban vertical restraints associated with licensing of technology, such as tying, exclusive dealing, and export restrictions. In the end a consensus failed to develop and negotiations ultimately stalled over three issues: (1) whether to adopt a *per se* rule or a rule of reason, (2) whether to exempt restrictions between affiliated firms, and (3) whether to recognise certain justifiable export restraints. See "Report on Coordination and Convergence", see para. 2.135, n. 13, at 8.

Chapter Three

Trade and Competition Policy At the WTO: The Past and Present

I. The history of competition rules in the GATT-WTO system

A. The Havana Charter and the Stillborn International Trade Organisation

3.001 The General Agreement on Tariffs and Trade (GATT) traces its origins to 1944. In that year, a comprehensive economic and financial plan for post-World War II reconstruction and development was proposed by representatives from the United States and the United Kingdom at Bretton Woods, New Hampshire. A triad of international economic and financial institutions was envisioned. Two of them, the World Bank and the International Monetary Fund, were created to address development and monetary issues. Rounding out the institutional triad was the International Trade Organisation (ITO). The General Agreement on Tariffs and Trade was to serve as an interim agreement until the ITO and its founding document, the Havana Charter,[1] could be approved by national legislatures.[2]

3.002 In September 1946, the United States drafted a proposed Charter that became the basis for discussions at the First Session of the Preparatory Committee on the Havana Charter.[3] In order to expedite the start of

[1] See Havana Charter for an International Trade Organization, Mar. 24, 1948 Arts. 46–54, UN Doc. E/Conf. 2/78 (1948). See Robert E. Hudec, *The GATT Legal System and World Trade Diplomacy* (1990) 11–61; John H. Jackson, *World Trade and the Law of GATT* 35–57 (1969); World Trade Organization, "analytical Index: Guide to GATT Law and Practice", vol. 1, at (1995) 1–9 (hereinafter "Guide to GATT Law and Practice"); George Bronz, The International Trade Organization Charter, (1949) 62 Harv. L. Rev. 1089, 1116.

[2] For a complete history of GATT and the Bretton Woods system, see Armand Van Dormael, *Bretton Woods: Birth of a Monetary System* (1978). See also G.J. Lanjouw, *International Trade Institutions* (1995); Jackson, *supra* note 1; Kenneth W. Dam, *The GATT: Law and International Economic Organization* (1970); Olivier Long, *Law and Its Limitations in the GATT Multilateral Trade System* (1985) 4–6; Hudec, *supra* note 1; *The GATT Legal System and World Trade Diplomacy* (1990); Gerald A. Bunting, "GATT and the Evolution of the Global Trade System: A Historical Perspective", (1995) 11 St. John's J. Legal Comment. 505.

[3] The members of the Preparatory Committee were Australia, Belgium, Luxembourg, Brazil, Canada, Chile, China, Cuba, Czechoslovakia, France, India, Lebanon, the Netherlands, New Zealand, Norway, South Africa, the USSR, the UK and the United States. With the exception of the former Soviet Union, all of these countries became GATT contracting parties under Protocols of Provisional Application.

international negotiations on tariff reductions and their implementation pending approval of the Havana Charter, GATT was approved provisionally by national representatives, effective January 1, 1948. President Truman approved it on behalf of the United States pursuant to authority granted under the Reciprocal Trade Agreements Act of 1934.

GATT Article XXIX makes plain that GATT was not intended by its drafters to function on a permanent basis. It was contemplated that once the Havana Charter entered into force and with it the ITO, Part II of GATT that contains the bulk of the international legal commitments (other than the MFN obligation and tariff commitments) would be suspended.[4] The Havana Charter was a far more complete document than GATT. It contained provisions relating to employment, economic development, restrictive business practices, foreign investment, and dispute resolution under ITO auspices.

3.003 Finally, as is well known, the Havana Charter never entered into force. In fact, no acceptance of the Charter was ever received by the United Nations: the depositary for Charter accessions. Once it became clear that the Havana Charter had no chance of being approved by the neo-isolationist U.S. Senate—in part because of objections to its competition law provisions[5]—the State Department issued a statement that the Charter would not be submitted again to Congress. As a consequence, GATT was pressed into service by default to fill the institutional and legal vacuum. Although the Havana Charter devoted an entire chapter to the subject of restrictive business practices,[6] GATT barely speaks to the issue of competition policy.[7]

3.004 Against this backdrop, the Havana Charter did include several broad provisions on the regulation of restrictive business practices. First,

---

[4] GATT Article XXIX provides in pertinent part: "2. Part II of this Agreement shall be suspended on the day on which the Havana Charter enters into force. 3. If by September 30, 1949, the Havana Charter has not entered into force, the contracting parties shall meet before December 31, 1949, to agree whether this Agreement shall be amended, supplemented or maintained".

[5] See U.S. Dep't of State, Pub. No. 3206, "Havana Charter for an International Trade Organization" 114 (1948).

[6] See "Final Act and Related Documents, United Nations Conference on Trade and Employment, Havana, Cuba" Nov. 21, 1947 to Mar. 24, 1947 UN Doc. ICITO/1/4 (1948). .

[7] Although it served as the leading international trade agreement and institution for close to half a century, paradoxically GATT 1947 never entered into force. In order for that to happen, GATT Article XXVI:6 required definitive acceptances from the countries listed in Annex H to GATT 1947, and the countries accepting also had to represent at least 85% of total world trade. In the end, GATT 1947 was accepted definitively only by Liberia and Haiti. See Guide to "GATT Law and Practice", *supra* note 1, at 6–7. GATT was applied provisionally by the contracting parties (as the signatories to GATT 1947 were called) under Protocols of Provisional Application or Protocols of Accession to the General Agreement. For an analysis of the Protocol of Provisional Application, see "Guide to GATT Law and Practice", see para. 3.001, n. 1, vol. 2, at 1071–84. All Protocols of Provisional Application and of Accession grandfathered pre-existing national legislation that was inconsistent with Part II of GATT. These laws consisted primarily of national laws that discriminated against imports *vis-à-vis* the like domestic product, and national laws authorising import quotas. GATT's legal status in the United States always was murky. GATT never was approved by the Senate as an Article II, s. 2 treaty, nor was it submitted for approval by the full Congress as a congressional-executive agreement. Not until 1994, when Congress enacted s. 101(a) of the Uruguay Round Agreements Act, were GATT and the Uruguay Round multilateral trade agreements elevated from provisional to definitive status. See generally John H. Jackson, "The General Agreement on Tariffs and Trade in United States Domestic Law", (1967) 66 Mich. L. Rev. 249.

Article 46: *General Policy Towards Restrictive Business Practices* would have required ITO members to take "appropriate measures" against RBPs affecting international trade

> which restrain competition, limit access to markets, or foster monopolistic control, whenever such practices have harmful effects on the expansion of production of trade. . . .[8]

Article 46 further provided that an ITO investigation could be conducted following a member's complaint of the following restrictive business practices:[9]

(1) Fixing prices, terms or conditions to be observed in dealing with others in the purchase, sale or lease of any product;

(2) Excluding enterprises from, or allocating or dividing, any territorial market or field of business activity, or allocating customers, or fixing sales quotas or purchase quotas;

(3) Discriminating against particular enterprises;

(4) Limiting production or fixing production quotas;

(5) Preventing by agreement the development or application of technology or invention whether patented or unpatented;

(6) Extending the use of rights under patents, trade marks or copyrights granted by any Member to matters which, according to its laws and regulations, are not within the scope of such grants, or to products or conditions of production, use or sale which are likewise not the subjects of such grants;

(g) Any similar practices which the Organisation may declare, by a majority of two-thirds of the Members present and voting, to be restrictive business practices.[10]

3.005 In short, the prohibited RBPs targeted by Chapter V include price fixing, division of markets, cartel activity and abuse of intellectual property rights. The third RBP in this group, cartels (the prohibited RBPs identified in (2) and (4)) is today addressed in part by the Agreement on Safeguards. This prohibits voluntary export restraint agreements (export quotas) concluded by

---

[8] Havana Charter, Art. 46.1.

[9] Art. 46.2 provided: "In order that the Organization may decide in a particular instance whether a practice has or is about to have the effect indicated in paragraph 1, the Members agree, without limiting paragraph 1, that complaints regarding any of the practices listed in paragraph 3 shall be subject to investigation in accordance with the procedure regarding complaints provided for in Articles 48 and 50, whenever (a) Such a complaint is presented to the Organization, and (b) The practice is engaged in, or made effective, by one or more private or public commercial enterprises or by any combination, agreement or other arrangement between any such enterprises, and (c) Such commercial enterprises, individually or collectively, possess effective control of trade among a number of countries in one or more products".

[10] Havana Charter, Art. 46.3.

WTO members on behalf of domestic producers, unless the requirements of the Safeguards Agreement are strictly observed.[11] The last in this group of prohibited RBPs concerning intellectual property rights (those identified in (5) and (6)) are today taken up in Articles 8.2 and 40 of the TRIPS Agreement (discussed below). Interestingly, the six specific RBPs were not deemed to be *per se* violations of the Havana Charter. Instead, the signatories to the Havana Charter

> clung to their respective sovereignty by agreeing only to 'take full account' of all ITO decisions or requests and in addition to 'take in the particular case the action it considers appropriate having regard to its obligations under this Chapter.'[12]

A complaint from an ITO member would only result in a prima facie justification for an ITO investigation.

3.006 Articles 47 and 48 of the Havana Charter would have established a consultation, complaint, and investigation mechanism. The Article 47 consultation procedure is a familiar one: it finds its modern-day analogue in Article XXII of GATT and in Article 4 of the WTO Dispute Settlement Understanding.[13] The Article 48 complaint and investigation procedure would have created a weak dispute settlement mechanism pursuant to which the ITO could issue declaratory rulings on whether nationals of a member have engaged in the RBPs listed in Article 46.[14] Article 48 called upon the disputing

[11] Art. 11.1(b) of the Safeguards Agreement provides in part: "[A] Member shall not seek, take or maintain any voluntary export restraints, orderly marketing arrangements or any other similar measures on the export or import side. Footnote 4 of the Agreement gives as examples, "export moderation, export-price or import-price monitoring systems, export or import surveillance, compulsory import cartels and discretionary export or import licensing schemes, any of which afford protection."

[12] Earl W. Kintner, Mark R. Joelson & Peter J. Vaghi, "Groping for a Truly International Antitrust Law", (1973) 14 Va. J. Int'l L. 75, 88 (quoting Art. 50(4) of the Havana Charter).

[13] Art. 47 of the Havana Charter provided: "Any affected Member which considers that in any particular instance a practice exists (whether engaged in by private or public commercial enterprises) which has or is about to have the effect indicated in paragraph 1 of Article 46 may consult other Members directly or request the Organization to arrange for consultation with particular Members with a view to reaching mutually satisfactory conclusions. If requested by the Member and if it considers such action to be justified, the Organization shall arrange for and assist in such consultation. Action under this Article shall be without prejudice to the procedure provided for in Article 48".

[14] Article 48 provided in part: "1. In accordance with paragraphs 2 and 3 of Article 46, any affected Member on its own behalf or any Member on behalf of any affected person, enterprise or organization within that Member's jurisdiction, may present a written complaint to the Organization that in any particular instance a practice exists (whether engaged in by private or public commercial enterprises) which has or is about to have the effect indicated in paragraph 1 of Article 46. . ." 4. If the Organization decides that an investigation is justified, it shall inform all Members of the complaint, request any Member to furnish such additional information relevant to the complaint as the Organization may deem necessary, and shall conduct or arrange for hearings on the complaint. Any Member, and any person, enterprise or organization on whose behalf the complaint has been made, as well as the commercial enterprises alleged to have engaged in the practice complained of, shall be afforded reasonable opportunity to be heard. 7. If the Organization decides that in any particular case the conditions specified in paragraphs 2 and 3 of Article 46 are present and that the practice in question has had, has or is about to have the

members to provide information to the ITO upon request. Although disputing members would have been required to provide information requested by the ITO in its Article 48 investigation, that obligation was not absolute.[15]

In the absence of a complete factual record, it is questionable whether ITO's investigation would have been credible. Article 48 did not establish any deadlines for the completion of an investigation. Given the prolix nature of antitrust litigation in the United States[16] (where compulsory discovery is available), whether the ITO's record have been any better on this score. At the end of an investigation, if the ITO concluded that Article 46 had been violated, it could recommend that the responding member take

> every possible remedial action, and may also recommend to the members concerned remedial measures to be carried out in accordance with their respective laws and procedures.[17]

Article 48 was silent on the question of what was to be done in a situation where national enforcement authorities previously investigated the same matter and found no cause to proceed. Nor did Article 48 say anything about the status of settlements entered into between national enforcement authorities and antitrust defendants.

3.007 What of a merger with cross-border effects that was approved by a national enforcement agency but challenged by another ITO member as being a violation of Article 46? Again, Chapter V of the Havana Charter was silent on this question. In this connection Article 50 of the Charter obligated members to take the remedial action recommended by the ITO but again that obligation was not hard and fast. Article 50 provided in part:

---

effect indicated in paragraph 1 of that Article, it shall request each Member concerned to take every possible remedial action, and may also recommend to the Members concerned remedial measures to be carried out in accordance with their respective laws and procedures. 10. The Organization shall report to all Members and make public the remedial action which has been taken by the Members concerned in any particular case".

[15] Article 50.3 provided: "Each Member shall furnish to the Organization, as promptly and as fully as possible, such information as is requested by the Organization for its consideration and investigation of complaints and for its conduct of studies under this Chapter; Provided that any Member on notification to the Organization, may withhold information which the Member considers is not essential to the Organization in conducting an adequate investigation and which, if disclosed, would substantially damage the legitimate business interests of a commercial enterprise. In notifying the Organization that it is withholding information pursuant to this clause, the Member shall indicate the general character of the information withheld and the reason why it considers it not essential".

[16] For examples of protracted antitrust litigation in the United States, see, *e.g. United States v. Microsoft Corp.*, 87 F. Supp. 2d 30 (D.D.C. 2000); *United States v. Amer. Tel. & Tel. Co.*, 401 F. Supp. 1310 (D. Minn. 1982); *United States v. Int'l Bus. Machines, Inc.*, 887 F. Supp. 591 (S.D.N.Y. 1982).

[17] Havana Charter, art. 48(7). The U.S. proposal would have required the responding ITO member to "take action." See "Suggested Charter for An International Trade Organization of the United Nations", Dep't of State Pub. No. 2598, Commercial Policy Series 93, art. 37(5) (1946). For an analysis of the U.S. draft of the Havana Charter's competition law provisions, see Corwin Edwards, *Control of Cartels and Monopolies: An International Comparison* (1967) 228–31; American Bar Ass'n, "Report of the Sections on Antitrust Law and International Law and Practice on the Internationalization of Competition Law Rules: Coordination and Convergence" 2–4 (2000) (hereinafter "Report on Coordination and Convergence").

> 4. Each Member shall take full account of each request, decision and recommendation of the Organization under Article 48 and, in accordance with its constitution or system of law and economic organization, take in the particular case the action it considers appropriate having regard to its obligations under this Chapter.
> 5. Each Member shall report fully any action taken, independently or in concert with other Members, to comply with the requests and carry out the recommendations of the Organization and, when no action has been taken, inform the Organization of the reasons therefor and discuss the matter further with the Organization if it so requests.

Article 50.1 of the Havana Charter imposed an affirmative obligation on ITO members to prosecute firms that engaged in prohibited RBPs. Members would have been required to

> take all possible measures by legislation or otherwise, in accordance with its constitution or system of law and economic organization, to ensure, within its jurisdiction, that private and public commercial enterprises do not engage in practices which are as specified in paragraphs 2 and 3 of Article 46 and have the effect indicated in paragraph 1 of that Article, . . .

Article 53 was a special provision dealing with services that would have obliged members to ensure that RBPs in services sectors that directly impact trade in goods (*e.g.* transportation, telecommunications) not be tolerated. Article 53 finds its analogue in part in GATS Articles VIII and IX, the GATS Understanding on Financial Services, the GATS Annex on Telecommunications, and the Reference Paper on competition principles annexed to the 1997 Agreement on Basic Telecommunications (each of these provisions are discussed below).

3.008 The balance of Chapter V were four articles that:

(1) called for RBP studies (Article 49),

(2) authorised mutual co-operation agreements among ITO members (Article 51),

(3) clarified that nothing in Chapter V prevents national enforcement of RBP laws (Article 52), and

(4) provided definitions of key terms (Article 54).

Just how Chapter V would have worked in practice is impossible to say. Nevertheless, I would speculate that it either would have been a disaster, or that it would have been largely ignored, or both. First, the Article 47 dispute settlement mechanism is frighteningly similar to the GATT dispute settlement mechanism which, by all accounts, was an abysmal failure.[18] Secondly, the assumption that the ITO would have been competent to resolve factually complex and politically sensitive antitrust issues was certainly a leap of faith, even for multilateralists.

3.009 A postscript to the stillborn Havana Charter—when by 1951 the Havana Charter had failed to obtain the necessary ratifications, a second attempt was made to revive Chapter V as a free-standing legal instrument under the auspices of the United Nations Economic and Social Council (ECOSOC). In May 1953, ECOSOC established an ad hoc committee which presented a report recommending the adoption of a draft Convention on Restrictive Business Practices. The committee's report failed to attract sufficient interest. As a consequence, the project was abandoned in 1955.[19]

B. Competition Policy under GATT 1994

1. *Provisions in GATT 1994 Relating to Competition Policy*

3.010 Despite that fact that GATT 1994 deals primarily with restrictions on trade imposed by governments, several GATT provisions bear, directly and

[18] Criticisms of the dispute settlement process under GATT 1947 are legion. The most frequently recurring complaints about dispute settlement under GATT 1947 included the following:

- GATT lacked an integrated dispute settlement procedure, with the Tokyo Round Codes containing separate dispute settlement mechanisms.
- GATT disputes were sometimes resolved through the grant of waivers.
- small countries were handicapped in achieving effective results against large countries.
- the GATT panel process was lengthy and subject to delaying tactics.
- GATT contained no provision for the automatic establishment of a panel.
- inadequate staff and experts often hamstrung panels in their fact finding.
- the insistence on approval of panel reports by consensus permitted the losing country to block adoption of reports.
- effective enforcement and sanctions were almost nonexistent, with the exception of bilateral retaliation.
- GATT did not require notification of the implementation of a panel recommendation.

The Uruguay Round Understanding on Rules and Procedures Governing the Settlement of Disputes (the Dispute Settlement Understanding or DSU) addresses almost all of these criticisms. For an analysis of the DSU, see Raj Bhala & Kevin Kennedy, *World Trade Law: The GATT-WTO System, Regional Arrangements, and U.S. Law* (1998) 26–49. For an analysis of dispute settlement under GATT 1947 and criticisms of that process, see Robert E. Hudec, *Enforcing International Trade Law: The Evolution of the Modern GATT Legal System* (1993); John H. Jackson, *Restructuring the GATT System* (1990); U.S. Int'l Trade Comm'n, "Review of the Effectiveness of Trade Dispute Settlement Under the GATT and the Tokyo Round Agreements" (USITC Pub. 1793 1985); Pierre Pescatore, *Handbook of GATT Dispute Settlement* (1992); Robert E. Hudec, "A Statistical Profile of the GATT Dispute Settlement Cases: 1948–1989", (1993) 2 Minn. J. Global Trade 1; William J. Davey, "The GATT Dispute Settlement System: Proposals for Reform in the Uruguay Round", in *Workshop on the Multilateral Trade Negotiations of GATT* (1992); William J. Davey, "Dispute Settlement in GATT", (1987) 11 Fordham Int'l L.J. 51; Rosine Plank, "An Unofficial Description of How a GATT Panel Works and Does Not", (Dec. 1987) J. Int'l Arb. 53.

[19] The 1953 UN Draft Convention is discussed in Chap. Two. See Diane P. Wood, "The Impossible Dream: Real International Antitrust", 1992 U. Chi. Legal F. 277, 284 (noting that the Eisenhower administration preferred a national approach) (hereinafter Wood, "The Impossible Dream"]; Sigmund Timberg, "An International Antitrust Convention: A Proposal to Harmonize Conflicting National Policies Towards the Multi-National Corporation", (1973) 30 J. Int'l L. & Econ. 157 (discussing the 1953 UN Draft Convention).

indirectly, on private business practices.[20] These provisions include Articles II:4, III, X, XI, XVII, XX(d), XXIII:1(b), and XXVIII:1(c).

3.011 **a. Article II:4.** Article II:4 provides:

> If any contracting party establishes, maintains or authorizes, formally or in effect, a monopoly of the importation of any product described in the appropriate Schedule annexed to this Agreement, such monopoly shall not, except as provided for in that Schedule or as otherwise agreed between the parties which initially negotiated the concession, operate so as to afford protection on the average in excess of the amount of protection provided for in that Schedule. . . .

The fundamental object and purpose of Article II:4 is to ensure the integrity of market access commitments against erosion by certain forms of internal market structure. Article II:4 proscribes conduct by an import monopoly that operates to afford protection "on the average" in excess of that provided for by the applicable tariff binding for that product. This proscription applies where a contracting party "establishes, maintains or authorizes" the import monopoly "formally or in effect." This provision was drafted to address "behind the border" practices that raise the level of protection against imports beyond what is reflected in a contracting party's Schedule of Concessions for the specific imported product.[21] Its aim is to discipline those practices so that tariff bindings are not circumvented.

3.012 What kinds of practices are covered by Article II:4? The 1988 GATT panel report on: *Canada—Import, Distribution and Sale of Alcoholic Drinks by Canadian Provincial Marketing Agencies*[22] is informative. The panel examined the practices of provincial liquor boards with respect to alcoholic beverages where the liquor boards used different mark-ups on imported as opposed to domestic alcoholic beverages. Canada's Schedule of Concessions included tariff bindings on all imported alcoholic drinks. Ottawa had also authorised a monopoly of the importation of alcoholic beverages. Thus, the amount of protection permissible under Article II:4 was either the amount specified in Canada's Schedule of Concessions or "as otherwise agreed between the parties which had initially negotiated the concession." The panel found that there was no other agreement between the parties which had

[20] See OECD, "Joint Group on Trade and Competition, Competition Elements in International Trade Agreements": A Post-Uruguay Round Overview of WTO Agreements (1999).
GATT 1994 consists collectively of the following legal instruments: GATT 1947, as amended and modified; waivers granted under GATT 1947 and still in force on the date of entry into force of the WTO Agreement; the Marrakesh Protocol, to which the WTO Members' schedules of market access commitments are appended; and the 6 Uruguay Round Understandings included in Annex 1A that amend and clarify GATT 1947.

[21] See "Guide to GATT Law and Practice", see para. 3.001, n. 1, at 88.

[22] See "Report of the GATT Panel, Canada—Import, Distribution and Sale of Alcoholic Drinks by Canadian Provincial Marketing Agencies", BISD, 35th Supp. 37 (adopted Mar. 22 1988) (hereinafter "Canada—Import, Distribution and Sale of Alcoholic Drinks").

initially negotiated the concession,[23] therefore, the mark-up differential could only be justified to the extent that the differential was commensurate with different costs of marketing the imported products. In responding to Canada's argument that the differential was warranted on grounds of "normal commercial considerations," the panel considered what would constitute the normal commercial behaviour of firms and normal conditions of competition:

> The Panel noted Canada's statement that, in some instances, the differential mark-ups also reflected a policy of revenue maximisation on the part of provincial liquor boards. These charged higher mark-ups on imported than on domestic alcoholic beverages because they marketed imported products as premium products and exploited less price elastic demand for these products. This policy was in accordance with the General Agreement because revenue maximisation was justified by normal commercial considerations.
>
> The Panel considered that a monopoly profit margin on imports resulting from policies of revenue maximisation by provincial liquor boards could not normally be considered as a "reasonable margin of profit" in the sense of Article II:4, especially if it were higher on imported products than on domestic products.
>
> The Panel considered that "a reasonable margin of profit" . . . was a margin of profit that would be obtained under normal conditions of competition (in the absence of the monopoly). The margin of profit would have on the average to be the same on both domestic and the like imported products so as not to undermine the value of tariff concessions under Article II.[24]

The panel recognised that certain practices inside the border that reflect market structure—in this case, exploitation of monopoly power—have to be taken into account when assessing whether market access is being denied and trade obligations violated.

3.013 Article II:4 covers monopolies, public or private, where monopoly rights are granted by *formal* governmental legislation or regulations. Whether the absence of formal governmental action would shield certain exclusive distribution and retailing networks for imported products from the obligations of Article II:4 is an open question. However, based on the phrase "in effect," the provision arguably applies to situations where, even though there is not formal governmental authorisation, a monopoly is effectively established, authorised, or maintained *de facto* through government inaction.

3.014 Although Article II:4 appears to be limited to monopolies for the importation of goods and not their distribution, the requirement that

[23] Canada argued that an agreement did exist. In the Tokyo Round, it had submitted a document to the European Communities on behalf of the provinces (Provincial Statement of Intentions with Respect to Sales of Alcoholic Beverages by Provincial Marketing Agencies in Canada) that set out specific undertakings with respect to mark-ups, listing and distribution practices. The panel found that Canada's emphasis on the non-binding nature of the undertakings contained in the Statement indicated that it was not meant to affect Canada's rights and obligations under Art. II:4. See "Canada—Import, Distribution and Sale of Alcoholic Drinks", *supra* note 22, at 85–86, paras. 4.5–4.8.

[24] *id.* at 87, paras. 4.13–4.15.

"protection" may not be increased above the bound duty rate is not restricted to any particular class of conduct. In another GATT panel report on minimum pricing practices of Canadian provincial liquor boards,[25] the panel found that the practice violated the national treatment obligation of Article III, even though the minimum pricing regulation applied equally to domestic and imported beer. The minimum pricing regulation went beyond recovering the additional costs necessarily associated with marketing and distributing imported beer, and thus operated in a way that prevented the imported product from competing with the domestic product on the basis of price.

3.015 b. Article III. GATT Article III's general theme is to prohibit members from circumventing tariff concessions through non-tariff barriers to import trade that might undermine the benefit of a tariff reduction. Like its MFN counterpart, national treatment is a nondiscrimination obligation, but imposed at the national level. Once imports have entered a member's territory,

(1) internal taxes must be applied equally to imports and the like domestic product, and
(2) national regulations must not treat imports "less favorably" than similar domestic goods.

The broad purpose of the Article III national treatment obligation is to avoid protectionism in the application of internal taxes and regulatory measures. Article III ensures that internal measures are not applied to imported or domestic products in a way that affords protection to domestic products. To that end, WTO members are obligated to provide equality of competitive conditions—a level playing field—for imported goods *vis-à-vis* domestic like products, regardless of actual trade effects.

3.016 Several GATT panel reports illuminate the point about equality of competitive conditions in import markets. First, in *United States—Taxes on Petroleum and Certain Imported Substances (Superfund)*,[26] the panel found that an excise tax on petroleum was imposed at a higher rate on imported products than on the like domestic product, and was therefore inconsistent with the first sentence of Article III:2.[27] The United States argued that the tax differential of 3.5 cents per barrel was so small that it did not nullify or impair benefits accruing to Canada, the E.U. and Mexico under GATT. The panel noted with respect to Article III:2:

> Article III:2, first sentence, obliges contracting parties to establish certain competitive conditions for imported products in relation to domestic

[25] See "Report of the GATT Panel, Canada—Import, Distribution and Sale of Alcoholic Drinks by Canadian Provincial Marketing Agencies", BISD, 39th Supp. 27 (adopted Feb. 18, 1992).
[26] "Report of the GATT Panel, United States—Taxes on Petroleum and Certain Imported Substances", BISD, 34th Supp. 136 (adopted June 27, 1987).
[27] Art. III:2, first sentence, provides: "The products of the territory of any contracting party imported into the territory of any other contracting party shall not be subject, directly or indirectly, to internal taxes or other internal charges of any kind in excess of those applied, directly or indirectly, to like domestic products".

> products. Unlike some other provisions in the General Agreement, it does not refer to trade effects. . . Article III:2, first sentence, cannot be interpreted to protect expectations on export volumes; it protects expectations on the competitive relationship between imported and domestic products. A change in the competitive relationship contrary to that provision must consequently be regarded ipso facto as a nullification or impairment of benefits accruing under the General Agreement. A demonstration that a measure inconsistent with Article III:2, first sentence, has no or insignificant effects would therefore in the view of the Panel not be a sufficient demonstration that the benefits accruing under that provision had not been nullified or impaired even if such a rebuttal in principle were permitted.[28]

3.017 Secondly, Article III:4, the source of national treatment commitments with respect to internal regulations affecting imports, applies "in respect of all laws, regulations and requirements *affecting* their internal sale, offering for sale, purchase, transportation, distribution or use."[29] GATT panel reports interpreting the term "affecting" have given it a generous construction. For example, in *Italian Discrimination against Imported Agricultural Machinery*,[30] the panel examined an Italian law providing special credit terms to farmers for the purchase of agricultural machinery, conditional on the purchase of machinery manufactured in Italy. The panel found:

> [T]he text of paragraph 4 referred . . . to laws and regulations and requirements *affecting* internal sale, purchase, etc., and not to laws, regulations and requirements governing the conditions of sale or purchase. The selection of the word "affecting" would imply, in the opinion of the Panel, that the drafters of the Article intended to cover in paragraph 4 not only the laws and regulations which directly governed the conditions of sale or purchase but also any laws or regulations which might adversely modify the conditions of competition between the domestic and imported products on the internal market.[31]

3.018 The key term in Article III:4—"affecting"—thus is a broad term that includes internal regulations that not only govern the sale, purchase, or distribution of imported products, but also those which have a negative effect on the competitive opportunities enjoyed by imports *vis-à-vis* the domestic

---

[28] *id.* at 158, para. 5.1.9. "Accord Report of the GATT Panel, United States—Measures Affecting Alcoholic and Malt Beverages", BISD, 39th Supp. 206, 270–71, para. 5.6 (adopted June 19, 1992)("Article III:2, first sentence, is not conditional on a 'trade effects test' nor is it qualified by a *de minimis* standard").

[29] GATT 1994, art. III:4 (emphasis added). Article III:4 provides in full: "The products of the territory of any contracting party imported into the territory of any other contracting party shall be accorded treatment no less favorable than that accorded to like products of national origin in respect of all laws, regulations and requirements affecting their internal sale, offering for sale, purchase, transportation, distribution or use. The provisions of this paragraph shall not prevent the application of differential internal transportation charges which are based exclusively on the economic operation of the means of transport and not on the nationality of the product".

[30] "Report of the GATT Panel, Italian Discrimination against Imported Agricultural Machinery", BISD, 7th Supp. 60 (adopted Oct. 23, 1958).

[31] *id.* at 64, para. 12 (emphasis in original).

like product in the importing member's home market. For example, a 1984 GATT panel report condemned the Canadian Foreign Investment Review Act for violating the national treatment obligation because it conditioned government approval of a foreign investment upon purchases of local as opposed to foreign-sourced inputs. Unless the foreign investor agreed to purchase goods of Canadian origin in preference to imports, provided the former were "competitively available," its investment would not be approved.[32] Even though the obligation was imposed on investors and not importers, the regulation was nevertheless held to violate Article III:4.

3.019 Regulations that favour imports in some instances but discriminate against them in others also violate Article III:4. In this connection, in section 337 of the Tariff Act of 1930,[33] the GATT panel rejected the contention that a balancing test should be used under which administrative proceedings in the United States that were less favourable to some imported products could be offset by ones that treated other imported products more favourably.[34] The panel noted:

> If this notion were accepted, it would entitle a contracting party to derogate from the no less favourable treatment obligation in one case, or indeed in respect of one contracting party, on the ground that it accords more favourable treatment in some other case, or to another contracting party. Such an interpretation would lead to great uncertainty about the conditions of competition between imported and domestic products and thus defeat the purposes of Article III.[35]

The upshot of the panel's decision is that just as tariff bindings afford exporters a minimum level of certainty regarding pricing, the national treatment obligation prevents importing countries from using internal regulations in a way that impede market access by impairing exporters' ability to reasonably assess the legal and regulatory climate in a target export market.

3.020 Are national competition laws "laws, regulations, or requirements" within the meaning of Article III:4? Based on the foregoing panel reports, the answer would appear to be an unequivocal "yes." If so, are there situations where those laws can affect the internal sale, offering for sale, purchase, transportation, distribution, or use of imports? Again, the answer would appear to be an unequivocal "yes." If so, would the national treatment obligation be breached in a situation where, as a matter of fact, those laws

---

[32] See "Report of the GATT Panel, Canada—Administration of the Foreign Investment Review Act", BISD, 30th Supp. 140, 159–61, paras. 5.7–5.11 (adopted Feb. 7, 1984). "Accord Report of the GATT Panel, EEC—Regulations on Imports of Parts and Components", BISD, 37th Supp. 132, 197, paras. 5.20–5.21 (1990) ("[N]ot only requirements which an enterprise is legally bound to carry out, . . . but also those which an enterprise voluntarily accepts in order to obtain an advantage from the government constitute 'requirements' . . .").

[33] "Report of the GATT Panel, United States—Section 337 of the Tariff Act of 1930", BISD, 36th Supp. 345 (adopted Nov. 7, 1989) (hereinafter "Section 337 of the Tariff Act of 1930").

[34] *id.* at 387, para. 5.14. "Accord Report of the GATT Panel, United States—Denial of Most-Favoured-Nation Treatment as to Non-Rubber Footwear from Brazil", BISD, 39th Supp. 128, 151, para. 6.10 (1992).

[35] Section 337 of the Tariff Act of 1930, see para. 3.019, n. 33, at 387, para. 5.14.

favour domestically produced goods over imports? Again, the answer would be "yes," based on the foregoing panel reports, if the manner in which the competition law or regulation itself is applied affects the competitive relationship between imported and domestically produced goods.

3.021 **c. Article VI.** In one of the few GATT provisions to address private conduct, GATT Article VI exhorts the contracting parties to condemn private-firm dumping—pricing exports below the home-market price or below the cost of production—"if it causes or threatens material injury to an established industry . . ."[36] However, it is left to the country of importation to respond to injurious dumping by imposing a duty "not greater in amount than the margin of dumping . . ."[37] Article VI imposes no affirmative obligation on the country of exportation to prevent or punish alleged dumping by firms within its territory. The clash of the antidumping duty law and the unfair pricing laws is analysed below in connection with the WTO dispute involving the U.S. Antidumping Act of 1916.

3.022 **d. Article X.** There can be little question that the smooth functioning of a multilateral trade system requires transparency of the trade regulations and measures adopted by its members. To that end, GATT Article X, *Publication and Administration of Trade Regulations*, provides in part:

> 1. Laws, regulations, judicial decisions and administrative rulings of general application, made effective by any contracting party, pertaining

[36] GATT Article VI:1. Under the Uruguay Round Antidumping Agreement (formally known as the Agreement on Implementation of Article VI of the General Agreement on Tariffs and Trade 1994), the basic test for imposing antidumping duties remains the same as under former law: a duty equal to the margin of dumping may be imposed on dumped imports that cause injury or threaten injury to a domestic industry producing the like product. The standard for determining if imports have been dumped is whether the product's export price is less than its normal value. The term "normal value" is defined as the market price for the product when sold in the country of exportation, (*i.e.* the home market price). In the event that home market sales are few or at prices that are less than the cost of production, then third-country market prices or constructed value may be used. Constructed value represents the cost of producing the product plus a reasonable amount for administrative and selling expenses, and for profit.

In administering the injury phase of an antidumping investigation, national authorities are permitted to cumulate imports from all countries that are subject to an investigation. Art. 3.5 requires that national authorities establish a causal link between the dumped imports and injury to the domestic industry. They are also required to examine factors other than dumped imports that may be the cause of injury to the domestic industry. In making a threat of injury determination, national authorities must base their determinations on facts, not on conjecture.

The Antidumping Agreement adds other important procedural rules to the antidumping administrative process. First, petitions submitted to national authorities must contain relevant evidence that substantiates claims of dumping and injury. National authorities are to examine the accuracy and sufficiency of this information. Secondly, Art. 5.4 establishes a predictable, two-step standard for determining industry support for a petition: (1) domestic producers accounting for more than 25% of total domestic production must expressly support a petition; and (2) of those domestic producers expressing a view on the petition, more domestic producers must support than oppose the petition. Thirdly, an investigation must be terminated if either (1) the margin of dumping is *de minimis* (less than 2% of the export price); or (2) the volume of imports is negligible (less than 3% of the volume of total imports). Fourthly, Art. 11.3 creates a sunset provision that obligates national authorities to terminate an antidumping order after 5 years, unless termination of the order would be likely to lead to the continuation or recurrence of dumping or injury.

[37] GATT 1994, Art. VI:2.

> to the classification or the valuation of products for customs purposes, or to rates of duty, taxes or other charges, or to requirements, restrictions or prohibitions on imports or exports or on the transfer of payments therefor, or affecting their sale, distribution, transportation, insurance, warehousing, inspection, exhibition, processing, mixing or other use, shall be published promptly in such a manner as to enable governments and traders to become acquainted with them. . .
> 3. (a) Each contracting party shall administer in a uniform, impartial and reasonable manner all its laws, regulations, decisions and rulings of the kind described in paragraph 1 of this Article.

3.023 The GATT panel interpretations of Article X have been a mixed bag. In a 1989 panel report, *Restrictions on Imports of Apples*,[38] the panel examined the legality of import quotas imposed by the EEC on apples, both in terms of the allocation of the quotas among supplying countries and the manner in which the quotas were notified retroactively. The quota allocation was announced in April 1988, but covered a period which began in February 1988 and ended in August 1988. The panel found that since the EEC had given public notice of the quota allocation two months after the quota period had begun, the EEC was in breach of Article X which, the panel concluded, prohibits back-dated quotas. However, in the 1992 GATT panel report *Import, Distribution and Sale of Certain Alcoholic Drinks by Provincial Marketing Agencies*,[39] the United States complained that the liquor board of British Colombia had shared information with domestic brewers relating to pricing policy before that information was available to U.S. authorities. The United States also claimed that the Ontario legislative assembly had announced a new pricing policy for beer only five days before its entry into force in violation of Article X. The panel concluded that Article X's requirement to publish trade regulations promptly did not require contracting parties to make information affecting trade available to domestic and foreign suppliers precisely at the same time and did not require contracting parties to publish trade regulations in advance of their entry into force.

3.024 In the Uruguay Round the trade ministers recommended the adoption of the Decision on Notification Procedures in order to strengthen and improve the transparency commitment of Article X. In the Decision, WTO members reaffirm their commitment to notify and publish measures affecting the operation of GATT 1994 and create a central registry for filing notifications. The Decision contains an Annex, *Indicative List of Notifiable Measures*, which is a non-exhaustive list of the types of measures subject to notification. The list includes tariffs; tariffs quotas and surcharges; quantitative restrictions, including voluntary export restraints and orderly marketing arrangements affecting imports; other non-tariff measures, such as licensing, mixing requirements, and variable levies; customs valuation; rules of origin;

[38] See "Report of the GATT Panel, EEC—Restrictions on Imports of Apples", BISD, 36th Supp. 135, 166–67, paras. 5.20–5.23 (1989).

[39] See "Canada—Import, Distribution and Sale of Certain Alcoholic Drinks by Provincial Marketing Agencies", see para. 3.014, n. 25, at 85–86, para. 5.34.

government procurement; technical barriers; safeguard actions; anti-dumping actions; countervailing actions; export taxes; export subsidies, tax exemptions, and concessionary export financing; free-trade zones, including in-bond manufacturing; export restrictions, including voluntary export restraints and orderly marketing arrangements; other governmental assistance, including subsidies and tax exemptions; the role of state-trading enterprises; foreign exchange controls related to imports and exports; government-mandated countertrade; and any other measure covered by the WTO agreements. Given the breadth of Article X's commitment, competition laws undoubtedly qualify as "laws . . . affecting the sale [and] distribution" of products.

3.025 **e. Article XI.** GATT Article XI, *General Elimination of Quantitative Restrictions*, is straightforward in stating the rule respecting quantitative restrictions (*i.e.* quotas):

> No prohibitions or restrictions other than duties, taxes or other charges, whether made effective through quotas, import or export licences or other measures, shall be instituted or maintained by any contracting party on the importation of any product of the territory of any other contracting party or on the exportation or sale for export of any product destined for the territory of any other contracting party.

The prohibition on quantitative restrictions is broad. First, both import and export quotas are prohibited. Secondly, any type of government measure that may lead to the imposition of a quota is prohibited. The GATT panel report in *Semi-Conductors*[40] rejected Japan's argument that "administrative guidance" by the government to Japanese semi-conductor producers did not fall within the Article XI prohibition because it was not legally binding or mandatory. The panel noted that Article XI:1, unlike other GATT provisions, does not refer solely to laws or regulations, but rather more broadly to "measures". Therefore, any measure maintained by a WTO member that restricts exports effectively is prohibited under Article XI:1, regardless of the legally binding status of the measure. The panel noted further, however, that not all types of government action—such as "jawboning" by government officials—necessarily comes within the scope of Article XI:1. Two criteria must be met:

(1) there are reasonable grounds to believe that sufficient incentives or disincentives exist for non-mandatory measures to take effect; and

(2) the operation of the measures to restrict exports below certain prices requires government action or intervention.[41]

This formulation leaves the question unanswered of what kind of measure, other than formal legislation, would be sufficient to amount to an export restriction prohibited under Article XI.

---

[40] See "Report of the GATT Panel, Japan—Trade in Semi-Conductors", BISD, 35th Supp. 116, 153–55, paras. 104–09 (adopted May 8, 1988).
[41] *id.* at 155, para. 109.

3.026 As is the case with alleged national treatment violations, whether a quantitative restriction has actual trade effects is irrelevant. The existence of a quantitative restriction, regardless of whether it actually impedes imports or exports, violates Article XI:1 because it affects the conditions of competition.[42] In the context of competition policy, government-sanctioned export cartels, which limit the quantity or fix the price of products destined for foreign markets, would appear to violate the express terms of Article XI, as would government-condoned domestic import cartels.

3.027 f. Article XVII. Article XVII:1(a) commits state trading enterprises—government-owned or government-controlled purchasing monopolies and sales monopolies—to act on an MFN basis in all their purchases and sales.[43] Article XVII also covers any enterprise that has been given exclusive or special buying or selling privileges, "formally or in effect". Article XVII:1(b) requires that state trading enterprises make their purchases and sales

> solely in accordance with commercial considerations, including price, quality, availability, marketability, transportation and other conditions of purchase or sale, and shall afford the enterprises of other contracting parties adequate opportunity, in accordance with customary business practice, to compete for participation in such purchases or sales.

The competition policy message of Article XVII is clear: If countries create or authorise state trading enterprises, they must not allow those enterprises to abuse their monopoly buying and purchasing power. No GATT panel has ever found a measure to be in violation of Article XVII *per se*, although, as noted above in connection with the Canadian provincial liquor board panel proceedings, state trading enterprises have been found to violate the national treatment and other GATT obligations.[44]

3.028 g. Article XX(d). Article XX is the general exceptions provision of GATT. The chapeau or preamble to Article XX provides:

---

[42] *See* "Report of the GATT Panel, EEC—Payments and Subsidies Paid to Processors and Producers of Oilseeds and Related Animal-Feed Proteins", BISD, 37th Supp. 86, 130, para. 150 (1991) (hereinafter "EEC—Oilseeds").

[43] Art. XVII:1(a) provides: "Each contracting party undertakes that if it establishes or maintains a State enterprise, wherever located, or grants to any enterprise, formally or in effect, exclusive or special privileges, such enterprise shall, in all its purchases or sales involving either imports or exports, act in a manner consistent with the general principles of non-discriminatory treatment prescribed in this Agreement for governmental measures affecting imports or exports by private traders". Some developed countries and many developing countries, as well as economies in transition, still maintain state trading enterprises. Under the Uruguay Round Understanding on the Interpretation of Article XVII of the General Agreement on Tariffs and Trade 1994, WTO members are obligated to notify all state trading enterprises to the Council for Trade in Goods.

[44] See also "Report of the GATT Panel, Thailand—Restrictions on Importation of and Internal Taxes on Cigarettes", BISD, 37th Supp. 200, 226, para. 80 (adopted Nov. 7, 1990) ("[t]he Thai government may use this monopoly to regulate the overall supply of cigarettes, their prices and their retail availability provided it thereby does not accord imported cigarettes less favourable treatment than domestic cigarettes"). See generally "Guide to GATT Law and Practice", see para. 3.001, n. 1, at 472–82.

> Subject to the requirement that such measures are not applied in a manner which would constitute a means of arbitrary or unjustifiable discrimination between countries where the same conditions prevail, or a disguised restriction on international trade, nothing in this Agreement shall be construed to prevent the adoption or enforcement by any contracting party of [the following] measures: . . .

Any member invoking an Article XX exception must satisfy the two preconditions set out in the chapeau. First, the member must show that its measure is not applied in a manner that constitutes a means of arbitrary or unjustifiable discrimination between countries where the same conditions prevail. Secondly, any such measure must not amount to a disguised restriction on trade.

3.029 Subject to the conditions laid out in the chapeau, Article XX(d) permits members to adopt measures "necessary to secure compliance with laws or regulations which are not inconsistent with the provisions of this Agreement, including those relating to . . . the enforcement of monopolies operated under paragraph 4 of Article II and Article XVII, . . ." This exception was examined in the 1988 panel report on *Restrictions on Imports of Certain Agricultural Products.*[45] In response to Japan's invocation of the Article XX(d) exception in justification of import restrictions administered by an import monopoly, the panel found that:

> Article XX(d) only exempts from the obligations under the General Agreement measures necessary to secure compliance with those laws and regulations 'which are not inconsistent with the provisions of [the General] Agreement.' Article XX(d) therefore does not permit contracting parties to operate monopolies inconsistently with the other provisions of the General Agreement.[46]

The panel concluded that the enforcement of laws and regulations providing for an import restriction made effective through an import monopoly that was inconsistent with Article XI:1 could not be justified under Article XX(d).

3.030 h. Article XXIII:1(b). Article XXIII:1(b), dealing with GATT dispute settlement, permits a contracting party to bring a complaint if it "should consider that any benefit accruing to it directly or indirectly under this Agreement is being nullified or impaired . . . as a result of the application by another contracting party of any measure, whether or not it conflicts with the provisions of this Agreement . . ." The gravamen of an Article XXIII:1(b) non-violation nullification or impairment complaint is that GATT benefits accruing to the complaining member have been nullified or impaired by a measure of another member, but that the measure itself does not violate

[45] "Report of the GATT Panel, Japan—Restrictions on Imports of Certain Agricultural Products", BISD, 35th Supp. 163 (1988).
[46] *id.* at 230, para. 5.2.2.3.

GATT.[47] The underlying purpose of Article XXIII:1(b) was cogently explained by the GATT panel in *EEC -Oilseeds*:

> The idea underlying [Article XXIII:1(b)] is that the improved competitive opportunities that can legitimately be expected from a tariff concession can be frustrated not only by measures proscribed by the General Agreement but also by measures consistent with that Agreement. In order to encourage contracting parties to make tariff concessions they must therefore be given a right of redress when a reciprocal concession is impaired by another contracting party as a result of the application of any measure, whether or not it conflicts with the General Agreement. . . The Panel considered that the main value of a tariff concession is that it provides an assurance of better market access through improved price competition. Contracting parties negotiate tariff concessions primarily to obtain that advantage. They must therefore be assumed to base their tariff negotiations on the expectation that the price effect of the tariff concessions will not be systematically offset. If no right of redress were given to them in such a case they would be reluctant to make tariff concessions and the General Agreement would no longer be useful as a legal framework for incorporating the results of trade negotiations.[48]

3.031 The following example illustrates non-violation nullification or impairment. Assume that Country A agrees to duty-free treatment of widgets imported from Country B and Country B gives a reciprocal concession to Country A on the latter's exports of cogs. Further assume that Country A thereafter makes certain domestic subsidies generally available to all its manufacturers, including its widget manufacturers, thereby permitting its widget manufacturers to lower the price of domestic widgets *vis-à-vis* the price of imported widgets. Country A has not violated any GATT obligations, but it has nullified or impaired the benefit of its duty-free concession it made to Country B on cogs.[49]

3.032 In GATT jurisprudence, most non-violation nullification or impairment cases have arisen where a country, which made a tariff concession thereafter, acted in a way that frustrated the reasonable expectations created by the concession, usually by granting a GATT-consistent domestic subsidy to domestic producers.[50] Besides the outright grant of a subsidy, is there other government action or inaction that constitutes "measures" for purposes of Article XXIII:1(b)? In the 1998 WTO panel report in *Japan—Measures*

---

[47] In a nullification or impairment complaint, a WTO member alleges that it has been denied some or all of the market access it was promised as a quid pro quo for concessions it made to other WTO members in prior GATT trade negotiations due to a violation of a GATT obligation by a member. A nullification or impairment complaint would be brought under GATT Art. XXIII:1(a). For more on the concept of nullification or impairment, see Robert E. Hudec, "A WTO Perspective on Private Anti-Competitive Behavior in World Markets" (1999) 34 New Eng. L. Rev. 79.

[48] "EEC—Oilseeds", see para. 3.026, n. 42, at 128–129, paras. 144, 148.

[49] See generally "Guide to GATT Law and Practice", see para. 3.001, n. 1, at 657–68.

[50] See, *e.g.* "EEC—Oilseeds", see para. 3.026, n. 42, at 86, para. 148. See also Patricia Isela Hansen, "Antitrust in the Global Market: Rethinking 'Reasonable Expectations'", (1999) 73 S. Cal. L. Rev. 276.

Affecting Consumer Photographic Film and Paper,[51] the United States complained that Japan had tolerated and/or actively supported a distribution system for film that amounted to a vertical restraint of trade and unlawfully excluded Eastman Kodak from the Japanese market. In considering the meaning of governmental "measures," the panel offered the following views:

> Whether assistance is financial or non-financial, direct or indirect, does not determine whether its effect may offset the expected result of tariff negotiations. Thus, a Member's industrial policy, pursuing the goal of increasing efficiency in a sector, could in some circumstances upset the competitive relationship in the market place between domestic and imported products in a way that could give rise to a cause of action under Article XXIII:1(b). In the context of a Member's distribution system, for example, it is conceivable that measures that do not infringe GATT rules could be implemented in a manner that effectively results in a disproportionate impact on market conditions for imported products. In this regard, however, we must also bear in mind that tariff concessions have never been viewed as creating a guarantee of trade volumes, but rather . . . as creating expectations as to competitive relationships.[52]

The panel thus made clear that the non-violation nullification or impairment remedy may apply to other types of governmental actions, including the failure to enforce competition laws and not just to the governmental provision of a domestic subsidy to local producers.

3.033 **i. Article XXIII:1(c).** Under Article XXIII:1(c), if benefits accruing to a WTO member under GATT or any WTO agreement are being nullified or impaired "as the result of the existence of any other situation," a WTO member may initiate a panel proceeding and the panel may circulate its report to WTO members. However, none of the other Dispute Settlement Understanding (DSU) procedures apply (*e.g.* rejection of the report by consensus) and none of the DSU remedies are available.

An example of a GATT Article XXIII:1(c) complaint is the 1983 complaint by the E.C. against Japan that the benefits of successive negotiations with Japan had not been realised due to factors peculiar to the Japanese economy that had resulted in a lower level of imports as compared with other industrial countries.[53] The E.C. complaint ultimately was not pursued. In the competition policy context, the United States has levelled similar charges against the structural impediments to market access created by the Japanese *keiretsu* system of vertical integration and interlocking directorships. These charges were in part the subject of the *Kodak-Fuji Film* dispute.

C. Proposals to Add Competition Policy Provisions to GATT 1947

3.034 Even though it is generally recognised that private anti-competitive behaviour can threaten and undermine global trade liberalisation,[54] a proposal

[51] "Report of the WTO Panel, Japan—Measures Affecting Consumer Photographic Film and Paper", WT/DS44/R (adopted Apr. 22, 1998) (hereinafter "Kodak-Fuji Film Dispute").
[52] *id.* at para. 10.38.
[53] See "Guide to GATT Law and Practice", see para. 3.001, n. 1, at 670–71.
[54] See, e.g. "WTO Cites Need for Competition Rules for Business Practices that Restrict Trade", (1997) 14 Int'l Trade Rep. (BNA) 2221.

to add the provisions of Chapter V of the Havana Charter dealing with cartels to GATT 1947 died in 1955 after a consensus failed to build for the proposal at the 1954–55 Review Session of the GATT Contracting Parties.[55] In 1958 the Contracting Parties adopted a resolution on restrictive business practices and appointed a group of experts "to study and make recommendations with regard to whether, to what extent if at all, and how the Contracting Parties should undertake to deal with restrictive business practices in international trade."[56] The expert group's 1960 report concluded and recommended:

> that the Contracting Parties should now be regarded as an appropriate and competent body to initiate action in the field . . . and should encourage direct consultations between contracting parties with a view to the elimination of the harmful effects of particular restrictive practices.[57]

Interestingly, however, the experts group was divided over what to recommend in the way of future measures and the applicability of the GATT dispute settlement mechanism contained in Article XXIII:

> The majority felt that, as experts on restrictive business practices rather than on the legal aspects of GATT, the Group were not competent to judge whether restrictive business practices were a matter that could be deemed to fall under any specific provisions of GATT—for example, whether the provisions of Article XXIII would be applicable. However, the majority were convinced that, regardless of the question whether Article XXIII could legally be applied, they should recommend to the Contracting Parties that they take no action under this Article. Such action would involve the grave risk of retaliatory measures under the provisions of paragraph 2 of that Article, which would be taken on the basis of judgments which would have to be made without adequate factual information about the restrictive business practices in question.
>
> The minority hold the view that [when consultations fail to lead to voluntary settlements] the provisions of paragraph 2 of Article XXIII are applicable. According to the first part of this paragraph the Contracting Parties shall, when matters are referred to them, make appropriate recommendations to the contracting parties concerned. While referring to these provisions, the minority advise against the use by the Contracting Parties of the authority conferred upon them under the second part of paragraph 2.[58]

3.035 In response to this recommendation and to the lack of consensus among the GATT Contracting Parties on a multilateral antitrust agreement, in

[55] See "Guide to GATT Law and Practice", see para. 3.001, n. 1, (1995) vol. 2, at 650–51. The GATT Contracting Parties is the predecessor of the WTO Ministerial Conference which is composed of representatives of all WTO members and has ultimate responsibility for carrying out the functions of the WTO. See "Agreement Establishing the World Trade Organization", art. IV:1.

[56] Resolution of Nov. 5, 1958 on "Restrictive Business Practices—Appointment of Group of Experts," BISD, 7th Supp. 29 (1958).

[57] GATT, L/1015, BISD, 9th Supp. 170, 171 (1960).

[58] *id.* at 172, para. 8; 177, para. 18.

1960 the Contracting Parties adopted a Decision on Arrangements for Consultations on Restrictive Business Practices.[59] The 1960 Decision exhorts the Contracting Parties to consult over RBPs. The Decision recommends in pertinent part:

> [A]t the request of any contracting party a contracting party should enter into consultations on such practices on a bilateral or multilateral basis as appropriate. The party addressed should accord sympathetic consideration to and should afford adequate opportunity for consultations with the requesting party, with a view to reaching mutually satisfactory conclusions, and if it agrees that such harmful effects are present it should take such measures as it deems appropriate to eliminate these effects, and Decide that:
>
> (a) If the requesting party and the party addressed are able to reach a mutually satisfactory conclusion, they should advise the secretariat of the nature of the complaint and the conclusions reached;
> (b) If the requesting party and the party addressed are unable to reach a mutually satisfactory conclusion, they should advise the secretariat of the nature of the complaint and the fact that a mutually satisfactory conclusion cannot be reached;
> (c) The secretariat shall convey the information referred to under (a) and (b) to the Contracting Parties.[60]

The Group of Experts concluded that the complexities of international antitrust enforcement and the difficulty of obtaining complete and accurate information on private business activities made it impracticable to create GATT procedures for investigating and resolving individual cases. Therefore, the Decision did not provide for any participation by advisory expert panels or groups, nor did it refer to the GATT Article XXIII dispute settlement mechanism.[61] The consultative mechanism has been invoked only once in 40 years and then in connection with the U.S.-Japan dispute over market access for photographic film.[62] However, bilateral consultations between the United States and Japan never got under way.[63] In 1961 GATT convened a group of experts to study and report on the feasibility of an international antitrust agreement again. That expert group reported that an insufficient lack of consensus exists in the world community about what kind of practices are anti-competitive and, therefore, merit attention from antitrust enforcement authorities.[64]

[59] "Decision on Restrictive Business Practices: Arrangements for Consultations", BISD, 9th Supp. 28 (1960).
[60] *id.* at 28–29.
[61] See GATT, L/1015, BISD, 9th Supp. 172, para. 8; 177, para. 18. See also Kintner, et al., see para. 3.005, n. 12, at 90 (the Decision "represents the first commitment actually reached among nations to cooperate in curbing the admitted evil of restrictive business practices.").
[62] See Office of the USTR, Press Release, "Acting U.S. Trade Representative Charlene Barshefsky Announces Action on Film" (June 13, 1996).
[63] See Merit E. Janow, "Unilateral and Bilateral Approaches to Competition Policy Drawing on the Trade Experience", in *Brookings Trade Forum 1998*, (Robert Z. Lawrence ed. 1988) at 253, 261–62 & n. 17.
[64] See "Report of the Group of Experts on Restrictive Business Practices: Arrangements for Consultations", BISD, 9th Supp. 170 (1961).

D. GATT Dispute Settlement Proceedings involving Competition Policy Issues

3.036 Within GATT the issue of restrictive business practices and international trade entered into a period of dormancy during the 1960s and 1970s. In the 1980s the issue of restrictive business practices and their effect on international trade once again surfaced in the context of GATT dispute settlement proceedings.

1. The Canadian Foreign Investment Review Act Dispute

3.037 In 1984, a GATT panel examined, among other things, the consistency of Canada's Foreign Investment Review Act *vis-à-vis* the national treatment obligation and the GATT Article XI prohibition on quantitative restrictions of imports and exports. Under the Foreign Investment Review Act (since replaced by the Investment Canada Act), the Canadian government could require that foreign investors agree to source inputs locally as a condition to approving certain large foreign direct investments in the country. Addressing the anti-competitive effects that written undertakings between the Canadian government and an investor could have, the panel was not moved by Canada's argument that such undertakings were private contractual obligations on which GATT was silent:

> The Panel carefully examined the Canadian view that the purchase undertakings should be considered as private contractual obligations of particular foreign investors via-a-vis the Canadian government. The Panel recognized that investors might have an economic advantage in assuming purchase undertakings, taking into account the other conditions under which the investment was permitted. The Panel felt, however, that even if this was so, private contractual obligations entered into by investors should not adversely affect the rights which contracting parties, including contracting parties not involved in the dispute, possess under Article III:4 of the General Agreement [national treatment] and which they can exercise on behalf of their exporters. This applies in particular to the rights deriving from the national treatment principle, which—as stated in Article III:1—is aimed at preventing the use of internal measures "so as to afford protection to domestic producers.[65]

3.037/1 The 1994 Uruguay Round TRIMs Agreement was negotiated in partial response to the government practice of imposing local content requirements on investors, both foreign and domestic, by prohibiting WTO members from requiring:

> the purchase or use by an enterprise of products of domestic origin or from any domestic source, whether specified in terms of particular products, in terms of value of products, or in terms of a proportion of volume or value of its local production; . . .[66]

[65] "Report of the GATT Panel, Canada—Administration of the Foreign Investment Review Act", BISD, 30th Supp. 140, 159, para. 5.6 (1984).

[66] TRIMs Agreement, Annex 1(a).

2. *The Copper Cartel Dispute*

3.038 In 1986 the E.C. requested that a GATT working party be established to examine whether an alleged producers' cartel on refined copper and copper concentrates existed in Japan. The E.C. claimed that their copper smelting and refining industry had serious difficulties in obtaining adequate supplies of copper concentrates at competitive prices. The E.C. smelters and refiners claimed that their Japanese counterparts offered prices for copper concentrates higher than what the E.C. smelters and refiners offered, thus enabling the Japanese smelters and refiners to obtain disproportionately large shares of concentrates. The E.C. smelters and refiners alleged that the high domestic price of refined copper in Japan made it possible for Japanese smelters in turn to offer high prices for concentrates. This ability on the part of Japanese smelters was attributed in part to high Japanese tariffs on imports of refined copper, concealed import restrictions, possibly hidden domestic subsidies and a price cartel operated by the Japanese producers.[67]

The Personal Representative of the Director-General issued a report in 1989, concluding that:

> Japan has not violated any of its GATT obligations. Nor was any evidence presented of the existence of a producers' cartel. Although certain kinds of government assistance (research funds, aid for stockpiling, unemployment aids etc.) have been extended in both Japan and the EEC, these do not appear to be of the sorts or amounts that have had any significant impact on the competitive position of the industry in either Japan or the EEC.[68]

Thus, the E.C. failed to produce evidence of a government-supported producers' cartel. The E.C. was to have better success in 1988 in the dispute settlement proceeding involving semiconductors from Japan.

3. *The Semiconductors Dispute*

3.039 Bilateral trade in semiconductors between the United States and Japan were covered by an arrangement first negotiated in 1986, renewed in modified form in 1996.[69] The arrangement grew out of a settlement of an antidumping complaint filed by U.S. semiconductor producers against Japanese semiconductor manufacturers. The 1986 arrangement was in essence a government-sanctioned, market-sharing agreement under the terms of which

[67] See "Good Offices Report of the Personal Representative of the Director-General", BISD, 36th Supp. 199, 200, para. 1 (1989), reprinted in part in "GATT Analytical Index", see para. 3.001, n. 1, at 652.

[68] *id.* at 201, para. 4.

[69] The 1996 agreement creates a forum for co-operative efforts in areas such as standards, intellectual property protection, and trade liberalisation. Texts of the arrangements and agreements are available from the web site of the Electronic Industries Association of Japan (EIAJ) at http://www.eiaj.org. For additional reading on the U.S.-Japan semiconductor trade regime, see Robert Carr, "Evolution of the U.S.-Japanese Semiconductor Trade Regime", Industry, Trade, & Tech. Rev. 45 (USITC Jan. 1997); Office of the USTR, "Semiconductor Market Share in Japan Reaches 29.4% in the Fourth Quarter", Press Release (May 1, 1997).

(1) Japan guaranteed access to U.S. producers of a share of the Japanese semiconductor market;

(2) Japanese producers would raise their semiconductor prices; and

(3) Japan would restrict exports of Japanese semiconductors to the U.S. market.

Concerned that excess capacity in Japan would lead to dumping of semiconductors in the E.C. market, the E.C. filed a GATT complaint.

3.040 In the panel proceeding, Japan claimed that there were no governmental measures limiting the right of Japanese producers and exporters to export semiconductors at any price they wished. Exports were limited, Japan argued,

> by private enterprises in their own self-interest and such private action was outside the scope of Article XI:1 [prohibiting government quotas on exports and imports].[70]

The panel rejected Japan's contention, finding that:

> an administrative structure has been created by the Government of Japan which operated to exert maximum possible pressure on the private sector to cease exporting at prices below company-specific costs. . . [T]he complex of measures exhibited . . . the essential elements of a formal system of export control.[71]

4. *Japanese Keiretsu*

3.041 Finally, the Japanese *keiretsu* system of vertical integration among manufacturing assemblers, their suppliers, and banks (bolstered by cross-ownership of shareholdings) has been a continuing source of friction between Japan and both the E.U. and the United States. Although never formally the subject of a GATT panel proceeding, the existence of *keiretsu* has been a lightening rod. For example, the inability of U.S. automobile parts suppliers to sell in the Japanese market has been attributed to *keiretsu*. It has been a focal point of U.S. demands for more aggressive enforcement by the Japan Fair Trade Commission of Japan's antitrust laws.[72]

II. WTO RULES ON COMPETITION POLICY

3.042 The GATT-WTO system in the main targets market access barriers to trade in goods and services that are the result of *government*, not private,

[70] "Report of the GATT Panel, Japan—Trade in Semi-Conductors", BISD, 35th Supp. 116, 153, para. 102 (1988).

[71] *id.* at 157–58, para. 117.

[72] See generally Kinya Kubo, "Distribution *Keiretsu* and Competition Policy in Japan", in *International Harmonization of Competition Laws* 75 (Chia-Jui Cheng, Lawrence S. Liu, & Chih-Kang Wang eds. 1995); Jiro Tamura, "Foreign Firm Access to Japanese Distribution Systems: Trends in Japanese Antitrust Enforcement", in *Antitrust: A New Trade Remedy?* (John O. Haley & Hiroshi Iyori eds. 1995) 267.

measures. Generally, the WTO does not regulate, prohibit, or condemn private anti-competitive behaviour that impedes market access. Viewed broadly, however, most WTO agreements could be regarded as related to competition policy in that they limit the ability of governments to impose trade measures that would have the effect of restraining or distorting competition from foreign sources in markets for goods and services.[73]

3.043 Nevertheless, the removal of government trade barriers may provide only limited market access where monopolies dominate a foreign market or horizontal and vertical restraints restrict access of foreign-source goods and services to a domestic market. This is certainly a legitimate concern in a number of services sectors, of which basic telecommunications is the clearest example. In situations where liberalisation has already taken place through the removal of tariff and non-tariff barriers to trade, private business practices can have the effect of replacing traditional tariff and other non-tariff barriers to foreign markets. Some practices can be subtle and appear benign, such as standards set by industry associations or non-governmental standards-setting organisations that are then promulgated by governments as mandatory measures. They may have the effect of restricting market access. The *raison d'être* of the GATT-WTO system is to open markets to the cross-border movement of goods and services, therefore, a number of WTO agreements address the issue of private restrictive business practices, albeit ever so lightly.

A. Competition Policy Issues addressed in the Uruguay Round Agreements

3.044 Seven Uruguay Round agreements address the issue of restrictive business practices to varying degrees:

(1) the TRIPS Agreement;

(2) the GATS and three GATS-related agreements,
   (a) the 1994 Understanding on Financial Services,
   (b) the GATS Annex on Telecommunications, and
   (c) the 1997 Basic Telecoms Agreement;

(3) the TRIMs Agreement; and

(4) and the Safeguards Agreement.

A handful of other competition policy-related provisions are sprinkled throughout a number of Uruguay Round agreements as well.

1. *The TRIPS Agreement*

3.045 Among the signal achievements of the Uruguay Round, the TRIPS Agreement ranks high among them. The TRIPS Agreement is one of two

[73] WTO, "Working Group on the Interaction between Trade and Competition Policy, Report to the General Council", WT/WGTCP/2, at 21, para. 58 (Dec. 8, 1998) (hereinafter "WGTCP 1998 Report").

Uruguay Round Agreements—the other being the General Agreement on Trade in Services—that breaks new ground by not dealing with trade in goods, GATT's traditional sphere of competence. The TRIPS Agreement takes the GATT-WTO system into uncharted territory.[74] Some consider the TRIPS Agreement the most remarkable achievement of the entire Uruguay Round.[75] It fills the intellectual property right (IPR) gap within GATT by establishing minimum levels of protection for copyrights, trademarks, geographical indications, industrial designs, patents, plant varieties, computer chip layout designs and trade secrets. It couples these IPR protections with the requirement that WTO members adopt effective enforcement mechanisms. Unlike other GATT commitments, which mainly obligate members to refrain from taking certain proscribed actions, the TRIPS Agreement obligates members to take affirmative action by adopting both minimum standards of IPR protection and domestic enforcement mechanisms. Not only is the TRIPS Agreement important in its own right for the competition policy provisions within it, but the TRIPS Agreement also has been cited by proponents of a WTO competition policy agreement as a possible model for a framework competition policy agreement. Therefore, it is useful to review the TRIPS Agreement and the other intellectual property provisions of GATT 1994.

3.046 Outside of the TRIPS Agreement, the subject of intellectual property rights receives only passing mention in GATT. First, GATT Article IX, *Marks of Origin*, directs the contracting parties to

> co-operate with each other with a view to preventing the use of trade names in such manner as to misrepresent the true origin of the product, to the detriment of such distinctive regional or geographical names of products of the territory of a contracting party as are protected by its legislation.[76]

[74] For a summary of the Uruguay Round negotiations leading to the TRIPS Agreement, see Carlos A. Primo Braga, "Trade-Related Intellectual Property Issues: The Uruguay Round Agreement and Its Economic Implications", in *The Uruguay Round and the Developing Countries* (Will Martin & L. Alan Winters eds. 1995) 381, 384; John Croome, *Reshaping the World Trading System: A History of the Uruguay Round* (1995) 130, 251, 283; Ernest H. Preeg, *Traders in a Brave New World: The Uruguay Round and the Future of the International Trading System* (1995). See generally *Edmond McGovern, International Trade Regulation*, (1995) ch. 21; *The Uruguay* Round Trade Agreements, Statement of Administrative Action, H.R. Doc. No. 316, vol. 1, 103d Cong., 2d Sess. 981 (1994); L. Peter Farkas, "Trade-Related Aspects of Intellectual Property", in *The World Trade Organization: Multilateral Framework for the 21st Century and U.S. Implementing Legislation* (Terence P. Stewart ed. 1996) 463; Frederick M. Abbott, "The Future of the Multilateral Trading System in the Context of TRIPS", (1997) 20 Hastings Int'l & Comp. L. Rev. 661; J.H. Reichman, "Universal Minimum Standards of Intellectual Property Protection under the TRIPS Component of the WTO Agreement", (1995) 29 Int'l Law. 345; J.H. Reichman, "The TRIPS Component of the GATT's Uruguay Round: Competitive Prospects for Intellectual Property Owners in an Integrated World Market", (1993) 4 Fordham Intell. Prop., Media & Entertainment L.J. 171; Ralph Oman, "Intellectual Property After the Uruguay Round", (1994) 42 J. Copyright Soc. 18; Jeffrey A. Divney & Gary J. Connell, "Intellectual Property Provisions of the GATT", (1994) 23 Colo. L. Rev. 1069; Hans Ullrich, "TRIPS: Adequate Protection, Inadequate Trade, Adequate Competition Policy", (1995) 4 Pac. Rim L. & Pol'y J. 153; Michael L. Doane, "TRIPS and International Intellectual Property Protection in an Age of Advancing Technology", (1994) 9 Am. U.J. Int'l L. & Pol'y 465.

[75] See, *e.g.* McGovern, *supra* note 74, s. 21.211.

[76] GATT art. IX:6.

Article IX further provides that when importing members adopt laws and regulations relating to marks of origin, they balance the burden such laws and regulations may impose on exporting countries against "the necessity of protecting consumers against fraudulent or misleading indications."[77]

3.047 Secondly, Article XII, *Restrictions to Safeguard the Balance of Payments*, provides that if an importing country imposes quantitative restrictions for balance-of-payments (BOP) purposes, it "not apply restrictions which would . . . prevent compliance with patent, trade mark, copyright, or similar procedures."[78] A parallel prohibition is found in Article XVIII:10 for developing countries that impose quantitative restrictions for BOP purposes.

3.048 Thirdly, Article XX, *General Exceptions*, authorises members to adopt trade measures that are necessary to secure compliance with domestic laws and regulations for "the protection of patents, trade marks and copyrights, and the prevention of deceptive practices."[79] Two leading examples of such laws and regulations in the United States are section 337 of the Tariff Act of 1930, which authorises the International Trade Commission (ITC) to ban the importation of goods that infringe IPRs owned by U.S. nationals, and Customs Service regulations on the importation of grey market goods.

3.049 In addition to the few GATT Articles dealing with IPRs, two GATT panels have concluded that national patent laws are internal regulations that are subject to Article III's national treatment obligation.[80] These original GATT provisions were neither intended nor designed to be a comprehensive international IPR legal regime. First steps toward addressing the problem of counterfeit goods were taken in the Tokyo Round in the form of a proposed Anti-Counterfeiting Code. A consensus failed to build for its adoption. The Quad members (Canada, the E.U., Japan and the United States) continued to press for adoption of such a code within GATT in the 1980s, but they faced strong opposition from Brazil and India.[81]

Developed countries recognised the IPR-protection gap in GATT insofar as minimum IP standards and effective IPR protection against counterfeit goods were concerned. They were also frustrated with the World Intellectual Property Organisation's (WIPO) lack of significant progress in securing universal participation in IPR conventions and effective international IPR protection. Consequently, developed countries—the Quad members in particular[82]—

[77] *id.* art. IX:2.

[78] *id.* Art. XII:3(c)(iii).

[79] *id.* Art. XX(d).

[80] See "Report of the GATT Panel, United States—Section 337 of the Tariff Act of 1930", BISD, 36th Supp. 402 (1989); "Report of the GATT Panel, United States—Imports of Certain Automotive Spring Assemblies", BISD, 30th Supp. 107 (1984).

[81] The GATT discussions on IPR protections that occurred between the Tokyo and Uruguay Rounds are summarised in Primo Braga, see para. 3.045, n. 74, at 384.

[82] The USTR released a statement in 1986 that the United States would seek to conclude "an enforceable multilateral trade agreement against trade-distorting practices arising from inadequate protection of intellectual property." Office of the U.S. Trade Representative, "Administration Statement on the Protection of U.S. Intellectual Property Rights Abroad", (1986) at 4.

When Congress passed the Omnibus Trade and Competitiveness Act of 1988, that included fast-track negotiating authority for the President in the Uruguay Round, it listed among its 16 trade negotiating objectives adequate, substantive intellectual property protection within the GATT system. See 19 U.S.C. 2901(b)(10).

pushed hard for including IPR protection in the Uruguay Round agenda. Many developing countries resisted, most notably the so-called Group of 10.[83] They argued that IPRs were within the exclusive jurisdiction of WIPO in the international arena and that IPR negotiations under GATT auspices were thus inappropriate.[84] In the end, of course, the developed countries' position prevailed.

3.050 As a result of the pioneering efforts at the Uruguay Round to formally link IPR protection to trade under the TRIPS Agreement, the World Trade Organisation now assumes some of the functions formerly performed by WIPO. More importantly, through the dispute settlement provisions of the WTO Dispute Settlement Understanding, the WTO wields an IPR enforcement club that WIPO does not have and never has had.[85]

3.051 As is the case with most international agreements, the TRIPS Agreement represents a series of compromises. The Agreement gives developed countries the substantive minimum standards and procedural protections they wanted. At the same time, the Agreement accommodated developing countries to some extent by giving them generous transition periods. The Agreement does not achieve all the goals that some developed countries sought. For example, the 10-year transition period given to all members within which to adopt laws providing for the patentability of drugs was criticised by the U.S. pharmaceutical industry. Conversely, developing countries criticised the Agreement's restrictions on the use of compulsory licencing. The TRIPS Agreement is primarily concerned with trade, not competition.[86] Nevertheless, the Agreement contains three provisions on IPRs and competition law:

---

[83] The Group of 10 developing countries were Argentina, Brazil, Cuba, Egypt, India, Nicaragua, Nigeria, Peru, Tanzania and the former Yugoslavia.

[84] See Alan S. Gutterman, "The North-South Debate Regarding the Protection of Intellectual Property Rights", (1993) 28 Wake Forest L. Rev. 89. When Congress approved fast-track negotiating authority for the President in connection with the Uruguay Round, it addressed this concern by providing that the inclusion of intellectual property protections within the GATT system was "without prejudice to other complementary initiatives undertaken in other international organizations." See Omnibus Trade and Competitiveness Act of 1988, 19 U.S.C. s. 2901(b)(10)(C).

[85] In 1995, the WTO and WIPO concluded a co-operation agreement covering various administrative matters. See "Agreement Between the World Intellectual Property Organisation and the World Trade Organisation", Dec. 22, 1995 reprinted in 35 Int'l Legal Materials (1996) 754. The text of the Agreement is available from the WTO's website at http://www.wto.org/wto/intellec/17–wipo.htm.

As events in late 1996 demonstrated, WIPO continues to be the premier international forum within which to negotiate international conventions on IPR protection. In Dec. 1996, negotiations were conducted under WIPO auspices on three new treaties covering copyright of music and artistic works, copyright of computer software, and copyright of computer databases on the Internet. Two treaties were successfully concluded: the Treaty on Copyright Law, and the Treaty on Performers and Phonograms. The Copyright Treaty expands on the Berne Convention in two respects. First, it recognises a right of reproduction and communication. Secondly, it establishes a right of making available to the public. Both rights are recognised under current U.S. copyright law under the right of distribution. The Performers and Phonograms Treaty closes another gap in the Berne Convention by extending copyright protection to sound recordings. The text of these treaties is available from the WIPO website at http:www.wipo.org/eng/iplex/index.htm. See "WIPO Delegates Agree on Two Copyright Treaties", (1997) 14 Int'l Trade Rep. (BNA) 11.

[86] See Hans Ullrich, "TRIPS: Adequate Protection, Inadequate Trade, Adequate Competition Policy", in *Antitrust: A New Trade Remedy?* (John O. Haley & Hiroshi Iyori eds. 1995) 153.

(1) WTO members are free to adopt measures to prevent the abuse of intellectual property rights;[87]
(2) members are limited in the conditions they may impose on compulsory licencing;[88] and
(3) members are free to adopt measures regulating anti-competitive practices under licencing agreements.[89]

3.052 **a. Abuse of IPRs.** Article 7, *Objectives*, and Article 8, *Principles*, may serve an important interpretative function in dispute settlement proceedings under the Agreement, especially in proceedings between developed and developing countries. Article 7 provides:

> The protection and enforcement of intellectual property rights should contribute to the promotion of technological innovation and to the transfer and dissemination of technology, to the mutual advantage of producers and users of technological knowledge and in a manner conducive to social and economic welfare, and to a balance of rights and obligations.

3.053 Building on these broad principles, Article 8.1 permits members to adopt measures to protect public health and nutrition, and to promote the public interest in sectors of vital importance to their socio-economic and technological development, provided such measures are consistent with the Agreement. Article 8.2 further recognises that national measures may be needed to prevent

(1) the abuse of IPRs by IPR owners, or
(2) the resort to practices that unreasonably restrain trade or adversely affect international technology transfer.[90]

This last provision was drafted to address concerns raised by developing countries that most IPRs are owned by nationals of developed countries who allegedly use the exclusive rights conferred by IPRs to engage in anti-competitive practices to the detriment of the economic interests of developing countries. However, the proviso in Article 8.2, "provided they are consistent with this Agreement," makes clear that the Article is not a general exceptions clause. Rather, it has been suggested that action to prevent abuse of IPRs is limited to those specifically provided for in the TRIPS Agreement, such as Article 40 on the control of anti-competitive practices in licencing agreements or Article 31 on compulsory licencing.[91]

---

[87] See TRIPS Agreement Art. 8.
[88] See *id.* Art. 31.
[89] See *id.* Art. 40.
[90] Art. 8.2 of the TRIPS Agreement provides: "Appropriate measures, provided they are consistent with the provisions of this Agreement, may be needed to prevent the abuse of intellectual property rights by right holders or the resort to practices which unreasonably restrain trade or adversely affect the international transfer of technology".
[91] See Competition Elements in International Trade Agreements, see para. 3.010, n. 20, at 14–15.

3.054 b. Anti-Competitive Licencing Agreements. Article 40, *Control of Anti-Competitive Practices in Contractual Relations*,[92] addresses the control of anti-competitive practices in contractual licences. It recognises that abuses of IPRs can have an adverse effect on competition. Article 40 permits members to adopt appropriate measures to prevent or regulate licensing practices that restrain competition and that, accordingly, constitute an abuse of IPRs.

3.055 A non-exhaustive list of practices that members may prevent or control include the following:

(1) exclusive grantback conditions that force a licensee to grant the licensor a licence to any spin-off patents that a licensee may acquire during the term of a technology transfer agreement,

(2) contract terms that prevent challenges to the validity of a patent, and

(3) coercive package licensing (*i.e.* unlawful tying arrangements that require that the licensee purchase goods and services from the licensor).[93]

Article 40 also requires members to consult with one another upon request when a national of another member is charged with engaging in anti-competitive licensing practices. Together, Articles 8 and 40 ensure that developed and developing countries are not hamstrung in their ability to address anti-competitive business practices associated with the use of IPRs.

Article 40 is silent with regard to contract terms designed to prevent grey market or parallel imports from a licensee to the licensor's home market. In addition, Article 6 provides "nothing in this Agreement shall be used to address the issue of the exhaustion of intellectual property rights." The doctrine of exhaustion has a direct bearing on the issue of grey market goods, discussed below.

3.056 c. Deceptive Practices. In the case of trademarks, Article 16 confers on the owner of a registered trademark the exclusive right to prevent all third parties not having the owner's consent from using identical or similar signs for goods or services that are identical or similar to those for which the trademark is registered. Where identical marks are used on identical goods or services, a likelihood of confusion is presumed. Limiting protected rights

---

[92] Art. 40 of the TRIPS Agreement provides the following in connection with anti-competitive licensing practices: "1. Members agree that some licensing practices or conditions pertaining to intellectual property rights which restrain competition may have adverse effects on trade and may impede the transfer and dissemination of technology. 2. Nothing in this Agreement shall prevent Members from specifying in their legislation licensing practices or conditions that may in particular cases constitute an abuse of intellectual property rights having an adverse effect on competition in the relevant market. . . . [A] Member may adopt . . . appropriate measures to prevent or control such practices, which may include for example exclusive grantback conditions, conditions preventing challenge to validity and coercive package licensing . . . . 3. Each Member shall enter, upon request, into consultations with any other Member which has cause to believe that an intellectual property right owner that is a national or domiciliary of the Member to which the request for consultations has been addressed is undertaking practices in violation of the requesting Member's laws and regulations. . . "

[93] See *id.* Art. 40.2.

under trademark to cases where confusion exists reflects a fair competition and consumer protection rationale.

In the case of geographical indications, Article 22 defines "geographical indications" as indications that identify a good as originating in the territory, region, or locality of a member, where a particular quality, reputation, or other characteristic of the good is essentially attributable to its geographic origin (*e.g.* a Swiss watch, French champagne, or Colombian coffee). Article 22.2 requires members to provide interested parties the legal means by which to prevent the use of product descriptions that mislead the public regarding the geographic origin of a good or that constitute an act of unfair competition within the meaning of Article 10 *bis* of the Paris Convention. Article 22.3 further requires members to refuse registration or invalidate trademark registrations for goods that use product descriptions that mislead the public regarding the geographic origin of a good. Also prohibited are geographic indications that, although literally true as to the territory, region, or locality in which the goods originate, falsely represent to the public that the goods originate in another territory (*e.g.* a geographical indication that perfume is from Paris, but fails to mention that the place is Paris, Michigan, not Paris, France).[94]

3.057 **d. Compulsory Licensing.** In order to shield patent owners from excessive government encroachment on their exclusive rights, Article 31 tightly regulates any compulsory licence system (euphemistically referred to in the Agreement as "other use without authorization of the right holder") that is used by a member to force a patent owner to license a government entity or a third party designated by the member.

Circumstances in which a compulsory licence may be authorised in countries with such measures include situations where the owner fails to work the invention within a certain period of time after receiving a patent, or to prevent or remedy other anti-competitive practices that might result or have resulted from the exercise of the exclusive patent rights by the owner.[95]

3.058 When authorising a compulsory licence, a member's action is circumscribed in the following respects:

(1) Authorisation of such use must be considered on its individual merits.

(2) Unless it is to remedy an anti-competitive practice, such use may only be permitted if the proposed user has made efforts to obtain authorisation from the patent owner on reasonable commercial terms and conditions and that such efforts have not been successful within a reasonable period of time.[96]

[94] See TRIPS Agreement Art. 22.4.

[95] U.S. law authorises the issuance of compulsory licenses under the Atomic Energy Act, the Clean Air Act, and the Energy Policy Act. See "Statement of Administrative Action", see para. 3.045, n. 74, at 1005. Regulations governing the grant of compulsory licences comply with the TRIPS Agreement criteria, with the exception of the restrictions on the compulsory licensing of semiconductor technology, which were amended. See *id.*

[96] This requirement may be waived by a Member in cases of national emergency, circumstances of extreme urgency, or public non-commercial use. See TRIPS Agreement Art. 31(b).

(3) The scope and duration of such use shall be limited to the purposes for which it was authorised.[97]

(4) Such use shall be non-exclusive.

(5) Such use shall be non-assignable, except with that part of the enterprise or goodwill which enjoys such use.

(6) Unless it is to remedy an anti-competitive practice, any such use must be authorised predominately for the supply of the domestic market of the Member authorising such use.[98]

(7) Authorisation for such use is subject to termination when a change in the circumstances which led to it no longer exist.

(8) The patent owner must be paid adequate remuneration. The need to correct any anti-competitive practices may be taken into account in determining the amount of the remuneration.

(9) The validity of any decision relating to the authorisation or to the remuneration shall be subject to judicial or other independent review by a higher authority within the Member.

(10) Where such use is authorised to permit the exploitation of a patent ("the second patent") which cannot be exploited without infringing another patent ("the first patent," which is the subject matter of the compulsory licence),

(a) the invention claimed in the second patent shall involve an important technical advance of considerable economic significance in relation to the invention claimed in the first patent,

(b) the owner of the first patent shall be entitled to a cross-licence on reasonable terms to use the invention claimed in the second patent, and

(c) the use authorised in respect of the first patent shall be non-assignable except with the assignment of the second patent.

3.059 Article 5 of the Paris Convention adds two important qualifications regarding compulsory licences. First, no proceedings for the forfeiture or revocation of a patent may be instituted before the expiration of two years from the grant of the first compulsory licence. Secondly, a compulsory licence may not be applied for on the ground of failure to work or insufficient working of the invention before the expiration of a period of four years from the date of filing of the patent application or three years from the date of the grant of the patent, whichever period expires last.

2. *The GATS*

3.060 The GATS contains several general obligations and disciplines with respect to anti-competitive activities of private business that bind all WTO

[97] A special requirement for semiconductor technology provides that the scope of the use shall be only for public non-commercial use (*e.g.* educational use) or to remedy a practice determined after judicial or administrative process to be anti-competitive. See TRIPS Agreement Art. 31(c).

[98] In the case of a customs union such as the E.U., it is an open question whether the relevant market is the entire territory of the customs union or the territory of an individual Member State.

members, regardless of the specific market access commitments made in their Schedule of Commitments. The GATS also imposes obligations and disciplines applicable solely to services sectors for which a member has made a specific market access commitment.

First, as a threshold matter, GATS Article I:1 provides that "[t]his Agreement applies to measures by Members affecting trade in services." Article I:3 in turn defines "measures by Members" to include measures taken by "non-governmental bodies in the exercise of powers delegated by central, regional or local governments or authorities," thus covering private conduct.

3.061 Secondly, with respect to general obligations and disciplines binding on all members regardless of market access commitments, Article VII encourages the mutual recognition of licences and certificates issued by other members—that is, to give full faith and credit to other members' licences and certificates. Article VII is designed to prevent the use of licencing and certification as a barrier to market access by foreign service suppliers. Bilateral, plurilateral, and multilateral mutual recognition agreements also are encouraged, provided that other WTO members are given adequate opportunity to become parties to such agreements.[99] Members are required to notify the Council for Trade in Services of any new recognition measures or agreements or any existing ones that they have in place.[1] Wherever appropriate, recognition should be based on multilaterally agreed-upon criteria.[2]

3.062 Article VIII, *Monopolies and Exclusive Service Suppliers*, obligates members to ensure that any monopoly service supplier in its territory, whether public or private, does not act in a manner inconsistent with the GATS Article II MFN requirement, that is, does not discriminate against foreign firms in the provision of services. That Article further requires that with respect to service sectors covered in a member's schedule of commitments, members ensure that when a monopoly supplier, as well as an exclusive service supplier whose rights are granted by the government, competes in the supply of a service outside the scope of its monopoly rights, it does not abuse its monopoly position by acting in a manner inconsistent with that member's commitments on national treatment and market access for foreign service suppliers. Article VIII also obligates members to consult with each other regarding restrictive business practices of certain incumbent service suppliers.[3]

---

[99] See GATS Art. VII:2. On May 29, 1997, the Council for Trade in Services adopted "Guidelines for Mutual Recognition Agreements or Arrangements in the Accountancy Sector". The text of the Guidelines is available from the WTO's web site http://www.wto.org.

[1] See GATS Art. VII:4. For example, on Feb. 10, 1997 the United States filed notifications under GATS Article VII:4 regarding mutual recognition agreements with Canada on certifications, accreditations, and educational equivalency for architects, and with Australia, Hong Kong, Ireland, New Zealand, South Africa and the United Kingdom for engineers. See Notification Pursuant to Article VII.4 of the General Agreement on Trade in Services, United States, Architecture, S/C/N/52 (1997); Notification Pursuant to Article VII.4 of the General Agreement on Trade in Services, United States, Engineering, S/C/N/53 (1997).

[2] See GATS Art. VII:5.

[3] Arts VIII provides in part: "1. Each Member shall ensure that any monopoly supplier of a service in its territory does not, in the supply of the monopoly service in the relevant market, act

GATS Article IX, *Business Practices*, provides that "certain business practices of service suppliers, other than the practices mentioned in Article VIII, may restrain competition and thereby restrict trade in services." Members are, therefore, under an obligation to enter into consultations with any other member with a view to eliminating such RBPs. It also imposes a duty to co-operate by providing non-confidential information of relevance to the matter in issue.

3.063 **a. The GATS Telecoms Annex.** The telecommunications sector serves a dual role as both a distinct sector of economic activity and as the means of delivery for other economic activities. Recognising this duality, the GATS Annex on Telecommunications was negotiated to ensure that in its role as the means of delivery, access to telecommunication networks does not turn into a non-tariff barrier to trade.

3.064 The Annex applies to all measures that affect access to and use of public telecommunication transport networks and services, but does not apply to measures affecting cable or broadcast distribution of radio or television programming.[4] Every member must ensure that the obligations of the Annex are applied to their own suppliers of public telecommunication transport networks and services by whatever means necessary. Unless a member has scheduled a specific commitment that requires access or use, nothing in the Annex requires a member to authorise a service supplier of any other member to establish, construct, acquire, or otherwise supply telecommunication transport networks or services.[5] Likewise, much to the relief of developing countries, the Annex does not require a member to acquire, lease, or build a telecommunications network or supply telecommunication services that are not offered to the public generally.[6] Paragraph 4 of the Annex on transparency obligates members to make publicly available all relevant information on conditions affecting access to and use of the networks and services.

3.065 The heart of the Annex is Paragraph 5. Its heading could easily serve as the sub-title of the Annex: *Access to and Use of Public Telecommunications Transport Networks and Services*. Paragraph 5(a) provides in pertinent part that "[e]ach Member shall ensure that any service supplier of any other Member is accorded access to and use of public telecommunications transport networks and services on reasonable and non-discriminatory terms and conditions, for the supply of a service included in its Schedule." A

in a manner inconsistent with that Member's obligations under Article II [the MFN commitment] and specific [market access] commitments. 2. Where a Member's monopoly supplier competes, either directly or through an affiliated company, in the supply of a service outside the scope of its monopoly right and which is subject to that Member's specific commitments, the Member shall ensure that such a supplier does not abuse its monopoly position to act in its territory in a manner inconsistent with such commitments".

[4] See GATS Annex on Telecommunications para. 2(a). Public telecommunications transport service means service that a member requires to be offered to the public generally (thus, they may be privately owned) and include telegraph, telephone, telex and data transmission. Public telecommunication transport network means the infrastructure that permits telecommunications between defined network termination points. *id.* para. 3(a), (c).

[5] See *id.* para. 2(c)(i).

[6] See *id.* para. 2(c)(ii).

footnote clarifies that the term "non-discriminatory" refers to MFN and national treatment as defined in the GATS.[7] It adds that sector-specific usage of the term means "terms and conditions no less favourable than those accorded to any other user of like public telecommunications transport networks or service under like conditions." This language strongly suggests that no derogations from the MFN or national treatment obligations may be listed in a member's schedule of commitments regarding access to or use of public telecommunication networks or services.

3.066 The specific access and use rights accorded foreign service suppliers include:

(1) the right to purchase or lease and attach terminal or other equipment that is necessary to supply services,

(2) the right to interconnect private leased or owned circuits with public networks or services,

(3) the right to use operating protocols of the supplier's choice in the supply of any service, and

(4) the right to use networks and services for the movement of information within and across borders, subject to reasonable measures necessary to ensure security and confidentiality (*e.g.* encryption requirements).[8]

3.067 A member may impose three general types of measures on access and use. First, a member may impose measures necessary to ensure that public service suppliers are able to make their networks or services available to the public generally. Secondly, a member may impose measures necessary to protect the technical integrity of networks or services. Thirdly, a member may impose measures necessary to ensure that service suppliers are providing only services for which the member has scheduled a commitment.[9] Provided that they fall within one of the three types of permissible measures just described, a member may impose specific conditions on access and use. These conditions include:

(1) restrictions on resale or shared use,

(2) requirements to use specified technical interfaces and protocols for inter-connection with such networks and services,

(3) approval of terminal or other equipment that interfaces with the network,

(4) restrictions on inter-connection of private leased or owned circuits with such networks or services, and

[7] See *id.* para. 5(a) n.2.
[8] See *id.* para. 5(b)–(d).
[9] See *id.* para. 5(e).

(5) requirements on registration and licensing.[10]

Developing countries are given a special dispensation that allows them to protect ("strengthen" in the words of the Annex) their domestic telecommunications infrastructure and service capacity through reasonable conditions on access and use, notwithstanding the limitations imposed on members by paragraph 5 in that connection.[11] Any such conditions must be specified in the developing-country member's schedule (no member has done so). The Annex also encourages technical co-operation between developed and developing countries.[12]

3.068 Finally, recognising the importance of international standards for global compatibility and inter-operability of telecommunication networks and services, members agree in paragraph 7 to promote such standards through appropriate international organisations. Such organisations include the International Telecommunication Union and the International Organisation for Standardisation. Members also agree to engage relevant NGOs by making arrangements with them for consultation on matters arising from the implementation of the Annex.

3.069 In May, 1998, the United States and the E.U. concluded a mutual recognition agreement on conformity assessment procedures covering several sectors, including telecommunications equipment. In June, 1998, the 21 members of the APEC Forum concluded a mutual recognition arrangement on telecommunications equipment that will streamline the conformity assessment procedures for a wide range of telecommunications equipment. Once it is fully implemented, the mutual recognition arrangement will facilitate trade in telecommunications and telecommunications-related equipment among the APEC members.

3.070 b. The Uruguay Round Understanding on Financial Services. The Understanding on Commitments on Financial Services, incorporated in the Final Act Embodying the Results of the Uruguay Round,[13] was intended to harmonise the structure of the market access commitments agreed to by the members during the post-Round financial services negotiations. It supplements, but does not conflict with, Part III of the GATS on specific commitments in two areas: market access and national treatment. It serves an important function in restraining anti-competitive business practices in the financial services sector. First, the Understanding contains a standstill restriction that provides that members will only inscribe conditions, limitations, and qualifications to their specific commitments to the extent of *existing* nonconforming measures.[14] Under Part III of the GATS, in contrast, it also is

[10] See *id.* para. 5(f).
[11] See *id.* para. 5(g).
[12] See *id.* para. 6.
[13] See Final Act Embodying the Results of the Uruguay Round of Multilateral Trade Negotiations, para. 1. The Understanding is not binding on all WTO Members either because it was not made an integral part of the WTO Agreement, having been excluded from the Annex 2 list of Uruguay Round Understandings. The Understanding was the work product of the OECD-member countries and was intended to bind them only.
[14] See Understanding on Financial Services, para. A.

possible for a member to inscribe *future* non-conforming measures in a member's schedule of commitments.

3.071 Second, regarding market access commitments, members agree to the following eight rules:[15]

(1) Members must list in their schedule of financial service commitments existing monopoly rights and shall endeavour to eliminate them or reduce their scope.[16]

(2) Notwithstanding GATS Article XIII on government procurement, members agree to accord MFN and national treatment to non-resident financial service suppliers in the purchase or acquisition of financial services by public entities.

(3) Members must permit the cross-border delivery and purchase of insurance services relating to

(a) maritime shipping, commercial aviation, and space launching;
(b) reinsurance; and
(c) financial information and data processing.

(4) Members must grant non-resident financial service suppliers the right to establish a commercial presence within their territory, including through the acquisition of existing enterprises, subject to terms, conditions, and procedures for authorisation of the establishment of a commercial presence that are otherwise consistent with the GATS.[17]

(5) Members must permit financial service suppliers of any other member established in the former's territory to offer any new financial service.[18]

(6) Members must not take measures that prevent transfers of information or the processing of information that are necessary for the conduct of ordinary business of a financial service supplier, subject to the right to protect personal data and privacy and the confidentiality of individual records and accounts.

(7) Members must permit the temporary entry of personnel from a financial service supplier that has established a commercial presence in the territory of a member, including senior managerial personnel possessing proprietary information essential to the service supplier,

[15] See *id.* paras. B.1–.11.
[16] This obligation extends to "other public entities" that are otherwise excluded from GATS coverage under the Annex on Financial Services, para. 1(b)(iii),
[17] Commercial presence includes wholly- or partly-owned subsidiaries, joint ventures, partnerships, sole proprietorships, franchising operations, branches, agencies, representative offices or other organisations. See Understanding on Financial Services, para. D.2.
[18] A new financial service includes the delivery of new and existing products that are not supplied by any financial service supplier in the territory of a particular Member but are supplied in the territory of another Member. See *id.* para. D.3.

specialists in the operation of the supplier and, subject to the availability of qualified personnel within the member's territory, computer and telecommunications specialists, actuarial specialists and legal specialists.

(8) Members commit to remove or limit any significant adverse effects on other members' financial service suppliers of:

(a) non-discriminatory measures that prevent other members' financial service suppliers from offering all the financial services permitted by the member,

(b) non-discriminatory measures that limit the expansion of financial service activities into a member's entire territory,

(c) measures that apply to both banking and securities services when the financial service supplier concentrates its activities in securities services,

(d) and other measures that adversely affect the ability of financial service suppliers to operate, compete, or enter a member's market. Members need not, however, discriminate against their own financial service suppliers in honouring this commitment.

3.072 Thirdly, regarding national treatment, members agree to provide financial service suppliers of other members access to payment and clearing systems operated by public entities and to official funding and refinancing facilities available in the ordinary course of business, other than the facilities of a member's lender of last resort.[19] When membership or participation in any self-regulatory body, securities or futures exchange, or any other organisation is required by a member as a condition of supplying a particular financial service on an equal footing with resident financial service suppliers, members must ensure that such entities accord national treatment to non-resident financial service suppliers.[20]

3.073 **c. The 1997 Agreement on Basic Telecommunications Services.** Basic telecommunication services account for 85 per cent of total global trade in telecommunication services (enhanced telecommunication services account for the balance). Differences between the United States and the other Quad members over their respective regulatory environments for basic telecommunication services made agreement on market openings in this sector impossible to achieve during the Uruguay Round negotiations.Three years after the conclusion of the Uruguay Round, on February 15, 1997 69 developed and developing countries from 55 WTO members (54 governments plus the 15 E.U. Member States) successfully concluded an agreement on basic telecommunication services that entered into force on February 1, 1998.[21]

[19] See *id.* para. C.1.

[20] See *id.* para. C.2.

[21] The "Agreement became the Fourth Protocol to the General Agreement on Trade in Services". For the text of the Agreement and the country schedules of commitments, see World Trade Organisation, "Agreement on Telecommunications Services" (Fourth Protocol to General Agreement on Trade in Services), Feb. 15, 1997, 36 Int'l Leg. Materials 354 (1997).

Not only were the number of offers broader than those previously made in April 1996 (55 versus 34) but they were deeper, covering services not previously scheduled by members in April 1996.

3.074 In addition to reaching agreement on significant market access openings, the 1997 basic telecoms agreement includes important terms on competition policy. Effective competition laws can be an immeasurable aid to investors by preventing local monopolies from abusing their position toward new entrants. This is especially true for network industries, such as basic telecoms, where an investor may have to rely on local transmission facilities to provide a competitive service. Basic telecommunications networks are also frequently government-owned or government-authorised monopolies, therefore, certain competition rules had to be agreed upon in order for market access commitments to be meaningful. In recognition of this market reality, under the rubric of regulatory principles, the Negotiating Group on Basic Telecommunications developed an Annex, known as the Reference Paper, on competition principles.[22] The Reference Paper requires national telecom regulators to be established (if they do not already exist) and to take appropriate measures to prevent major suppliers[23] from engaging in anti-competitive conduct. The national regulators are to referee interconnection with former or existing telecom monopolies. The Reference Paper also describes the following measures national regulators are to take with regard to anti-competitive conduct by major suppliers:

- adopt safeguards against anti-competitive practices by major suppliers, such as cross-subsidisation, withholding technical and commercial information, or using information obtained from competitors with anti-competitive results.
- require cost-based and timely interconnection on non-discriminatory terms, rates, and quality.
- adopt transparent and non-discriminatory universal service requirements (*i.e.* requirements that mandate basic telecommunication service for every citizen at affordable prices).
- adopt transparent and publicly available licensing criteria, including a statement of reasons for licencing denial.
- maintain the independence of regulators from suppliers of basic telecommunications services.
- adopt transparent and non-discriminatory rules for the allocation of scarce resources, such as radio spectrum frequencies.
- require publication of international accounting rates.

[22] The Reference Paper is based on the U.S. Telecommunications Act of 1996. See World Trade Organisation, "Report of the Group on Basic Telecommunications", S/GBT/4 (Feb. 15, 1997), reprinted in (1997) 36 Int'l Leg. Materials 367 (hereinafter "Reference Paper").

[23] A "major supplier" is defined as "a supplier which has the ability to materially affect the terms of participation (having regard to price and supply) in the relevant market for basic telecommunications services as a result of (a) control over essential facilities, or (b) the use of its position in the market". "Reference Paper", see para. 3.074, n. 22, at 367.

3.075 With respect to dispute settlement under the Basic Telecommunications Agreement, the Reference Paper distinguishes between disputes about anti-competitive practices and disputes about interconnection. With regard to the former, the Reference Paper offers no specific dispute settlement mechanism for resolving alleged anti-competitive practices of major suppliers. With respect to interconnection, the Reference Paper points to dispute settlement before national regulatory authorities with the power to resolve disputes regarding the appropriate terms, conditions and rates of interconnection within a reasonable period of time.

3.076 Sixty-three of the 69 participating governments, covering 94 per cent of WTO members' total basic telecommunication services revenue, inscribed commitments on regulatory principles in the "Additional Commitments" column of their national schedules. Of these, 57 committed to the Reference Paper by inscribing it in whole or in part in their schedule of commitments, including the Quad members and Mexico. Bangladesh, Brazil, Mauritius, Morocco, Turkey and Venezuela deferred the date of entry into force of the regulatory principles but Bolivia, India, Malaysia, Pakistan and the Philippines adopted them in part.

By one estimate, the provisions of the Reference Paper "amount, in effect, to a world competition policy for the industry in embryo."[24] However, another observer has warned that although the Reference Paper represents a breakthrough by extending competition rules to international trade in services:

> it also contains some dangers if it spawns a raft of other sector-specific agreements, each with its own set of competition rules. . . [S]ectoral regulators are significantly more prone to capture by industry interests than competition offices having an economy-wide, competition encouraging, rather than regulation-based, mandate.[25]

Whether the Reference Paper could serve as a model for addressing anti-competitive practices that threaten trade either generally or in other sectors is unclear.

3. *The TRIMs Agreement*

3.077 The Agreement on Trade-Related Investment Measures (the TRIMs Agreement) represents a modest attempt to reinforce GATT rules respecting national treatment and the prohibition on import quotas in the investment context. The TRIMs Agreement builds on GATT Article III, which requires Members to provide national treatment to imported products, and GATT Article XI, which prohibits Members from imposing quantitative restrictions

[24] Guy de Jonquieres, "Financial Times Survey: The World Trading System at 50", *Financial Times*, May 18, 1988 at 1. For an excellent analysis of telecommunications services negotiations, see Marco C.E.J. Bronckers & Pierre Larouche, "Telecommunications Services and the World Trade Organization", (1997) 31 J. World Trade 5.

[25] See Joanna Shelton, "Competition Policy: What Chance for International Rules?" (1999) 2 OECD J. Competition L. & Pol'y 59, 62.

on the importation or exportation of goods. However, the Agreement falls far short of being a comprehensive set of rules regulating either international investment or restrictive business practices.[26] Although GATT Articles III:4, III:5, and III:7 do apply to certain aspects of investment laws, the GATT panel decision involving the Canadian Foreign Investment Review Act[27] spotlighted the need for Article III repair through the adoption of specific and unambiguous rules on certain trade-distorting investment measures, in particular local content requirements.[28]

3.078 What is a trade-related investment measure or "TRIM"? A TRIM is any measure imposed by a government (usually but not exclusively a developing country) on a foreign investor (often but not always a multinational enterprise) as a condition for investing in the host country. TRIMs can be positive or negative. Examples of positive TRIMs include financial incentives, such as tax holidays or subsidies, to invest within the host country generally or within certain economically depressed regions of the host country specifically.[29] Negative TRIMs include local equity requirements, licencing requirements, profit remittance restrictions, foreign exchange restrictions, transfer-of-technology requirements, domestic sales requirements, trade-balancing requirements, local-content requirements, export requirements and import-substitution requirements.[30] The TRIMs Agreement deals exclusively with negative TRIMs and addresses only a handful of the most egregious trade-related investment measures. The Agreement has three main features.

3.079 First, it identifies certain types of investment measures that are inconsistent with GATT 1994. Article 2.1 of the TRIMs Agreement stipulates that "no Member shall apply any TRIM that is inconsistent with the provisions of Article III or Article XI of GATT 1994." Article 2.2 refers to the illustrative list of TRIMs that are inconsistent with GATT Articles III:4 and XI:1. The TRIMs Annex provides that measures must be mandatory, that is, enforceable under domestic law or under administrative rulings, or compliance with which is necessary to obtain an advantage. Next, these mandatory measures are prohibited if they require the purchase or use of domestic products (*i.e.* local content requirements), limit the purchase or use of imported products to an amount related to the volume or value of local products that are exported (*i.e.* trade-balancing requirements), or tie access to foreign exchange to an investor's foreign exchange earnings (*i.e.* foreign exchange balancing restrictions). The prohibited measures listed in the

[26] See Daniel M. Price & P. Bryan Christy III, "Agreement on Trade Related Investment Measures (TRIMS): Limitations and Prospects for the Future", in *The World Trade Organization: The Multilateral Trade Framework for the 21st Century and U.S. Implementing Legislation* (Terence P. Stewart ed. 1996) 439.

[27] See "Report of the GATT Panel, Canada—Foreign Investment Review Act", BISD, 30th Supp. 140 (adopted Feb. 7, 1984).

[28] See "Canada—Administration of the Foreign Investment Review Act", *supra* n. 27.

[29] For a list of typical TRIMs, see UNCTAD, *World Investment Report 1996: Investment, Trade and International Policy Arrangements* (1996) 181; Patrick Low & Arvid Subramanian, "TRIMs in the Uruguay Round: An Unfinished Business?" in *The Uruguay Round and the Developing Economies* (Will Martin & L. Alan Winters eds. 1995) 417.

[30] For an illustrative list of local content requirements in 27 developing countries, see Low & Subramanian, *supra* n. 29, at 419–20.

illustrative Annex to the TRIMs Agreement underscore the close link between foreign investment and international trade. The prohibitions of the TRIMs Agreement apply equally to measures imposed on domestic firms, not just on foreign investments, and cover both new and existing investments.

3.080 Secondly, the Agreement requires that all inconsistent TRIMs be notified and eliminated in two years in the case of developed countries (by 1997), five years in the case of developing countries (by 2000), and seven years in the case of least-developed countries (by 2002).[31] In order not to disadvantage established enterprises that are subject to a TRIM *vis-à-vis* new investments that are exempt from it, Members may apply the same TRIM to new investments during the transition period, where the existing and new investment manufacture like products.[32]

3.081 Thirdly, in a small victory for developing-country members, the Council for Trade in Goods was to review the operation of the TRIMs Agreement by the end of 1999. As part of the Council's review, the Council was to "consider whether the Agreement should be complemented with provisions on investment policy and competition policy."[33]

3.082 The TRIMs Agreement is the first successful attempt made within the GATT-WTO system to facilitate foreign investment by eliminating non-tariff barriers to trade in goods associated with foreign investment. The Agreement is designed to ensure that governments do not apply measures to foreign investment that create restrictions on trade in goods. It gives investors the assurance that they may freely buy, sell, import, and export goods that are produced in countries outside the country in which their investment is located. At the same time, however, the TRIMs Agreement may have been a solution in search of a problem. It is reported, for example, that only 6 per cent of all overseas affiliates of U.S. companies are affected by TRIMs.[34] It is also reported that most TRIMs have little effect on managers' behaviour because they would have made most of the same decisions with or without local investment measures to influence or guide their decision-making.[35]

The TRIMs of greatest concern to the United States going into the Uruguay Round covered only a small amount of total foreign investment and existed mainly in developing countries.[36] Ironically, developing countries were granted a waiver under Article 4 of the TRIMs Agreement for balance-of-payment purposes.

3.083 Overall, the TRIMs Agreement is an unbalanced document that reflects the bargaining positions of the E.U. and developing countries in the Uruguay Round negotiations.[37] What the United States wanted in a TRIMs

[31] See TRIMs Agreement art. 5.2. Art. 6.2 further provides for notification to the WTO Secretariat of publications in which information on TRIMs can be found.

[32] See *id.* Art. 5.5.

[33] *id.* Art. 9. See generally Harvey M. Applebaum, "Relationship of the Trade Laws and the Antitrust Laws", in *The GATT, the WTO and the Uruguay Round Agreements Act* (Harvey M. Applebaum & Lyn M. Schlitt eds. 1995) 537.

[34] See Philip Evans & James Walsh, *The EIU Guide to the New GATT* (1994) 32.

[35] See *id.* at 33.

[36] See *id.*

[37] See *id.* at 34, 36.

Agreement was a comprehensive investment code. What the United States got was something far more modest in scope. The TRIMs Agreement became a bargaining chip for the United States that it wagered in order to secure gains in the areas of intellectual property protection and trade in services.

3.084 The two areas where a TRIMs Agreement was arguably most needed, *i.e.* restrictive business practices and positive TRIMs, are the very areas where the TRIMs Agreement is virtually silent. And the practices that the TRIMs Agreement does address could have been dealt with under existing GATT rules. All of the legal tools necessary to curb the use of the negative TRIMs listed in the Annex were in place under GATT 1947. The negative TRIMs listed in the Illustrative Annex all violate Articles III and XI with or without a TRIMs Agreement stating that they do. The absence of a strong dispute settlement mechanism in GATT 1947 probably explains why a TRIMs Agreement was considered necessary in the first place and why more TRIMs weren't challenged under GATT 1947.[38]

3.085 The TRIMs Agreement addresses at least one point where Foreign Direct Investments, (FDI) and international competition policy intersect, *i.e.* multinational enterprises (MNEs) and intra-firm agreements affecting market and product allocation. For example, parent companies may impose export restrictions on their foreign subsidiaries in order to reap the benefits of specialisation and maximise profits. However, these export restrictions could conflict with export promotion policies of host countries. Consequently, as a condition of approving a foreign investment, some host countries imposed performance requirements in the form of local content or export requirements to counteract intra-firm trade restrictions. Recognising that performance requirements themselves could distort trade flows and competition in national and international markets, the TRIMs Agreement bans requirements imposed as a condition of approval of a foreign investment that limit a firm's use of imported products to an amount related to the volume or value of local products that it exports.[39]

3.086 In sum, the TRIMs Agreement deals with some governmental measures restricting investment, but the Agreement fails to cover private business practices that restrict competition. Article 9 of the TRIMs Agreement provides that as part of its five-year review of the operation of the Agreement (at the end of 1999), the Council for Trade in Goods was to consider whether the Agreement should be complemented with provisions on investment and competition policy. No consensus was reached on either question. However, the five-year review has dovetailed into the work of the Working Group on the Relationship Between Trade and Investment and the Working Group on the Interaction between Trade and Competition Policy. The work of the latter Working Group is discussed in the next Chapter.

4. *The Safeguards Agreement*

3.087 One of the most serious threats to competition in the global marketplace during the period from the late 1960s to the early 1990s were

[38] The U.S. complaint against Canada's Foreign Investment Review Act is a notable exception.
[39] See TRIMs Agreement, Annex 1(b).

voluntary export restraint agreements (VRAs or VERs), also known euphemistically as "managed trade." Designed to protect domestic producers from import competition, VRAs were the direct product of government intervention in the market that took the form of specific and detailed undertakings, pursuant to which countries party to the VRA would limit their export of goods subject to the VRA.

3.088 One of the best examples of such an undertaking is the Multifiber Arrangement on textiles and clothing. A less detailed VRA is the 1986 U.S.-Japan Semiconductor Agreement.[40] The differences are largely ones of form rather than effect. Other examples of VRAs include the 1981 agreement between the United States and Japan to reduce the latter's export of automobiles to the United States by 7.7 per cent from 1980 levels and the agreement reached in 1969 among Japan, the EEC, and the United States limiting steel exports to the United States. The automobile VRA followed an unsuccessful attempt by the United Auto Workers and Ford Motor Company to obtain safeguards relief from the U.S. International Trade Commission. The Commission found that Japanese imports were not a substantial cause of serious injury to the U.S. auto industry.[41] Other goods that have been the subject of VRAs include agricultural products, televisions, machine tools and footwear.

3.089 By reducing the volume of exports, VRAs lead to higher prices for imports and allow domestic firms in the importing country to raise their prices as well. VRAs can have adverse effects among firms in the exporting country by reducing the incentive for exporting firms to innovate because their share of the foreign market has been fixed by a quota. Although it is difficult to quantify the economic impact of VRAs because of lack of transparency and government reporting, it is clear that whatever the economic cost of VRAs to consumers, they were staggering.[42] For example, the cost to U.S. consumers of the automobile VRA was estimated at $5.8 billion in 1984 alone; the cost to U.S. consumers of each auto worker job saved by the VRA was $105,000 in 1984, in an industry where workers earn far more than the average U.S. purchaser of automobiles.[43] Similarly, the steel VRAs cost U.S. consumers $6.9 billion in 1984, with a price tag to consumers for each steelworker's job saved of $750,000 in 1984.[44]

[40] See Laura D'Andrea Tyson, *Who's Bashing Whom? Trade Conflict in High-Technology Industries* (1992) 109–10. For additional reading on the U.S.-Japan semiconductor trade regime, see Robert Carr, "Evolution of the U.S.-Japanese Semiconductor Trade Regime", Industry, Trade, & Tech. Rev. 45 (USITC Jan. 1997); Office of the USTR, "Semiconductor Market Share in Japan Reaches 29.4% in the Fourth Quarter", Press Release, (May 1, 1997), available at http://www.ustr.gov.

[41] See "Certain Motor Vehicles and Certain Chassis and Bodies Therefor, Inv. No. TA-201–44" (USITC Pub. 1110 1980). A majority of the Commission found the decline in demand for new cars and lightweight trucks to be attributable to general recessionary conditions in the United States, as well as to a shift in consumer tastes to smaller, more fuel-efficient models. See *id.* at 35.

[42] For the economic consequences of VRAs, see Ulrich Immenga, "Export Cartels and Voluntary Export Restraints Between Trade and Competition Policy", in *Antitrust: A New Trade Remedy?* 93, 129–35 (John O. Haley & Hiroshi Iyori eds. 1995).

[43] See "The High Cost of Protectionism and What Can Be Done About It", Christian Sci. Monitor, Mar. 20, 1986, at 23.

[44] See *id.*

3.090 The pattern for concluding a VRA followed a well-worn script: as a result of pressure from an importing country or countries, a foreign government typically agreed to orchestrate a limit on the price and/or volume of its manufacturers' exports of certain merchandise to the importing country for a fixed time period. Extortion played a significant role in explaining the "success" of VRAs. In the words of a 1984 GATT Report on the subject of VRAs:

> [E]xporting countries which accepted so-called "grey-area" actions did so primarily because, even if they were satisfied that the requirements of the GATT safeguard provisions had been met [entitling the exporting country to compensation in the form of reduced tariffs on other unrelated products of export interest to that country], they felt that they had little choice and the alternative was, or would have been, unilateral action in the form of quantitative restrictions, harassment by antidumping investigations, countervailing action, enforcement by pricing mechanisms, etc., involving greater harm to their exports in terms of both quantity and price. The time factor played an important role—the exporting countries concerned had not sought a remedy under the GATT dispute settlement procedures, e.g., Article XXIII, because these were considered cumbersome and time-consuming and there was fear that the industries involved could suffer serious, and perhaps irreparable, damages in the meantime.[45]

In short, for exporting countries half a loaf was preferable to no loaf at all.[46]

3.091 The resort to VRAs was in part attributable to their uncertain legal status under GATT; hence the name, "gray area" measure. While the question is now purely academic in light of the Safeguards Agreement it is arguable, nevertheless, that they were a blatant violation of three core GATT principles. First, they violated the MFN clause by permitting discrimination among suppliers. Secondly, they flouted the GATT prohibition against quotas and thirdly, they undercut the GATT principle of assured market access through tariff bindings. In addition, contrary to GATT multilateralism, VRAs were either bilateral or plurilateral.

3.092 The Director-General of GATT did not mince words over the legal status of VRAs *vis-à-vis* GATT when he stated that:

> "voluntary" export restraints are clearly contrary to the present rules of the General Agreement and are only "outside the General Agreement" in the sense that governments have not brought them formally to the GATT for examination.[47]

---

[45] "Report of the Chairman of the Safeguards Committee", BISD, 30th Supp. 216, 218 (1984).

[46] Domestic legal challenges in the United States to VRAs on the grounds, *inter alia*, that they were *ultra vires* the President's authority delegated to him by Congress, proved unsuccessful in U.S. courts. They were defended on the ground that because they were voluntary and therefore not enforceable, they did not represent an unlawful exercise of power by the President. See, *e.g. Consumer Union of U.S., Inc. v. Kissinger*, 506 F.2d 136 (D.C. Cir. 1974), cert. denied, 421 U.S. 1004 (1975).

[47] "Report of the Chairman of the Safeguards Committee", BISD, 30th Supp. 216, Annex at 4 (1984).

The legal status of VRAs under national competition law was also fuzzy at best. However, with the imprimatur of national authorities placed on VRAs, exporters were assured that national enforcement authorities would not pursue an antitrust action against them. With regard to private antitrust actions, exporters arguably were shielded from legal attack under the defence of foreign sovereign compulsion.[48]

3.093 GATT Article XIX on safeguards actions had become virtually a dead letter through circumvention and the use of VRAs. According to the U.S. International Trade Commission:

> Countries have often found the "escape" clause discipline of article XIX a prohibitively costly means of securing import relief because compensation must be paid to all affected members on a nondiscriminatory basis. As a result, countries have at times employed a safeguard-like mechanism, "voluntary export restraints (VERs)," which are outside GATT disciplines. VERs typically commit an exporting country to restrict the export of an offending product for a certain period of time during which the domestic industry can restructure.[49]

3.094 The Agreement on Safeguards breathes new life into moribund GATT Article XIX. The preamble to the Agreement states that members recognise "the importance of structural adjustment and the need to enhance rather than limit competition in international markets." To that end, Article 11.1(b) of the Safeguards Agreement prohibits resort to grey area measures in the future.[50] Such measures include "export moderation, export-price or import-price monitoring systems, export or import surveillance, compulsory import cartels and discretionary export or import licensing schemes, any of which afford protection" to the importing country's industry.[51]

Secondly, WTO members were required to terminate any outstanding VRAs by the end of 1998.[52] Thirdly, members must not encourage or support the adoption by public and private enterprises of non-governmental measures equivalent to VRAs.[53] What would amount to encouragement or support remains an open question. The GATT panel report on *Semi-Conductors*[54] could be instructive, however. The panel there rejected Japan's argument that

[48] See Donald deKieffer, "Antitrust and the Japanese Auto Quotas", (1982) 8 Brooklyn J. Int'l L. 59–63.

[49] "U.S. Int'l Trade Comm'n, The Year in Trade 1993: Operation of the Trade Agreements Program 19" (USITC Pub. 2769 1994).

[50] Art. 11.1(b) provides in part: "[A] Member shall not seek, take or maintain any voluntary export restraints, orderly marketing arrangements or any other similar measures on the export or the import side".

[51] Agreement on Safeguards, Art. 11.1(b) n. 4.

[52] See *id.* Art. 11.2. Each WTO member was permitted to grandfather one outstanding VRA through 1999. The EU VRA on Japanese automobiles was the only VRA which was grandfathered until December 31, 1999. *id.* Annex.

[53] See *id.* Art. 11.3.

[54] See "Report of the GATT Panel, Japan—Trade in Semi-Conductors", BISD, 35th Supp. 116, 153–55, paras. 104–09 (adopted May 8, 1988).

"administrative guidance" by the government to Japanese semi-conductor producers did not fall under the Article XI prohibition against export quotas because it was not legally binding or mandatory. The panel noted that Article XI:1, unlike other GATT provisions, does not refer solely to laws or regulations, but rather more broadly to "measures."

Finally, any safeguards measure that is imposed must be done in strict compliance with GATT Article XIX and the Safeguards Agreement, *i.e.* that a product is being imported in such increased quantities and under such conditions as to cause or threaten to cause serious injury to the domestic industry that produces the like or directly competitive product.[55]

5. *The Agreement on Government Procurement*

3.095 Another important WTO plurilateral agreement that enhances competition in the market for government purchases of goods and services is the Agreement on Government Procurement. It improves on its predecessor agreement, the Tokyo Round Government Procurement Code, in three respects.[56] First, the Code's rules on bid challenge procedures and dispute resolution are strengthened. Secondly, the new Agreement expands the Code vertically by covering sub-central levels of government and central government-owned utilities and transportation facilities. Thirdly, the new Agreement expands the Government Procurement Code horizontally by covering government procurement of services and construction contracts. Besides these achievements, the Uruguay Round negotiators added an important new member, Korea. The Government Procurement Agreement addresses anti-competitive practices in several articles.

3.096 First, in cases of procurement through selective tendering rather than open tendering, Article X governs the selection procedure. To ensure optimum effective international competition under selective tendering procedures, procuring entities must invite tenders from the maximum number of domestic and foreign suppliers consistent with the efficient operation of the procurement system. Participating suppliers are to be selected in a fair and non-discriminatory manner. If permanent lists of qualified suppliers are maintained, suppliers invited to participate may be selected from those lists, subject to allowing equitable opportunities for other suppliers on the lists. Qualified suppliers or suppliers who will qualify in time may request to participate in a particular procurement, are to be permitted to submit a tender

[55] See *id.* Art. 2.1.

[56] Agreement on Government Procurement, Apr. 15, 1994, Marrakesh Agreement Establishing the World Trade Organisation, Annex 4. The Agreement on Government Procurement had twelve signatories as of the end of 2000: Aruba, Canada, the E.C., Hong Kong, Israel, Japan, Korea, Liechtenstein, Norway, Singapore, Switzerland and the United States. Iceland will become the 13th member in 2001. See "WTO, Report (2000) of the Committee on Government Procurement", GPA/44 (Nov. 2, 2000). For an overview of the Agreement on Government Procurement, see Bhala & Kennedy, see para. 3.008, n. 18, at 1311–28; Jean Heilman Grier, "Japan's Implementation of the WTO Agreement on Government Procurement", (1996) 17 U. Pa. J. Int'l Econ. L. 605, 606–20.

and must be considered, subject to the efficient operation of the procurement system.

3.097 Secondly, Article XV provides that limited tendering procedures may be used, provided that limited tendering is not used with a view to avoiding maximum possible competition or in a manner which would constitute a means of discrimination among suppliers of other Parties or protection to domestic producers or suppliers. Limited tendering is permitted, for example, "when the tenders submitted have been collusive".

6. *Other WTO Provisions*

3.098 Provisions in other Uruguay Round agreements address private conduct that has the potential for being anti-competitive. First, the Agreement on Technical Barriers to Trade provides that the preparation, adoption, and application of technical regulations, standards, and conformity assessment procedures by non-governmental bodies must be consistent with the MFN and national treatment obligations and must not be more trade restrictive than necessary.[57] Secondly, virtually the entire Agreement on Preshipment Inspection deals with regulating the activities of preshipment inspection firms. Thirdly, Article 15.5 of the Agreement on Subsidies and Countervailing Measures requires an examination of other factors besides subsidised imports that may be the cause of injury to a domestic industry, including "trade restrictive practices and competition between foreign and domestic producers."

7. *Summary*

3.099 The preceding survey of GATT-WTO provisions addressing competition policy issues shows that these provisions do in fact deal with the trade-competition policy interface, but that they do not deal with private anti-competitive practices in a comprehensive fashion. In some cases, the provisions are skeletal with many interstices. In other cases, the provisions are more fully elaborated and fleshed out, such as the Reference Paper to the Agreement on Basic Telecommunications. In cases involving detailed commitments on regulating anti-competitive practices, the RBPs in question could be a violation of a WTO agreement, such as the GATS provision on monopoly service suppliers. In all other cases, the coverage of GATT and the WTO agreements extends potentially to all RBPs that prevent market access or adversely affect the conditions of competition. At a minimum, the toleration by a WTO member of RBPs within its market that prevent market access suggests a basis for a possible non-violation nullification or impairment complaint. The discussion that follows of the *Kodak-Fuji Film* panel report examines this last point. The foregoing discussion shows that the WTO membership has not shied away from addressing specific anti-competitive

[57] See Agreement on Technical Barriers to Trade Arts. 3.1, 3.4, 4.1 & 8.1.

conduct at least on a sectoral basis, even though that conduct is not governmental but private in nature.

B. Competition Policy Disputes in the WTO

3.100 Two WTO dispute settlement proceedings have been brought involving competition policy issues. In the first proceeding, the United States was the complainant, charging Japan with violating GATT by not having in place an aggressive antitrust enforcement policy to combat alleged private barriers to import trade. The WTO panel found no violation of GATT. In the second proceeding, the United States was the respondent, with the E.U. and Japan complaining that a U.S. antitrust law—the Antidumping Act of 1916—violates GATT and the WTO Antidumping Agreement in several respects. Specifically, they charged that the Antidumping Act of 1916 violates Articles VI:1 of GATT by not requiring the existence or threat of material injury to a domestic industry as a prerequisite to the imposition of antidumping remedies; that the 1916 Act violates GATT Article VI:2 which provides that antidumping duties are the remedy for a dumping violation; and that the 1916 Act violates Articles 1, 4, and 5.5 of the WTO Antidumping Agreement concerning procedures governing the imposition of antidumping measures. Despite the fact that 1916 Antidumping Act was rarely used and had slipped into virtual desuetude, the E.U. and Japan brought their WTO complaints. The WTO panel and Appellate Body agreed that the Antidumping Act of 1916 does violate GATT.

1. *The Kodak-Fuji Film Dispute*

3.101 The 1998 WTO dispute between the United States and Japan over access to Japan's photographic film market is the most high profile case involving restrictive business practices to have ever reached either a GATT or WTO dispute settlement panel. The dispute formally began on May 18, 1995 when Eastman Kodak Company (Kodak) lodged a complaint with the U.S. Trade Representative's Office, pursuant to section 301 of the Trade Act of 1974.[58] Kodak alleged that "anticompetitive rebate schemes, resale-price

[58] See 19 U.S.C. ss. 2411–2421. Under s. 301, the USTR may threaten the imposition of prohibitive duties on imports from a target country unless that country reaches a satisfactory resolution with the United States of a trade dispute. In 1988 amendments to s. 301, the USTR is authorised to investigate "toleration by a foreign government of systematic anti-competitive activities." 19 U.S.C. s. 2411(d)((3)(B)(i)(IV). See Bhala & Kennedy, see para. 3.008, n. 18, at 1009–1080; William H. Barringer & James P. During, "Out of Focus: The Use of Section 301 to Address Anticompetitive Practices in Foreign Markets", (1996) 1 U.C.L.A. J. Int'l L. & For. Aff. 99; Judith Hipler Bello & Alan Holmer, "The Heart of the 1988 Trade Act: A Legislative History of the Amendments to Section 301", (1988) 25 Stan. J. Int'l L. 2. The USTR maintains a list of all s. 301 petitions at http://www.ustr.gov.

maintenance, and horizontal price-fixing" prevented Kodak from penetrating the Japanese film market.[59] Kodak further alleged that acts, policies, and practices of the Japanese government with respect to the sale and distribution of consumer photographic film in Japan restricted access to imported film.[60]

3.102 Specifically, Kodak's petition alleged that Fujifilm's non-price vertical restraints allowed it to obtain as exclusive distributors the principal wholesalers of film in the Japanese market. Kodak contended that its exclusion from the wholesale channel of distribution blocked its access to the majority of Japanese retailers. Kodak also alleged that Fujifilm's vertical integration into photo processing further excluded Kodak from the colour paper market. It asked the USTR to lodge a complaint with the Japanese and start the process of imposing sanctions.[61]

3.103 The gravamen of the U.S. complaint with Japan was that because Fuji controlled the distribution system for consumer photographic film, it was able to exclude Kodak from the wholesale distribution channel. This situation forced Kodak to sell directly to retailers, an inefficient vehicle for market penetration. However, because GATT 1994 only addresses government measures that block market access, the USTR had to recast Kodak's complaint for purposes of the WTO dispute settlement proceeding. As a consequence, the U.S. complaint filed with the WTO was that the Japanese government established and tolerated a market structure that impeded U.S. film exports to Japan and this market structure nullified and impaired the benefit of tariff concessions that the United States had negotiated with Japan in three earlier rounds of multilateral trade negotiations (*i.e.* the Kennedy, Tokyo, and Uruguay Rounds).[62] As summarized by the WTO panel, the complaint filed with the WTO focused on Japan's administration of its competition law in three respects:

(1) distribution measures, which allegedly encouraged and facilitated the creation of market structures for film and paper in which imports are excluded from traditional distribution channels;
(2) the Large Stores Law, which allegedly restricted the growth of an alternative distribution channel for film; and

[59] See Wendy Bounds & Bob Davis, "Kodak Charges Japan and Fuji on Trade Issues", Asian Wall St. J., May 19, 1995, at A2.

[60] Under the Japanese Antimonopoly Law, any private party may petition the (JFTC) alleging a violation of that Law. The JFTC must then conduct a preliminary investigation to determine whether there is probable cause to proceed with an enforcement action. Kodak did not file a petition with the JFTC before filing its s. 301 petition with the USTR, claiming that such action would have been futile. See William H. Barringer, "Competition Policy and Cross Border Dispute Resolution: Lessons Learned from the U.S.-Japan Film Dispute", (1998) 6 Geo. Mason L. Rev. 459, 463–64. Eventually, Kodak did file a complaint with the JFTC. See "Kodak Files Protest With Japan Agency In Dispute With Fuji", Wall Street Journal, Aug. 8, 1996, at B5.

[61] See Charles A. Brill & Brian A. Carlson, "U.S. and Japanese Antimonopoly Policy and the Extraterritorial Enforcement of Competition Laws", (1998) 33 Int'l Law. 75, 114–15.

[62] See "Statement by Ambassador Charlene Barshefsky Regarding the WTO Dispute on Photographic Film and Paper", Office of the USTR, Press Release 97–102 (Dec. 5, 1997). Following the panel report, the United States sought consultations with Japan on whether the Japanese Large Scale Retail Store Law violates the General Agreement on Trade in Services by blocking market access for Kodak film. Those consultations were inconclusive, and the USTR did not pursue the matter further.

(3) restrictions on premiums and misleading representations under the Premiums Law, which allegedly disadvantaged imports by restricting sales promotions.[63]

Japan countered that it neither restricted foreign imports of photographic film not did it tolerate restrictive business practices by private firms that would have a similar result.[64] Japan added that the control by Fuji of wholesale networks was irrelevant because most of the retailers it served also bought imported film.

3.104 At the core of the first allegation was the Japanese distribution system. Nearly 70 per cent of the photographic products sold in Japan pass through one of four distributors, called *tokuyakuten*.[65] Kodak claimed that Fuji maintained exclusive agreements with the distributors that bind them to Fuji by "financial, operational and technical" means. For example, Fuji owns stock in two of the four distributors and also owns stock in the banks that lend to all of them.[66] Furthermore, Fuji offers large year-end rebates to the distributors and the stores that carry the film. Kodak contended that the rebates encourage wholesalers to purchase greater volume from fewer suppliers. Fuji for its part blamed Kodak for the lack of distribution channels, saying that Kodak had not even attempted to have the four major distributors carry Kodak film in 20 years. Kodak denied a lack of effort on its part and claimed to have contacted one of the distributors in the past year.

3.105 The second allegation addressed legal restrictions on foreign access to Japanese retail service establishments under Japan's Large-Scale Retail Store Laws. The United States claimed that these laws block access to the Japanese market by limiting the growth of large stores, which could offer the best chance for an alternative channel of distribution for foreign products. The third allegation charged that Premium Laws and certain private-sector business practices were discriminatory and exclusionary, and that some administrative decisions were not made public as required. These actions allegedly denied Kodak the expected benefit from later trade concessions and agreements.

The United States reworked Kodak's three allegations into a GATT-based complaint that charged the Japanese government with the following:

(1) the Japanese "measures" constituted a non-violation nullification or impairment of GATT benefits under GATT Article XXIII:1(b);

(2) the distribution measures violated the national treatment provision of GATT Article III:4; and

(3) the Japanese government had issued unpublished guidance requiring that applicants for large store permits co-ordinate their plans with

[63] See "Report of the WTO Panel, Kodak-Fuji Film Dispute", see para. 3.032, n. 51, para. 4.1.

[64] See Office of the USTR, "USTR and Department of Commerce Announce Next Steps on Improving Access to the Japanese Market for Film", Press Release 98–10 (Feb. 3, 1998).

[65] See Wendy Bounds & Helene Cooper, "Kodak Wants U.S. to Force Japan to Open Film Market", Asian Wall Street Journal, June 2, 1995, at A1.

[66] See Wendy Bounds, "Film Exposures: Fuji, Accused by Kodak of Hogging Markets, Spits Back: 'You Too'", Wall Street Journal, July 31, 1995, at A1.

local competitors before seeking governmental approval, in violation of the transparency requirements of GATT Article X.[67]

3.106 In a 477 page report, *Japan—Measures Affecting Consumer Photographic Film and Paper*,[68] the panel ruled in favour of Japan on all counts. The panel faced a threshold question of jurisdiction because the essence of the U.S. complaint was directed against private-sector actions in Japan. The United States finessed this problem, however, by claiming that at least some of Fuji's actions were "conducted with the knowledge and participation of the government of Japan."[69] This allegation was that in the 1970s, when Japan promised to open its markets to foreign film, officials at MITI conspired with Fuji to create *boeiki shohon jiyuka taisaku*, or "liberalization countermeasures."[70] In order to find jurisdiction, the panel applied a broad definition of the term "measure" used in the GATT articles. For example, the panel noted that the Japanese government acts through non-binding administrative guidance.[71] The panel added that, depending on the circumstances, administrative guidance and policy statements by various government officials and agencies would be considered measures under Articles III:4 and XXIII:1(b) of GATT:[72]

> In our view, a government policy or action need not necessarily have a substantially binding or compulsory nature for it to entail a likelihood of compliance by private actors in a way so as to nullify or impair legitimately expected benefits within the purview of Article XXIII:1(b). Indeed, it is clear that non-binding actions, which include sufficient incentives or disincentives for private parties to act in a particular manner, can potentially have adverse effects on competitive conditions of market access. . . [W]here there is a high degree of cooperation and collaboration between government and business . . . even non-binding, hortatory wording in a government statement of policy could have a similar effect on private actors to a legally binding measure or what Japan refers to as regulatory administrative guidance.[73]

3.107 Having resolved the threshold jurisdictional question in favour of the United States, the panel proceeded to the merits. First, it rejected the U.S. claims that Japan's photographic film market was closed to imports in

---

[67] See "Report of the Panel, Kodak-Fuji Film Dispute", paras. 7.9–7.15, 7.78, 10.33.
[68] "Report of the WTO Panel, Japan—Measures Affecting Consumer Photographic Film and Paper", WT/DS44/R (1998). The United States did not appeal to the Appellate Body. For additional analyses of the dispute, see Norio Komuro, "Kodak-Fuji Film Dispute and the WTO Panel Ruling", (1998) 32 J. World Trade 161, 188–91; David A. Gantz, "Lessons from the United States-Japan Semiconductors Dispute", (1999) 16 Ariz. J. Int'l & Comp. L. 91, 116–19; Sara Dillon, "Fuji-Kodak, The WTO, and the Death of Domestic Political Constituencies", (1999) 8 Minn. J. Global Trade 197.
[69] See "U.S. Will Investigate Kodak's Allegations Against Fuji Photo", Asian Wall St. J., July 4, 1995, at A2.
[70] See *id.*
[71] See "Kodak-Fuji Film Dispute", para. 10.44.
[72] See *id.* paras. 10.42–10.44, 10.376.
[73] See *id.* at 385.

violation of the national treatment clause and the transparency provisions of GATT Article X:1.[74] The panel found that three of the four distributors were already single-brand distributors two years before the issuance of the MITI guidelines complained of by the United States.[75] The fourth became a single-brand distributor only after Kodak refused to deal with it directly.

3.108 Second, the panel rejected the U.S. argument that government measures instituted by Japan in connection with the retail distribution of photographic film gave rise to a claim of non-violation nullification or impairment under GATT Article XXIII:1(b).[76] Simply stated, the timing of the alleged Japanese measures relative to the tariff concessions did not match up. The United States also claimed that eight distribution measures in Japan accord less favourable treatment to imported photographic film than to like domestic film in the Japanese market.[77] Rejecting the U.S. arguments, the panel found that:

> none of the eight distribution "measures" cited by the United States has been shown to discriminate against imported products, either in terms of a *de jure* discrimination (a measure that discriminates *on its face* as to the origin of products) or in terms of a *de facto* discrimination (a measure that in its application upsets the relative competitive position between domestic and imported products, as it existed at the time when a relevant tariff concession was granted).[78]

Accordingly, the panel dismissed claims by the United States that Japan's measures governing distribution violated Article III:4 because the United States had failed to demonstrate that any of the distribution measures in issue accords less favourable treatment to imported film than to film of Japanese origin.[79]

3.109 In disposing of the U.S. claim that Japan violated GATT Article X:1 by allegedly failing to publish administrative rulings dealing with

(1) enforcement actions taken by the JFTC that establish or modify rules applicable in future actions, and

---

[74] *See id.* paras.10.403–.404.
[75] See *id.* paras. 4.4, 4.9.
[76] See *id.* at 476, para. 10.402. As Professor Paul Stephan explains, in an Art. XXIII:1(b) non-violation complaint: "[A] WTO member's application of any governmental measure that nullifies or impairs a benefit enjoyed by another member as a result of the GATT justifies relief, whether or not the member's measure violates any provision of the GATT. The GATT, in other words, does more than impose a set of positive rules of conduct. It also obligates its members to deal with each other in a manner that does not frustrate legitimate expectations formed in the process of GATT bargaining". Paul B. Stephan, "Sheriff or Prisoner? The United States and the World Trade Organization", (2000) 1 Chi. J. Int'l L. 49, 58. For an analysis of an Article XXIII:1(b) non-violation claim in the context of the *Kodak-Fuji Film* dispute, see generally Sung-joon Cho, "GATT Non-Violation Issues in the WTO Framework: Are They the Achilles' Heel of the Dispute Settlement Process?" (1998) 39 Harv. Int'l L.J. 311.
[77] See "Kodak-Fuji Film Dispute", at 470, para. 10.378.
[78] id. at 471, para. 10.380.
[79] See *id.* at 471, para. 10.382.

(2) guidance to regional MITI offices and local authorities on the administration of the Large Stores Law,[80]

the panel noted that the publication requirement of Article X:1 does not extend to administrative rulings addressed to specific individuals or entities.[81] Moreover, there was a total absence of evidence that the unpublished JFTC enforcement actions effected changes in JFTC enforcement criteria.[82] Likewise in connection with the Large Stores Law claim, the panel found no evidence showing that such guidance established or modified criteria applicable to future cases.[83] Therefore, the panel concluded, the United States failed to provide sufficient evidence of a violation of Article X:1.

3.110 In sum, the panel held that the Japanese distribution system did not exclude imports as a result of any government policy. Significantly, the panel noted that:

> single-brand wholesale distribution is the common market structure—indeed the norm—in most major national film markets, including the US market. While the United States responded that the U.S. market structure was the result of private and not governmental actions, it is unclear why the same economic forces acting in the United States would not also exist in Japan.[84]

In the immediate aftermath of the panel report, the United States and Japan launched the Enhanced Initiative on Deregulation and Competition Policy. The USTR also established a monitoring and enforcement committee to monitor developments in the Japanese photographic materials market.[85]

3.111 The aggressive, results-oriented style of the USTR's office is in sharp contrast to the cautious, co-operative, consensus-building approach of the DOJ in these matters.[86] Although the USTR's office regularly accuses Japanese *keiretsu* of excluding foreign goods, there is no consensus among economists or lawyers about whether such vertical arrangements are anti-competitive. From a competition law standpoint, this is the key question, not whether foreign firms have a share of a foreign market that they consider fair, reasonable, or adequate. The USTR is focused on U.S. producer welfare, not on the welfare of Japanese consumers. The *Kodak-Fuji Film* dispute probably says more about the unresolved tension between trade policy and competition policy than it does about any gap in coverage of restrictive business practices that exists in GATT 1994 or the WTO agreements.

---

[80] See *id.* at 471–72, para. 10.383.

[81] The panel cited in support the WTO panel report in "United States—Restrictions on Imports of Cotton and Man-Made Fibre Underwear", WT/DS24/R, para. 7.65 (1997).

[82] See "Kodak-Fuji Film Dispute", at 475, para. 10.396.

[83] *See id.* at 476, para. 10.309.

[84] See *id.* para. 10.173.

[85] See "USTR and Department of Commerce Announce Next Steps on Improving Access to the Japanese Market for Film", Office of the USTR, Press Release 98–10 (Feb. 3, 1998).

[86] See Barringer, see para. 3.101, n. 58, at 460.

2. *The Antidumping Act of 1916 dispute*

3.112 The Antidumping Act of 1916 makes the systematic dumping of goods in the United States with the intent to injure a U.S. industry illegal and provides for an award of treble damages, the imposition of fines, and/or imprisonment.[87] (The USTR's Office prefers to refer to the 1916 Antidumping Act as the "U.S. Revenue Act of 1916.")[88] Representing a blend of antidumping and antitrust concepts, the 1916 Act has never been fully adjudicated in any U.S. court, probably owing to the fact that the *scienter* element is so difficult to prove.[89] Fewer than 20 civil actions had been filed under the 1916 Act prior to 1997.[90] In 1997, the federal district court for the district of Utah stated in a case involving imports of carbon steel plate that the 1916 Act "is not limited only to antitrust injury or predatory price discrimination. It is also designed to protect U.S. industry."[91] Accordingly, in denying defendant's motion to dismiss, the court ruled that plaintiffs did not have to show

[87] The Anti-Dumping Act of 1916 provides in pertinent part: "It shall be unlawful for any person importing or assisting in importing any articles from any foreign country into the United States, commonly and systematically to import, sell or cause to be imported or sold such articles within the United States at a price substantially less than the actual market value or wholesale price of such articles, at the time of exportation to the United States, in the principal markets of the country of their production, or of other foreign countries to which they are commonly exported after adding to such market value or wholesale price, freight, duty, and other charges and expenses necessarily incident to the importation and sale thereof in the United States: *Provided*, That such act or acts be done with the intent of destroying or injuring an industry in the United States, or of preventing the establishment of an industry in the United States, or of restraining or monopolizing any part of trade and commerce in such articles in the United States". 15 U.S.C. s. 72. Thus, the business activity which the 1916 Act prohibits is a form of international price discrimination, which has two basic components: (1) an importer must have sold a foreign-produced product within the United States at a price which is "substantially less" than the price at which the same product is sold in the country of the foreign producer; and (2) the importer must have undertaken this price discrimination "commonly and systematically." See Note, "Rethinking the 1916 Antidumping Act", (1997) 110 Harv. L. Rev. 1555. A closely-related price discrimination law, the Robinson-Patman Act, provides in pertinent part: "It shall be unlawful for any person engaged in commerce, in the course of such commerce, either directly or indirectly, to discriminate in price between different purchasers of commodities of like grade and quality, where either or any of the purchasers involved in such discrimination are in commerce, where such commodities are sold for use, consumption, or resale within the United States . . . and where the effect of such discrimination may be substantially to lessen competition or tend to create a monopoly in any line of commerce, or to injure, destroy, or prevent competition with any person who either grants or knowingly receives the benefit of such discrimination or with customers of either of them". 15 U.S.C. s. 13(a). To establish price discrimination in a Robinson-Patman Act action, there first must be evidence of two actual sales at different prices, with each sale occurring in interstate commerce. The Robinson-Patman Act does not apply to cross-border price discrimination. See *Brooke Group Ltd. v. Brown & Williamson Tobacco Corp.*, 509 U.S. 209, 222–23 (1993).

[88] See Office of the USTR, "WTO Appellate Body Upholds Panel Ruling Against U.S. Revenue Act of 1916", Press Release 00–59 (Aug. 28, 2000). The Antidumping Act if 1916 was enacted as Title VIII of the Revenue Act of 1916, Chap. 463, 39 Stat. 798 (1916).

[89] See Applebaum, see para. 3.08, n. 33, at 486. The Act was discussed and upheld against a constitutional challenge in *Zenith Radio Corp. v. Matsushita Elec. Indus. Co.*, 402 F. Supp. 244 (E.D. Pa. 1975).

[90] See *Geneva Steel Co. v. Ranger Steel Co.*, 980 F. Supp. 1209, 1214 (D. Utah 1997).

[91] *Geneva Steel Co. v. Ranger Steel Co.*, 980 F. Supp. 1209, 1215 (D. Utah 1997). But see *Zenith Radio Corp. v. Matsushita Elec. Indus. Co.*, Ltd., 494 F. Supp. 1190 (E.D. Pa.1980) (this section is an antitrust law, not a protectionist statute).

antitrust predatory intent in pursuing relief under the Act.[92] This ruling stoked the fires of the E.U. and Japan which pressed claims against the 1916 Act in the WTO on the grounds, *inter alia*, that the Act violates GATT Article VI and the WTO Antidumping Agreement. It provides treble damages recovery and criminal penalties, forms of relief for injurious dumping that is not prescribed in either the Antidumping Agreement or GATT Article VI.

3.113 The E.U. complained that the Antidumping Act of 1916 violates several GATT 1994 provisions and WTO Agreements, including Articles VI and III of GATT 1994, and the WTO Anti-Dumping Agreement.[93] First, with regard to proof of injury, Article VI:1 of GATT 1994 requires the establishment of material injury or a threat thereof. The 1916 Act does not expressly refer to material injury or threat of material injury or material retardation of the establishment of a domestic industry but rather to "the *intent* of destroying or injuring an industry in the United States, or of preventing the establishment of an industry in the United States." However, the panel noted, identifying an "intent" may not always require a finding of actual injury or actual threat of injury,[94] and reading the "intent" requirement out of the 1916 Act would be contrary to the plain language of the Act. For that reason,

[92] The district court also ruled that mere knowledge on the part of importers of foreign steel that their sales would take business away from U.S. steel firms was insufficient to demonstrate intent to injure the entire U.S. steel industry and, therefore, was inadequate to establish a violation of the Antidumping Act of 1916. See *Geneva Steel*, 980 F. Supp. at 1224.

Wheeling-Pittsburgh Steel Corp. also filed an Antidumping Act of 1916 complaint against three Japanese importers of hot-rolled steel in 1998. See *Wheeling-Pittsburgh Steel Corp. v. Mitsui & Co. (U.S.A.), Inc.*, No. 98–01122 (S.D. Ohio 1998). In addition to suing to recover treble damages and attorneys' fees, Wheeling-Pittsburgh sought injunctive relief barring defendants from importing or selling hot-rolled steel at prices substantially less than its actual market value. On appeal from the district court's denial of Wheeling-Pittsburgh's motion for injunctive relief, the Sixth Circuit affirmed. See *Wheeling-Pittsburgh Steel Corp. v. Mitsui & Co. (U.S.A.), Inc.*, 2000 U.S. App. LEXIS 17759 (6th Cir. July 27, 2000). In a case of first impression, the court noted that Congress expressly provided for treble damages, attorneys' fees, and costs, but made no provision for injunctive relief. The court concluded, therefore, that injunctive relief is not available under the 1916 Act. See *id.* at 6–7. The court added that injunctive relief under the 1916 Act might impede Commerce Department and ITC investigations under the antidumping duty law of Title VII of the Tariff Act of 1930, 19 U.S.C. ss. 1671a, 1673. See *id.* at 9–12.

[93] See "Report of the WTO Panel, United States—Anti-Dumping Act of 1916", WT/DS136/R (2000) (hereinafter "United States—Antidumping Act of 1916"). The same panel of three persons issued a report in a companion case filed by Japan. See "Report of the WTO Panel, United States—Anti-Dumping Act of 1916", WT/DS162/R (2000). The two panel reports, while not identical, are alike in all major respects. Japan complained that the Anti-Dumping Act of 1916 violates the national treatment obligation of Article III:4, *inter alia*, because imported products could be the subject of a U.S. legal proceeding alleging price discrimination under either a trade law remedy (*i.e.* the antidumping duty law), under a competition law remedy (*i.e.* the Anti-Dumping Act of 1916), or both, whereas domestic firms would only be subject to an action for price discrimination under the Robinson-Patman Act. In addition, Japan claimed that the 1916 Act violates Art. III:4 of the GATT 1994 to the extent that it provides less favourable treatment to imported goods than is granted to U.S. goods under the Robinson-Patman Act in terms of the difference in (1) pleading requirements, (2) the use of the intent requirement in the 1916 Act instead of a requirement of "effect" under the Robinson-Patman Act, (3) the cost recoupment requirement, (4) the statutory defences available under the Robinson-Patman Act and not expressly provided for in the 1916 Act, and (5) the conduct subject to penalties. In exercising the principle of judicial economy, the panel disposed of the dispute in favour of Japan on other grounds and declined to examine the question whether the 1916 Act violates the national treatment obligation. See *id.* paras. 6.270–6.272.

[94] See "United States—Antidumping Act of 1916", *supra* n. 93, para. 6.180.

the panel found that the 1916 Act, to the extent that it provides for the identification of an "intent" by the defendant, rather than for the injury requirement of Article VI, is not compatible with Article VI:1 of GATT 1994.[95] The panel also agreed with the E.U. that Article VI:2 provides the exclusive remedy, *i.e.* anti-dumping duties, that may be applied to counteract dumping as such and that, by providing for the imposition of fines, imprisonment, and/or the recovery of treble damages, the 1916 Act violates Article VI:2 of GATT 1994.[96]

In a consolidated appeal to the Appellate Body, the United States renewed its argument that Article VI of GATT 1994 does not provide the exclusive remedy for dumped imports and that only when a WTO member imposes antidumping duties—as opposed to damages, fines and imprisonment—are the provisions of Article VI triggered.[97] The United States added as a corollary argument that the 1916 Act is an antitrust law that targets predatory pricing, not an antidumping law that targets dumping. The Appellate Body rejected both of these contentions.

3.114 In connection with the claim that the 1916 Act does not target dumping, the Appellate Body found that the express language of the Act provides for the recovery of damages and the imposition of criminal penalties when persons import products for sale at a price less than the price for which the products are sold in the country of export or, in certain cases, a third-country market. "In other words," the Appellate Body concluded, "the civil and criminal proceedings and penalties contemplated by the 1916 Act require the presence of the constituent elements of 'dumping,'" thus making GATT Article VI:1 applicable to the 1916 Act.[98] The Appellate Body also rejected the contention that the 1916 Act's *scienter* requirement—an antitrust-type intent—somehow transforms the Act and takes it outside the scope of Article VI. Even though the 1916 Act contains an intent element not found in Article VI:1, the 1916 Act is nevertheless "a specific action against dumping" within the meaning of Article 18.1 of the WTO Antidumping Agreement.[99]

3.115 Having concluded that the 1916 Act is within the scope of Article VI, the Appellate Body agreed with the panel that by providing for the imposition of fines, imprisonment, and an award of treble damages—remedies not available under Article VI:2—the 1916 Act violates Article VI:2.[1] Because the appeal was disposed of under Article VI, the Appellate Body did not address the national treatment claims of Japan and the E.U. Had it considered the national treatment claim in the *Antidumping Act of 1916* case, the

[95] See *id.*
[96] See *id.*, para. 6.204.
[97] See "Report of the Appellate Body, United States—Antidumping Act of 1916", WT/DS136/AB/R, WT/DS162/AB/R, paras. 16–18 (2000) (hereinafter "Report of the Appellate Body, Antidumping Act of 1916").
[98] "Report of the Appellate Body, Antidumping Act of 1916", *supra* note 97, para. 130.
[99] See *id.* para. 132.
[1] See *id.* para. 138. With regard to the E.U.'s and Japan's claim of a national treatment violation, the Appellate Body declined to rule on that claim because it was conditioned on a reversal of the panel's Art. VI findings that the 1916 Act falls within the scope of Art. VI of GATT 1994. See *id.* para. 153.

Appellate Body would probably have concluded that the Act does violate the national treatment obligation of Article III:4 as well. This issue is explored in Chapter Six.

III. Cautious steps forward on competition policy negotiations at the WTO

3.116 Against this backdrop of sector-specific competition policy provisions and a few broad competition policy provisions contained in the TRIPS Agreement and GATS, the WTO largely is silent—and based on the panel report in the *Kodak-Fuji Film* dispute, ambivalent—on whether or how to address the issue of private RBPs that restrict international trade. In an effort to clarify this situation, the E.U. has taken the lead in launching the initiative to examine the question of trade and competition policy under WTO auspices. Prior to the conclusion of the Uruguay Round negotiations in 1994, European Competition Commissioner Sir Leon Brittan called for a WTO agreement on international competition rules.[2] His successor, Karl van Miert, commissioned a Group of Experts to consider this question. The Group of Experts reported back in 1995 that the existing network of bilateral and regional legal regimes on competition law enforcement was not up to the task of resolving all RBPs. They suggested that international antitrust enforcement was being impeded by bilateral antitrust co-operation agreements, differences among national competition laws and the absence of competition laws altogether in some countries.[3] On the basis of the Experts' report, Brittan and van Miert prepared an official communication seeking a WTO agreement that would include an obligation on WTO members to adopt competition rules that would meet a minimum international standard and an obligation to enforce them and to co-operate in such enforcement.[4]

3.117 While the E.U., and later Japan, expressed interest in developing multilateral rules to address cross-border RBPs under WTO auspices, the

---

[2] See Leon Brittan, "A Framework for International Competition", Address Delivered to the World Competition Forum, Davos, Switzerland (Feb. 3, 1992).

[3] See European Commission, "Report by the Group of Experts, Competition Policy in the New Trade Order: Strengthening International Cooperation and Rules" (July 1995).

[4] See Communication to the Council, submitted by Sir Leon Brittan and Karl van Miert, "Towards An International Framework of Competition Rules", COM (96) 296 final (June 18, 1996).

At about this same time, the American Bar Association was examining the issue of a multilateral antitrust agreement. In 1995, an ABA Section Report considered the possibility of using international antitrust rules to open foreign markets. See ABA, Section of International Law and Practice, Report to the House of Delegates, "Using Antitrust Laws to Enhance Access of U.S. Firms to Foreign Markets", (1995) 29 Int'l Law. 945. It found that some business conduct, such as vertical restraints and unilateral refusals to deal, may bar market access without violating U.S. antitrust laws. It noted that suggestions to negotiate multilateral rules to prevent such conduct, however, raise "serious policy issues . . . . The idea of challenging access-restricting private conduct without an antitrust rationale raises the risk of prohibiting efficiency enhancing conduct." The Report therefore recommended that the U.S. government first identify whether such business activities were a significant concern, and, if so, then "study from a policy standpoint whether there is a principled basis to prohibit some of these restraints." The Report noted, however, that "[s]uch an analysis should be informed by competition policy principles and should focus on assuring that efficiency-enhancing conduct is not proscribed." *id.* at 956.

official position of the United States was to participate in such discussions to the extent they identify specific problems that lead to specific solutions to RBPs affecting trade. However, antitrust officials at the DOJ remained sceptical, to say the least, of any multilateral antitrust agreement for fear in part that the end product would reflect the lowest common denominator insofar as prohibited RBPs are concerned.[5] Speaking for the Justice Department, Assistant Attorney General Joel Klein worried that establishing an international antitrust legal regime would slow future developments in the field and inhibit flexibility to adjust policies to changing business conditions. He advocated a bottom up, rather than a top down, approach to the question of an international antitrust legal regime. In that way, antitrust laws might converge naturally and eventually lead to a high-quality, multilateral agreement.

3.118 On a more conciliatory, if not overly enthusiastic, note on behalf of the United States, U.S. Trade Representative Charlene Barshefsky announced at the first WTO Ministerial meeting in Singapore in December 1996 that the United States was "willing to go along with others who wish to begin a modest work program in the areas of investment and competition, as part of a balanced overall agenda for the WTO."[6]

With no strong opposition to the suggestion of at least putting competition policy on the WTO's agenda, the WTO membership accepted an E.U. proposal to form a Working Group to study the relationship between trade and competition policy. As developed in the next Chapter, the enthusiastic search for convergence has exposed the painful reality of divergence.

[5] See Joel I. Klein, Assistant Attorney General, U.S. Dep't of Justice, "A Note of Caution with Respect to a WTO Agenda on Competition Policy", Remarks Before the Royal Institute of Int'l Affairs, London, Eng. (Nov. 18, 1997) ("we must guard against a lowest-common-denominator outcome in the development of competition rules by the WTO"), htt://www.usdoj.gov/atr/speeches/jikspch.htm; Charles S. Stark, Chief, Foreign Commerce Section, U.S. Dep't of Justice, "Enhancing Market Access Through Trade and Antitrust Law", Remarks Before the Section of Int'l Law & Practice, Amer. Bar Ass'n, (Aug. 8, 1995), htt://www.usdoj.gov/atr/speeches/chicago.ccs; "U.S. Opposes Plan to Negotiate Agreement in WTO, Officials Say",(1997) 14 Int'l Trade Rep. (BNA) 2034.

[6] Statement by the Hon. Charlene Barshefsky, WT/MIN(96)/ST/5 (Dec. 9, 1996), http://www.wto.org/archives/st5.htm.

Chapter Four

The Search for Convergence, The Reality of Divergence

I. The WTO work programme on competition policy

4.001 Two WTO Working Groups were established in 1997 to examine the relationship between trade and investment and between trade and competition policy. The Ministerial Declaration issued at the conclusion of the 1996 Singapore Ministerial Conference directed as follows:

> Having regard to the existing WTO provisions on matters related to investment and competition policy and the built-in agenda in these areas, including the TRIMs Agreement, and on the understanding that the work undertaken shall not prejudge whether negotiations will be initiated in the future, we also agree to:
>
> –establish a working group to examine the relationship between trade and investment; and
>
> –establish a working group to study issues raised by Members relating to the interaction between trade and competition policy, including anti-competitive practices, in order to identify any areas that may merit further consideration in the WTO framework.[1]

The Working Group on the Interaction between Trade and Competition Policy (WGTCP) was established concurrently with the Working Group on the Relationship between Trade and Investment. The purpose of the WGTCP is to examine the interaction between trade and competition policy, with the long-term goal of determining how the WTO could move towards a greater convergence between these two policies. The many contributions of the participants in the WGTCP reveal that there are points of convergence, matched by even more points of divergence, in national competition legislation, practice, and policy.

A. The WGTCP's 1997 Work Programme

4.002 The bulk of WTO members' submissions to the WGTCP in 1997 was devoted to suggestions for a work programme. Participation was open to all WTO members and several international organisations and regional

[1] Singapore Ministerial Declaration, adopted on Dec. 13, 1996 WT/MIN(96)/DEC, para. 20.

arrangements with a special interest in international antitrust. APEC, ASEAN, the OECD, the World Bank and the United Nations were among the participants in this latter group.[2] It was a year marked by drift and lack of direction. No sooner did the WGTCP hold its first meeting in July 1997 than a dispute broke out over whether reform of the antidumping (AD) laws should be on the agenda. On this question, the United States was joined by the E.U. in opposing consideration of reform of the AD laws by the Working Group. Japan, Hong Kong and Korea argued that any study of the relationship between trade and competition policy would be incomplete if it did not include an examination of the operation of the AD laws. In the end, the topic was discussed by the participants. Although the Working Group assumed the task of finding whatever common ground it could on the issues of trade and its relationship with competition policy, this episode highlights the lack of consensus on at least one critical aspect of the trade and competition policy relationship, namely the fit of the AD laws with competition law.

Several members made submissions during 1997 suggesting possible areas of study for the WGTCP.

Australia.

4.003 Possible issues for discussion that Australia thought important were:

(1) transparency of domestic regulations,

(2) appropriate minimum standards of regulation,

(3) whether a common understanding on concepts in trade and competition policy can be reached, and

(4) structural reform of state monopolies.[3]

Canada.

4.004 Canada suggested the Working Group undertake:

(1) an assessment of the contribution of competition policy to economic growth and development,

(2) a survey of the treatment of competition policy in WTO agreements,

(3) an analysis of the linkages between competition policy and foreign investment, and

(4) an examination of the impact of private RBPs on markets, producers, and consumers.[4]

[2] See, *e.g.* WTO, "Working Group on the Interaction between Trade and Competition Policy, Communication from ASEAN", WT/WGTCP/W/19 (July 3, 1997); WTO, "Working Group on the Interaction between Trade and Competition Policy, Communication from the World Bank", WT/WGTCP/W/22 (July 9, 1997).

[3] See WTO, "Working Group on the Interaction between Trade and Competition Policy, Communication from Australia", WT/WGTCP/W/8 (June 19, 1997).

[4] See WTO, "Working Group on the Interaction between Trade and Competition Policy, Communication from Canada", WT/WGTCP/W/7 (June 19, 1997).

Egypt.

4.005 Egypt viewed the mission of the WGTCP as largely educational. It suggested that the Working Group undertake three major studies on:

(1) the elements of an effective competition policy,

(2) the development dimension of competition policy, and

(3) the relevant provisions of the Uruguay Round agreements related to competition.[5]

European Union.

4.006 The E.U. suggested that the WGTCP examine five areas:

(1) identify the main anti-competitive practices that restrict international trade,

(2) examine the feasibility of all WTO members adopting a competition law and enforcement mechanism,

(3) examine how the WTO can support co-operation among national enforcement authorities,

(4) identify core common principles of competition law that might be adopted at the international level, and

(5) examine the extent to which WTO dispute settlement might be used to ensure compliance with a multilateral agreement.[6]

Hong Kong.

4.007 Hong Kong proposed that the WGTCP:

(1) study the objectives of trade policy and competition policy;

(2) take stock of existing WTO provisions relevant to competition issues;

(3) examine areas of potential inconsistencies between trade and competition policies, such as antidumping duties on low-priced imports; and

(4) examine the relationship between competition and development.[7]

India.

4.008 India suggested a broad, three-part framework to guide the WGTCP's discussions:

[5] See WTO, "Working Group on the Interaction between Trade and Competition Policy, Communication from Egypt", WT/WGTCP/W/9 (June 19, 1997).
[6] See WTO, "Working Group on the Interaction between Trade and Competition Policy, Communication from the European Community", WT/WGTCP/W/1 (June 11, 1997).
[7] See WTO, "Working Group on the Interaction between Trade and Competition Policy, Communication from Hong Kong", WT/WGTCP/W/15 (June 26, 1997).

(1) study the relationship between trade and competition policy;

(2) examine the linkages among development, trade, and competition policy; and

(3) study existing WTO provisions with a bearing on competition policy.[8]

Japan.

4.009 The suggested work program proposed by Japan included:

(1) a stocktaking of existing WTO, regional, bilateral, and national rules on competition policy;

(2) an analysis of the interaction between trade and competition policy, including the effects of cartels, predatory pricing, and mergers with cross-border effects on trade flows; and

(3) case studies on the interaction between trade and competition policies, such as the experience in the E.U. and ANZCERTA.[9]

Mexico.

4.010 Mexico's position was that the WGTCP should analyse:

(1) the convergence and divergence in existing competition laws and policies,

(2) the effects of competition policy on market access,

(3) the practicability of all WTO members adopting and enforcing a competition law, and

(4) the international co-operation mechanisms for improving coherence between trade and competition policy.[10]

Norway.

4.011 Norway suggested that the Working Group answer the following five questions:

(1) what are the main RBPs restricting international trade?

(2) what are the restrictive effects of trade measures on international competition?

(3) to what extent are the foregoing covered by existing WTO provisions?

[8] See WTO, "Working Group on the Interaction between Trade and Competition Policy, Communication from India", WT/WGTCP/W/24 (July 10, 1997).
[9] See WTO, "Working Group on the Interaction between Trade and Competition Policy, Communication from Japan", WT/WGTCP/W/4 (June 19, 1997).
[10] See WTO, "Working Group on the Interaction between Trade and Competition Policy, Communication from Mexico", WT/WGTCP/W/13 (June 25, 1997).

(4) which are the common elements of national and regional competition rules currently in force? and

(5) is it feasible to identify common competition principles?[11]

Pakistan.

4.012 Pakistan's suggestions for a WGTCP work programme included an examination of:

(1) competition policy in developing countries that highlights their special needs for institutional capacity-building,

(2) how RBPs adversely impact developing countries,

(3) the relationship of competition policy and development,

(4) the appropriateness of competition law as it exists in developed countries for developing countries, and

(5) the ability of developing countries to combat the RBPs of multinational firms.[12]

Switzerland.

4.013 Switzerland recommended that the WGTCP proceed in three stages. Stage 1 would identify anti-competitive practices affecting international trade. Stage 2 would analyse WTO coverage of the practices identified in Stage 1. On the basis of the results of the first two stages, Stage 3 would determine the future work programme of the WTO.[13]

United States.

4.014 The United States offered an approach to the WGTCP's discussions that was more focused on competition law *per se*. It suggested that the Working Group begin by examining the history and current treatment of competition law in the GATT–WTO system. That examination would be followed by a review of national competition laws, including the core elements of competition law, its economic underpinnings and institutions of enforcement. Finally, the WGTCP should study the international dimensions of competition law and policy, including areas where increased co-operation could be beneficial.[14]

4.015 As reflected in its 1997 report to the General Council, the WGTCP attempted to synthesise these diverse suggestions and provide some focus to

---

[11] See WTO, "Working Group on the Interaction between Trade and Competition Policy, Communication from Norway", WT/WGTCP/W/12 (June 23, 1997).

[12] See WTO, "Working Group on the Interaction between Trade and Competition Policy, Communication from Pakistan", WT/WGTCP/W/10 (June 19, 1997).

[13] See WTO, "Working Group on the Interaction between Trade and Competition Policy, Communication from Switzerland", WT/WGTCP/W/2 (June 17, 1997).

[14] See WTO, "Working Group on the Interaction between Trade and Competition Policy, Communication from the United States", WT/WGTCP/W/6 (June 19, 1997).

future discussions by issuing the following checklist of issues suggested for study:

- What are the main anti-competitive practices that restrict international trade?
- Is it feasible for all WTO umembers to adopt domestic competition laws and enforcement mechanisms?
- How can the WTO promote co-operation between national enforcement authorities?
- Is there a core of common competition policy principles that might be adopted at the international level?
- What is the relationship of restrictive business practices with foreign direct investment, especially in the area of mergers and acquisitions?
- How do restrictive business practices of multinational enterprises inhibit developing-country economic development?[15]

B. The WGTCP's 1998 Work Programme

4.016 As part of its work programme for 1998, the WGTCP examined

(1) the relationship between the objectives, principles, concepts, scope, and instruments of trade and competition policy;

(2) existing instruments regarding trade and competition policy;

(3) the impact of trade policy on competition;

(4) the impact of anti-competitive practices of enterprises on international trade; and

(5) the impact of regulatory practices, state monopolies, and exclusive rights on competition and international trade.[16]

The relationship between the objectives, principles, concepts, scope, and instruments of trade and competition policy.

4.017 Written submissions on the subject of the relationship between trade and competition policy were provided by Canada, the E.U., Hong Kong,

[15] See WTO, "Working Group on the Interaction between Trade and Competition Policy, Report (1997) to the General Council", WT/WGTCP/W/49 (Nov. 25,1997). For other WTO member submissions on a study agenda for the WGTCP, see WTO, "Working Group on the Interaction between Trade and Competition Policy, Communication from Nigeria", WT/WGTCP/W/16 (July 2, 1997); WTO, "Working Group on the Interaction between Trade and Competition Policy, Communication from New Zealand", WT/WGTCP/W/20 (July 4, 1997); "WTO, Working Group on the Interaction between Trade and Competition Policy, Communication from Poland", WT/WGTCP/W/23 (July 9, 1997); WTO, "Working Group on the Interaction between Trade and Competition Policy, Communication from Venezuela", WT/WGTCP/W/14 (June 25, 1997).

[16] See generally WTO, "Working Group on the Interaction between Trade and Competition Policy, Report to the General Council", WT/WGTCP/2 (Dec. 8, 1998) (hereinafter "WGTCP 1998 Report"). See also Joseph P. Griffin, "The WTO Study of the Interaction Between Trade and Competition Policy: Timely and Controversial", (1997) 145 Corp. Couns. Int'l Adviser 10; Robert E. Hudec, "A WTO Perspective on Private Anti-Competitive Behavior in World Markets", (1999) 34 New Eng. L. Rev. 79 (hereinafter Hudec, "A WTO Perspective").

Japan, Mexico, Morocco, New Zealand, Pakistan, Peru, Romania, Singapore, Turkey, the United States and ASEAN.[17] The participants disagreed on whether the term "competition policy" necessarily embraces a competition law. Members noted that trade and competition policy can be and usually are mutually reinforcing, interdependent, and complementary. Both policies contribute towards making domestic markets more competitive, thus improving the allocation of resources, promoting efficiency and enhancing consumer welfare.[18] The view was offered that neither policy could achieve its goal without the other, given that trade policy's focus generally is government conduct at the border, whereas competition policy's focus is private conduct within a domestic market. Members also stated that from a development viewpoint, the two policies should be adopted simultaneously. In this way, competition policy would act as a catalyst for economic reform and development based on market principles.[19]

4.018 Participants noted the divergence between trade and competition policy when restrictive trade measures are tolerated that block market access, thereby

(1) limiting competition in the domestic market by curtailing market access for foreign goods and services, and
(2) facilitating anti-competitive behaviour by domestic firms.

Likewise, exclusions or exemptions from competition law, as well as lack of enforcement, can have a negative impact on trade. It was also noted that the two policies can diverge in their overall goals. Competition policy's goal is to protect competition and thereby enhance consumer welfare. Other goals include promoting international competitiveness and preserving opportunities for small and medium-size enterprises (SMEs) to participate in the national economy.[20] Trade policy, on the other hand, focuses on protecting competitors, promoting exports, raising revenue and enhancing producer welfare, thus making it susceptible to capture by special interest groups.[21] At the same time, competition policy gives excessive weight to the welfare of domestic consumers by its indifference to anti-competitive domestic conduct that only harms foreign consumers. This preference for domestic consumers is evidenced in the exemptions for export cartels found in many national competition laws.

4.019 The participants conceded that it is unrealistic to expect a convergence of the objectives of trade and competition policy.[22] While competition policy focuses on efficiency and consumer welfare, trade policy's objective is to protect and advance the interests of domestic producers. This divergence can yield a determination, for example, that a given vertical

[17] See "WGTCP 1998 Report", *supra* note 16, at 7.
[18] See *id.* at 8, paras. 21–23.
[19] See *id.* at 8, para. 24.
[20] See *id.* at 18, para. 48.
[21] See *id.* at 8, para. 26.
[22] See *id.* at 9, para. 27.

restraint is acceptable under competition policy because there are a sufficient number of competing domestic firms, but is unacceptable under trade policy if it blocks market access to foreign producers.[23]

On the question of whether one policy is substitutable for another, some participants suggested that the antidumping duty law might be replaced by competition law on discriminatory pricing.[24] With the lifting of trade barriers, unfairly priced imports could be shipped directly back to the country of exportation. Thus, removal of barriers to market access in the country of exportation, coupled with arbitrage, would eliminate the need for an anti-dumping duty law.[25] Several submissions were critical of the AD law from a competition standpoint in that AD duties can be imposed in a case of price discrimination that is in fact pro-competitive or beneficial to consumers in the importing country.[26]

Stocktaking of existing instruments regarding trade and competition policy.

4.020 Twenty-four members made submissions analysing their national competition policies, laws, and legal instruments as they relate to international trade.[27] In the discussions among members on this point, some members indicated that they were committed to maintaining a vigorous competition policy, but had found it unnecessary to enact a comprehensive competition law.[28] Other members responded that while it might be possible to have a competition policy without also having a competition law, the benefits of having a competition law included greater consistency in enforcement proceedings across sectors, giving competition policy enforceability and stability and reducing the danger of capture of a competition authority by special interest groups.[29]

4.021 Working Group participants also discussed a number of important aspects of competition policy analysis, including market definition, the distinction between *per se* rules and the rule of reason, and the extraterritorial application of competition law. With regard to market definition, defining the relevant market is important in competition cases. The relevant market has a product and geographic dimension. In connection with the product dimension, the inquiry is with which other products and services does a particular product compete? With regard to the geographic dimension of market definition, the focus is on the geographic area within which competition

[23] See *id.*
[24] See, *e.g.* WTO, "Working Group on the Interaction between Trade and Competition Policy, Submission from Mexico", WT/WGTCP/W/58 (Dec. 19, 1997).
[25] See "WGTCP 1998 Report", see para. 4.016, n. 16, at 9, para. 28.
[26] See, *e.g.* WTO, "Working Group on the Interaction between Trade and Competition Policy, Communication from Japan", WT/WGTCP/W/32, at 2–3 (Sept. 26, 1997) (criticising abuse of AD law); WTO, "Working Group on the Interaction between Trade and Competition Policy, Communication from New Zealand", WT/WGTCP/W/30, at 3 (Sept. 15, 1997) (noting anti-competitive effects of AD orders).
[27] See "WGTCP 1998 Report", see para. 4.016, n. 16 , at 17, Table 1.
[28] See *id.* at 18, para. 46.
[29] See *id.* at 18, para. 47.

occurs. The relevant geographic market traditionally has been local or national in scope, but with increased integration of national economies through the process of globalisation, the geographic market could be international. This development suggested to some participants the need for greater co-operation among national enforcement authorities.[30]

4.022 With regard to *per se* rules and rules of reason, the participants could find no common ground, first of all, on which practices are anti-competitive; and, secondly, of the practices that are anti-competitive, which should be subject to a *per se* rule or a rule of reason.[31] As the Working Group report notes,

> [p]ractices subject to the former approach, *at least in some jurisdictions*, included horizontal price fixing, bid rigging and market allocation. Practices subject to the latter approach (again, *in some jurisdictions*) included vertical agreements and single-firm exclusionary conduct.[32]

4.023 Finally, regarding the extraterritorial application of competition law, the participants noted the potential for conflict between jurisdictions when national competition laws are applied to conduct occurring abroad that causes harmful effects in the territory of the country of enforcement. It was agreed that co-operation agreements that include principles of traditional comity and positive comity can be useful in minimising conflicts.[33] Canada and the United States cautioned that positive comity requests are limited to a violation of the competition laws in the country where the anti-competitive practices are occurring, and that the alleged conduct must violate the law of the requested country in most cases. If, due to an exception or exclusion, the alleged conduct does not violate the requested country's law, no enforcement action in that country is possible in most circumstances.[34]

The impact of private anti-competitive practices on international trade.

4.024 In this phase of the Working Group's discussions, participants presented national experiences with actual cases of private, anti-competitive practices that had an impact on international trade. These actual cases were supplemented by hypothetical ones to illustrate related concerns.

The first category of RBPs considered by the WGTCP were practices affecting market access. The list of practices include import cartels, international cartels that allocate national markets among participating firms,

---

[30] See *id.* at 20, para. 54.

[31] Under a *per se* rule, practices are treated as objectionable without the necessity of showing harmful effects; hence, the *per se* label. Under a rule of reason, anti- and pro-competitive effects are weighed and balanced against each other in a specific case.

[32] "WGTCP 1998 Report", see para. 4.016, n. 16, at 20, para. 55 (emphases added, footnote omitted).

[33] See *id.* at 20, para. 56.

[34] See WTO, "Working Group on the Interaction between Trade and Competition Policy, Communication from Canada", WT/WGTCP/W/72, at 6 (Apr. 6, 1998); WTO, "Working Group on the Interaction between Trade and Competition Policy, Communication from the United States", WT/WGTCP/W/67, at 4–5 (Mar. 26, 1998). As noted in Chap. Two, some MLATs dispense with the dual criminality requirement.

restrictions on parallel imports, control over import facilities, abuse of a dominant position through exclusionary practices, vertical restraints that foreclose markets to competitors, private standards-setting activities, vertical integration by manufacturers into distribution, exclusive dealing and sole distribution contracts, and predatory pricing.[35] The observation was made that although vertical arrangements can be used for market foreclosure purposes, they can also be efficiency enhancing and pro-competitive, necessitating an evaluation on a case-by-case basis.[36] Argentina and Peru presented case studies showing that despite trade liberalisation in their respective countries, specific markets within their economies were not competitive owing to private RBPs within their countries.[37]

4.025 A second category of RBP examined by the Working Group was any practice affecting different countries in largely the same way, the foremost example being international cartels on price and output for multiple-country markets. For example, international cartelisation could be forced upon a firm through industry associations which threaten the exporters of other countries with an antidumping petition and thereafter extort a price undertaking (*i.e.* suspension agreement) from them.[38]

4.026 A third category of RBP examined by the WGTCP with a differential impact on affected countries was export cartels. The extent of such cartels is difficult to know because most countries do not require registration of such cartels but instead turn a blind eye.[39] The Working Group also discussed government policies that could facilitate anti-competitive practices, such as the failure to have a comprehensive competition law and policy, and the failure to adequately enforce existing competition laws where they do exist.

4.027 A proposal was made for work to be done on the following five anti-competitive practices, based on the degree of consensus that the WGTCP believed exists with respect to each practice and their importance for international trade:[40]

(1) Hard-core cartels. Given the high degree of consensus to eliminate hard-core cartels, the prospects for adoption of a common enforcement principle and a framework for co-operative enforcement among the WTO members seems good, according to the WGTCP. However, some members are of the view that domestic competition laws are adequate to respond to hard-core cartels.

(2) Export cartels. The WGTCP suggested that consideration be given as to how to strengthen the application of competition law in this area. Some participants agreed that inter-agency co-operation could be helpful in addressing export cartels, but that mutual confidence building was needed first.

---

[35] See "WGTCP 1998 Report", see para. 4.016, n. 16, at 28, para. 84.
[36] See *id.* at 29, para. 86.
[37] See *id.* at 28–29, para. 85.
[38] See *id.* at 29–30, para. 87.
[39] See *id.* at 30, para. 89.
[40] See *id.* at 32, para. 93.

(3) Vertical restraints. It is generally recognised that the rule of reason applies to most vertical restraints, but a list of factors used by national enforcement authorities when balancing the anti- and pro-competitive effects of a vertical agreement needs to be developed. Some participants believed that the most that can be hoped for in this category of RBP is consultation between countries with overlapping interests. They added that it is inevitable that different jurisdictions will reach different conclusions regarding the anti-competitive effects of a vertical arrangement in a particular case.

(4) Abuse of a dominant position. The WGTCP suggested that it develop

(a) a list of abusive practices that could foreclose market access, and
(b) a set of criteria to be used in identifying a dominant position in a market.

(6) Mergers. The WGTCP suggested examining the possibility for convergence on procedural requirements and enhanced cross-border co-operation among enforcement authorities.

The impact of regulatory practices, state monopolies, and exclusive rights on competition and international trade.

4.028 The potential anti-competitive effects of state monopolies is widely recognised. However, while some countries apply competition rules to state monopolies or to enterprises enjoying exclusive rights, other governments exempt them in whole or in part.[41] Some members noted a gap in coverage of GATT Article XVII, dealing with state trading enterprises, but not with the operation of private firms that can have similar effects on market access.

The impact of trade policy on competition.

4.029 The WGTCP noted that any trade measure that effectively protects domestic markets from foreign competition could contribute to concentration in a domestic market and lead to a possible abuse of a dominant position to the detriment of consumers.[42] Such trade-restrictive measures include high tariffs, export and domestic subsidies, product standards and testing requirements, safeguards, discriminatory rules on government procurement, import quotas, and discriminatory rules of origin.

In connection with the fit of the antidumping duty law and competition policy, some participants asserted that the imposition of antidumping duties can be detrimental to competition and consumer welfare.[43] The mere filing of an antidumping duty petition can be used by domestic firms for its *in terrorem*

[41] See *id.* at 34, para. 101.
[42] See *id.* at 43–44, para. 136.
[43] See *id.* at 22–23, para. 60; WTO, "Working Group on the Interaction between Trade and Competition Policy, Communication from Japan", The Impact of Trade Policy on Competition, WT/WGTCP/W/92 (Sept. 21, 1998).

effect to restrain or eliminate foreign competition by inducing exporters to unilaterally reduce their exports, raise their prices (thereby encouraging cartelisation), or switch production locations.[44]

Recommendations for the future work programme.

4.030 The Working Group stated at the end of 1998 that it intended to continue the educative work it has undertaken by focusing on

(1) the relevance of fundamental WTO principles of national treatment, MFN treatment, and transparency to competition policy;

(2) approaches to promoting co-operation and communication among members; and

(3) the contribution of competition policy to achieving the objectives of the WTO.[45]

C. The WGTCP's 1999 Work Programme

4.031 The Singapore Ministerial Declaration directed the General Council to determine after two years, *i.e.* at the end of 1998, whether and how the work of the two Working Groups should proceed. In December 1998, the General Council extended the term of the WGTCP indefinitely, but directed the WGTCP to focus its discussions on three items:

(1) the relevance of fundamental WTO principles of national treatment, transparency, and most-favoured-nation treatment to competition policy and vice versa;

(2) approaches to promoting co-operation and communication among members, including in the field of technical co-operation; and

(3) the contribution of competition policy to achieving the objectives of the WTO, including the promotion of international trade.[46]

The relevance of fundamental WTO principles to competition policy.

4.032 Participants expressed the general view that adherence to the fundamental WTO principles of MFN treatment, national treatment, and transparency was not just important but essential to the sound application, effectiveness, impartiality, and credibility of competition law.[47] Competition

[44] See "WGTCP 1998 Report", see para. 4.016, n. 16, at 46, para. 140.
[45] See *id.* at 50, para. 154. See generally F.M. Scherer, *Competition Policies for An Integrated World Economy* (Brookings 1994).
[46] See WTO, Decision of the General Council, WT/GC/M/32, at 52 (Dec. 1998).
[47] See WTO, "Working Group on the Interaction between Trade and Competition Policy", (1999) "Report of the Working Group on the Interaction between Trade and Competition Policy to the General Council", WT/WGTCP/3, at 4, para. 11 (Oct. 11, 1999) (hereinafter "WGTCP 1999 Report); WTO, "Working Group on the Interaction between Trade and Competition Policy, Communication from the European Community and Its Member States", *The relevance of fundamental WTO principles of national treatment, transparency and most-favoured-nation treatment to competition policy and vice versa*, WT/WGTCP/W/115, at 1–4 (May 25,1999).

policy and the principles of MFN and national treatment share an intrinsic relationship in that they seek to ensure equal competitive opportunities to foreign competitors.[48] They each protect competition, not competitors, given that the nationality of individual competitors is irrelevant under all three.[49] In a submission to the WGTCP, the United States observed that private discrimination does not violate competition law unless it causes injury, whereas government discrimination that violates either the national treatment or MFN commitments is a GATT violation regardless of injury. This divergence raises the question whether the focus should be on market access (a concern of trade policy) or on the ability of firms to compete (the concern of competition policy).[50]

The fit of bilateral co-operation agreements and mutual legal assistance treaties with the MFN commitment was touched upon, but not satisfactorily resolved. The United States suggested that the MFN commitment is not a straitjacket that precludes differentiated results, only differentiated treatment.[51]

Approaches to resolving anti-competitive practices in the trade context.

4.033 Three possible approaches were suggested for addressing anti-competitive practices that adversely affect international trade. First, WTO members could attempt to eliminate these practices through national trade and competition legislation (a unilateral approach). The shortcoming of the unilateral approach is that it often provokes jurisdictional conflicts. Secondly, a bilateral approach could be used that involves greater resort to co-operative arrangements. Bilateral approaches tend to be limited to countries with deep experience in competition law enforcement, however. Alternatively, and third, a multilateral approach could be pursued.[52]

4.034 The elements of a multilateral approach would include the adoption in each member country of a competition law that addresses at a minimum the most trade-distorting RBPs: anti-competitive horizontal restraints, vertical restraints and abuses of a dominant position.[53] Merger control should be applied in a transparent and non-discriminatory manner. Exclusions from the scope of competition law should be restricted to a minimum. Secondly, affected countries should deal with export cartels in a co-operative manner. Thirdly, measures should be taken to promote the

---

[48] See "WGTCP 1999 Report", *supra* n. 47, at 21, para. 66.

[49] See WTO, "Working Group on the Interaction between Trade and Competition Policy, Note by the Secretariat", *Fundamental WTO Principles of National treatment, Most-Favoured-Nation Treatment and Transparency*, WT/WGTCP/W/114, at 7–8 para. 29 (April 14, 1999).

[50] See WTO, "Working Group on the Interaction between Trade and Competition Policy, Communication from the United States", *Relevance of Fundamental WTO Principles to Competition Policy*, WT/WGTCP/W/131, at 1 n. 2 (July 13, 1999).

[51] See *id.* at 8, para. 21.

[52] See *id.* at 8, para. 24.

[53] See *id.* at 8, para. 26; WTO, "Working Group on the Interaction between Trade and Competition Policy, Communication from the European Community and Its Member States", *The relevance of fundamental WTO principles of national treatment, transparency and most-favoured-nation treatment to competition policy and vice versa*, WT/WGTCP/W/115, at 1–4 (May 25, 1999).

institutional capacities of competition authorities, including their advocacy role, effective and transparent enforcement powers and mechanisms for protecting confidential information.[54] Fourthly, the aim should be to eventually converge national competition laws. A number of objections were raised to these suggestions. Some participants disagreed, first of all, that a multilateral approach was either appropriate or needed. The participants affirmed that in the case of their own competition laws, the principles of MFN treatment, national treatment and transparency were already a part of those laws.[55] As such, from a WTO standpoint, no action was needed at the multilateral level in this regard. In addition, some participants questioned whether a competition law was needed at all. Singapore and Hong Kong were cited as examples of two countries regarded as being among the most competitive in the world, despite the fact that neither country has a comprehensive competition law.[56] Moreover, requiring a comprehensive competition law as part of WTO commitments fails to take into account the diversity of legal systems and the state of development of individual WTO members.

4.035 It was suggested that in lieu of a multilateral agreement mandating specific competition legislation, a multilateral or plurilateral framework agreement could be negotiated that did not specify or require individual members to introduce comprehensive competition legislation. In the case of a plurilateral agreement, a framework agreement would merely prescribe principles to be followed if a member were to introduce national competition legislation.[57] Against the backdrop of more than 80 countries now having enacted competition legislation, representing 86 per cent of world trade,[58] to some the prospects seem better than ever for reaching a consensus on core competition principles.[59]

Despite the enthusiasm shown by some participants for launching negotiations on a multilateral competition policy agreement, these participants were reminded that the Working Group is "in an exploratory and educative process and was still a long way off from the point where it could be in a position to gauge the need for multilateral rules."[60]

---

[54] See "WGTCP 1999 Report", see para. 4.032, n. 47, at 8, para. 24.

[55] See *id.* at 6, para. 16.

[56] See *id.* at 10, para. 30.

[57] See *id.* at 11, para. 34.

[58] See WTO, "Working Group on the Interaction between Trade and Competition Policy, Communication from the European Community and Its Member States", *A Multilateral Framework Agreement on Competition Policy*, at 2, WT/WGTCP/W/152 (Sept. 25, 2000).

[59] See *id.* at 11, para. 35; WTO, "Working Group on the Interaction between Trade and Competition Policy, Communication from the United States", *Relevance of Fundamental WTO Principles to Competition Policy*, WT/WGTCP/W/131, at 3, para. 7 (July 13, 1999). But see A.E. Rodriguez & Malcolm B. Coate, "Limits to Antitrust Policy for Reforming Economies", (1996) 18 Hous. J. Int'l L. 311, 327–29 (authors note that one unifying characteristic of the new competition laws of Albania, Bulgaria, the Czech Republic, Estonia, Hungary, Latvia, Lithuania, Poland, Romania, Russia, Slovakia and Slovenia is a desire to support a pro-market model of privatisation).

[60] "WGTCP 1999 Report", see para. 4.032, n. 47, at 12, para. 37.

Approaches to promoting co-operation and communication among members.

4.036 The benefit of co-operation among members from a trade perspective is that if market access is restricted due to private anti-competitive practices, co-operation with foreign competition authorities could help resolve the problem. From a competition policy perspective, co-operation among WTO members can improve the co-ordination of national competition policies and help to avoid jurisdictional conflicts.[61]

The participants discussed the merits of positive comity agreements. Practical experience with positive comity is limited.[62] They noted that while such agreements have merit, they are unlikely to work in situations where the requested country is being asked to enforce its competition law at the expense of a domestic industry and where the requesting country will be the primary beneficiary of the enforcement action. They also noted the limitations of positive comity as a tool for combating export cartels. The exporting country/ requested country will not find it in its interest to take action against the export cartel and may not be able to take action if the export cartel's activities are lawful in the requested country.[63]

4.037 The participants noted the limitations of bilateral co-operation agreements. For one, bilateral co-operation agreements tend to be concluded between countries that are economically interdependent and that have had a similar level of experience in competition laws enforcement.[64] For another, co-operation under these agreements is ad hoc, on a case-by-case basis. They do not address in a comprehensive manner broader questions of competition policy.[65] With regard to regional co-operation efforts, the WGTCP concluded that harmonisation of national competition laws depends on the level of economic integration among the countries to the regional arrangement. In this regard, the contrasting styles of different regional arrangements were noted, with the E.U. having supranational competition law enforcement in place, in contrast to NAFTA's decentralised approach.[66]

---

[61] See *id.* at 12, 13, paras. 39, 41.

[62] See WTO, "Working Group on the Interaction between Trade and Competition Policy, Communication from the United States", *Approaches to Promoting Cooperation and Communication among Members including in the Field of Technical Cooperation*, WT/WGTCP/W/129, at 6 (May 25, 1999). The onc case where a positive comity provision in a bilateral co-operation agreement has been invoked is the referral by the U.S. Department of Justice to the E.U. involving allegations that anti-competitive conduct by European airlines prevented entry by U.S.-based airline computer reservation systems known as SABRE. See *id.* at 6; U.S. Dep t of Justice, Press Release, "Justice Department Asks European Communities to Investigate Possible Anticompetitive Conduct Affecting U.S. Airlines Computer Reservations Systems" (Apr. 28, 1997). See also "U.S. Industries Urge Justice to Take Action on Antitrust in Japan's Glass, Paper Sectors", 16 Int'l Trade Rep. (BNA) 817 (May 12, 1999) ("Assistant Attorney General Joel I. Klein . . . said positive comity is a process that can work,' but he cautioned that it is not going to be a panacea for all trade problems.").

[63] See "WGTCP 1999 Report", see para. 4.032, n. 47, at 13, para. 42, WTO, "Working Group on the Interaction Between Trade and Competition Policy" (2000), *Report of the Working Group to the General Council*, WT/WGTCP/4, at 6–30 (Nov. 30, 2000).

[64] See WTO, "Working Group on the Interaction between Trade and Competition Policy, Communication from the Republic of Korea", *International Cooperation and Competition Policy: Bilateral, Regional and Multilateral Approaches*, WT/WGTCP/W/124, at 1 (May 31, 1999).

[65] See "WGTCP 1999 Report", see para. 4.032, n. 47, at 14, para. 44.

[66] See *id.* at 14–15, para. 46.

4.038 It was noted that co-operation at the multilateral level is limited and consists mainly of the work of the OECD and UNCTAD with the World Bank playing a minor role in providing policy advice, giving technical assistance, and preparing specialised studies. The E.U. and Korea contend that while the work of the OECD is a positive development, a more coherent and comprehensive approach is necessary because of increased globalisation of business activities and the concomitant increase in RBPs with cross-border effects.[67]

4.039 With regard to the role that the WTO might play in this connection, the participants considered several possible models for a WTO agreement on competition policy. An agreement could consist of uniform substantive and procedural competition norms, with a supranational competition authority. The 1993 Munich Draft Code (analysed in Chapter One) was suggested as a drafting model. Given the differences in objectives, priorities, rules, procedures and institutions in the competition law regimes of WTO members, however, it was suggested that this diversity called for the adoption of broad competition principles in a multilateral framework agreement rather than harmonisation of members' competition rules.[68] This option would be a TRIPS-type agreement under which every member would be required to incorporate substantive competition norms into domestic law, and to establish independent administrative and judicial bodies to oversee implementation and enforcement. Principles on transparency and non-discrimination would be an essential part of any framework agreement.[69] The agreement would include common rules on anti-competitive practices affecting international trade, at least where a consensus exists. For example, hard-core cartels—agreements among competitors involving price fixing, bid rigging, output restrictions or market allocation—would be addressed under a common rule.[70] Other RBPs,

[67] See WTO, "Working Group on the Interaction between Trade and Competition Policy, Communication from the European Community and Its Member States", *Approaches to promoting cooperation and communication among WTO Members, including in the field of technical cooperation*, WT/WGTCP/W/129, at 8 (July 12,1999); WTO, "Working Group on the Interaction between Trade and Competition Policy, Communication from the Republic of Korea", *International Cooperation and Competition Policy: Bilateral, Regional and Multilateral Approaches*, WT/WGTCP/W/124, at 3 (May 31, 1999).

[68] See "WGTCP 1999 Report", see para. 4.032, n. 47, at 24, para. 75; WTO, "Working Group on the Interaction between Trade and Competition Policy, Communication from the Republic of Korea", *International Cooperation and Competition Policy: Bilateral, Regional and Multilateral Approaches*, WT/WGTCP/W/124, at 3 (May 31, 1999); WTO, "Working Group on the Interaction between Trade and Competition Policy, Communication from Japan", *Observation on the possible WTO framework on competition*, WT/WGTCP/W/119, at 3 (May 27, 1999); WTO, "Working Group on the Interaction between Trade and Competition Policy, Communication from the European Community and Its Member States", *The contribution of competition policy to achieving the objectives of the WTO, including the promotion of international trade*, WT/WGTCP/W/130, at 4 (July 12, 1999).

[69] See WTO, "Working Group on the Interaction between Trade and Competition Policy, Communication from the United States", *Relevance of Fundamental WTO Principles to Competition Policy*, WT/WGTCP/W/131 (July 13, 1999).

[70] See WTO, "Working Group on the Interaction between Trade and Competition Policy, Communication from Japan", *Relationship between Cartels and International Trade*, WT/WGTCP/W/135 (May 31, 1999); WTO, "Working Group on the Interaction between Trade and Competition Policy, Communication from the European Community and Its Member States", *The contribution of competition policy to achieving the objectives of the WTO, including the promotion of international trade*, WT/WGTCP/W/130, at 4 (July 12,1999).

such as abuse of a dominant position or vertical restraints, were not good candidates for a common rule given their rule-of-reason treatment under national competition laws.[71] The agreement would also include provisions on co-operation, notification and traditional comity, but would exclude provisions on positive comity, exchange of information and merger control.[72] Violations of the substantive norms would be resolved through WTO dispute settlement procedures, but in no event would dispute settlement involve a review of individual decisions taken by national competition law enforcement authorities.[73]

4.040 Some participants were opposed to a multilateral agreement on competition policy as being both premature and unwarranted for several reasons. For one, because a large percentage of WTO members have not enacted competition legislation or established a competition authority, proposals for a multilateral agreement are premature. For another, with regard to whether a multilateral agreement is warranted, in some countries the adoption of measures liberalising trade and investment flows would be an adequate competition policy.[74] The opponents of a multilateral agreement added that requiring multilateral notifications of every investigation that might affect the interests of another WTO member would be burdensome and unworkable. Such notifications require confidentiality and secrecy. Notifying upcoming enforcement actions on a multilateral basis would be inconsistent with the requirements of confidentiality and could seriously compromise the effectiveness of enforcement actions.[75]

Regardless of whether a multilateral agreement on competition policy materialises, the suggestion was made that regular reviews in the area of competition policy should take place at the WTO, although perhaps by a body other than the Trade Policy Review Body.[76]

---

[71] See "WGTCP 1999 Report", see para. 4.032, n. 47, at 26, para. 79; WTO, "Working Group on the Interaction between Trade and Competition Policy, Communication from the European Community and Its Member States", *The contribution of competition policy to achieving the objectives of the WTO, including the promotion of international trade*, WT/WGTCP/W/130, at 4 (July 12,1999).

[72] See "WGTCP 1999 Report", see para. 4.032, n. 47, at 16–17, 26, paras. 51–52, 79–80; WTO, "Working Group on the Interaction between Trade and Competition Policy, Communication from the Republic of Korea", *Multilateral Framework on Competition Policy: Issues and Suggestions*, WT/WGTCP/W/133, at 4–5 (July 15, 1999). The E.U. believes that a multilateral framework agreement should include a provision on positive comity. See WTO, "Working Group on the Interaction between Trade and Competition Policy, Communication from the European Community and Its Member States", *Approaches to promoting cooperation and communication among WTO Members, including in the field of technical cooperation*, WT/WGTCP/W/129, at 10 (July 12,1999).

[73] See "WGTCP 1999 Report", see para. 4.032, n. 47, at 26, para. 79; WTO, "Working Group on the Interaction between Trade and Competition Policy, Communication from the European Community and Its Member States", *The relevance of fundamental WTO principles of national treatment, transparency and most-favoured-nation treatment to competition policy and vice versa*, WT/WGTCP/W/115 (May 25,1999).

[74] See "WGTCP 1999 Report", see para. 4.032, n. 47, at 17, para. 54.

[75] See *id.* at 18, para. 56.

[76] See *id.* at 19, para. 58.

The contribution of competition policy to achieving the objectives of the WTO.

4.041 The WGTCP noted that some WTO rules that permit trade measures restricting imports and exports work in an anti-competitive manner by protecting domestic producers from import competition. It was suggested that before any multilateral framework on competition policy is introduced into the GATT-WTO system, WTO rules first be reformed in order to be made more consistent with the broad competition principles of open markets, non-discriminatory conditions of competition and consumer welfare.[77]

4.042 First on the list of candidates for reform would be the antidumping duty law. Some participants suggested that GATT Article VI be amended to limit the imposition of antidumping duties to cases involving predatory intent, thus bringing the AD law into line with competition law.[78] The mere filing of an AD petition can have trade distortive effects by causing exporting firms to raise their prices or to exit the market. As part of this reform process, therefore, the AD petition process should also be reviewed from a competition policy perspective. Other participants objected to this proposal on the bases, *inter alia*, that:

(1) such reform proposals went beyond the WGTCP's mandate, and

(2) such a WTO review, if it was to be undertaken, should be holistic and non-discriminatory as between WTO provisions.[79]

4.043 Realising that an impasse existed on the issue of reforming the AD law, the participants shifted focus to an area where they might find common ground, namely, cartels. The impact of import, export, and international cartels on international trade was fairly obvious to all. Import cartels restrict competition in domestic markets between domestic and foreign suppliers by limiting imports of goods and services. Export cartels restrict competition in foreign markets where exports are destined. International cartels prevent competition in global markets, thus harming consumers in the domestic market by raising the price of goods and services sold there. Thus, there was general agreement that such hard-core cartels were significant from both a trade and competition policy viewpoint.[80]

D. The WGTCP 2000 Work Programme

4.044 On March 27, 2000 the WGTCP decided to continue its educative work programme along the lines of the December 1998 General Council

[77] See "WGTCP 1999 Report", see para. 4.032, n. 47, at 21, para. 66.
[78] See *id.* at 22, para. 67; WTO, "Working Group on the Interaction between Trade and Competition Policy, Communication from Mexico", *Anti-dumping Measures and Competition*, WT/WGTCP/W/136 (July 15, 1999); WTO, "Working Group on the Interaction between Trade and Competition Policy, Communication from Japan", *Response to U.S. Views on Anti-dumping*, WT/WGTCP/W/123 (May 28, 1999); WTO, "Working Group on the Interaction between Trade and Competition Policy, Communication from Japan", *The Contribution of Competition Policy to Achieving the Objectives of the WTO, including the Promotion of International Trade*, WT/WGTCP/W/122, at 3 (May 28, 1999).
[79] See "WGTCP 1999 Report", see para. 4.032, n. 47, at 23, para. 69.
[80] See *id.* at 23, para. 70.

mandate. Submissions to the WGTCP in 2000 focused on the issues involved in enacting competition legislation and establishing an enforcement agency. Of special interest was how best to assist developing countries with capacity building.

Capacity building in developing countries.

4.045 Australia shared its experience that the effectiveness of co-operation activities varies with the country's stage of development. For example, in-country training appears to be most effective once competition legislation is in place. Prior to that, when countries are in the exploratory stage of competition policy development, Australia has found it most effective to bring officials to Australia to examine legislation and regulatory structures first hand.[81] In terms of the size and composition of incoming delegations, Australia has found that small groups from different countries are the most effective mode of exchange of information and experiences.[82]

4.046 In its submission the United States examined some of the issues involved in drafting a competition law. One of the most important threshold issues concerns the scope of a competition law, *i.e.* should certain sectors or activities be exempted from coverage?[83] Once a country decides to enact competition legislation, it must also establish enforcement agencies. It is generally agreed that competition law enforcement agencies should be independent, *i.e.* that their actions are based on the facts and the law, not on political considerations, and their decisions should not discriminate in favour of local firms or against foreign ones.[84] Independence has its limits, however. In order for enforcement agencies to be both accountable in a democratic society and to be properly funded, they usually are part of the executive branch of government.[85] A third significant issue in drafting a competition law is whether to provide private persons aggrieved by anti-competitive conduct with a right to seek relief before an administrative agency or the courts.

4.047 The United States pointed out the many thorny issues facing a country that does decide to enact competition legislation and establish an enforcement agency. First is the question of adequate funding of the agency (a major problem for small countries). Next is the issue of proper staffing: how many employees should an agency have and what should their qualifications be? In the United States, for example, the Department of Justice and the FTC have a combined staff of 1,000 attorneys and economists working on antitrust law enforcement; Japan has approximately 530 such employees; the E.U., 500 (including generalists), and Canada has 250.[86] A related issue is retention of

---

[81] See WTO, "Working Group on the Interaction between Trade and Competition Policy, Communication from Australia", *Australia's Experience in Competition Policy Development Assistance and Some Best-Practice Indicators,* WT/WGTCP/W/148, at 2–3 (Aug. 3, 2000).

[82] See *id.* at 4.

[83] See WTO, "Working Group on the Interaction between Trade and Competition Policy, Communication from the United States", *Creating a Culture of Competition: Issues Involved in Establishing an Effective Antitrust Agency*, WT/WGTCP/W/142, at 4 (Aug. 3, 2000) (hereinafter *Creating a Culture of Competition*).

[84] See *id.* at 5.

[85] See *id.*

[86] See *id.* at 7.

qualified staff once they are hired, given that salaries in the private sector for attorneys and economists are generally higher than in government service.

4.048 The United States also noted that an agency's procedures have to be transparent and consistent with due process if the agency is to be effective, achieve public respect and make a significant contribution to creating a competition culture over time. New competition agencies will have to educate the general public and the courts about the new legislation and about the agency's priorities. Adequate training of agency staff is also important. In this connection, the United States has sent roughly 220 missions to dozens of countries to work with officials of new competition law enforcement agencies and has hosted foreign delegations.

The benefits of a competition legal regime for developing countries.

4.049 In the case of small developing countries that are mainly monoculture producers, export-oriented and import dependent, a competition legal regime can yield many benefits. Having an open trade policy can certainly discipline local firms that might otherwise engage in RBPs but trade cannot prevent anti-competitive conduct in non-tradable sectors. In addition, for developing countries dependent on imports, export cartels can have an especially negative impact on a small country's economy. Moreover, even if small developing countries have an open investment climate, MNEs nevertheless tend to dominate their economies. Consequently, abuse of dominance can be prevalent. In short, small developing countries can benefit from a competition legal regime.[87]

E. Other WTO Activities on Trade and Competition Policy

4.050 In addition to the work of the WGTCP, the WTO held four trade and competition policy symposia over the course of 1997, 1998 and 1999. The symposia addressed a range of subjects, including the relationship of competition policy, international trade, and economic development; the relationship of competition policy and the multilateral trading system; the relevance of fundamental WTO principles, international co-operation and the contribution of competition policy to WTO objectives; and a dialogue with civil society on competition policy and the multilateral trading system.[88] Against the backdrop of submissions by WTO members to the WGTCP, what conclusions can be drawn about the points of convergence and divergence of WTO members' competition laws and policies?

II. AREAS OF CONVERGENCE AND DIVERGENCE: THRESHOLD ISSUES

4.051 The areas where countries' competition laws and policies converge, at least outwardly, is not insignificant. Certainly, the points of convergence

[87] See, *e.g.* WTO, "Working Group on the Interaction between Trade and Competition Policy, Communication from Trinidad and Tobago", *Developing and Implementing a Competition Regime: Challenges Faced by Small Open Economies*, WT/WGTCP/W/143, at 3 (Aug. 2, 2000).
[88] See "WGTCP 1998 Report", see para. 4.016, n. 16, at 4, para. 8; "WGTCP 1999 Report", see para. 4.032, n. 47, at 3, para. 7.

are sufficient to give the proponents of a multilateral competition law agreement reason for optimism.[89] To generalise, it has been observed that nearly all of the approximately 85 national competition laws include, in some form, four basic substantive elements: provisions dealing with horizontal agreements, vertical agreements, abuses of a dominant position/unlawful monopolisation and anti-competitive mergers.[90] Countries in the main have used either the U.S. antitrust laws or the E.U. competition rules as drafting models, although the E.U. rules "have attracted many more adherents than the US model."[91] But, as the United States has noted in this regard:

> This apparent convergence on broad substantive elements, however, conceals a wide range of significantly divergent views among nations concerning the proper objectives of antitrust law.[92]

The points of divergence among WTO members in their national competition laws are thus numerous as well, making harmonisation a difficult task. While the focus here is on the points of convergence and divergence in WTO members' competition laws, it is impossible to divorce law from policy and economics.

4.052 First, European, Japanese and American approaches to competition policy have marked differences. For the United States, the courts have viewed U.S. antitrust law as a tool for promoting economic efficiency. However, articulating a coherent competition policy goal in the United States has been marked by "eloquent indecision," in the words of one commentator.[93] Different elements of competition policy often appear together, as U.S. policy makers are reluctant to admit priorities.[94] The pole star for U.S. antitrust law is keeping markets competitive, but other articulated goals include promoting consumer welfare, protecting the competitive process and enhancing economic efficiency, all of which are generally consistent with one another.[95] The

[89] See Eleanor M. Fox, "Toward World Antitrust and Market Access", (1997) 91 Am. J. Int'l L. 1 (hereinafter Fox, "Toward World Antitrust"); Gary M. Horlick & Michael A. Meyer, "The International Convergence of Competition Policy", (1995) 29 Int'l Law. 65, 66. A similar assessment was made more than 25 years ago. See Earl W. Kintner, Mark R. Joelson & Peter J. Vaghi, "Groping for a Truly International Antitrust Law", (1973) 14 Va. J. Int'l L. 75, 96 (an international standard as to what private restrictive practices should be controlled or prohibited appears to be slowly emerging); Richard I. Fine, "The Control of Restrictive Business Practices in International Trade—A Viable Proposal for an International Trade Organization", (1973) 7 Int'l Law. 635, 637. For a collection of competition laws from around the world, see *World Antitrust Law and Practice*.

[90] See WTO "Annual Report for 1997, Special Study on Trade and Competition Policy" 12–14 (1997); *Creating a Culture of Competition*, see para. 4.046, n. 83, at 2; American Bar Ass'n, "Report of the Sections of Antitrust Law and International Law and Practice on the Internationalization of Competition Law Rules: Coordination and Convergence 17–19" (2000) (hereinafter "Report on Coordination and Convergence").

[91] "Report on Coordination and Convergence", *supra* n. 90, at 19.

[92] See *Creating a Culture of Competition*, see para. 4.046, n. 83, at 2.

[93] Michael Wise, "Review of United States Competition Law and Policy", (1999) 1 OECD J. Competition L. & Pol'y 7, 14.

[94] See *id.*

[95] See *id.*; WTO, "Working Group on the Interaction between Trade and Competition Policy, Communication from the United States", WT/WGTCP/W/35, at 2 (Oct. 1, 1997).

U.S. Supreme Court has stated that competition policy and U.S. antitrust laws are based

> on the premise that the unrestrained interaction of competitive forces will yield the best allocation of our economic resources, the lowest prices, the highest quality and the greatest material progress, while at the same time, providing an environment conducive to the preservation of our democratic political and social institutions.[96]

The Supreme Court has stressed that "[t]he antitrust laws were enacted for 'the protection of competition, not competitors.'"[97]

4.053 In other countries, other economic goals as well as social, cultural and political goals inform national competition policy.[98] Canadian competition law, for example, encourages SMEs.[99] In the E.U., concerns about fairness can be more important that fostering competition. The Treaty of Rome conditionally prohibits imposing dissimilar conditions in equivalent transactions in situations where persons are placed at a competitive disadvantage.[1] Article 81 of the E.C. Treaty provides further that agreements containing such dissimilar conditions may be valid if they are shown to improve the production or distribution of goods, or to promote technical or economic progress, provided consumers receive a fair share of these benefits. In Japan, the Antimonopoly Law is interpreted against the background of Japanese industrial policy.[2] Competition policy may force inefficient firms out of business, therefore social policy measures may be introduced to develop new industries, to promote the mobility of human resources and to provide

---

[96] *Northern Pac. Ry. v. United States*, 356 U.S. 1, 4 (1958). *Accord NCAA v. Bd. of Regents of Univ. of Okla.*, 468 U.S. 85, 104 n.27 (1984).

[97] *Atlantic Richfield Co. v. USA Petroleum Co.*, 495 U.S. 328, 300 (1990) (quoting *Brown Shoe Co. v. United States*, 370 U.S. 294, 320 (1962)).

[98] See, *e.g. Global Competition Policy* (Edward M. Graham & J. David Richardson eds. 1997 34); Tony A. Freyer, "Restrictive Trade Practices and Extraterritorial Application of Antitrust Legislation in Japanese-American Trade", (1999) 16 Ariz. J. Int'l & Comp. L. 159, 168–69; Eleanor M. Fox, "The End of Antitrust Isolationism: The Vision of One World", (1992) U. Chi. Legal F. 221, 223–25 (examining differences between U.S. and E.U. antitrust policy); Joseph P. Griffin, "EC/U.S. Antitrust Cooperation Agreement: Impact on Transnational Business", (1993) 24 L. & Pol'y Int'l Bus. 1051 (hereinafter Griffin, "EC/U.S. Antitrust Cooperation Agreement"); Nina Hachigan, "Essential Mutual Assistance in International Antitrust Enforcement", (1995) 29 Int'l Law. 117, 123–25 (citing examples from the UK and Japan); Diane P. Wood, "The Impossible Dream: Real International Antitrust", (1992) U. Chi. Legal F. 277, 304 (describing differences among the antitrust policies of Canada, the E.U., and the United States); WTO, Working Group on the Interaction between Trade and Competition Policy, Communication from Hong Kong, China, "Contribution of Competition Policy to Achieving the Objectives of the WTO", WT/WGTCP/W/118, at 2, para. 4 (May 26,1999).

[99] See Competition Act, R.S.C., Chap. C–34, s. 1.1 (1995) (The purpose of this Act is to maintain and encourage competition in Canada in order to . . . ensure that small and medium-sized enterprises (SMEs) have an equitable opportunity to participate in the Canadian economy . . . .). Canada also uses a strict efficiency (*i.e.* total surplus) test for evaluating mergers.

[1] See Treaty of Rome, Arts. 85(1) (d) & 86(c).

[2] See Mitsuo Matshushita, *Introduction to Japanese Antimonopoly Law* (1990) 3; Daniel J. Gifford & Mitsuo Matsushita, "Antitrust or Competition Laws Viewed in a Trading Context: Harmony or Dissonance?", in 2 *Fair Trade and Harmonization: Prerequisites for Free Trade?* 317, app. A (Jagdish Bhagwati & Robert E. Hudec eds., 1996).

relief to the jobless under Japan's Industrial Renewal Policy introduced in 1999.[3]

4.054 In small countries, in order for an industry to achieve economies of scale, it may be necessary to tolerate a greater degree of market power than would be the case in a larger country. Thus, the benefits of competition might be outweighed by the need to achieve economies of scale.[4] In addition, while the goal of competition policy in some developed countries is to maximise consumer welfare (*e.g.* in the United States under the Clinton administration), newly industrialised countries and other developed countries might implement their competition law so as to maximise total (*i.e.* consumer plus producer) welfare. As a consequence, countries will nurture a few large domestic industries as "national champions," which may result in sacrificing consumer welfare maximisation in favour of producers, assuming such national champions are shielded from import competition.[5] To generalise, competition policies are usually multi-faceted in nature. Efficiency goals (*e.g.* productive and allocative efficiency, consumer welfare, promoting competition) and non-efficiency goals (*e.g.* exemptions of sectors for economic and political reasons) are common features of national competition policies.[6]

4.055 Secondly, economic theory can play a key role in shaping a country's competition legal regime. Many writers argue that the sole goal of competition policy should be the promotion of economic efficiency.[7] Consider two examples in the context of monopolisation. The giant of economic theory Joseph Schumpeter, argued somewhat counterintuitively that a monopoly could stimulate innovation through a process he called "creative destruction."[8] His theory was that once an innovative firm wins a monopoly, complacency sets in and the monopolist is displaced by a more nimble competitor. Another economic theory known as "contestable markets"[9] contends in a similar vein that a monopolist who becomes inefficient or overprices will induce rivals to enter the market. More efficient rivals may in turn drive the monopolist out of the market. Thus, the theory runs, highly concentrated markets will function as if they were competitive if entry and

---

[3] See WTO, "Working Group on the Interaction between Trade and Competition Policy, Communication from Japan", *Japan's Discussion Paper for Trade and Competition*, at 2–3, WT/WGTCP/W/145 (Sept. 11, 2000).

[4] See Andrew T. Guzman, "Is International Antitrust Possible?", (1998) 73 N.Y.U.L. Rev. 1501, 1539–40.

[5] See R. Shyam Khemani, The Instruments of Competition Policy and Their Relevance for Economic Development 2 (1996), available at http://www.oecd.ord/daf/clp/non-member—activities/dnme04.htm; WTO, Working Group on the Interaction between Trade and Competition Policy, Note by the Secretariat", *Synthesis Paper on the Relationship of Trade and Competition Policy to Development and Economic Growth*, WT/WGTCP/W/80, at 3, 6–7, paras. 10, 20 (Sept. 18, 1998).

[6] See WTO, "Working Group on the Interaction between Trade and Competition Policy, Communication from Hong Kong, China", WT/WGTCP/W/141, at 3 (Aug. 2, 2000).

[7] See, *e.g.* Richard A. Posner, *Antitrust Law: An Economic Perspective* (1976) 3–4, 8–35 (sole goal of antitrust policy should be the promotion of economic efficiency); Eleanor M. Fox & Lawrence A. Sullivan, *Cases and Materials on Antitrust* (1989) 2–3, 10–11, 845–51 (economic efficiency is an important competition policy goal).

[8] See Joseph A. Schumpeter, *Capitalism, Socialism, and Democracy* (3d ed. 1950) 81.

[9] See William J. Baumol, John C. Panzar & Robert D. Willig, *Contestable Markets and the Theory of Industrial Structure* (1982).

exit are free enough that the potential entry of competitors will force incumbents to behave as if they were price takers in a highly competitive market. Because potential competition can bring economic efficiency, the theory concludes that the degree of actual concentration in the market should not be the sole criterion in judging the competitive conditions of the market.

However, as India has observed in a submission to the WGTCP, "[w]ith developing countries, the dangers of the doctrine of contestability of markets eroding their ability to take domestic social and economic action are even greater."[10]

4.056 Clearly, if national competition enforcement authorities adopted either the "creative destruction" or "contestable markets" economic theory, the result would influence, if not dictate, when, if ever, the anti-monopoly provisions of national competition law would be enforced. Some enforcement authorities presume that markets will function to discipline dominant firms. Others are openly suspicious of MNEs and assume that they will abuse their dominant position.[11] The point is bridging the gap in economic theory among national enforcement authorities can present a formidable obstacle to the creation of a transnational or international antitrust legal regime.

Against this policy and economic backdrop, the following discussion examines the convergence and divergence of national competition laws in the areas of horizontal restraints, vertical restraints, unlawful monopolisation (abuse of a dominant position), and mergers and acquisitions.[12]

III. HORIZONTAL RESTRAINTS

4.057 Broadly, horizontal restraints of trade involve collective conduct that weakens or restrains competition among firms in the same market. Horizontal restraints include agreements among competitors in which they restrict their freedom to compete in agreed-upon ways. The focus is on collusive behaviour among competitors. In the context of international trade, two of the more important types of horizontal restraints are:

(1) price fixing, and

(2) export and import cartels through which territories are allocated.

4.058 Most competition laws treat naked agreements to fix prices, rig bids, limit output or divide markets very harshly and as illegal *per se*.[13] The

[10] WTO, "Working Group on the Interaction of Trade and Competition Policy, Communication from India", *The Relationship Between Trade Liberalization and Competition Law and Policy*, WT/WGTCP/W/11, at 1, para. 2 (Nov. 16, 1998).

[11] See "Report on Coordination and Convergence", see para. 4.051, n. 90, at 20.

[12] For examples of divergences between U.S. and E.U. competition law, see "Report on Coordination and Convergence", see para. 4.051, n. 90, at 52–57.

[13] See, *e.g.* WTO, "Working Group on the Interaction between Trade and Competition Policy, Note by the Secretariat", *Synthesis Paper on the Relationship of Trade and Competition Policy to Development and Economic Growth*, WT/WGTCP/W/80, at 10, para. 32 (Sept. 18, 1998);

reason for this harsh treatment is that when competitors agree to act co-operatively they have, in effect, the same power as a monopolist, so that consumer welfare is likely to be reduced. Other horizontal agreements, including co-operation on product standards and research, may have positive effects for consumers because they enhance efficiencies. As a consequence, most competition laws deal with these types of horizontal arrangements less aggressively because they may have beneficial effects for consumers and instead assess them in light of their benefits and harms—in the U.S. antitrust parlance, under a rule of reason. In other countries, horizontal non-price restraints are evaluated in the light of efficiency, industrial policy, trade and the public interest.[14] Special leniency may be shown for co-operation among SMEs.[15] For example, in Korea competition legislation provides for three-year programmes for sunset industries and growing sunrise industries that allows firms in these industries to enter into horizontal agreements for the purpose of industrial rationalisation.[16]

A. Cartel Activity

1. *Introduction*

4.059 A cartel has been defined as "an arrangement in which competing firms have substituted an agreement on price, output, or related matters for independent decision making."[17] Cartels are formed for the purpose of engaging in one or more naked restraints, *i.e.* restraints whose sole purpose is to affect price and output. Any such agreement among competitors on price, market allocation or output restriction is generally treated as *per se* illegal,[18] although cartels can be treated under either a *per se* rule or a rule of reason depending upon the jurisdiction.[19] The rationale for the *per se* treatment of cartels is straightforward:

Hartford-Empire Co. v. United States, 323 U.S. 386, 406–07 (1945) (agreement to limit production and set quotas *per se* unlawful); *Palmer v. BRG of Georgia, Inc.* 498 U.S. 46, 49–50 (1990) (allocation of markets *per se* unlawful); Ley Federal de Competencia Economica (Federal Law of Economic Competition), Diario Ofical de La Federacion (Official Gazette of the Federation), art. 9 (Dec. 24, 1992) (price fixing, output restrictions, market allocation, and bid rigging treated as *per se* illegal) (hereinafter LCFE).

[14] UNCTAD, Revised Study by the UNCTAD Secretariat, Review of All Aspects of the Set of Multilaterally Agreed Equitable Principles and Rules for the Control of Restrictive Business Practices, "The role of competition policy in economic reforms in developing and other countries" 26, TD/RBP/CONF.4/2 (May 26, 1995).

[15] See *id.*

[16] See *id.*

[17] 2 Phillip E. Areeda & Donald F. Turner, *Antitrust Law* (1978) 280.

[18] See Thomas Kauper, "The Treatment of Cartels Under the Antitrust Laws of the United States", in *International Harmonization of Competition Laws* (Chia-Jui Cheng, Lawrence S. Liu, & Chih-Kang Wang eds. 1995) 75 (hereinafter Kauper).

[19] See WTO, "Working Group on the Interaction between Trade and Competition Policy, Report (1999) of the Working Group on the Interaction between Trade and Competition Policy to the General Council", WT/WGTCP/3, at 20, para. 61 (Oct. 11, 1999). Many competition laws provide for administrative or civil remedies rather than criminal penalties for cartel activity. Penalties differ significantly in jurisdictions that have active enforcement programs against cartel activity. See "International Competition Policy Advisory Committee to the Attorney General and Assistant Attorney General for Antitrust, Final Report" 186, Annex 4–B (2000) (hereinafter "ICPAC Final Report").

> [It] rests on the determination that price-fixing and related cartel conduct will almost invariably have adverse price and output consequences, when compared to a fully competitive market outcome, and that cartels seldom, if ever, result in true efficiencies or, if they do, that such efficiencies will be small compared with the conduct's adverse effects. . . . A cartel, *if successful*, will approximate the price and output decisions of a single firm monopolist.[20]

By some estimates, international cartels controlled as much as 40 per cent of world trade between 1929 and 1937.[21]

4.060 In the United States, cartel activity can be a criminal violation of the antitrust laws.[22] Criminal prosecutions and civil actions were brought by the Justice Department against a broad spectrum of international cartels in the 1940s and 1950s.[23] During the 1990s the Justice Department prosecuted a large number of international cartels—approximately 25 per cent of the more than 625 criminal cases filed—across of wide range of sectors.[24] Canada and the E.U. have also been active in investigating and prosecuting cartels.[25] In short,

> it appears that interest in enforcement [against international cartels] is growing in many jurisdictions around the world and the U.S. experiences are receiving close scrutiny."[26]

2. *An example of Prohibited Cartel Activity: Price Fixing*

4.061 Price fixing is condemned because it enables producers in a competitive or non-monopolistic market to mimic the behaviour of a monopolist by forcing buyers to pay higher prices for an artificial short supply of a product. In order to enforce their agreement, competitors may exchange sensitive business information and engage in boycotts to prevent outside firms from competing and to discipline firms that do not co-operate.

An economic rationale for price fixing is that it

(1) reduces buyers' transaction costs of searching for lower-priced goods and

(2) promotes product standardisation.

---

[20] Kauper, see para. 4.059, n. 18, at 77 (emphasis in original).
[21] See, *e.g.* Helga Nussbaum, "International Cartels and Multinational Enterprises", in *Multinational Enterprises in Historical Perspective* (Alice Teichova, Maurice Levy-Leboyer & Helga Nussbaum eds. 1986) 131, 134.
[22] See 15 U.S.C. s. 1.
[23] See, *e.g.* Wilbur L. Fugate, 1 *Foreign Commerce and the Antitrust Laws* s. 2.21 (5th ed. 1996); Barry Hawk, *United States, Common Market and International Antitrust: A Comparative Guide* (2d ed. 1996) 1–28; Spencer Weber Waller, 1 *Antitrust and American Business Abroad* ss. 2:13–2:16 (3d ed. 1997).
[24] See "ICPAC Final Report", see para. 4.059, n. 19, at 167. For a list of 23 Justice Department international cartel prosecutions from 1995–1999, see *id.* Annex 4 A. See also A. Paul Victor, "The Growth of International Criminal Enforcement", (1998) 6 Geo. Mason L. Rev. 493.
[25] See "ICPAC Final Report", see para. 4.059, n. 19, at 187–89.
[26] *id.* at 190.

Nevertheless, competitors have little incentive to fix prices below the monopoly price. Moreover, insofar as price fixing might shield producers from competition risks, that is true only for the least efficient producers, the most efficient probably surviving or thriving in a competitive market in any event.

4.062 Most developed countries condemn horizontal price fixing as being a *per se* violation of the antitrust laws. In the United States, for example, horizontal price fixing is *per se* unlawful, regardless of whether the fixed price is reasonable.[27] The *per se* rule has also been applied by U.S. courts to horizontal agreements that did not involve the ultimate price, such as market allocation agreements.[28] Mexico also treats price fixing as *per se* illegal if it involves cartel activity,[29] and most of its enforcement actions involve price fixing between competing suppliers.[30] Japan has shown a slightly more relaxed attitude toward bid rigging in the context of major construction contracts.[31]

4.063 A few countries, however, use the rule of reason or some modified version of it in judging the anti-competitive effects of price fixing agreements. In Canada, for example, it is illegal to fix prices.[32] However, section 45 of the Canadian Competition Act employs the adverb "unduly" to modify the conduct that is prohibited by the Act (to "[l]imit *unduly* the facilities for . . . manufacturing . . . any product;" "[p]revent, limit or lessen, *unduly*, the manufacture or production of a product;" "[p]revent or lessen, *unduly*, competition in the in the production, manufacture, purchase, . . . [or] sale . . . of a product" [emphasis added]). The Supreme Court of Canada has described "undueness" in terms of a serious or significant effect on competition.[33] The Court used a market power test to assess undueness but observed that only a moderate degree of market power is required to trigger the proscriptions of section 45.[34] As noted by the International Antitrust Committee of the American Bar Association,

> The presence of the "undueness" qualification prevents the judicial development of *per se* offenses under Section 45, such as those for price fixing and price maintenance under Section 1 of the Sherman Act. Indeed, the Supreme Court has indicated that Section 45 lies somewhere on the continuum between a per se rule and a rule of reason.[35]

Bid rigging, however, is *per se* illegal in Canada, being the subject of a different section of the Competition Act which does not use the qualifier "unduly."[36]

---

[27] See, *e.g. United States v. Socony Vacuum Oil Co.*, 310 U.S. 150, 225 n.59 (1940).
[28] See, *e.g. United States v. Brown*, 936 F.2d 1042, 1045 (9th Cir. 1991).
[29] See LCFE, see para. 4.058, n. 13, art. 9.
[30] See American Bar Ass'n, "The Competition Laws of NAFTA, Canada, Mexico, and the United States, A Practitioner's Guide" (1997) 63.
[31] See Naoaki Okatani, "Regulations on Bid Rigging in Japan, the United States and Europe", in *Antitrust: A New Trade Remedy?* (John O. Haley & Hiroshi Iyori eds. 1995) 249.
[32] See Competition Act, s. 45.
[33] See *R. v. Nova Scotia Pharmaceutical Society*, 2 S.C.R. 606 (1992).
[34] See *id.* at 654.
[35] The "Competition Laws of NAFTA", see para. 4.062, n. 30, at 58.
[36] See Competition Act, s. 47.

3. *Problems in Policing Export Cartel Activity*

4.064 Practices involving collusion are the result of agreement among competitors in the domestic market (*e.g.* export or import cartels) or among competitors in the domestic market and a foreign country (international cartels) with the purpose of increasing market power by dividing markets or fixing output and prices. This type of practice is difficult to counteract because it is achieved by taking advantage of a position of immunity with respect to competition laws. Even assuming the existence of competition laws in the countries adversely affected, when such practices are detected within a foreign country, it is difficult to attack them. It is a jurisdictional problem with which competition enforcement authorities are not unfamiliar in other contexts.

For example, in connection with monopolistic practices that harm consumers or producers in an importing country, competition enforcement authorities in the importing country have to verify the existence of monopolistic practices in some other jurisdiction. When monopolistic practices cannot be verified in the country where the distortion was created, firms may be able to act freely. In connection with price discrimination, if discriminatory prices are detected in the importing country, competition laws are largely irrelevant because first, jurisdictional problems may exist and secondly, such prices have no anti-competitive impact on the domestic market of the exporting country. Indeed, the peculiarity of this kind of discrimination is to distort only the conditions of production in the importing country but not in the trading partner's market where competition law could be applied.

4.065 The case of collusive agreements presents the same enforcement problems, or even greater difficulties if the practices in question are implemented by certain firms, *e.g.* state monopolies, export cartels or other enterprises in sectors or activities that have been shielded by rules that exclude them from the reach of competition law.

Certain export associations among competing firms may have the earmarks of an export cartel but still are benign to the country of importation and beneficial to the home country. For example, individual firms may be deterred from expanding their business to foreign markets because of the high transaction costs and lack of expertise. Export arrangements among competing firms can offer small and medium-size firms efficiencies of scale, expertise in penetrating foreign markets, familiarity with foreign markets, promotional assistance, and channels of distribution. From a trade point of view, many governments view their own export arrangements as an excellent vehicle for export promotion and expansion. For this reason, certain export trading arrangements among competing firms have been approved by governments, subject to certain restrictions on, for example, price fixing and market sharing.[37]

4.066 Export cartels remain one of the most controversial issues under trade and competition policy. Unlike import cartels whose anti-competitive

[37] See, *e.g.* Webb-Pomerene Act, Pub. L. No. 65–126, 40 Stat. 516 (1918), codified at 15 U.S.C. ss. 61–66.

effects are felt in the market where the anti-competitive conduct takes place, export cartels enjoy considerable freedom from the application of the exporting country's competition laws. One explanation for this effective immunity is that export cartels often have anti-competitive effects only in foreign markets and thus do not trigger concerns about harm to consumer welfare in the exporting country.[38] In 1991, the ABA Special Committee on International Antitrust offered the following economic critique of export cartels:

> [E]ven if any individual nation were to benefit from its export cartels, these benefits may be outweighed by welfare losses to that country's consumers resulting from export cartels of its trading partners directed against that nation, either through short-term higher prices, or through predatory practices that may injure or eliminate the local industry, allowing supracompetitive prices in the future. Although the victim country could theoretically prosecute the export cartel members under its competition laws, there are enormous procedural and jurisdictional obstacles to such lawsuits. . . . Thus, mutual elimination of export cartel immunity among the major participants in a trading system should confer net welfare benefits on the countries in the trading system.[39]

Thus, while export cartels are generally viewed as a positive arrangement in the home country, in the target market export cartels can, in theory, be challenged under the competition laws of the country of importation, but in practice the cartel activity may go unpunished even if challenged.

4.067 There is an active debate over whether export cartels should be permitted as a means of penetrating foreign markets or prohibited because they are likely to lead to collusive arrangements adversely affecting the domestic market. Thus, the potential for conflict exists between the trade policies of the home country and the competition laws of the importing country. Moreover, if foreign producers agree to enter into a cartel independently of government influence, support or compulsion, this conduct could be challenged under the antitrust laws of the target market.[40] However, government measures that require conduct having a restrictive effect on competition are usually not subject to foreign or domestic competition law under the doctrine of foreign sovereign compulsion.

4.068 To the extent that an export cartel's *raison d'être* is to foreclose non-cartel competitors from the members' individual markets through the division of world markets into shares for its members, the fixing of prices or

[38] See OECD, "Trade and Competition: Frictions After the Uruguay Round 9" (1996) ("Pure export cartels, directed exclusively at foreign markets, enjoy considerable freedom from the application of competition laws."); Barry E. Hawk, "Overview", in *Antitrust and Market Access: The Scope and Coverage of Competition Laws and Implications for Trade* (OECD 1996) 33; ABA Section of Antitrust Law, "Report of the Special Committee on International Antitrust 8" (1991) (hereinafter "ABA Special Committee Report").

[39] ABA "Special Committee Report", see para. 4.066, n. 38, at 84.

[40] For examples of Department of Justice antitrust actions against international cartels in 1998 for price fixing and market allocation, see Arthur J. Burke, Gabriel Castaneda, et al., "International Antitrust", (1999) 33 Int'l Law. 277, 280.

the imposition of limits on output, such cartels are widely—although not universally—condemned under WTO members' competition laws.[41] Still, most countries' competition laws do not apply to cartels whose only anti-competitive effect occurs in other countries. A smaller number of countries also exempt cartels that are concerned solely with imports.[42] Many WTO members exempt export cartels from the scope of their competition laws provided their activities do not adversely affect the domestic market.[43] There are important differences among countries' exemptions, however. For example, Australia, Germany, Japan and the United States extend a statutory exemption only to export cartels that meet specific requirements.[44] The requirements include the notification or registration of the cartel to national enforcement authorities.

4.069 In Canada export cartels are exempt from prosecution under the competition laws for conspiracy. Section 45(5) of the Competition Act provides that a court "shall not convict the accused if the conspiracy, combination, agreement or arrangement relates only to the export of products from Canada." However, the export cartel exception is limited by section 45(6) which provides that a person may be prosecuted for anti-competitive export cartel activity where the arrangement

(1) has resulted in or is likely to result in a reduction or limitation of the real value of exports of a product;

(2) has restricted or is likely to restrict any person from entering into or expanding the export of products from Canada; or

(3) has prevented or lessened competition unduly in the supply of services facilitating the export of products from Canada.

4.070 In Mexico, Article 6 of the Ley Federal de Competencia Economica[45] (LCFE) mirrors the language of Article 28 of the Mexican Constitution by providing that export cartels that sell their products abroad do not constitute illegal monopolies, provided:

(1) their goods are not essential staples;

(2) their goods are not sold or distributed in Mexico;

(3) members are free to join or resign; and

[41] See generally OECD, "Recommendation Concerning Effective Action Against 'Hard Core' Cartels", Mar. 3, 1998, http://www.oecd.org/daf/ccp/rec9com.htm; OECD, "Report of the Committee of Experts on Restrictive Business Practices, Export Cartels" (1974); Philip Marsden, "Antitrust at the WTO", 13 *Antitrust* 28 (1999).

[42] See "Conference on Trade and Competition Policies: Exploring the Ways Forward, Summary", (1999) 1 OECD J. Competition L. & Pol'y 7, 25.

[43] See "ABA Special Committee Report", see para. 4.066, n. 38, at 61–73.

[44] For additional reading on the export cartel laws of Germany, Japan and the U.K., see "ABA Special Committee Report", see para. 4.066, n. 38, at 61–73.

[45] Ley Federal de Competencia Economica (Federal Law of Economic Competition), Diario Oficial de La Federacion (Official Gazette of the Federation), Art. 6 (Dec. 24, 1992).

(4) the export association is authorised by the local legislature.

Given these strict requirements, the application of the export cartel exemption is extremely limited.

4.071 In the United States, there are three ways that an export cartel can escape the reach of U.S. antitrust law. First, under the 1918 Webb-Pomerene Act,[46] export trade associations that register with the Federal Trade Commission receive an automatic exemption from the Sherman Act and section 7 of the Clayton Act if they are formed "for the sole purpose of engaging in export trade" and actually engage solely in export trade, subject to two conditions:

(1) the export trade association must not restrain trade within the United States or restrain the export trade of any domestic competitor of the association; and
(2) the export trade association may not enter into any agreement which increases or depresses prices within the United States of the class of goods exported.[47]

In addition, the Webb-Pomerene Act prohibits export trade associations from engaging in "unfair methods of competition" as used in the Federal Trade Commission Act, even when such conduct occurs outside the territory of the United States. Such associations may not enter into agreements with foreign firms on fixing prices or allocating markets.[48] Thus, it is theoretically possible under U.S. law for members of an export association to enter into a price-fixing agreement *inter se* directed solely at exported products or services and escape the reach of the U.S. antitrust laws.[49]

4.072 As the FTC registration defines the scope of the trade association's immunity and because nothing prevents private parties or the Justice Department from proceeding against Webb-Pomerene trade association for exceeding its grant of immunity, Webb-Pomerene associations never gained wide popularity with the exporting business community.[50] Moreover, nothing shields an export trade association from action against it by a foreign enforcement authority if its activities have the requisite adverse effects. Indeed, the *Wood Pulp* case decided by the European Court of Justice in 1988[51] involved a U.S. trade association of wood pulp exporters registered under the Webb-Pomerene Act.

[46] Pub. L. No. 65–126, 40 Stat. 516 (1918), codified at 15 U.S.C. ss. 61–66. For an overview of the Webb-Pomerene Act, see "ABA Special Committee Report", see para. 4.066, n. 38, at 49–56. See also A Paul Victor, "Export Cartels: An Idea Whose Time Has Passed", (1992) 60 Antitrust L.J. 571, 572.

[47] See 15 U.S.C. ss. 62, 65. See also "Guidelines for the Issuance of Export Trade Certificate of Review" (1985), *reprinted in* 4 Trade Reg. Rep. (CCH) 13,300.

[48] See *United States v. U.S. Alkali Export Ass'n*, 325 U.S. 196 (1945).

[49] Cf. *United States v. Minnesota Mining & Manufacturing Co.*, 92 F. Supp. 947 (D. Mass. 1950) (Act does not extend to an association which jointly operated manufacturing facilities abroad and restricted its exports from the United States in order to make sales from its overseas facility).

[50] See John F. McDermid, "The Antitrust Commission and the Webb-Pomerene Act: A Critical Assessment", (1980) 37 Wash. & Lee L. Rev. 105.

[51] The *Wood Pulp* case is discussed in Chap. Two.

4.073 A second U.S. law that attempts to encourage the use of export cartels is Title III of the Exporting Trading Company Act of 1982.[52] Under the Act, a firm may apply for and receive a Certificate of Review from the Secretary of Commerce if it demonstrates that its activities will not have harmful effects in the United States. While the Certificate does not cloak the firm with complete immunity, it does shield it from treble damage awards and criminal liability, as well as creating a presumption of legality *vis-à-vis* the antitrust laws for any activity covered by the Certificate.

4.074 Thirdly, the 1982 Foreign Trade Antitrust Improvements Act amends the Sherman Act to exempt export activities of businesses from the reach of the antitrust laws unless those activities produce a "direct, substantial, and reasonably foreseeable" effect on domestic commerce, on import commerce or on export commerce of a U.S. person insofar as the activity injures that person's export business.[53]

4.075 In the E.U., against the backdrop of the implicit approval of the effects doctrine by the Court of Justice under its *Wood Pulp* implementation test, an export cartel that is engaged solely in export activity from the E.U. "to a non-member country, is not in itself likely to restrict or distort competition within the common market," and thus does not violate Article 81.[54]

4.076 As noted in the 1984 OECD Report of the Committee of Experts, only four OECD member countries require that export cartels register with or notify national authorities of their existence.[55] What information does exist on export cartels indicates that their numbers are few and that they account for a small fraction of total export trade in the countries where they have been formed. Given the incomplete data, any conclusions about the trade impact of export cartels are purely speculative. It could be the case that the threat of antitrust proceedings being brought against an export cartel in its export markets has acted as a deterrent on their formation. If this speculation is accurate, national competition laws may in fact be acting as a restraint on, or deterrent to, anti-competitive behaviour in international markets without the aid of a multilateral agreement on the subject, notwithstanding that *de jure* the U.S. antitrust exemptions for export cartels permit an exporter to engage in practices that would not otherwise be tolerated if committed within the domestic market.[56]

---

[52] Pub. L. No. 97–290, 96 Stat. 1233–45, *codified at* 15 U.S.C. ss. 4001–4021. By the early 1980s the Webb-Pomerene Act was not receiving much use and was considered ineffective. In response, Congress enacted the Export Trading Company Act in 1982. See For an overview of the Webb-Pomerene Act, see "ABA Special Committee Report", see para. 4.066, n. 38, at 56–61; George E. Garvey, "Exports, Banking and Antitrust: The Export Trading Company Act—A Modest Tool for Export Promotion, 5 Nw. J. Int'l L. & Bus. 818 (1983); Donald Zarin, *The Export trading Company Act: Reducing Antitrust Uncertainty in Export Trade*", (1983) 17 Geo. Wash. J. Int'l L. & Econ. 297; Dennis Unkovic, "Joint Ventures and the Export Trading Company Act", (1985) 5 J.L. & Com. 373.

[53] Pub. L. No. 97–290, 96 Stat. 1246–47, codified at 15 U.S.C. ss. 6a, 45(a)(3).

[54] See *Bulk Oil v. Sun International*, [1986] E.C.R. 559, 589; [1986] 2 C.M.L.R. 732.

[55] See "Report of the Committee of Experts", see para. 4.068, n. 41, at 32, para. 53.

[56] For more on antitrust exemptions for cartels under U.S. law, see Kauper, see para. 4.059, n. 18. Other U.S. laws that exempt specific industries and activities in whole or in part from the

4. *The OECD Recommendation on Hard-core Cartels*

4.077 As discussed in Chapter Two, the OECD Recommendation of the Council Concerning Effective Action Against Hard Core Cartels is the first consensus document on an approach to policing international cartels. The Recommendation encourages OECD members

(1) to co-operate with each other, given their common interest in preventing hard-core cartels;

(2) to enter into mutual assistance agreements that permit information exchanges between national enforcement authorities; and

(3) to adopt competition legislation that prohibits and deters hard-core cartels.

B. Import Cartels

4.078 Import cartels are the buyers' equivalent of an export cartel. Are import cartels a serious threat to competition? The OECD Committee of Experts stated in 1984 that:

> it would seem that import cartels do not present serious problems as regards manufactured goods. . . . [T]he conditions for an import cartel to be established and sustained will not be very commonly realised; and where they are, the cartel is likely to come to the attention of the competition authorities in the importing country because of the likely adverse effects on competition in that country.[57]

However, with the progressive lowering of barriers to international trade, domestic firms have an increased incentive to form import cartels that exclude foreign firms from selling their goods in the domestic market. Import cartels consist of an agreement among importers/buyers within a country to co-ordinate the purchase and importation into the country of a good or service. Import cartels are defended by some to the extent they enable small and medium-size firms to achieve economies of scale in terms of bulk discounts, insurance, storage, and related costs associated with the purchase of foreign inputs.

---

reach of the antitrust laws include the Capper-Volstead Act, 7 U.S.C. s. 291 (agriculture and fish co-operatives); Bank Merger Act of 1960, 12 U.S.C. s. 1828 (banking); McCarran-Ferguson Act, 15 U.S.C. ss. 1011–1015 (insurance); National Co-operative Research Act of 1984, 15 U.S.C. ss. 4301–4305 (research joint ventures); National Co-operative Research and Production Act of 1993, 15 U.S.C. s. 4301 (extending the antitrust protection of the 1984 version of the Act to joint ventures involving products, processes, or services); Norris LaGuardia Act, 29 U.S.C. ss. 101–115, and 15 U.S.C. s. 17 (labour unions); 42 U.S.C. s. 6272 (international energy agreements); Shipping Act of 1984, 46 U.S.C. ss. 1701–1720 (international ocean shipping); Communications Act of 1934, 47 U.S.C. ss. 151–156 (international communications); 49 U.S.C. ss. 1382, 1384 (international aviation); Defence Production Act of 1950, 50 U.S.C. s. 2158a(j) (national defence programs). See also Dep't of Justice, "Antitrust Guidelines Concerning Research Joint Ventures", Antitrust & Trade Reg. Rep (BNA), No. 992, Special Supp. (Dec. 4, 1980).

[57] "Report of the Committee of Experts", see para. 4.068, n. 41, at 36.

4.079 Import cartels have also been established at times in response to export cartels. By pooling the purchasing power of importers of certain products, the leverage to set favourable prices that an export cartel might otherwise have is minimised or eliminated. For example, in response to a U.S. cartel of sulphur exporters called SUXELCO, import cartels were established in Australia, New Zealand and the U.K. to negotiate lower price increases than those sought by SUXELCO.[58]

In the United States, section 1 of the Sherman Act is supplemented by the Wilson Tariff Act[59] on import cartels which makes them illegal.[60] The competition laws of the U.K., Germany and Spain, on the other hand, provide for the exemption or approval of import cartels that are considered necessary to counteract sellers' market power.[61]

C. Trading Companies

4.080 Trading companies are created to conduct trade in goods and services on both the export and import side of the ledger. They can assist domestic firms in both selling their goods overseas through distribution channels established by the trading company, as well as assist foreign firms eager to sell in the trading company's home market. In the United States, legislation has been enacted to promote the creation of trading companies. First, the Export Trading Company Act of 1982 exempts qualified export trading companies from a Justice Department antitrust enforcement action in order to encourage small and medium-size companies to sell their goods and services abroad (the Webb-Pomerene Act applies only to transactions in goods). The Act also authorises the issuance of export trade certificates of review[62] that shields the holder from government antitrust lawsuits and from private treble damages actions.[63]

4.081 Despite the existence of jurisdiction over domestic enterprises that have formed an export trading company, most countries as a policy matter only prosecute conduct that causes anti-competitive effects in the domestic market. Nevertheless, although the export activities of trading companies tend to be of little concern to the home country, their activities can be of interest to the importing country. For example, if trading companies acquire

[58] *See* "Report of the Committee of Experts", see para. 4.068, n. 41, at 27.

[59] See 15 U.S.C. ss. 8–11.

[60] The Wilson Act provides in pertinent part that every combination, conspiracy, trust, agreement or contract made by or between two or more persons either of whom . . . is engaged in importing any article from any country into the United States . . . is illegal and void if intended to operate in restraint of trade or to increase the market price of any imported article in any part of the United States or of any manufacture into which such article enters or is intended to enter. 15 U.S.C. s. 8.

[61] See "Report of the Committee of Experts", see para. 4.068, n. 41, at 35.

[62] To qualify for a certificate of review, the applicant's conduct must not: (1) substantially lessen competition or restrain trade in the United States or restrain the export trade of a U.S. competitor, (2) unreasonably enhance, stabilise, or depress proces in the United States, (3) be an unfair method of competition against export competitors, and (4) reasonably be expected to result in a resale in the United States of the exported goods or services. See 15 U.S.C. 4013(a).

[63] A private person may sue for actual damages and injunctive relief if the certified conduct is inconsistent with the statutory standards for exemption.

and exercise dominant market power in the purchase of goods for export, thus eliminating competitive sources of supply from foreign sellers, an importing country may be concerned about predatory pricing designed to drive its domestic producers out of business. Here, however, the antidumping duty law stands ready to cut down attempts to unfairly undersell competitors in the importing country.

IV. VERTICAL RESTRAINTS

4.082 A vertical restraint may be defined as a practice that confines, constrains or inhibits the action of two or more parties at different stages of the production or distribution chain, such as manufacturer-distributor relationships.[64] Vertical agreements, in essence, attempt to control the distribution of goods and services but they typically involve less danger of creating monopoly power. National competition enforcement authorities' concern with such agreements is their potential for raising prices, lowering the quality and quantity of goods, or preventing market entry and innovation. Typical vertical restraints include price and non-price terms and conditions imposed on the sale of goods along the chain of distribution from manufacturer to retailer to restrain the conduct of the downstream purchaser.

4.083 The anti-competitive effects of vertical agreements can be even more complex than those of horizontal agreements, therefore the legal treatment of vertical agreements varies more than that of horizontal agreements among countries with competition legislation. Most of the competition law conflicts among OECD countries centre on vertical restraints because there is little agreement on if and when they are harmful. These restraints are only condemned, if at all, after an intensive analysis of their anti- and pro-competitive effects in a specific case.[65] Although U.S. antitrust statutes do not distinguish between horizontal and vertical restraints (which is the case for the texts of most competition laws, including Article 81 of the E.C. Treaty), as a matter of administrative practice and decisional law a sharp line is drawn between the two in the case of non-price restraints. In the United States, most vertical price agreements are condemned as illegal *per se*. Vertical non-price agreements, however, are generally lawful in the United States unless they violate the rule of reason.[66]

4.084 There is close to universal agreement among economists and some government officials that vertical restraints in the abstract are in most cases efficient and pro-competitive, at least when such restraints are used by firms that lack market power.[67] The Chicago School, for example, argues that vertical restraints are almost never harmful. Conversely, there is similar

[64] See George A. Hay, "Vertical Restraints", in *International Harmonization of Competition Laws*, see para. 4.059, n. 18, at 189.
[65] See Hawk, see para. 4.066, n. 38, at 12.
[66] See, *e.g. Business Elecs. Corp. v. Sharp Elecs. Corp.*, 485 U.S. 717, 724 (1988); *Continental T.V., Inc. v. GTE Sylvania, Inc.*, 433 U.S. 36, 59 (1977).
[67] See "Conference on Trade and Competition Policies", see para. 4.068, n. 42, at 26.

agreement that vertical restraints can be inefficient and anti-competitive when used by firms that possess market power.[68] However, there is virtually no consensus on when a vertical restraint is or is not anti-competitive in any given case. In addition, there is no consensus on the competition policy implications of exclusivity arrangements, with some viewing exclusive dealing agreements as pro-competitive and other as anti-competitive.[69]

Given this lack of consensus, it seems highly doubtful that any international agreement could be reached on a clear set of rules governing all types of vertical restraints. As Professor Eleanor Fox points out, even if different jurisdictions adopted identical statutory language, judicial and administrative interpretations could easily differ depending on the weight given the factors that make up the economic and legal analysis.[70]

A. Resale Price Maintenance

4.085 A classic vertical price restraint is a resale price maintenance agreement (*i.e.* vertical price fixing), where a supplier sells to a distributor on the condition that the distributor sells at a price dictated by the supplier. In the case of vertical agreements on pricing practices, the competition rules on resale price maintenance set the limits on the retail prices that manufacturers/distributors can set for goods and then force downstream retailers to charge.

4.086 In most OECD countries, resale price maintenance agreements are illegal, although some countries authorise the practice if the beneficial effects can be shown to outweigh the detrimental ones.[71] Even though a resale price maintenance agreement could have pro-competitive effects by facilitating market entry and penetration, it is nevertheless treated as illegal *per se* in the United States in the case of minimum resale price fixing.[72] In 1997 however, in *State Oil Co. v. Khan*,[73] the U.S. Supreme Court rejected *per se* treatment of maximum resale price maintenance agreements as having an insufficient economic justification.

Despite the *per se* label for minimum price agreements, resale price maintenance is not treated like horizontal price fixing in terms of remedy and enforcement. The Justice Department rarely brings a civil action and virtually never brings a criminal proceeding, leaving enforcement largely to private parties.[74]

---

[68] See *id.*

[69] See *id.* at 27.

[70] See Eleanor M. Fox, "Toward World Antitrust and Market Access", (1997) 91 Am. J. Int'l L. 1, 16–17.

[71] See OECD, "Resale Price Maintenance", CDE/GD(97)229, at 10 (1997) (illegal in most OECD countries with the exception of newspapers and books).

[72] See, *e.g. Dr. Miles Medical Co. v. John D. Park & Sons Co.*, 220 U.S. 373 (1911); *Kiefer-Stewart Co. v. Joseph E. Seagram & Sons, Inc.*, 340 U.S. 211 (1951); *Atlantic Richfield Co. v. USA Petroleum Co.*, 495 U.S. 328 (1990) (proof of predatory pricing required for a competitor to have a private claim for vertical maximum resale price fixing); 324 *Liquor Corp. v. Duffy*, 479 U.S. 335, 341–43 (1987); *Monsanto v. Spray-Rite Serv. Corp.*, 465 U.S. 752, 761 (1984); Wise, see para. 4.052, n. 93, at 21.

[73] 522 U.S. 3, 18 (1997). See "*Symposium: State Oil Co. v. Khan*, Albrecht Overruled at Last", (1998) 66 Antitrust L.J. 537.

[74] See Wise, see para. 4.052, n. 93, at 21.

4.087 In Canada, pursuant to section 61 of the Competition Act, minimum and maximum resale price maintenance is a criminal offence.[75] Mexico, on the other hand, treats resale price maintenance as a "relative monopolistic practice" (*prácticas monopólicas relativas*) that is subject to an economic analysis similar to the U.S. rule of reason.[76] Germany, Japan and the U.K. relax their competition rules governing resale price maintenance with respect to books and publishing.[77]

B. Vertical Non-Price Restraints

4.088 Vertical non-price restraints include contract terms on exclusive dealing, refusals to deal, territorial restraints, tying, full-line forcing, and abuse of negotiating position. Thus, for example, in the sale or distribution of goods manufacturers might restrict wholesalers and retailers by requiring them to enter into exclusive dealing arrangements that forbid the latter from dealing in the products of a competitor. Two of these non-price restraints, exclusive dealing and territorial restraints, can have pro-competitive effects by promoting interbrand competition. Accordingly, these restraints are not treated as *per se* violations by most national antitrust enforcement authorities.

4.089 Vertical non-price restraints have the potential for stimulating interbrand competition so they are generally analysed under the rule of reason test.[78] Vertical non-price restraints can, of course, be anti-competitive depending on the circumstances. For example, an exclusive dealing arrangement could be anti-competitive if it results in substantial foreclosure of the relevant market to competitors of the licensor. Similarly, grantback clauses in a licensing agreement, while they may promote innovation based on information provided by the licensee to the licensor, may also adversely affect competition by reducing a licensee's incentive to engage in research and development, thereby limiting competition in the market.

4.090 The United States and Canada generally apply the rule of reason in the case of exclusive dealing arrangements and territorial restrictions in licensing agreements.[79] The rule of reason balances the pro-competitive effects of territorial and other restrictions on intellectual property licences, thereby protecting legitimate interests of businesses in penetrating a market and creating interbrand competition within that market, on the one hand, against

[75] See Competition Act, s. 61(1)(a).

[76] See LCFE Art. 10. See also "The Competition Laws of NAFTA", see para. 4.062, n. 30, at 64–66.

[77] See Hawk, see para. 4.066, n. 38, at 15.

[78] See, *e.g. Business Elecs. Corp. v. Sharp Elecs. Corp.*, 485 U.S. at 724; *Continental T.V., Inc. v. GTE Sylvania, Inc.*, 433 U.S. 51, 52 n.19, 54 (1977). See also Michael A. Carrier, "The Real Rule of Reason: Bridging the Disconnect", (1999) B.Y.U.L. Rev. 1265.

[79] See, *e.g. Continental TV v. GTE Sylvania*, 433 U.S. at 51–59; Competition Act, s. 77; "The Competition Laws of NAFTA", see para. 4.062, n. 30, at 60–61. Under the joint Department of Justice/Federal Trade Commission Antitrust Guidelines for the Licensing of Intellectual Property, it is ordinarily considered illegal to use territorial restraints in licensing agreements between competitors because it is considered a device for dividing global markets. See Dep't of Justice & Federal Trade Comm'n, "Antitrust Guidelines for the Licensing of Intellectual Property" s. 5.1, Horizontal Restraints (1995), available at http://www.usdoj.gov/atr/public/guidelines/ipguide.htm.

the inhibiting effects of such agreements on intrabrand competition, on the other. In the United States so long as its potential pro-competitive effects are not outweighed by any substantial foreclosure of competition in the relevant market, an exclusive dealing agreement will pass muster under the antitrust laws.[80] In Canada, if the market restriction is engaged in by a major supplier of a product so that the restriction is likely to lessen competition in relation to the product, the Canadian Competition Tribunal may prohibit any or all suppliers of the product from engaging in the market restriction.[81] The E.U., on the other hand, prohibits vertical non-price restraints of intrabrand competition, such as grants of exclusive territories, regardless of their overall effect on interbrand competition or efficiency.[82]

C. Abuse of Intellectual Property Rights in Vertical Agreements

4.091 A 1989 OECD study of members' competition laws on the abuse of IPRs in licensing agreements reveals a wide disparity in the legal treatment that certain vertical agreements and clauses receive under national competition laws.[83] Some licensing restrictions are treated as *per se* unlawful under various members'competition laws, while other members analyse them on a case-by-case basis for their anti-competitive effects.

Article 8.2 of the TRIPS Agreement highlights the abuse of IPRs as one area where appropriate measures may be needed to prevent the abuse of IPRs or the resort to practices that unreasonably restrain trade. While a vertical territorial restriction in a technology licensing agreement is not inherently suspect, territorial restrictions in horizontal agreements between competitors to divide markets are. An example of a vertical restraint that could constitute an abuse of a patent right would be a condition that as part of a patent licensing agreement the licensee agrees to buy other products of the supplier that are not the subject matter of the patent. This would be an example of an illegal tying arrangement or full-line forcing—a form of tying.

4.092 In the United States, these abuses are generally addressed under the antitrust laws. In 1995, the Department of Justice and the Federal Trade Commission published joint Antitrust Guidelines for the Licensing of Intellectual Property.[84] The Guidelines provide that in the vast majority of cases restraints in technology transfer licensing agreements will be evaluated under the rule of reason.[85] In analysing an agreement under the rule of reason, the inquiry is whether the restraint in question is likely to have anti-competitive effects and if so, whether the restraint is reasonably necessary to achieve pro-competitive benefits that outweigh those anti-competitive effects. The touch-

[80] See, *e.g. Standard Oil Co. v. United States*, 337 U.S. 293 (1949); *Tampa Electric Co. v. Nashville Coal Co.*, 365 U.S. 320 (1961).
[81] See The "Competition Laws of NAFTA", see para. 4.062, n. 30, at 61.
[82] See *Consten & Grundig v. Commission*, [1966] E.C.R. 299.
[83] See OECD, "Competition Policy and Intellectual Property Rights" (1989) 98–104. See also "Report of the OECD Secretariat, Competition Policy and Vertical Restraints: Franchising Agreements" (1993) 16 (recognising that there is a wide range of possible rules, and that the same rules may not be the most efficient in all jurisdictions).
[84] "Antitrust Guidelines for the Licensing of Intellectual Property", see para. 4.090, n. 79.
[85] See *id.* Guideline 3.4.

stone is whether the restraint in question achieves an efficiency-enhancing integration of economic activity.

In general, licensing arrangements promote such integration because they facilitate the combination of the licensor's intellectual property with the complementary factors of production owned by the licensee. Restraints in the licensing agreement may promote such integration by aligning the incentives of the licensor and licensee to promote the development and marketing of the licensed technology or by reducing transaction costs.

4.093 The Guidelines further provide that a horizontal relationship between a licensor and licensee does not, in itself, indicate that an arrangement is anti-competitive. Such arrangements may be efficiency-enhancing and pro-competitive when they result in economies of scale and integrate complementary research and development, production, and marketing capabilities.[86] Accordingly, they are also generally evaluated under the rule of reason. However, in the case of agreements to fix prices, allocate markets, or reduce output the *per se* rule is applied.

The Antitrust Licensing Guidelines establish a safe harbour or "safety zone" (comparable to the block exemptions promulgated by the European Commission) whereby the Justice Department and the FTC will not challenge a restraint in an intellectual property licensing agreement. This is provided the restraint is not *per se* anti-competitive and the licensor and licensee collectively account for no more than 20 per cent of the relevant market affected by the restraint.[87]

4.094 In the European Union, Article 81 of the Treaty of Rome prohibits anti-competitive agreements, decisions, and concerted practices. All agreements, decisions, or concerted practices prohibited under Article 81(1) are void pursuant to Article 81(2), at least to the extent the anti-competitive provisions are non-severable from the balance of the agreement, decision, or practice. Under Article 81(3), an agreement, decision, or concerted practice may be exempted from the prohibition of paragraph 1 if it contributes to improving the economic welfare of consumers.

The Commission has the power to grant "block" or "group" exemptions for classes of agreements. The block exemptions are in essence a codification of the rule of reason for a given class of agreements. The block exemption dispenses with the requirement of notifying the Commission of each proposed agreement.[88] Provided the agreement meets the criteria outlined in the Commission's regulations for qualifying for the block exemption, it is presumptively valid under Article 81. The Commission has issued regulations on granting block exemptions for exclusive distributorships, exclusive purchasing, group research and development projects, patent licensing, know-

---

[86] See *id.* Guideline 5.1.

[87] See *id.* Guideline 4.3.

[88] For background on the Commission's group or block exemptions, see Chap. Two. An unresolved issue is whether an affirmative duty exists to seek an exemption. See, *e.g.* Valentine Korah, *Introductory Guide to EEC Competition Law and Practice*, s. 6.3 (1990).

how licensing, and franchises.[89] In each of the regulations on these block exemptions, the Commission lists permitted and prohibited contract terms.[90]

4.095 On January 31, 1996 the Commission adopted a regulation, effective April 1, 1996 that combines Regulation 2349/84, exempting certain patent licensing agreements, and Regulation 556/89, exempting certain know-how licensing agreements. To generalise, the Know-How Regulation was more liberal than the Patent Regulation in that it had a longer list of permitted clauses in licensing agreements and a shorter list of prohibited clauses. By adopting Regulation 240/96, the Commission eliminated most of the different treatment that patent and know-how licensing agreements received under the former Patent and Know-How Regulations.[91] The list of prohibited clauses that will prevent a patent or know-how licensing agreement from qualifying for the group exemption include:

(1) restrictions regarding the determination of prices or discounts,[92]

(2) restrictions on parallel imports within the E.U.,[93]

(3) restraints on output,[94] and

(4) grantback clauses.[95]

D. Grey Market Goods and the Doctrine of Exhaustion

4.096 Another example of a vertical restraint that represents a blend of competition and intellectual property law—and thus has an impact on international trade flows—involves grey market goods. This is another area where WTO members' competition laws diverge. Manufacturers might enter into a trademark licensing agreement with wholesalers or distributors that includes a clause not to resell in other territories or to re-export the goods to the manufacturer's home market, thereby preventing parallel importation and avoiding being undercut through arbitrage of the manufacturer's own product in its home market. Similarly, in a technology transfer or licensing agreement, licensors may attempt to exploit IPRs by limiting the territorial scope of the licensee's market by prohibiting the sale or export of goods bearing the

[89] See Chap. Two.

[90] See, *e.g.* Commission Regulation 1983/83, June 30, 1983 [1983] O.J. L173/1 (exclusive distribution agreements); Commission Regulation 1984/83, June 30, 1983 [1983] O.J. L173/5 (exclusive purchasing agreements); Commission Regulation 418/85, Feb. 22, 1985 [1985] O.J. L53/5 (joint research and development); Commission Regulation 2349/84, Aug. 16, 1984 [1984] O.J. L219/15; Apr. 26, 1985 [1985] O.J. L113/34 (patent licensing); Commission Regulation 556/89, Mar. 4, 1989 [1989] O.J. L61/1 (know-how licensing); Commission Regulation 4087/88, Dec. 28, 1988 [1988] O.J. L359/46 (franchise agreements).

[91] For an analysis of the Regulation 240/96, see Pierre V.F. Bos & Marco M. Slotboom, "The EC Technology Transfer Regulation—A Practitioner's Perspective", (1998) 32 Int'l Law. 1.

[92] See Regulation 240/96, Art. 3(1).

[93] See *id.* Art. 3(3).

[94] See *id.* Art. 3(5).

[95] See *id.* Art. 3(6).

licensed trademark or manufactured through the licensed technology to buyers outside of a designated geographic area, for example.

4.097 Grey market goods begin their distribution cycle as goods manufactured and sold abroad that lawfully bear a trademark identical to a trademark used in the import market. These goods are genuine goods but become "grey market" goods when they are imported into an unauthorised market that was reserved either for the licensor or a different licensee under a separate licensing agreement. From the licensor's perspective, grey market goods present the problem of the free rider who trades on the goodwill of the licensor in a particular market without having paid for it. From a consumer perspective, grey market goods generate intrabrand competition that translates into lower prices.[96]

4.098 An importer's motivation for exporting grey market goods is purely profit driven. Goods manufactured abroad may be cheaper than the identical or comparable product manufactured, for example, in the United States because of the strength of the U.S. dollar relative to foreign currencies. If arbitrage can be prevented and the lower-priced, grey market goods can be kept out of the U.S. market, then the U.S. manufacturer and distributor may have more profit to share between them. In addition, by keeping grey market goods out of the U.S. market, importers are prevented from enjoying a free-ride on the goodwill generated by the U.S. manufacturer and distributor. Such goodwill can take the form of advertising and after-sale warranties and service, for which neither the importer nor the foreign manufacturer paid, but from which they may derive economic benefit.[97] The United States thus applies a policy of national exhaustion, allowing IPR owners to block grey market imports at the border.

4.099 In many countries, including Japan, New Zealand and the E.U., the doctrine of exhaustion,[98] sometimes referred to as the "first sale" doctrine, prevents a trademark owner from controlling the resale of goods bearing a genuine mark, provided there is no consumer confusion as to the source of

[96] See generally Shashank Upadhye, "Rewriting the Lanham Trademark Act to Prohibit the Importation of All Gray Market Goods", (1996) 20 Seton Hall Legis. J. 59; Lucy J. Minehan, "The Gray Market: A Call for Greater Protection of Consumers and Trademark Owners", (1991) 12 U. Pa. J. Int'l Bus. L. 457; Harry Rubin, "Destined to Remain Gray: The Eternal Recurrence of Parallel Imports", (1992) 26 Int'l Law. 597; Soojin Kim, "In Pursuit of Profit Maximization by Restricting Parallel Imports: The U.S. Copyright Owner and Taiwan Copyright Law", (1995) 5 Pac. Rim. L. & Pol'y J. 205; Robert K. Hahm, "Gray Market Goods: Has A Resolution Been Found?", (1991) 81 Trademark Rep. 58.

[97] See generally Sam J. Alberts, "Trademarks and Gray Market Goods: Why U.S. Trademark Holders Should Be Held Strictly Liable for Defective Gray Market Goods", (1992) 25 Geo. Wash. J. Int'l L. & Econ. 841.

[98] See Jacques Picard, "The Legality of International Gray Marketing: A Comparison of the Position in the United States, Canada, and the European Union", 26 Canadian Bus. L.J. 422 (1995–96); Yun-Peng Chu, "Towards the Establishment of an Order of Competition for the International Economy: With References to the Draft International Antitrust Code, The Parallel Imports Problem, and the Experience of Taiwan, ROC", in *International Harmonization of Competition Laws,* see para. 4.059, n. 18, at 453, 459–63. Article 6 of the TRIPS Agreement takes no position on the doctrine of exhaustion, thus leaving the matter for resolution under national law.

the goods.[99] The IPR owner loses the right to control or prevent the resale of such goods once those goods have entered the stream of commerce. The exhaustion doctrine states that the owner's trademark rights have been exhausted after the first authorised sale of the marked goods. The underlying rationale for the doctrine of exhaustion is the notion that the allocation of markets between licensor and licensee is anti-competitive. On the subject of grey market goods within the E.U., the E.U. Trademark Directive 89/104/EEC provides that a trademark owner's rights are exhausted and may not be exercised to prevent articles from being placed on sale anywhere within the E.U. Thus, in the E.U., parallel imports are subject to a doctrine of regional exhaustion. Some E.U. members (*e.g.* Austria) had drafted their national laws to extend the Directive's exhaustion principle to articles sold outside the E.U. and then imported back into the E.U. The European Court of Justice ruled in 1998 that such national laws violate the trademark directive. The Court held that E.U. trademark owners have the right to block grey market imports into the E.U. of goods they originally sold outside the E.U.[1] The decision will prevent importers from purchasing branded merchandise sold outside the E.U. at lower prices and then importing them into the higher-priced E.U. market, thereby exploiting the price difference.[2]

1. *The Regulation of Grey Market Goods in the United States*

4.100 The history of the regulation of grey market goods in the United States is a tortured but interesting one. It demonstrates the complexity of the issue and the obstacle it places in the way of bridging the gap with the E.U. and other countries which follow the doctrine of exhaustion. In the United States, the federal government did not regulate the importation of grey market goods before 1922. This laissez-faire attitude existed even in cases where a foreign manufacturer exported grey market goods to the United States in breach of a licensing agreement to refrain from engaging in such conduct. However, in 1922, Congress passed legislation to block the importation of grey market goods.[3]

4.101 Today, a U.S. trademark owner does have some ability to prevent the importation of grey market and parallel imports, including the right to

[99] See generally Kaoru Takakmatsu, "Parallel Importation of Trademarked Goods: A Comparative Analysis", (1982) 57 Wash. L. Rev. 433.

[1] See C–355/96 (1998) *Silhouette Int'l Schmied GmbH & Co. KG v. Hartlauer Handelsgesellschaft mbH*. The opinion is available at http://europa.eu.int. Under the Australia-New Zealand Closer Economic Relations Agreement, parallel importation restrictions were repealed in 1999. Additional information is available at http://www.accc.gov.au/docs/speeches/ipsanz98.html.

[2] See "A grey area", *The Economist*, June 13, 1998 at 61–62.

[3] Congress was spurred by the Second Circuit's decision in *A. Bourjois & Co. v. Katzel*, 275 F.2d 539 (1921), *rev d*, 260 U.S. 689 (1923). There, the court refused to enjoin the importation of grey market goods shipped to the United States by a foreign manufacturer which had licensed a U.S. person to use the former's trademark in the United States.

enlist the assistance of the Customs Service to that end, under section 526 of the Tariff Act of 1930, the Genuine Goods Exclusion Act.[4] The Genuine Goods Exclusion Act provides a blanket prohibition on the unauthorised importation into the United States of foreign-manufactured goods bearing a registered trademark that is owned by a U.S. national without the owner's written consent. In addition, any goods entered in violation of section 526 are subject to seizure and forfeiture. An importer who violates section 526 is subject to a civil damages action and may be enjoined to re-export, destroy, or obliterate the trademark on the infringing merchandise.[5]

4.102 Although the Act makes no exceptions, it is important to recall that Congress enacted section 526 as a narrow response to the Second Circuit's *Katzel* decision. There, the Second Circuit permitted a foreign trademark licensor to import into the United States foreign-manufactured goods in purported breach of a licensing agreement with a U.S. licensee.[6] When it first promulgated its section 526 implementing regulations, the Customs Service carved out two exceptions to section 526's prohibition on the unauthorised importation of articles bearing recorded trademarks and trade names:

(1) a common-control exception (sometimes referred to as the affiliation exception[7]), and

(2) an authorised-use exception.[8]

The common-control exception was sustained and the authorised-use exception invalidated by the U.S. Supreme Court in 1988 in *K Mart Corp. v. Cartier, Inc.*[9]

---

[4] 19 U.S.C. s. 1526. Section 526 was originally enacted in 1922 as part of the Tariff Act of 1922. The Genuine Goods Exclusion Act provides in part: (a) Importation Prohibited—. . . [I]t shall be unlawful to import into the United States any merchandise of foreign manufacture if such merchandise, or the label, sign, print, package, wrapper, or receptacle, bears a trademark owned by a citizen of, or by a corporation or association created or organized within, the United States, and registered in the Patent and Trademark Office by a person domiciled in the United States, . . ., and if a copy of the certificate of registration of such trademark is filed with the Secretary of the Treasury, unless written consent of the owner of such trademark is produced at the time of making entry. (b) Seizure and Forfeiture—Any such merchandise imported into the United States in violation of the provisions of this section shall be subject to seizure and forfeiture for violation of the customs laws. (c) Injunctions and Damages—Any person dealing in any such merchandise may be enjoined from dealing therein within the United States or may be required to export or destroy such merchandise or to remove or obliterate such trademark and shall be liable for the same damages and profits provided for wrongful use of a trademark, under the provisions of sections 81 to 109 of Title 15.

[5] See 19 U.S.C. s. 526(a)(c).

[6] For background on the enactment of s.526, see Michael B. Weicher, "*K Mart Corp. v. Cartier, Inc.*: A Black Decision for the Gray Market", (1989) 38 Am. U.L. Rev. 463.

[7] See Rubin, see para. 4.097, n. 96, at 599.

[8] See *K Mart Corp. v. Cartier, Inc.*, 486 U.S. 281 (1988). The practical effect of the Customs Service's position was to allow the importation of most grey market goods into the United States.

[9] 486 U.S. 281 (1988). The authorised use exception, which was invalidated by the Supreme Court and formerly found at 19 C.F.R. s. 133.21(c)(3), permitted the importation of grey market goods if the foreign manufacturer was authorised to use the mark by a U.S. trademark owner. See Weicher, see para. 4.102, n. 6.

4.103 Customs' common-control exception provides that the restriction on importation of articles bearing a recorded trademark or trade name is not applicable when:

> (1) [b]oth the foreign and the U.S. trademark or trade name are owned by the same person or business entity; [or] (2) [t]he foreign and domestic trademark or trade name owners are parent and subsidiary companies or are otherwise subject to common ownership or control.[10]

Accordingly, the Customs Service will seize grey market goods only when the trademark rights are not under common ownership or control.

4.104 Alternatives to section 526 for preventing the importation of grey market goods can be found in the Lanham Act and the Copyright Act. First, in connection with the Lanham Act, section 42 of the Act prohibits the importation of merchandise that copies or simulates a registered U.S. trademark.[11] In addition, under section 32 of the Act, a U.S. owner of a registered trademark may seek damages and injunctive relief from persons who, without authorisation, use a reproduction, counterfeit, copy or colourable imitation of the mark in a way that is likely to cause confusion, to cause mistake, or to deceive.[12]

4.105 U.S. courts are split on the question whether grey market imports can be excluded from entry into the United States under these two Lanham Act provisions. Some courts conclude that no relief is available under section 42 because with genuine goods there is no likelihood of consumer confusion.[13] Other courts have held that relief is available against grey market goods under section 42 when the imports materially differ in physical characteristics from the trademarked goods sold in the United States.[14] In 1998 the Customs Service drafted a rule to implement a 1993 decision of the District of Columbia Court of Appeals, *Lever Bros. Co. v. U.S.*[15] The court in *Lever Bros.* struck down the Customs' affiliate exception as inconsistent with section 42 of the Lanham Act. Under the affiliate exception, Customs will not

[10] 19 C.F.R. s. 133.21(c)(1)(2). The regulations define "common ownership" as "individual or aggregate ownership of more than 50 percent of the business entity". "Common control" means "effective control in policy and operations and is not necessarily synonymous with common ownership". *id.* s. 133.2(d)(1)–(2). See *United States v. Eighty-Three Rolex Watches*, 992 F.2d 508 (5th Cir. 1993) (strictly construing the "common control" regulation).

[11] See 15 U.S.C. s. 1124. The Customs Service implementing regulation can be found at 19 C.F.R. s. 133.21(a). Customs applies the common-control exception to both s. 526 and s. 42 imports. See 19 C.F.R. s. 133.21(c).

[12] See 15 U.S.C. s. 1114.

[13] See, *e.g. Weil Ceramics & Glass, Inc. v. Dash*, 878 F.2d 659 (3d Cir.), cert. denied, 493 U.S. 853 (1989); *Monte Carlo Shirt v. Daewoo Int'l (America) Corp.*, 707 F.2d 1054 (9th Cir. 1983); *Bell & Howell: Mamiya Co. v. Masel Supply Co.*, 719 F.2d 42 (2d Cir. 1983); *NEC Electronics v. CAL Circuit Abco*, 810 F.2d 1506 (9th Cir.), cert. denied, 484 U.S. 851 (1987).

[14] See, *e.g. Lever Bros. Co. v. United States*, 877 F.2d 101 (D.C. Cir. e1989); *Societe Des Produits Nestle, S.A. v. Casa Helvetia, Inc.*, 982 F.2d 633 (1st Cir. 1992); *Original Appalachian Artworks v. Granada Elec., Inc.*, 816 F.2d 68 (2d Cir.), cert. denied, 484 U.S. 847 (1987). For an analysis of the *Lever Brothers* decision, *see* "*Theodore H. Davis, Lever Bros. v. United States* and the Legality of Gray Market Imports: A New Shield for United States Trademark Owners in Transnational Markets", (1993) 28 Wake Forest. L. Rev. 571.

[15] 981 F.2d 1330 (D.C. Cir. 1993).

seize imports bearing a mark identical to the mark owned by a U.S. firm if the foreign and domestic companies are parent and subsidiary or otherwise under common control. Under the proposed rule, in order to protect against consumer confusion Customs will seize genuine imported goods sold by a foreign affiliate if the goods are materially and physically different from goods authorised by the U.S. trademark owner.[16]

4.106 Secondly, for grey market goods that infringe a copyright, section 602(a) of the Copyright Act[17] states that the importation into the United States of copies or sound recordings of a work acquired outside the United States without authorisation of the copyright owner is an infringement of the exclusive right to distribute copies or sound recordings. Such copies or sound recordings are subject to seizure and forfeiture.[18] An important qualification to the owner's right to exclude grey market goods that infringe a copyright is contained in section 109(a) of the Copyright Act.[19] Among a copyright owner's basket of rights is the right of distribution but that right is limited to the first sale. Under the "first sale" doctrine—analogous to the doctrine of exhaustion—the owner may lose the right to control sales of copies of copyrighted works after the first sale. Therefore, in *Quality King Distributors, Inc. v. L'Anza Research Int'l, Inc.*,[20] the Supreme Court held that under the "first sale" doctrine of the Copyright Act, copyright law does not prohibit a purchaser from importing that product back into the United States, even without the copyright owner's permission, once the owner sells its product in a foreign market.[21] The Court rejected the copyright owner's argument that under section 602(a) of the Copyright Act, the owner could have the products excluded from entry into the United States. Construing the first sale defence of section 109 with section 602's provisions on the exclusion of genuine goods, the Court stated that the right granted to distribute a copyrighted product is a limited right. Thus, the distribution right granted under section 602 is limited by other provisions of the Copyright Act, including section 109(a), which plainly states that an owner of a product "is entitled without the authority of the copyright owner, to sell" that product.[22]

4.107 As the U.S. experience with grey market goods and parallel imports illustrates, the law on this issue is complex. So too is the economics. Economists argue that as long as a producer faces interbrand competition, exclusive arrangements that prohibit intrabrand competition are irrelevant. In developing countries the major brands may be owned or controlled by a single firm or a *de facto* cartel. In that situation, with the doctrine of exhaustion being inapplicable and with exclusive distributor agreements being lawful, consumer welfare may suffer.

---

[16] See "Customs Seeks Comments on Gray Market Goods Proposal", (1998) 15 Int'l Trade Rep. (BNA) 581.
[17] See 17 U.S.C. s. 602.
[18] The Customs Service implementing regulations can be found at 19 C.F.R. ss. 133.42–133.47.
[19] 17 U.S.C. s. 109(a).
[20] 118 S. Ct. 1125 (1998).
[21] See *id.* at 1128–30.
[22] See *id.* at 1131–32.

E. Parent-Subsidiary Relationships

4.108 Issues arise in the field of competition law enforcement with respect to the liability of foreign entities for the conduct of their domestic affiliates and vice versa. Under the alter ego theory or control test, resolution of these questions of vicarious liability depends to a large extent on the degree of control exercised by the parent over the subsidiary.[23] While an enterprise is subject to the laws of the country in which it does business, it may also find itself subject to the laws of other countries in which its affiliates are located if those countries use an alter ego or control test of corporate liability.

4.109 Most countries consider a subsidiary incorporated under the laws of the country where it does business to be a legal citizen of that country. However, in cases where a domestic parent company exercises sufficient control over the activities of its foreign subsidiary and the conduct abroad causes adverse effects on the domestic market, the parent may be held responsible under the competition laws of some countries. In the United States, for example, domestic parent companies of multinational enterprises have been held liable for the restrictive business practices of their foreign subsidiaries when those practices have the requisite effect on the U.S. market.[24]

4.110 In the E.U., the European Court of Justice has stated that

> [t]he fact that a subsidiary has a separate legal personality is not sufficient to exclude the possibility of imputing its conduct to the parent company.[25]

Thus, if a parent company and its subsidiary form an economic entity, an E.U. subsidiary may be held responsible under E.U. competition law for the conduct of the parent company organised under the laws of and located in a non-Member State.[26] In order to find a single economic entity under E.U. law two conditions must be met:

(1) the parent firm must have the power to control the subsidiary, such as through share ownership; and

(2) both firms must have a uniform approach to business which suggests that the subsidiary is dependent on the directives of the parent.[27]

---

[23] U.S. courts may find that a parent company and its subsidiary are a single, integrated enterprise based on 4 factors: (1) the interrelation of operations, (2) centralized control of operations, (3) common management, and (4) common ownership or financial control. See *United States v. Scophony Corp. of America*, 333 U.S. 795, 813–16 (1948); *Cook v. Arrowsmith Shelburne, Inc.*, 69 F.3d 1235, 1240 (2d Cir. 1995); *Velandra v. Regie Nationale des Usines Renault*, 336 F.2d 292, 296 (6th Cir. 1962); *GAVCO, Inc. v. Chem-Trend Inc.*, 81 F. Supp. 2d 633 (W.D.N.C. 1999); *Atlantic City Coin & Slot Service Co. v. IGT*, 14 F. Supp. 2d 644 (D.N.J. 1998).

[24] See, *e.g. Continental Ore Co. v. Union Carbide & Carbon Corp.*, 370 U.S. 690 (1962); *O.N.E. Shipping Ltd. v. Flota Mercante Grancolombia, S.A.*, 830 F.2d 449, 453 (2d Cir. 1987); *Hunt v. Mobil Oil Corp.*, 550 F.2d 68, 74 (2d Cir. 1977).

[25] *Imperial Chemical Industries v. Commission* (Case 48/69), [1972] E.C.R. 619, 662; [1972] C.M.L.R. 557.

[26] See *Commercial Solvents v. Commission*, [1974] E.C.R. 223, 254, 256.

[27] See Ivo E. Schwartz, "The International Antitrust Law of the European Community", in *International Harmonization of Competition Laws*, see para. 4.059, n. 18, at 97, 104.

Countries which observe the territoriality principle of prescriptive jurisdiction strictly might object to any legal responsibility of companies incorporated under their laws on the basis of an alter ego or control test of corporate liability, particularly where the company has not violated the domestic laws of the state of incorporation.

V. ABUSE OF DOMINANT POSITION (UNLAWFUL MONOPOLISATION)

4.111 Anti-monopoly law generally forbids unfair conduct through which a firm achieves or maintains a monopoly, primarily by excluding other efficient competitors. In the United States, the Sherman Act does not prohibit being a monopolist or even acting like one by reducing output or earning supranormal profits. What the Act does prohibit are practices by which a firm achieves monopolist status.

While abuse of a dominant position (which is roughly analogous but not identical to unlawful monopolisation) is expressly prohibited in the E.U. under Article 82 of the E.C. Treaty, the European Commission and courts within the E.U. often define markets more narrowly than their U.S. counterparts do, find dominance to exist at lower levels of market share and have declared that dominant firms have a duty to deal with competitors and downstream firms.[28] Thus, one point of divergence centres on the definition of the relevant market in the context of dominance (*e.g.* regional, national, international?). Closely related is the question of market share. A second point of divergence focuses on predatory conduct. While it is generally agreed, for example, that predatory pricing is to be condemned, there is less agreement on what constitutes predation. A third point of divergence, closely related to the second point above, concerns the fit of the unfair pricing laws and the antidumping duty law.[29]

A. Definition of the Relevant Market

4.112 The relevant market for purposes of competition policy is different from the market firms refer to when describing the area where they sell their goods or services, or the industry or sector to which they belong. Market definition in the competition policy context is a tool for drawing the boundaries of competition between firms. Its purpose is to identify the competitive constraints that firms face. To that end, the relevant market is defined in terms of both product and geography in order to identify those competitors who are actually capable of constraining the behaviour of the firms which are parties to a competition law proceeding and of preventing

[28] See Lawrence A. Sullivan & Warren S. Grimes, "The Law of Antitrust: An Integrated Handbook 997" (2000).

[29] For a review of the divergences in OECD members competition laws in the area of abuse of a dominant position, see OECD, "Abuse of Dominance and Monopolisation", OCDE/GD(96)131 (1996); Sally Van Siclen, "Background Note: Abuse of Dominance and Monopolization", (1999) 1 OECD J. Competition L. & Pol'y 170.

them from acting independently of any effective competitive pressure.[30] Market definition makes it possible, for example, to calculate the size of market share that would translate into market power for the purpose of assessing whether a firm has a dominant position, the anti-competitive effects of a proposed merger or the anti-competitive effects of horizontal or vertical agreements.[31] The relevant geographic market can be local, national, international or even global. Given the globalisation of international trade and the increased integration of national economies, markets that were once local or national in scope are increasingly becoming international.[32]

4.113 In the E.U., for example, the relevant product market is defined as:

> all those products and/or services which are regarded as interchangeable or substitutable by the consumer, by reason of the products' characteristics, their prices and their intended use.[33]

The relevant geographic market is defined as:

> the area in which the undertakings concerned are involved in the supply and demand of products or services, in which the conditions of competition are sufficiently homogeneous and which can be distinguished from neighboring areas because the conditions of competition are appreciably different in those areas.[34]

The scope of the relevant geographic market starts at the national level and might expand to include the Community-wide level.[35]

4.114 In defining the relevant market, the United States, like the E.U., requires the identification of the firms that are competitors in a given product in a given geographic area.[36] After defining the relevant market, the United States and the E.U. evaluate market shares and consider barriers to market entry. However, the European Commission's market definitions, in the opinion of some commentators, "tend to be more consonant with views of practical business people, less theoretically rigorous than U.S. [market] definitions."[37]

4.115 The 1992 DOJ/FTC Horizontal Merger Guidelines define the relevant market in terms of product and geographic markets. In determining the product market the Guidelines direct the agencies to evaluate the buyers'

---

[30] See "WGTCP 1998 Report", see para. 4.016, n. 16, at 20, para. 54.

[31] See Van Siclen, see para. 4.111, n. 29, at 171; Chien-Te Fan, "Market Definition and the Application of the ROC Fair Trade Law", in *International Harmonization of Competition Laws*, see para. 4.059, n. 18, at 381, 382–83.

[32] "WGTCP 1998 Report", see para. 4.016, n. 16, at 20, para. 54.

[33] Commission Notice on the definition of the relevant market for the purposes of Community competition law, (1997) O.J. C-372, at 2, available at http://europa.eu.int/comm/competition.

[34] *id.* at 2.

[35] See *id.* at 5.

[36] See *Brown Shoe Co. v. United States*, 370 U.S. 294, 324 (1962).

[37] Sullivan & Grimes, see para. 4.111, n. 28, at 200. The authors add that [t]his distinction may fade in response to DG–IV's 1997 statement on relevant market definition, which in many respects emulates the approach to market definition set forth in U.S. horizontal merger guidelines. *id.* (footnote omitted).

and sellers' perceptions of the substitutability of two products; a comparison of the products in terms of design, physical composition and other characteristics; and a comparison of price movements over the prior one-year period.[38] In defining the geographic market, the Guidelines give weight to, *inter alia*, the shipment patterns of the merging firms and of competing firms; a comparison of price movements of the relevant product in different geographic areas over a period of a year; transportation costs; and excess capacity of firms outside the market.[39] Products are included in the same market if they are interchangeable in use.[40] The relevant geographic market is one that "correspond[s] to the commercial realities" of the industry and is "economically significant."[41]

4.116 Once the relevant product and geographic markets are determined, market share of the firm or firms under review or investigation is determined. Whether a firm enjoys a dominant position in a relevant market depends on its share of that market. Market share, coupled with the ease or difficulty of entry into a market, is used as a surrogate for determining a firm's monopoly power. In the E.U., a 50 per cent and sometimes 40 per cent market share translates into dominance, especially if the next largest firm lags far behind.[42] The E.U. takes the view that a dominant position can generally exist when a firm has a market share of 40–45 per cent, although dominance may exist even if the market share is 20–40 per cent.

4.117 The United States, unlike the E.U., measures market power and its possible increase microeconomically by considering the relevant factors in the specific context.[43] The Supreme Court has held, however, that monopoly power could be inferred from a market share of 80 per cent.[44] Where barriers to market entry are high, other courts have required less market share for a finding of monopoly power.[45] In the United States, courts consistently find that a market share of less than 70 per cent is insufficient to establish dominance, and that a market share of less than 40 per cent virtually precludes a finding of monopoly.[46]

4.118 In Canada, in the context of a predatory pricing investigation, the Predatory Pricing Enforcement Guidelines (PPEG) issued by the Director of Investigation and Research in 1992 note that "it is unlikely that an alleged

[38] See "U.S. Dep t of Justice/Federal Trade Comm'n, Horizontal Merger Guidelines, with April 8, 1997 Revisions to Section 4 on Efficiencies", reprinted in 4 Trade Reg. Rep. 13,104, available at http://www.ftc.gov/bc/docs/horizmer.htm, (hereinafter "Horizontal Merger Guidelines").

[39] See "Horizontal Merger Guidelines", see para. 4.115, n. 38, at s. 1.2.

[40] See, *e.g. United States v. E.I. du Pont Nemours & Co.*, 351 U.S. 316 (1961).

[41] *Brown Shoe*, 370 U.S. at 336–37.

[42] See "ICPAC Final Report", see para. 4.059, n. 19, at 48. In the *Boeing/McDonnell Douglas* merger, for example, Boeing increased its market share from 64% to 70% after merging with McDonnell Douglas, thus being deemed dominant by the European Commission. See *Boeing/McDonnell Douglas*, E.C. Case No. IV/M.877, & 29 (July 30, 1997).

[43] See "ICPAC Final Report", see para. 4.059, n. 19, at 48. For additional differences between U.S. and E.U. merger review, see *id.* at 48–49.

[44] See *Eastman Kodak Co. v. Image Technical Servs.*, 504 U.S. 451 (1992).

[45] See, *e.g. United States v. Syufy Enters.*, 903 F.2d 659, 664–69 (9th Cir. 1990); *United Air Lines v. Austin Travel Corp.*, 867 F.2d 737, 742 (2d Cir. 1989) (31% market share insufficient where barriers to market entry were low).

[46] See Van Siclen, see para. 4.111, n. 29, at 172.

predator with a market share of less than 35% would have the ability to unilaterally affect pricing."[47] Pursuant to the PPEG, the first step in a predatory pricing claim is to define the relevant product and geographic market.[48] However, it has been observed that:

> the PPEG are only guidelines that are not binding on courts. Consequently [*sic*], the Canadian definition of . . . markets in judicially considered predatory pricing cases may not be clearer than in the United States.[49]

In determining if a firm has market power, the Competition Tribunal also examines market share and entry barriers.[50] The Tribunal has noted that a firm's market share, the number of competitors and their respective market shares, excess capacity in the market and the ease of entry into the market are all factors that are taken into account in determining market power.[51]

4.119 When national competition authorities ostensibly use the same criteria for determining the relevant market, reasonable minds may still differ over the definition of the relevant market. Even when national competition authorities agree on the relevant market—as the European Commission and the FTC did in the *Boeing/McDonnell Douglas* merger where they agreed that the relevant market was the worldwide market for large civil aircraft—they can still reach conflicting results about the ant-competitive effects of business behaviour.[52]

When deciding whether a firm is engaged in unlawful monopolisation practices, if a country has implemented a liberal trade policy, there should be less need to tolerate firms with monopoly power in the domestic market because trade increases the size of the relevant market and thereby allows firms to achieve economies of scale without also possessing excessive market power. In addition, because many markets cross national borders in an open trade environment, there would seem to be some wisdom in creating a supranational competition law enforcement mechanism that employs international rules that define the relevant market in terms broader than just national markets.[53]

---

[47] Director of Investigation and Research, Supply and Services Canada, "Predatory Pricing Enforcement Guidelines" 6–7 (1992).

[48] See *id.* at 6.

[49] The "Competition Laws of NAFTA", see para. 4.062, n. 30, at 91. The DOJ/FTC Horizontal Merger Guidelines are not binding on courts either.

[50] See *Director of Investigation & Research v. The Nutrasweet Co.*, (1990) 32 C.P.R. (3d) 1, 28.

[51] See *Director of Investigation and Research v. Laidlaw Waste Systems, Ltd.*, (1992) 40 C.P.R. (3d) 289, 325. ANZCERTA has defined the relevant geographic market as the trans-Tasman market. The term trans-Tasman market covers conduct outside New Zealand by any person resident or carrying on business in Australia to the extent such conduct affects a market in New Zealand, and vice versa.

[52] See Joel I. Klein, "Anticipating the Millennium: International Antitrust Enforcement at the End of the Twentieth Century", 1997 Fordham Corporate L. Inst. 1, 8 (1998).

[53] Even in the E.U.'s highly-integrated market, with its community-wide competition enforcement legal regime, each of its members has retained competition law enforcement authority for national markets.

B. Predatory Pricing

4.120 There is no generally accepted legal or economic definition of predatory conduct. A distinction is drawn in the literature and the cases between price and non-price predatory conduct.[54] Both forms of predatory conduct have relevance, of course, to international trade, the concern being that a dominant firm will exclude new market entrants through anti-competitive acts of predatory conduct.

4.121 The OECD has defined predatory pricing as "the use of short-run price-cutting in an effort to exclude rivals on a basis other than efficiency in order to gain or protect market power," and as "pricing so low that competitors quit rather than compete, permitting the predator to raise prices in the long run."[55] In the United States, Judge Easterbrook has described predatory pricing as "an investment in a future monopoly, a sacrifice of today's profits for tomorrow's."[56] In short, the predator foregoes short-term profits in exchange for future long-term gains.

Price predation has two distinct phases. In the first phase the alleged predator engages in temporary low pricing to drive out competitors and to discourage any new entrants. In the second phase the alleged predator recoups lost profits in a market now devoid of competitors. A consensus runs through the American, Canadian and E.U. economics literature that the predator is already a dominant firm that is able to absorb any self-imposed losses during phase one.[57] However, consensus breaks down in the case law and the literature on the issue of predatory intent. Some writers would require a showing of a specific intent to destroy as evidenced by conduct that would not be employed in the normal course of competition.[58] Others reject this view and any requirement of a showing of predatory intent, instead looking to the actual market effect on competition.[59] Under this view, a predatory pricing plaintiff may lose business on pricing grounds because the defendant has engaged in aggressive, but lawful price competition, not because of anti-competitive predatory pricing. Distinguishing between the two has spawned a number of tests that turn on an analysis of below-cost pricing.[60]

---

[54] See Kerrin M. Vautier, "Trans-Tasman Trade and Competition Law", in *CER and Business Competition Australia and New Zealand in a Global Economy* (1990) 73, 92.

[55] OECD, "Predatory Pricing 81" (1989), available at http://www.oecd.org/daf/clp/publications/preda.pdf.

[56] *AA Poultry Farms, Inc. v. Rose Acre Farms, Inc.*, 881 F.2d 1396, 1401 (7th Cir. 1989).

[57] See Vautier, see para. 4.120, n. 54, at 94.

[58] See, *e.g.* Robert Bork, The Antitrust Paradox (1978) 144.

[59] See, *e.g. AA Poultry Farms*, 881 F.2d at 1401–02.

[60] See Vautier, see para. 4.120, n. 54, at 96–104 (price discrimination alone is not necessarily anti competitive under ANZCERTA competition rules); Phillip Areeda & Donald F. Turner, Antitrust Law (1978) 723–33 (pricing is predatory *per se* if prices are below either average variable cost or short-run marginal cost); Frederic M. Scherer, "Predatory Pricing and the Sherman Act: A Comment", (1976) 89 Harv. L. Rev. 869, 873 (advocating a case-by-case rule-of-reason approach); Oliver E. Williamson, "Predatory Pricing: A Strategic and Welfare Analysis", (1997) 87 Yale L.J. 284 (advocating output restriction rule); Donald G. McFetridge & Stanley Wong, "Predatory Pricing in Canada: The Law and Economics", (1985) 63 Canadian B. Rev. 685, 733

4.122 Under U.S. antitrust law, below-cost pricing without price discrimination can be the basis of an antitrust lawsuit based on an attempt to monopolise a market in violation of section 2 of the Sherman Act. According to the U.S. Supreme Court, a "plaintiff seeking to establish competitive injury from a rival's low prices must prove that the prices are below an appropriate measure of its rival costs."[61] However, because the parties agreed that the relevant measure of cost was average variable cost, the Court declined "to resolve the conflict among the lower courts over the appropriate measure of costs."[62] A plaintiff must also demonstrate that its rival had a "dangerous probability of recouping its investment in below-cost prices."[63]

4.123 Canadian courts have held that under section 50(1)(c) of the Competition Act one may not infer from a price-cost relationship alone that a price is unreasonably low. Even in instances of below-cost pricing, Canadian courts have held that other competitive factors could justify such prices.[64] According to the 1992 Predatory Pricing Enforcement Guidelines issued by the Director of Investigation and Research, the Director will recommend enforcement action by the Attorney General if the firm under investigation is pricing below average variable cost.[65]

4.124 Non-price predatory conduct is aimed at raising rival firms' costs through, for example, the filing of baseless complaints with governmental or judicial authorities against competitors. Such baseless complaints could be a device for creating a *de facto* international cartel. In an antidumping duty case, for example, an importing firm might raise its prices in response to a dumping complaint and enter into a price undertaking agreement with trade authorities rather than fight the charges. For firms that prefer to fight, in the United States the *Noerr-Pennington* doctrine addresses such abuses.[66] Another

("Given the difficulty experienced in defining what is a predatory price, we are sceptical that the development of a workable jurisprudence in the area of abuse of dominant position is a reasonable prospect."); William J. Baumol, "Predation and the Logic of the Average Variable Cost Test", (1996) 39 J.L. & Econ. 49.

[61] *Brooke Group, Ltd. v. Brown & Williamson Tobacco Corp.*, 509 U.S. 209, 222 (1993). See "Symposium: Predatory Pricing After *Brooke Group*", (1994) 62 Antitrust L.J. 537.

[62] Brooke Group, 509 U.S. at 223 n.1. See "ABA Special Committee Report", see para. 4.066, n. 38, at 150 (noting split among the circuits and citing court of appeals' cases).

[63] Brooke Group, 509 U.S. at 224. See *Spectrum Sport, Inc. v. McQuillan*, 506 U.S. 447 457–58 (1993).

[64] See, *e.g. Director of Investigation and Research v. Hoffman-La Roche*, (1980), 28 O.R. (2d) 164, 200, *aff'd* (1981), 33 O.R. (2d) 694 (Ont. C.A.); Director of *Investigation and Research v. Consumers Glass Co.*, (1981), 33 O.R. (2d) 228 (Ont. HCJ). For a comparison of Canadian, Mexican, and U.S. laws on predatory pricing and price discrimination, see "ABA Special Committee Report", see para. 4.066, n. 38, at 148–56.

[65] See Director of Investigation and Research, "Predatory Pricing Enforcement Guidelines, Corporate and Consumer Affairs, Canada", (1992) at 10–11.

[66] The so-called *Noerr-Pennington* doctrine generally shields firms from Sherman Act liability for competitive advantages obtained through lobbying or petitioning state or federal authorities. See *United Mine Workers of America v. Pennington*, 381 U.S. 657 (1965); *Eastern R.R. Presidents Conf. v. Noerr Motor Freight*, 365 U.S. 127 (1961). However, under the sham exception to that doctrine, persons who use governmental processes for the purpose of filing objectively baseless claims as an anti-competitive weapon are not shielded from antitrust liability. See Professional *Real Estate Investors, Inc. v. Columbia Pictures Industries, Inc.*, 508 U.S. 49 (1993); *City of Columbia v. Omni Outdoor Advertising, Inc.*, 499 U.S. 365, 380 (1991); *Chemicor Drugs, Ltd. v.*

example of non-price predatory conduct is an exclusionary contract pursuant to which a purchasing firm forces its input suppliers to refuse to deal with the purchaser's rivals on equal terms.[67]

C. The fit of the Price Discrimination Laws and the Antidumping Duty Law

4.125 International price discrimination is the setting of prices in the export market below those of the national market. Firms do this usually with the aim of penetrating new markets. Such practices are facilitated by structural barriers that prevent market access to imported goods from other countries, or by anti-competitive practices that prevail in the firm's home market.

4.126 Under Article 82(c) of the E.C. Treaty,[68] the Commission has challenged pricing practices of firms exporting to the E.U. where different prices are charged to different distributors along E.U. Member State lines.[69] The 1997 OECD Guidelines for Multinational Enterprises also provides that MNEs should refrain from:

> discriminatory (i.e., unreasonably differentiated) pricing and using such pricing transactions between affiliated enterprises as a means of affecting adversely competition outside these enterprises.[70]

While the European Union and the Australia-New Zealand free trade area have abandoned their antidumping laws with respect to members *inter se*, many regional trade arrangements retain the right to use antidumping laws against members, including NAFTA, MERCOSUR and the various E.U.-EFTA Agreements.

Where antidumping legislation has been retained, it is seen by domestic producers who are threatened with import competition as a defence against what appears to be some form of predatory pricing or other anti-competitive practice. However, anti-dumping legislation itself can be used to preserve anti-competitive situations (*e.g.* maintaining a domestic industry's dominant share of the domestic market) and encourage anti-competitive behaviour (*e.g.*

Ethyl Corp., 168 F.3d 119 (3d Cir. 1999). See also *Music Center S.N.C. Di Luciano Pisoni & Cia. v. Prestini Musical Instruments Corp.*, 874 F. Supp. 543 (E.D.N.Y. 1995) (antidumping petitions were not shown to constitute "sham litigation" within Noerr-Pennington immunity exception).

[67] See Vautier, see para. 4.120, n. 54, at 102–04; Thomas G. Krattenmaker & Steven C. Salop, *Anticompetitive Exclusion: Raising Rivals' Costs*, 96 Yale L.J. 209 (1986).

[68] Art. 82(c) makes it an abuse of a dominant position for a firm to apply dissimilar conditions to equivalent transactions with other trading parties, thereby placing them at a competitive disadvantage.

[69] See, *e.g. United Brands Co. v. Commission* (Case 27/76), [1978] E.C.R. 207; [1978] 1 C.M.L.R. 429.

[70] OECD, "Guidelines for Multinational Enterprises", *Competition* 1(e) (1997). The 2000 OECD Guidelines dropped the discriminatory pricing proscription. See OECD, "Guidelines for Multinational Enterprises, Part IX", *Competition* (2000), available at http://www.oecd.org/daf/investment/guidelines/mnetext.htm.

price fixing and cartelisation).[71] Thus, the accelerating debate on multilateral competition rules has a direct bearing on the future of antidumping legislation.

4.127 Until recently, antidumping duties were applied by an exclusive club of developed countries (with the one exception of Mexico). With the adoption of AD legislation in many developing countries, coupled with the view that antidumping measures are a legitimate response to low-priced imports because antidumping duties are a WTO-approved "trade remedy" under GATT Article VI and the WTO Antidumping Agreement, the widespread resort to antidumping actions is proving to be a major challenge for the WTO.[72]

4.128 The AD law and antitrust laws target the same anti-competitive practice in one instance, *i.e.* predatory pricing practices, making the AD law redundant in the eyes of some observers.[73] Otherwise, the two bodies of law are misfits. Antitrust rules on discriminatory pricing regulate the extent to which manufacturers and suppliers can offer goods at different prices to competitors' customers. In the United States, the Robinson-Patman Act prohibits price discrimination by domestic producers that is intended to eliminate competition in a domestic market.[74] On the other hand, the Antidumping Act of 1916, as noted in Chapter two, targets predatory pricing, *i.e.* pricing designed to eliminate competition, but in the case of imported goods only and also requires a showing of predatory intent. Within their respective spheres, both laws are intended to protect competition and promote consumer welfare.

4.129 The policy of the AD law, in contrast, is to protect domestic producers and workers from import competition—in effect, to close off

[71] The literature on the AD law is vast. Suffice it to say that the AD law has no shortage of critics. For criticisms of the AD law *vis-à-vis* the antitrust law, see Wesley A. Cann, Jr., "Internationalizing Our Views Toward Recoupment and Market Power: Attacking the Antidumping/Antitrust Dichotomy Through WTO-Consistent Global Welfare Theory", (1996) 17 U. Pa. J. Int'l Econ. L. 69, 127–28; Ernest-Ulrich Petersmann, "International Competition Rules for Governments and for Private Business: A 'Trade Law Approach' for Linking Trade and Competition Rules in the WTO, (1996) 72 Chi.-Kent L. Rev. 545, 574; Ronald A. Cass, "Price Discrimination and Predation Analysis in Antitrust and International trade: A Comment", (1993) 61 U. Cin. L. Rev. 877; Richard D. Boltuck & Seth Kaplan, "Conflicting Entitlements: Can Antidumping and Antitrust Regulation Be Reconciled?", (1993) 61 U. Cin. L. Rev. 903; Spencer Weber Waller, "The Collusive Settlement of International Trade Cases", (1986) 16 J. Reprints Antitrust L. & Econ. 505; Bernard Hoekman & Peter C. Mavroidis, "Dumping, Antidumping and Antitrust", (1996) 30 J. World Trade 27.

[72] In 1990, there were 405 antidumping duty order in place worldwide, with only 4 of those issued by a developing country (Mexico). By 1997, there were 832 AD orders in force, and of that total 244 30% were issued by 15 developing countries. See WTO "Annual Report 1999", (2000), at 3. At the end of June 1999, a total of 1,097 AD orders were in place, including 435 nearly 40% issued by developing countries. See WTO, "Annual Report 1999", at 47 (2000). In the first 7 months of 2000, 259 antidumping actions were reported to the WTO. The United States was the leading nation in the number of antidumping actions taken (145). The E.U. was second with 35, Mexico third with 26 actions, and Canada fourth with 11 actions. See Daniel Pruzin, "WTO Figures Show U.S. Far Ahead in Year 2000 Antidumping Actions", (Aug. 17, 2000) 17 Int'l Trade Rep. (BNA) 1265.

[73] But see James C. Hartigan, "An Antidumping Law Can Be Procompetitive", (2000) 5 Pac. Econ. Rev. 1.

[74] See 15 U.S.C. s. 13(a).

market access to foreign goods. Economists generally agree that, in the absence of predatory intent, dumping is essentially harmless for the importing country because the welfare gains for consumers from low-priced imports more than offset any harm to producer welfare in the country of importation.[75] Given that the AD policy seeks to raise both the price of imported goods and domestic producers' profits, the AD law is less concerned, if it is concerned at all, with consumer welfare and the competitive process. Consequently, it is irrelevant whether lower priced imports enhance consumer welfare. It is equally irrelevant whether foreign producers are or are not engaged in predatory pricing, that is, pricing below average variable cost or marginal cost that is intended to destroy competition. The AD law targets pricing practices that fail to recover the total cost of production.

4.130 Antitrust law, on the other hand, as an outward looking, offensive tool, focuses on the maintenance of open markets, the promotion of competition, and the maximisation of consumer welfare. Only when pricing practices threaten to destroy the competitive process, such as through predatory pricing, is antitrust law triggered. Some might argue that if AD policy was concerned with economic efficiency,[76] rather than protecting domestic producers, then the AD law would target predatory pricing, a practice already banned by antitrust law.[77] But the AD law goes well beyond targeting just predatory pricing. The AD law also reaches sporadic dumping where the exporter may have no hope or desire of gaining market share or power but may simply wish to unload overproduction in a foreign market at the end of a production run. The antitrust laws do not reach this type of dumping, and yet such dumping could well cause injury to domestic firms.

4.131 Beyond these policy differences, there are significant procedural and substantive differences between the two laws, at least insofar as they are administered in the United States.[78] The Commerce Department and the International Trade Commission are charged with the enforcement of the AD law, with judicial review in the Court of International Trade and the Court of Appeals for the Federal Circuit.[79] The administrative process is informal, expedited, and not subject to the rigors of the Administrative Procedure Act (APA). The remedy for the successful AD petitioner is the prospective assessment of antidumping duties on future imports of the subject merchandise from the date of the AD final order. In critical circumstances, the

[75] See "WGTCP 1999 Report", see para. 4.032, n. 47, at 22, para. 67.

[76] Economists distinguish the terms consumer welfare and economic efficiency, equating economic efficiency with total welfare (total welfare being the sum of consumer welfare plus producer welfare). I have followed Judge Bork's lead and have equated the two terms. See Robert Bork, *The Antitrust Paradox: A Policy at War With Itself* (1978) 107–08.

[77] See John R. Morris, "International Trade and Antitrust: Comments", (1993) 61 U. Cin. L. Rev. 945, 948.

[78] For a defence of the AD law, see Greg Mastel, *Antidumping Laws and the U.S. Economy* (1998) (and sources cited therein); Clarisse Morgan, "Competition Policy and Anti Dumping: Is it Time for a Reality Check?", (1996) 30 J. World Trade 61, 62–68; Terence P. Stewart & Timothy C. Brightbill, "Some "Heretical" Observations on the Interaction of U.S. Trade and Competition Laws: A Defense of U.S. Antidumping and Countervailing Duties", (1996) 4 U.S.-Mex. L. J. 35.

[79] For an analysis of the substance and procedure of the U.S. AD law, see Raj Bhala & Kevin Kennedy, *World Trade Law: The GATT-WTO System, Regional Arrangements, and U.S. Law* (1998) 489–766.

assessment may be retroactive 90 days before the date of a Commerce Department preliminary affirmative dumping determination. The petitioner receives no compensatory damages for an injury caused by the dumped imports, although if the margin of dumping is sufficiently high, the foreign producer may be forced to exit the U.S. market.

The antitrust laws are administered by the Department of Justice, the Federal Trade Commission, state attorneys-general and private parties. The Federal Trade Commission conducts its investigations pursuant to the APA, which is a regularised, adjudicatory process. Actions brought by the Justice Department and private litigants are filed in federal district court, with appeal to the U.S. Courts of Appeals. Remedies include compensatory damages, treble damages, injunctive relief, divestiture and, in appropriate cases, criminal fines and prison sentences.

4.132 The substantive differences between the AD and antitrust laws are threefold: the standards for determining injury, causation, and unlawful pricing. With regard to injury and causation, an AD petitioner must show that dumped imports cause or threaten to cause material injury.[80] The AD law provides an unedifying definition of material injury as "harm which is not inconsequential, immaterial, or unimportant."[81] The AD law does not require that a petitioner show that dumped imports are the sole, principal or even substantial cause of injury.[82] The antitrust laws require a different and greater showing of causation and injury. With regard to injury, the antitrust laws require a showing of an unreasonable restraint of trade (which can be *per se* in the case of, for example, price fixing) or a substantial lessening of competition. The anti-competitive conduct must be the cause of plaintiff's injury.[83] The Robinson-Patman Act (the antitrust price discrimination law) makes an important defence available that is unavailable under the AD law—the "meeting competition" defence.[84]

4.133 The respective approaches of the AD and antitrust laws on the issue of what constitutes unlawful pricing is a point of great controversy and contention. First, the AD law, unlike the antitrust laws, does not require a showing of predatory intent.[85] Congress made this difference clear in the Omnibus Trade Act of 1988 where it clarified in the legislative history that a showing of predatory intent is not required in an AD case.[86] Secondly, under the AD law, even if sales in the United States are above average variable cost, the Commerce Department will find dumping if the price of the imported goods is either below the total cost of production or if the price of the imported goods is below the price of those goods when sold in the home market. Under the antitrust laws, in order for a court to find predatory intent,

[80] The statute requires the ITC to determine that a domestic industry is materially injured "by reason of" dumped imports. 19 U.S.C. s. 1673(2).
[81] 19 U.S.C. s. 1677(7)(A).
[82] See, *e.g. British Steel Corp. v. United States*, 593 F. Supp. 405, 413 (CIT 1984).
[83] See, *e.g. Brunswick Corp. v. Pueblo Bowl-O-Mat, Inc.*, 429 U.S. 477 (1977).
[84] See 15 U.S.C. s. 13(a), (b).
[85] See, *e.g. Brooke Group, Ltd. v. Brown & Williamson Tobacco Co.*, 509 U.S. 209 (1993).
[86] See H.R. Conf. Rep. No. 576, 100th Cong., 2d Sess.. Part I.C.2.17.b (1988), *reprinted in* 1988 U.S.C.C.A.N. 1547, 1650.

the price of goods must be below either marginal cost or average variable cost.[87] Moreover, below-cost pricing alone is insufficient to establish predatory intent unless it also can be shown that the defendant was capable of eventually recovering its lost profits on the below-cost sales.[88]

4.134 As noted previously, the Working Group on the Interaction between Trade and Competition Policy received proposals that the AD law be repealed and replaced by antitrust law, or at the least amended to better reflect a competition policy perspective. While there are many strong economic arguments in support of this position, the practical consequences and difficulties in doing so are many, assuming that the goal is to put in place an effective remedy against discriminatory pricing.

4.135 First, gathering proof of international price discrimination would be difficult for national enforcement authorities, in the absence of a co-operation or mutual assistance agreement that would facilitate discovery. Even the best co-operation agreement still retains provisions against disclosure of information deemed confidential. The difficulties in international evidence gathering that national authorities would face would only be compounded in a private party enforcement action.

4.136 Second, in either an Antidumping Act of 1916 price discrimination case or a section 2 Sherman Act monopolisation case, predatory intent must be established. In order to prove predatory intent, current jurisprudence at the courts of appeals requires a showing of below-cost sales, which is either sales at prices below marginal cost or average variable cost. And even if such below-cost sales are shown to exist, the Supreme Court has held that predatory intent requires proof that the defendant was eventually able to recoup its lost profits.[89] In addition, even if a plaintiff can successfully prove the requisite below-cost sales element, formidable hurdles await in connection with proof of injury and causation.

4.137 Not only may the AD law be working at cross purposes with the antitrust laws by preventing market access in the country of importation, the AD administrative process offers opportunities for collusive behaviour among the firms that comprise the petitioning domestic industry and among the domestic industry and its foreign competitors. An AD petition contains business confidential information about sales, profits, capacity, and expenses of the firms within the domestic industry. Although that confidential information is protected from disclosure to competing foreign firms, there is no bar to the domestic firms sharing this information *inter se*. Such information

[87] See, *e.g. Henry v. Chloride, Inc.*, 809 F.2d 1334, 1346 (8th Cir. 1987); *O. Hommel Co. v. Ferro Corp.*, 659 F.2d 340, 352 (3rd Cir. 1981).

[88] See *Brooke Group, Ltd. v. Brown & Williamson Tobacco Co.*, 509 U.S. 209, 224 (1993).

[89] See Brook Group, 509 U.S. at 224; Robert Bork, *The Antitrust Paradox* (1978) 145. In *Matsushita Elec. Indus. Co. v. Zenith Radio Corp.*, 475 U.S. 574 (1986), the Court stated in the context of a Sherman Act s.1 conspiracy claim, "A predatory pricing conspiracy is by nature speculative. . . . The foregone profits may be considered an investment in the future. For the investment to be rational, the conspirators must have a reasonable expectation of recovering, in the form of later monopoly profits, more than the losses suffered." *Matsushita Elec. Indus. Co.*, 475 U.S. at 588–89. See Harry First, "An Antitrust Remedy for International Price Predation: Lessons from" *Zenith v. Matsushita*, in *Antitrust: A New Trade Remedy?*, see para. 4.062, n. 31, at 211.

exchange is probably protected in the United States under the *Noerr-Pennington* doctrine and the constitutionally protected rights of free speech and to petition the government for a redress of grievances, but such information exchanges among business rivals would in any other context raise the eyebrows of competition law enforcement authorities.[90]

Opportunities for collusion also exist with the settlement of AD cases through price undertakings. Although voluntary settlements are between foreign firms and government authorities, price undertakings require that the foreign exporters raise their prices and refrain from future dumping, creating a *de facto* price-fixing agreement between the foreign and domestic competitors by establishing a floor price for imported goods.[91]

4.138 While some participants in the Working Group see the adoption of a multilateral competition policy agreement as an opportunity for the eventual elimination of domestic antidumping laws, or at least the rationalisation of the antidumping and antitrust laws, the United States and the E.U. quashed that hope. The United States made clear that the Working Group's charge was restricted to addressing antitrust issues and did not extend to domestic antidumping standards and rules.[92] In the view of the United States, if AD rules are to be discussed, the proper forum is the WTO Anti-Dumping Committee, not the WGTCP.[93] On the other hand, many WTO members will not agree to a WTO competition policy agreement unless and until AD laws are repealed or substantially amended and made rational *vis-à-vis* competition laws.[94]

The economic argument for repeal is that geographic price discrimination can have a legitimate basis, such as the necessity to gain market entry by lowering prices, different structures of demand in the home market versus the export market in terms of elasticity or buying power and different business cycles. The contra argument is the slow pace of antitrust proceedings and the failure of antitrust law to successfully deal with predatory pricing. The streamlined and somewhat over-compensatory AD administrative proceeding and the AD law's more relaxed definition of price discrimination, provide injured domestic industry with a remedy before the industry is destroyed by unfair pricing practices.

---

[90] Several lower courts have held that the *Noerr-Pennington* doctrine does not shield from antitrust liability efforts to influence foreign governments. See, *e.g. Bulkferts, Inc. v. Salatin, Inc.*, 574 F. Supp. 6 (S.D.N.Y. 1983); *Occidental Petroleum Corp. v. Buttes Gas & Oil Co.*, 331 F. Supp. 92, 107–08 (C.D. Cal. 1971), *aff'd*, 461 F.2d 1261 (9th Cir.), *cert. denied*, 409 U.S. 950 (1972).

[91] See Mitsuo Matsushita, "A Critical Review of the Enforcement of Antidumping Laws in the Context of Competition Policy", in *Antitrust: A New Trade Remedy*?, see para. 4.062, n. 31, at 327.

[92] See Office of the USTR, "Statement on Competition Policy in the World Trade Organization", Press Release 96–95 (Dec. 13, 1996), available at http://www.ustr. gov/releases/1996/12/96–95.htm

[93] See "WGTCP 1999 Report", see para. 4.032, n. 47, at 29, para. 89.

[94] See William H. Barringer, "Competition Policy and Cross-Border Dispute Resolution: Lessons Learned from the U.S.–Japan Film Dispute", (1998) 6 Geo. Mason L. Rev. 459, 476.

4.139 There is an ideological clash here, however the solution could be improved market access in the home country of the alleged dumper. Moreover, in a world of free trade, the need for an AD law would vanish because geographic price discrimination would be absent. Without a protected home market to prevent arbitrage (*i.e.* reimportation into the country of exportation), a foreign firm cannot successfully subsidise exported products with higher-priced home-market sales of the same product. If market access is blocked by private conduct, then a more aggressive application of competition law by the national authorities of the country of exportation could remove this impediment to trade. On the other hand, to the extent the AD law defines dumping as both geographic price discrimination and as sales at below cost, then home prices and export prices could be the same but a dumping duty nevertheless could still be assessed, rendering arbitrage and improved market access irrelevant.

4.140 Professor Alan Sykes has concluded that "[a]ntitrust and antidumping law come from the same family tree, but the two branches have diverged widely."[95] In noting how highly resistant the AD law is to reform, he wonders what, if anything, is possible with regard to changing the AD law:

> The fact that antidumping law sweeps far beyond what is necessary to achieve the stated objectives of its original sponsors has not threatened its political popularity. Commentators have advocated its modification or repeal for years, with no apparent effect on its ability to survive in the global political equilibrium. The reasons for the stability of this equilibrium are not entirely clear, and it remains to be seen whether the equilibrium can be constructively perturbed.[96]

One possible explanation for the AD law's resilience in the face of repeated calls for its reform is that it fulfils a role in the balance of concessions offered by WTO members, so that any attempt to refashion the AD rules would upset the existing balance that has been struck in the GATT-WTO system.[97]

4.141 In sum, how to deal with dumping practices legally, economically and politically remains an extremely complex problem. The alternatives are:

(1) repeal the AD law and substitute competition law,

(2) reform the AD law in light of competition policy principles, or

(3) continue with parallel, but separate, legal regimes, to the extent they address related, but different, practices.

---

[95] Alan O. Sykes, "Antidumping and Antitrust: What Problems Does Each Address?", in *Brookings Trade Forum: 1998* (Robert Z. Lawrence ed. 1998) 1, 42. See also Spencer Weber Waller, "The Internationalization of Antitrust Enforcement", 77 B.U.L. Rev. (1997) 343, 402–03 (noting that entrenched political interests account for the resilience of the antidumping duty law to reform or repeal).

[96] Sykes, *supra* n. 95, at 43.

[97] See "WGTCP 1999 Report", see para. 4.016, n. 16, at 23, para. 69.

Repealing the AD law and substituting antitrust law would accomplish the goal of eliminating anti-competitive pricing practices. With regard to repealing the AD law, however, proponents of retaining the AD law—primarily the United States—point out that dumping is a private practice made possible by government policies and practices, those being the protection of the dumping firm from import competition.[98] Competition law thus does not reach this government-sanctioned, anti-competitive conduct.

4.142 Reforming the AD law to reflect a competition policy perspective would entail at least three changes. First, the price standard in AD cases should be average variable cost. Secondly, predatory intent and the probability of future success in predation would have to be proven. Thirdly, an affirmative injury determination could be made only if dumping was shown to have anti-competitive effects. This analysis would include an examination not only of producer interests but also of the benefits to consumers from low-priced imports, *i.e.* the imposition of AD duties would be assessed from the perspective of total welfare.[99] Finally, cumulatively applying antitrust and antidumping rules to deal with the same imported goods would appear to be prohibited after the *Antidumping Act of 1916* WTO panel and Appellate Body reports, discussed in Chapter Two.

VI. MERGERS AND ACQUISITIONS

4.143 Global merger and acquisition activity increased from $100 billion in 1987 to $720 billion in 1999: an annual rate of increase of 42 per cent.[1] This phenomenal growth underscores the importance of multi-jurisdictional issues in the merger control area, which is another point of divergence and source of conflict. Mergers between firms with a resulting high market share can have anti-competitive effects not only in countries where the merging firms are domiciled but also in countries where the firms are not domiciled or do not have facilities. For this reason, national competition authorities want to be able to review a proposed merger that has cross-border effects, regardless of the domicile of the merging firms. Firms, on the other hand, want to minimise the number of competition authorities they must report to, not only to cut down on transaction costs but also to avoid inadvertently

[98] See WTO, "Working Group on the Interaction between Trade and Competition Policy, Communication from the United States", *Observations on the Distinctions between Competition Laws and Antidumping Rules*, WT/WGTCP/W/88, at 3–4 (Aug. 28, 1998).
[99] See "WGTCP 1998 Report", see para. 4.016, n. 16, at 47, para. 143; WTO, "Working Group on the Interaction between Trade and Competition Policy, Communication from the Republic of Korea", *Impact of Trade Policy on Competition: An Assessment of Anti-Dumping Rules*, WT/WGTCP/W/90, at 4–5 (Sept. 3, 1998); "WGTCP 1999 Report", see para. 4.032, n. 47, at 22, para. 67.
[1] See Daniel Pruzin & Diana I. Gregg, "UNCTAD Cites Merger, Acquisition Boom as Global FDI Expected to Hit $1 Trillion", (Oct. 12, 2000) 17 Int'l Trade Rep. (BNA) 1551.

failing to file a notification with an authority and being fined as a consequence.[2]

4.144 The number of countries with pre-merger notification laws is roughly 60 and growing.[3] Forty-nine of these countries have a mandatory pre-closing notification system.[4] The substantive standards found in national merger control legislation and regulations not only differ, reflecting divergent policy goals but are also vague, subjective and difficult to interpret.[5] The detailed level of information that some national pre-merger review authorities require at the initial filing stage can also be burdensome.[6] These differences, plus the extraterritorial application of merger control regulations by national reviewing authorities, present challenges and uncertainties for both the private and public entities involved in the merger transaction. Thus, in order to avoid inconsistent or conflicting rulings, the business community might welcome some type of "one-stop shopping" for multi-jurisdictional pre-merger review,[7] although concerns persist over the mishandling of business-confidential information by national enforcement authorities. Even though most mergers with a cross-border dimension are approved without conflict between the responsible national authorities, when jurisdictional conflicts do surface, they can be politically divisive and ultimately fatal to a transaction that is otherwise pro-competitive.[8]

---

[2] See Waller, see para. 4.140, n. 95, at 385–86. Professor Waller observes: "These various requirements make for fascinating work for competition lawyers, but great frustration for business planners. The differences and conflicts between national laws can doom a transaction for reasons unrelated to its competitive effects. . . . [T]he inability to close in a timely and certain manner can trigger an antitrust kick-out clause or cause one or both parties to withdraw from a deal." *Id.* at 386. In responses submitted to ICPAC, businesses reported that the transaction costs are sizeable. See "ICPAC Final Report", see para. 4.060, n. 19, at 91. Filing fees in the United States are $45,000; in Canada, they are C$25,000. For the filing fees of other jurisdictions, see *id.*, Annex 3–A. Intangible costs include the drain on senior officers' time. ICPAC concludes, however, that these are reasonable costs of doing business. See *id.* at 94–95.

[3] See "ICPAC Final Report", see para. 4.060, n. 19, at 37, 48. For a list of those countries as of early 2000, see *id.* Annex 2 C. See also Richard Whish & Diane P. Wood, "Merger Cases in the Real World: A Study of Merger Control Procedures (1994) 42 (authors note that the 1989 acquisition of Wilkinson by Gillette was reviewed by 14 competition law enforcement authorities); Howard Adler, Jr., Lynda Martin Alegi & David A. Clanton, *The Global Merger Notification Handbook* (1999).

[4] See "ICPAC Final Report", see para. 4.060, n. 19, Annex 2 C. Only 11 countries have a voluntary notification system. See *id.* Mandatory pre-merger notification is seen as useful to competition authorities for at least two reasons: (1) it avoids the necessity of "unscrambling the eggs" after an anti-competitive merger has been consummated; and (2) national competition authorities have neither the time nor resources to monitor all merger transactions and then to identify those that are potentially anti-competitive. See *id.* at 89.

[5] See *id.* at 41, 91.

[6] See *id.* at 116.

[7] But see Daniel K. Tarullo, "Norms and Institutions in Global Competition Policy", (2000) 94 Am. J. Int'l L. 478, 482 ("although proposals for harmonising pre-merger procedures go back at least a decade, they have never risen to the top of the corporate policy agenda" (footnote omitted)).

[8] For a thorough review of the issues surrounding multi-jurisdictional mergers, see "ICPAC Final Report", see para. 4.060, n. 19, at 41–162. As noted in the "ICPAC Final Report", "The cumulative effect of remedies imposed by various jurisdictions ultimately may outweigh the benefits the merging parties had hoped to attain, thereby forcing the parties to abandon the proposed transaction". *id.* at 53 (footnote omitted).

4.145 All three NAFTA parties and the E.U. prohibit anti-competitive mergers. Their respective laws provide for notification of mergers and for pre-merger review. Canada provides an express efficiencies defence where an otherwise anti-competitive merger will be approved if the efficiency gains outweigh the lessening of competition. Neither the United States nor Mexico expressly allow such a defence in their merger control legislation, although enforcement authorities have indicated that they will consider efficiency gains in merger reviews.[9] The E.C. Merger Control Regulation is likewise silent on efficiency gains as a defence when appraising a proposed merger.[10]

4.146 The standards for pre-merger review vary considerably among countries.[11] For example, the E.U., though not the United States, uses a worldwide revenue test regardless of the nexus of the parties to the E.U. The focus is on whether the merged firms will have an increased market share and thereby threaten SMEs, while in the United States the focus is on whether economies of scale outweigh the effect on prices following a reduction in competition.[12] The Commission retains exclusive jurisdiction to review mergers and acquisitions when the monetary thresholds that establish a "Community dimension" are met. These thresholds are based on worldwide and E.U. sales; a physical presence in the E.U. is not required in order to trigger the Commission's power. Pursuant to Regulation 4064, firms are under an affirmative duty to notify the Commission within one week of the signing of a merger or acquisition agreement, if either an initial test or a supplementary test is met.[13] Under the initial test, a merger has a "Community dimension" if:

(1) the undertakings concerned have combined worldwide sales of 5 billion Euros (approximately $5.75 billion), and

(2) at least two of the undertakings concerned each has sales in the E.U. of 250 million Euros (approximately $285 million).[14]

If each of the undertakings concerned makes more than two-thirds of its E.U. sales in only one Member State, then the merger does not have a Community dimension.

4.147 Under the supplementary test, a merger has a Community dimension if:

---

[9] See "The Competition Laws of NAFTA", see para. 4.062, n. 30, at 94.

[10] See Council Regulation No. 4064/89 (Dec. 21, 1989), as amended by Council Regulation No. 1310/97 (June 30, 1997), art. 2.

[11] See "ICPAC Final Report", see para. 4.060, n. 19, at 48–51; J. William Rowley & Donald Baker, *International Mergers: The Antitrust Process*, vols. 1, 2 (2d ed. 1996) (analyzing the merger control regimes of 30 countries); OECD, Merger Cases in the Real World: A Study of Merger Control Procedures (1994) (case studies of multi-jurisdictional merger reviews).

[12] See Barry E. Hawk & Henry L. Huser, *European Community Merger Control: A Practitioner's Guide* (1996); Russell J. Weintraub, "Globalization's Effect on Antitrust Law", (1999) 34 New Eng. L. Rev. 27, 35.

[13] See *id.* art. 1(2); Andre R. Fiebig, "Joint Ventures and Mergers", in *Introduction to European Law: How to Comply and Compete in the European Union* (Global Law and Policy Initiative 1999).

[14] See Council Reg. 4064/89, [1989] O.J. L395 1, *as amended*, [1990] O.J. L257 13, [1997] O.J. L180 1, [1998] O.J. L61, Art. 1(2).

(1) the undertakings concerned have combined worldwide sales of more than 2.5 billion Euros (approximately $3 billion);

(2) in each of at least three Member States the undertakings concerned have the combined sales of more than 100 million Euros (approximately $115 million);

(3) in each of at least three member states the aggregate sales of at least two of the undertakings concerned are more than 25 million Euros (approximately $30 million); and

(4) at least two of the undertakings concerned have aggregate E.U.-wide sales of more than 100 million Euros (approximately $115 million).

Once a proposed merger or acquisition is notified, its effective date is suspended while the Commission investigates the agreement. The Commission has four months within which to complete its investigation and challenge or approve the agreement.

4.148 The United States has a well-established history of exercising jurisdiction over mergers with cross-border effects.[15] A proposed merger is reportable under the Hart-Scott-Rodino Antitrust Improvements Act of 1976 (the HSR Act) if all of the following criteria are met:

(1) either the acquired or acquiring person is engaged in interstate commerce or in an activity affecting interstate commerce;

(2) the acquired or acquiring person has net sales or total assets of $100 million and the other has annual net sales or total assets of $10 million; and

(3) as a result of the merger, the acquiring person would hold either

(a) 15 per cent of either the voting securities or assets of the acquired person, or

[15] See U.S. Dep t of Justice/Federal Trade Comm'n, *Antitrust Enforcement Guidelines for International Operations* s. 3.14 (1995), reprinted in 7 Trade Reg. Rep. (CCH) 13,107 (1995). The Department of Justice and the Federal Trade Commission share power to review mergers and to formulate competition policy. The agencies use a clearance process, which is based on past experience and expertise, to determine which agency will be responsible for reviewing each proposed transaction. Overlapping jurisdiction is also an issue in connection with state attorneys general who have the power to review mergers. In addition, private parties are entitled to challenge mergers judicially. Finally, federal sectoral regulatory agencies in the communications, transportation, and defence sectors (the Federal Communications Commission, the Interstate Commerce Commission, the Department of Transportation, and the Department of Defence) also have the authority to impose conditions on proposed mergers of firms in their respective sectors. See "ICPAC Final Report", see para. 4.060, n. 19, at 144–45. For the role of competition policy advocacy by competition authorities *vis-à-vis* government regulators in the telecommunications industry, see WTO, "Working Group on the Interaction between Trade and Competition Policy, Communication from Canada", *The Significance of Competition Policy Advocacy*, WT/WGTCP/W/146 (Sept. 12, 2000).

(b) voting securities and assets of the acquired person with a total aggregate value of $15 million,[16] a figure described as "absurdly low."[17]

Although the HSR Act thresholds are lower than those of the E.C. Merger Control Regulation, the HSR criteria ensure that only parties to transactions with an appreciable nexus to the United States are required to notify U.S. antitrust authorities.[18] The HSR Act imposes a 30-day waiting period after filing a notification and report form during which the transaction may not be closed. If either the DOJ or the FTC desire to conduct a more thorough investigation, the waiting period may be extended an additional 20 days.[19]

In Canada, mergers and acquisitions are subject to a far less structured review process.[20] Unlike the E.U., which does not require any nexus of the parties with the E.U., pre-merger notification is required of proposed mergers meeting the following financial thresholds and Canadian nexus:

(1) the parties to the transaction have assets in Canada or annual gross revenues from sales in, from, or into Canada in excess of Can $400 million; and

(2) the value of the transaction itself must involve Canadian assets or annual gross revenues from sales in, from, or into Canada greater than Can $35 million.[21]

Proposed mergers are examined under a test of substantial prevention or lessening of competition.[22] Under Merger Enforcement Guidelines promulgated by the Director of Investigation and Research in 1991, the principal focus is the effect a merger will have on price.[23] A five per cent increase in price will generally be considered significant.[24] Even if a merger is likely to result in a substantial prevention or lessening of competition, an efficiency exception is available to block a challenge. Parties can elect to file a short form with a seven-day waiting period, or a long form with a 21-day waiting period.[25] Canadian authorities endeavour to clear a notified transaction in 14 days for noncomplex mergers, 10 weeks for complex mergers and five months

[16] See 15 U.S.C. s. 18a(a)(3). Under the FTC's implementing regulations, an acquisition of less than $15 million of the acquired person's voting securities is exempt unless it confers control of an acquired person with at least $25 million in annual net sales or total assets. See 16 C.F.R. ss. 801.1(b)(1) & 802.20.

[17] "The new enforcers", *The Economist*, Oct. 7, 2000, at 82.

[18] The DOJ/FTC Horizontal Merger Guidelines provide that U.S. antitrust authorities attempt to avoid unnecessary interference with the larger universe of either competitively beneficial or neutral mergers. See "Horizontal Merger Guidelines", see para. 4.115, n. 38, at 0.1.

[19] See 15 U.S.C. s. 18a(e).

[20] See generally Paul S. Crampton, *Mergers and the Competition Act* (1990).

[21] See Competition Act, s. 110.

[22] See *id.* s. 92(1).

[23] Director of Investigation and Research, Supply and Services Canada, Merger Enforcement Guidelines, at i (1991).

[24] See *id.* at iii.

[25] See Competition Act, ss. 120–22.

for very complex mergers.[26] The five-month review period is slightly longer than the E.U.'s four-month review period for second-phase investigations.

4.150 Several countries use a market-share test to determine whether a proposed merger is subject to notification requirements, including Brazil (20 per cent), Greece (25 per cent), Israel (50 per cent), Spain (25 per cent), and Taiwan (25 per cent). From the perspective of the merging firms, market-share tests suffer from the inherent subjectivity of market-share calculations (*i.e.* reasonable minds may differ concerning the definition of relevant markets) and from their inherent imprecision (*i.e.* market-share calculations require an estimate of the size of the relevant market).[27]

In connection with the triggering event for making a mandatory pre-merger notification, some jurisdictions allow a notification to be filed after a letter of intent has been signed (the United States and Canada), while other require that a definitive merger agreement first be executed (the E.U.).[28]

4.151 The record of co-operation in multi-jurisdictional mergers is mixed. An example of successful co-operation that is cited is E.U./U.S. co-operation in the 1998 *Dresser/Halliburton* merger.[29] However, concerns over national sovereignty and the protection of national champions can prevent a disinterested review of a proposed merger by national enforcement authorities. An example is the European Commission's review of the *Boeing/McDonnell Douglas* merger in 1997. Even though the Federal Trade Commission had approved the proposed merger, the Commission threatened to disapprove it unless Boeing addressed specific Commission concerns, including indirect subsidisation of Boeing through McDonnell Douglas' defence contracts. Rather than risk Commission fines of up to 10 per cent of its total revenues or worse, of being shut out of the E.U. market altogether, Boeing acceded to three Commission demands:

(1) it agreed not to abuse its position in the civil aircraft industry by maintaining the civil aircraft business of McDonnell Douglas as a separate entity for 10 years;

(2) it agreed to license any patents it obtains from McDonnell Douglas' defence contracts; and

---

[26] See "ICPAC Final Report", see para. 4.060, n. 19, at 134.

[27] See "ICPAC Final Report", see para. 4.060, n. 19, at 107–08.

[28] See *id.* at 110–11.

[29] See WTO, "Working Group on the Interaction between Trade and Competition Policy, Communication from the European Community and Its Member States", *Approaches to promoting cooperation and communication among WTO Members, including in the field of technical cooperation*, WT/WGTCP/W/129, at 2 (July 12, 1999). In the *Dresser/Haliburton* merger, however, the parties submitted 670 boxes of documents to the Justice Department, but only 4 boxes to Mexican authorities, 2 boxes to the European Commission, and 1 box to Canadian investigators. See "ICPAC Final Report", see para. 4.060, n. 19, at 138–39.

For additional examples of cooperation in the merger area between the United States and the E.U., Canada, Australia, and Mexico, see WTO, "Working Group on the Interaction between Trade and Competition Policy, Communication from the United States", *Approaches to Promoting Cooperation and Communication among Members including in the Field of Technical Cooperation*, WT/WGTCP/W/129, at 4 (May 25, 1999).

(3) it agreed not to enforce the 20-year exclusive supplier contracts it had with Delta, Continental and American Airlines, and not to conclude any future exclusive supplier contracts for 10 years.[30]

The E.U.'s conditions for approval of the merger are telling because they had little, if anything, to do with any anti-competitive effects of the merger. The Commission's concern with Boeing's sole-sourcing, exclusive supply contracts is that they risked excluding Airbus if they were not challenged. The concern was not that the merger would lead to higher prices for civil aircraft purchasers. These contractual arrangements were unrelated to the merger, therefore if they posed an anti-competitive threat to the E.U. they did so independent of the merger.

4.152 A valuable lesson to be learned from the *Boeing/McDonnell Douglas* merger is that the bilateral co-operation agreement between the E.U. and the United States was ineffective in preventing the dispute. It must be seriously questioned whether an international agreement would be any more effective than a bilateral agreement in forcing one of the parties to recede in a case where strong national or regional interests are at stake.

4.153 Even if the *Boeing/McDonnell Douglas* was *sui generis*, cross-border frictions may still arise, however, in multi-jurisdictional merger reviews in at least two general circumstances. First, international friction may arise because of adverse effects that are not addressed by a national reviewing agency.[31] For example, an approved merger may have the effect of increasing prices in another jurisdiction, while a blocked merger may have the effect of preventing consumers in another jurisdiction from enjoying lower prices. Frictions may also arise when mergers are either approved or blocked for policy reasons unrelated to competition, such as the positive effects a merger may have on employment, investment and economic growth in a domestic economy. Even if a merger is reviewed on competition policy grounds by different national reviewing authorities, it is still possible that one agency may find the proposed merger to be anti-competitive while the other deems it to be pro-competitive.[32]

4.154 A second source of friction in the merger review process concerns remedies that are imposed on proposed mergers that have extraterritorial effects. Such effects can be felt whenever one of the merging firms is foreign-based: a common occurrence with increased globalisation. In addition, both the United States and the E.U. have reviewed and taken enforcement action against a merger of foreign firms with no production facilities in the reviewing jurisdiction.[33]

4.155 Finally, convergence in the pre-merger review process appears to outweigh divergence, at least as measured by the number of consistent

[30] *See Boeing/McDonnell Douglas*, E.C. Case No. IV/M.877 (July 30, 1997); "*Boeing v. Airbus*, Peace in our time", *The Economist*, July 26, 1997, at 59–61.

[31] See "ICPAC Final Report", see para. 4.060, n. 19, at 54.

[32] See *id.*

[33] See, *e.g. Re Institut Merieux*, 113 F.T.C. 742 (1990) (consent decree requiring divestiture although neither party maintained production facilities in the United States); *Boeing/McDonnell Douglas*, E.C. Case No. IV/M.877 (July 30, 1997); *Gencor/Lonrho*, E.C. Case No. IV/M.619 (Apr. 24, 1996); *Anglo American Corp./Lonrho*, E.C. Case No. IV/M.754 (Apr. 23, 1997).

outcomes and compatible remedies that are more the rule than the exception in the multi-jurisdictional merger review process,[34] the *Boeing/McDonnell Douglas* merger notwithstanding.[35] In 1999, only 14 transactions of 292 notified were challenged or subjected to second-phase investigation by the European Commission. In the United States, of the 4,679 transaction notified during FY 1999, requests for additional information were made in 113 cases (2.4 per cent), and only 76 transactions (1.6 per cent) resulted in an enforcement action.[36]

4.156 Moreover, some of the gaps in substantive pre-merger review standards between national review authorities are slowly closing. The E.U., for example, has adopted aspects of market definition analysis traditionally employed by U.S. authorities.[37] Nevertheless, the possibility of divergent outcomes remains as long as national reviewing authorities use different substantive criteria for judging the anti-competitive effects of proposed mergers. While procedural differences exist among the merger control laws and regulations of developed countries, these laws and regulations share a common policy of preventing excessive concentrations of market power. Bridging at least the procedural gaps among these laws does not seem overly overambitious,[38] although some observers worry that harmonisation of procedural requirements could increase transaction costs by imposing more burdensome notification requirements than some jurisdictions currently require.[39] The work of the OECD on this subject has provided a valuable step in the direction of increased co-ordination among national enforcement authorities, if not actual harmonisation of substantive and procedural rules.[40] The International Competition Policy Advisory Committee (ICPAC), a blue-ribbon advisory panel of competition policy experts appointed by the Antitrust Division of the Department of Justice in 1998, has also made recommendations on rationalising the merger review process.[41] Despite these efforts, complete harmonisation and convergence of merger control regulations remain on the far-distant horizon.

---

[34] See "ICPAC Final Report", see para. 4.060, n. 19, at 56.

[35] It has been suggested that efficiency criterion be used as a basis for limiting the extraterritorial application of national competition laws in the context of multi-jurisdictional mergers and other transactions. See Daniel J. Gifford & E. Thomas Sullivan, "Can International Antitrust Be Saved for the Post-Boeing Merger World? A Proposal to Minimize International Conflict and to Rescue Antitrust from Misuse", (2000) 44 *Antitrust Bull.* 55.

[36] See "ICPAC Final Report", see para. 4.060, n. 19, at 96.

[37] See *id.* at 51.

[38] See James Halverson, "Harmonization and Coordination of International Merger Procedures", (1992) 60 Antitrust L.J. 531.

[39] See "ICPAC Final Report", see para. 4.060, n. 19, at 120. A survey of the transaction costs associated with complying with multiple merger control regimes is being undertaken by the International Bar Association and is to be completed by the end of 2001. See "IBA Begins Study of Costs Imposed by Merger Vetting", 17 Int'l Trade Rep. (BNA) 1474 (Sept. 28, 2000).

[40] See OECD Committee on Competition Law & Policy, "Report on Notification of Transnational Mergers", DAFFE/CLP(99)2/Final (Feb. 24, 1999) http://www.oecd.org/daf/clp/law_enforcement.htm. ICPAC has supported the OECD reform proposal. See "ICPAC Final Report", see para. 4.060, n. 19, at 158–59. However, former Assistant Attorney General James Rill has noted that the response of business and the antitrust bar to the OECD proposal has been "tepid." See "Merger Review Is Out of Control, Non-Government ABA Panelists Agree", (Apr. 22, 1999) 76 Antitrust & Trade Reg. Rep. (BNA) 418.

[41] See "ICPAC Final Report", see para. 4.060, n. 19, at 87–162.

VII. RESIDUAL ISSUES

4.157 In addition to the divergences among nations in the substantive provisions of their competition laws, a number of procedural and policy differences also exist making harmonisation a difficult task.

Private party enforcement v. national authority enforcement.

4.158 The overwhelming majority of antitrust cases filed in the United States are brought by private parties pursuant to section 4 of the Clayton Act, which authorises trebling of any award of compensatory damages.[42] The United States permits private actions, including class actions, with extensive pre-trial discovery (sometimes the target of blocking statutes), contingency-fee arrangements and jury awards of compensatory damages that are automatically trebled. The backlash in some countries to treble damage awards has resulted in the enactment of legislation preventing the enforcement of the trebled portion of the damages award. Interestingly, in Taiwan private parties who are injured by cartel activity may recover damages in a judicial proceeding and may be awarded treble damages in the discretion of the court, if the violation was intentional.[43]

In addition to government enforcement actions by the Justice Department and the Federal Trade Commission, state attorneys-general may bring antitrust actions under state statutes modelled after the Sherman and Clayton Acts.[44] Both the Justice Department and the FTC have policies on sharing information with state attorneys-general regarding possible antitrust violations affecting their respective states.[45] Neither the provinces of Canada nor the Mexican states have any authority to bring an antitrust action. That power is reserved to the federal government.

4.159 What this mix of federal, state and private party enforcement within the United States means is that there is no coherent pattern of antitrust enforcement in the United States.[46] What this means for an international agreement on competition policy is that it would be extremely difficult for the United States to assure other countries that like cases will be treated in a like

---

[42] See 15 U.S.C. s. 15(a). In addition, should the Justice Department bring a successful antitrust enforcement action, private parties may subsequently sue the defendant to recover treble damages without having to prove the elements of the antitrust violation. See, *e.g. Parklane Hosiery Co. v. Shore*, 439 U.S. 322 (1979) (nonmutual offensive use of collateral estoppel approved in securities fraud action).

[43] See Kauper, see para. 4.059, n. 18, at 96; Lawrence S. Liu, "Efficiency, Fairness, Adversary and Moralsuasion: A Tale of Two Chinese Competition Laws", in *International Harmonization of Competition Laws*, see para. 4.059, n. 18, at 317, 345–46 (hereinafter Liu).

[44] These state statutes are sometimes referred to as little Sherman and little Clayton Acts. For a compilation of state antitrust statutes and case law, see American Bar Ass'n, *State Antitrust Practice and Statutes* (2d ed. 1999).

[45] See American Bar Ass'n, *The Competition Laws of NAFTA, Canada, Mexico, and the United States, A Practitioner's Guide* (1997) 27–28 (hereinafter *The Competition Laws of NAFTA, Canada, Mexico, and the United States*).

[46] See Joseph P. Griffin, "United States Antitrust Laws and Transnational Business Transactions: An Introduction", (1987) 21 Int'l Law. 307, 312–24 (describing the web of federal, state, and private party antitrust enforcement in the United States).

manner, *e.g.* that foreign litigants will receive the same treatment as domestic litigants in similar circumstances. Even if Congress was to pre-empt antitrust lawsuits by state attorneys-general, the vagaries of jury awards alone make such assurances impossible.[47]

In the words of Professor Waller, "The private right of action . . . has failed to win many converts among nations."[48] Nevertheless, the United States has won some converts. Australia and New Zealand have a well-developed private right of action available to persons aggrieved by anti-competitive conduct; this right is independent of any action taken by national competition law enforcement authorities.[49] Class actions (called representative actions) may also be brought in Australia. A private right of action is also available in Ireland. It is anticipated that the courts will develop a private right of action in the United Kingdom pursuant to recently enacted legislation (the Competition Act 1998) that entered into force on March 1, 2000.[50]

4.160 In other OECD countries, the right to enforce competition laws is either reserved exclusively to the government or is much more limited in the hands of private parties.[51] Instead, many competition laws provide procedures whereby private persons may complain to the competition enforcement agency about alleged illegal conduct. In the E.U., for example, violations of Articles 81 and 82 are prosecuted by the European Commission, although a private person may petition the Commission to investigate an alleged competition law violation. The Commission may reject a complaint on the ground that no significant Community interests are at stake and that the issue can be settled satisfactorily in national courts. Private firms may then bring an action in the national courts of an E.U. Member State.[52] If the Commission rejects a complaint on the ground that there is insufficient evidence for initiating an investigation, it must inform the complainant of its reasons and fix a time limit for submitting additional comments in writing. The complainant is entitled to obtain a definitive decision from the Commission on its complaint and that decision may be challenged in an action for annulment before the Court of First Instance.[53]

---

[47] But see Kevin M. Clermont & Theodore Eisenberg, "Xenophilia in American Courts", (1966) 109 Harv. L. Rev. 1120 (the authors conclude that foreigners have higher success rates than American citizens in federal court).

[48] Waller, see para. 4.046, n. 83, at 393.

[49] See *Creating a Culture of Competition*, see para. 4.045, n. 83, at 5. For an exhaustive comparative analysis of private rights of action in Australia, Ireland, New Zealand, the UK and the United States, see R. Jack Roberts, International Comparative Analysis of Private Rights of Access (April 18, 2000) (study commissioned by the Canadian Competition Bureau), available at http://strategis.ic.gc.ca//SSG/ct01713e.html.

[50] See *id.*

[51] The competition laws of Japan, Peru and Thailand, for example, provide private rights of action in certain circumstances. See, *e.g.* Hiroshi Iyori & Akinori Uesagi, *The Antimonopoly Laws and Policies of Japan* (1994) 238–45; *Doing Business in Peru: The New Legal Framework* (Beatriz Boza ed. 1994) 289: Sutee Supanit, "Thailand: Implementation of Competition Law", (1999) 27 Int'l Bus. Law 497.

[52] See WTO, "Working Group on the Interaction between Trade and Competition Policy, Communication from the European Community and Its Member States", *The relevance of fundamental WTO principles of national treatment, transparency and most-favoured-nation treatment to competition policy and vice versa*, WT/WGTCP/W/115, at 8 (May 25,1999).

[53] See *id.*

4.161 In Canada, private parties who have suffered loss or damage have standing to bring an action with respect to conduct that is contrary to the criminal provisions of the Competition Act, or in violation of an order of the Competition Tribunal or of a court under the Act.[54] Damages may not exceed an award of single damages. It has been predicted that the number of such actions will increase given the liberalisation of the court rules governing class actions in Ontario.[55]

4.162 In Japan, Articles 25 and 26 of the Antimonopoly Law authorise a private plaintiff to sue for injury caused by monopolisation or unreasonable restraints of trade in the Tokyo High Court and to seek injunctive relief in some cases. However, a prerequisite for filing suit is that the JFTC has first acted against the alleged conduct and has rendered a final decision.[56] Professor Mitsuo Matsushita observes that "the rule regarding this proof [of causation] is quite stringent, and it is quite difficult for a plaintiff to meet this requirement."[57]

Civil versus criminal enforcement proceedings.

4.163 Another difference among some WTO members in competition law enforcement is that in some countries competition law proceedings are civil only and remedial relief prospective (an injunction against future violations).[58] In the E.U., for example, there are no criminal sanctions for a violation of Articles 81 or 82. The trend among the larger developed economies is to criminalise hard-core cartel activity. In the United States, for example, besides being the subject of a civil action by either the Justice Department or a private party, Sherman Act violations are felonies punishable by a fine of up to $350,000 and imprisonment of up to three years for an individual. A maximum fine of $10 million for a corporation is possible or, if greater, double the gross amount gained from the violation or lost by the victim.[59] Most of the Justice Department's criminal enforcement activities involve suspected violations of section 1 of the Sherman Act, such as horizontal agreements on price fixing and market allocation.

[54] Competition Act, s. 36. In 1989, the Supreme Court of Canada resolved the issue of the constitutionality of private causes of action in this area by upholding their constitutionality. See *General Motors of Canada Ltd. v. City National Leasing*, 1 S.C.R. 641 (1989).

[55] See "ABA Special Committee Report", see para. 4.066, n. 38, at 46.

[56] See Japan Fair Trade Commission, "Final Report on Improvement for Civil Remedy System to the Antimonopoly Act Violations" (Oct. 22, 1999, available at *http://www.jftc.admix.go.jp/e-page/press/1999/19991922.htm;* Mitsuo Matsushita, "Cartels Under the Japanese Antimonopoly Law", in *International Harmonization of Competition Laws*, see para. 4.059, n. 18, at 61, 69 (hereinafter Matsushita).

[57] Matsushita, *supra* note 56, at 69.

[58] See WTO, "Working Group on the Interaction between Trade and Competition Policy, Note by the Secretariat", *Overview of Members National Competition Legislation*, WT/WGTCP/W/128 (June 7, 1999) (noting that of the 27 WTO members submitting information, 16 did not criminalise competition law violations).

One exception to this remedial picture exists with merger control where enforcement authorities have the right to dissolve a merger found to be illegal or against the public interest. Because of the tremendous costs and wrenching dislocations that the dissolution of a merger can cause, the focus is on evaluation of a proposed merger before it is consummated.

[59] See 15 U.S.C. ss. 1, 2; 18 U.S.C. s. 3571.

4.164 In Canada, criminal charges may be brought for implementing in Canada agreements for carrying out an anti-competitive conspiracy entered into abroad, including price-fixing agreements, bid rigging and market-sharing cartels.[60] Fines of up to Can $10 million and a term of imprisonment of up to 5 years may be imposed.

In Japan, Article 89(1) of the Antimonopoly Law provides that an individual who has engaged in unlawful monopolisation or cartel activity is subject to a fine of up to 5 million Yen or imprisonment of up to three years. Corporations are subject to fines of up to 100 million Yen.[61]

In Taiwan, monopolisation and illegal cartels are subject to criminal fines of up to NT$1 million (less then $40,000) and imprisonment of up to three years.[62] Unreasonable vertical restraints are subject to fines of up to NT$500,000 (less than $20,000) and imprisonment of up to two years.[63] Taiwan's Code of Criminal Procedure follows the German approach and permits citizens' prosecution of a crime by the victim.[64]

4.165 Nine OECD-member countries have enacted criminal penalties for hard-core cartel activity. Firms and individuals are subject to criminal sanctions for such activity in Canada, Ireland, Japan, Korea, Norway and the United States. Individuals only are subject to criminal penalties for engaging in hard-core cartel activity in France, Greece, and Switzerland.[65]

Discretionary enforcement.

4.166 Another point of divergence among WTO members deals with competition law enforcement and the exercise of discretion. The legislation under which national enforcement authorities act, although often facially similar among countries, is invariably broad-brushed. Facially similar statutes may receive a different interpretation and construction in different countries. The details are left to the enforcement authorities to flesh out through administrative rulings and regulations. As a consequence, enforcement authorities are vested with a good deal of discretion in deciding whether to initiate an antitrust proceeding.

4.167 National self-interest may often inform an enforcement authority's decision whether to exercise its discretionary power. As noted by Judge

[60] See R.S.C. 1985, Chap. C–46, as amended, s. 45. Violations of s.45 are punishable by up to 5 years imprisonment and/or fines of up to Can$10 million. In 1993, Sumitomo Canada Ltd. entered a guilty plea in the Federal Court of Canada on a charge of having implemented a foreign-directed conspiracy contrary to s.46 of the Competition Act. See *The Competition Laws of NAFTA, Canada, Mexico, and the United States*, see para. 4.060, n. 19, at 37–38.

[61] See "ICPAC Final Report", see para. 4.060, n. 19, Annex 4–B; Matsushita, see para. 4.162, n. 56, at 68.

[62] See Kauper, see para. 4.059, n. 18, at 96; Liu, see para. 4.158, n. 43, at 346–47.

[63] See Liu, see para. 4.158, n. 43, at 347.

[64] See *id.* Horizontal price restraints are also a crime in Brazil and collusive tendering is criminal in Kenya. See UNCTAD, Revised Study by the UNCTAD Secretariat, Review of All Aspects of the Set of Multilaterally Agreed Equitable Principles and Rules for the Control of Restrictive Business Practices, *The role of competition policy in economic reforms in developing and other countries* 25, TD/RBP/CONF.4/2 (May 26, 1995).

[65] See Report by the OECD Competition Law and Policy Committee, "New Initiatives, Old Problems: A Report on Implementing the Hard Core Cartel Recommendation and Improving Co-operation, in OECD", (2000) Hard Core Cartels 26 n.13. For a list of the civil and criminal sanctions imposed by OECD member countries for hard-core cartel activity, see *id.* Annex A.

Wood, "If a country has autonomy over its competition policy, it has *de facto* power to make exceptions to even the strictest rule."[66] If a country's economy is highly vertically integrated, for example, it might be reluctant to enforce its competition laws against vertical restraints of trade, especially if the vertically integrated firms are major exporters. This type of discretionary authority has been a source of friction between the United States and Japan. The United States has on a number of occasions accused Japan of tolerating illegal vertical restraints practised by *keiretsu*, even though Japan's Antimonopoly Law restricts vertical integration.[67] Similar charges were brought by the United States against Japan in the WTO *Kodak-Fuji Film* dispute, discussed in Chapter Two.

4.168 In addition, WTO oversight of antitrust actions by national authorities would, in the view of Assistant Attorney General Joel Klein, be a non-starter:

> [Such oversight would] involve the WTO in second-guessing prosecutorial discretion in a complex evidentiary context—a task in which the WTO has no experience and for which it is not suited—and would inevitably politicize international antitrust enforcement in ways that are not likely to improve either the economic rationality or the legal neutrality of antitrust decision making.[68]

In a closely-related vein, national enforcement authorities do not have unlimited resources. Given a choice between prosecuting a horizontal price-fixing scheme with a direct and adverse effect on the welfare of domestic consumers, versus prosecuting an unlawful exclusive distribution agreement between a local manufacturer and a foreign distributor whose negative effects will be felt mostly by foreign consumers, the choice seems clear in a world of limited staff and thin financial resources.

Weak enforcement versus strong enforcement.

4.169 An issue closely related to discretionary enforcement is weak enforcement. Weak enforcement is a common complaint. Japan, for example, is frequently accused by the United States of not aggressively enforcing its Antimonopoly Law. Determining whether and when a country has a weak substantive law or is failing to enforce an otherwise serviceable competition law can be difficult to determine, especially with regard to vertical restraints and abuse of a dominant position. In those two areas, much ambiguity exists and different but reasonable economic and legal tests are used by national enforcement authorities.[69] It has been suggested that in the case of certain horizontal restraints, such as price fixing and market division, there is greater

[66] Wood, "The Impossible Dream", see para. 4.053, n. 98, at 306–07.
[67] See Michael J. Trebilcock & Robert Howse, *The Regulation of International Trade* (1995) 123.
[68] Joel I. Klein, "A Reality Check on Antitrust Rules in the World Trade Organization, and a Practical Way Forward on International Antitrust" in *Trade and Competition Policies: Exploring the Ways Forward* (OECD 1999) 37, 42.
[69] See Hawk, see para. 4.066, n. 38, at 12.

consensus and less ambiguity. Thus, any failure to apply competition laws to such practices would appear to be the result of weak enforcement rather than weak substantive rules.[70] The E.U. has made the further suggestion that transparency can expose weak or lax enforcement by requiring competition authorities to provide a fully reasoned decision concerning the enforcement of competition law.[71]

Exempted sectors.

4.170 OECD countries exempt in whole or in part a number of sectors of the economy from the reach of competition law, including:

(1) labour and employment-related activities,
(2) agriculture, fishing, and forestry,
(3) energy and utilities,
(4) postal services,
(5) transportation,
(6) communications,
(7) defence,
(8) financial services,
(9) media and publishing, and
(10) other miscellaneous sectors, such as natural resources.[72]

In addition, although the competition laws of most OECD countries apply to state enterprises, entities owned and operated by the U.S. government are immune from antitrust liability.[73]

Exempted conduct.

4.171 The state action doctrine protects from antitrust liability private action taken pursuant to a clearly articulated policy of one of the 50 states of the United States to substitute competition with regulation.[74] In order for

[70] See *id.* Professor Daniel Gifford and Mitsuo Matsushita have argued that the weakness or strength of national competition legislation should be measured according to the extent they further efficiency. See Daniel J. Gifford & Mitsuo Matsushita, "Antitrust or Competition Laws Viewed in a Trading Context: Harmony or Dissonance?" in *Harmonization and Fair Trade: Prerequisites for Free Trade?* (MIT Press 1996) 271, 279.

[71] See WTO, "Working Group on the Interaction between Trade and Competition Policy, Communication from the European Community and Its Member States", *The relevance of fundamental WTO principles of national treatment, transparency and most-favoured-nation treatment to competition policy and vice versa*, WT/WGTCP/W/115, at 6–7 (May 25, 1999).

[72] See *FTC v. Ticor Title Ins. Co.*, 504 U.S. 621 (1992); Hawk, see para. 4.066, n. 38, at 20.

[73] See *United States v. Rock Royal Co-op Ass'n*, 307 U.S. 533 (1939) (federal government cannot be held to violate the antitrust laws).

[74] See, *e.g. Parker v. Brown*, 317 U.S. 341 (1943); *Southern Motor Carriers Rate Conf. v. United States,* 471 U.S. 48 (1985). See also Dirk Ehle, "State Regulation Under the U.S. Antitrust State Action Doctrine and Under E.C. Competition Law: A Comparative Analysis", [1998] 6 E.C.L.R. 380; Eleanor M. Fox, "The Problem of State Action that Blesses Private Action that Harms 'the Foreigners'", in *Towards WTO Competition Rules: Key Issues and Comments on the WTO Report (1998) on Trade and Competition* (Roger Zäch ed. 1999) 325; Robert P. Inman & Daniel L. Rubinfeld, "Making Sense of the Antitrust State-Action Doctrine: Balancing Political Participation and Economic Efficiency in Regulatory Federalism", (1997) 75 Tex. L. Rev. 1203.

private conduct to qualify for immunity under the state action doctrine, the state must not only articulate a clear policy but it must also maintain active supervision and exercise independent control and judgment over the private conduct.[75] The doctrine extends to state executive, legislative, and judicial branches of government.

The E.U. has rejected the state action doctrine on the ground that E.U. competition law and policy has constitutional status and pre-empts any inconsistent competition legislation of an E.U. Member Country.[76]

Small and medium-size enterprises.

4.172 Although express exceptions for SMEs are rare, SMEs do receive *de facto* or *de jure* preferential treatment under competition laws in at least two respects. First, when such enterprises merge, they usually slip under the radar of merger control financial thresholds. Secondly, some competition laws are designed to favour SMEs.[77] For example, section 1.1 of the Canadian Competition Act provides in part that:

> [t]he purpose of this Act is to maintain and encourage competition in Canada . . . in order to ensure that small and medium-sized enterprises have an equitable opportunity to participate in the Canadian economy . . . .

VIII. SUMMARY

4.173 As the foregoing discussion has shown, domestic competition policies and legislation vary significantly across economies both in form, substance, interpretation, and administration. There are some points of convergence in WTO members' competition laws and policies, primarily with regard to horizontal restraints involving hard-core cartels. As observed by the ABA Sections of Antitrust Law and International Law and Practice in 2000:

> But there are differences. Nations accord different meanings to the word "anticompetitive." Also, they have different rules and thresholds for application of industrial policy. They diverge on the degree of intervention appropriate to make markets work better. They have somewhat different goals. Some pursue economic opportunity, diversity, and fairness to people without power. The EU stresses market integration. Some emphasize efficiency. Even when pursuing common goals of competitive markets and efficiency, nations often disagree on how best to achieve these objectives.[78]

Against this backdrop of divergence, it should come as no surprise that the WGTCP has been unsuccessful in bridging the many gaps that exist among

[75] See, *e.g. California Retail Liquor Dealers Ass'n v. Midcal Aluminum, Inc.*, 445 U.S. 97 (1980); *Patrick v. Burget,* 486 U.S. 94 (1988).
[76] See Hawk, see para. 4.066, n. 38, at 9.
[77] See *id.* at 31.
[78] "Report on Coordination and Convergence", see para. 4.051, n. 90, at 51.

WTO members regarding the efficacy or scope of a WTO competition policy agreement. Differences exist on so many facets of competition law—substantive and procedural rules on mergers, parallel imports, vertical restraints and abuse of a dominant position. These divergences reflect differences in objectives, priorities, the role of government in the economy, and discretion in the application of flexible rules such as the rule of reason. The literature and the reports submitted to the WTO Working Group do show, however, that there is near unanimity that horizontal agreements to fix prices and divide markets are anti-competitive and should be prohibited. The following Table summarises the degree of consensus on applicable legal standards, on regulation at the national level, and on regulation at the multilateral level:

Restrictive Business Practice	**Degree of Consensus to Eliminate/ Regulate Through National Competition Laws**	**Degree of Consensus on Applicable Legal Standard**	**Degree of Consensus to Eliminate/ Regulate Through Multilateral Agreement**
Hard-Core Cartels on Price Fixing, Bid Rigging, Output Restriction, and Market Allocation	High	High	Moderate to High
Export Cartels	High for Importing Countries, Low for Exporting Countries	High for Importing Countries, Low for Exporting Countries	Low to Moderate
Vertical Restraints	High	Low	Low
Abuse of a Dominant Position	High	Low	Low
Mergers	High	Low	Low

4.174 This table suggests that negotiating an international agreement on minimum standards or on core principles will be difficult, if not impossible. In June 1999, the OECD sponsored a conference attended by 200 trade and competition officials, academics, and business and labour groups from the 29 OECD-member countries and 30 non-member countries.[79] No consensus on the inclusion of competition policy in the next round of WTO multilateral trade negotiations emerged.[80] While the participants agreed that competition

[79] See "OECD Antitrust/Trade Conference Shows Disparate Approaches Toward Reconciliation", (July 8, 1999) 77 Antitrust & Trade Reg. Rep. (BNA) 41.
[80] See *Conference on Trade and Competition Policies*, see para. 4.068, n. 42, at 21–22.

laws should be transparent and non-discriminatory, there was no consensus on any substantive core principles.[81] In 1991, the American Bar Association's Special Committee on International Antitrust concluded that no global competition law standards are feasible.[82] This opinion was echoed in 2000 by ICPAC, the blue-ribbon advisory panel of competition policy experts appointed by the Antitrust Division of the Department of Justice.[83] Professor Daniel Gifford notes that:

> international discussions about harmonizing competition laws presents a substantial challenge, since the participants are likely to approach the subject with preconceptions arising out of their differing cultural experiences.[84]

Professor Eleanor Fox has added that:

> when nations continue to have different rules (leading to conflict), despite the enormous amount of cross-fertilization that occurs, that tends to indicate rooted differences in countries' preferences, which in turn may indicate a low feasibility for convergence.[85]

Another authority on the subject, Bernard Hoekman, has observed that the possible outcomes may vary from doing nothing to adopting a fully harmonised international antitrust code.[86] In short, building a broad consensus continues to be a work in progress. Assuming that at least a partial consensus does eventually build, the next Chapter examines what shape a potential multilateral agreements on competition policy might take.

---

[81] See *id.* at 22; "OECD Antitrust/Trade Conference Shows Disparate Approaches Toward Reconciliation", (July 8, 1999) 77 Antitrust & Trade Reg. Rep. (BNA) 41.
[82] See "ABA Special Committee Report", see para. 4.066, n. 38, at 294.
[83] See "ICPAC Final Report", see para. 4.060, n. 19, at 271.
[84] See Daniel J. Gifford, "Antitrust and Trade Issues: Similarities, Differences, and Relationships", (1995) 44 DePaul L. Rev. 1049; Daniel J. Gifford, "The Draft International Antitrust Code Proposed at Munich: Good Intentions Gone Awry", (1997) 6 Minn. J. Global Trade 1, 3.
[85] Eleanor M. Fox, "Comments", in *Brookings Trade Forum 1998*, see para. 4.140, n. 94, at 376.
[86] See Bernard Hoekman, "Harmonizing Competition Policy in the WTO System", (1977) 1 World Econ. Affairs No. 2.

CHAPTER FIVE

Trade and Competition Policy At the WTO: The Future

I. A WTO MULTILATERAL AGREEMENT ON COMPETITION POLICY

5.01 As the previous Chapter shows, GATT 1994 and the WTO multilateral trade agreements contain a patchwork of provisions dealing with restrictive business practices. The most ambitious action that the WTO members could take to rationalise and make this patchwork quilt of provisions more coherent would be to negotiate either a multilateral framework agreement on core principles or a multilateral agreement on harmonised, minimum competition policy standards.[1] Given the lack of a broad, international consensus on minimum RBP standards, as well as a lack of support from some national competition enforcement agencies for a multilateral agreement on harmonised, minimum RBP standards, a framework agreement would appear to have better prospects for near-term success.[2] Both approaches are discussed in the following sections, beginning with a multilateral agreement on minimum RBP standards.

A. A Multilateral Agreement on Minimum RBP Standards

5.02 Although a framework agreement based on broad, core principles might be more politically palatable to WTO members, an agreement based on harmonised national laws offer advantages not possible in a framework agreement on core principles.[3] First, multinational firms operate in a number

[1] See, *e.g.* Edward M. Graham & J. David Richardson, *Global Competition Policies: An Agenda* (Institute for Int'l Econ. 1997); Frederic M. Scherer, *Competition Policies for an Integrated World Economy* (Brookings 1994); J. David Richardson, "Multilateralizing Conventions", in *Brookings Trade Forum*: 1998, (Robert Z. Lawrence ed. 1998) at 366–74; Peter Lloyd, "Multilateral Rules for International Competition Law?", (1998) 21 World Economy 1029; Bernard Hoekman, "Harmonising Competition Policy in the WTO System", World Econ. Affairs 39 (Winter 1997) (hereinafter Hoekman I).

[2] See Peter Morici, *Antitrust in the Global Trading System: Reconciling U.S., Japanese and European Approaches* (Economic Strategy Institute 2000) http://www.econstrat.org/ECONSTRAT/antitrust.htm. But see Spencer Weber Waller, "The Internationalization of Antitrust Enforcement", (1997) 77 B.U.L. Rev. 343, 394 ("Harmonization of competition law is only possible in an economic system that is deeply integrated globally or regionally.").

[3] See generally Eleanor M. Fox, "Toward World Antitrust and Market Access", (1996) 91 Am. J. Int'l L. 1; Eleanor M. Fox, The End of Antitrust Isolationism: The Vision of One World, (1992) U. Chi. Legal F. 221.

of jurisdictions. The uncertainties created by variations in national competition laws can impose significant costs on firms. Harmonisation helps businesses by providing a certain legal environment throughout the global marketplace. A set of harmonised, transparent rules governing business conduct would, therefore, be of direct benefit to firms engaged in cross-border trade. Secondly, increased co-operation in the merger control area would also reduce the cost of doing business for firms acquiring assets in other jurisdictions. Thirdly, harmonisation of national competition laws would promote international trade by removing some or all of the differences in enforcement among national authorities that act as a non-tariff barrier to trade.

Whereas most of the provisions in GATT and the other WTO agreements are prohibitions on government conduct that inhibits trade flows, the TRIPS Agreement imposes affirmative obligations on WTO members to enact minimum intellectual property protections and to provide effective domestic IPR enforcement mechanisms. Therefore, a model for a WTO agreement on minimum competition policy standards could be the TRIPS Agreement.[4] Like the TRIPS Agreement, the proposed WTO agreement on competition policy would set out minimum competition policy standards that all WTO members would be obligated to enact as part of their national competition legislation and to provide for effective national enforcement mechanisms.[5] The agreement would consist of four parts:

[4] See Brian Hindley, "Competition Law and the WTO: Alternative Structures for Agreement", in 2 *Fair Trade and Harmonization: Prerequisites for Free Trade?* (Jagdish Bhagwati & Robert Hudec eds. 1996) 333 (expressing scepticism about the attainability and value of such an agreement); Robert E. Hudec, "A WTO Perspective on Private Anti-Competitive Behavior in World Markets", (1999) 34 New Eng. L. Rev. 79, 86–87 (hereinafter Hudec, "A WTO Perspective"). Although this type of agreement modelled after the TRIPS Agreement has been described as a framework agreement, see Hudec, "A WTO Perspective", *supra* this note, more accurately such an agreement would be a minimum standards agreement because, like the TRIPS Agreement, specific commitments would be made as to which business practices are unacceptable from a competition law standpoint and those commitments would then take immediate effect. An example of a framework agreement within the GATT–WTO context is the General Agreement on Trade in Services. Under GATS, WTO members agreed to a general framework of legal obligations that would apply to whatever market access commitments, if any, they made in 12 different services sectors. The follow-on negotiations that began in 2000 look to expand market access in these services sectors, subject to the general obligation of the framework agreement of GATS.

Outside of the GATT–WTO context, another example of a framework multilateral convention is the Convention on the International Trade in Endangered Species (CITES) regulating the international trade in certain threatened and endangered species of flora and fauna. CITES sets forth the manner in which signatories are to treat endangered and threatened species of flora and fauna, but does not itself identify which species are endangered or threatened. Instead, the flora and fauna that receive protection under CITES are the subject of continuing negotiation and listed in appendices to the Convention.

[5] In keeping with the theme of using acronyms as titles for WTO agreements—TRIMs, TRIPS, GATT, and GATS—writers have suggested titles for the new competition policy agreement using acronyms such as "TRAMS" (the Agreement on Trade—Related Antitrust Measures), "TRACLAP" (the Agreement on Trade-Related Aspects of Competition Law and Policy), and "TRAPS" (the Agreement on Trade-Related Antitrust Principles"). I leave it to others more clever than I to invent a suitable acronym.

1. *Minimum Standards on Anti-Competitive Conduct.*

5.03 Part I would contain provisions on agreed minimum standards and enforcement commitments. Members would agree to a harmonisation programme by enacting national competition laws or amending existing laws so that these agreed minimum standards become part of national legislation. The process would be analogous to the legislative process in the E.U. where the Commission issues a directive but leaves it to Member State legislatures to enact appropriate legislation. E.U. directives are addressed to one or more Member States. Member States, in turn, are obligated to implement the subject matter of the directive. Article 189 of the Treaty of Rome provides, however, that it is left to the national governments of the Member States to select the form and method by which the provisions in the directive are to be fulfilled. Thus, harmonisation would not require that countries enact identical competition laws. In addition to adopting minimum RBP standards, WTO members would enact minimum standards on enforcement of competition law to ensure effective action against RBPs and remedies adequate both to compensate for past violations and to deter future violations. Articles 41--50 of the TRIPS Agreement, dealing with civil and administrative procedures and remedies and provisional measures, could serve as a blueprint.[6]

5.04 Harmonisation's goal is to promote convergence of national competition laws, both substantive and procedural, not to establish uniformity of national laws. While differences do exist among national competition laws in the areas of vertical restraints (*e.g.* the treatment of exclusive territory clauses), abuse of a dominant position (*e.g.* defining the relevant market for the purpose of determining market power), and mergers (*e.g.* factoring efficiencies into the assessment of the anti-competitive effects of a proposed merger), there are many points of convergence as well.

5.05 An ambitious list of minimum standards and enforcement commitments would draw from the submissions to the WTO Working Group on Trade and Competition Policy and from the OECD's Joint Group on Trade and Competition. A consensus exists—although this assertion is made with trepidation given the many thorny issues involved in this supremely delicate undertaking—that price-based restraints (horizontal and vertical), bid-rigging, market allocation and restrictions on output are *per se* anti-competitive and should, accordingly, be dealt with severely. Non-price restraints are generally subject to a rule of reason. This category of RBPs would include vertical non-price restraints, such as exclusivity clauses in supplier-distributor arrangements. Here, competition law enforcement that would be considered satisfactory to all concerned members could easily break down, for what is one national enforcement authority's reasonable restraint is another's competition law violation. In addition, because vertical RBPs committed in Country A, but with adverse effects in Country B, tend to be of little interest to the enforcement authorities of Country A, principles of positive comity would be

[6] For a description and analysis of the TRIPS Agreement's domestic enforcement provisions, see Raj Bhala & Kevin Kennedy, *World Trade Law: The GATT–WTO System, Regional Arrangements, and U.S. Law* (1998) 1117–22.

an essential element of an agreement. Abuse of a dominant position would be a third category of RBP, although defining and broadening the relevant market to take into account international market factors could be problematic.

5.06 A fourth category of competition law standards would govern mergers and acquisitions that threaten to destroy competition. The differences among national laws regarding notification requirements, notification thresholds, waiting periods, and decision making criteria, however, should not be minimised.[7] It is probably premature to expect across-the-board harmonisation in the area of merger control and therefore, advisable to seek agreement on harmonising WTO members' merger control procedures (reporting requirements, thresholds, and time limits); to require co-operation, information exchange and mutual assistance between national enforcement authorities; but to postpone negotiations on matters of substantive merger control law.

5.07 Several conceptual obstacles exist with respect to harmonising national laws through minimum standards. Take, for example, the case of vertical and horizontal restraints of trade. National antitrust enforcement authorities apply a rule of reason, rather than a *per se* rule, when assessing the anti-competitive effects of many non-price vertical and horizontal restraints. The rule of reason has been criticised at the WTO, however, for failing to take into account the adverse effects of exclusionary business conduct on foreign producers who are denied market access. The WTO's mission has been to ensure effective market access for foreign firms. That goal has guided the thinking of WTO officials with respect to competition policy analysis in the context of vertical restraints of trade. Former Director-General Renato Ruggiero asked rhetorically:

> How should the situation be handled where there is an increasing reliance on a 'rule of reason' approach which requires an assessment of the balance of pro- and anti-competitive effects of a practice to be made and yet national law does not require the effects on other trading partners to be taken into account?[8]

Mr. Ruggiero's Deputy, Anwarul Hoda, added:

> [U]se of the rule of reason approach at the multilateral level would involve considerations quite different from those arising in national jurisdictions, for example, on standards, enforcement and remedies. Thus, if it were decided to employ a rule of reason in any multilateral competition rules, considerable work would be required to adapt this approach to that particular context.[9]

[7] See, *e.g.* Andre Fiebig, "A Role for the WTO in International Merger Control", (2000) 20 Nw. J. Int'l L. & Bus. 233; Eleanor M. Fox, "Mergers, Market Access and the Millennium", (2000) 20 Nw. J. Int'l L. & Bus. 203; George N. Addy, "International Harmonization and Enforcement Cooperation: The Canadian Experience", in *International Harmonization of Competition Laws* (Chia-Jui Cheng, Lawrence S. Liu, & Chih-Kang Wang eds. 1995) 399, 401.

[8] Closing Address of Renato Ruggiero, Conference on Antitrust: Rules, Institutions and International Relations, at 9 (Nov. 21, 1995).

[9] Comments by Anwarul Hoda, "Trade, Competition Policy and the World Trade Organization", Global Forum on Competition and Trade Policy Conference, at 8 (Mar. 17–19, 1997).

In 1997, the WTO Secretariat agreed with Mr. Ruggiero, concluding that:

> [T]he criteria commonly employed by competition authorities in 'rule of reason' cases may make relief more difficult to obtain in cases involving foreclosure of access for foreign suppliers . . . This is because, in weighing the costs and benefits under the rule-of-reason, enforcement actions relating to vertical restraints may not take into account the adverse effects of such restraints on foreign producers.[10]

The WTO Secretariat's assessment of the rule of reason, however, fails to take into account the enhancement of consumer welfare. For instance, it concludes that a merger between two domestic firms may be approved by national enforcement authorities, even though it shifts profits from foreign firms to the merging firms.[11] Suggesting that such a merger ought to be disapproved under a trade policy analysis, the Secretariat's analysis does not take into account the fact that considerations of consumer welfare and prices play an important role in the rule-of-reason analysis. The Secretariat appears to view national competition law enforcement as being an exercise in creating profit opportunities for domestic firms at the expense of competing foreign firms, with no mention of consumer welfare considerations.[12] The Secretariat's approach is decidedly weighted by a trade policy bias. Such a bias has also manifested itself within U.S. government circles.

5.08 Within the United States there is a lack of congruence between the U.S. Justice Department's position on non-price vertical restraints, which requires a rule-of-reason analysis of whether vertical restraints enhance efficiency, on the one hand, and the approach taken by the USTR toward vertical restraints, which takes a one-dimensional analysis of whether market access by U.S. firms is impeded, on the other. For example, when challenging Japanese *keiretsu* on the ground that they are a vertical restraint that blocks market access, the USTR has never asked whether vertical arrangements such as *keiretsu* enhance efficiency and, therefore, achieve a pro-competitive purpose. Similarly, in the *Kodak-Fuji Film* dispute, the USTR did not address the question whether Fuji's alleged vertical restraints created allocative efficiencies, instead applying in effect a *per se* rule to Fuji's activities. A gaping hole in the U.S. case against Japan from an antitrust enforcement perspective was a failure of proof of exclusivity agreements between Fuji and its distributors. What is more, the fact that Fuji offered volume-based rebates would not normally raise an antitrust red flag in U.S. practice.

5.09 The result is the application of a double standard, one applicable to the Japanese market under a trade policy approach and the other applicable to the U.S. market under a competition policy approach. This disconnect between U.S. trade and antitrust authorities not only makes concluding bilateral antitrust co-operation agreements problematic, but it also dims any

[10] WTO Secretariat, "WTO Annual Report" 1997, *Special Topic: Trade and Competition Policy* (Dec. 1997) 56.
[11] See *id.* at 52.
[12] See *id.* at 30, 55.

prospects of concluding a multilateral antitrust agreement as envisioned by some proponents.[13]

If a WTO agreement on competition policy was to be negotiated, would it measure the adequacy of antitrust law and enforcement against the yardstick of market access only? If certain vertical restraints or mergers received national antitrust enforcement authority approval or did not warrant the authority's scrutiny pursuant to published guidelines, would a WTO member be entitled to complain, pursuant to the enforcement provisions of a WTO agreement on competition policy, that such restraints and mergers are GATT illegal because they deny market access to foreign firms, regardless of efficiency gains and the maximisation of consumer welfare?[14] Under such an agreement, the United States could have made out a prima facie case of a GATT nullification and impairment in the *Kodak-Fuji Film* dispute simply by showing that Kodak had been denied access to the Japanese film market.

5.10 Given these realities, a less ambitious list of minimum RBP standards would limit the targeted practices to those bearing most directly on denial of market access to foreign goods and services. Candidate practices would be the so-called "hard-core" agreements on price fixing, bid rigging, output restriction and market division.[15] In dealing with export cartels, national enforcement authorities tend to neglect them because they do not have an important impact on the national market, even though they contravene the letter and the spirit of the GATT–WTO trading system by being a "beggar-thy-neighbour" policy.[16] The broader global interest reflected in a multilateral agreement on competition policy should require members to ban such cartels.[17] Expecting countries to ban export cartels under their national legislation without a reciprocal agreement from other countries to do the same—in effect, to unilaterally disarm—would run counter to the mercantilist philosophy that is at the core of most countries' trade policies. A multilateral solution would thus seem to be the only viable course of action.[18] However, given the

[13] See Daniel J. Gifford, "Antitrust and Trade Issues: Similarities, Differences and Relationships", (1995) 44 DePaul L. Rev. 1049, 1062–63.

[14] See Philip Marsden, "'Antitrust' at the WTO", 13 (1999) Antitrust 28, 31.

[15] See WTO, "Working Group on the Interaction between Trade and Competition Policy, Communication from Switzerland", *Promoting Cooperation and Communication in Competition Policy at the Multilateral Level: Possible Elements*, WT/WGTCP/W/151, at 2 (Sept. 22, 2000); OECD, Recommendation Concerning Effective Action Against "Hard Core" Cartels, OECD C(98)35/Final, Part I.A.2(b) (March 30, 1998), available at http://www.oecd.org/daf/clp/Recommendations/Rec9com.htm; Hudec, "A WTO Perspective", see para. 5.03, n. 4, at 79; Sir Leon Brittan, "The Need for a Multilateral Framework of Competition Rules", in *Trade and Competition Policies: Exploring the Ways Forward* (OECD 1999) 29, 34.

[16] See Waller, see para. 5.01, n. 2, at 398.

[17] See Waller, see para. 5.01, n. 2, at 397 (author proposes an international agreement banning cartels and requiring non-discriminatory enforcement); Auke Haagsma, "An International Competition Policy As a Means to Create An Open Global Market Place", in *International Harmonization of Competition Laws*, see para. 5.06, n. 7, at 409, 425.

[18] But see Waller, see para. 5.01, n. 2, at 398 n.284 (suggesting that the United States could benefit from unilaterally eliminating its legislation authorizing export cartels); Daniel K. Tarullo, "Norms and Institutions in Global Competition Policy", (2000) 94 Am. J. Int'l L. 478, 491 ("The problem of international cartels can be resolved more directly by creating cooperative arrangements that provide enforcers with . . . evidence than by initiating a WTO action for nonenforcement of another country's anti-cartel law.").

embedded nature of export cartels and the reality that certain export association agreements are authorised under national competition laws, the path of least resistance might be to agree

(1) that a WTO member where an export association is located and under whose laws an export association is organised would not be obligated to take action against such an export association, but

(2) that another WTO member adversely affected by the conduct of such an association would have the right to bring an enforcement action against the export association.

This is currently the way in which injurious dumping is handled under GATT Article VI and the Antidumping Agreement.

2. *Non-Discrimination and Transparency.*

5.11 Part II would cover basic WTO commitments on MFN and national treatment. Provisions on transparency of national competition laws, regulations, and enforcement mechanisms would be essential features in order to ensure due process and predictability.

3. *Dispute Settlement.*

5.12 Part III would cover dispute settlement (alternatives to binding dispute settlement under the DSU are examined in connection with a framework competition policy agreement, discussed later in this Chapter.) Leaving resolution of cross-border competition law disputes over market access to a neutral, international forum would address the problem of mistrust that foreign businesses and national enforcement authorities seem to have of the decisions of other national enforcement authorities.[19] Kodak's and the USTR's reaction to the JFTC's determination that Fuji had not engaged in any impermissible vertical restraints is just one example of this mistrust. If binding WTO panel review is the preferred dispute resolution mechanism then the issue of remedies also has to be sorted out in trade-competition policy disputes.

5.13 The hierarchy of remedies for a violation of GATT or a WTO agreement is:

(1) remove the offending measure,

(2) compensate the aggrieved member with offsetting trade concessions, and

(3) in the event that compensation is not given, retaliate by suspending trade concessions in an amount equal to the value of the trade lost due to the offending measure.[20]

---

[19] See Eleanor Fox, "Competition Law and the Agenda for the WTO: Forging the Links of Competition and Trade", in *Antitrust: A New Trade Remedy?* (John O. Haley & Hiroshi Iyori eds. 1995) 1, 15.

[20] See DSU Art. 22.

In a non-violation case where no GATT–WTO obligation has been violated, but an aggrieved member alleges that it has not received the benefit of the bargain that was to flow from making trade concessions because of some action taken by a responding member, the offending measure need not be withdrawn, thus paring down the list of available remedies to compensation or suspension of concessions.[21]

5.14 The suggestion has been made that in order to move negotiations on a WTO competition policy agreement down the road to completion, it would be preferable to treat alleged violations of a WTO agreement premised on private, anti-competitive conduct as non-violation nullification or impairment.[22] Thus, for example, if a private RBP was shown to prevent market access in violation of GATT 1994 or a WTO agreement, the responding member would not be obligated to prosecute the anti-competitive conduct. Although Professor Hudec characterises this as a weaker remedy,[23] it is not clear how, as a practical matter, the remedy in non-violation cases differs from that in violation cases. In violation cases, although the preferred outcome is removal of the offending measure, a WTO member cannot be forced to do so. In fact, the *Hormone Beef*[24] and *Bananas*[25] disputes both involved violations of GATT obligations, yet the offending measures were not removed in either case and the aggrieved members ended up retaliating by suspending trade concessions.[26]

5.15 Is an international enforcement authority, such as the WTO pursuant to the DSU, really needed?[27] It seems fanciful to believe that by the mere stroke of a pen a finding of a competition law violation by a supranational authority will suddenly be respected and observed at the national level. A necessary pre-condition to having some assurance that WTO panel and Appellate Body reports will be abided by is a showing that national enforcement authorities are able to work co-operatively with their sister agencies in other countries to avoid jurisdictional conflicts by observing principles of traditional comity and positive comity. Without this pre-

[21] See *id.* Art. 26.1(b).

[22] See Hudec, "A WTO Perspective", see para. 5.03, n. 4, at 95–96. For an argument that non-violation complaints should be strictly limited, see Sung-joon Cho, "GATT Non-Violation Issues in the WTO Framework: Are they the Achilles Heel of the Dispute Settlement Process?" (1998) 39 Harv. Int'l L. J., 311, 321–26.

[23] See Hudec, see para. 5.039, n. 4 at 96.

[24] See Report of the Appellate Body, "European Communities—Measures Concerning Meat and Meat Products (Hormones)", WT/DS26/AB/R (1998).

[25] See Report of the Appellate Body, "European Communities—Regime for the Importation, Sale and Distribution of Bananas", WT/DS27/AB/R (1997).

[26] See Office of the U.S. Trade Representative, "USTR Announces Final Product List in Beef Hormones Dispute", Press Release 99–60 (July 19, 1999); Office of the U.S. Trade Representative; "WTO Finds U.S. Trade Damages by EU Beef Import Ban", Press Release 99–58 (July 12, 1999); Office of the U.S. Trade Representative, "WTO Finds EU Banana Regime Hurts U.S. Trade", Press Release 99–31 (April 6, 1999); Office of the U.S. Trade Representative, "USTR Announces Final Product List in Bananas Dispute", Press Release 99–35 (April 9, 1999); Office of the U.S. Trade Representative, "WTO Authorizes U.S. Retaliation", Press Release 99–38 (April 19, 1999); Elizabeth Olson, "U.S. and Canada Get $125 Million Ruling on Europe Beef Ban", *New York Times*, July 13, 1999, s. C, at 4.

[27] See Topic Four, "Is an International Enforcement Authority Needed?" in *Antitrust: A New Trade Remedy?*, see para. 5.12, 19, at 1, 15.

condition in place, moving such unresolved bilateral disputes into an international forum is a prescription for disaster. Rather than ameliorate international tensions over jurisdictional conflicts, it will only exacerbate them. Even then, considering that application of the principles of traditional comity and positive comity entails assessments of reasonableness and national interests, it seems misguided to refer such matters to a WTO dispute settlement panel for resolution.

Insofar as a country permits private antitrust suits, proper consideration of the jurisdictional rule of reason by the courts becomes important because private parties have no interest in the international repercussions of extraterritorial exercises of competition law jurisdiction. As noted in Chapter Two, under the 1982 Australia–U.S. bilateral co-operation agreement, the United States has agreed to intervene in private party suits or to submit *amicus* briefs regarding the possible adverse effects of the action on the national interests of Australia.[28] This provision could be a model for a parallel provision in any WTO competition policy agreement.

4. *Developing Countries.*

5.16 Finally, Part IV would address the special needs of developing. For developing countries and for countries with economies in transition, enacting and implementing competition legislation can be a formidable task.[29] The many hurdles facing developing countries in implementing a competition law regime include developing a skilled staff and securing the financial resources needed to administer and implement competition legislation. Small developing countries face a scarcity of skilled human resources, making it difficult for them to participate in international meetings and negotiating fora in which they must be present simultaneously. Developing a culture of competition also presents a challenge for businesses with little or no knowledge of competition law and its impact. They must be educated.[30]

5.17 As part of a multilateral competition policy agreement, developed countries would commit to providing developing countries and LDCs with

[28] See "Agreement Between the Government of the United States of America and the Government of Australia Relating to Co-peration on Antitrust Matters", At. 6, done at Washington, D.C., June 29, 1982, available at htt://www.usdoj.gov, reprinted in (1984) 21 Int'l Leg. Materials 275. The 1984 Canada-U.S. Memorandum of Understanding had a similar commitment. See "Agreement Between the Government of the United States of America and the Government of Canada Regarding the Application of Their Competition and Deceptive Marketing Practices Laws", art. 11, Mar. 9, 1984, U.S.-Canada, reprinted in (1984) 23 Int'l Leg. Materials 275.

[29] See, *e.g.* William E. Kovacic, "Getting Started: Creating New Competition Policy Institutions in Transition Economies", (1997) 23 Brooklyn J. Int'l L. 403; William E. Kovacic, "Designing and Implementing Competition and Consumer Protection Reforms in Transitional Economies: Perspectives from Mongolia, Nepal, Ukraine, and Zimbabwe", (1995) 44 DePaul L. Rev. 1197; Donald I. Baker, "Building a Competition Law that Works", (Oct.-Nov. 1999) Global Comp. Rev.; OECD, *Competition Law and Policy in the Baltic Countries* (1999).

[30] See, *e.g.* WTO, "Working Group on the Interaction between Trade and Competition Policy, Communication from Trinidad and Tobago", *Developing and Implementing a Competition Regime: Challenges Faced by Small Open Economies*, WT/WGTCP/W/143 (Aug. 2, 2000).

technical assistance.[31] The modalities of technical assistance would be tuned to the stage of development of the recipient country. For developing countries with no or little competition law experience, officials from the developing country would visit a host country to see legislative and regulatory structures first-hand. For developing countries with competition law and enforcement machinery in place, local training in a host country would be most effective. Programmes that brought together officials from developing countries could be fruitful in terms of information and experience sharing and networking. Technical assistance can be mutually beneficial. Developing countries receive assistance in ensuring that an effective competition legal regime is established in their market, and developed countries increase their sensitivity to the concerns and conditions of developing countries in the field of competition law.[32]

5.18 In addition, the suggestion was made in the WGTCP that developing countries should receive special consideration in four areas.[33] First, if developing countries are expected to enact or amend competition legislation, their different economic realities and degrees of economic development need to be considered, for example, with regard to the question of the breadth of exemptions from competition law that would be appropriate in particular economies. Secondly, the different cultural conditions that prevail in developing countries need to be considered when introducing a competition policy. Its introduction can cause far-reaching social and economic changes.[34] Thirdly, differences in resource endowments means more human and material resources are required for development, a fact to which competition policy in developing countries must be sensitive. Fourthly, recognising the different degrees of institutional development among developing countries, any multilateral agreement on competition policy should include transition periods, progressivity of commitments and technical co-operation. For example, developing countries could be required to enact legislation prohibiting RBPs that are deemed *per se* illegal before tackling those practices that are subject to a rule of reason.

[31] Developed countries have committed to provide technical assistance to developing countries, for example, in the SPS Agreement (Art. 9) and the TRIPS Agreement (Article 67). See also WTO, Council for Trade-Related Aspects of Intellectual Property Rights, WTO Secretariat Technical Co-operation in the TRIPS Area, IP/C/W/201 (Aug. 30, 2000). For a list of developing countries seeking technical assistance at the end of 1998 from UNCTAD and other organisations on how to deal with RBPs, see Susan K. Sell, *Power and Ideas: North-South Politics of Intellectual Property and Antitrust* (1998) 202–03.

Exempting LDCs from the agreement is an alternative, although they were not given such a blanket exemption under the TRIPS Agreement which requires enacting and enforcing sophisticated laws and regulations on intellectual property protection. Under the TRIPS Agreement, developing countries were given a 5 year transition period, and LDCs an eleven-year transition period. See TRIPS Agreement arts. 65.2, 66.1.

[32] See WTO, "Working Group on the Interaction between Trade and Competition Policy, Report (1999) of the Working Group on the Interaction between Trade and Competition Policy to the General Council", WT/WGTCP/3, at 13–14, para. 43 (Oct. 11, 1999) (hereinafter "WGTCP 1999 Report").

[33] See "WGTCP 1999 Report", at 10, para. 29.

[34] See WTO, "Working Group on the Interaction between Trade and Competition Policy, Note by the Secretariat", *Synthesis Paper on the Relationship of Trade and Competition Policy to Development and Economic Growth*, WT/WGTCP/W/80, at 14–16, paras. 37–43 (Sept. 18, 1998).

5.19 As evidenced by their support of the UNCTAD Restrictive Business Practices Code, developing countries seem to prefer the multilateral regulation of RBPs. Developing countries fear multinational enterprises (MNEs) and their dominance in local markets. It is argued—chiefly by developing countries—that MNEs are able to engage in restrictive business practices in host countries which result in monopoly profits, lower efficiency and barriers to entry by potential domestic competitors. The WTO Secretariat has argued to the contrary that the entry of an MNE:

> might have the effect of breaking up a comfortable domestic oligopolistic market structure and stimulating competition and efficiency. . . . The empirical evidence, however, points strongly to pro-competitive effects.[35]

For example, with open investment rules in place, an exporter who finds himself unable to penetrate a foreign market because incumbent wholesalers and retailers are owned or controlled by local producers of competing goods who will not handle his goods could establish a new distribution channel or purchase an existing one, thereby eliminating the local distribution bottleneck. A liberal investment policy, in short, can simultaneously promote competition and trade in the host-country market and perhaps in the global market as well.

5.20 Whether a potential host country has in place and actively enforces antitrust laws is part of the mix of local business laws that foreign investors consider when asking, "Does a fair and predictable legal environment for doing business exist in the host country?" If competition laws are in place and are regularly enforced, then potential investors will have at their disposal the means of combating local cartels or monopolies which abuse their position. Likewise, local firms will have the same ability to prevent abuses by foreign investors. Conversely, if antitrust law does not exist in a potential host country, or if it is loosely or discriminatorily enforced, then potential investors might look elsewhere to make their investment.

Some developing countries, bucking the law of comparative advantage, have used investment screening laws to force investors to make specific commitments on performance requirements. While the WTO Agreement on Trade-Related Investment Measures (TRIMs) bans the use of certain performance requirements primarily tied to the purchase of local versus foreign-source goods, many other performance requirements, such as requiring technology transfer, mandating the use of local business partners, or preventing the free repatriation of profits, are not the subject of the TRIMs Agreement. Such performance requirements are likely to deter, not attract FDI and associated technology, thereby preventing increased competition in

[35] "Report of the WTO Secretariat, Trade and Foreign Direct Investment" 16 (1998) (citing in support Richard E. Caves, *Multinational Enterprises and Economic Analysis* (1982), and Edward M. Graham, *Global Corporations and National Governments* (1996)).

local markets.[36] National laws and regulations that discriminate against foreign direct investment distort international trade in much the same way as do tariffs, quotas, and other non-tariff barriers to trade. By favouring domestic investors or discriminating against foreign investors, the most efficient producers may be not be able to penetrate a market due to government interference in the market.

5.21 Besides MNEs dominating local markets, developing countries have expressed concerns about subsidiaries of MNEs that purchase inputs from their parent, rather than source locally, and parent-imposed restrictions on the subsidiary's export markets in order to segment world markets.[37] A multilateral regulatory scheme would thus serve as a counterweight to the power of MNEs. In addition, developing countries are even less able to combat export cartels than are developed countries. Developing countries may stand to gain from a WTO agreement that prohibits such cartel activity and that takes developing-country interests into account when cross-border mergers are reviewed. Thus, the need may exist from a developing country perspective for an international competition policy agreement with a binding dispute settlement mechanism. As far as what would be in the best interests of developing countries, Bernard Hoekman has advocated a competition policy agreement that:

(1) bans horizontal restraints on price fixing and market sharing, including export cartels;

(2) replaces antidumping duty laws with competition laws; and

(3) provides for binding WTO dispute settlement.[38]

Of the more than 80 countries that have enacted some form of competition law, nearly 40 of these are developing countries and countries with economies

[36] As noted in a U.S. submission to the WTO Working Group on Trade and Investment: "Sometimes these investment screening regimes have even been given a competition policy rationale, one based on concern that efficient new market entrants could harm existing local competitors and perhaps achieve a local monopoly. In our view, these concerns are largely misplaced, especially if foreign entry is by way of "greenfield" investment rather than through acquisition of a local competitor. On the conceptual level, competition policies that attempt to protect (established) competitors, rather than consumers, are inherently suspect; after all, competition laws should protect competition, not competitors. While other rationales are sometimes asserted for maintaining such protective policies, competition rarely is enhanced by them". Relationship between Investment and Competition Policy, Communication from the United States, WTO Working Group on the Relationship between Trade and Investment, at 5, WT/WGTI/W/55 (Sept. 25, 1998).

[37] See Sung-joon Cho, "GATT Non-Violation Issues in the WTO Framework: Are They the Achilles' Heel of the Dispute Settlement Process?" (1998) 39 Harv. Int'l L.J. 311, 328.

[38] See, *e.g.* Bernard Hoekman, "Competition Policy and the Global Trading System: A Developing-Country Perspective" 16 (World Bank Policy Research Paper No.1735 1997) (hereinafter Hoekman II). But see Bernard Hoekman & Peter Holmes, *Competition Policy, Developing Countries and the WTO* (1999) (authors argue that developing countries are better off pursuing an active domestic competition law independently of the WTO, given the WTO's focus on eliminating border measures that prevent producers from gaining market access, rather than on promoting consumer welfare through enforcement of competition laws); Ignacio de Leon, "An Alternative Approach to Policies for the Promotion of Competition in Developing Countries", (1999) 6 Sw. J.L. & Trade Am. 85.

in transition.[39] The United Nations Conference on Trade and Development has concluded that:

> there would be substantial benefits to be obtained from strengthening the application of competition law and policy in developing and least developed countries and countries in transition in terms of greater production, allocative and dynamic efficiency, welfare and growth.[40]

Those developing countries which do have competition laws in place are typically unable to apply them extraterritorially.[41] In addition, having a competition law on the books and having an effective national enforcement mechanism in place are not the same thing. Developing countries which have enacted competition legislation may lack the resources and expertise to implement an effective legal regime, although a lack of capacity to pursue investigations and to bring enforcement actions is not universally the case.[42] Nevertheless, competition law enforcement actions are expensive whenever they are brought. Moreover, broadly drafted legislation, coupled with agency discretion, creates an environment of legal uncertainty for businesses.

5.22 Developing countries might lack the expertise and other resources necessary to implement a comprehensive competition policy all at once, therefore the suggestion has been made that a phased approach to the implementation of a competition law is appropriate for developing countries.[43] Under this incremental approach, national competition authorities would focus first on eliminating horizontal cartels—the most unambiguously harmful RBP—and on basic competition advocacy relating to market reforms.[44] Once competition authorities have gained experience in these areas, they would then assume additional responsibilities, such as merger review and dealing with anti-competitive vertical restraints.

---

[39] See "Conference on Trade and Competition Policies: Exploring the Ways Forward, Summary", (1999) 1 OECD J. Competition L. & Pol'y 7, 8. For a list of 37 developing countries and countries with economies in transition that have enacted a competition law, and 21 that are in the process of adopting such legislation, see Hoekman II, see para. 5.21, n. 38, at 16.

There is an ongoing, but quiet, debate over whether traditional competition laws are appropriate for developing countries and economies in transition. See, *e.g.* A.E. Rodriguez & Mark D. Williams, "The Effectiveness of Proposed Antitrust Programs for Developing Countries", 19 N.C.J. Int'l L. & Com. Reg. 209 (1994); Craig W. Conrath & Barry T. Freeman, "A Response to 'The Effectiveness of Proposed Antitrust Programs for Developing Countries,'" (1994) 19 N.C.J. Int'l L. & Com. Reg. 233.

[40] UNCTAD, Report by the UNCTAD Secretariat, "Empirical Evidence of the Benefits from Applying Competition Law and Policy Principles to Economic Development in Order to Attain Greater Efficiency in International Trade and Development 2", TD/B/COM.2/EM/10/Rev.1 (May 25, 1998).

[41] See Andrew T. Guzman, "Is International Antitrust Possible?", (1998) 73 N.Y.U.L. Rev. 1501, 1537.

[42] For a review of competition law enforcement activities of several Latin American countries (Argentina, Brazil, Colombia, Costa Rica, Jamaica, Mexico, Panama, Peru and Venezuela), see "Organization of American States, Report on Developments and Enforcement of Competition Policy and Laws in the Western Hemisphere", FTAA.ngcp/inf/04/Cor.1 (Oct. 25, 1999).

[43] See WTO, "Working Group on the Interaction between Trade and Competition Policy, Report to the General Council", WT/WGTCP/2, at 19, para. 51 (Dec. 8, 1998) (hereinafter "WGTCP 1998 Report").

[44] See *id.*

5.23 Alternatively, one of the cheapest and most effective pro-competitive devices available to any government is to adopt a liberal trade policy that will bring competitive pressure to bear on local monopolies in the form of imports. Equally important in the promotion of competition in national markets is the encouragement of foreign direct investment. The overall focus for developing countries, then, should be on a competition policy that promotes competition in local markets, rather than competition law that seeks to punish anti-competitive conduct. In short, competition in local markets can be promoted "on the cheap" through liberal trade and foreign investment policies at the national level.[45] UNCTAD has warned, however, that:

> [t]rade and foreign investment liberalization, while increasing international competition in many sectors, may enhance the incentive for firms to resort to RBPs to maintain their marker position . . .[46]

Therefore, it may too facile to conclude that developing countries need only be concerned with competition policy and not also with competition law enforcement.

5.24 Although these last observations suggest that developing countries have little to gain from a multilateral competition law agreement, two issues of interest to developing countries are merger control and export cartels; two areas of competition law that local competition law cannot satisfactorily address.[47] Developing countries would benefit from an international rule that requires home countries of merging firms to take into account the interests of developing countries when reviewing a proposed merger with potential cross-border effects. Devising meaningful standards that would account for and accommodate developing-country interests is problematic. A positive comity analysis is a close analogue, but positive comity is a relatively untested concept in practice. When a traditional comity analysis has been used, rarely have the interests of affected countries prevented the exercise of extraterritorial jurisdiction.

5.25 Similarly, a multilateral agreement that makes export cartels illegal would benefit developing countries. However, recalling that the members of the OECD were unable to reach a consensus on making export cartels *per se* illegal as recently as 1998,[48] the prospects for doing so under WTO auspices are not good. In this connection, the structure of negotiations is critical. Developing countries must be prepared to make major concessions in areas of export interest to developed countries in order to overcome the resistance of

[45] See *id.* at 13, para. 37.
[46] UNCTAD, Revised Study by the UNCTAD Secretariat, Review of All Aspects of the Set of Multilaterally Agreed Equitable Principles and Rules for the Control of Restrictive Business Practices, "The role of competition policy in economic reforms in developing and other countries" 7, TD/RBP/CONF.4/2 (May 26, 1995). *See* WTO, "Working Group on the Interaction between Trade and Competition Policy, Report to the General Council", WT/WGTCP/2, at 14, para. 38 (Dec. 8, 1998)
[47] See "Conference on Trade and Competition Policies: Exploring the Ways Forward, Summary", see para. 5.21, n. 39, at 15–16.
[48] See Recommendation Concerning Effective Action Against "Hard Core" Cartels, see para. 5.10, n. 15.

politically powerful interest groups in developed countries. Preparatory to the launch of any negotiations on a competition policy agreement, a thorough educative process needs to be concluded for the benefit of developing countries.[49]

5.26 Assuming negotiation of a modest WTO agreement on core principles, developing countries that have not already done so may be expected to enact a competition law or amend an existing one to incorporate these core principles. A developing country which has enacted a comprehensive competition law is Mexico. It could serve as a model for other developing countries, especially as the latter deal with developed countries in cross-border enforcement proceedings. As is true with most developing economies, competition policy had not been a major area of concern in Mexico. In fact, although Mexico has had antitrust legislation for almost 60 years, antitrust enforcement is a relatively new concept in Mexico because the Mexican government had never enforced the statute.[50] Prior to the enactment of the Federal Law on Economic Competition of 1993 (the Competition Law),[51] no antitrust enforcement agency or right to bring a private antitrust action existed.[52]

5.27 The Competition Law provides for free economic competition through the elimination of monopolies, monopolistic practices, restraints of trade and other anti-competitive market practices.[53] The Competition Law does not apply to constitutional monopolies, such as the petroleum industry, basic petrochemicals, satellite communications and railroads. The Competition Law clearly prohibits monopolistic practices and distinguishes between absolute monopolistic practices and relative monopolistic practices. Horizontal, anti-competitive agreements (*i.e.* absolute monopolistic practices) are defined in the Competition Law as agreements among competitors to fix prices, restrict output and distribution of goods or services, divide markets, or otherwise manipulate the public bidding process. If one of the above is proven in a Mexican court, it is deemed illegal *per se* and can result in severe civil penalties.[54]

However, the Competition Law permits most vertical restraints of trade (*i.e.* relative monopolistic practices), except those made with the intent of effectively driving competitors from the market or otherwise impeding their access to it.[55] Such vertical agreements may include:

[49] See WTO, Working Group on the Interaction between Trade and Competition Policy, Report (1999) to the General Council, WT/WGTCP/3, at 25, para. 78 (Oct. 11, 1999).

[50] See Sergio Garcia-Rodriguez, "Mexico's New Institutional Framework for Antitrust Enforcement", (1995)44 DePaul L. Rev. 1149.

[51] See Ley Federal de Competencia Economica (Federal Law of Economic Competition), Diario Oficial de La Federacion (Official Gazette of the Federation) (Dec. 24, 1992). For an analysis of Mexico's competition law, see Michael O. Wise, "Review of Competition Law and Policy in Mexico", (1999) 1 OECD J. Competition L. & Pol'y 43. For an English translation of the Mexican competition law, see "Report of the ABA Antitrust Section Task Force on the Competition Dimension of the North American Free Trade Agreement", Appendix Two (1994) (hereinafter "Report of the ABA Task Force").

[52] See Garcia-Rodriguez, see para. 5.26, n. 50, at 190.

[53] See Mexican Competition Law, see para. 5.26, n. 51, Art. 2. For an overview of the Mexican Competition Law, see "Report of the ABA Task Force", see para. 5.26, n. 51, at 47–58.

[54] See Rogelio Lopez-Velarde, *Mexico's New Antitrust Law* (1993) 5.

[55] See Lopez-Velarde, see para. 5.27, n. 54, at 5.

(1) geographical distribution restrictions;

(2) resale price maintenance;

(3) tying and other after-market agreements;

(4) reciprocal dealing, exclusive dealing, or otherwise refusal to deal;

(5) agreements not to compete; and

(6) any other practices that illegitimately impede or affect competition.[56]

In order to determine whether such vertical agreements are unlawful under the Competition Law, Mexican courts must undertake an economic analysis similar to that employed by U.S. courts.[57]

5.28 The Competition Law also introduces provisions on mergers and acquisitions (concentrations). A concentration is defined as any merger, acquisition, consolidation or any other act that combines corporations, associations, shares, assets, or trusts between competitors, customers, suppliers, or other business entities.[58] The elements of proof necessary to characterise a concentration as anti-competitive turn on the existence of substantial power over the relevant market, the degree of concentration in the relevant market, and other factors to be included in the Competition Law regulations.[59]

Finally, the Competition Law creates the Federal Competition Commission (FCC), an independent administrative enforcement agency charged with conducting investigations, issuing administrative rulings and enforcing the

[56] See Mexican Competition Law, see para. 5.26, n. 51, Art. 10.

[57] See "Report of the ABA Task Force", see para. 5.26, n. 51, at 61–62. Elements of proof include: (i) that the alleged company or person had substantial power over the relevant market, and (ii) that the company or person intended to harm the competition processes in Mexico. "Substantial power" is determined by factors such as: (i) market share and whether the entity has the ability to engage in unilateral price fixing or to otherwise restrict access to the market without actual or potential competitors being able to refute that ability; (ii) the existence of barriers to market entry and possibilities of altering those barriers; (iii) the existence of and relative market power of the competitors; (iv) the parties' access to sources of input; (v) recent activity and conduct; and (vi) other criteria to be established in the Competition Law Regulations. Mexican Competition Law, see para. 5.26, n. 51, Art. 13. "Relevant market" is determined by: (i) the potential of substituting the good or service through other suppliers, whether foreign or national, and considering technological aspects, consumer input in the substitute good or service, and the time required to effectuate the substitution; (ii) the cost of moving substitute goods across geographic areas and the time required for them to enter a market; (iii) the costs of potential buyers to reach other markets; and (iv) tariffs or other trade restrictions that limit consumer access to alternative sources of supply or limit the provider's access to other customers. *id.* Art. 12.

[58] See Mexican Competition Law, see para. 5.26, n. 51, Art. 16. See also Leonel Pereznieto Castro, "Comments on Mexican Economic Competition Legislation with Regard to Monopolistic Practices and Mergers",(1999) 6 Sw. J.L. & Trade Am. 307.

[59] See Mexican Competition Law, see para. 5.26, n. 51, Art. 18. The Competition Law contains notification procedures for: (1) any merger, consolidation, or acquisition that exceeds $55 million or more, (2) transactions involving the acquisition of 35% or more of the assets or shares of another entity with assets or sales in excess of $55 million, or (3) when the merging entities' joint assets or annual sales exceed $220 million and the transaction involves the additional accumulation of assets or shares of $22 million or more. See *id.* Art. 20. See also Rogelio Lopez-Velarde and Augustin Berdega-Prieto, "Antitrust Enforcement in Mexico", Int'l Fin. L. Rev., Sept. 1994, at 34–35.

Competition Law.[60] The FCC is empowered to impose civil penalties and enjoin anti-competitive market practices without intervention of the Mexican courts. FCC rulings may be challenged through judicial review.

Of additional value to developing countries and LDCs looking to adopt competition legislation is the work of UNCTAD on its model law on competition, together with commentaries.[61]

B. A WTO Framework Agreement on Core Principles

5.29 Harmonisation of substantive competition laws may be a laudable goal, but it will be politically impossible to achieve in the near term and would be unenforceable without binding WTO dispute settlement. The practical difficulties of harmonisation are noted in the 2000 Report by the ABA Sections of Antitrust law and International Law and Practice:

> [T]here is a real risk that an ambitious harmonization project might fail to produce consensus as to any common standard. Alternatively, the need to achieve consensus in the face of real differences in views might result in adopting principles of such a level of generality as to be meaningless. Potentially more troubling, nations that effectively enforce their competition laws in a manner designed to maximize consumer welfare might find themselves pressured to accept principles of law with which they do not agree; if they acceded, this would degrade their national laws or lead to non-compliance.
>
> In other words, "harmonization" may not be a good in and of itself. The benefits of harmonization we have considered all have assumed that the single law is optimal. That assumption does not necessarily hold. Some would argue that an optimal law should be neither unduly regulatory nor insufficiently interventionist, and the procedural system employed should be the least costly alternative consistent with those goals. That is not the necessary result of harmonization efforts, as recent experience confirms.[62]

Moreover, changing the law is not enough to eliminate international tensions over cross-border competition law disputes. Competition law is more than just the text of a statute, a code provision, or an administrative regulation. Competition law outcomes

> are also the result of the interweaving of . . . the means of handling work, doing analyses, and interacting with sister agencies. Thus, changing the law is not enough to accomplish full harmonization because the 'production technology' of antitrust policy is not solely contained in the law.[63]

[60] See Mexican Competition Law, see para. 5.26, n. 51, Art. 23. The FCC is comprised of 5 commissioners appointed by the Chief Executive for 10 year terms, subject to renewal, and is vested with broad powers to enforce the Competition Law. See *id.* Arts. 24–26.

[61] The UNCTAD Model Law is available at http://www.unctad.org/en/subsites/cpolicy/index.htm.

[62] American Bar Ass'n, *Report of the Sections of Antitrust Law and International Law and Practice on the Internationalization of Competition Law Rules: Coordination and Convergence* 69 (2000) (hereinafter Report on Coordination and Convergence).

[63] Dennis A. Yao & Joseph G. Krauss, "Prospects for Harmonization of United States and European Union Antitrust Laws Concerning International Strategic Alliances", in *International Harmonization of Competition Laws*, see para. 5.06, n. 7, at 427, 451.

5.30 A less ambitious, but perhaps more realistic, alternative to a WTO agreement on the harmonisation of national competition laws with minimum RBP standards and binding supranational dispute settlement would be a framework agreement based on core principles without binding dispute settlement.[64] A framework agreement would not specify or require WTO members to introduce any comprehensive competition legislation or specific rules, but would instead prescribe principles to be followed when a member introduces competition legislation. Under a framework agreement on core principles, WTO members would be required to:

(1) enact competition legislation reflecting specific core principles on competition policy;

(2) establish an independent, properly staffed, and adequately funded national enforcement authority whose processes are transparent; and

(3) abide by the GATT core non-discrimination principles of MFN treatment, national treatment, and transparency.

The framework agreement would borrow from bilateral co-operation agreements and the work of the OECD by including provisions on traditional comity and positive comity, notification of investigations, international co-operation in cross-border investigations and the exchange of information.[65] There would be no dispute settlement at the supranational level, although the non-adversarial review processes under the Trade Policy Review Mechanism and/or by Working Parties could prove useful.[66]

Specifically, the framework agreement would contain the following non-exhaustive list of core principles:

1. National treatment.

5.31 Competition laws, their enforcement and their administration would not discriminate, *de facto* or *de jure*, between domestic and foreign firms' goods, services, or investments.

[64] See, *e.g.* WTO, "Working Group on the Interaction between Trade and Competition Policy, Communication from the European Community and Its Member States", *A Multilateral Framework Agreement on Competition Policy*, WT/WGTCP/W/152 (Sept. 25, 2000). Regarding the nomenclature, an agreement based on core principles, as opposed to an agreement on core or minimum standards, would delineate fundamental principles of general application. A core or minimum standards agreement, on the other hand, would set forth detailed, specific competition law commitments that must be applied by members and the manner in which they are to be applied. Between core principles and core standards is a middle position described as a core approach that lists criteria or objectives without delineating how they would be applied. See OECD, Joint Group on Trade and Competition, "Outline of (A) Core Principles, Common Approaches and Common Standards and (B) Bilateral and Multilateral Approaches", at 4–5, COM/TD/DAFFE/CLP(98)97/Final (Oct. 13, 1999) [hereinafter "Outline of Core Principles"]. Of course, a competition policy agreement could be a blend of core principles, standards, and approaches.

[65] For a similar proposal, see Fox, see para. 5.02, n. 3, at 30–31.

[66] For a description of a model multilateral framework agreement, see "Outline of Core Principles", see para. 5.30, n. 64, at 12.

2. *Most-favoured-nation treatment.*

5.32 Competition laws, their enforcement, and their administration would not discriminate, *de jure*, among foreign firms' goods, services or investments. Given the discretionary nature of competition law enforcement, *de facto* discrimination would not be prohibited. It would seem to be the case that the unconditional MFN obligation would automatically extend the commitments made in bilateral antitrust co-operation and mutual assistance agreements on traditional comity and positive comity; co-operation in and co-ordination of competition law enforcement; and exchange of information, including confidential information, to all WTO members not parties to the bilateral agreement. The same would be true for regional agreements unless excepted under some provision analogous to GATT Article XXIV or GATS Article V on customs unions and free trade areas. Consequently, whether and how bilateral agreements, as well as regional competition policy agreements, should be blended or folded into a multilateral WTO competition policy agreement through unconditional MFN deserves careful consideration.

5.33 The alternatives to absorbing bilateral co-operation agreements into a multilateral agreement are either:

(1) to grandfather bilateral agreements, or

(2) make the MFN commitment conditional, so that members who are not parties to a bilateral agreement can only complain of an MFN violation if they have first made reciprocal commitments *vis-à-vis* the responding member.

Similarly, the alternatives to a multilateral agreement that absorbs regional antitrust co-operation agreements are either:

(1) to make the MFN commitment conditional, or

(2) to exempt regional agreements by extending GATT Article XXIV to include competition policy agreements.

3. *Transparency.*

5.34 The term "transparency" refers to the degree to which WTO members make publicly available their rules and regulations affecting trade, the method by which those rules and regulations are promulgated and the manner in which internal rules and regulations are enforced. There can be little question that the smooth functioning of a multilateral trade system requires transparency of the trade regulations and measures adopted by its members. To that end, GATT Article X, *Publication and Administration of Trade Regulations*, requires the prompt publication of all laws, regulations, administrative rulings, and judicial decisions of general application affecting trade.[67] The obligation applies both *ex ante*, so that businesses know under what legal conditions they must operate before they enter a market, and *ex post*, so that they are made aware of enforcement decisions.

In addition to the general obligations contained in GATT Article X, the following transparency provisions should be made explicit in a competition policy framework agreement:

- Laws and regulations on restrictive business practices, including cartels, horizontal agreements, vertical relationships, abuse of dominant position, and mergers and acquisitions, are to made publicly available and a designated contact or enquiry point within the country is to be established. Modifications or amendments to laws and regulations are to be published regularly. Administrative guidelines on enforcement policy and enforcement priorities are to be published.
- All industries, sectors, or activities exempted from the competition laws or subject to special rules are to be identified and exemption criteria published. If current competition law has any gaps in coverage, such gaps are to be identified.
- All dispositive administrative decisions by national enforcement authorities and relevant judicial opinions are to be published.
- Consistent with Article X:1, business confidential information and trade secrets gathered during an investigation are to be protected from unauthorised disclosure.

4. *The Content and Coverage of Competition Laws.*

5.35 While avoiding the detail of an agreement on minimum RBP standards, the framework agreement would nevertheless require the adoption and implementation of a comprehensive national competition law regime. WTO members would be required to enact the following:

- As part of a competition law package, members must enact a competition law or amend existing law stating that the objectives of

[67] In the *Kodak-Fuji Film* dispute, the United States maintained that Japan enforced the Premiums Law and the Retailers Fair Competition Code, as well as the Large Stores Law, primarily through informal, unpublished enforcement actions in a manner inconsistent with Article X:1. The panel noted: "In our view, it stands to reason that inasmuch as the Article X:1 requirement applies to all administrative rulings of general application, it also should extend to administrative rulings in individual cases where such rulings establish or revise principles or criteria applicable in future cases. At the same time, we consider that it is incumbent upon the United States in this case to clearly demonstrate the existence of such unpublished administrative rulings in individual matters which establish or revise principles applicable in future cases". Report of the WTO Panel, "Japan—Measures Affecting Consumer Photographic Film and Paper", WT/DS44/R, para. 10.388 (adopted April 22, 1998) (hereinafter "*Kodak-Fuji Film Dispute*"). The panel found "that the United States has failed [to] demonstrate the existence of any such administrative rulings by any of the councils, establishing or modifying criteria applicable in future cases, the non-publication of which could be viewed as a violation of Article X:1." *id.* para. 10.396.

the law are, *inter alia*, to ensure market access for goods and services regardless of origin, and identifying categories of anti-competitive practices to which the law applies, namely, horizontal restraints (especially hard-core cartels [68]), vertical restraints, abuse of a dominant position and mergers and acquisitions. Here, the distinction between a framework agreement and a minimum standards agreement blurs if the framework agreement sets forth specific criteria for judging the anti-competitive effects of certain proscribed conduct, *e.g.* vertical restraints that restrict market access, unless they are reasonably related to the lawful realisation of cost-reducing or output-enhancing efficiencies; and mergers and acquisitions that threaten to substantially weaken or destroy competition.[69] To the extent that agreement can be reached on specific RBPs beyond the four broad categories described above, the WTO members should do so.

Competition legislation must include provisions on remedies that are adequate to compensate for past violations, and penalties that are adequate to deter future violations. Certain anti-competitive conduct should be criminalised, such as horizontal restraints involving price fixing, bid rigging, output restrictions, and division of markets.[70]

- Members commit to a standstill on new sectoral exclusions and to rollback existing exclusions. Government-owned monopolies and state-authorised monopolies are to be identified and made subject to a requirement that they not abuse their dominant position in the provision of their monopoly good or service by discriminating among purchasers. Regulated industries that are exempt from competition laws must also be identified.
- Competition authorities are to be independent, provided with adequate and competent staff and resources and empowered to seek and demand information necessary for a complete investigation of anti-competitive practices.
- Subject to specific exceptions, competition legislation applies equally to privately and publicly owned enterprises.

5. *Effective Enforcement Procedures and Meaningful Remedies.*

5.36 Effective enforcement mechanisms are a hedge against the risk of under-enforcement or non-enforcement by national competition law enforcement authorities. The following provisions would be included in the framework agreement:

[68] See Recommendation Concerning Effective Action Against "Hard Core" Cartels, see para. 5.10, n. 15.

[69] For a criticism that a multilateral framework approach to competition policy as described here as being unduly vague, see Tarullo, see para. 5.10, n. 18, at 490 ("A rule stating that 'anticompetitive vertical restraints should be prohibited' fails to deal with the important question of what specific behavior should be prohibited.").

[70] TRIPS Art. 61 obligates members at a minimum to adopt criminal procedures and penalties in cases of wilful trademark counterfeiting or copyright piracy on a commercial scale. Penalties must be meaningful, with fines and/or imprisonment sufficient to serve as a deterrent, "consistently with the level of penalties applied for crimes of a corresponding gravity." *id.*

- Each WTO member must provide fair and transparent enforcement procedures, including access by foreign firms to effective judicial procedures for competition law enforcement. Foreign firms are to have access to domestic administrative agencies and courts on a non-discriminatory basis. This obligation does not require that members establish a judicial system for competition law enforcement distinct from general law enforcement, however.[71] Such procedures must not erect unreasonable time limits, cause unwarranted delays, or be unnecessarily complicated or costly.[72]
- Foreign firms and WTO members have the right to petition enforcement authorities for an explanation of why action has not been taken on specific matters affecting international trade and market access.
- Foreign firms have standing to bring suit in national courts to seek remedies for injury suffered as a result of RBPs. Remedies are to be expeditious and meaningful, so that current RBPs are prevented and future RBPs are deterred.[73] Available remedies are to include injunctive relief, the award of compensatory damages and the award of attorneys' fees. In the case of abuse of judicial procedures, defendants are to be provided a remedy if they were wrongfully enjoined or were wrongfully sued by another private party.
- All parties to administrative and judicial proceedings are to have certain minimum due process guarantees, including:
  (1) a means to identify and protect confidential information from unauthorised disclosure;[74]
  (2) timely written notice to defendants of the claims made;[75]
  (3) the right to be represented by independent legal counsel;[76]
  (4) mandatory production of evidence in the possession of an opposing party,[77] with administrative and judicial authorities being empowered to render a decision on the basis of the evidence presented by the complaining party in the event of non-production by the responding party;[78] and
  (5) the right to a reasoned administrative decision or judicial opinion.[79]

Decisions on the merits are to be in writing and based solely on evidence with regard to which parties were afforded an opportunity to be heard.

[71] Compare TRIPS Art. 41.5.
[72] Compare TRIPS Art. 41.2.
[73] A possible drafting model is TRIPS Art. 41.1, which provides in part: "Members shall ensure that enforcement procedures . . . are available under their law so as to permit effective action against any act of infringement of intellectual property rights covered by this Agreement, including expeditious remedies to prevent infringements and remedies which constitute a deterrent to further infringements".
[74] Compare TRIPS Art. 42.
[75] Compare *id.*
[76] Compare *id.*
[77] Compare TRIPS Art. 43.1.
[78] Compare TRIPS Art. 43.2.
[79] Compare TRIPS Art. 41.4.

- In the case of final administrative determinations, there must be an opportunity for judicial review.[80] If initial decisions are made by a member's courts, there must be at least one opportunity for appellate review of legal issues involving the merits that were decided in that initial judicial proceeding.

6. *International Co-operation and Co-ordination.*

5.37 Borrowing from bilateral co-operation agreements, WTO members would commit to co-operating in cross-border investigations by exchanging information and to co-ordinating enforcement activities. Such co-operation would be both case-specific and general, and would include the following:

- In connection with the principle of traditional comity, members agree:
  (1) to notify other members when an enforcement proceeding may have an effect on the other member's important interests, and
  (2) to give full and sympathetic consideration to ways of fulfilling its enforcement mandate without harming those important interests. Members would also agree to give consideration to adopting other comity principles.[81]
- Members agree to adopt the principle of positive comity and
  (1) give full and sympathetic consideration to another member's request that it open or expand an investigation in order to remedy conduct that is occurring in the requested member's territory and that is having a substantial and adverse effect in the requesting member's territory, and
  (2) take whatever remedial action the requested member deems appropriate, considering its legitimate interests.
- Members agree to co-operate with other members in cross-border investigations by sharing confidential information, subject to safeguards against unauthorised disclosure to third parties and consistency of the request with the requested member's national interests.

[80] Compare *id.*

[81] For example, Article VI(3) of the 1991 E.U.-U.S. Antitrust Co-operation Agreement lists the following 6 factors to guide the parties' comity analysis: (1) the relative significance to the anti-competitive activities involved of conduct within the enforcing party's territory as compared to conduct within the other party's territory; (2) the presence or absence of a purpose on the part of those engaged in the anti-competitive activities to affect consumers, suppliers, or competitors within the enforcing party's territory; (3) the relative significance of the effects of the anti-competitive activities on the enforcing party's interests as compared to the effects on the other party's interests; (4) the existence or absence of reasonable expectations that would be furthered or defeated by the enforcement activities; (5) the degree of conflict or consistency between the enforcement activities and the other party's laws or articulated economic policies; and (6) the extent to which enforcement activities of the other party with respect to the same person, including judgments or undertakings resulting from such activities, may be affected. See "Agreement between the Government of the United States and the Commission of the European Communities Regarding the Application of Their Competition Laws", art. VI(3), Sept. 23, 1991,U.S.-E.C., reprinted in (1991) 30 Int'l Legal Materials 1491.

7. Developing Countries and Economies in Transition.

5.38

- Developed countries would commit to providing technical assistance to developing countries and countries with transition economies.[82]
- Developing countries and transition economies would agree to the core principles, but their commitments would be staged over an appropriate transition period.[83]

8. Dispute Settlement.

5.39 At a minimum, a member would be required to consult with any other member upon request concerning measures affecting the operation of the agreement. This obligation would include a duty to consult in the event of an alleged failure of a member to adopt and/or enforce any of the core principles of the agreement. Whether unresolved disputes over the alleged failure to adopt or enforce core principles should then be referred to a WTO dispute settlement panel under the Dispute Settlement Understanding would be one of the more contentious issues facing negotiators. On the one hand, it would be a fairly straightforward matter to determine whether a member had or had not enacted national legislation in conformity with the agreement. However, resolving questions of an alleged failure to enforce competition law in individual cases will often turn on the determination of highly fact-intensive, complex issues of competition law, *e.g.* determining whether a firm, such as Microsoft, has abused its dominant position, or whether a vertical or horizontal restraint satisfies the rule of reason. Such panel proceedings would involve developing sufficient facts to establish a competition law violation, a necessary predicate to proving a member's failure to enforce.

5.40 Not only are WTO panels ill-equipped to handle this type of inquiry but an affirmative WTO panel ruling would rub a sensitive national nerve; could effectively eviscerate any discretionary authority that national enforcement authorities retain over whether or not to proceed with an investigation in a particular case; and would mean second-guessing their performance in cases where an investigation was undertaken, but insufficient evidence of prohibited anti-competitive practices was uncovered. It is difficult to imagine any country which would be willing to accept the judgment of a WTO panel that national competition law enforcement authorities botched an investigation in any given case. The OECD's Joint Group on Trade and Competition concurs, concluding in 1999 that:

---

[82] TRIPS Art. 67 obligates developed countries to render technical assistance to developing countries in bringing the latter's laws into compliance with the Agreement.

[83] Developing countries received special transition periods in several of the Uruguay Round multilateral trade agreements. For example, Art. 14 of the Agreement on Sanitary and Phytosanitary Measures gave developing and least-developed countries extended transition periods of 2 years and 5 years, respectively, within which to bring their domestic measures affecting importation or imported products into compliance with that Agreement. Under Art. 5.2 of the Agreement on Trade-Related Investment Measures, developing countries were given 5 years to eliminate all prohibited TRIMs, and least-developed countries were given 7 years.

> [t]here is now consensus that dispute settlement should not be available to review individual cases. . . . [N]o competition agency has supported having individual competition case decisions being reviewed under the WTO's dispute settlement mechanism.[84]

Participants in a 1999 OECD conference on trade and competition policy agreed that a multilateral dispute settlement process is not appropriate for the review of individual competition law cases due to problems of national sovereignty, the complex and fact-intensive nature of individual competition cases and the application of judgment in the assessment of those facts.[85] Two national enforcement authorities could legitimately reach different conclusions even when applying similar methodologies or norms.

5.41 In the *Kodak-Fuji Film* dispute, for example, if a WTO agreement on competition policy had been in place, would the Japan Fair Trade Commission (JFTC) have had the burden of showing that it was unable to uncover the existence of any RBPs by Fuji? As noted in the WTO panel report in *Kodak-Fuji Film*,

> single brand wholesale distribution is the common market structure—indeed the norm—in most major national film markets, including the US market. It is unclear why the same economic forces acting to promote single brand wholesale distribution in the United States would not also exist in Japan.[86]

Would the JFTC have the burden of showing that single-brand film distribution resulted in efficiency savings? In addition, the JFTC's hypothetical investigation would undoubtedly have included obtaining business confidential documents from Fuji. Because those documents could not be disclosed, would the JFTC be able to meets its burden? If the dispute resolution provisions of a WTO competition policy agreement required that confidential business information be disclosed to a WTO dispute settlement panel, the business community would probably balk.[87]

---

[84] "Outline of Core Principles", see para. 5.30, n. 64, at 4, 6. See Brittan, see para. 5.10, n. 15, at 35 ("it would be inappropriate to introduce a dispute settlement review of individual cases"). It also is highly doubtful that the current DSU timetable of 9 to 12 months for the issuance of a panel or Appellate Body report would be adequate in these circumstances. See DSU Art. 20.

[85] See "Conference on Trade and Competition Policies: Exploring the Ways Forward, Summary", see para. 5.21, n. 39, at 22.

[86] "*Kodak-Fuji Film Dispute*", see para. 5.34, n. 67, para. 10.381.

[87] See Marsden, see para. 5.09, n. 14, at 31–32. Professor Marsden offers the following hypothetical case under a WTO competition policy agreement based on market access principles: "A multilateral standard to enforce one's antitrust laws in accordance with market access principles might have allowed the EU to complain to the WTO that American toleration of Boeing's long-term supply agreements was preventing Airbus Industrie from accessing the major American airlines. There would be no need for the EU to wait for Boeing to acquire another supplier and thereby trigger European jurisdiction under the Merger Control Regulation. Faced with such a complaint, American antitrust authorities would have to explain why they allowed the agreements. Unlike Europe, however, where vertical restraints of this magnitude have to be cleared in advance by the Commission, the U.S. authorities might not even have a file to show the WTO. The FTC might have to scramble to produce evidence of the estimated savings these contracts produced for Boeing and the airlines and thus explain why no challenge was brought under American law. Win or lose, governments around the world would take note and realize that it would be in their interest to tighten up their approach to such conduct. Regulatory scrutiny of many methods of vertical integration might increase without any evidence of a change in the nature or effect of the practices themselves, let alone another evolution in economic analysis. *id.* at 32.

5.42 At least two ways of cutting this Gordian knot have been suggested. The first alternative is substantive. Rather than obligate members to investigate and prosecute every alleged instance of an RBP that inhibits or prevents cross-border trade, a WTO framework agreement on competition policy could merely require that members enact a comprehensive competition law regime, establish an enforcement authority to administer the law and enforce the law in good faith instead.[88]

The difficulty with this proposal, however, in the case of bad faith enforcement is whether the complainant's prima facie case would include a showing, for example, that the JFTC has acted in bad faith with regard to pursuing an alleged RBP by Fuji? How does one prove a negative? Or would good faith be an affirmative defence that Japan would have the burden of proving?[89] From an evidentiary standpoint it makes a difference. Assuming a satisfactory answer to this important burden-of-proof question, adopting a good faith enforcement standard would defuse certain intractable cases, such as those where the rule of reason is applied. Reasonable minds can differ, and two national competition law enforcement authorities can legitimately disagree whether a given restraint's pro-competitive benefits outweigh its anti-competitive effects. Even if two national enforcement authorities apply the same or similar methodologies and norms, the conclusions they reach can differ.

5.43 The second alternative is a procedural one. It would establish non-binding peer review of members' competition laws under the Trade Policy Review Mechanism and non-binding resolution by a WTO Working Party assisted by a panel of competition law experts of alleged private anti-competitive conduct that prevented market access.[90] This suggestion, in essence, creates a competition advocacy role for the WTO, but does not entrust it with any authority to resolve disputes. The General Council, serving in its capacity as the Trade Policy Review Body (TPRB), would carry out trade and competition policy reviews.[91] The frequency of such reviews depends on the member's share of world trade in a recent representative period. Members

[88] See Hudec, "A WTO Perspective", see para. 5.03, n. 4, at 95.

[89] The issue of proving bad faith versus proving good faith is important enough to have been decided by U.S. Supreme Court in the civil rights context. See, *e.g. Gomez v. Toledo*, 446 U.S. 635 (1980) (good faith is an affirmative defence that defendant must plead).

[90] See Trade Policy Review Mechanism, Annex 3 of the Agreement Establishing the World Trade Organisation. Annex 3 of the Agreement Establishing the World Trade Organisation (the WTO Agreement) creates the Trade Policy Review Mechanism (TPRM). The TPRM continues the surveillance mechanism of national trade policies provisionally established in 1988 during the Uruguay Round and made permanent by the WTO Agreement. See WTO Agreement art. III:4 & Annex 3. The purpose of the TPRM is to ensure members' adherence to the rules, disciplines, and commitments made under the WTO multilateral trade agreements and, where applicable, the plurilateral trade agreements. See Trade Policy Review Mechanism s. A(i). The TPRM's *raison d'être* is enhanced transparency of members' trade policies and calls for the regular review of all WTO members' trade policies to assess their impact on the functioning of the GATT—WTO system. It is not an enforcement or dispute settlement mechanism.
The E.U. has made a similar proposal. See WTO, Working Group on the Interaction between Trade and Competition Policy, Communication from the European Community and Its Member States, "A Multilateral Framework Agreement on Competition Policy", at 10, WT/WGTCP/W/152 (Sept. 25, 2000).

[91] See TPRM s. C(i).

that rank in the top four on the basis of this criterion are subject to bi-annual reviews. These four countries are, of course, the Quad members. The next 16 are reviewed every four years. The remaining members are reviewed every six years, although a longer period may be fixed for least-developed country members.[92]

5.44 Members are required to report regularly to the TPRB describing the members' trade policies and practices. This report could be expanded to describe the members' competition laws and enforcement record during the review period. Reviews are conducted on the basis of a member's policy statement and a report prepared by the Secretariat's Trade Policy Review Division. The report examines the member's trade policies and practices and describes the member's institutions responsible for trade policy. The report would be expanded to describe the member's institutions responsible for competition law enforcement. A review meeting then is held with the TPRB. The member's policy statement, the Secretariat's report, the minutes of the TPRB meeting, and the Chairperson's concluding remarks are delivered at the meeting and are published thereafter.[93]

As a corollary to TPRM review, and to improve transparency of members' trade regulations, WTO members are required to notify the WTO Secretariat of the adoption of trade measures affecting the operation of GATT 1994.[94] The Indicative List of Notifiable Measures lists 20 different types of trade measures that are to be notified to the Secretariat and recorded in a Central Registry of Notifications. To this list could be added members' competition laws and policies.

5.45 In addition to periodic TPRM check-ups, non-binding resolution of specific trade-competition law claims would be referred to a Working Party following a member's complaint that private anti-competitive conduct in an export market has prevented market access. Unlike a WTO panel proceeding which is adversarial, a Working Party is an ad hoc inquisitorial body open to all interested WTO members and established to study and report on the issues submitted to it for its consideration. It submits a report of its investigation to the General Council. A Working Party has been used in the past to resolve a non-violation nullification or impairment dispute.[95]

5.46 Although non-binding review by a Working Party or the TPRB would not be an enforcement mechanism, bringing to light inadequate competition law enforcement in a non-adversarial setting might prod national enforcement authorities into pursuing the RBPs in question. The odds of a positive response from competition enforcement authorities is, of course, impossible to predict. WTO second-guessing might be completely unacceptable to some national enforcement authorities because it would be anathema

---

[92] See *id.* s. C(ii).

[93] Trade policy reviews are available from the WTO's website at http://www.wto.otg/wto/Trade_Reviews/tp.htm.

[94] See WTO General Council, "Decision on Notification Procedures" (1995). See also "Report of the Working Group, Notification Obligations and Procedures", G/L/112 (1996).

[95] See "Report of the Working Party, Australian Subsidy on Ammonium Sulphate", BISD II/188, 191, para. 8 (1950).

to the deeply-seated concept of prosecutorial discretion. Nevertheless, the resources needed to undertake such a review successfully would not be greater, and could be substantially less, than those needed to prosecute a trade-competition law dispute before a WTO panel or the Appellate Body.[96]

Assuming that a critical mass of support builds for a multilateral framework agreement, it is far from clear that a framework agreement would be effective in remedying international competition law disputes or in defusing international tensions. The inclusion or exclusion of a binding supranational dispute settlement mechanism may be the Achilles' heel of any multilateral agreement proposal. Leaving it exclusively to national authorities to determine whether to bring an enforcement action would defuse the issues of national sovereignty and prosecutorial discretion, but would open the door to charges of under-enforcement or non-enforcement. The suggestion to permit aggrieved WTO members and foreign firms to petition national enforcement authorities to take action against an alleged RBP is one way of responding to the issue of under-enforcement. This suggestion is, of course, at the heart of positive comity. A variation on this theme would give either or both the aggrieved WTO member and/or foreign firm the right to bring an enforcement action in the courts of the country where the alleged RBPs have occurred.[97]

5.47 The first suggestion is of questionable efficacy. On this score, the lesson of the *Kodak-Fuji Film* dispute is instructive. Under the Japanese Antimonopoly Law, any private party may petition the JFTC alleging a violation of that Law. The JFTC must then conduct a preliminary investigation to determine whether there is probable cause to proceed with an enforcement action. Kodak did not file a petition with the JFTC before filing its section 301 petition with the USTR, claiming that such action would be futile.[98] Eventually, Kodak did file a complaint with the JFTC, but the JFTC found no evidence of a competition law violation.[99] Despite this report, at the urging of Kodak the USTR pursued the WTO panel proceeding to conclusion.

5.48 What if the JFTC had refused to conduct an investigation of Kodak's petition, citing a case overload, or did conduct an investigation that Kodak considered to be superficial or perfunctory? The suggestion has been made

[96] It has been suggested that the panel's terms of reference would be (1) whether the alleged RBPs exist, (2) whether national enforcement authorities have a history of enforcing competition laws in the industry in question, (3) whether the competitive conditions in the industry being investigated were more exclusionary than in other countries, (4) whether market access is blocked due to the alleged RBPs or because of other factors, such as a foreign firm's lack of competitiveness in the industry, and (5) whether the alleged RBPs are lawful in other countries with antitrust laws and enforcement machinery. See William H. Barringer, "Competition Policy and Cross Border Dispute Resolution: Lessons Learned from the U.S.-Japan Film Dispute", (1998) 6 Geo. Mason L. Rev. 459, 476.

[97] See Joanna Shelton, "Competition Policy: What Chance for International Rules?" (1999) 2 OECD J. Competition L. & Pol'y 57, 64.

[98] See Barringer, see para. 5.46, n. 96, at 463–64.

[99] See "Kodak Files Protest With Japan Agency In Dispute With Fuji", *Wall Street Journal*, Aug. 8, 1996, at B5; Toshio Aritake, "Japan Film Market Passes JFTC Muster; But U.S. Is Pursuing Its Case at WTO", (July 30, 1997) 14 Int'l Trade Rep. (BNA) 1319; Toshio Aritake, "Japan Fair Trade Agency to Conduct Follow-Up Survey of Photo Film Market", (April 22, 1998) 15 Int'l Trade Rep. (BNA) 679.

that such a refusal to conduct an investigation should be subject to judicial review in the courts of the national enforcement authority.[1] What would be the standard of review? Assuming the standard of review is abuse of discretion, it is hard to imagine any national court second-guessing a decision not to proceed by the agency charged with the responsibility of administering the national competition laws, not to mention completely undermining the principle of prosecutorial discretion.

5.49 The alternative suggestion to, in effect, privatise competition law enforcement is more promising. Such privatisation already exists in the United States[2] and in other OECD countries where private parties—foreign and domestic—have standing to bring a private antitrust action in national courts. In countries where a private right of action does not currently exist, it will be necessary to overcome the notion that competition law enforcement is an exercise of governmental power reserved exclusively to government officials. While the right to file a private competition law action is not universal, it could be included in the core principles of the framework agreement.

5.50 At first glance, allowing private persons injured by anti-competitive practices to sue in the national courts of the alleged violator would seem to offer one of the best methods for addressing RBPs. If the economic stakes are high enough, then foreign firms would seem to have the economic incentive to bring a private enforcement action. However, the realities are much different. The alleged victim of RBPs has the burden of proving the unlawful RBP. As noted in connection with the resolution of individual competition law cases by WTO dispute panels, competition law cases are prolix, fact-intensive inquiries that involve complex economic and legal issues. Evidence of certain types of RBPs, *e.g.* collusive behaviour, is difficult to obtain, particularly for private parties filing suit in countries other than the United States where pre-trial discovery is limited. Even with the availability of pre-trial discovery, as is known in the American system of civil justice, proof is still not easy. Closely related to the problem of proving the existence of unlawful conduct is the problem of proving damages.

If a private action is brought following a successful proceeding by national enforcement authorities, then the private party should only have to prove injury and causation, formidable obstacles in themselves to overcome.

C. The Structure of Negotiations on a Multilateral Competition Policy Agreement

5.51 Given the wide divergence among national competition laws and policies, the prospects for successfully negotiating any type of WTO agreement on competition policy seem remote, at best, if the negotiations deal exclusively with the subject of a competition policy agreement. The structure

---

[1] See Shelton, see para. 5.46, n. 97, at 64 ("a refusal to investigate could be subject to appeal in the courts"); Brittan, see para. 5.10, n. 15, at 33–34. A variation of this theme this involves positive comity. Rather than the foreign firm petitioning directly to the national enforcement agency, the firm would instead approach its own government and request that it espouse its claim before those national authorities. See *id.* at 65.

[2] See 15 U.S.C. ss. 12–27.

of negotiations has to be wide ranging so that negotiators who want such an agreement are in a position to offer concessions on other items in exchange for competition policy concessions. Unless negotiations on a competition policy agreement are bundled with other substantive negotiations on issues of cross-cutting interest, negotiations on a multilateral WTO agreement are doomed. Some countries will have much to gain from such an agreement, but other countries will undoubtedly perceive that they have much to lose. As noted by Professor Guzman, "These potential losers will refuse to join a cooperative agreement unless they receive some form of compensation."[3] Substantial cross-linkages are thus required if negotiations are to have any chance for success.

Linkage was certainly one of the hallmarks of the Uruguay Round negotiations, which explains how agreements could be reached on topics as diverse as trade in services and intellectual property rights; two areas that were completely outside the traditional GATT–WTO portfolio. In short, a condition precedent to a WTO agreement on competition policy is the launch of a WTO multilateral trade negotiation (MTN) round with an agenda that is modestly ambitious but that also includes bargaining chips.

5.52 With the failed launch of a new MTN round in Seattle in December 1999, one way to make negotiations on a competition policy agreement a part of a broader agenda is to fold the negotiations on trade in services and agricultural trade that are underway into a new trade round that includes competition policy on the agenda. If a new MTN round is launched eventually, then the advocates of a WTO competition policy agreement should renew their efforts to make competition policy an agenda item, just as they did prior to the debacle in Seattle.

5.53 It is important to remember, however, that the *raison d'être* of the GATT–WTO system is market access. Enhanced consumer welfare ideally will be a by-product of increased market access but the two are not necessarily in a cause-effect relationship. For example, exclusive distribution arrangements may be efficient and may enhance consumer welfare, but they also limit or foreclose the market access of competitors. Thus, serious doubts must be raised regarding the suitability of the WTO as a forum for negotiating an agreement on competition policy that would in the end be welfare enhancing not only for producers but for consumers as well.[4]

II. A WTO PLURILATERAL AGREEMENT ON COMPETITION POLICY

5.54 Any programme of competition law harmonisation at the multilateral level could be facilitated by prior, incremental steps at the plurilateral level. Negotiations on a plurilateral agreement are more likely to succeed than

[3] Guzman, see para. 5.21, n. 41, at 1542.
[4] See Bernard Hoekman, "Competition Policy and the Global Trading System", (1997) 20 World Economy 383.

a multilateral initiative if for no other reason than that the number of participating countries is fewer and the interests of the negotiating countries more closely aligned. A more modest co-operation initiative will make it easier for countries to find common ground and bridge gaps in areas of divergence regarding the goals and scope of competition policy and its implications for removing barriers to international trade.

A clear, but controversial, precedent for negotiating a WTO plurilateral agreement on competition policy is to be found in the Tokyo Round codes. As part of the Tokyo Round, nine side agreements or "codes" were concluded to which only a handful of GATT contracting parties acceded.[5] Most of those agreements were folded into the WTO and became part of the single undertaking or package deal approach of the WTO. Four exceptions were the Dairy, Bovine Meat, Civil Aircraft and Government Procurement Agreements. Of those four, only the Civil Aircraft and Government Procurement Agreements survive.

5.55 In lieu of attempting to conclude a multilateral agreement on competition policy, then, an alternative would be the plurilateral side agreement approach. A plurilateral agreement that required participation by WTO members accounting for 75 per cent of total world trade in goods and services, plus participation by all four Quad members, would include the important players in world trade and would remove the thorny issue of concluding a multilateral agreement with a host of developing and less-developed countries.[6] Building on the network of bilateral co-operation agreements that have been concluded between the United States and Canada, Japan and the E.U., a plurilateral approach could produce a coherent set of rules on conduct, as well as common procedural rules and enforcement standards to be applied by an international dispute settlement body. The final result would be a common approach on how best to address anti-competitive practices that threaten international trade, including horizontal and vertical restraints, abuse of a dominant position and common methodologies for merger evaluation.

5.56 Borrowing from the MERCOSUR experience and the U.S. bilateral antitrust co-operation agreements, an alternative plurilateral approach under WTO auspices would involve a co-operation programme with three implementation stages at the national level. The first stage would be the enactment of national competition laws containing the provisions required by the plurilateral agreement. That stage has been reached by the Quad. The second stage would be the creation of an autonomous and properly staffed national

[5] For a list of the Tokyo Round code signatories at the end of the Uruguay Round, see *U.S. Int'l Trade Comm'n, The Year in Trade 1993: Operation of the Trade Agreements Program* (USITC Pub. 2769 1994) 43–45.

[6] The Quad members accounted for 62% and 64% of total world trade in goods and services, respectively, in 1997. See "WTO Focus Newsletter", March 1998, at 6. Under Art. 18.2 of the UN Draft Convention on Restrictive Business Practices, the Draft Convention would not have entered into force until it had been accepted either by (a) 20 or more countries accounting for 65% or more of the total value of world imports and exports, or (b) countries accounting for 65% or more of the total value of world imports and exports, including six countries which individually accounted for 3% or more of such total value.

enforcement authority. Again, that stage has been reached by the Quad. The third stage would involve the establishment of transparent procedures and rules by national enforcement authorities, such as the publication of annual reports, guidelines for the private sector and consistent enforcement criteria. After those national laws and procedures are firmly in place, the parties would then implement the co-operation provisions of their agreement, the essentials terms of which would model the bilateral antitrust co-operation agreements entered into between the United States and Australia, Canada, the E.U. and Japan.

III. AN OECD AGREEMENT ON COMPETITION POLICY

5.57 An alternative to negotiating a plurilateral competition policy agreement under WTO auspices would be to negotiate such an agreement in the OECD. When trade figures for all OECD member countries were calculated, OECD countries accounted for 70 per cent of total world trade in goods in 1997, and 68.5 per cent of trade in services. Thus, while not accounting for all global trade in goods and services, OECD-member countries do account for a majority of all such trade.[7] More importantly, U.S. merchandise trade with the other three Quad members in 1998 accounted for over half (53 per cent) of its total merchandise trade in exports. When Mexico is included, that percentage increases to 64 per cent. On the import side of the merchandise trade ledger, the percentage of U.S. merchandise import trade with the other three Quad members in 1998 was 52 per cent. Adding Mexico, the percentage increases to 62 per cent. In addition, of the world's 100 largest non-financial transnational corporations, close to 90 per cent are located in the E.U., Japan and the United States.[8] Membership on the list of the 100 largest MNEs has changed little since 1990. Only five are not headquartered in Canada, the E.U., Japan, Mexico or the United States: Nestle, Roche Holding AG and Novartis in Switzerland; Daewoo Corp. in Korea; and Petroleos de Venezuela S.A. in Venezuela.[9] As a consequence, it seems natural that those countries with the most at stake in the international trade game would find it in their self-interest to attempt to strike a plurilateral deal on competition policy under OECD auspices.[10]

5.58 Given the strong business and trade relationship of OECD member countries, coupled with the large volume of studies and reports generated by the OECD on the relationship between trade and competition policy, the OECD would be a natural forum for undertaking negotiations on a multilateral competition policy agreement. The OECD's great strength in the

[7] See *U.S. Int'l Trade Comm'n, The Year in Trade 1998: Operation of the Trade Agreements Program 18* (USITC Pub. 3192 1999).
[8] See *UNCTAD, World Investment Report 1999*, at xvii.
[9] See UNCTAD, *World Investment Report 1998*, at 35–37, Table II.1.
[10] See Diane P. Wood, "The Impossible Dream: Real International Antitrust", (1999) U. Chi. Legal F. 277, 313 (proposing a trilateral antitrust co-operation agreement among Canada, the E.U., and the United States as an initial framework for a multilateral agreement). Some observers are sceptical that even a scaled—down, plurilateral antitrust agreement among economically advanced countries is feasible. See Barringer, see para. 5.46, n. 96, at 476.

competition policy field is its ability to encourage soft harmonisation of competition law and policies among the OECD members. Unlike the WTO, the OECD would have the advantage of not being plagued with a market-access mandate that would muddy competition policy norms.[11]

One obvious institutional weakness of the OECD is that it lacks any enforcement mechanism.[12] As a consequence, any OECD competition policy agreement would use a consultative process to hash out competition law and policy disputes among the parties to it. Another weakness is the perception among non-member nations—chiefly developing countries—that the OECD is a rich countries' club. Moreover, the inability of the OECD to deliver the Multilateral Agreement on Investment "may have cast a shadow over its ability to serve as a forum for negotiating international agreements."[13] Despite this setback, the OECD is far and away the most experienced international organisation at addressing international competition policy issues.

[11] For the view that this would work to the OECD's disadvantage and create legitimacy problems, see Tarullo, see para. 5.10, n. 18, at 498 ("a different kind of legitimacy problem could arise, as companies [allegedly denied market access] complained that there was no effective institutional response to their difficulties").

[12] For further analysis of the pros and cons of an OECD agreement on competition policy, see Tarullo, see para. 5.10, n. 18, at 494–99.

[13] *International Competition Policy Advisory Committee to the Attorney General and Assistant Attorney General for Antitrust, Final Report* (2000) 258.

CHAPTER SIX

The Limits of Multilateralism

I. PRECONDITIONS TO NEGOTIATIONS ON A WTO AGREEMENT ON COMPETITION POLICY

6.01 Are existing GATT–WTO provisions on competition policy and anti-competitive conduct, complemented by the multilateral and plurilateral work of UNCTAD and the OECD, respectively, and supported by the growing network of bilateral antitrust co-operation agreements among the Quad members, adequate to ensure that private RBPs do not threaten the free flow of goods and services across national borders? Or are existing legal instruments so inadequate that a comprehensive approach is required? If a comprehensive, multilateral approach is needed, how can bilateral and regional co-operation agreements be used to facilitate and guide negotiations on a multilateral or plurilateral competition policy agreement? If a comprehensive, multilateral approach is required, should the WTO, the OECD, or some other international organisation sponsor the negotiations and administer the agreement?

6.02 Although a multilateral agreement on competition policy negotiated under the auspices of and administered by the WTO has its advocates, at present it remains an open question whether anti-competitive business practices that have international trade effects should be subject to WTO disciplines and referred to the WTO for resolution. Only after a consensus builds for a WTO-sponsored agreement on trade-related aspects of competition policy will it be appropriate and fruitful for the WTO members to tackle this subject. Not until the question shifts from whether the WTO should address this issue to how the WTO should deal with these issues will the time be ripe to broach the subject of negotiating a WTO multilateral agreement on competition policy.

6.03 Assuming that a consensus does eventually build for such an agreement, is a WTO competition policy agreement a solution in search of a problem? What practical problems are the proposed WTO competition rules supposed to solve? To what extent are purely private RBPs a significant barrier to market access? Are anti-competitive practices with cross-border effects all that prevalent? The scholarship on this question is divided and the evidence is largely anecdotal and conclusion drawing. For example, the 1998 WGTCP Report states that "[a] large number of specific examples of anti-competitive practices that affected international trade were provided by

Members and observer intergovernmental organizations."[1] That Report continues by citing examples of practices affecting market access, including

> actual cases of import cartels, international cartels that allocated national markets among participating firms, the unreasonable obstruction of parallel imports, control over importation facilities, exclusionary abuses of a dominant position and vertical market restraints that foreclosed markets to competitors, certain private standard-setting activities and other anti-competitive practices involving industry associations.[2]

One year later, however, the 1999 WGTCP Report added an important qualification to its 1998 assessment: "A few well-publicized multi-jurisdictional cases did not make such problems global nor did they make a case for a global solution."[3] The OECD Secretariat in1999 also cited the absence of reliable data on the scope of this problem:

> Given the lack of any measure or systematic data, anecdotes are relied upon. The survey data that was presented at the conference involved only a small number of respondents and could not be extrapolated. Given the lack of data, some suggested that there should be no presumption that the current regime is bad or needs changing.[4]

6.04 Scholarship is also divided, for example, over whether there has been an increase in international cartel activity since World War II or merely better detection of cartel behaviour by national enforcement authorities.[5] ICPAC concludes that whether RBPs with cross-border effects, especially international cartel activity, has increased or decreased during the twentieth century is not clear.[6] ICPAC adds that "[t]he clandestine nature of cartels makes it impossible to determine the truth, but the record shows that international cartels remain a real problem at this time."[7] Regardless of what the data reveal, ICPAC concludes that "seeking a binding world antitrust code and dispute resolution system is neither achievable nor advisable."[8]

---

[1] WTO, "Working Group on the Interaction between Trade and Competition Policy, Report (1998) of the Working Group on the Interaction between Trade and Competition Policy to the General Council", WT/WGTCP/2, at 28, para. 83 (Dec. 8, 1998) (hereinafter "WGTCP 1998 Report").

[2] *id.* at 28, para. 84.

[3] WTO, "Working Group on the Interaction between Trade and Competition Policy, Report (1999) of the Working Group on the Interaction between Trade and Competition Policy to the General Council", WT/WGTCP/3, at 18, para. 55 (Oct. 11, 1999) (hereinafter "WGTCP 1999 Report").

[4] OECD Secretariat, "Summary", in *Trade and Competition Policies: Exploring the Ways Forward* (OECD 1999) 12.

[5] Compare Kurt Rudolph Mirow & Harry Maurer, *Webs of Power: International Cartels and the World Economy* (1982) 8–9, and Maurice Guerrin & Georgios Kyriazis, "Cartels: Proof and Procedural Issues", (1993) 16 Fordham Int'l L.J. 266, 269, with Richard Caves, *Multinational Enterprises and Economic Analysis* (2d ed. 1996) 92–93.

[6] See *International Competition Policy Advisory Committee to the Attorney General and Assistant Attorney General for Antitrust, Final Report* (2000) 164, 175 (hereinafter "ICPAC Final Report").

[7] *id.* at 176.

[8] *id.* at 58.

Proponents of a multilateral agreement insist that anti-competitive practices increasingly have an international dimension and therefore, affect the interests of many WTO members. Proponents add that the notion that anti-competitive practices are unimportant is inaccurate considering the frequent occurrence of anti-competitive practices with cross-border effects, investigations against international cartels, and merger reviews involving more than one jurisdiction.[9] Nevertheless, the evidence remains anecdotal.[10] ICPAC concludes that "[m]easurements of the costs to the global economy of these alleged anticompetitive or exclusionary practices are not available now nor likely to be in the foreseeable future."[11] The Justice Department reports that in some investigations more than $1 billion per year of U.S. commerce is adversely affected by international cartel activity.[12] One billion dollars is not insignificant. To put the number in perspective, it represents approximately 0.5 per cent of total U.S. trade in goods and services in 1998, or 0.011 per cent of U.S. GDP in 1999.[13] More importantly, none of these figures provide any empirical proof of the magnitude of the effects of these antitrust cases on global trade or the global economy.

6.05 Is there even such a phenomenon as a purely private RBP? The available evidence suggests that in many instances anti-competitive business practices by private firms receive either active or tacit government support. Private restraints may be encouraged by government regulators, for example, through lack of enforcement of competition laws. Where government support of private restraints does exist, such exclusionary practices that are neither purely private nor purely governmental have been described as "hybrid restraints."[14] When asked to provide examples of the interaction between trade and competition policies as part of an OECD survey, the issues listed by the responding governments did not involve strictly private arrangements but rather arrangements in which government was an essential participant.[15] In the case of domestic hard-core cartels on price fixing, output allocation, and market division, for example, such cartel activity raises prices in the domestic

[9] See "WGTCP 1999 Report", see para. 6.03, n. 3, at 18, para. 57.

[10] See American Bar Ass'n, *Report of the Sections of Antitrust Law and International Law and Practice Concerning Private Anticompetitive Practices as Market Access Barriers* (2000) 3 (hereinafter Report Concerning Private Anticompetitive Practices); WTO, "Working Group on the Interaction between Trade and Competition Policy, Communication from the European Community and Its Member States", *Impact of Anti-competitive Practices on Trade*, WT/WGTCP/W/62 (March 5, 1998) (citing case examples); WTO, "Working Group on the Interaction between Trade and Competition Policy, Communication from Norway", *Impact of Anti-Competitive Practices of Enterprises and Associations on International Trade*, WT/WGTCP/W/73 (March 30, 1998) (same); "ICPAC Final Report", see para. 6.04, n. 6, at 211–19.

[11] "ICPAC Final Report", see para. 6.04, n. 6, at 211.

[12] See *id.* at 168.

[13] In 1998 the United States exported $949 billion in goods and services, and imported over $1 trillion worth of goods and services. Its GDP was $9.2 trillion in 1999. See OECD, *OECD in Figures Statistics on the Member Countries* (2000) 12–13, 60–61. The Justice Department estimates that the figure is closer to $500 million in other investigations, or 0.25% of total U.S. exports of goods and services. See "ICPAC Final Report", see para. 6.04, n. 6, at 168.

[14] For a description of some of the anecdotal evidence, see "Report Concerning Private Anticompetitive Practices", see para. 6.04, n. 10, at 3–4.

[15] See OECD, "Cases of Interaction between Trade and Competition Policy", COM/TD/DAFFE/CLP (92)50 (1992).

market, which in turn will attract entry by foreign firms. Thus, in order to be successful, a domestic cartel may require government assistance in the form of measures, such as tariffs and non-tariff barriers, that exclude foreign companies from the domestic market. Some members of the business community maintain that there is little or no evidence of private anti-competitive acts that have not received the imprimatur of government or cannot be dealt with by domestic competition legislation. Other segments of the business community assert that purely private exclusionary practices are a barrier to access to foreign markets.[16]

6.06 Another possibility is that government assistance plays no role in domestic firms' ability to exclude foreign competitors simply by controlling the channels of distribution in the domestic market. Even in this case, WTO members may still be protecting domestic firms even after dismantling tariff and other barriers to trade, either by failing to enact effective competition laws and enforcement mechanisms, or simply by deliberate non-enforcement of otherwise seeming adequate competition laws. These lapses—the classic "beggar-thy-neighbour" policy—create a market advantage over countries with stricter competition rules.

If in fact most private RBPs are government supported, does the WTO provide an adequate mechanism for addressing them? As explained more fully below, a GATT Article XXIII:1(a) nullification or impairment complaint could be brought against private RBPs that receive active government support. A GATT Article XXIII:1(b) non-violation nullification or impairment complaint would provide a means of challenging private RBPs that receive tacit government support, such as through weak or lax competition law enforcement.[17]

6.07 Besides government support of private RBPs, government barriers to market access are arguably much more important trade barriers than private RBPs. Even after full implementation of the Uruguay Round agreements, a substantial number of high tariffs and non-tariff barriers to trade will remain in place, especially in sectors of export interest to developing countries, such as agricultural trade, textiles and clothing, and footwear and leather goods. In most other trade sectors, competition will be enhanced more by trade liberalisation than by the introduction of competition law reforms in the WTO or by greater international co-operation among national enforcement authorities. Even though border measures are waning as barriers to market entry for trade in most goods, they have not disappeared.

6.08 Government measures, such as product standards, safeguards measures to protect domestic industries from import competition, subsidies to domestic producers, and restricted market access for services trade, to name just a few, are arguably more important barriers to trade than are private RBPs. International trade continues to be hampered by governmental market distortions, such as government procurement policies that discriminate against

[16] See "ICPAC Final Report", see para. 6.04, n. 6, at 225.

[17] See Bernard Hoekman & Peter C. Mavroidis, "Competition, Competition Policy and the GATT", (1994) 17 World Econ. 121.

foreign goods and services and trade distortions flowing from regional trade arrangements. Further trade liberalization and a recommitment to the core non-discrimination principles of most-favoured-nation and national treatment offer more effective means for reducing barriers to trade and promoting competition.

6.09 Even if one concludes that it would be premature, unwise and unnecessary to launch negotiations on a WTO multilateral agreement on competition policy, two anti-competitive practices of foreign firms that distort competitive conditions in an export market illustrate the need for greater co-operation among trading nations and perhaps at some later date, for multilateral prescriptions. These anti-competitive practices are price discrimination and collusive behaviour through export cartels. The first is dealt with under the antidumping duty laws and the price discrimination rules of competition law. The fit of the two bodies of law, as has been exhaustively explored in the literature, is poor, but at least there are in place WTO-approved rules regulating the use of antidumping measures.

6.10 Export cartels, however, pose barriers to market access but WTO rules have no mechanism in place to deal with this anti-competitive practice, other than a GATT Article XXIII:1(b) non-violation nullification or impairment complaint. Export cartels may reduce the welfare of consumers in the foreign market, but they increase the welfare of producers in the country of exportation. In the absence of an agreement on positive comity, export cartels cannot be disciplined because the jurisdiction able to investigate effectively and gather evidence is unwilling to do so, and the jurisdiction with the incentive to investigate is prevented from doing so because of its inability to collect information.

6.11 A third area of friction with an international dimension involves multi-jurisdictional conflicts over proposed mergers with cross-border effects. As desirable as harmonised substantive and procedural rules on pre-merger review would be, however, ICPAC concludes that:

> [t]he development of a substantive [pre-merger review] code, for example, has been criticized as unworkable or overly ambitious at this juncture, in large part because of the difficulties of reconciling the numerous substantive and procedural variations of disparate merger review systems.[18]

Despite these three areas where multilateral rules negotiated under the aegis of the WTO might be desirable, existing WTO provisions on trade-related competition policy issues—Article IX of GATS, Article 40 of the TRIPS Agreement, and Article 9 of the TRIMS Agreement—recognise the sovereign right of WTO members to regulate RBPs without prescribing substantive rules. This decentralised approach is a reflection of the lack of consensus on competition rules and legal instruments for dealing with RBPs, which

[18] See "International Competition Policy Advisory Committee to the Attorney General and Assistant Attorney General for Antitrust, Final Report" (2000) 57 (hereinafter "ICPAC Final Report").

contrasts with the general consensus among economists and government officials that liberalisation of government barriers to trade leads to beneficial welfare effects. In addition, a proposal for a multilateral WTO competition policy agreement is inconsistent with the culture of the WTO.

6.12 In the GATT–WTO system, members are required to ensure that their domestic laws are in conformity with the rights and obligations of the relevant WTO Agreements. The WTO Agreements are largely proscriptive, not prescriptive in nature. For example, the Antidumping Agreement circumscribes the action that members may take in response to injurious dumping, but no member is required to enact AD legislation. Even where a WTO Agreement is prescriptive, such as the TRIPS Agreement, the WTO leaves it to the individual member to determine how it should give effect to GATT–WTO prescriptions in its domestic legislative or administrative process.

6.13 One experienced hand has approached the question of whether and how international rules on competition policy should be negotiated from a legal framework, *i.e.* an intellectual property law approach, a trade law approach or a competition policy approach.[19] The competition policy approach tackles its subject matter head-on with a multilateral agreement on competition policy. The intellectual property law and the trade law approaches envision international codes whose broad subject matter is intellectual property, *e.g.* the TRIPS Agreement, or trade law regulation, *e.g.* the GATT–WTO agreements, at the international level, but in which are embedded competition rules intended to buttress the larger project. Examples include the TRIPS Agreement and the GATS, as well as intellectual property treaties such as the Paris Convention on Protection of Industrial Property.

6.14 The trade law approach would draw upon and enhance the fundamental WTO principles and basic objectives of competition policy, including non-discrimination, *i.e.* MFN and national treatment, economic efficiency and consumer welfare. This approach can be defended on the economic ground that competition would be enhanced more by trade liberalisation than by the introduction of new WTO rules relating to national competition laws and international co-operation. It can be defended on the legal ground that the traditional GATT–WTO portfolio has been to focus on governmental measures affecting conditions of competition.

6.15 The legal and economic framework within which international rules on competition policy would be negotiated and agreed upon is an important one, but equally if not more important is the political context. A WTO approach to trade and competition policy, as just described, is preferable to an agreement on competition policy on the political grounds that the time is not ripe for detailed discussions under WTO auspices on the harmonisation of national competition laws and policies.[20] Do countries have the political will and desire to reach agreement on international competition policy? The United States opposes any agreement on competition policy negotiated under

[19] See, *e.g.* Ernest-Ulrich Petersmann, "International Competition Rules for Governments and for Private Business: A 'Trade Law Approach' for Linking Trade and Competition Rules in the WTO", (1996) 72 Chi.-Kent L. Rev. 545.

[20] See "WGTCP 1998 Report", see para. 6.01, n. 1, at 25–26, para. 75.

WTO auspices, while the E.U. is its chief proponent.[21] At an OECD conference on trade and competition policy held in June 1999, experts from nearly 60 countries, including representatives of government, academia, business, labour, and NGOs could not agree on the need for or desirability of a multilateral agreement on competition policy.[22] So where do the parties go from here?

6.16 From the foregoing discussion, it can be safely said that if market access is prevented by restrictive business practices, then those practices have cross-border effects and consequently such practices pose a threat to international competition. Is the harm sufficient that an international response is warranted? Are national competition laws inadequate for the task of addressing the problem?[23] Assuming aggressive enforcement by national authorities, their focus will tend to be on the national impact of anti-competitive business practices, not on their international ramifications.

6.17 An example of the inconsistent treatment caused by this myopic perspective is the *Boeing/McDonnell Douglas* merger in 1995. The FTC gave unqualified approval to the merger, yet the E.C. Commission attached several conditions to its approval. Interestingly, the Boeing/McDonnell Douglas merger was not a consequence of the growth of international trade or of foreign direct investment. Yet certain conflicts of jurisdiction in the area of competition law enforcement arise as a direct consequence of the growth of international trade and of foreign direct investment. Moreover, a single country's competition law may be impotent in the face of cross-border RBPs, because much of the relevant information is inaccessible and some of the parties are located abroad. That shortcoming in national law suggests that the proper prescription is increased bilateralism, not necessarily increased multilateralism

In addition, the countries most vulnerable to restrictive business practices are also the countries least capable of combating them: developing countries. Although more and more developing countries and transition-economy countries have adopted competition laws, most of them have not. One defensive (and cheap) response has been to protect local firms and infant industries by restricting access of foreign investors and foreign traders to their markets. The upshot is the impoverishment of the protected economy, damage to international competition, and an overall decline in aggregate world wealth.

6.18 On the other hand, national regulation of restrictive business practices—augmented by bilateral co-operation agreements—while perhaps not a model of efficiency, is arguably a more effective way to address the problem of cross-border antitrust violations. Regulation at the international

---

[21] See "U.S. Opposes Plan to Negotiate Agreement in WTO, Officials Say", (1997) 14 Int'l Trade Rep. (BNA) 2034. See generally Eleanor M. Fox, "Toward World Antitrust and Market Access", (1997) 91 Am. J. Int'l L. 1.

[22] See "Conference on Trade and Competition Policies: Exploring the Ways Forward, Summary", (1999) 1 OECD J. Competition L. & Pol'y 7, 18, 20–21 (noting that since market access cases have involved only a few countries, there is no need for a multilateral framework).

[23] These questions are posed by Professor David J. Gerber in "Intellectual Property Rights, Economic Power, and Global Technology Integration", (1996) 72 Chi.-Kent L. Rev. 463, 470.

level creates additional transaction costs, raises concerns of political legitimacy within the country where business conduct is being challenged and thus could strain international relations.

While bilateral agreements achieving harmonisation and co-operation between countries are useful, the ultimate goal (as developed in the preceding Chapter) could be a multilateral agreement harmonising the antitrust laws of all nations. Harmonisation, however, is a lofty goal—some would say utopian—especially against the backdrop of the repeated failures to conclude an international competition policy agreement under the auspices of the League of Nations, the stillborn International Trade Organisation, GATT, and the UN. Additional to this string of failures is the fact that the WTO Dispute Settlement Body is an untested forum for resolving competition policy disputes at any level. Therefore, one must pause to consider if the quest for harmonisation of competition law is quixotic.

6.19 Despite these inconvenient realities, some argue that globalisation is so intertwining the world's economies that the same competition laws must apply to all, or they will be effective for none. Vigorous but fair global competition in which the same rules apply to every market participant assures the best utilisation and allocation of the world's resources. From an efficiency standpoint alone, proponents of an international competition policy agreement ask if international regulation of restrictive business practices would avoid duplication of effort at the national level by several national authorities. The answer offered by Judge Diane Wood is that:

> the existence of many authorities does not itself make the case for internationalization, because competition cases in the end deal with competitive conditions in particular countries.[24]

Professor Waller adds that harmonisation of competition law is not simply an exercise in reducing transaction costs: "Competition law has potent historical, economic, political, and social roots that make it a market nation's ultimate form of public law."[25]

6.20 The legal approach taken by the GATT and WTO agreements in addressing the trade–competition policy relationship has been anything but coherent or comprehensive, but this matters very little if the political will is lacking to conclude an international agreement. Moving the key players to the point where they perceive it to be in their national interest to have such international rules is the crucial first step. At present, a near consensus appears to exist that having a national competition law of some sort is a good idea. Even here some countries, for example, Hong Kong and China, question the need for competition legislation as such. There also seems to be a consensus that if a country does have a competition law, it should be transparent and applied in a non-discriminatory manner.

[24] Diane Wood, "A Cooperative Framework for National Regulation", (1996) 72 Chi.-Kent L. Rev. 521, 524 (hereinafter Wood, "A Cooperative Framework").

[25] Spencer Weber Waller, "The Internationalization of Antitrust Enforcement", (1997) 77 B.U.L. Rev. 343, 395.

6.21 If and when a consensus is reached on the details of international competition policy—a big "if," considering the inability of even the OECD to close the many gaps among its relatively homogenous membership—then the question of the legal vehicle by which to negotiate these rules can be explored, whether as a stand-alone international convention, such as the ill-fated OECD Multilateral Agreement on Investment, or under the auspices of another international organisation, such as the WTO. It might be superficially tempting to point to the Havana Charter as an example of a multilateral trade agreement that included comprehensive provisions on restrictive business practices and state, "if it was done once, then it can be done again." Before citing Chapter V of the Havana Charter as a model for a multilateral agreement on restrictive business practices, however, it is worth remembering several important facts.

6.22 First, the Havana Charter never entered into force. An unratified treaty serves as a poor example of what is possible when countries put their collective minds to it. Secondly, the United States failed to ratify the Havana Charter at least in part because of the Charter's provisions on restrictive business practices that, it was felt in some quarters, would place intolerable restrictions on U.S. antitrust enforcement activities.[26] Thirdly, only 19 countries participated in the drafting of the Havana Charter (in the end, only 23 countries were original signatories to GATT). Given the small number of countries participating in the negotiations which, of course, excluded Germany and Japan, it was a far more manageable affair than would be a WTO multilateral trade negotiation round with 140 participants.

6.23 Fourthly, the major participants in the Havana Charter negotiations were allies during the War and therefore flush with victory over the Axis powers. Excepting the former Soviet Union, which participated in the negotiations but, being suspicious of the West, never signed the Charter or GATT, there were no deep ideological divides separating the participants. Fifthly, the United States dominated the negotiations, being the only major power left virtually unscathed by the war and therefore it became the world's economic powerhouse by default. The imminent adoption of the Marshall Plan only served to solidify the leadership role assumed by the United States in the Havana Charter negotiations *vis-à-vis* the United Kingdom and France.

6.24 Sixthly, and most importantly, even if Chapter V of the Havana Charter had entered into force, as explained in Chapter Three, the RBPs prohibited in Chapter V would obviously have to have been interpreted in the context of specific cases. Even after an ITO investigation of a private firm found to have committed a prohibited RBP, the member where that firm was located was only obligated to take full account of the decision and recommendation of the ITO and take the action it considered appropriate. It would seem that Chapter V is more hortatory than mandatory. Consequently, even had it entered into force, it is not obvious that much would have come of it.

[26] See "Hearings on H.R.J. Res. 236 Before the House Comm. On Foreign Affairs", 81st Cong., 2d Sess. (1950); Earl W. Kintner, Mark R. Joelson & Peter J. Vaghi, "Groping for a Truly International Antitrust Law", 14 Va. J. Int'l L. 75, 86–89 (1973).

If a multilateral competition policy agreement is to be negotiated and is to enter into force, close attention must be paid to whether it makes economic, legal and political sense to negotiate it within a broader international legal regime, such as the GATT–WTO system; as a regional agreement, such as the NAFTA and ANZCERTA chapters on investment and antitrust; or as a stand-alone agreement negotiated under the auspices of the United Nations or the OECD. Fortunately, we have real-world experiences by which to judge the success of bilateral and regional agreements on competition policy. However, elevating those bilateral and regional efforts to the multilateral plane takes us into uncharted waters. A large body of scholarship and studies has accumulated over the last 10 years that advocates adoption of multilateral competition rules under WTO auspices. Powerful WTO members, most notably the E.U., have weighed in favour of a WTO agreement on competition policy. Before WTO members undertake negotiations on a competition policy agreement, at least eight conditions must first be met.

(1) Condition 1.

6.25 The first condition is a consensus among policy makers as to what constitutes prohibited, anti-competitive behaviour by private firms. The major players in the international trade arena—the E.U., Japan and the United States—have in place competition law regimes that at least textually resemble each other. However, a great deal of divergence exists among those systems in the details of what conduct is deemed anti-competitive. As Professor Spencer Weber Waller observes:

> National competition laws do not easily transfer from place to place, and there is insufficient international consensus on the details of competition law and enforcement to make the search for an international code a worthwhile exercise. The prospects for such a code are either outright failure or the creation of a lowest common denominator code meaning all things to all people.[27]

Due to different political and economic philosophies among WTO members as to the proper role of government in the national economy and in regulating private business behaviour, a consensus is lacking as to what types of business behaviour should constitute a *per se* violation of competition laws and what conduct should be subject to a balancing test (a rule of reason) that weighs the pro-competitive benefits of business behaviour against its anti-competitive effects.

(2) Condition 2.

6.26 The second condition is a consensus on the optimal legal instrument for promoting competition policy. Here again, issues of national sovereignty, especially within the United States, point in the direction of national rules

[27] Waller, see para. 6.19, n. 25, at 348.

enforced extraterritorially and bilateral legal instruments to address trans-border antitrust problems. Closely related to the national sovereignty hurdle blocking a multilateral competition policy agreement are powerful, and too often underestimated, sentiments of nationalism and national pride that prevent a consensus from building on a multilateral agreement. This sentiment runs deep especially when the topic is protecting national champions from being out-competed by foreigners. These strong nationalistic proclivities undermine efforts to conclude a multilateral competition policy agreement, either under WTO auspices or in any other international forum.

(3) Condition 3.

6.27 The third condition is a consensus on the best forum for negotiating multilateral rules on competition policy and the structure of those negotiations. Many solid arguments can be made for holding such negotiations in the WTO. Even better arguments can be made for assigning responsibility for developing international competition rules to the OECD which has studied this question extensively. Its outstanding expert analyses and recommendations on the subject of competition policy, together with a membership that is roughly economically homogenous, make it an ideal forum for further discussions on the internationalisation of competition policy.[28]

6.28 Moreover, assigning to the WTO the task of policing private conduct would expand its portfolio substantially. The WTO and its predecessor, GATT, have had as their *raison d'être* the elimination of *government* barriers to international trade and, under the GATS, services as well. This historical fact does not necessarily dictate that the WTO's competency and focus remain permanently fixed on government barriers to trade to the exclusion of private anti-competitive conduct. Nevertheless, until the WTO has fulfilled its primary mandate, that is, until it has completed the unfinished business of eliminating the many government-supported barriers to market access—barriers that are far and away more important economically and politically than any purely private barriers to market access[29]—it would be premature, ill-advised and dangerous to the health of the institution to expand its mandate. Despite the tremendous strides made in the Uruguay Round to further liberalise international trade, many items of export interest to developing countries, *e.g.* textiles, clothing, shoes and leather goods, will remain subject to high tariffs even after the Uruguay Round commitments are fully implemented. In addition, liberalising trade in services, trade in agricultural products, and government procurement policies remain works in progress at the WTO. State trading is also an area that merits closer scrutiny by WTO members. Moreover, behind-the-border government measures involving product standards are a growing non-tariff barrier to trade.

[28] See Gabrielle Marceau, *Anti-Dumping and Anti-Trust Issues in Free-Trade Areas* (1994) 302 (OECD the best of the existing institutions for developing international competition policy agreements); Waller, see para. 6.19, n. 25, at 391 ("Japan and the United States . . . favor the OECD for its moderate, consensus-oriented approach").

[29] See, *e.g.* Friedl Weiss, "From World Trade Law to World Competition Law", (2000) 23 Fordham Int'l L.J. 250, 269 ("governmental access barriers are of incomparably greater importance than purely private RBPs").

6.29 While the WTO is not *in extremis*, neither is it sufficiently robust to resolve satisfactorily individual competition policy disputes between members. The WTO might indeed be a natural forum for negotiating such an agreement, as suggested by some scholars,[30] because of the opportunities for using bargaining chips and making trade-offs among and between trade sectors. However, the single undertaking, "package deal" approach that characterised the Uruguay Round agreements, *i.e.* no country could opt out of any of the Uruguay Round agreements if it wanted to become a WTO member, makes the WTO a far less promising forum for successfully negotiating a competition policy agreement whose terms would be acceptable to all WTO members. On the other hand, if the structure of negotiations is one that includes many agenda items, the opportunity then has been created for compensating a WTO member with a concession in the services sector, for example, in exchange for a concession it makes in competition policy negotiations.

(4) Condition 4.

6.30 A fourth condition to the launch of competition policy negotiations at the WTO is a consensus that a comprehensive, global approach to addressing restrictive business practices under WTO auspices is preferable to deepening and broadening the existing patchwork of bilateral and regional agreements, complemented by the restrictive business practice provisions in several WTO agreements. As Professor Merit Janow notes:

> While the soft harmonization of competition laws is occurring to some degree at the international level, . . . neither the need nor the requisite trust for formal harmonization of competition laws is apparent.[31]

The submissions to the Working Group on Trade and Competition Policy bear out this observation. While more bilateral agreements could not be a bad development, bilateral co-operation agreements do not address the issues of countries with no competition law or of countries where competition laws are either not enforced or are under-enforced.[32] Regional agreements based on minimum RBP standards work best among countries with common cultures, histories and legal traditions, ANZCERTA and the E.U. being prime examples. In fact, such commonalities may be necessary conditions. Moreover, the justification for a multilateral agreement standardising countries' laws and

[30] See, *e.g.* Ernest-Ulrich Petersmann, "International Competition Rules for Governments and for Private Business: A "Trade Law Approach" for Linking Trade and Competition Rules in the WTO", (1996) 72 Chi.-Kent L. Rev. 545. 560–61.

[31] Merit E. Janow, "Unilateral and Bilateral Approaches to Competition Policy Drawing on the Trade Experience", in *Brookings Trade Forum* 1998, at 253, 282 (Robert Z. Lawrence ed. 1998). See also Merit E. Janow, "International Competition Policy in the WTO", in *The Uruguay Round and Beyond: Essays in Honor of Arthur Dunkel* (Jagdish N. Bhagwati & Mathias Hirsch eds. 1998)

[32] For a criticism of bilateral co-operation agreements as a limited tool, given that the parties to these agreements are not required to co-operate when their national interests are adversely affected, see Waller, see para. 6.19, n. 25, at 400.

practices in the area of competition law and policy is not self-evident. There is nothing inherently offensive or inappropriate about 80 or more competition laws in the world.[33]

6.31 Although WTO RBP provisions are sectoral and incremental, they may represent the camel's nose under the tent. For example, the TRIPS Agreement and the GATS both address, in a modest way, the subject of private restrictive business practices that could threaten market access for goods and services. The consultation provision contained in GATS Article IX requires a member to give "full and sympathetic consideration" to requests from another member when private business practices restrain competition and thereby restrict trade in services. This "soft" positive comity principle, as yet untested, nevertheless has the potential for resolving cross-border disputes over private RBPs that affect services trade.

Neither of these WTO agreements, however, deal with international antitrust issues in a comprehensive fashion. Should the WTO members take the plunge then and launch negotiations on a comprehensive WTO agreement on competition policy? Given the many linkages between trade and competition policy, the WTO is in many ways a natural forum for negotiating a multilateral competition policy agreement. Nevertheless, there is nothing in the WTO's constitution that makes a WTO agreement on this subject essential, necessary, inexorable or preordained. Indeed, the absence of such an agreement, regardless of the negotiating forum, is not evidence of a WTO lacuna or failure, but rather some rather compelling evidence that a critical mass of political will among nations has failed to build since the end of World War II to reach a multilateral agreement on this subject. A multilateral agreement on competition policy has not materialised for lack of discussion. On the contrary, it has been much discussed and debated in other international platforms, including the OECD and the United Nations, for close to half a century. The conclusion to be drawn from these discussions and negotiations is that the world is not ready for, does not want or does not need a multilateral agreement on competition policy.

(5) Condition 5.

6.32 A fifth condition is a consensus that it is in every country's economic self-interest to conclude a multilateral agreement on competition policy. Such a consensus unquestionably developed in the case of trade in goods, as evidenced by the broad-based membership in the WTO. But it took more than 50 years for the GATT–WTO system to grow from a membership of 23 to its current membership base of 140 countries. Even so, many countries' commitment to the goal of free trade has been less than unflagging over the past 50 years. The consensus for liberal trade promotion, such as it is, took over 200

[33] In the area of merger control, increased transactions costs associated with simultaneously complying with several countries' merger control laws—the direct legal, consultancy, and filing fee costs, plus the indirect costs of executive time and delays in implementing efficiencies—suggests closer co-operation among national enforcement authorities in merger control. Just what those costs are is a matter of speculation, but the subject is under study. See "IBA Begins Study of Costs Imposed by Merger Vetting", (Sept. 28, 2000) 17 Int'l Trade Rep. (BNA) 1474.

years to develop from the time Adam Smith and David Ricardo first wrote on the economic benefits of liberal trade. It could be argued, however, that such a consensus is not necessary, based on the Uruguay Round negotiations on trade in services. Although no consensus existed on trade in services negotiations, with developing countries being either hostile or indifferent to such negotiations, they used it as a bargaining chip to force agreement form developed countries on the phase-out and eventual elimination of import quotas on textiles and clothing.

(6) Condition 6.

6.33 A sixth condition is a consensus that an international agreement on RBPs would eliminate or at least reduce the friction that a unilateral approach, supported by the growing network of bilateral and regional competition policy arrangements, generate. One of the oft-repeated political reasons offered in support of a WTO agreement on competition policy is to reduce the friction caused by the extraterritorial application of national antitrust laws. As noted in a 1984 OECD Report on Competition and Trade Policies:

> Although there seems to be growing observance of moderation and self-restraint, in the absence of multilaterally agreed upon criteria, unilateral approaches are not likely to be successful in resolving all conflicts which may arise.[34]

That assessment begs the question. At present, international antitrust enforcement in today's global economy is characterised by three features:

(1) the extraterritorial application of a country's antitrust laws to conduct occurring wholly or partly outside a country where such conduct causes anti-competitive effects in that country;

(2) co-operation between national authorities in the enforcement of their competition laws; and

(3) the adoption of principles on positive comity to avoid disputes arising from a country's failure to prevent RBPs that occur in its territory that cause injury in another country.[35]

The current legal regime for cross-border enforcement of competition law—largely bilateral, less often regional—is not without friction. If developing and applying international rules on competition policy are the preferred solution for resolving cross-border antitrust disputes, how are such international rules to be enforced? Are lapses in enforcement to be punished

[34] OECD, *Competition and Trade Policies: Their Interaction* (1984) 119.

[35] See Crystal L. Witterick, "Regulation of Competition in the Canada/U.S. Context—Extraterritorial Reach of U.S. Antitrust Law—A Canadian Perspective", (1998) 24 Can.-U.S. L.J. 299, 300.

through trade sanctions? Would the imposition of trade sanctions be consistent with the WTO's mission of promoting liberal trade? Would such an international sanctioning mechanism reduce international friction or exacerbate it?

6.34 The WTO as a forum for sorting out questions of conflicting and overlapping jurisdiction between national enforcement authorities is no panacea, for at least three reasons. First, the benefits of co-operation under WTO auspices could easily outweigh the costs entailed in achieving the commonality of approach required to ensure the success of multilateral co-operation. WTO members will only be prepared to co-operate if they share a perception of common interest and mutual benefit. ICPAC notes in this regard that:

> it is fanciful to imagine that jurisdictions with established competition policy regimes would be prepared to cede national authority to review cases that adversely affect them to a new supranational authority. To establish such a body requires a shared vision and commitment to economic integration that does not currently exist among nations.[36]

6.35 Secondly, the experience under the WTO Agreement on the Application of Sanitary and Phytosanitary Measures suggests that a multilateral agreement does not always generate the expected benefits and that the realisation of such benefits may hinge upon the establishment of bilateral agreements.[37] Indeed, to the extent that rules on competition law enforcement are multilateralised under WTO auspices, the greater the risk of heightened global tensions among WTO members. Thirdly, the WTO dispute settlement mechanism cannot itself eliminate or reduce political friction. The experience from the protracted *Hormone Beef* and *Bananas* disputes should signal that the WTO dispute settlement process, much improved as it is from its GATT predecessor, has not been the silver bullet that its supporters thought it would be. As Professor Russell Weintraub notes, "Folks who cannot prevent the banana war between the United States and the European Union are not ready for so ambitious a project as unifying antitrust law."[38] On the contrary, the WTO dispute settlement mechanism has at times increased trade tensions. The dispute settlement mechanism might give the victorious WTO member

---

[36] "ICPAC Final Report", see para. 6.04, n. 6, at 271.

[37] See Kevin C. Kennedy, "Resolving International Sanitary and Phytosanitary Disputes in the WTO: Lessons and Future Directions", (2000) 55 Food & Drug L.J. 81. In connection with the controversy over genetically-modified organisms (GMOs), in November 1999, the United States and the E.U. discussed the formation of an *ad hoc* scientific panel to resolve GMO issues. In June 2000, the two parties agreed to continue government-to-government talks aimed at improving market access for U.S. biotechnology products by establishing the U.S.-E.U. Biotechnology Consultative Forum. See Clinton, "Prodi Vow to Ease WTO Differences, Create Temporary Scientific Panel on GMOs", (1999) 16 Int'l Trade Rep. (BNA) 1776; "U.S., EU to Begin Talks Aimed at Settling Row Over EU Ban on GMO Imports", (1999) 16 Int'l Trade Rep. (BNA) 1862; Gary G. Yerkey, "U.S., EU Agree to Pursue High-Level Talks on Biotech Trade as New Group Is Set Up", (June 8, 2000) 17 Int'l Trade Rep. (BNA) 886. Thus, despite the existence of the multilateral SPS Agreement, a bilateral approach is being used to resolve the GMO controversy.

[38] Russell J. Weintraub, "Globalization's Effect on Antitrust Law", (1999) 34 New Eng. L. Rev. 27, 35 (footnote omitted).

international bragging rights, but that will do nothing to reduce friction and might instead inflame the losing party. The wrenching experience of the *Hormone Beef* and *Bananas* disputes, coupled with the seemingly pointless *Antidumping Act of 1916* complaint and dispute settlement proceeding, provides ample support for the view that the WTO cannot be expected to act as the parent that disciplines the unruly child whenever it misbehaves. In the end, experience shows that the good will of the disputing parties is the essential ingredient to bringing a WTO dispute to a mutually satisfactory conclusion. In the end, some country has to be big.

6.36 Even if WTO members were to take a minimalist approach and agree to certain common rules on restrictive business practices, asking the WTO to step in to resolve an international antitrust dispute would not necessarily reduce international friction. On the contrary, it could exacerbate tensions if it meant condemning an antitrust enforcement action that the WTO member deemed to be in its national interest. If a WTO agreement on competition policy was adopted, how would the alleged failure of a WTO member to enforce its national antitrust laws be satisfactorily resolved? Can WTO panelists—even competition law experts—fully appreciate a WTO member's national competition laws and the policies that inform it? If competition law enforcement is turned over to the traders, will the focus on enforcement shift from protecting competition and consumers to protecting domestic producers from import competition?

6.37 A good international trade agreement (and by "good" I mean a trade agreement that liberalises trade and opens markets) may reduce international friction by integrating national economies into a global economy of mutual dependency. A good international trade agreement on competition policy, however, may increase political tensions in both the near term and long term. Again, the experience to date of the WTO dispute settlement process provides ample support for the view that closer economic integration is not a course that always runs smooth. Should non-enforcement of national competition laws constitute GATT nullification or impairment? Is a WTO panel competent to judge what constitutes an appropriate exercise of discretion by national antitrust enforcement agencies? The WTO lacks the authority and competence to adjudicate individual competition cases and to enforce antitrust laws.[39]

6.38 The obstacles to reaching a multilateral agreement on conduct deemed anti-competitive, coupled with the difficulties of presenting sufficient evidence in a WTO panel proceeding, threaten to undermine the integrity and acceptance of the results of the WTO dispute settlement process. Clear, bright-line legal standards of what is or is not a prohibited anti-competitive practice are an absolute necessity if the WTO is to assume the role of global

[39] See James Rill, "Comments", in *Brookings Trade Forum: 1998*, at 382; "ICPAC Final Report", see para. 6.04, n. 6, at 57 ("differing substantive legal standards and underlying merger policies, national sovereignty issues, and enforcement mechanisms would all present insuperable obstacles to any *supra* national arbitration process, even assuming a consensus could ever be achieved as to the identity or composition of such a body").

competition law adjudicator. That kind of global consensus across a broad spectrum of RBPs, however, is not even on the distant horizon. As noted by Assistant Attorney General Joel Klein:

> if we try to run before we have learned to walk, we will stumble and badly injure what we all have been trying to promote—sound antitrust enforcement.[40]

6.39 Assuming that an adequately robust and credible dispute settlement process exists or can be fashioned at the WTO to resolve trade-related competition law disputes, do the WTO members have the will to abide by adverse dispute settlement decisions?[41] Given the WTO's track record to date of panel and Appellate Body reports being ignored by the losing WTO member, the precondition of a robust and credible dispute settlement mechanism has not been satisfied. It is ironic that the chief advocate of a WTO competition policy agreement, the E.U., is also the WTO member with arguably the worst record of compliance with WTO panel and Appellate Body rulings. The E.U. has raised the practice of footdragging to an art form, given its record of non-compliance with the WTO's rulings in the *Bananas* and *Hormone Beef* disputes. Its behaviour in bringing WTO dispute settlement proceedings challenging the U.S. Antidumping Act of 1916 and section 301 of the Trade Act of 1974 has been nothing short of reckless. In fairness to the E.U., the same could be said of the United States in bringing the *Bananas* complaint in the first place. The incessant bickering between the United States and the E.U. has put tremendous stress on the WTO dispute settlement mechanism.[42]

6.40 As an alternative to binding dispute resolution, it has been suggested that simply exposing anti-competitive business practices is itself sufficient to bring about a change in firm behaviour. In Sweden, for example, under its 1946 competition law, enforcement authorities had investigatory powers and could announce their findings, but had no authority to prosecute violators. Making information public about these firms and their RBPs was deemed sufficient to convince them to respect the law and desist from their anti-competitive practices.[43] In short, the most effective policy for combating RBPs

[40] Joel I. Klein, "A Reality Check on Antitrust Rules in the World Trade Organization, and a Practical Way Forward on International Antitrust", in *Trade and Competition Policies: Exploring the Ways Forward* (OECD 1999) 37, 42.

[41] See, *e.g.* Janow, see para. 6.30, n. 31, at 282 n.67 ("An international body such as the WTO reviewing merger cases under binding dispute settlement procedures is even harder to imagine.").

[42] See Gary G. Yerkey, "Farmers Urge USTR to Hit New Countries in Disputes with Europe over Beef, Bananas", (June 8, 2000) 17 Int'l Trade Rep. (BNA) 884; Daniel Pruzin, "EU Initiates WTO Complaint Against U.S. Carousel Retaliation", (June 8, 2000) 17 Int'l Trade Rep. (BNA) 884; Joe Kirwin & Gary G. Yerkey, "EU Proposes Amended Legislation to Outlaw Growth Hormone; Seeks Lifting of Sanctions", (June 1, 2000)17 Int'l Trade Rep. (BNA) 854; "USTR Steps Up Pressure on EU to Comply with Beef and Banana Rulings", (June 1, 2000) 17 Int'l Trade Rep. (BNA) 853; Jane Winebrenner, "No Progress Made at EU-U.S. Summit on FSC Proposal, Beef, and Bananas", (June 1, 2000) 17 Int'l Trade Rep. (BNA) 852.

[43] See Yves Bourdet, "Policy Toward Market Power and Restrictive Practices", in *Internationalization, Market Power and Consumer Welfare*, (Y. Bourdet ed. 1992) at 301.

might be a policy of competition advocacy, which promotes transparency, rather than competition enforcement.[44]

(7) Condition 7.

6.41 If merger review is to be included as part of any WTO competition policy negotiations, then a seventh condition is a consensus that it is necessary and practical to give the WTO jurisdiction over cross-border merger activity. In the area of mergers and acquisitions, having more than one jurisdiction examine the anti-competitive effects of a merger increases the transactions costs of the parties and adds to legal uncertainty. One of the rationales for the 1989 E.U. Merger Control Regulation was to eliminate the transaction costs associated with multiple filings with E.U. Member State enforcement authorities by giving the European Commission exclusive jurisdiction over mergers with a "Community dimension."[45]

At a minimum the costs of the pre-merger reporting and notification requirements are increased because firms are required to make multiple filings with several different competition authorities under penalty of fines and other sanctions. Just how onerous these multiple pre-merger notification filings are is the subject of some anecdotal dispute. Although it may not be true across the board, firms engaged in large M&As will generally be sophisticated enough to retain knowledgeable counsel for whom multiple pre-merger filings are routine. Of course, being routine does not mean cost-free. As a percentage of the deal, however, the transaction costs associated with multiple pre-merger notifications are often *de minimis*. Moreover, given that national competition authorities will be asking for much of the same information in most cases, the information that is collected for one pre-merger notification can be used for all others.

6.42 The legal uncertainty associated with multiple M&A filings presents a concern of a slightly different dimension. It is possible that one national authority will approve a proposed merger unconditionally, while another will impose conditions or reject it altogether. The *Boeing/McDonnell Douglas* merger illustrates the point, with the Federal Trade Commission giving its unconditional approval to the merger and the European Commission balking unless Boeing agreed to several conditions.

Overlapping jurisdiction because of extraterritorial enforcement of antitrust law not only can create legal uncertainty, but can also be a source of political friction. That said, it does not necessarily follow that the only possible solution to this predicament is a multilateral one in the form of a WTO competition policy agreement. The cure of a multilateral mechanism for resolving such conflicts may be worse than the disease. The heavy mix of law and policy when national authorities evaluate a merger implicates deep-rooted feelings of national sovereignty.

[44] See Jose Tavares de Araujo & Luis Tineo, "The Harmonization of Competition Policies Among Mercosur Countries", (1998) 24 Brooklyn J. Int'l L. 441.

[45] In the first recital of its preamble, the Merger Control Regulation provides that "multiple notification of the same transaction increases legal uncertainty, effort and cost for companies and may lead to conflicting assessments." Council Reg. 4064/89, 1989 [1989] O.J. L395 1, as amended, 1990 [1990] O.J. L257 13, and 1997 [1997] O.J. L180 1.

6.43 Reformers ignore this inconvenient but critical fact at their peril. Rather than reach for a multilateral solution, bilateral solutions that take the form of mutual co-operation agreements, or unilateral solutions in the form of comity and wise self-restraint, are immediately "doable." For example, when Congress enacted the Hart-Scott-Rodino Antitrust Improvements Act of 1976, amending the Sherman Act and requiring pre-merger notification, the law was essentially unlimited in its jurisdictional reach. Subsequent DOJ/FTC regulations tempered the Act's reach by introducing principles of comity in the exercise of jurisdiction under the Act.[46] Bilateral and unilateral solutions also take better account of the legal and political realities that a multilateral solution either ignores or papers over.

(8) Condition 8.

6.44 An eighth condition is a consensus that responsibility for international competition policy should be placed in the hands of trade officials. Taking such a step has potentially adverse consequences for competition policy. Although the purpose of trade law and competition law is broadly the same—to open markets, enhance efficiencies, and promote consumer welfare—the two bodies of law and their underlying policies are not entirely congruent. For example, the antidumping duty law punishes conduct that would be considered lawful under the predatory pricing law. To take a second example, trade policy officials may deem all vertical restraints that block or impede market access unlawful without asking, as would national antitrust enforcement authorities, whether such restraints create efficiencies that, on balance, maximise consumer welfare.

6.45 It has been suggested that trade policy officials should encourage and cajole competition policy officials to use their competition laws more forcefully.[47] The argument is that

> trade policy officials view private trade barriers as a current problem [that] indicates a perception that, on the whole, competition laws in many countries are not presently addressing such private conduct in a sufficiently effective manner.[48]

Should competition law officials pander to trade law officials simply because the latter equate denial of market access with private anti-competitive behaviour, in the absence of some showing that market foreclosure is the result of an obvious government-imposed barrier to trade? Professors Lawrence Sullivan and Warren Grimes are unequivocal in their view that trade policy makers should not be allowed to hijack competition policy:

> As trading nations respond to globalization, one of the risks to antitrust is that it will be increasingly treated as an aspect of trade policy. That risk is

[46] See 43 Fed. Reg. 33,497 (1978).
[47] See Robert E. Hudec, "A WTO Perspective in Private Anti-Competitive Behavior in World Markets", (1999) 34 New Eng. L. Rev. 79, 84.
[48] *id.*

probably no greater in the EU than it is in the United States. It should be resisted everywhere.[49]

6.46 Although calls for greater assertiveness in competition law enforcement may in itself be harmless enough, how are developing countries with no competition law in place supposed to respond? How are countries with a competition law in place, but with insufficient resources to investigate and prosecute all allegations of private anti-competitive behaviour, supposed to respond? Moreover, demands by trade officials for more aggressive competition law enforcement may not be so harmless if it draws attention away from the real reasons why a domestic firm cannot penetrate a foreign market. The latter could include a lack of competitiveness on the part of domestic producers and exporters in world markets, a charge that elected officials are reluctant to level at their own constituents. Or foreign markets may be closed to imports because of government barriers to trade erected by importing countries, not by private persons. Removing government barriers to trade remains the WTO's *raison d'être* and its unfinished business.[50] Focusing on private barriers to trade is a red herring that could lure the WTO away from completing the job for which it was created, namely, to remove government barriers to trade. It probably should be competition law enforcement authorities cajoling trade officials to reform or repeal the trade remedy laws, especially the antidumping and countervailing duty laws, because of their anti-competitive and protectionist effects.

6.47 Trade and competition policy share the same goal of ensuring that anti-competitive activity does not distort the efficient operation of markets. Traditionally, trade officials have been concerned about the effect that public protectionist measures have on market forces between countries and competition law officials have been concerned about exertions of market power within countries and with allocative efficiencies and consumer welfare within national markets.[51] As globalisation blurs the boundaries of markets, however, so does it blur the borders between these areas of policy. Effective international competition law enforcement can and does complement liberal trade policy. However, those who seek to reconstitute competition law as a new trade remedy may be forgetting that market access is a means to an end and not an end in itself. One lowers trade barriers to increase the efficient operation of market forces; one does not break up efficient market structures to increase trade flows.

6.48 Work at the WTO on international competition rules might have a greater chance of moving forward if such work is informed by one competition policy principle in particular: a concern for consumer welfare. This is not

[49] Lawrence A. Sullivan & Warren S. Grimes, *The Law of Antitrust: An Integrated Handbook* 996 (2000).

[50] See, *e.g.* Weiss, see para. 6.28, n. 29, at 269–70.

[51] The ABA Sections on Antitrust Law and International Law and Practice have concluded that "there seems to be no reasonable prospect in the foreseeable future" of re-orienting competition enforcement authorities to focus on global efficiencies and global consumer welfare, rather than solely on national market efficiencies and national consumer welfare. See "Report Concerning Private Anticompetitive Practices", see para. 6.04, n. 10, at 33.

expressly recognised in any of the WTO agreements, as it is apparently assumed that efficiency savings from reduced barriers to international trade will trickle down ultimately to the consumer. It is possible for market-opening initiatives to have inefficient outcomes, however. This is particularly the case with attempts to manage trade by balancing the market share and profit opportunities of international rivals. Allowing market access principles to override or ignore antitrust's core concern with consumer welfare may put efficient market structures at risk and provide more opportunity for powerful competitors to distort the independence and impartiality of antitrust enforcement. Professor Daniel Tarullo is critical of proposals to negotiate a multilateral competition policy agreement that would be administered by the WTO. He states:

> Housing a competition arrangement in the WTO would inevitably favor the trade norms [of market access over the consumer-welfare norm of competition policy] where the two conflict.[52]

6.49 Until such time as trade law and policy reflect a full understanding that not all denials of market access by private actors are *per se* unlawful, competition law and policy should be left to the competition enforcement authorities. Edward Graham asks, "Will the circle ever be complete, such that competition polices meet trade policies to act jointly to make markets more internationally contestable?"[53] In the United States, the process-oriented approach adopted by the Justice Department and the FTC in concluding bilateral co-operation and mutual assistance agreements with major trading partners (Canada, the E.U. and Japan), with minor trading partners (Australia and Israel) and with developing countries (Brazil and Mexico) has created a forum for the exchange of views about national antitrust enforcement activities when those activities cross national borders. The results-oriented approach of the USTR, adversarial and confrontational in nature, is at odds with a conciliatory, co-operative approach that seeks mutually satisfactory resolution of these sensitive policy questions. The answer to Dr. Graham's query whether the trade-competition policy circle will ever be complete has to be, "not any time soon in the United States."

6.50 The Working Group on Trade and Competition Policy has provided a useful first step for the exchange of views by trade and competition policy officials on overlapping trade-competition policy issues. While progress was made on achieving a better understanding of WTO members' positions on these issues, much still divides them. WTO Working Groups are ad hoc bodies with no permanent mandate, therefore, it might be appropriate to institutionalise the process by creating a permanent consultative body within the WTO.[54]

---

[52] Daniel K. Tarullo, "Norms and Institutions in Global Competition Policy", (2000) 94 Am. J. Int'l L. 478, 479.

[53] Edward M. Graham, "Comments", in *Brookings Trade Forum 1998*, (Richard Z. Lawrence ed. 1998) at 290.

[54] A similar proposal was made in 1998 as part of a trade-competition policy symposium. See Hudec, "A WTO Perspective", see para. 6.45, n. 47, at 85.

First, the 1960 GATT Decision on Arrangements for Consultations on Restrictive Business Practices—invoked only once in its 40–year history in the *Kodak-Fuji Film* dispute—should be resurrected and re-invigorated.[55] Next, a standing committee on Trade and Competition Policy would be created that reports directly to the General Council.[56] The Trade and Competition Policy Committee would in effect continue the work started by the Working Group by:

(1) identifying problems of divergence among national competition laws and policies,

(2) advising developing countries on the enactment and enforcement of competition laws, and

(3) identifying areas of convergence on competition policy that might be suitable candidates for addition to the General Agreement or other WTO agreements, as appropriate.

The Trade and Competition Policy Committee should be directed to co-ordinate its work with the OECD, which has made important contributions to the trade-competition policy interface.[57] Its approach to the trade-competition policy relationship should be results-oriented rather than instrument-oriented with a view to identifying specific anti-competitive practices that bear directly on international trade liberalisation, and then exploring possible multilateral solutions to those practices, including closer co-operation among national enforcement authorities and technical assistance to developing countries.

II. ADDRESSING PRIVATE RBPS UNDER EXISTING GATT–WTO RULES

6.51 A final option is to do nothing more substantively in the WTO context, with the possible exception of introducing more competition principles into existing WTO agreements *à la* GATS Article IX.[58] The

[55] "Decision on Restrictive Business Practices: Arrangements for Consultations", BISD, 9th Supp. 28 (1960).

[56] WTO standing committees that report directly to the General Council include the Trade and Development Committee, the Trade and Environment Committee and the Regional Trade Agreements Committee.

[57] For a similar proposal, see Joel L. Klein, "Time for a Global Competition Initiative?" (speech delivered at E.C. Merger Control Conference, Sept. 14, 2000, available at www.usdoj.gov). See, *e.g.* OECD, Joint Group on Trade and Competition, "Outline of (A) Core Principles, Common Approaches and Common Standards and (B) Bilateral and Multilateral Approaches" (Oct. 13, 1999); "Competition Elements in International Trade Agreements: A Post-Uruguay Round Overview of WTO Agreements" (Jan. 29, 1999); "Complementarities Between Trade and Competition Policies" (Jan. 29, 1999); "Consistencies and Inconsistencies Between Trade and Competition Policies" (Feb. 25, 1999). These documents are available at http://www.oecd.org/daf/clp.

[58] See Bernard Hoekman, "Harmonising Competition Policy in the WTO System" (Winter 1997) 39 World Econ. Affairs.

argument in favour of maintaining the status quo at the WTO *vis-à-vis* private RBPs is simple and straightforward: the WTO's priorities should be on removing government barriers to trade, including restrictions on foreign direct investment. Trade and investment liberalisation, the argument runs, are the most powerful pro-competitive instruments available.[59] In addition, as previously noted, a WTO agreement on competition policy could be a solution in search of a problem. With the exception of the *Kodak-Fuji Film* dispute, the absence of competition law issues in GATT–WTO jurisprudence implies that anti-competitive practices are not a significant issue in the context of international trade and market access.[60]

Moreover, the GATT–WTO system offers more to its members than just a forum for consulting *inter se* on the trade and competition policy relationship. Existing GATT–WTO instruments contain the bases for making legal challenges to private RBPs affecting trade. GATT Article XXIII:1 provides that a contracting party may initiate a dispute settlement proceeding if it

> should consider that any benefit accruing to it directly or indirectly under this Agreement is being nullified or impaired or that the attainment of any objective of the Agreement is being impeded as the result of
>
> (a) the failure of another contracting party to carry out its obligations under this Agreement,
> (b) the application by another contracting party of any measure, whether or not it conflicts with the provisions of this Agreement, or
> (c) the existence of any other situation, . . .

6.52 The threshold question in determining which type of Article XXIII proceeding may properly be brought is whether private RBPs that restrict trade constitutes a violation of GATT 1994 or of a WTO Agreement, or whether they instead come under the heading of non-violation nullification or impairment. As explained more fully below, each type of Article XXIII:1 proceeding carries with it distinct procedures and remedies.[61]

A. An Article XXIII:1(a) Nullification or Impairment Complaint

6.53 If a WTO panel or the Appellate Body finds that a WTO member has breached one of its GATT obligations by, for example, imposing a six per cent tax on imported products but a four per cent tax on sales of the like domestic product and that report is adopted by the Dispute Settlement Body, then the offending member is to bring the measure into compliance with GATT. If the offending member fails to withdraw the measure, then the

[59] See *id.*

[60] See *id.* In an evaluation of s.301 cases, a 1994 study concludes that antitrust violations have not been a factor in the filing of s.301 petitions. See J. Michael Finger & K.C. Fung, Can "Competition Policy Control 301?," (1994) 49 Aussenwirtschaft 379.

[61] For additional analyses of Article XXIII:1, see Sung-joon Cho, "GATT Non-Violation Issues in the WTO Framework: Are They the Achilles' Heel of the Dispute Settlement Process?" (1998) 39 Harv. Int'l L.J. 311; Hudec, *A WTO Perspective*, see para. 6.45, n. 47, at 89–91.

aggrieved member is entitled to compensation from the offending member in the form of additional trade concessions in an amount equal to the value of lost trade. If the parties cannot agree on compensation, then the aggrieved member may retaliate by suspending concessions in an amount determined by the original panel equal to the trade lost by the offending measure.[62]

6.54 Outside of the specific contexts of a WTO agreement with competition law commitments, *e.g.* the TRIPS Agreement and its provisions an abuse of IPRs in licensing agreements, or the GATS and the competition policy principles agreed to in the Reference Paper to the Agreement on Basic Telecommunications, a WTO member would have a difficult, if not impossible, task in establishing that another member has violated its WTO obligations either by failing to enact or to enforce competition laws. No specific provision of GATT 1994 imposes a general obligation on WTO members to enact, maintain, or enforce a national competition law. Nevertheless, there are several situations involving a question of competition law in which a WTO member arguably could be found to be in violation of a GATT 1994 article or one of the WTO agreements with competition policy provisions.

1. *An Article II:4 Import Monopoly Complaint.*

6.55 First, if a WTO member has authorised a private firm to act as an import monopoly, such a monopoly would violate GATT Article II:4 if it treated imports in such a way "so as to afford protection on the average in excess of the amount of protection provided for" in the member's tariff binding for that imported product. Thus, for example, if an import monopoly were to mark-up the price of imported goods on grounds other than "normal commercial considerations," such a price mark-up would violate Article II:4,[63] regardless of whether the imports were still competitive with the like domestic product despite the price mark-up.

6.56 Could an import cartel or an exclusive distribution network be found to violate Article II:4? Recall that Article II:4 provides, "If any contracting party establishes, maintains or authorizes, formally or *in effect*, a monopoly of the importation of any product . . . [emphasis added]." If an import cartel or exclusive distribution network refused to deal in the goods of foreign producers or exporters and a contracting party failed to take action against the cartel or network, would not the toleration of that anti-competitive activity violate Article II:4? Despite the fact that there would be an absence of formal government authorisation of the anti-competitive activity, by the importing country's toleration of that activity, the member arguably would *in effect* establish, authorise or maintain an import monopoly. The cartel's or distribution network's refusal to deal would be the functional equivalent of a trade-prohibitive tariff and would clearly frustrate the benefit

[62] See Dispute Settlement Understanding art. 22. See also Raj Bhala & Kevin Kennedy, *World Trade Law: The GATT-WTO System, Regional Arrangements, and U.S. Law* (1998) 40–41.
[63] See "Report of the GATT Panel, Canada—Import, Distribution and Sale of Alcoholic Drinks by Canadian Provincial Marketing Agencies", BISD, 35th Supp. 37, 85–86, paras. 4.5–4.8 (adopted Mar. 22 1988).

of the bargain reflected in the tariff binding listed in the importing member's schedule of tariff concessions. The language of Article II:4 is certainly broad enough to include types of "protection" other than price mark-ups; "such monopoly shall not . . . operate *so as to afford protection* on the average in excess of the amount of protection provided for in that Schedule" [emphasis added].

In this connection, the Interpretative Note to Article II:4 is instructive. It states that Article II:4 is to be interpreted in light of the provisions of Article 31 of the Havana Charter. Article 31:5 provides that import monopolies are to import and offer for sale such quantities of the product as are sufficient to satisfy the full domestic demand for the imported product. Therefore, the obligations of Article II:4 arguably cover conduct that denies imported goods the opportunity to compete with domestic goods.[64]

2. *A National Treatment Complaint.*

6.57 Secondly, the national treatment obligation of GATT Article III:4 requires that imported products receive treatment no less favourable than the like domestic product in connection with national "laws, regulations or requirements *affecting* their internal sale, offering for sale, purchase, transportation, distribution or use . . . [emphasis added]." It is worth recalling that the GATT drafters did not use the word "governing," implying that Article III:4 covers laws and regulations that might adversely affect the conditions of competition between the domestic and imported products in the internal market.[65]

6.58 Competition law obviously is such a national law, regulation, or requirement within the meaning of Article III:4.[66] Article III:4 could, therefore, be the basis of an Article XXIII:1(a) complaint if an importing country's competition laws discriminated against imported goods *vis-à-vis* the like domestic product either *de facto* (a measure that in its application upsets the competitive relationship between domestic and imported goods as it existed at the time when a relevant tariff concession was granted) or *de jure* (a measure that on its face discriminates against imported products).[67] The subject matter of the complaint would not be private anti-competitive behaviour, but rather the discriminatory application of national competition law to imports compared to domestic products in a manner that upsets the competitive relationship between the two. Article III does not employ a trade effects test; instead, the inquiry is whether national legislation upsets "effective equality of

---

[64] See, *e.g.* "Report of the GATT Panel, Republic of Korea—Restrictions on Imports of Beef", BISD, 36th Supp. 202, 229, para. 106 (adopted Nov. 7, 1989) ("an import monopoly was not to charge on the average a profit margin which was higher than that which would be obtained under normal conditions of competition (in the absence of the monopoly)").

[65] This point is made in "Report of the GATT Panel, Italian Discrimination against Imported Agricultural Machinery", BISD, 7th Supp. 60, 64, para. 12 (adopted Oct. 23, 1958).

[66] See "Report of the WTO Panel, United States—Anti-Dumping Act of 1916", WT/DS162/R, para. 6.69 (2000) (ruling that Anti-Dumping Act of 1916 is an internal law within the scope of Art. III:4) (hereinafter "Anti-Dumping Act of 1916").

[67] See Report of the WTO Fund, "Japan—Measures Affecting Consumer Photographic Film and Paper", WT/DS44/R, para. 10.20 (hereinafter "Kodak-Fuji Film Dispute").

competitive opportunities."[68] Such discrimination covers not only the substantive provisions of competition law, but also its procedural provisions.[69] Thus, for example, if a country's competition law gave domestic firms a right to file a private antitrust lawsuit against anti-competitive conduct within their national market, but denied such a right to foreign firms whose exports to that market were being blocked by anti-competitive behaviour within that market, a prima facie case of GATT nullification or impairment would be made out under Article III:4.

6.59 Similarly, if competition laws were enacted that targeted foreign firms and their imported products, but without any parallel legislation in place targeting domestic firms, an Article III:4 claim might exist. In the 2000 panel and Appellate Body reports on *United States—Anti-Dumping Act of 1916*,[70] Japan and the E.U. complained that the Anti-Dumping Act of 1916 violates Article III:4, *inter alia*, because imported products could be the subject of a U.S. legal proceeding alleging price discrimination under a trade law remedy, *i.e.* the antidumping duty law[71], or under a competition law remedy, *i.e.* the Anti-Dumping Act of 1916[72], whereas domestic firms would only be subject to an action for price discrimination under the Robinson-Patman Act.[73] In addition, Japan and the E.U. claimed that the 1916 Act violates Article III:4 of GATT 1994 to the extent that it provides less favourable treatment to imported goods than is granted to U.S. goods under the Robinson-Patman Act in terms of the difference in:

(1) pleading requirements,
(2) the use of the intent requirement in the 1916 Act instead of a requirement of "effect" under the Robinson-Patman Act,
(3) the cost recoupment requirement,
(4) the statutory defences available under the Robinson-Patman Act and not expressly provided for in the 1916 Act, and
(5) the conduct subject to penalties.[74]

In exercising the principle of judicial economy, the panel and Appellate Body disposed of the dispute in favour of Japan and the E.U. on other grounds and declined to examine the question whether the 1916 Act violates the national treatment obligation.[75] Nevertheless, as following analysis shows, the 1989

[68] See *id.*
[69] See "Report of the GATT Panel, United States—section 337 of the Tariff Act of 1930", BISD, 36th Supp. 345, 385–86, para. 5.10. (1989).
[70] See "Anti-Dumping Act of 1916", see para. 6.58, n. 66; Report of the Appellate Body, United States—Antidumping Act of 1916, WT/DS136/AB/R, WT/DS162/AB/R (2000).
[71] See 19 U.S.C. ss. 1673–1673g.
[72] See 15 U.S.C. ss. 71–74.
[73] See 15 U.S.C. s. 13(a).
[74] See "Anti-Dumping Act of 1916", see para. 6.58, n. 66, para. 6.7.
[75] See *id.* paras. 6.270–6.272. The Appellate Body also declined to examine Japan's national treatment claim.

GATT panel report in *Section 337 of the Tariff Act of 1930* is instructive and strongly suggests that Japan and the E.U. had a compelling Article III:4 claim.

6.60 Following a complaint by the European Community, in January 1989, a GATT panel issued a report in which it agreed with the E.C. that section 337[76] does violate the national treatment obligation of GATT Article III:4.[77] The panel found that, prior to amendments in 1994, section 337 discriminated against imported articles *vis-à-vis* the like domestic product in six respects.[78] First, a section 337 complainant had a choice of two platforms—the ITC or federal district court—in which to challenge imported articles, whereas articles manufactured domestically in the United States could only be challenged in federal court. Secondly, foreign producers and importers of challenged products were at a potential disadvantage *vis-à-vis* their U.S. domestic counterparts, given the strict time limits applicable in section 337 proceedings, with no corresponding time limits applicable in federal court actions.

6.61 Thirdly, a section 337 respondent could not bring a counterclaim (*e.g.*, a counterclaim alleging an antitrust violation by the complainant for abusing its exclusive rights under a patent, trademark or copyright), whereas a federal court defendant had that option. Fourthly, relief in the form of a general exclusion order against infringing imports was available in a section 337 proceeding. In contrast, no corresponding remedy was available against infringing articles of U.S. origin in a federal court proceeding. Fifthly, exclusion orders were automatically enforced by the U.S. Customs Service, whereas any injunctive relief ordered by a federal court in a private civil action required for its enforcement separate contempt proceedings brought by

[76] Section 337(a) of the Tariff Act of 1930, 19 U.S.C. s. 1337(a), generally makes unlawful unfair methods of competition and unfair acts in the importation of articles into the United States, or in their sale, the effect or tendency of which is (1) to destroy or substantially injure an industry in the United States, (2) prevent the establishment of such an industry, or (3) restrain or monopolise trade and commerce in the United States. In a non-IPR s.337 investigation, the complainant must prove the existence of (a) unfair methods of competition or other unfair acts that (b) tend to substantially injure or destroy an American industry. Besides the general prohibition against unfair methods of competition, the most important provisions of s.337 also declare unlawful the importation or sale of articles that infringe: (1) a valid and enforceable patent or patent process, (2) a valid and enforceable copyright, (3) a valid and enforceable trademark, or (4) a registered semiconductor mask work. For this separate class of unfair import practice, the importation or sale of infringing articles is unlawful without proof of injury to a U.S. industry. Such injury is presumed, unlike the case with non-IPR violations. However, a U.S. industry must exist or be in the process of being established that is connected with the imported article and the IPR that is allegedly being infringed.

[77] See "House Comm. on Ways and Means, Overview and Compilation of U.S. Trade Statutes", H.R. Doc. No. 6, 104th Cong., 1st Sess. 93 (1995). For background on the s.337 proceedings leading up to the E.C.'s complaint, an analysis of the panel report, and proposals for legislative reform of s. 337, see Robert G. Krupka, Philip C. Swain & Russell E. Levine, "Section 337 and the GATT: The Problem or the Solution?", 42 Am. U.L. Rev. 779 (1993); Jeffrey S. Neeley & Hideto Ishida, "Section 337 and National Treatment Under GATT: A Proposal for Legislative Reform", (1989–90) 13 Fordham Int'l L.J. 276; Anne L. Spangler, "Intellectual Property Protection and Import Trade: Making Section 337 Consistent with the General Agreement on Tariffs and Trade", (1991) 43 Hastings L.J. 217; Lisa Barons, "Amending Section 337 to Obtain GATT Consistency and Retain Border Protection", (1991) 22 Law & Pol'y Int'l Bus. 289; Kenneth W. Abbott, "GATT Dispute Settlement Panel", (1990) 84 Am. J. Int'l L. 274 (1990).

[78] See "Report of the GATT Panel, United States—Section 337 of the Tariff Act of 1930", (1989) BISD, 36th Supp. 345.

the successful plaintiff. Sixthly, and finally, foreign producers and importers of challenged imports faced the prospect of defending parallel or successive administrative and judicial proceedings. In contrast, products of U.S. origin were not exposed to the same gauntlet.[79]

6.62 The panel recommended that the United States amend section 337 to remedy the inconsistencies with Article III:4. Although it took over six years, Congress finally did amend section 337 in December 1994 to remedy the national treatment violations.[80]

6.63 Applying the GATT panel's analysis to the Anti-Dumping Act of 1916, given that a domestic firm facing below-cost import competition has available two platforms in which to proceed against such imported goods (*i.e.* an administrative as well as judicial forum), whereas below-cost, domestically-produced goods can only be the subject of legal proceedings filed in a judicial forum, Japan and the E.U. certainly had a colourable national treatment claim against the Anti-Dumping Act of 1916. Moreover, if as alleged, the Anti-Dumping Act of 1916 subjects foreign defendants accused of price discrimination to more onerous legal requirements compared to similarly circumstanced domestic defendants accused of price discrimination under the Robinson-Patman Act, then such a disparity in competitive conditions would likewise draw into question whether the 1916 Act is consistent with the national treatment obligation.[81]

3. *An Article XI Quantitative Restriction Complaint.*

6.64 If a government's toleration or encouragement of an import monopoly, import cartel, or exclusive distribution network could be the basis for a GATT nullification or impairment complaint under Article II:4, could a government's toleration or encouragement of a private export cartel be the basis of a GATT Article XXIII:1(a) complaint under Article XI which prohibits import and export quotas? Assume that a group of firms within a country manufacture the same product for which the supply is insufficient to meet total world demand. They agree upon their respective market shares and

[79] See "Section 337 of the Tariff Act of 1930", see para. 6.58, n. 69, at 391, para. 5.20.

[80] As part of the 1994 Uruguay Round Agreements Act, Congress amended s.337 in several important respects in response to the 1989 GATT panel report. In addition, although not specifically addressed in the 1989 GATT panel report, Congress amended title 28 of the United States Code regarding district court practice in the context of s.337 IPR infringement proceedings. Section 321(a) of the URAA amends s.337 with regard to: (1) time limits for completing investigations, (2) a respondent's ability to bring a counterclaim, (3) the issuance of exclusion orders, (4) ITC practice on bonding requirements and deference to arbitration proceedings, and (5) the persons who may have access to business confidential information in the course of ITC proceedings. For an assessment of the 1994 amendments to s.337, see F. David Foster & Joel Davidow, "GATT and Reform of U.S. Section 337", (1996) 30 Int'l Law. 97; Tom M. Schaumberg, "A Revitalized Section 337 to Prohibit Unfairly Traded Imports", in *The GATT, The WTO and the Uruguay Round Agreements Act* (Practising Law Institute 1995) 487.

[81] A more difficult case to prove, but one which would implicate a national treatment violation as well, would be one claiming that national competition law enforcement authorities have exercised their discretionary enforcement authority in a discriminatory manner by bringing price discrimination cases against foreign exporters, while consistently declining to investigate or institute proceedings against domestic firms accused of the same or similar anti-competitive conduct in the domestic market.

further agree to limit the supply of the product exported to foreign markets in order to keep prices artificially high and thereby reap supranormal profits. National enforcement authorities might not have sufficient incentive to take action against the export cartel, so long as consumer welfare in their country is not being reduced. Would the failure of national antitrust enforcement authorities to break up the export cartel violate the Article XI prohibition on quantitative restrictions?

6.65 Article XI:1 is directed at governmental restrictions or prohibitions on imports or exports, "whether made effective through quotas, import or export licenses or other measures." It does not discipline purely private conduct. A distinction could be drawn between government toleration of export cartel activity and government encouragement of such activity. While the former might escape challenge under Article XI:1 successfully, the latter could be the basis for a GATT complaint. The 1988 GATT panel in *Trade in Semi-Conductors* ruled that "measures" include government conduct that is not legally binding or mandatory. In determining that "administrative guidance" from the Japanese government to Japanese exporters of semi-conductors was a "measure" for purposes of Article XI:1, the panel recognised that not all non-mandatory governmental requests to restrict exports could be regarded as measures within the meaning of Article XI:1. The panel noted:

> Government-industry relations varied from country to country, from industry to industry, and from case to case and were influenced by may factors. There was thus a wide spectrum of government involvement ranging from, for instance, direct government orders to occasional government consultations with advisory committees.[82]

6.66 The reach of the *Semi-Conductors* ruling was tested in the *Kodak-Fuji Film* dispute. The United States did not allege that Japan's toleration of allegedly anti-competitive behaviour by private actors violated GATT. Instead, the United States argued that Japan promoted the establishment of the exclusive distribution network for film.[83] The United States attempted to link several seemingly unrelated acts by the Japanese government as proof of an Article XI:1 "measure." While the panel did not fault the United States' legal argument, it was unable to make the connection between the acts of the Japanese government and the establishment of the exclusive distribution network.[84]

In light of the *Semi-Conductors* case, active government encouragement in the form of legislation immunising the hypothetical export cartel from competition law scrutiny (*e.g.* in the United States the Webb-Pomerene Act or the Export Trading Company Act of 1982) would arguably be a "measure"

---

[82] See "Report of the GATT Panel, Japan—Trade in Semi-Conductors", BISD, 35th Supp. 116, 155, para. 108 (1988).

[83] See "Kodak-Fuji Film Dispute", see para. 6.58, n. 67, at paras. 6.243–6.247, 6.609–6.612, 10.22.

[84] See "Kodak-Fuji Film Dispute", see para. 6.58, n. 67, at 10.39, 10.204.

that violates Article XI:1. However, Article XI:1 speaks in terms of affirmative government conduct that restricts or prohibits exports. Therefore, unless the mere acquiescence in such cartel activity would qualify as a "measure," government toleration of or acquiescence in an export cartel that divided markets and restricted the supply of its products for export to foreign markets would not violate Article XI:1.

6.67 GATT 1994 generally limits governments in the action they may take to restrict trade flows and does not impose an affirmative obligation to take positive steps to promote trade flows on them. However, as discussed in the following sections, GATT 1994 and other WTO agreements do direct WTO members to restrict the activities of monopolies in at least four situations when those monopolies abuse their dominant position by restricting or preventing market access.

4. *Private import or export Monopolies established under GATT Article XVII.*

6.68 Article XVII does not prohibit a member from establishing import or export monopolies but it does regulate their operation and effect on trade when they make purchases or sales. Although no GATT or WTO panel has ever found a measure to be in violation of Article XVII itself, GATT panels have found that Article XVII state trading enterprises have violated the Article XI prohibition on import or export quotas and the national treatment obligation.[85]

6.69 Article XVII:1(b) also requires government-authorised import and export monopolies to:

> afford enterprises of the other contracting parties adequate opportunity, in accordance with customary business practice, to compete for participation in [the monopoly's] purchases or sales.

Thus, a WTO member which has authorised a private import or export monopoly could be found to be in violation of GATT if it allowed such a monopoly to, in effect, abuse its dominant position by acting in a manner inconsistent with the Article I most-favoured-nation obligation or the national treatment obligation of Article III.[86]

---

[85] See, *e.g.* "Report of the GATT Panel, Canada—Import, Distribution and Sale of Alcoholic Drinks by Canadian Provincial Marketing Agencies", BISD, 35th Supp. 37, 90, para. 4.27 (adopted March 22, 1988) (Article XI violated); "Report of the GATT Panel, Republic of Korea—Restrictions on Imports of Beef", BISD, 36th Supp. 268, 301–02, paras. 114–15 (adopted Nov. 7, 1989) (Article XI violated).

[86] See, *e.g.* "Report of the GATT Panel, Canada—Import, Distribution and Sale of Alcoholic Drinks by Canadian Provincial Marketing Agencies", BISD, 39th Supp. 27, 85, paras. 5.31 (adopted Feb. 18, 1992); "Report of the GATT Panel, Thailand—Restrictions on Importation of and National Taxes on Cigarettes", BISD, 37th Supp. 200, 223–26, paras. 76–81 (adopted Nov.7, 1990).

Arguments have also made that the national treatment commitment is incorporated by reference in Article XVII. However, GATT panels have either declined to rule that the national treatment obligation is part of Article XVII or have suggested that it is not. See, *e.g.* "Report of the GATT Panel, Belgian Family Allowances", BISD, 1st Supp. 59, 60, para. 4 (adopted Nov. 7, 1952) (national treatment obligation not part of Article XVII); "Report of the GATT Panel, Canada—Import, Distribution and Sale of Alcoholic Drinks by Canadian Provincial Marketing Agencies", BISD, 35th Supp. 37, 90, para. 4.27 (adopted March 22, 1988) (complaint disposed of on other grounds).

5. *GATS Competition Policy Commitments.*

6.70 The few instances where a WTO member has an affirmative obligation to take action against private anti-competitive behaviour are to be found in the GATS and its subsidiary agreements.

6.71 **a. Abuse of dominant position by monopoly service suppliers generally.** GATS Article VIII: *Monopolies and Exclusive Service Suppliers*, obligates members to ensure that any monopoly services supplier in its territory, whether public or private, does not act in a manner inconsistent with the GATS Article II MFN requirement—it does not discriminate among foreign firms in the provision of services. That Article further requires that with respect to services sectors covered in a member's schedule of market access commitments, members ensure that when a monopoly supplier or an exclusive service supplier whose rights are granted by the government compete in the supply of a service outside the scope of their government-granted rights, they do not abuse their monopoly position by acting in a manner inconsistent with that member's commitments on national treatment and market access for foreign service suppliers.[87] The operative phrase in Article VIII is "[e]ach Member shall ensure," language that is mandatory, not hortatory. The failure to observe these Article VIII commitments could be the basis for an Article XXIII:1(a) nullification or impairment complaint.

6.72 **b. Abuse of dominant position by a monopoly service supplier in the basic telecommunications sector.** Effective antitrust laws can be an immeasurable aid to investors by preventing local monopolies from abusing their position toward new entrants. This is especially true for network industries, such as basic telecoms, where an investor may have to rely on local transmission facilities, typically owned by state monopolies, to provide a competitive service.

6.73 The 1997 WTO Agreement on Basic Telecommunications contains important competition rules, the violation of which could be the basis for an Article XXIII:1(a) nullification or impairment complaint. As explained in Chapter Three, the Negotiating Group on Basic Telecommunications developed a Reference Paper on competition principles that requires national telecom regulators to be established and to referee interconnection with former or existing telecom monopolies. In the context of a WTO member's duty to regulate anti-competitive behaviour, the Reference Paper contains two highly relevant provisions:

(1) those WTO members which have agreed to the terms of the Reference Paper must maintain appropriate measures for the purpose of preventing specific anti-competitive practices by major

[87] Articles VIII provides in part: (1) Each Member shall ensure that any monopoly supplier of a service in its territory does not, in the supply of the monopoly service in the relevant market, act in a manner inconsistent with that Member's obligations under Article II [the MFN commitment] and specific [market access] commitments. (2) Where a Member's monopoly supplier competes, either directly or through an affiliated company, in the supply of a service outside the scope of its monopoly right and which is subject to that Member's specific commitments, the Member shall ensure that such a supplier does not abuse its monopoly position to act in its territory in a manner inconsistent with such commitments.

suppliers, such as cross-subsidisation, withholding technical and commercial information, or using information obtained from competitors with anti-competitive results; and

(2) WTO members must ensure that interconnection is cost-based, timely, and on non-discriminatory terms, rates, and quality.

This second provision is probably the most important one affecting market access because without interconnection customers of one service supplier cannot communicate with the customers of others. Although the Reference Paper identifies three types of conduct that may be anti-competitive—cross-subsidisation, withholding technical information, and misusing competitors' information—it does not define the term "anti-competitive". In the case of anti-competitive cross-subsidisation, for example, it would occur presumably if a major service supplier who has market power were to use the supranormal profits it earns from that segment of the market to sustain a loss-making operation in a segment of the market where there is competition.[88] However, this is only speculation.

6.74 What would constitute anti-competitive behaviour in situations involving withholding technical information and misuse of competitors' information is not clear. In addition, the Reference Paper does not specifically obligate members to prevent these anti-competitive practices, but only to adopt appropriate measures for the purpose of preventing them. This might put too fine a point on it. Without an obligation to take effective action to prevent these RBPs, the commitments made in the Reference Paper would ring very hollow indeed. GATT and WTO panels have seldom hesitated to give terms in GATT a generous reading that serve to promote the goal of market access.

6.75 Commentators have suggested that in order for the Reference Paper to be effectively implemented, a necessary precondition is the conclusion of a WTO agreement on competition standards—in effect, a reference paper for the Reference Paper.[89] Others believe that such an auxiliary WTO competition principles agreement is not essential and place their faith in the ability of WTO panels to develop such competition principles.[90] Panels would draw from core competition law principles in ruling on whether private conduct is anti-competitive. In addressing private conduct where consensus on competition law principles breaks down, panels would presumably be guided by the basic objective of the Reference Paper and of the Basic Telecoms Agreement itself which is, of course, market access. Professor Robert Hudec is sanguine. He writes:

> Whatever the answers are [from WTO panels], they will only be answers for this one area of government-to-government legal relations, affecting

[88] See OECD, Joint Group on Trade and Competition, "Competition Elements in International Trade Agreements: A Post-Uruguay Round Overview of WTO Agreements" (1999) 14.

[89] See Marco C.E.J. Bronckers & Pierre Larouche, "Telecommunications Services and the World Trade Organization", (1997) 31 J. World Trade 5, 26–28.

[90] See Hudec, "A WTO Perspective", see para. 6.45, n. 47, at 93.

> only the private firms involved in that sector of the economy. There would seem to be no good reason why the answers given by dispute settlement panels would be any less acceptable than in any other area of WTO law. There is no threat here to the integrity, and sovereignty, of national competition laws. Just a slight dent, perhaps, in their pretensions as exclusive arbiter.[91]

This "one area of government-to-government legal relations, affecting only the private firms involved in that sector of the economy," as Professor Hudec describes it, was a $600 billion industry in 1997 and, by one estimate, is expected to double or triple over 10 years.[92] In 1999, world export trade in commercial services was $1.34 trillion.[93] His assessment may also underestimate the power of competition law enforcement authorities and their sensitivity to "turf" issues. And although he does not spell out what the objectives of the Reference Paper are that would guide WTO panels in their formulation of competition law principles in non-core competition policy areas, it is worth remembering that market access *über alles* is the trade policy mantra. Efficient markets in the service of consumer welfare is the competition policy pole star. This is a critical policy difference, one where trade policy and competition policy are a poor fit. The seeds of conflict may be sown if mediating this tension is left to WTO panels.

6.76 **c. Denial of market access to the financial services sector by government-authorised monopolies and other private organisations.** Pursuant to the GATS Understanding on Commitments in Financial Services, members are obligated to list in their schedule of financial services commitments existing monopoly rights and "shall endeavor to eliminate them or reduce their scope."[94] Regarding national treatment violations by private organisations, when membership or participation in any self-regulatory body, securities or futures exchange, or any other organisation is required by a member as a condition of supplying a particular financial service on an equal footing with resident financial service suppliers, members must ensure that such entities accord national treatment to non-resident financial service suppliers.[95]

These are two of the rare instances where GATT–WTO provisions impose an affirmative competition policy obligation on WTO members to ensure market access by eliminating or reducing the market power of financial services monopolies, public or private, and to ensure that foreign financial services suppliers have access to membership in private exchanges and other self-regulatory bodies.

---

[91] Hudec, "A WTO Perspective", see para. 6.45, n. 47, at 93–94.

[92] See Statement of Ambassador Charlene Barshefsky, Basic Telecom Negotiations, Feb. 17, 1997 http://www.ustr.gov/agreements/telecom/barshefsky.html ("Today, telecommunications is a $600 billion industry; under this agreement it will double or even triple over the next ten years.").

[93] See *World Trade Organization, Annual Report 1999*, (2000) at 9.

[94] Understanding on Commitments in Financial Services, para. B.1.

[95] See *id.* para. C.2.

6. *Abuse of Intellectual Property Rights.*

6.77 Articles 8 and 40 of the TRIPS Agreement permit WTO members to take action against licensing practices that restrain competition and other measures against the abuse of intellectual property rights, respectively. The TRIPS Agreement does not require the adoption of laws to prevent such abuses, however. If a member has such competition laws and proceeded against what it considered to be an abuse of IPRs, another member would have a basis for an Article XXIII:1(a) complaint if the member's measures are inconsistent with the other provisions of the TRIPS Agreement.[96]

B. An Article XXIII:1(b) Non-Violation Nullification or Impairment Complaint

6.78 Although the overwhelming majority of GATT and WTO panel proceedings involve alleged breaches of GATT–WTO legal obligations, a WTO member may nevertheless complain that GATT benefits that were to accrue to it have been nullified or impaired because of GATT-legal conduct by another member or of any other situation. Although the non-violation remedy has been an accepted tool of GATT–WTO dispute settlement for over 50 years, few non-violation cases have been decided and those that have have all been decided under Article XXIII:1(b), not under Article XXIII:1(c).[97] This suggests that both the GATT contracting parties and WTO members have approached this remedy with caution and, indeed, have treated it as an exceptional instrument of dispute settlement. The panel reports in the *EEC—Oilseeds* case and the *Kodak-Fuji Film* dispute confirm that the non-violation nullification or impairment remedy should be approached with caution and treated as an exceptional concept.[98] The reason for this caution is straightforward: Members negotiate the rules that they agree to follow and only in the

[96] See TRIPS Agreement, Art. 8.1.

[97] There have been ten cases in which panels or working parties have substantively considered Article XXIII:1(b) claims. See "Report of the Working Party, Australian Subsidy on Ammonium Sulphate", BISD, II/188 (adopted April 3, 1950); "Report of the GATT Panel, Treatment by Germany of Imports of Sardines", BISD, 1st Supp.53 (adopted Oct. 31,1952); "Report of the GATT Panel, Uruguayan Recourse to Article XXIII", BISD, 11th Supp. 95 (adopted Nov. 16, 1962); "Report of the GATT Panel, EC—Tariff Treatment on Imports of Citrus Products from Certain Countries in the Mediterranean Region", GATT Doc. L/5576 (unadopted, Feb. 7, 1985); "Report of the GATT Panel, EEC—Production Aids Granted on Canned Peaches, Canned Pears, Canned Fruit Cocktail and Dried Grapes", GATT Doc. L/5778 (unadopted, Feb. 20, 1985); "Report of the GATT Panel, Japan—Trade in Semi-conductors", BISD, 35th Supp.116 (adopted May 4,1988); "Report of the GATT Panel, EEC—Oilseeds", BISD, 37th Supp. 86 (adopted Jan. 25, 1990); "Report of the GATT Panel, United States—Agricultural Waiver", BISD, 37th Supp. 228 (adopted Nov. 7, 1990); "Kodak-Fuji Film Dispute", see para. 6.58, n. 67; "Report of the WTO Panel, European Communities—Measures Affecting Asbestos and Asbestos-Containing Products", WT/DS135/R, Part F (Sept. 18, 2000), appeal pending before Appellate Body as of December 1, 2000. See also Cho, see para. 6.52, n. 61, at 316–21; Ernst-Ulrich Petersmann, "Violation Complains and Non-Violation Complaints in Public International Trade Law", (1991) 34 German Y.B. Int'l L. 175, 192.

[98] In *EEC—Oilseeds*, the United States stated that it "concurred in the proposition that non-violation nullification or impairment should remain an exceptional concept. Although this concept had been in the text of Article XXIII of the General Agreement from the outset, a cautious approach should continue to be taken in applying the concept." *EEC—Oilseeds*, BISD, 37th Supp. 86, 118, para. 114. The EEC in that case stated that "recourse to the 'non-violation'

rarest of cases would expect to be challenged for actions not in contravention of those rules.

6.79 A claim of Article XXIII:1(b) non-violation nullification or impairment has three elements. A complaint must allege that:

(1) benefits accruing to the complaining member under GATT or a WTO agreement have been

(2) nullified or impaired

(3) "by the application of another contracting party of any measure," although that measure is not prohibited under GATT or any WTO agreement. The complaining party must submit a detailed justification in support of its complaint.[99]

In GATT practice, non-violation nullification or impairment claims have arisen where a country which made a tariff concession thereafter acted in a way that frustrated the reasonable expectations of market access created by the concession.[1] The reasonable expectations element is a temporal element: a comparison must be made of the competitive relationship between the domestic and imported products at the time when a relevant tariff concession was made and at the current time. In order for a non-violation claim to succeed, the action taken by the responding member could not have been reasonably anticipated by the complaining member at the time the concession was first negotiated.[2]

6.80 The formal remedy that is available in an Article XXIII:1(b) proceeding differs slightly from the Article XXIII:1(a) remedy. The WTO DSU provides special procedures applicable to disputes involving non-violation nullification or impairment complaints. Under DSU Article 26.1, following a successful Article XXIII:1(b) complaint, the panel or Appellate Body is to recommend that the parties reach a mutually satisfactory adjustment of their dispute. The losing party is under no obligation to withdraw the offending measure or practice, but it must make "a mutually satisfactory adjustment" and compensation may be part of the final settlement.[3] A successful Article XXIII:1(b) complainant is thus entitled to compensation and may retaliate if suitable compensation is not forthcoming.[4]

---

concept under Article XXIII:1(b) should remain exceptional, since otherwise the trading world would be plunged into a state of precariousness and uncertainty". *id.* para. 113. See "Kodak-Fuji Film Dispute", see para. 6.58, n. 67, para. 10.36. See also Edmond McGovern, *International Trade Regulation* s. 2.27, at 2.27–1 ("If these provisions were taken literally their potential scope would be enormous.").

[99] See DSU Art. 26.1(a).

[1] See, *e.g.* "Report of the GATT Panel, EEC—Payments and Subsidies Paid to Processors and Producers of Oilseeds and Related Animal-Feed Proteins", BISD, 37th Supp. 86, para. 148 (1991). See generally World Trade Organization, *Analytical Index: Guide to GATT Law and Practice*, vol. 2, at 657–68 (1995) (hereinafter "Guide to GATT Law and Practice").

[2] See, *e.g.* "Kodak-Fuji Film Dispute", see para. 6.58, n. 67, at para. 10.76.

[3] DSU Art. 26.1(b), (d).

[4] See Hudec, "A WTO Perspective", see para. 6.45, n. 47, at 90. It has also been suggested that the a non-violation complaint proceeding can be a valuable transparency device. See Bernard Hoekman & Peter C. Mavroidis, "Competition, Competition Policy and the GATT", (1994) 17 World Economy 121.

6.81 In the context of an RBP complaint, a generalised Article XXIII:1(b) complaint that a member's failure to maintain or enforce competition legislation, which failure has left unchecked private RBPs within that member's territory that have in turn prevented market access, probably would not be cognisable as an Article XVIII:1(b) claim. First, an Article XXIII:1(b) complainant must present "a detailed justification" in support of its claim that the responding member's measure has upset the competitive position of the imported products in issue.[5] The complainant must establish the existence of a concession and then identify specific, affirmative conduct by another member—in the words of Article XVIII:1(b), "the application of another contracting party of any measure"—that has denied the complainant of the benefits of the concession, *i.e.* has put the imported products in issue at a competitive disadvantage. Thus, a causal connection must be established between the measure and the injury.

6.82 Secondly, in proving nullification or impairment of a benefit in the context of private anti-competitive conduct, the complaining member would have to show that it had a reasonable expectation that, at the time it negotiated trade concessions with the responding member, the responding member would enforce its competition laws to prevent private barriers to market access.[6] On the other hand, if the private barriers were known to exist at the time the trade concessions were negotiated, then the complaining member is in effect estopped from complaining about them later on the ground that the complaining member should have specifically negotiated for their removal at the earlier negotiations.[7]

6.83 In evaluating whether a member's expectations are reasonable, the matter is straightforward at the polar extremes—the complained-of measure was either in effect at the time the concession was negotiated or it was not even contemplated. In a panel proceeding involving facts in between these two extremes, a GATT panel concluded that because of public discussions during the Tokyo Round negotiations of E.C. tariff preferences for citrus products from Mediterranean countries, the United States must have been aware that the value of the tariff concessions it received from the E.C. for such products would be adversely affected.[8] In a variation on these facts, in the *Kodak-Fuji Film* dispute the panel concluded that a measure that is introduced after the close of tariff negotiations is presumptively unanticipated, but this presumption can be rebutted if the responding member shows that the new measure was clearly contemplated on the basis of a measure in place prior to the negotiations. Measures introduced before the close of

[5] See McGovern, see para. 6.78, n. 98, s. 2.273, at 2.27–5, 2.27–6.

[6] See, *e.g.* "Report of the Working Party, Australian Subsidy on Ammonium Sulphate", BISD, II/188 (1952).

[7] See Hudec, "A WTO Perspective", see para. 6.45, n. 47, at 98–99 ("barriers cannot be considered a breach of expectations unless they were in fact not known at the time the bargain was actually made, on the theory that known hazards are always discounted in the prices paid in a deal").

[8] See "Report of the GATT Panel, EC—Tariff Treatment on Imports of Citrus Products from Certain Countries in the Mediterranean Region", GATT Doc. L/5576, para. 4.34 (unadopted, Feb. 7, 1985).

negotiations, however, give rise to the opposite presumption. In that event, the complaining member is on notice of such measures from the date of their publication and can only rebut the presumption by showing that it could not have reasonably anticipated their effect.[9]

6.84 Regarding the third element of a "measure," the failure to investigate or prosecute anti-competitive conduct within a member's territory would in all likelihood not qualify as a "measure," unless that failure or refusal was based on a regulation or guideline promulgated by national enforcement authorities stating that certain conduct was exempt under the national competition laws. In this connection, the following statement by the panel in the *Kodak-Fuji Film* report is worth noting:

> [A] Member's industrial policy, pursuing the goal of increasing efficiency in a sector, could in some circumstances upset the competitive relationship in the market between domestic and imported products in a way that could give rise to a cause of action under Article XXIII:1(b).[10]

The panel generally favoured an expansive interpretation of the term. Thus, the term "measure" is much broader than the term "requirement" used in Article III:4.

Professor Hudec is undoubtedly correct when he states that:

> [d]oing nothing would not normally be considered a 'measure,' and on this point WTO tribunals are certain to require strict conformity with the words of the [non-violation nullification or impairment] remedy, given its exceptional character.[11]

6.85 When, if ever, could government inaction give rise to an Article XXIII:1(b) non-violation complaint? Consider, first, GATT Article VI on dumping. It does not obligate members from whose territory dumped exports are shipped to prevent such dumping.[12] As a practical matter this makes sense, considering that it is only injurious dumping that is condemned. The country of importation is in a much better position to investigate and access the injurious impact of dumped imports than is the country of exportation. Nevertheless, Article VI:1 does state that:

> contracting parties recognize that dumping . . . is to be condemned if it causes or threatens material injury to an established industry in the territory of a contracting party.

Therefore, it is arguable that upon presentation of satisfactory evidence by the importing member that such injurious dumping is occurring or has occurred, an Article XXIII:1(b) case could possibly be made out.

[9] See "Kodak-Fuji Film Dispute", see para. 6.58, n. 67, paras. 10.79–10.81, 10.103.
[10] *id.* para. 10.38.
[11] Hudec, "A WTO Perspective", see para. 6.45, n. 47, at 99.
[12] See "Report of the GATT Panel, Canada—Foreign Investment Review Act", BISD, (adopted Feb. 7, 1984). 30th Supp. 140, 163, para. 5.18.

6.86 Next consider GATS Article IX, *Business Practices*. That Article provides in part that "certain business practices of service suppliers, other than the practices mentioned in Article VIII, may restrain competition and thereby restrict trade in services." GATS Article IX places upon WTO members an obligation to enter into consultations with any other member with a view to eliminating such RBPs. It also imposes a duty to co-operate by providing non-confidential information of relevance to the matter in issue. Thus, analogous to the American labour law rule that employers have a duty to bargain with unions but no duty to agree, WTO members have a duty to consult and co-operate, but no duty to eliminate offending RBPs.

C. An Article XXIII:1(c) Non-Violation Nullification or Impairment Complaint

6.87 The other non-violation complaint provision, Article XXIII:1(c), permits a complaint to be brought if benefits accruing to a member under GATT or a WTO agreement are being nullified or impaired "as the result of the existence of any other situation." A nullification or impairment complaint based upon a government's failure to take action against private RBPs could be the subject of an Article XXIII:1(c) complaint.

As rare as Article XXIII:1(b) complaints are, Article XXIII:1(c) complaints are even rarer. An example of a GATT Article XXIII:1(c) situation is a 1983 complaint by the E.C. against Japan that the benefits of successive negotiations with Japan had not been realised due to factors peculiar to the Japanese economy that had allegedly resulted in a lower level of imports. Ultimately, the E.C. did not pursue its complaint.[13]

6.88 DSU Article 26.2 sets out special procedures applicable to GATT Article XXIII:1(c) complaints. The normal DSU procedures apply only up to the point where the panel report is circulated to the members. Beyond that point, the dispute settlement rules and procedures contained in the Decision of April 12, 1989 on Improvements to the GATT Dispute Settlement Rules and Procedures apply to issues of adoption, surveillance, and implementation of recommendations.[14] This means that in GATT Article XXIII:1(c) cases, there is no Appellate Body review and the GATT 1947 practice of adoption of panel reports by consensus, as opposed to the DSU rule of rejection by consensus, applies.[15]

6.89 In the context of competition law complaints, as noted above, the failure or refusal of a member to either enact or enforce competition laws would probably not qualify for an Article XXIII:1(b) complaint because the member has not engaged in any affirmative conduct. However, that failure or refusal would certainly amount to "the existence of any other situation" under Article XXII:1(c). Resolving the issue of nullification or impairment of

---

[13] See *Guide to GATT Law and Practice*, see para. 6.79, n. 1, at 670–71. The only other Article XXIII:1(c) complaint is Uruguayan Recourse to Article XXIII, BISD, 11th Supp. 95 (1963); Uruguayan Recourse to Article XXIII, BISD, 13th Supp. 35, 45 (1965).

[14] BISD, 36th Supp. 61 (1989).

[15] Compare *id.* at G.3, with DSU Art. 16.4.

a GATT benefit would require an examination of what the parties knew at the time they negotiated trade concessions about private conduct restricting market access. It would be incumbent about the complaining member to show that it had no knowledge of such anti-competitive conduct and a reasonable expectation that none would occur to block market access on products for which it had successfully negotiated tariff concessions.

6.90 In either type of non-violation complaint, the resources and capacity of the WTO dispute settlement mechanism would be severely tested. The private parties themselves would not be on trial in a WTO dispute settlement proceeding, therefore many due process guarantees could be dispensed with in order to expedite the proceeding. Nevertheless, proving that private parties have violated competition laws can be a formidable task. Competition law enforcement proceedings brought in national courts are prolix, complex, and expensive.[16] Economics and economists play a major role in competition cases. Discovery of confidential business information is facilitated in court proceedings through protective orders and the threat of contempt sanctions for violating that order. But what assurances would businesses have that their confidential information would remain confidential if disclosed to a WTO panel?

More importantly, what would the "reasonable expectations" standard be for showing nullification or impairment of a GATT benefit in either an Article XXIII:1(b) or (c) non-violation case? That the responding member would enact and aggressively enforce competition laws? That it would enact such laws and make a good faith effort to enforce them? Either of these standards would make it difficult to prove a non-violation claim, for under either standard the responding member could successfully defend where it thoroughly investigated the RBP claim and found no cause to proceed.

6.91 It has been suggested that the standard should be simply that an exporting country has a reasonable expectation that private barriers to trade will not exist in export markets for which trade concessions have been negotiated.[17] Even with this relaxed reasonable expectation standard, a complaining member would still have to prove the existence of a prohibited RBP. In the case of core competition law principles where some consensus has been reached, such as hard-core horizontal restraints, there would be an agreed-upon legal norm against which the private conduct could be measured. In the case of most vertical restraints, however, even when agreement ostensibly exists on the governing legal standard, *e.g.* the rule of reason, reasonable minds may differ on whether a vertical restraint is, on balance, efficiency enhancing. Nevertheless, formidable proof problems would persist, once again drawing into question the capacity of the WTO dispute settlement mechanism to handle such disputes. In cases where consensus does not exist on a legal norm, how would a WTO panel be expected to rule in the absence

[16] See OECD, "Judicial Enforcement of Competition Laws", OCDE/GD(97)200 (1997).

[17] See Hudec, "A WTO Perspective", see para. 6.45, n. 47, at 101. For an argument that non-violation cases should be abolished because they are not rules-based, see Cho, see para. 6.52, n. 61.

of a WTO agreement on competition policy? In the end, perhaps the best solution after all is said and done is to leave the resolution of international competition law disputes to national enforcement authorities.

6.92 A reasonable expectations standard that asks whether private RBPs in an export market are preventing market access looks like a no-fault approach to the issue. The complaining member is not formally accusing the responding member of having failed to take action not otherwise required under GATT–WTO agreements. It would be surprising, however, if responding members—encouraged by their proud competition law enforcement authorities and the concerned domestic firms—did not take umbrage at the insinuation that they were not enforcing their competition laws. One would expect responding members in most cases to vigorously defend against the charge that they in effect tolerated anti-competitive behaviour in their domestic market, as well as to champion the cause of their domestic firms by coming to their defence. Besides questions of lost pride, responding members stand to lose trade benefits if a complaining member is successful in its non-violation, competition policy complaint.

D. A Postmortem on and Lessons from the *Kodak-Fuji Film* Dispute

6.93 The *Kodak-Fuji Film* dispute teaches several lessons. One of the more important is that bringing a successful, non-violation nullification or impairment complaint is difficult. A second lesson, which the panel report puts in high relief, is the different perspective of trade officials and competition law enforcement authorities regarding vertical restraints of trade. A third broad lesson is that Japan and the United States have competition laws that, while quite similar on the surface, are on occasion applied in very different ways.

6.94 Differences in the historical development of the two countries' economies, societal values and the independence of the enforcement and judicial branches of the two governments all combine to create substantially divergent systems of competition law. Each country has a unique perspective on the proper role of co-operation and competition among related businesses and industries, which likely results from each nation's unique viewpoint on the role of the individual in society. While U.S. firms are restricted by punitive laws from engaging in collective behaviour that is arguably efficient, Japanese companies are encouraged to take advantage of the enhanced efficiency derived from co-operation and are gently prodded back into line if the co-operation is excessive. These two systems collide, as is inevitable in a global economy. While the U.S. government complains to Japan about the resulting trade imbalance, the Japanese government naturally views U.S. competition laws as part of the problem.

6.95 Although the two systems are incompatible enough that a complete harmonisation of laws cannot occur in the foreseeable future, each government can begin to eliminate the behaviour that is most offensive to the other. For Japan, this means taking serious efforts to end cartels, combines, inefficient *keiretsu* and changing prevailing societal attitudes that prevent foreign access to the domestic market. For the United States, this means elimination of the treble damages penalty, which arguably has a chilling effect on efficient legal behaviour; greater consideration for Japan's sovereignty, which should increase trust and mutual respect between the two countries; and respect for the decisions of international bodies such as the WTO, which should increase the legitimacy of the WTO in future disputes.

III. SUMMARY AND CONCLUSIONS

6.96 Assuming the utility of international rules to regulate private RBPs, the WTO is not the ideal international organisation for negotiating or developing such rules, or for policing such practices. The GATT–WTO system is less concerned about economic efficiency than it is about market access, less concerned about enhancing total welfare (consumer plus producer welfare) in markets than it is about ensuring that producers have access to export markets. The GATT–WTO system is, at its core, a forum with a mercantilist approach to multilateral trade negotiations—that is, a system that is market-access oriented and that promotes global trade through reciprocal trade concessions. In that capacity the GATT–WTO system plays an important role in making markets more competitive by reducing government tariff and non-tariff barriers to trade. It has been successful in that role it for over 50 years.

Despite more than 50 years of effort toward trade liberalisation, however, the restrictive and distortive effects of government measures, especially trade remedies, still appear to be more harmful to trade and competition than the effects of private RBPs.[18] Would not further work by the WTO toward completing its unfinished agenda of opening markets to foreign goods and services be a more effective means of promoting the contestability of markets? The closer countries move toward open market access, the less opportunity there will be for RBPs to be pursued in domestic and international markets. Accordingly, the WTO should stick to its traditional role by completing the unfinished agenda of reducing and eliminating government barriers to trade in goods and services. Promoting liberal trade, coupled with fostering an open investment climate, should be the WTO's focus. These goals in themselves are part of competition policy, although they go by different names.

6.97 The WTO may be a victim of its own success. Measured against its mandate to reduce the very high tariffs that existed at the end of World War II, to eliminate the quotas on imports that were rampant after the War and otherwise to liberalise international trade, the WTO and its predecessor, the GATT, have been hugely successful. With its rules-based legal regime for conducting international trade, backed by an re-invigorated dispute settlement mechanism, it is understandable why proponents of a multilateral agreement on competition policy have turned to the WTO as the forum for negotiating and administering such an agreement. Their reasons and motives differ little

[18] See "WGTCP 1998 Report", see para. 6.01, n. 1, at 21, para. 59.

from those of environmentalists who push for reform of WTO agreements so that those agreements better accommodate environmental goals. With improved rules in place, the WTO is the only international organisation with an effective intergovernmental dispute settlement mechanism of any kind to enforce those rules.

6.98 While the links between trade and competition policy are undeniable, those links are not without kinks and breaks. To press the WTO into service as the forum for repairing the breaks and taking out the kinks would be misguided for at least two reasons. For one, the institutional costs to the WTO would be high. The WTO's plate is full, its agenda unfinished and its authority fragile. The WTO dispute settlement mechanism is under tremendous stress. To saddle the Organisation with yet another hot-button issue—a virtual lightening rod planted on its institutional head—would do little but further undermine the WTO's status and drain valuable and scarce institutional resources away from its primary mission of promoting liberal trade by eliminating government barriers to trade.[19] From a GATT–WTO perspective, maintaining the status quo in the area of competition policy, coupled with further research on the subject, is the only unambiguously beneficial course of action for the WTO to pursue. The WTO can perform ably as an educational body in the near term, and perhaps as a deliberative and negotiation forum in the long term.

6.99 A second reason for not adding competition policy to the WTO's agenda is that while a commitment to further trade liberalisation under WTO auspices clearly exists—although at times it is a wavering commitment—the same level of commitment does not exist for international competition policy and rules. A consensus exists among economists and some government officials that the GATT–WTO rules and agreements on trade liberalisation generate mutually beneficial welfare effects for importing and exporting nations. No similar consensus exists among economists or government officials regarding the effects of proposed international competition rules. Until such a consensus emerges, it is only sensible to continue with the current decentralised, bilateral approach on competition law enforcement and the multilateral, WTO approach to trade liberalisation and to leave for another day negotiation of a multilateral competition policy agreement. Until then, increased use of bilateral agreements can help build toward a plurilateral or multilateral agreement on competition policy by increasing trust and building confidence in competition law cases with cross-jurisdictional implications.

In sum, the economic arguments for government intervention to correct market failures brought on by restrictive business practices may be strong but those arguments do not necessarily lead inexorably to the conclusion that a multilateral agreement on competition norms and enforcement is the optimal response. Forcing the bitter pill of international regulation of competition policy down the throats of countries that are neither prepared nor willing to accept such rules is a formula for disaster. Developed countries might bully

[19] For additional institutional arguments against housing a multilateral agreement on competition policy in the WTO, see generally Tarullo, see para. 6.48, n. 52.

less-powerful developing countries into entering into such agreements as the price of continued WTO membership, but adherence to the commitments made in such agreements will be begrudging and cheating at the margins widespread. In order to be durable, robust and successful, international agreements must be perceived by the parties as being in their self-interest.

Index

Abuse of dominant position, 2.105, 2.106, 4.111–4.112
- abuse, meaning, 2.106
- antidumping duty law, 4.125–4.142
  - adoption of, 4.127
  - alternatives, 4.141
  - antitrust laws compared, 4.131–4.142
  - collusive behaviour, and, 4.13
  - forum for discussion, 4.138
  - free trade, and, 4.139
  - injury and causation, 4.132
  - policy, 4.129
  - purpose, 4.126
  - reform, 4.142
  - repeal, proposal for, 4.134
  - resistance to reform, 4.140
  - target, 4.128
  - United States, 4.131
  - unlawful policy, 4.133
- **antitrust law**, and, 4.130–4.142
- **Article 82, E.C. Treaty**, 2.105–2.106
- **dominant position, meaning**, 2.106
- **European Union**, 4.111
- **market share**, 4.116–4.118
  - Canada, 4.118
  - European Union, 4.116
  - United States, 4.117
- predatory pricing, 4.120–4.124. *See also* **Predatory pricing**
- price discrimination laws, 4.125–4.142
- proof of international price discrimination, 4.135
- relevant geographic market, 4.113, 4.114
- relevant market, definition, 4.112–4.119
- differences as to, 4.119
  - DOJ/FTC Horizontal Merger Guidelines, 4.115
- relevant product market, 4.113

Abuse of intellectual property rights, 4.091–4.095
- European Union, 4.094, 4.095
- legal treatment, 4.091
- United States, 4.092, 4.093

Act of state doctrine, 2.025

Addressing private RBPs under existing GATT-WTO rules, 6.51– 6.95
- abuse of intellectual property rights, 6.77
- argument for maintaining status quo, 6.51

Addressing private RBPs under existing GATT-WTO rules—*cont.*
- Article II:4 import monopoly complaint, 6.55, 6.56
- Article XI quantitative restriction complaint, 6.64–6.67
  - aim, 6.65
  - *Kodak-Fuji Film* dispute, 6.66
- Article XXIII: 1(a) nullification or impairment complaint, 6.53, 6.54
- Article XXIII: 1(b) non-violation nullification or impairment complaint, 6.78–6.86
  - business practices, 6.86
  - elements, 6.79
  - failure to investigate, 6.84
  - formal remedy, 6.80
  - proof, 6.82
- Article XXIII: 1(c) non-violation nullification or impairment complaint, 6.87–6.92
  - dispute settlement mechanism, and, 6.90
  - reasonable expectation standard, 6.91, 6.92
  - special procedures, 6.88
- GATS competition policy commitments, 6.70–6.76
  - abuse of dominant position by monopoly service suppliers generally, 6.71
  - abuse of dominant position by monopoly service supplier in basic telecommunications sector, 6.72–6.75
  - denial of market access to financial services sector by government-authorised monopolies and other private organisations, 6.76
- *Kodak-Fuji Film* dispute
  - lessons from 6.93–6.95
- national treatment complaint, 6.57–6.63
  - subject matter, 6.58
  - U.S. legal proceedings, and, 6.59–6.63
- private import or export monopolies established under GATT Article XVII, 6.68–6.69

Agreement in Government Procurement, 3.095–3.097
- limited tendering procedures, 3.097
- selection procedure, 3.096

Antidumping Act of 1916 dispute, 3.112–3.115
aim of Act, 3.112
findings of Appellate Body, 3.113, 31.114, 3.115
findings of panel, 3.113
violation of GATT provisions and WTO agreements, 3.113
Asia-Pacific Economic Co-operation forum (APEC), 2.172–2.177
annual workshop, 2.176
background, 2.172
competition policy, 2.175–2.177
individual action plans, 2.174
informality, 2.172
membership, 2.172
Osaka Action Agenda, 2.174
permanent Secretariat, 2.173
Australia-New Zealand Closer Economic Relations Trade Agreement, 2.088–2.090
background, 2.088
"effects test", and, 2.089
significance, 2.089
Australia-U.S. Antitrust Co-operation Agreement 1982, 2.044–2.046

Bilateral approaches to competition policy, 2.037–2.090
Australia and New Zealand, 2.071
Australia-U.S. Antitrust Co-operation Agreement, 2.044–2.046
bilateral agreements on antitrust enforcement under IAEAA, 2.077–2.090
Australia-New Zealand Closer Economic Relations Trade Agreement, 2.088
Australia-U.S. Agreement 1999, 2.083–2.086
background, 2.077–2.079
benefits of information sharing, 2.082
confidentiality, and, 2.078
disclosure of evidence, 2.079
exceptions, 2.081
future agreements, 2.087
bilateral co-operation agreements on competition law enforcement, 2.041–2.071
Brazil-U.S. Antitrust Co-operation Agreement, 2.068
Canada-E.U. Co-operation Agreement 1998, 2.070
Canada-U.S. Co-operation Agreements, 2.047–2.051. *See also* **Canada-U.S. Co-operation Agreements**

Bilateral approaches to competition policy—*cont.*
E.U.-Eastern and Central Europe Co-operation Agreements, 2.069
E.U.-U.S. Co-operation Agreements, 2.052–2.055. *See also* **E.U.-U.S. Co-operation Agreements**
E.U., within, 2.071
Germany-U.S. Antitrust Accord, 2.042, 2.043
Israel-U.S. Antitrust Co-operation Agreement, 2.063
Japan-U.S. Antitrust Co-operation Agreement, 2.064–2.067
Mutual Legal Assistance treaties (MLATs), 2.072–2.087
scope, 2.072, 2.073
need for, 2.038
non-enforceability, 2.039
Treaty of Mutual Legal Assistance in Criminal Matters 1985, 2.074–2.076
types of agreement, 2.040
Blocking statutes, 2.029–2.031
Brazil-U.S. Antitrust Co-operation Agreement, 2.068
Canada
effects test, 2.008
Canada-E.U. Co-operation Agreement 1998, 2.070
Canada-U.S. Co-operation Agreements, 2.047–2.051
enforcement co-operation, 2.048
factors, 2.049, 2.050
enforcement of deceptive marketing practices laws, 2.051
notification obligation, 2.047
CARICOM, 2.149
Cartel activity, 4.059–4.077
collusive, 4.065
criminal law, and, 4.060
export cartels, 4.066–4.076. *See also* **Export cartels**
import cartels, 4.078–4.079
meaning, 4.059
OECD Recommendation on Hard-core Cartels, 4.077
price fixing, 4.061–4.063
problems in policing, 4.064–4.077
trading companies, 4.080, 4.081
Chile
MERCOSUR, and, 2.120
Civil enforcement proceedings, 4.163–4.165
criminal proceedings, and, 4.163–4.165
Clawback statutes, 2.029–2.031

Comity, 2.013–2.021
jurisdictional rule of reason, and, 2.014, 2.015
Antitrust Enforcement Guidelines for International Operations 1995, 2.019–2.020
applicability, 2.016
balancing of interests, and, 2.015
U.S. Clayton Act, 2.017, 2.018
U.S. Foreign Trade Antitrust Improvements Act, 2.017
"true conflict", and, 2.016
Kodak-Fuji Film dispute, 2.021
meaning, 2.013
sensitivity towards interests of other countries, 2.014
Competition policy. *See also* **Trade and competition policy**
consumer welfare, and, 1.17
government-condoned business practices, 1.19
maintenance of competitive markets, and, 1.24
national concerns, and, 1.18
national policies, 1.14
predatory pricing, and, 1.26
WTO, and. *See* **WTO**
Convention on international competition rules, prospects for, 1.52
Convergence of competition laws and policies threshold issues, 4.051–4.056
Criminal enforcement proceedings, 4.163–4.165
Canada, 4.164
civil proceedings, and, 4.163–4.165
Japan, 4.164
OECD member countries, 4.165
Taiwan, 4.164
Discretionary enforcement, 4.166–4.168
national self-interest, and, 4.167
oversight by national authorities, 4.168
Divergence of competition laws and policies
Canada, 4.053
degree of consensus, 4.173
economic theory, and, 4.055, 4.056
European Union, 4.053
future prospects, 4.174
small countries, 4.054
threshold issues, 4.051–4.056
United States, 4.052
Draft International Antitrust Code, 2.178–2.187
abuse of dominant position, 2.185
abuse of intellectual property rights, 2.182
contents, 2.179
Draft International Antitrust Code—*cont.*
"Control of Concentration and Restructuring", 2.184
future development, 2.186
"Horizontal and Vertical Restraints", 2.180–2.183
minimum standards approach, 2.187
principles, 2.178
prohibition against inflicting disadvantage, 2.183
"Public Undertakings and State Authorisation", 2.186
vertical restraints, 2.181, 2.182
E.U.-Eastern and Central Europe Co-operation Agreements, 2.069
E.U.-U.S. Co-operation Agreements, 2.052–2.055
Antitrust Agreement of 1991, 2.052–2.055
Boeing/ McDonnell Douglas case, 2.055
co-ordination of enforcement activities, 2.054
factors to guide comity analysis, 2.052
notifications of merger and enforcement activities, 2.053
Positive Comity Agreement 1998, 2.056–2.062
effect, 2.056
enforcement proceedings, 2.057
E.U.'s motives, 2.060
investigations, 2.058, 2.059
potential efficacy, 2.062
purported benefits of positive comity, 2.061
European Union, 2.091–2.116
Article 81 on restrictive agreements, 2.094–2.104
agreements of minor importance, 2.098
block exemptions, 2.097, 2.100–2.103
fines, 2.099
individual exemptions, 2.095, 2.096
reforms of 1999–2000 affecting vertical restraints, 2.100–2.103
reforms of 2001 affecting Regulation No.17, 2.104
Article 82 on abuse of dominant position, 2.105, 2.106. *See also* **Abuse of dominant position**
Article 86 on government-induced distortions of competition, 2.107
European Commission, 2.092
extraterritoriality and comity, 2.115
"implemented" test, 2.116
regulation of mergers and acquisitions, 2.108–2.114
Boeing/McDonnell Douglas case, 2.112

European Union—*cont.*
regulation of mergers and acquisitions—*cont.*
Community dimension, 2.109, 2.110
extraterritorial enforcement power, 2.112–2.114
investigation by Commission, 2.111
MCI/WorldCom merger, 2.113
notification thresholds, 2.109
statistics, 2.114
Title V, E.C. Treaty, 2.093
Exempted conduct, 4.171
Exempted sectors, 4.170
Export cartels, 4.066–4.076
Canada, 4.069
condemnation under WTO members' competition laws, 4.068
European Union, 4.075
Exporting Trading Company Act 1982, 4.073
Foreign Trade Antitrust Improvements Act 1982, 4.074
immunity of, 4.066
Mexico, 4.070
OECD, 4.076
United States, 4.071–4.074
Webb-Pomerene Act, 4.071, 4.072

Foreign nondisclosure laws, 2.029–2.031
Foreign sovereign compulsion, 2.026
Foreign sovereign immunity, 2.022–2.024
"commercial" activity, 2.024
restrictive immunity, 2.023
Free Trade Area of the Americas (FTAA), 2.137–2.148
background, 2.137
Belo Horizonte Summit 1997, 2.143
antidumping laws, 2.145
areas of divergence, 2.144
Costa Rica meeting, 2.146, 2.147
Declaration of Principles, 2.138
labour and the environment, 2.140
Miami Summit Action Plan 1994, 2.139
negotiating group on competition policy, 2.142–2.147
recommendations, 2.143
negotiations, 2.140, 2.141
policy statements, 2.148

GATS, 3.060–3.076
business practices, 3.062
"measures by Members", meaning, 3.060
monopolies and exclusive service suppliers, 3.062

GATS—*cont.*
private restrictive business practices, and, 1.34
recognition measures, 3.061
Telecoms Annex, 3.063–3.069
access to and use of public telecommunications transport networks and services, 3.065–3.069
types of measures, 3.067
General Agreement on Tariffs and Trade (GATT) 1994, 3.010–3.033
Article II.4, 3.011–3.014
minimum pricing practices, 3.014
monopolies, 3.013
object and purpose, 3.011
practices covered, 3.012
reasonable margin of profit, 3.012
Article III, 3.015–3.020
"affecting", meaning, 3.017, 3.018
equality of competitive conditions in import markets, 3.016
"laws, regulations or requirements", 3.020
purpose, 3.015
Tariff Act 1930, and, 3.019
Article VI, 3.021
Article X, 3.022–3.024
panel interpretations, 3.023
Uruguay Round, 3.024
Article XI, 3.025, 3.026
quantitative restrictions, 3.025, 3.026
Article XVII, 3.027
Article XX, 3.028, 3.029
Article XXIII:1(c), 3.033
Article XXIII:1(b), 3.030–3.032
non-violation nullification or impairment, 3.030–3.032
open trade, and, 1.06
provisions relating to competition policy, 3.010
reduction of tariffs and non-tariff barriers, 1.07
GATT-WTO system, 3.001–3.040
Canadian Foreign Investment Review Act dispute, 3.037
competition policy under GATT 1994, 3.010–3.033. *See also* **GATT 1994**
copper cartel dispute, 3.038
GATT dispute settlement proceedings involving competition policy issues, 3.036–3.040
Havana Charter 3.001–3.009. *See also* **Havana Charter**
history of competition rules, 3.001–3.040
Keiretsu, 3.041

GATT dispute settlement proceedings involving competition policy issues—*cont.*
nature of, 6.96
proposals to add competition policy provisions to GATT 1947, 3.034, 3.035
Decision on Arrangements for Consultation on Restrictive Business Practices, 3.035
semiconductor dispute, 3.039
Germany-U.S. Antitrust Accord 1976, 2.042, 2.043
Grey area measures. *See* **Voluntary export restraint agreements**
Grey market goods, 4.096–4.107
exhaustion, doctrine of, 4.099
meaning, 4.097
motivation for exporting, 4.098
regulation in United States, 4.100–4.107
common-market exceptions, 4.103
Copyright Act, 4.106
Customs Service, and, 4.101
Katzel decision, and, 4.102
Lanham Act, 4.104, 4.105
Hard-core cartel
meaning, 2.164
Havana Charter, 1.51, 3.001–3.009
Article 46, 3.004
Article 47, 3.006
Article 48, 3.006
Article 50, 3.007
Article 53, 3.007
background, 3.001, 3.002
Chapter V, 3.008, 3.009
prohibited RBPs, 3.005
regulation of restrictive business practices, 3.004
Horizontal restraints, 4.057–4.081
cartel activity, 4.059–4.077. *See also* **Cartel activity**
meaning, 4.057
treatment by competition laws, 4.058
Import cartels, 4.078–4.079
International Competition Policy Advisory Committee (ICPAC)
extraterritoriality, on, 2.012
Israel-U.S. Antitrust Co-operation Agreement 1999, 2–063
Japan-U.S. Antitrust Co-operation Agreement 1999, 2.064–2.067
Agreement on Importance of Co-operation, 2.066
background, 2.064
Japan-U.S. Antitrust Co-operation Agreement 1999—*cont.*
Conflict Avoidance, 2.066
Consultations and Exchange of Information, 2.066
Enforcement Co-operation and Co-ordination, 2.066
Enhanced Initiative on Deregulation and Competition Policy June 1997, 2.065
Notification of Enforcement Activities, 2.066
Positive Comity, 2.066
preamble, 2.066
traditional comity factors, 2.067

Keiretsu, 1.15
disputes as to, 3.041

Limits of multilateralism, 6.01–6.99
Medium-size enterprises, 4.172
MERCOSUR, 2.117–2.128
arbitral panel, 2.119
Chile, 2.120
competition policy, 2.122–2.128
goal, 2.118
membership, 2.120, 2.121
Protocol of the Defence of Competition, 2.122
co-operation and consultation mechanism, 2.128
enforcement, 2.124
sanctions, 2.125–2.127
types of conduct constituting prohibited restrictive business practice, 2.123
size of market, 2.118
Treaty of Asuncion, 2.117
key obligations, 2.119
Mergers and acquisitions, 4.143–4.156
Boeing/McDonnell Douglas merger, 4.151, 4.152
Canada, 4.149
"Community dimension", 4.146, 4.147
convergence in pre-merger review process, 4.155
co-operation in multi-jurisdictional mergers, 4.151
cross-border frictions, 4.153, 4.154
European Union, 4.145
ICPACrecommendations, 4.156
market-share test, 4.150
multi-jurisdictional issues, 4.143
NAFTA, 4.145
pre-merger notification laws, 4.144
remedies, 4.154

Mergers and acquisitions—*cont.*
standards for pre-merger review, 4.146
statistics, 4.143
substantive pre-merger review standards, 4.156
United States, 4.148
Mexico
effects test, 2.008
Multilateral agreement on minimum RBP standards, 5.02–5.28
developing countries, 5.16–5.28
enforcement, and, 5.21
exemptions, 5.18
export cartels, 5.25
investment screening laws, and, 5.20
liberal trade policy, 5.23
merger control, 5.24
Mexico, 5.26–5.28
multilateral regulation of RBPs, 5.19
phased approach, 5.22
special consideration, 5.18
subsidiaries of MNEs, 5.21
technical assistance, 5.17
dispute settlement, 5.12–5.15
international enforcement authority, 5.15
non-violation cases, 5.14
remedies, 5.12, 5.13
violation cases, 5.14
goal of harmonisation, 5.04
harmonised national laws, 5.02
minimum standards on anti-competitive conduct, 5.03–5.10
challenges to *Keiretsu*, and, 5.08, 5.09
conceptual obstacles, 5.07
existing consensus, 5.05
"hard-core" agreements, and, 5.10
Kodak-Fuji Film dispute, 5.08, 5.09
mergers and acquisitions, 5.06
non-discrimination, 5.11
proposals for, 5.02–5.28
transparency, 5.11
TRIPS Agreement as model, 5.02
Multilateral approaches to competition policy, 2.188–2.198
Multilateral solutions
scepticism as to, 1.53

NAFTA, 2.129–2.136
background, 2.129
Chapter 15, 2.130
control of abusive or anti-competitive practices or conditions, 2.134
co-operation in competition law enforcement, 2.131
NAFTA—*cont.*
designation of state monopolies, 2.132
state enterprises, 2.133
U.S. dominance, 2.136
Working Group, 2.135
National competition laws, 1.02, 1.03
Negotiations on multilateral competition policy agreement, 5.51–5.53
Noerr-Pennington doctrine, 1.23
Official protests, 2.029–2.031
Open trade
meaning, 1.06
Organisation for Economic Co-operation and Development (OECD), 2.151–2.171
background, 2.151
expansion of anti-cartel programme, 2.166
Guidelines for Multinational Enterprises, 2.154–2.159
categories of horizontal and vertical restraints, 2.155
conflicting jurisdiction, 2.157
cross-border trade and investment, 2.159
goal of competition policy, 2.158
restrictive agreements, 2.156
revision, 2.157
Joint Group on Trade and Competition, 2.152
MAI, 1.42, 1.44
notification of transnational mergers, 2.167–2.169
benefits, 2.167
differences in national competition laws, 2.168
model form, 2.169
Recommendation on action against hard-core cartels, 2.164–2.166
boycotts, 2.166
common interest of members, 2.165
hard-core cartel, meaning, 2.164
Recommendation on Co-operation on Anti-Competitive Practices, 2.160–2.163
consultation, 2.162
cross-border conflict, and, 2.161
domestic confidentiality laws, and, 2.163
notification, 2.162
studies and recommendations on trade and competition policy, 2.152, 2.153
technical assistance to developing countries, 2.170
OECD Agreement on Competition Policy, 5.57, 5.58
business and trade relationship of member countries, 5.58
enforcement mechanism, 5.58

Parent-subsidiary relationships, 4.108–4.110
European Union, 4.110
United States, 4.109
Plurilateral approaches to competition policy, 2.151–2.187
APEC, 2.172–2.177. *See also* **Asia-Pacific Economic Co-operation forum**
Draft International Antitrust Code, 2.178–2.187. *See also* **Draft International Antitrust Code**
Organisation for Economic Co-operation and Development, 2.151–2.171. *See also* **Organisation for Economic Co-operation and Development**
Predatory pricing, 4.120–4.124
Canada, 4.123
competition law, and, 1.26
meaning, 4.120, 4.121
non-price predatory conduct, 4.124
phases, 4.121
United States antitrust law, 4.122
Price fixing, 4.061–4.063
Canada, 4.063
Private party enforcement, 4.158–4.162
Canada, 4.161
European Union, 4.160
Japan, 4.162
national authority enforcement, and, 4.158–4.162
United States, 4.158, 4.159

Regional approaches to competition policy, 2.091–2.150
CARICOM, 2.149
European Union, 2.091–2.116. *See also* **European Union Free Trade Area of the Americas,** 2.137–2.148. *See also* **Free Trade Area of the Americas**
MERCOSUR, 2.117–2.128. *See also* **MERCOSUR**
NAFTA. *See* **NAFTA**
Relevant market. *See* **Abuse of dominant position**
Resale price maintenance, 4.085–4.087
Canada, 4.087
legality, 4.086
Restrictive business practices
definition, 2.193
trade policy, and, 1.28

Safeguards Agreement, 3.087–3.094
preamble, 3.094
VRAs, and, 3.087–3.093. *See also* **Voluntary export restraint agreement**
Small enterprises, 4.172
Trade and competition policy, 1.01–1.53
allocative efficiency, and, 1.15
antidumping duty law, and, 1.20
antidumping law, and, 1.25
common objectives, 1.10
competition policy, aim of, 1.08
complementaries, 1.06–1.12
divergences, 1.13–1.26
economics of, 1.10
efficient allocation of resources, and, 1.11
integration, 1.16
interests intended to be protected, 1.21
Keiretsu, and, 1.15
Noerr-Pennington doctrine, 1.23
relationship, 1.05–1.30
removal of barriers, objective of, 1.12
shared common themes, 1.27
trade policy, aim of, 1.09
transnational mergers and acquisitions, and, 1.29
Trade policy. *See also* **Trade and competition policy**
abuse by domestic producers, 1.22
consumer welfare, and, 1.17
protectionism, and, 1.30
restrictive business practices, and, 1.28
usual concerns of, 1.15
Trading companies, 4.080, 4.081
Treaty of Mutual Legal Assistance in Criminal Matters 1985 between U.S. and Canada, 2.074–2.076
TRIMS Agreement, 3.077–3.086
aim, 3.082
extension of mandate, proposal for, 1.33
investment measures inconsistent with GATT 1994, 3.079
multinational enterprises, and, 3.085
notification and elimination, 3.080
omissions, 3.084–3.086
review of operation of, 3.081
TRIM, meaning, 3.078
unbalanced document, as, 3.083
TRIPS Agreement, 3.045–3.059
abuse of IPRs, 3.052, 3.053
anti-competitive licensing agreements, 3.054, 3.055
balance of payments, 3.047
compromises, 3.051
compulsory licensing, 3.057–3.059
counterfeit goods, 3.049
deceptive practices, 3.056
geographical indications, 3.056
general exceptions, 3.048
intellectual property rights, 3.046

TRIPS Agreement—*cont.*
objectives, 3.052
principles, 3.052
private restrictive business practices, and, 1.34

UNCTAD Principles on Restrictive Business Practices, 2.193– 2.198
aim, 2.193
antitrust laws, and, 2.197
Intergovernmental Group, 2.197, 2.198
monopolistic practices, 2.196
principles on competition, 2.195
recommendations, 2.194
restrictive business practice, definition, 2.193
Unilateral approaches to competition policy, 2.002–2.036
act of state doctrine, 2.025
anti-competitive conduct that may go unchallenged, 2.027, 2.028
Canada, 2.028
domestic market, and, 2.027
Export Trading Company Act 1982, 2.028
clawback statutes, 2.029–2.031
comity, 2.013–2.021. *See only* **Comity**
effects test
infringement on state sovereignty, and, 2.032
extraterritorial application of U.S. antitrust law, 2.012
extraterritoriality, and, 2.009–2.012
foreign nondisclosure laws, 2.029–2.031
foreign sovereign compulsion, 2.026
foreign sovereign immunity, 2.022–2.024. *See also* **Foreign sovereign immunity**
implementation test, 2.005
effects test, and, 2.007
imposition of U.S. competition policy principles on other nations, 2.033
incentives for co-operation, and, 2.034
International Competition Policy Advisory Committee, and, 2.036
jurisdictional nexus, 2.006
limits, 2.032–2.036
official protests, 2.029–2.031
policy conflict in cross border competition law, 2.011
reactions to, 2.029–2.031
responsibility of national authorities, 2.004
self-restraint, 2.013–2.021
territoriality principle, 2.002
effects test, 2.003, 2.004, 2.005
United Nations Draft Convention on Restrictive Business Practices, 2.189–2.192
alienation of U.S. business community, 2.192
investigating authority, 2.191
limitation on scope, 2.190
objectives, 2.189
United States
attitude to WTO negotiations over competition rules, 1.40
enforcement mechanisms, 1.39
Uruguay Round Understanding on Financial Services, 3.070–3.072
Agreement on basic telecommunications services 1997, 3.073–3.076
"Additional Commitments", 3.076
dispute settlement, 3.075
Reference Paper on communication principles, 3.074
aim, 3.070
market access commitments, 3.071
national treatment, 3.072

Vertical non-price restraints, 4.088–4.090
Canada, 4.090
effects, 4.089
examples, 4.088
United States, 4.090
Vertical restraints, 4.082–4.110
abuse of intellectual property rights, 4.091–4.095. *See also* **Abuse of intellectual property rights**
effect, 4.084
grey market goods, 4.096–4.107. *See also* **Grey market goods**
legal treatment, 4.083
meaning, 4.082
parent-subsidiary relationships, 4.108–4.110
resale price maintenance. *See* **Resale price maintenance**
vertical non-price restraints, 4.088–4.090. *See also* **Vertical non-price restraints**
Voluntary export restraint agreements (VERs) or (VRAs), 1.50, 3.087–3.093
aim, 3.087
effect, 3.089
GATT Article XIX, and, 3.093
"gray area" measures, 3.091
legal status, 3.092
pattern concluding, 3.090

Weak enforcement, 4.169

Working Group on the Interaction between Trade and Competition Policy (WGTCP), 4.001–4.049
Work Programme 1997, 4.002–4.015
Australia, submissions by, 4.003
Canada, submissions by, 4.004
checklist of issues suggested for study, 4.015
Egypt, submissions by, 4.005
European Union, submissions by, 4.006
Hong Kong, submissions by, 4.007
India, submissions by, 4.008
Japan, submissions by, 4.009
Mexico, submissions by, 4.010
Norway, submissions by, 4.011
Pakistan, submissions by, 4.012
Switzerland, submissions by, 4.013
United States, submissions by, 4.014
Work Programme 1998, 4.016–4.030
impact of private anti-competitive practices on international trade, 4.024–4.027
impact of regulatory practices, state monopolies, and exclusive rights on competition and international trade, 4.028
impact of trade policy on competition, 4.029
recommendations for future work programme, 4.030
relationship between objectives, principles, concepts, scope and instruments of trade and competition policy, 4.017–4.019
stocktaking of existing instruments regarding trade and competition policy, 4.020–4.023
Work Programme 1999, 4.031–4.043
approaches to promoting co-operation and communication among members, 4.036–4.040
approaches to resolving anti-competitive practices in trade context, 4.033–4.035
contribution of competition policy to achieving objectives of WTO, 4.041–4.043
relevance of fundamental WTO principles to competition policy, 4.032
Work Programme 2000, 4.044–4.049
benefits of competition legal regime for developing countries, 4.049
capacity building in developing countries, 4.045–4.048

World Trade Organisation (WTO), 3.001–3.118. *See also* **GATT-WTO system**
agreements addressing private conduct, 3.098
anti-competitive behaviour, and, 1.38
Antidumping Act of 1916 dispute, 3.112–3.115. *See also* **Antidumping Act of 1916 dispute**
arguments in favour of multilateral framework agreement, 1.43
benefits of multilateral agreement on competition policy, 1.41
competition policy, 1.31–1.53
competition policy disputes, 3.100–3.115
competition policy negotiations
cautious steps forward, 3.116–3.118
fragility of, 1.46
framework agreement on competition law, 1.36
government conduct, and, 1.32
government trade barriers, and, 3.043
grey area measures, and, 1.50
international merger and acquisition activity, and, 1.35
Kodak-Fuji Film dispute, 3.101–3.111
exclusion of Kodak from wholesale distribution channel, 3.102, 3.103
GATT-based complaint, 3.105
Japanese distribution system, 3.104
Japanese large-scale retail store laws, 3.105
merits, 3.107
panel's rulings, 3.106–3.111
timing of alleged Japanese measures, 3.108
unpublished enforcement actions, 3.109
minimum standards, requirement of, 1.35
multilateralism, and, 1.45
opposition to competition policy negotiations, 1.37
primary goal, 1.31
private anti-competitive practices, and, 1.01
reasons for not adding competition policy to agenda, 6.98, 6.99
rules binding rich and poor countries alike, 1.47
rules on competition policy, 3.042–3.115
significance of governmental barriers to market access, and, 1.48, 1.49
success of, 6.97
trade and competition policy: overview, 1.01–1.53

World Trade Organisation (WTO)—*cont.*
trade and competition policy symposia, 4.050
Uruguay Round Agreements, 3.044–3.099
VERS, and, 1.50
WTO Agreement on Competition Policy
preconditions to negotiations, 6.01–6.50
adverse dispute settlement decisions, 6.39, 6.40
benefits of multilateral agreement, and, 6.35
consensus as to anti-competitive behaviour, 6.25
consensus as to global approach, 6.30, 6.31
consensus on best forum, 6.27–6.29
consensus on optimal legal instrument, 6.26
consumer welfare, 6.48
developing countries, 6.17
domestic laws, and, 6.12
economic self-interest, 6.32
examples of practices affecting market access, 6.03
export cartels, 6.10
global consensus, 6.38
globalisation, and, 6.19
government barriers to market access, and, 6.07, 6.08
harmonisation as goal, 6.18
Havana Charter, and, 6.21–6.24
increase in cartel activity, whether, 6.04
increased bilateralism, 6.17
legal framework, 6.13
legal vehicle, 6.21
permanent consultative body, 6.50
political context, 6.15
political tensions, and, 6.37
political will, 6.20
price discrimination, 6.09
proposed mergers with cross-border effects, 6.11
purely private RBP, whether, 6.05, 6.06
reduction of friction, 6.33–6.40
responsibility to be placed in hands of trade officials, 6.44–6.50
role of WTO, and, 6.02
WTO Agreement on Competition Policy—*cont.*
preconditions to negotiations—*cont.*
threat to international competition, and, 6.16
trade law approach, 6.14
WTO jurisdiction over cross-border merger activity, 6.41– 6.43
WTO Framework Agreement on Core Principles, 5.28–5.50
bilateral co-operation agreements, and, 5.33
content and coverage of competition laws, 5.35
core principles, on, 5.30
developing countries, 5.38
difficulties of harmonisation, and, 5.29
dispute settlement, 5.39–5.50
burden of proof, and, 5.41, 5.42
competition policy reviews, 5.43
comprehensive regime, 5.42
consultation, 5.39
effectiveness, 5.46
investigations, 5.39, 5.40
Kodak Fuji Film dispute, 5.47
privatisation of enforcement, 5.49
proceedings in national courts, 5.50
referring complaints to Working Party, 5.45
refusal to conduct investigation, 5.48
reports, 5.44
effective enforcement procedures, 5.36
international co-operation and co-ordination, 5.37
meaningful remedies, 5.36
most-favoured nation treatment, 5.32, 5.33
national treatment, 5.31
proposal for, 5.28–5.50
transparency, 5.34
WTO multilateral agreement on competition policy, 5.01–5.53
proposals for, 5.01–5.53
WTO Plurilateral Agreement on Competition Policy, 5.54–5.56
implementation stages, 5.56
Tokyo Round codes, and, 5.54
WTO Work Programme on Competition Policy, 4.001–4.050